# THE LIVES OF LESBIANS, GAYS, AND BISEXUALS

▼

## Children to Adults

### Ritch C. Savin-Williams

Cornell University

### Kenneth M. Cohen

Cornell University

**Harcourt Brace College Publishers**

Fort Worth   Philadelphia   San Diego   New York   Orlando   Austin   San Antonio
Toronto   Montreal   London   Sydney   Tokyo

Publisher            Ted Buchholz
Editor in Chief      Christopher P. Klein
Project Editor       Deanna M. Johnson
Production Manager   Diane Gray
Art Director         Jim Dodson

Cover Image     © Ei Kuriki / Photonica

ISBN: 0-15-501497-8
Library of Congress Catalog Card Number: 95-76861

*Address for Editorial Correspondence:* Harcourt Brace College Publishers,
301 Commerce Street, Suite 3700, Fort Worth, TX 76102.

*Address for Orders:* Harcourt Brace & Company, 6277 Sea Harbor Drive,
Orlando, FL 32887-6777. 1-800-782-4479, or 1-800-433-0001 (in Florida).

Printed in the United States of America
5 6 7 8 9 0 1 2 3   016   9 8 7 6 5 4 3 2 1

*This book is dedicated to our parents*
*Joy J. Williams, Marilyn and Norman Cohen*
*and grandmother, Sarah Moscovitch*

# PREFACE

In undertaking the publication of this text our primary intent is to promote an increased awareness and understanding of the lives of lesbian, gay, and bisexual individuals and their development from conception through old age. To this end, we solicited 20 original chapters that draw on the most up-to-date research and literature on the lives of lesbians, gays, and bisexuals. Although the chapters were written explicitly for *college and university students* enrolled in undergraduate and graduate level courses that discuss human diversity and sexual-minority issues, we have also designed this book to appeal to *educated laypersons, psychologists, counselors, social workers, psychiatrists, community psychologists, educators, medical personnel,* and *researchers* who seek to better understand the development of lesbians, bisexuals, and gays. We believe this book will benefit the lives of young adults as they attempt to understand their personal and sexual identity within the context of modern North American culture.

To enhance the accessibility of this volume to non-academicians, authors use empirical and theoretical literature as well as "data" not usually included in scholarly volumes. To illustrate particular points, chapter authors incorporate reflections from the lives of lesbians, gays, and bisexuals who have thought deeply and poetically regarding what it means to be a sexual minority. Examples include interviews, life stories, and anecdotes derived from both popular and personal biographical and autobiographical accounts. Several chapters review resources and support services for gays, lesbians, and bisexuals as well as for those who want to assist them. Advice that will benefit clinicians and mental health professionals is also integrated throughout the textbook. Although developmental and clinical psychology are the primary orientations of the text, multiple disciplines—including sociology, anthropology, biology, education, law, and history—are also well represented within the chapters.

Chapters in this text repeatedly highlight two paradoxical facts: Although bisexuals, gays, and lesbians experience the same fundamental human needs, desires, and aspirations that typify their heterosexual peers, they are in significant ways also distinct from heterosexuals in their developmental pathways. These differences are likely the result of both their biological heritage and their experiences of growing up in a culture that does not fully accept its sexual-minority members.[1]

Second, despite the tendency to speak of bisexuals, lesbians, and gays as representing a singular "lifestyle" or "community," they are a very diverse, heterogeneous assembly with often discrepant aspirations and lifestyles. There is no single "gay lifestyle," no simple way to conceptualize all sexual-minority individuals, and no coherent group that forms a community of like-minded individuals. Despite cultural stereotypes, many lesbians, gays, and bisexuals vote Republican, believe they differ from heterosexuals only in terms of the sex of the person they choose to love, and desire to live in life-long monogamous relationships.

Stereotypes serve a function: They portray bisexuals, lesbians, and gays in a manner that is understandable to the majority culture, thus rendering those with same-sex attractions predictable and less threatening. Many well-meaning individuals are seduced by the security and parsimony afforded when complex systems are reduced to simple, formulaic elements. The stereotypes to which heterosexuals as well as sexual minorities frequently subscribe are challenged and often repudiated by the empirical research and life stories reported in this text.

Increased understanding is needed both by "heterosexual allies"—those who are apparently accepting of sexual diversity yet subscribe to stereotypes and prejudices because they are often unknowingly influenced by the teachings of the majority culture—and by those who dislike sexual minorities or the sexual behaviors in which they engage. The latter cannot be forced to embrace gays, lesbians, and bisexuals or their "lifestyles," but they can be encouraged to *question their beliefs and challenge their assumptions.* By becoming familiar with research-derived evidence for the normalcy and diversity of same-sex attractions and behaviors, an objective and empathic understanding about the life-course development of sexual minorities becomes possible.

Psychologist Ervin Staub insisted, "In a pluralistic society different orientations can counterbalance each other, but dominant values and views tend to result in overall biases, limiting the picture of reality" (p. 272).[2] Thus, even individuals who believe that they are nonracist, nonsexist, and nonhomophobic are, by virtue of being raised in the majority culture, subject to subtle, often unconscious biases and stereotypes. Psychotherapists Derald Wing Sue and David Sue concurred, adding that benevolence and empathy are not sufficient attributes for working with minority individuals; concrete information about the culture or group must be acquired *and* assimilated in order to better appreciate their unique experiences, needs, motivations, psychosocial development, stresses, and modes of communications.[3] We want this book to serve these educational functions.

## ORGANIZATION OF THE BOOK

To normalize lives and illustrate diversity, we approach the study of gays, lesbians, and bisexuals from a developmental perspective. Chapter writers—many of whom are the preeminent authorities in their field—examine the psychological, biological, social, political, and legal forces that impact sexual-minority individuals from conception to death. The book is organized into four sections, three of which address development from a particular time in life: prenatal development and childhood, adolescence, and adulthood and aging. The final section examines cultural and mental health issues.

The first four chapters explore the etiology of homosexuality and early childhood experiences. In chapter 1, Lee Ellis considers the prevalence of homosexuality and the prominent psychosocial and biological theories proposed to account for its genesis. Ellis's second chapter reviews the role of perinatal factors in determining sexual orientation. Discussed are genetics, prenatal stress, prenatal drug exposure, and immunological factors, with particular emphasis on the perinatal hormone theory. In chapter 3, J. Michael Bailey examines the first manifestations of an eventual sexual identity among a significant number of gays, bisexuals, and lesbians—early childhood gender atypical behaviors. Ritch C. Savin-Williams concludes this section with a chapter that recounts the memories of gay and bisexual male youths regarding their same-sex attractions and desires during their childhood and early adolescent years.

The second section of the book is devoted to issues usually experienced during adolescence. Chapter 5, written by Kenneth M. Cohen and Savin-Williams, addresses factors that contribute to and result from coming out as lesbian, gay, or bisexual to self and others. Particular emphasis is placed on coming-out models, psychological defenses and repercussions, self-esteem, and disclosure to parents. Experiences that are unique to ethnic- and sexual-minority youth follow in chapter 6 by Savin-Williams. Issues such as racism in lesbian and gay communities, homophobia in ethnic communities, and the importance of family relationships are explored. Chapter 7, also by Savin-Williams, considers the unique challenges lesbian, gay, and bisexual youth encounter when attempting to date and establish romantic relationships with other same-gendered individuals. In chapter 8, Savin-Williams and Cohen report that the psychosocial consequences of harassment and physical violence that some lesbian, bisexual, and gay youth experience from parents, peers, and teachers include quitting school, running away from home, and attempting suicide. Nancy J. Evans and Anthony R. D'Augelli present in chapter 9 the experiences of young adults who come of age in college. They address personal identity development, mental health, dual minority status, relationships, and harassment; they conclude with suggestions for creating a supportive environment for lesbian, gay, and bisexual students.

Developmental concerns that pertain to adulthood and aging are introduced in the third section of the book. Carla Golden reviews feminist debates about sexual identity and presents empirical data in support of multiple pathways to identity formation. Issues of choice, fluidity, social construction, and biology are considered. In chapter 11, Letitia Anne Peplau, Rosemary C. Veniegas, and Susan Miller Campbell summarize and interpret research on the love relationships of lesbians and gay men. They examine power structures, partitioning of labor, difficulties, dissolution, and alternate forms of couples therapy. In chapter 12, Charlotte J. Patterson surveys the ways in which sexual-minority individuals become parents and examines the psychological health of children raised in nontraditional families. Services for lesbian and gay families and directions for research, service, and advocacy conclude the chapter. In chapter 13, Virginia Casper and Steven Schultz tackle the problems of communication between gay and lesbian parents and their children's school teachers and administrators. They highlight the challenges of parenthood, the experiences of educators, and the sometimes arduous process gay and lesbian parents face coming out to educators. The legal implications of adult activities such as marriage, sexual activity, child rearing, housing, and employment are addressed by William B. Rubenstein in chapter 14. He examines their relationship to sodomy laws, family rights, and nondiscrimination policies. Sharon Jacobson and Arnold H. Grossman conclude the section on adulthood and aging with an exploration of older lesbians and gays. The authors report the disparate means by which these individuals developed a lesbian or gay identity, address stereotypes about aging sexual-minority individuals, and conclude with a discussion of services for elderly sexual minorities and suggestions for future research and services.

The final section of the text addresses cultural and mental health issues. Chapter 16, by Kristin Gay Esterberg, considers the myriad communities built by lesbian, gay, and bisexual individuals as well as the ways in which their social and political identities have changed over time. Reviewed is the establishment of the homophile movement, gay liberation, and a growing bisexual community. In chapter 17, Martin F. Manalansan IV explores several Latino, Black, and Asian communities and the marginality of their members who engage in same-sex activity, some of whom do not consider themselves to be "gay." Walter L. Williams reviews the prevalence of gender nonconformity behavior and same-sex activity among Native American and Native Hawaiian youths in chapter 18. Referring to these individuals as "two-spirit persons," Williams explores the special, often highly esteemed position homoerotically inclined persons hold in these and other cultures. In chapter 19, Jay P. Paul tackles the complexities of bisexuality. He addresses myths, stereotypes, and difficulties faced by individuals who are attracted to members of both genders and makes suggestions for clinicians who support bisexual people. The final chapter in the book, written by John C. Gonsiorek, addresses the relationship between sexual orientation and mental health from historic and contemporary perspectives. He concludes with the presentation of models that help explain the link between mental health concerns and sexual orientation.

## ACKNOWLEDGMENTS

We wish to thank several people who have been helpful in making this project a reality. First and foremost, we are indebted to the chapter authors. They were willing to summarize the major findings in their area of expertise in a format that would be comprehensible to the rest of us. Without them we could not have produced a text of this quality. Second, we will always be grateful to Eve Howard, Senior Editor, for her initial enthusiasm for this text and for her unwavering commitment to its publication. We also wish to thank the anonymous reviewers for their insight and helpful suggestions on an earlier draft of the book. Finally, we appreciate and will miss Deanna Johnson's warmth, good humor, optimism, and daily phone calls as she moved the book through production.

Ithaca, New York                                                      Ritch C. Savin-Williams
February 14, 1995                                                    Kenneth M. Cohen

## ENDNOTES

1. This book does not explicitly address the issues or concerns of all sexual-minority groups. In particular, we have neglected the growing transgendered movement. We hope, nevertheless, that the chapters provide support for all sexual-minority individuals and guidance to those who provide services and advocacy to them.

2. Staub, E. (1989). *The roots of evil: The origins of genocide and other group violence.* Cambridge: Cambridge University Press.

3. Sue, D. W., & Sue, D. (1990). *Counseling the culturally different: Theory and practice* (2nd ed.). New York: John Wiley & Sons. Sue and Sue are referring specifically to clinical work with racial-/ethnic-minority individuals. Their insights, nonetheless, readily generalize to working with sexual minorities.

# TABLE OF CONTENTS

# PART TWO • ADOLESCENCE                            111

## PART THREE • ADULTHOOD AND AGING    227

# PART FOUR • CULTURAL AND MENTAL HEALTH ISSUES 375

# INTRODUCTION

Kenneth M. Cohen
&
Ritch C. Savin-Williams

## INCREASED VISIBILITY AND ACCEPTANCE

During no other time in history have lesbians, gays, and bisexuals been the recipients of so much overt attention, scrutiny, and unprecedented acceptance and inclusion into mainstream American culture. Although it may be argued that the historical tolerance for unmarried persons, many of whom were homoerotically inclined, constitutes a level of acceptance, it pales in comparison to today's acknowledgement or endorsement of alternative forms of sexuality. Even the ancient Greeks stopped short of endorsing the "highest form of love between two men" as a substitute to heterosexual marriage.

Life has not always been good for individuals inclined toward same-sex attractions. In fact, the greatest advances for the homophile movement occurred only recently, following the Stonewall riots in 1969 (see Esterberg, this volume). The pre-Stonewall period in the U.S. was often characterized by secrecy, fear, isolation, and invisibility. For example, gay and lesbian organizations held clandestine meetings for fear of being discovered or exposed publicly, and thus risk its members' losing jobs, family, and friends. Frequent police raids on bars patronized by lesbians, gays, bisexuals, and transsexuals fueled these fears. In pre-Stonewall America, the mere disclosure of homoerotic attractions to employers or coworkers invited threats, personal injury, or job firing. Although pockets of gay life flourished in large urban areas, sexual minorities were largely invisible to most of the country beyond those ghettos. These conditions are recounted by historians D'Emilio (1983), Timmons (1990), and Chauncey (1994) and captured on celluloid in films such as *Before Stonewall* and *Word Is Out*.

Although we do not wish to imply that our culture has matured to the point where it entirely embraces or endorses homosexuality, North American society has evolved considerably since the Stonewall riots. This is evident in recent polls of United States citizens. For example, in a 1994 election night exit poll, 70% of those surveyed believed that lesbians, gays, and bisexuals "should not face unfair job discrimination and should have 'equal rights in hiring and firing'" (Walsh, 1994, p. 14). Twice as many voters "worried" more about the religious right agenda than the "gay agenda." A further study found that over 70% of New York State voters felt that a candidate's sexual orientation would make "no difference" in how they voted ("Gay Candidates," 1994). Two thirds of the respondents of a poll commissioned by *New York* magazine reported that the partners of gay city employees should receive full spousal benefits. Furthermore, most respondents (81%) maintained that gays and lesbians should be permitted to hold any occupation ("Will All the Homophobes," 1994).

This "acceptance" of lesbian, bisexual, and gay people is, however, circumscribed. For example, by a four to one margin, New York City residents believed that gay people should be permitted to become doctors—but nearly half of these "liberal" residents reported that they would also feel uncomfortable going to a gay doctor. Living next door to a gay couple was okay, but they should not hold hands or kiss in public. The message, according to this survey, was "Be whatever you want—just keep it to yourself" ("Will All the Homophobes," 1994, p. 39). Another source reported that according to *Who's Who Among American High School Students,* prejudice against gays was twice as frequent among students than against African Americans, Hispanics, or Asian Americans ("High Achieving Students," 1994, p. 16).

Amidst this atmosphere of relative acceptance in public domains, significant progress has been made among gays, bisexuals, and lesbians in accepting and supporting themselves. Today, there are literally thousands of groups for individuals who are lesbian, gay, or bisexual—not to mention transgender, sexually questioning, asexual, or transsexual. Organizations that are committed to the spiritual, psychological, athletic, social, or political enhancement of individuals with homoerotic attractions and desires are present throughout North America. They consist of high school and university student organizations; athletic leagues; political groups; professional organizations (e.g., for nurses, teachers, lawyers, physicians, and psychologists); 12-step support groups; parent support groups; and a vast array of HIV positive/AIDS counseling/support services.

Books, magazines, and newsletters written for and about lesbians, gays, and bisexuals have also flourished. Many professional and paraprofessional organizations have newsletters and/or computer bulletin boards for their sexual-minority members. For instance, psychologists have a gay and lesbian newsletter as well as an e-mail discussion group for graduate students in psychology; Unitarians/Universalists publish the newsletter *Interweave World;* and youth have *Crossroads* to address their unique needs. Most major metropolitan areas have a gay-oriented newspaper, including Chicago's *Windy City Times,* Minneapolis's *Equal Times,* San Francisco's *Bay Area Reporter,* Boston's *Gay Community News,* Washington, D.C.'s the *Washington Blade,* and central New York's *Stonewall News.* National magazines such as *The Advocate, Out and About,* and *10 Percent* provide news, art, entertainment, fashion, and travel coverage of sexual minorities. Books are available on nearly every sexual minority topic conceivable. There are encyclopedias (Dynes, Johansson, Percy, & Donaldson, 1990), fact and statistical books

(Singer & Deschamps, 1994), biographies (White, 1993), readers (Abelove, Barale, & Halperin, 1993), and anthologies (Beck, 1989). Books have been published on major topics such as bisexuality (Weinberg, Williams, & Pryor, 1994), public policy (Gonsiorek & Weinrich, 1991), psychotherapy (Silverstein, 1991), biology (Hamer & Copeland, 1994; LeVay, 1993), and psychological theory and research (D'Augelli & Patterson, 1995; Garnets & Kimmel, 1993; Greene & Herek, 1994), and on specialized topics such as gays in Thailand (Jackson, 1989), same-sex activities among pirates and sea rovers (Burg, 1983), Nazi treatment of lesbians and gays (Plant, 1986), lesbian nuns (Curb & Manahan, 1985) and gay priests (Wolf, 1989), gay men and lesbians serving in World War II (Berube, 1990), and a gay baseball umpire (Pallone & Steinberg, 1990).

In this atmosphere of tolerance and visibility, increasing numbers of actors, singers, writers, politicians, and sports figures are proclaiming their homoerotic attractions and offering support to those who desperately desire to come out of the closet. Among these are young lesbians, gays, and bisexuals—formerly unrecognized groups (see Cohen & Savin-Williams, "Coming Out," this volume). The result is that gay, bisexual, and lesbian youths are coming to terms with their same-sex attractions and disclosing their sexual identity to others at increasingly early ages and with fewer negative psychological repercussions.

Furthering public awareness of the prevalence and contributions of people with same-sex desires are social functions such as the 1993 March on Washington; the Stonewall 25 celebration in New York City; and the 1994 Gay Games IV, modeled after the Olympics. In addition, issues such as AIDS, adoption and parenting rights, and gays in the military are regularly discussed in the newspaper and movies and on the radio and television. Exposure by the media has brought issues of homosexuality to the forefront of North American awareness.

For example, for several months before this book was sent to production, the *New York Times* published numerous stories about the ways in which gay, lesbian, and bisexual issues have permeated our culture. In May 1994, a story appeared about the unconditional acceptance MacNeil/Lehrer news anchor Robert MacNeil has for his gay son, Ian, and Ian's partner—Robert MacNeil's "son-in-law" (Dullea, 1994). In August, Solomon (1994) noted the active presence of lesbians and gays in Deaf Culture; in September, De Witt (1994) wrote about the revival of many decaying urban neighborhoods by lesbians, bisexuals, and gays who had moved to formally undesirable areas of the city, rebuilt the homes, and stabilized the economy. On the sports pages, Frey (1994) described the coming out and medical decline due to AIDS of Los Angeles Dodger Glenn Burke; on the religious pages, Niebuhr (1994) wrote about the 1,400 congregants of the Cathedral of Hope gay church in Dallas. In November, Sheila James Kuehl, the actress who played Zelda on the late 1950s/early 1960s television show *The Many Loves of Dobie Gillis*, became the first openly lesbian candidate to win a seat in the California Legislature (Dunlap, 1994). Even the Speaker of the U.S. House of Representatives, Newt Gingrich, consented to an interview on gay-related issues, during which he reflected on the causes of homosexuality; his gay Republican friend, Representative Steve Gunderson; and gay couples (Burr, 1994).

Gone, at least for the present time, are the days when homosexuality was unquestioningly classified by the majority heterosexual culture as deviant, pathological, and amoral. Today, a sizable number of mental health professionals (e.g., psychologists, psychiatrists, social workers), medical personnel (e.g., physicians and nurses), researchers, and academicians profess to owning homoerotic feelings. Many in our increasingly educated and sophisticated society no longer accept scientifically unverified or untested claims based on single-case reports or "intuition" that lesbians, gays, and bisexuals are mentally ill or depraved *simply because* of their sexual orientation. Indeed, a growing body of empirical research attests to the stability, benevolence, and health of their lives, relationships, and careers (see Gonsiorek, this volume; Peplau, Veniegas, & Campbell, this volume).

## UNIQUENESS AND SAMENESS

That which we hope to present is a portrayal of a heterogeneous group of people who can be characterized as much by their *uniqueness* and *diversity* as by their *sameness*. Their lives are thus *normalized* as well as *individualized*. Perhaps most importantly, they are made recognizable.

In significant ways the basic needs, aspirations, desires, and relationships of bisexuals, lesbians, and gays are more typical of the girl/boy next door than the clichés that typecast their lives. A recent letter to the *New York Times* illustrates the "commonality" of gay men;

> Most of us do not want to be women or anything like women. We do not live lives like operas any more than straight men do. We have no more facility or talent for the arts than the heterosexual community. Many of us pump gas at service stations or drive trucks. (Orlov, 1993, p. H4)

Despite the basic human qualities that sexual minorities share with heterosexuals, there are many unique issues that characterize the development of lesbians, gays, and bisexuals. For example, scholars in this volume suggest that there are several milestones that are characteristic of lesbian, bisexual, and gay development, the negotiation of which *may* hinder development in other areas. For instance, gay, lesbian, or bisexual youths who behave in a gender-atypical manner may be subjected to relentless ridicule and/or violence by peers and family. The result may be withdrawal from social interactions, which would thus hinder the development of intimacy, trust, and interpersonal relationships. Some youths repress their homoerotic attractions; all too often this results in a temporary, though often protracted, moratorium of the development of a sexual identity and intimate relationships with same-sex youths. For youths who acknowledge their same-sex desires to self but conceal them from others, life consists of lies, half-truths, and concealment—all of which may interfere with the development of self-consistency, self-concept, and self-esteem (see Cohen &

Savin-Williams, "Coming Out," this volume). Although not all gays and lesbians experience these issues, many do.

These developmental challenges are resolved in a variety of ways that contribute to the diversity of lesbians, bisexuals, and gays. To ignore these variations is to simplify the lives of sexual minorities. Lesbian, gay, and bisexual individuals are not a monolith: Some are artistic and others are pedantic; some are revolutionaries and others are reactionaries; some are peace activists and others are military personnel. They also vary in the degree to which they are out to themselves and others, when they come out, and to whom they come out. Some proudly engage in same-sex relationships in junior and senior high school; others declare their sexual identity on their deathbed. Many crave parenting children and others are satisfied to let heterosexuals raise the next generation. Some gay and lesbian youths are models of psychological health and fortitude while others attempt to end their lives prematurely. Although few would suggest that all heterosexuals have identical thoughts, feelings, or needs, too frequently people assume that all lesbians and gays are identical.

## CONCLUSION

We hope that this book will help to answer questions, dispel myths, and relieve apprehensions about gays, lesbians, and bisexuals. Homoeroticism has long intrigued yet frightened people. It has been a taboo topic, the serious discussion of which often evoked terror by those who feared being implicated. Consequently, it has remained wrapped in a shroud of mystery and stigma. We wish to *normalize* the lives of those who own homoerotic attractions as well as highlight the *diversity* that exists among them. Our ambition is also to *sensitize* so that when the time comes, as it inevitably will, when the reader learns that a best friend, coworker, parent, child, or grandchild is a lesbian, gay, or bisexual individual, she or he will not react with anger, shame, or fear but with understanding, acceptance, and pride.

There are many ways to help better the lives of sexual minorities, reduce discrimination, and eliminate violence against those whose only "crime" is to love another. Education is one such way, for *the path to acceptance is knowledge and understanding.*

We embrace that which Robert Kennedy said in 1966 during a speech to students in South Africa: "Each time a man [woman] stands for an ideal, or acts to improve the lot of others, or strikes out against injustice, he [she] sends forth a tiny ripple of hope." *We wish to inculcate tolerance and appreciation for a pluralistic society.* This aim can only be achieved by examining and continually monitoring the ways in which we treat those who are different from us. This point is made by Staub in his book *The Roots of Evil: The Origins of Genocide and Other Group Violence:*

Parents, schools, and universities can teach children to recognize in themselves and others the psychological processes that lead to destructive acts. To realize that seeing others as of lesser value or blaming them might represent devaluation and scapegoating is significant progress. Further progress is achieved by learning to catch oneself devaluing others or deflecting self-blame to others and by acquiring the capacity to become an observer not only of others' but of one's own psychological processes. (1989, p. 281)

This book is fundamentally a call for introspection. Without confronting our own indifference, latent prejudices, and passivity, we are helpless before sexual-minority individuals who would gladly embrace our efforts.

## ▼   REFERENCES   ▼

Abelove, H., Barale, M. A., & Halperin, D. M. (Eds.). (1993). *The lesbian and gay studies reader.* New York: Routledge.

Beck, E. T. (Ed.). (1989). *Nice Jewish girls: A lesbian anthology* (Rev. ed.). Boston: Boston Press.

Berube, A. (1990). *Coming out under fire: The history of gay men and women in World War Two.* New York: Free Press.

Burg, B. R. (1983). *Sodomy and the pirate tradition: English sea rovers in the seventeenth-century Caribbean.* New York: New York University Press.

Burr, C. (1994, November 25). Newt Gingrich speaks out. *Washington Blade,* pp. 1, 27, 29.

Chauncey, G. (1994). *Gay New York: Gender, urban culture, and the making of the gay male world, 1890–1940.* New York: Basic Books.

Curb, R., & Manahan, N. (Eds.). (1985). *Lesbian nuns: Breaking silence.* Tallahassee, FL: Naiad Press.

D'Augelli, A. R., & Patterson, C. J. (Eds.). (1995). *Lesbian, gay and bisexual identities over the lifespan: Psychological perspectives on personal, relational, and community processes.* New York: Oxford University Press.

D'Emilio, J. (1983). *Sexual politics, sexual communities: The making of a homosexual minority in the United States, 1940–1970.* Chicago: University of Chicago Press.

De Witt, K. (1994, September 6). Gay presence leading a revival of many urban neighborhoods. *New York Times,* pp. A1, A12.

Dullea, G. (1994, May 5). A father and a son, growing up again. *New York Times,* pp. C1, C8.

Dunlap, D. W. (1994, November 20). Zelda's unwavering love is no longer unrequited. *New York Times,* p. A24.

Dynes, W. R. (Ed.); Johansson, W., & Percy, W. A. (Associate Editors); & Donaldson, S. (Assistant). (1990). *Encyclopedia of homosexuality* (two volumes). New York: Garland.

Frey, J. (1994, October 18). A boy of summer's long, chilly winter: Once a promising ballplayer, Glenn Burke is dying of AIDS. *New York Times,* pp. B15, B19.

Garnets, L. D., & Kimmel, D. C. (1993). *Psychological perspectives on lesbian and gay male experiences.* New York: Columbia University Press.

Gay candidates: Could attacks backfire? (1994, October 13). *New York Times,* p. B1.

Gonsiorek, J. C., & Weinrich, J. D. (Eds.). (1991). *Homosexuality: Research implications for public policy.* Newbury Park, CA: Sage.

Greene, B., & Herek, G. M. (Eds.). (1994). *Lesbian and gay psychology: Theory, research, and clinical application.* Thousand Oaks, CA: Sage.

Hamer, D., & Copeland, P. (1994). *The science of desire: The search for the gay gene and the biology of behavior.* New York: Simon & Schuster.

High achieving students see much prejudice. (1994, November 25). *Washington Blade,* p. 16.

Jackson, P. A. (1989). *Male homosexuality in Thailand: An interpretation of contemporary Tai sources.* Elmhurst, NY: Global Academic Publishers.

LeVay, S. (1993). *The sexual brain.* Cambridge: MIT Press.

Niebuhr, G. (1994, October 30). Biggest gay church finds a home in Dallas. *New York Times,* p. 16.

Orlov, C. (1993, April 18). Perpetuating myths: Letter to the Editor. *New York Times,* p. H4.

Pallone, D., & Steinberg, A. (1990). *Behind the mask: My double life in baseball.* New York: Viking.

Plant, R. (1986). *The pink triangle: The Nazi war against homosexuals.* New York: Henry Holt.

Silverstein, C. (Ed.). (1991). *Gays, lesbians, and their therapists: Studies in psychotherapy.* New York: W.W. Norton & Company.

Singer, B. L., & Deschamps, D. (Eds.). (1994). *Gay and lesbian stats: A pocket guide of facts and figures.* New York: New Press.

Solomon, A. (1994, August 28). Defiantly deaf. *New York Times Magazine,* pp. 66–68.

Staub, E. (1989). *The roots of evil: The origins of genocide and other group violence.* Cambridge: Cambridge University Press.

Timmons, S. (1990). *The trouble with Harry Hay: Founder of the modern gay movement.* Boston: Alyson.

Walsh, S. (1994, November 25). Post-election poll reveals voters' stance. *Washington Blade,* p. 14.

Weinberg, M. S., Williams, C. J., & Pryor, D. W. (1994). *Dual attractions: Understanding bisexuality.* New York: Oxford University Press.

White, E. (1993). *Genet: A biography.* New York: Alfred A. Knopf.

Will all the homophobes please stand up? (1994, June 20). *New York,* pp. 39, 42–45.

Wolf, J. G. (1989). *Gay priests.* San Francisco: Harper & Row.

# - Part One -

# *BEGINNINGS AND CHILDHOOD*

# *Chapter 1*

▼

# THEORIES OF HOMOSEXUALITY

---

# Lee Ellis[1]

*Why are some people sexually drawn to members of their own sex? Is it possible for science to shed light on such an intimate personal question? This chapter summarizes the many efforts of scientists to unravel the mysteries of sexual orientation. Before examining their proposals, it should be noted that many people have misgivings about scientific efforts to understand homosexuality.[2] Some, for example, view homosexuality as a religious issue, not a scientific one. Evangelist Jerry Falwell has asserted that, unlike race or ethnicity, homosexuality is "a lifestyle choice" (Martin, 1982, p. 35). According to those who espouse this view, because sexual orientation is a matter of choice, there are likely to be no objective, scientific causes of homosexuality to identify. Others have attributed homosexuality to a host of causes, including genetic defects, hormone imbalances, dysfunctional families, childhood sexual abuse, and even the work of the devil.*

*Opposition to the scientific study of homosexuality is also expressed by gay and lesbian supporters. Many fear that scientists view homosexuality as an illness or abnormality that is in need of treatment and prevention (DeCecco, 1987; Schmidt, 1984, p. 127; Sigusch, Schorsch, Dannecker, & Schmidt, 1982). Thus, many who support gay and lesbian rights would rather have scientists identify the causes of homophobic intolerance rather than the causes and cures for homosexuality. As one proponent stated, "Homosexuality needs no explanation . . . it exists as a moral right" (see Money, 1990, p. 407).*

*Before surveying the various theories of sexual orientation, it is helpful to consider the proportions of people who are gay or lesbian.*

## THE PREVALENCE OF HOMOSEXUALITY

Prior to the advent of social science surveys, it was virtually impossible to accurately assess the number of people who were gay, lesbian, or bisexual. All that was available was a vague recognition that homosexuality was "out there" and included such reputed "homosexuals" as Plato, Michelangelo, and Leonardo da Vinci (Riess & Safer, 1979, p. 261). The percentage of today's adult Americans who are gay or lesbian depends on the definition of *homosexuality* that is used.

Three major obstacles confront those who seek estimates of sexual orientation. One obstacle is that some people are hard to classify, because either they have attractions for both sexes (i.e., some degree of bisexuality), or their sexual attractions change over time. A second obstacle regards uncertainty about whether sexual orientation refers to sexual preferences or to behavior. Third, it is difficult to obtain information from representative samples of adults who are willing to answer intimate questions about their sexuality (Bailey & Pillard, 1991; McConaghy, Armstrong, Birrell, & Buhrich, 1979).

Nevertheless, sufficient research has recently been conducted to justify rough estimates of the prevalence of homosexuality based on the following three overlapping criteria: (a) fantasies about same-sex relationships, (b) engagement in intimate same-sex relationships, and (c) exclusive long-term preference for same-sex relationships.

When a homosexual sexual orientation is defined in terms of ever having had a same-sex fantasy or a sexual desire for a member of the same sex, between 25% and 40% of males and 10% and 20% of females are classified as gay or lesbian (Kinsey, Pomeroy, & Martin, 1948; Kinsey, Pomeroy, Martin, & Gebhard, 1953; McConaghy, 1987; Voeller, 1990). When a homosexual sexual orientation is defined as ever having had a same-sex erotic experience to the point of orgasm, the percentage of gay males is 5% to 10% (Fay, Turner, Klassen, & Gagnon, 1989; Rogers & Turner, 1991; Simon, 1989), and the percentage of lesbians is 1% to 3% (Simon, 1989). When having a more or less exclusive erotic preference for one's own sex is the focus of interest, the proportion of adults who are gay or lesbian is from 1% to 4% for males (Berrios, Hearst, & Perkins, 1992; Billy, Tanfer, Grady, & Klepinger, 1993; Diamond, 1993; Michael, Lauman, Gagnon, & Smith, 1988; Pool, 1993, p. 291; Rogers & Turner, 1991) and well under 1% for females (Gebhard, 1972; Michael et al., 1988).

Thus far, only one study has seriously attempted to address the question of whether these figures have changed appreciably over the years. It identified roughly comparable figures for males from 1970 to 1990. The study concluded that male homosexuality had remained essentially stable throughout this time period (Rogers & Turner, 1991).

While comparable survey data are limited, cross-cultural studies reveal similar findings on all three measures of homosexuality for both sexes as the aforementioned studies documented in the United States. This is the case for England (Wellings, Wadsworth, Johnson, & Bradshaw, 1990; Wilson, 1987), Australia (McConaghy, 1987; Ross, 1988), Germany (Hirschfeld, 1920), China (see Ruan & Bullough, 1992, p. 224), and Malaysia (Buhrich, Armstrong, & McConaghy, 1982). According to an extensive literature review by Diamond (1993), surveys in Denmark, Japan, the Netherlands, the Philippines, and Thailand also suggest that exclusive homosexuality is characteristic of about 5% of males and substantially less than that for females.

Overall, while occasional same-sex interests are fairly common, more or less exclusive lifelong same-sex preferences appear to characterize no more than 4% of all adults (Diamond, 1993). Throughout the world, same-sex behavior has been found to be at least twice as common among males as females (Gebhard, 1972; Kiernan, 1984, p. 263; Weinrich, 1987, p. 24), and more or less exclusive same-sex preferences may be as much as 10 times more common in males as in females (Kenrick, 1987, p. 23). It is not surprising, therefore, to find that most theories of homosexuality are primarily aimed toward explaining male homosexuality.

The prevalence of same-sex behavior in nonhumans varies, depending on the way in which homosexuality is defined and whether same-sex behavior in cages (where members of the same-sex exclusively cohabitate over long periods of time) is considered. For the present discussion, such instances of same-sex behavior are ignored. Also excluded from consideration are so-called pseudosexual acts, in which mounting and genital displays are part of the rituals used in several species for establishing and maintaining dominance (Ellis, 1993, p. 25).

Even with the aforementioned acts excluded, studies have found same-sex behavior to be fairly common in many species (see Denniston, 1980; Jezierski, Koziorowski, Goszcztnski, & Sieradzka, 1989; Nadler, 1990; Nadler & Phoenix, 1991). However, if the focus is only on long-term preferences for members of the same sex—rather than occasional sexual contacts, especially in the first year or two following puberty—the prevalence of homosexuality in most mammalian species is characteristic of only a small percentage of individuals.

There is at least one species in which the prevalence of almost exclusive homosexuality appears to rival the rates found in humans. Among domestic sheep, an estimated 9% of the rams exhibit almost exclusive same-sex preferences and an additional 23% exhibit bisexual preferences (Price, Katz, Wallach, & Zenchak, 1988; also see Katz, Price, Wallach, & Zenchak, 1988; Miller, 1990). Such males obviously are of little value to sheep breeders, thus they have been nicknamed "dud studs" (Miller, 1990). Two other species in which same-sex behavior has been observed at a fairly substantial level in both sexes are rhesus monkeys (Akers & Conway, 1979; Erwin & Maple, 1976; Michael, Wilson, & Zumpe, 1974) and pygmy chimpanzees (Kuroda, 1980; Thompson-Handler, Malenky, & Badrian, 1984).

Several researchers have expressed the view that the similarities between homosexuality in humans and other species may be more apparent than real (Dewsbury, 1984, p. 205; Feder, 1984; McGivern & Handa, 1994, p. 14; Mellen, 1981, p. 211). This view is difficult to defend or refute. Probably the only way it will ever be settled is if the exact causes of homosexuality in various species are found. Should the causes be the same across species, at that point it would be reasonable to argue that the behavior itself is indeed the same.

Scientists have proposed numerous causes for variations in sexual orientation. Although all theories pertain to humans, some researchers have attempted to test at least certain aspects of their proposals with other animals.

# SCIENTIFIC THEORIES OF HOMOSEXUALITY

Proposals by scientists to explain diversity in sexual orientation first began to appear near the end of the nineteenth century (Byne & Parsons, 1993, p. 228). Prior to that time, attempts to understand homosexuality were largely framed in religious terms. Drawing from a Biblical passage (Leviticus 18:22), Judeo-Christian tradition held that homosexuality was evil and a form of demonistic possession (Money, 1980, p. 59). Thus, the ultimate Western religious explanation for homosexuality has been in terms of evil supernatural forces.

Science is not able to test supernatural explanations. Therefore, scientific theories of homosexuality only identify and investigate natural (including social) causes of homosexuality.

The explanations to be reviewed will be called *theories,* even though some are so simple and straightforward as to be better categorized as *hypotheses* (see Ellis, 1994, p. 201).[3] Scientific theories of homosexuality can be grouped into two broad categories: environmental and biological. In turn, the numerous environmental theories can be subsumed under three headings: parent/child oriented, sexual interaction oriented, and gender role oriented. Thus far there are three biological theories: postpubertal hormonal, genetic, and perinatal hormonal. Each theory is described below.

## Parent/Child-Oriented Theories

### Psychoanalytic (Freudian) theory

Arguably, the first scientific explanations of homosexuality were proposed by Sigmund Freud (1905). He developed them in a very rudimentary form from several earlier proposals on the origin of homosexuality (Lewes, 1988). Freud theorized that people develop psychosexually through stages from infancy through adolescence, and he hypothesized that one of the psychosexual stages involves attraction to one's own sex. Freud contended that most people pass through this stage several years prior to puberty, but that "homosexuals" may either develop more slowly than normal or become "fixated" in the same-sex attraction stage. Although he did not dismiss hereditary factors, Freud thought that such a fixation was typically due to the presence of a domineering and overly protective mother and/or to the absence of a dominant, protective father. Focusing almost entirely on male homosexuality, most contemporary psychoanalytic explanations continue to emphasize the theme of a *romantic triad*—that is, an emotionally strong mother, a submissive or absent father, and the mother's favorite son (Bieber & Bieber, 1979; Socarides, 1968).

Some psychoanalytic explanations have also attributed homosexuality to seduction in early childhood by an older same-sex sibling, playmate, or adult, suggesting that this too could prematurely arrest psychosexual development (Cameron, 1963).

Research supporting psychoanalytic explanations primarily consists of evidence which indicates a greater number of unusually protective mothers and/or detached, unloving fathers among gay males relative to male and female heterosexuals (Bieber et al., 1962; Chang & Block, 1960; Saghir & Robins, 1973; Snortum, Gillespie, Marshall, & Mosberg, 1969; Thompson, Schwartz, McCandless, & Edwards, 1973; Van den Aardweg, 1984). As will be shown later, these parental characteristics could be reactions to the effeminate behavior of many "pre-gay" children, rather than causes of homosexuality.

### Inadequate parenting

During the middle of this century, several theorists asserted that homosexuality might result from several forms of inadequate parenting (Bakwin & Bakwin, 1953; Bene, 1965; Moore, 1945; Storr, 1964). These explanations shared elements with psychoanalytic perspectives but downplayed Freud's suggestion of a subconscious romantic triad pervading parent-child relationships. They shared with Freud the view that homosexuality represented an immature stage of psychosexual development but focused much more broadly than Freud did on intrafamily relationships.

These theorists hypothesized that psychosexual development can be prematurely arrested by many factors, including unhappy and broken homes, inadequate parenting, and inappropriate same-sex role models. Consistent with the theory, several studies have linked both male and female homosexuality to higher incidences of parental discord and divorce (reviewed by Coates, 1985).

## Sexual Interaction-Oriented Theories

### Sex segregation/heterosexual frustration theory

Noting that homosexuality seemed to be more prevalent in men than in women, Westermarck (1922) attributed the behavior in part to a shortage of eligible women (also see O'Kelly & Carney, 1986, p. 100). Conditions conducive to male homosexuality, therefore, could either be numeric shortages of women or excessive training of women in chastity, according to Westermarck.

Similarly, Gallup and Suarez (1983, p. 318) proposed that homosexuality often results from a particularly unpleasant heterosexual experience early in life. A survey among psychiatrists and other physicians in England revealed that over one half of respondents considered homosexuality largely due to a fear of heterosexual activity and/or unsuccessful heterosexual experiences (Bhugra, 1990). Given the popularity of this explanation, it is surprising that very little research has been done to test it.

At least one study called this explanation into question. Lesbians reported recalling no more traumatic experiences with men than was true of women who were heterosexual (Brannock & Chapman, 1990).

Regarding nonhuman animals, several experiments have been conducted in which male rats have been shocked every time they attempted to mate with a female. In one study, about one third of the males eventually exhibited same-sex behavior (Rasmussen, 1955), while in another study, none did (Hayward, 1957). In another experiment, male rats who had been shocked whenever they attempted to mate with a female only avoided doing so when they were in the training cage in which the shock had been inflicted. In all other enclosures, the males were just as likely to copulate with females as were males who had never been shocked (Zimbardo, 1958).

Studies among mammals have also assessed the effects of complete unisex rearing on choices of sex partners later in life. These studies showed that a lack of social experience with opposite-sex peers prior to the onset of puberty generally resulted in sexual ineptitude in adolescence and adulthood, especially for males (Dunlap, Zadina, & Gougis, 1978; Gerall, Hendricks, Johnson, & Bounds, 1967; Moore, 1985, p. 38; Price & Wallach, 1990). This ineptitude appears to be mainly due to few early life play opportunities with the opposite sex. Play provides mammals with experiences needed to learn (a) not to fear and, at the same time, not to frighten members of the opposite sex when in proximity to them; and (b) how to approach and coax conspecifics in ways that elicit cooperative responses, rather than withdrawal, or even attack, responses.

Despite their sexual ineptitude with members of the opposite sex, however, unisex-reared males became sexually aroused by the presence of females (Price & Wallach, 1990; Sackett, 1968). This suggested that a heterosexual orientation per se was not disrupted by unisex rearing, although the skills needed to express it were impaired.

Research with rhesus monkeys has found that female tendencies to mount and male tendencies to assume a receptive posture can be enhanced by manipulating the social environment. Specifically, unisex rearing of both male and female rhesus monkeys resulted in an unusually high rate of "playful" same-sex activities prior to puberty (Goldfoot, Wallen, Neff, McBrair, & Goy, 1984). When members of these unisex-reared monkeys were introduced into bisex enclosures shortly before puberty, most sexual overtures were directed toward same-sex, rather than opposite-sex, members. Over the next few years, however, heterosexual behavior gradually dominated, although to lesser degrees than in monkeys who had been reared in bisex conditions throughout childhood (D. A. Goldfoot, personal communication, May 1986).

Similar tendencies were reported for another monkey species. Three male stump-tailed macaques were reared together without contact with females for their first nine years of life. When finally allowed contact with other monkeys of both sexes, all three males preferred females as sex partners (Slob & Schenek, 1986).

In summary, experiments with nonhuman animals indicate that the probability of same-sex behavior can be enhanced by unisex rearing. Because exclusive same-sex rearing rarely occurs in humans, it is doubtful that this explains much homosexuality in humans.

## Imprinting theory

In the 1930s, researchers demonstrated a form of learning called *imprinting*. This concept principally referred to a tendency for newly hatched water fowl (e.g., ducklings and goslings) to develop an almost instantaneous emotional attachment to any moving object in their environment, and then to exhibit great distress when separated from the object (Gould, 1982, p. 50). Presumably, this completely automatic learned response evolved to insure that newly hatched ducklings and goslings maintain proximity to their mothers.

Subsequent to the discovery of imprinting, researchers suggested that similar learning processes might account for variations in sexual orientation (Kinsey, 1941; Smitt, 1952; Young, 1961). According to this theory, humans may have imprinting tendencies around the time of puberty, and possibly earlier, in terms of sexual attractions. Most of the time, opposite-sex members will be the object of the imprinting, but occasionally sexual bonds form with same-sex members. The nature of the experiences that cause same-sex imprinting was never explicated in these early proposals.

One possibility for the way in which an imprinting-like process could account for homosexuality was suggested more recently by Storms (1981; Wasserman & Storms, 1984). He reviewed evidence that gay males reach sexual maturity on average 6 to 12 months earlier than male heterosexuals. Based on these data, Storms theorized that early maturing males may be more likely than later maturers to experience sexual awakening at a time when they are spending most of their intimate moments with other males, rather than with females. As a result, early-maturing males are at an increased risk of cognitively associating their first intense sexual feelings with members of their own, rather than the opposite, sex.

One serious problem with this theory is that a sizable proportion of lesbians and gay men report being aware of their same-sex attractions long before reaching puberty (Savin-Williams, 1988, 1990).

## Sexual reinforcement theory

A popular perspective in psychology during the middle part of this century was behaviorism, a theory that focused more on the overt aspects of behavior than on internal cognitive motivations. This perspective gave rise to a learning theory of homosexuality that emphasized the reinforcing aspects of all sexual experiences (Acosta, 1975; Hacker, 1957; James, 1967; Kinsey, Reichert, Cauldwell, & Mozes, 1955). The sexual reinforcement theory held that same-sex preferences may come about from the reinforcing nature of one or more early same-sex sexual encounters that preceded opposite-sex sexual encounters.

Similarly, Gagnon and Simon (1973) maintained that sexual orientation could be explained in terms of varying schedules of rewards and punishments. Assuming that same-sex experiences are fairly common during childhood and early adolescence, Gagnon and Simon reasoned that to the degree these experiences were pleasurable, they would increase the probability of a homosexual orientation in adulthood.

# Sex Role-Oriented Theories

## Self-labeling theory

Without entirely discounting a genetic predisposition, East (1946) attributed homosexuality to confusion during the time an individual learns appropriate sex roles. East contended that to the degree a person's appearance or mannerisms resembled those of the opposite sex, the individual may gradually settle into a same-sex identity and lifestyle (also see Nasjleti, 1980). East's view was elaborated by Kagan (1964), who asserted that sexual orientation comes about as a result of self-labeling, which is reinforced by the impression of others about the appropriateness of someone's sex role behavior (also see Plummer, 1981).

More recently, Greenberg (1988) theorized that from early childhood all humans have the capacity to be sexually attracted to members of the same sex. He added that whether these feelings eventually lead to a lifelong same-sex identity depends on a complex array of social and cultural dynamics impinging on how people come to perceive themselves.

The strongest support for the self-labeling theory comes from evidence that gay males are much more likely than heterosexual males to exhibit effeminate behavior in childhood (Bailey, this volume; Bailey, Miller, & Wellerman, 1993; Green, 1985; Grellert, Newcomb, & Bentler, 1982; McConaghy et al., 1979; McConaghy & Silove, 1991; Money & Russo, 1979; Tuttle & Pillard, 1991; Whitam & Mathy, 1986; Zuger, 1984). Similar but less extreme tendencies toward tomboyism have been found among lesbians (Bailey, this volume; Bailey, Pillard, Neale, & Agyei, 1993; Blanchard & Freund, 1983; Grellert et al., 1982; Thompson et al. 1973; for partial replication see McConaghy & Silove, 1991).

## Inappropriate sex role training

Another social environmental explanation that focused attention outside the home was proposed by Kardiner (1963). He attributed male homosexuality to excessive societal demands on boys to be "masculine." Individuals who felt inadequate in complying with those demands were believed to sometimes seek refuge in female roles.

Storr (1964) essentially inverted Kardiner's theory. He asserted that homosexuality often resulted from exposure to inadequate sex role training or role models.

Most evidence linking sex role training and homosexuality is more consistent with Storr's than Kardiner's version. For example, one study found that mothers of boys who eventually become gay were unusually protective of them and encouraged them to exhibit that which would generally be considered feminine behavior (Coates, 1985). Also, the research cited earlier on the linkage between homosexuality and high rates of childhood effeminate behavior in boys and masculine behavior in girls supports Storr's version of the inappropriate sex role training theory.

Contrary to both versions of this theory, however, is evidence derived from studies of children reared by openly lesbian and gay couples. The rates of sex-atypical behavior and interests among these children do not differ from children reared by heterosexual parents (Green, 1978; Patterson, this volume).

# Biological Theories

## Postpubertal hormonal theory

The field of endocrinology (the study of hormones) emerged in the early decades of the twentieth century. This new scientific discipline led to the suggestion that sex hormones could be responsible for variations in sexual orientation (Forel, 1924; Hirschfeld, 1920). In particular, it was reasoned that gays and lesbians might have sex hormone levels that are more typical of the opposite sex than of their own sex. This proposal was carefully investigated, and support for it has been at best mixed. While some studies found slightly lower circulating testosterone levels among gay than heterosexual males, most found no significant differences (reviewed by Baucom, Paige, & Callahan, 1985; Meyer-Bahlburg, 1984; Tourney, 1980). Several other sex hormones and their metabolites have also been studied, again with equivocal results (Tourney, 1980).

At least one clinical experiment attempted to alter the sexual orientation of a group of gay males by injecting them with synthetic testosterone. No significant changes were observed in their orientation (Barahal, 1940; Gartrell, 1982).

Regarding females, the available evidence on testosterone as well as other sex hormones is also mixed. About one half of the studies have found no significant differences between lesbians and other women, while the other half have found significantly higher levels of testosterone in lesbians, although still far below the normal male range (reviewed by Dancey, 1990).

Overall, the evidence linking postpubertal sex hormones and homosexuality is at best only modestly encouraging (Savin-Williams, 1987; Tourney, 1980). If relationships exist, they are complex and may only apply to certain subgroups.

## The genetic theory (or hypothesis)

The possibility of genetic factors contributing to variations in sexual orientation was first investigated in the 1940s (e.g., Darke, 1948; Glass, DeVel, & Wright, 1940; Heston & Shields, 1968; Jensch, 1941; Lang, 1940; Witschi & Mengert, 1942). Basically, four types of studies have been undertaken to probe for genetic influences: pedigree (or general family) studies, twin studies, adoption studies, and studies designed to identify specific chromosomes or genes that may be linked to homosexuality. The results are briefly considered below.

**Pedigree studies.**     Studies that investigate traits "running in families" at unusually high rates are called *pedigree studies*. Although these studies obviously do not prove that genes are causing a particular trait, nevertheless, if a trait such as homosexuality is more prevalent in some families than in others, especially over several generations, this is at least consistent with a genetic hypothesis.

Over the years, several studies have indicated that homosexuality is more common in some families than in others (Dank, 1971; Pillard, Poumadere, & Carretta, 1982, 1986; Pillard & Weinrich, 1986). The latter of these studies reported that if one male in a family is gay, each of his brothers has about a 20% probability of being gay also, a much higher probability than is found in the general male population. Two more recent studies, however, found considerably lower tendencies for male homosexuality to run in families (Bailey & Pillard, 1991, p. 1089; Blanchard & Sheridan, 1992), although the rates were still about twice as high as those seen in the general male population.

Thus far, two pedigree studies have focused on lesbianism, both of which found that it tends to run in families (Bailey & Benishay, 1993; Pillard, 1988, p. 54). Regarding the question of whether lesbianism and male homosexuality are more heavily concentrated in the *same* families, some evidence is affirmative (Bailey & Bell, 1993; Pillard, 1988), while other evidence is somewhat equivocal (Bailey, Pillard, Neale, & Agyei, 1993).

**Twin studies.**    There are two main types of twins: identical twins, who share 100% of their genes in common, and fraternal twins, who on average share 50% of their genes in common (as is also the case for ordinary siblings). When twins are alike with respect to a trait, such as sexual orientation, researchers say they are *concordant*. Basically, the more a trait is influenced by genetics, the more the concordance for that trait should approach 100% for identical twins, and 50% or less for fraternal twins.[4]

Because twins are uncommon to begin with, and those in which at least one twin is lesbian or gay are rarer still, most of the studies have involved less than a dozen twin pairs (see Whitam, Diamond, & Martin, 1993). Two of these small studies have found little or no concordance for homosexuality in identical twins (Koch, 1965; Parker, 1964). Two large twin studies, however, found over 95% concordance for male homosexuality among identical twin pairs, as opposed to about 15% concordance for fraternal twins (Kallmann, 1952; Schlegel, 1962).

Since the mid-1980s, several new twin studies of homosexuality have been published. These studies found that if one male member of a twin pair is gay, the probability that his twin will also be gay or bisexual is between two and five times higher for identical twins than for fraternal twins (Bailey et al., 1993; Bailey & Pillard, 1991; Buhrich, Bailey, & Martin, 1991; Eckert, Bouchard, Bohlen, & Heston, 1986; King & McDonald, 1992; Whitam et al., 1993). However, none of these more recent studies have confirmed the near perfect concordance rates for identical twins reported by Kallmann and Schlegel.

One of the few recent studies to consider lesbianism in twins found 75% concordance for identical twins, although the sample size was small (Whitam et al., 1993). This study also compared females and males who had a gay male fraternal twin. For male twins, the rate of homosexuality was 27%; for female twins, 33%. These figures confirm an issue raised earlier: Male and female homosexuality tends to run in families.

Overall, the twin studies support the view that genetic factors contribute to homosexuality. Nevertheless, the failure of most studies to find anything close to 100% concordance in identical twins or close to 50% in fraternal twins suggests that nongenetic factors are also critical. Among the possibilities are social environmental factors considered in experiential theories previously reviewed. Prenatal environmental factors could also be involved. For example, because of their position in the womb, one twin member may have a superior placental connection to the mother's blood supply (Melnick, Myrianthopolos, & Christian, 1978). Supporting this is evidence that there can be significant differences in birth weights and postnatal rates of growth between identical twin pairs (Turner, 1994). Also, studies have shown that various genetically influenced twin characteristics, from major diseases to minor birthmarks and hair whorls, are substantially discordant among identical twins (Turner, 1994).

**Adoption studies.**    Research that can be particularly helpful in separating genetic influences from the effects of the home environment involve studying those who were adopted by nonrelatives at or near birth. Recently, an adoption study assessed the rates of homosexuality among biological and adopted brothers of gays. For the biological brothers of gay men, the rate of homosexuality was 9%, whereas among adopted brothers, the rate was 11% (Bailey & Pillard, 1991, p. 1089). While the sample sizes were small, this finding casts doubt on the genetic hypothesis (Byne & Parsons, 1993, p. 229).

**Studies designed to identify specific chromosomes and genes.**    A recent study conducted by a research team at the National Institute of Cancer found evidence that a gene located on the X chromosome was closely linked to male homosexuality (Hamer, Hu, S., Magnuson, Hu, N., & Pattatucci, 1993). Although the specific location of the gene is still being sought, the researchers were able to specify a fairly small region of the X chromosome by carefully noting family patterns in transmission over several generations. Besides being the first study to link a specific chromosome region to homosexuality, this study is especially fascinating because of the chromosome involved and the way in which it is transmitted. Males have only one X chromosome, which they receive from their mothers, to complement the Y chromosome from their fathers. Therefore, to the degree that a gene on the X chromosome is causing homosexuality, it should be transmitted primarily through the mother rather than the father (see Nimmons, 1994, p. 70; Pool, 1993, p. 291). Other genetic studies of homosexuality are more complicated and will be discussed in the following chapter.

At the present time, evidence suggests that genetic factors contribute to homosexuality. However, this evidence is not unanimous (Baron, 1993; Byne, 1994, p. 54). In succeeding years, it should be especially interesting to note the results of replication attempts of the adoption study, which did not support a genetic hypothesis, and the X-chromosome study, which did.

## Perinatal hormonal theory

In the 1960s, a new type of hormonal theory was proposed (Dorner, Docker, & Moustafa, 1968; Loraine, Ismail, Adamopoulos, & Dove, 1970; Saba, Salvadorini, Galeone, & Luisi, 1973). Rather than contending that the postpubertal hormone levels of lesbians and gays might be more typical of the opposite sex than of the same sex, this theory focused on hormone levels during fetal development, or within the first few months after birth, the *perinatal period*.

The theory proposes that during certain critical periods in perinatal development, the brain is irreversibly *sexed* (i.e., sexually differentiated) by the presence of sex hormones. If the hormones present during a particular critical period (sometimes lasting only a few days) are in the range more typical of the opposite sex than of an individual's own sex, a same-sex preference later in life is probable.

Much of the impetus for this theory was derived from research with rodents as well as other species. These studies demonstrated that animals could be made to exhibit same-sex behavior in adulthood by manipulating sex hormones perinatally (Beach & Kuehn, 1970; Levine, 1966; Phoenix, Goy, Gerall, & Young, 1959; Short, 1979; Ward, 1972a, 1972b; Ward & Renz, 1972; Young, 1961). A variety of techniques for altering perinatal sex hormones was developed. The earliest usually involved castrating male rat pups at birth (Harris, 1964). During the first week after birth, the rodent brain is still being sexed. As is discussed in chapter 2, humans may have a similar critical period.

In other experiments, expectant mother guinea pigs were injected with testosterone, much of which passes through the placental barrier and enters the blood system of her fetuses (Phoenix et al., 1959). This had little effect on the behavior of male offspring, but increased mounting attempts by female offspring when they reached puberty and lowered their tendencies to present their hindquarters to males (called the *lordosis response*).

Other researchers injected pregnant females with drugs that prevent the body from producing testosterone. These drugs also cross the placental barrier. The male offspring of these mothers often exhibited a lordosis response to other males and showed little interest in mounting females (Neumann, Elger, & von Berswordt-Wallrabe, 1967).

In most mammals, the genitals are sexually differentiated during the first half of gestation, whereas the brain is not sexed until the latter half of gestation, allowing for some "fine-tuning" following birth. If a male fetus is not exposed to sufficient amounts of testosterone or some closely related hormones in the latter half of gestation or a few days following birth, his brain fails to be masculinized. Later in life, his sexual behavior will resemble that of a female.

The opposite may occur in females. If a female fetus is exposed to high levels of testosterone in the latter half of gestation, her brain will function as a male brain. Following puberty, one manifestation of this male brain functioning will be a preference for female sex partners.

Several scientists have speculated that similar events may occur "naturally" in humans (reviewed by Ellis & Ames, 1987). Because of genetics or biochemical disturbances caused by drugs taken by women during fetal development, the brains of some human males may receive insufficient exposure to testosterone or chemically related hormones. Similarly, the brains of some human females may receive unusually high amounts of testosterone or chemically related hormones, resulting in masculine behavior later in life.

The perinatal hormone theory is unique in the degree to which it rests on experimental research with nonhuman animals. As further discussed in chapter 2, increasingly sophisticated versions of this theory have shown considerable promise in explaining some of the variation in human sexual orientation.

## WHAT DO MOST PEOPLE BELIEVE?

If the "(wo)man on the street" were asked what causes homosexuality, what would she or he say? In the largest survey conducted to date on this topic, only 30% of over 3,000 United States adults attributed homosexuality to being "born that way" (Levitt, Klassen, & Albert, 1974, p. 139). The remainder attributed homosexuality to experiences, such as "how their parents raised them" and the lure from older "homosexuals" (Levitt et al., 1974, p. 139). For example, 43% of Americans responding to this 1970 survey agreed that "young homosexuals became that way because of older homosexuals" (Klassen, Williams, & Levitt, 1989).

Subsequent surveys have found that considerably fewer than 30% of U.S. adults attribute homosexuality to biological factors. Specifically, nationwide surveys conducted in 1977 and 1982 by Gallup International reported 12% and 17% of the populace, respectively, attribute homosexuality to "being born that way" (Schneider & Lewis, 1984, p. 19). In 1983, another nationwide survey was conducted by the *Los Angeles Times*. Sixteen percent believed that homosexuality is biological rather than learned (Schneider & Lewis, 1984). The apparent drop in the 30% of Americans in 1970 who believed that homosexuality is due to biological factors is puzzling. Plausible explanations include subtle differences in the way questions were worded and in the samples selected.

Recently, a survey was conducted in four diverse regions of the world concerning causes of homosexuality. In all samples, only a minority of people thought gays and lesbians were born that way. The highest percentage (44%) attributing homosexuality to biology was in the Philippines. Otherwise, those favoring biology were 29% in Sweden, 27% in Arizona, and 15% in Hawaii (Ernulf, Innala, & Whitam, 1989).

These percentages are in the same range as the opinions offered by those in the scientific community. Two relevant surveys have recently been published. A study of sociologists asked each respondent to estimate the percentage of variation in homosexuality that they felt was attributable to biology as opposed to the environment. With wide-ranging disagreement, the average sociologist attributed 27% of same-sex tendencies to biology; the rest was attributed to the environment (Sanderson & Ellis, 1992).

A study of English physicians reported that 23% of general practitioners attributed homosexuality to biology; only 13% of psychiatrists did so (Bhugra, 1990). Thus, the scientific community is in agreement with the "common (wo)man;" both attribute homosexuality primarily to social experiences rather than to biology (Leo, 1979, p. 48).

This same survey also asked gay men what they thought caused homosexuality. Two groups were sampled: members of an association of gay physicians and gay men at large. Of those who offered an opinion, 36% of the gay physicians believed gay men are born that way, and 78% of gays in general thought so (Bhugra, 1988). Although a single survey is far from conclusive, there is a much greater tendency for gay men to attribute their orientation to biology than is true of either the scientific community or the general public.

Beliefs about the causes of homosexuality are associated with tolerance of gay and lesbian lifestyles. DeCecco (1987, p. 114) argued that believing biology plays an important part in determining sexual orientation fosters intolerance of homosexuality. Ironically, however, the opposite appears to be true. Five studies have found that those who believe lesbians and gay men are "born that way" were *more* tolerant and accepting of them than people who attributed homosexuality to learning or "free will" (Aguero, Bloch, & Byrne, 1984; Ernulf et al., 1989; Schmalz, 1993; Schneider & Lewis, 1984; Whitley & Bernard, 1990).

# Summary

Homosexuality has existed throughout history in virtually all societies. Estimates of its prevalence depend on the way in which the concept is defined. If homosexuality is considered in terms of an almost exclusive preference for members of the same sex, surveys in various countries indicate that 2% to 5% of males are gay and less than 1% of females are lesbian. Thus, in the United States alone there are at least 5 million gay males and 1 million lesbians, or there will be once they reach adulthood. If homosexuality is defined in terms of one ever having sexual attractions for someone of the same sex, as many as one third of all males and 15% of all females would be classified as gay or lesbian. Although these percentages appear to be fairly universal across societies and over time, there is clearly a need for more cross-cultural research in this regard.

Over the past century, considerable scientific research and theorizing have been aimed toward identifying the causes of homosexuality and of sexual orientation in general. This chapter reviewed the various scientific theories and the evidence bearing on the former. These theories can be subsumed under two broad categories: social learning (or experiential) and biological.

The social learning theories were grouped into the following three categories: those focused on parent-child relationships, early sexual experiences, and learning of sex roles.

The two *parent/child-oriented theories* are the psychoanalytic (Freudian) theory and the more general inadequate parenting theory. The first of these attributes homosexuality to childhood experiences in which parents disrupt a child's natural progression through stages of psychosexual maturation. The child is thought to be arrested during a developmental stage in which same-sex members become sexually attractive. Inadequate parenting theory resembles Freud's theory except that it places less emphasis on specific stages of psychosexual maturation and proposes that children sometimes use homosexuality as a refuge from poor parent-child relationships early in life.

The *sexual interaction-oriented theories* consist of sex segregation/heterosexual frustration theory, imprinting theory, and sexual reinforcement theory.

Sex segregation/heterosexual frustration theory maintains that reduced social interaction between the sexes prior to puberty and reduced sexual interaction between them following puberty serve to increase the probability of homosexuality in adolescence and adulthood.

According to imprinting theory, strong emotional bonds sometimes form between members of the same sex, and these bonds can lead to long-term same-sex preferences.

Sexual reinforcement theory contends that same-sex encounters increase the chances of developing a same-sex identity to the degree that the contacts are pleasurable and occur prior to the time an individual has pleasurable opposite-sex encounters.

*Sex role-oriented theories* include self-labeling theory and inappropriate sex role training theory. Each of these theories purports that lesbians and gays acquire a self-concept or learn sex roles that are socially inappropriate for their sex.

The self-labeling theory argues that children whose appearance and mannerisms resemble those of the opposite sex may develop confusion over their sexual identity, and this confusion increases their chances of being sexually attracted to members of their own sex.

Inappropriate sex role training theory attributes homosexuality to the way people are taught to think and behave as males or females in a particular culture. If the training is inadequate or confusing, the probability of same-sex preferences is increased.

The three *biological explanations* are the postpubertal hormone theory, the genetic theory, and the perinatal hormone theory.

The postpubertal hormone theory proposes that a sex hormone imbalance exists in gays and lesbians following the onset of puberty. The evidence is complex and contradictory.

Regarding the genetic hypothesis, the evidence is fairly supportive. Nevertheless, the connection between genes and sexual orientation is complex and may involve several genes expressing themselves only within certain environmental contexts. For example, genes may operate perinatally to affect the timing of the release of various hormones that help to sexually differentiate the brain.

The perinatal hormone theory contends that the level of sex hormones (especially testosterone) during and shortly after fetal development permanently sexes the brain. Normally the brain is sexed in ways that complement the sexing of the genitals. When this fails to occur, an individual who has the outward appearance of one sex will have the brain of the opposite sex. Assuming that the brain controls sexual behavior, such an individual will prefer same-sex members, rather than opposite-sex members, as sex partners.

Much of the support for the perinatal hormone theory has come from experiments with laboratory animals. Whether these experiments are relevant animal models for human sexual orientation, however, remains a point of contention. This is further discussed in chapter 2.

Of course, *there is no need to assume that only one theory of homosexuality is correct.* Several theories may be tapping different veins leading to the same outcome. Scientists are continuing to refine and test their theories.

## ▼    ENDNOTES    ▼

1. Gratitude is extended to Drs. Michael Bailey, Milton Diamond, Craig Kinsley, and Frederick Whitam and Mr. Jeff Hall for commenting on drafts of this and the subsequent chapter.

2. Note that throughout this chapter, the term *homosexuality* will include *bisexuality,* unless they are separately specified.

3. For other summaries of scientific theories of sexual orientation, see Ellis and Ames (1987), Ruse (1988), Savin-Williams (1988), Storms (1980), and West (1967).

4. This assumes that there are no difficulties in measuring the trait or in determining whether twin pairs are in fact identical versus fraternal. The reason genetically determined traits can sometimes be less than 50% concordant for fraternal twins involves recessive genes only being expressed when both genes for a trait are present at a particular location.

▼   **REFERENCES**   ▼

Acosta, F. (1975). Etiology and treatment of homosexuality: A review. *Archives of Sexual Behavior, 4,* 9–29.

Aguero, J., Bloch, L., & Byrne, D. (Eds.). (1984). *The relationships among sexual beliefs, attitudes, experience and homophobia.* New York: Haworth.

Akers, J. S., & Conway, C. H. (1979). Female homosexual behavior in *Macaca mulatta. Archives of Sexual Behavior, 8,* 63–80.

Bailey, J. M., & Bell, A. P. (1993). Familiality of female and male homosexuality. *Behavior Genetics, 23,* 313–322.

Bailey, J. M., & Benishay, D. S. (1993). Familial aggregation of female sexual orientation. *American Journal of Psychiatry, 150,* 272–277.

Bailey, J. M., Miller, J. S., & Wellerman, L. (1993). Maternally rated childhood gender nonconformity in homosexuals and heterosexuals. *Archives of Sexual Behavior, 22,* 461–469.

Bailey, J. M., & Pillard, R. C. (1991). A genetic study of male sexual orientation. *Archives of General Psychiatry, 48,* 1089–1096.

Bailey, J. M., Pillard, R. C., Neale, M. C., & Agyei, Y. (1993). Heritable factors influence sexual orientation in women. *Archives of General Psychiatry, 50,* 217–223.

Bakwin, H., & Bakwin, R. M. (1953). Homosexual behavior in children. *Journal of Pediatrics, 43,* 108–111.

Barahal, H. S. (1940). Testosterone in psychotic male homosexuals. *Psychiatric Quarterly, 14,* 319–330.

Baron, M. (1993). Genetics and human sexual orientation. *Biological Psychiatry, 33,* 759–761.

Baucom, D. H., Paige, B. K., & Callahan, S. (1985). Relation between testosterone concentrations, sex role identity, and personality among females. *Journal of Personality and Social Psychology, 48,* 1218–1226.

Beach, F. A., & Kuehn, R. E. (1970). Coital behavior in dogs. X. Effects of androgenic stimulation during development of female mating responses in females and males. *Hormones and Behavior, 1,* 347–367.

Bene, E. (1965). On the genesis of male homosexuality: An attempt at clarifying the role of the parents. *British Journal of Psychiatry, 111,* 803–813.

Berrios, D. C., Hearst, N., & Perkins, L. L. (1992). Antibody testing in young, urban adults. *Archives of Internal Medicine, 152,* 397–402.

Bhugra, D. (1988). Homosexuals' attitudes to male homosexuality—a survey. *Sexual and Marital Therapy, 3,* 197–204.

Bhugra, D. (1990). Doctors' attitudes to male homosexuality: A survey. *Sexual and Marital Therapy, 5,* 167–174.

Bieber, I., & Bieber, T. B. (1979). Male homosexuality. *Canadian Journal of Psychiatry, 24,* 409–421.

Bieber, I., Dian, H. J., Drellich, M. G., Dince, P. R., Grand, H. G., Gundlach, R. H., Kremer, M. W., Rifkin, A. H., Wilbur, C. B., & Bieber, T. B. (1962). *Homosexuality: A psychoanalytic study.* New York: Basic Books.

Billy, J. O., Tanfer, K., Grady, W. R., & Klepinger, D. H. (1993). The sexual behavior of men in the United States. *Family Planning Perspective, 25,* 52–60.

Blanchard, R., & Freund, K. (1983). Measuring masculine gender identity in females. *Journal of Consulting and Clinical Psychology, 51,* 205–214.

Blanchard, R., McConkey, J. G., & Steiner, B. W. (1983). Measuring physical aggressiveness in heterosexual, homosexual, and transsexual males. *Archives of Sexual Behavior, 12,* 511–524.

Blanchard, R., & Sheridan, P. M. (1992). Proportion of unmarried siblings of homosexual and non-homosexual gender-dysphoric patients. *Canadian Journal of Psychiatry, 37,* 163–167.

Brannock, J. C., & Chapman, B. E. (1990). Negative sexual experiences with men among heterosexual women and lesbians. *Journal of Homosexuality, 19,* 105–110.

Buhrich, N., Armstrong, M. S., & McConaghy, N. (1982). Bisexual feelings and opposite-sex behavior in male Malaysian medical students. *Archives of Sexual Behavior, 11,* 387–393.

Buhrich, N., Bailey, J. M., & Martin, N. G. (1991). Sexual orientation, sexual identity, and sex dimorphic behavior. *Behavioral Genetics, 21,* 75–96.

Byne, W. (1994, May). The biological evidence challenged. *Scientific American, 270,* 50–55.

Byne, W., & Parsons, B. (1993). Human sexual orientation: The biological theories reappraised. *Archives of General Psychiatry, 50,* 228–239.

Cameron, N. (1963). *Development and psychopathology.* Boston: Houghton-Mifflin.

Chang, J., & Block, J. A. (1960). A study of identification in male homosexuals. *Journal of Consulting Psychology, 24,* 307–310.

Coates, S. (1985). Extreme boyhood femininity: Overview and new research findings. In Z. DeFrier, R. C. Friedman, & R. Corn (Eds.), *Sexuality: New perspectives* (pp. 101–124). Westport, CT: Greenwood Press.

Dancey, C. P. (1990). Sexual orientation in women: An investigation of hormonal and personality variables. *Biological Psychology, 30,* 251–264.

Dank, B. M. (1971). Coming out in the gay world. *Psychiatry, 34,* 180–197.

Darke, R. A. (1948). Heredity as an etiological factor in homosexuality. *Journal of Nervous and Mental Disease, 107,* 251–258.

DeCecco, J. P. (1987). Homosexuality's brief recovery: From sickness to health and back again. *The Journal of Sex Research, 23,* 106–129.

Denniston, R. H. (1980). Ambisexuality in animals. In J. Marmor (Ed.), *Homosexual behavior* (pp. 25–40). New York: Basic Books.

Dewsbury, D. A. (1984). *Comparative psychology in the twentieth century.* Stroudsburg, PA: Hutchinson Ross.

Diamond, M. (1993). Homosexuality and bisexuality in different populations. *Archives of Sexual Behavior, 22,* 291–310.

Dorner, G., Docker, F., & Moustafa, S. (1968). Homosexuality in female rats following testosterone implantation in the anterior hypothalamus. *Journal of Reproduction and Sterility, 17,* 173–175.

Dunlap, J. L., Zadina, J. E., & Gougis, G. (1978). Prenatal stress interacts with prepubertal social isolation to reduce male copulatory behavior. *Physiology and Behavior, 21,* 873–875.

East, W. N. (1946). Sexual offenders. *Journal of Nervous and Mental Disease, 103,* 626–666.

Eckert, E. D., Bouchard, T. J., Bohlen, J., & Heston, L. L. (1986). Homosexuality in monozygotic twins reared apart. *British Journal of Psychiatry, 148,* 421–425.

Ellis, L. (1993). Operationally defining social stratification in human and nonhuman animals. In L. Ellis (Ed.), *Social stratification and socio-economic inequality, Volume 1: A comparative biosocial analysis* (pp. 15–35). Westport, CT: Praeger.

Ellis, L. (1994). *Research methods in the social sciences* (1st ed.). Dubuque, IA: Brown & Benchmark.

Ellis, L., & Ames, M. A. (1987). Neurohormonal functioning and sexual orientation: A theory of homosexuality-heterosexuality. *Psychological Bulletin, 101,* 233–258.

Ernulf, K. E., Innala, S. M., & Whitam, F. L. (1989). Biological explanation, psychological explanation, and tolerance of homosexuals: A cross-national analysis of beliefs and attitudes. *Psychological Reports, 65,* 1003–1010.

Erwin, J., & Maple, T. (1976). Ambisexual behavior with male-male anal penetration in male rhesus monkeys. *Archives of Sexual Behavior, 5,* 9–14.

Fay, R. E., Turner, C. F., Klassen, A. D., & Gagnon, J. H. (1989). Prevalence and patterns of same-gender sexual contact among men. *Science, 243,* 338–348.

Feder, H. H. (1984). Hormones and sexual behavior. *Annual Review of Psychology, 35,* 165–200.

Forel, A. (1924). *The sexual question.* New York: Physicians & Surgeons.

Freud, S. (1905). *Drei Abhandlungen zur Sexualtheorie* [Three essays on the theory of sexuality]. Leipzig, Germany: F. Deuticke.

Gagnon, J., & Simon, W. (1973). *Sexual conduct.* Chicago: Aldine.

Gallup, G. G., Jr., & Suarez, S. D. (1983). Homosexuality as a by-product of selection for optimal heterosexual strategies. *Perspectives in Biology and Medicine, 26,* 315–319.

Gartrell, N. K. (1982). Hormones and homosexuality. In W. Paul, J. D. Weinrich, J. C. Gonsiorek, & M. E. Hotvedt (Eds.), *Homosexuality: Social, psychological, and biological issues* (pp. 169–182). Beverly Hills: Sage.

Gebhard, P. H. (1972). *Incidence of overt homosexuality in the United States and Western Europe.* Washington, DC: U.S. Government Printing Office (HSM No. 72-9116).

Gerall, A. A., Hendricks, S. E., Johnson, L. L., & Bounds, T. N. (1967). Effects of early castration on male rats' adult sexual behavior. *Journal of Comparative and Physiological Psychology, 64,* 202–212.

Glass, J., DeVel, H. J., & Wright, C. A. (1940). Sex hormone studies in male homosexuality. *Endocrinology, 26,* 590–594.

Goldfoot, D. A., Wallen, K., Neff, D. A., McBrair, M. C., & Goy, R. W. (1984). Social influences on the display of sexually dimorphic behavior in rhesus monkeys: Isosexual rearing. *Archives of Sexual Behavior, 13,* 395–402.

Gould, J. L. (1982). *Ethology: The mechanisms and evolution of behavior.* New York: Norton.

Green, R. (1978). Sexual identity of 37 children raised by homosexual or transsexual parents. *American Journal of Psychiatry, 135,* 692–697.

Green, R. (1985). Gender identity in childhood and later sexual orientation: Follow-up of 78 males. *American Journal of Psychiatry, 142,* 339–341.

Greenberg, D. (1988). *The construction of homosexuality.* Chicago: University of Chicago Press.

Grellert, E. A., Newcomb, M. D., & Bentler, P. M. (1982). Childhood play activities of male and female homosexuals and heterosexuals. *Archives of Sexual Behavior, 11,* 451–479.

Hacker, H. M. (1957). The new burdens of masculinity. *Marriage and Family Living, 19,* 227–233.

Hamer, D. H., Hu, S., Magnuson, V. L., Hu, N., & Pattatucci, A. M. L. (1993). A linkage between DNA markers on the X chromosome and male sexual orientation. *Science, 261,* 321–327.

Harris, G. W. (1964). Sex hormones, brain development and brain function. *Endocrinology, 75,* 627–648.

Hayward, S. C. (1957). Modification of sexual behavior of the male albino rat. *Journal of Comparative and Physiological Psychology, 50,* 70–73.

Heston, L. L., & Shields, J. (1968). Homosexuality in twins: A family study and a register study. *Archives of Sexual Behavior, 18,* 149–160.

Hirschfeld, M. (1920). *Die Homosexualitat des Mannes und des Weibes.* [Homosexuality in men and women]. Berlin: Marcus.

James, B. (1967). Learning theory and homosexuality. *New Zealand Medical Journal, 66,* 748–751.

Jensch, K. (1941). Zur Genealogie der Homosexualitat. [Concerning the causes of homosexuality]. *Archive fur Psychiatrie und Nervenkrankheiten, 112,* 527–540.

Jezierski, T. A., Koziorowski, M., Goszcztnski, J., & Sieradzka, I. (1989). Homosexual and social behaviours of young bulls of different geno- and pheno-types and plasma concentrations of some hormones. *Applied Animal Behaviour Science, 24,* 101–113.

Kagan, J. (1964). Acquisition and significance of sex typing and sex role identity. In M. L. Hoffman & L. W. Hoffman (Eds.), *Review of child development research* (pp. 137–167). New York: Sage.

Kallmann, F. J. (1952). Comparative twin study on the genetic aspects of male homosexuality. *Journal of Nervous and Mental Disorders, 115,* 283–298.

Kardiner, A. (1963). The flight from masculinity. In H. M. Ruitenbeek (Ed.), *The problem of homosexuality in modern society* (pp. 17–39). New York: Dutton.

Katz, L. S., Price, E. O., Wallach, S. J., & Zenchak, J. J. (1988). Sexual performance of males reared with or without females after weaning. *Journal of Animal Science, 66,* 1166–1173.

Kenrick, D. T. (1987). Gender, genes, and the social environment. In P. Shaver & C. Hendrick (Eds.), *Sex and gender* (pp. 14–43). Newbury Park, CA: Sage.

Kiernan, J. G. (1984). Perverted sexual instinct. *Chicago Medical Journal and Examiner, 48,* 263–265.

King, M., & McDonald, E. (1992). Homosexuals who are twins: A study of 46 probands. *British Journal of Psychiatry, 160,* 407–409.

Kinsey, A. C. (1941). Homosexuality. *Clinical Endocrinology, 1,* 424–428.

Kinsey, A. C., Pomeroy, W. B., & Martin, C. E. (1948). *Sexual behavior in the human male.* Philadelphia: W. B. Saunders.

Kinsey, A. C., Pomeroy, W. B., Martin, C. E., & Gebhard, P. H. (1953). *Sexual behavior in the human female.* Philadelphia: W. B. Saunders.

Kinsey, A. C., Reichert, P., Cauldwell, D. O., & Mozes, E. B. (1955). The causes of homosexuality: A symposium. *Sexology, 21,* 558–562.

Klassen, A. D., Williams, C. J., & Levitt, E. E. (1989). *Sex and morality in the U.S.* Middletown, CT: Wesleyan University Press.

Koch, G. (1965). Die Bedeutung genetischer faktoren fur das menschliche verhalten. *Arztlich Proxis, 17,* 839–846.

Kuroda, S. (1980). Social behavior of the pygmy chimpanzees. *Primates, 21,* 181–197.

Lang, T. (1940). Studies on the genetic determination of homosexuality. *Journal of Nervous and Mental Disease, 92,* 55–64.

Leo, J. (1979, January 8). Homosexuality: Tolerance vs. approval. *Time,* pp. 48–49, 51.

Levine, S. (1966, April). Sex differences in the brain. *Scientific American, 214,* 84–90.

Levitt, E. E., Klassen, J., & Albert, D. (1974). Public attitudes towards homosexuality: Part of the 1970 national survey by the Institute for Sex Research. *Journal of Homosexuality, 1,* 129–142.

Lewes, K. (1988). *The psychoanalytic theory of male homosexuality.* New York: Simon & Schuster.

Loraine, J. A., Ismail, A. A., Adamopoulos, A. A., & Dove, G. A. (1970). Endocrine function in male and female homosexuals. *British Medical Journal, 4,* 406–409.

Martin, A. D. (1982). The minority question. *et cetera, 39,* 22–42.

McConaghy, N. (1987). Heterosexuality/homosexuality: Dichotomy or continuum. *Archives of Sexual Behavior, 16,* 411–424.

McConaghy, N., Armstrong, M. S., Birrell, P. C., & Buhrich, N. (1979). The incidence of bisexual feelings and opposite sex behavior in medical students. *Journal of Nervous and Mental Disease, 167,* 685–688.

McConaghy, N., & Silove, D. (1991). Opposite sex behaviours correlate with degree of homosexual feelings in the predominantly heterosexual. *Australian and New Zealand Journal of Psychiatry, 25,* 1–7.

McGivern, R. F., & Handa, R. J. (1994). *Prenatal exposure to drugs of abuse: Methodological considerations and effects on sexual differentiation.* Bethesda, MD: National Institute on Drug Abuse.

Mellen, S. L. W. (1981). *The evolution of love.* San Francisco: W. H. Freeman.

Melnick, M., Myrianthopolos, N. C., & Christian, J. C. (1978). The effects of chorion on variation in I.Q. in the NCPP twin population. *American Journal of Human Genetics, 30,* 425–433.

Meyer-Bahlburg, H. F. (1984). Psychoendocrine research on sexual orientation and future options. *Progressive Brain Research, 61,* 375–398.

Michael, R. P., Wilson, M. L., & Zumpe, D. (1974). The bisexual behavior of female rhesus monkeys. In R. Friedman, R. Richard, & T. van de Velde (Eds.), *Sex differences in behavior* (pp. 399–412). New York: Wiley.

Michael, R. T., Lauman, E. O., Gagnon, J. H., & Smith, T. W. (1988). Number of sex partners and potential risk of sexual exposure to human immunodeficiency virus. *Morbidity Morality Weekly Report, 37,* 565–567.

Miller, K. (1990). Is your ram a stud or dud? *National Wool Grower, 3,* 28–30.

Money, J. (1980). Genetic and chromosomal aspects of homosexual etiology. In J. Marmor (Ed.), *Homosexual behavior* (pp. 60–72). New York: Basic Books.

Money, J. (1990). Androgyne becomes bisexual in sexological theory: Plato to Freud and neuroscience. *Journal of the American Academy of Psychoanalysis, 18,* 392–413.

Money, J., & Russo, A. J. (1979). Homosexual outcome of discordant gender identity/role in childhood. *Journal of Pediatric Psychology, 4,* 29–41.

Moore, C. L. (1985). Another psychobiological view of sexual differentiation. *Developmental Review, 5,* 18–55.

Moore, T. V. (1945). The pathogenesis and treatment of homosexual disorders: A digest of some pertinent evidence. *Journal of Personality, 14,* 47–83.

Nadler, R. D. (1990). Homosexual behavior in nonhuman primates. In D. P. McWhirter, S. A. Sanders, & J. M. Reinisch (Eds.), *Homosexuality/heterosexuality: Concepts of sexual orientation* (pp. 138–170). New York: Oxford University Press.

Nadler, R. D., & Phoenix, C. H. (1991). Male sexual behavior: Monkeys, men and apes. In J. D. Loy & C. B. Peters (Eds.), *Understanding behavior: What primate studies tell us about human behavior* (pp. 152–189). New York: Oxford University Press.

Nasjleti, M. (1980). Suffering in silence: The male incest victim. *Child Welfare, 59,* 269–275.

Neumann, F., Elger, W., & Von Berswordt-Wallrabe, R. (1967). Intersexualitat mannlicher feten und hemmung androgenabhangiger funktionen bei erwachsenen tieren durch testosteron blocker. *Deutsche Medizinische Worhenschrift, 92,* 360–366.

Nimmons, D. (1994, March). Sex and the brain. *Discover,* pp. 64–71.

O'Kelly, C. G., & Carney, L. S. (1986). *Women and men in society* (2nd ed.). Belmont, CA: Wadsworth.

Parker, N. (1964). Homosexuality in twins: A report on three discordant pairs. *British Journal of Psychiatry, 110,* 489–495.

Phoenix, C. H., Goy, R. W., Gerall, A. A., & Young, W. C. (1959). Organizing action of prenatally administered testosterone propionate on the tissues mediating mating behavior in the female guinea pig. *Endocrinology, 65,* 369–382.

Pillard, R. C. (1988). Sexual orientation and mental disorder. *Psychiatric Annals, 18,* 52–56.

Pillard, R. C., Poumadere, J. I., & Carretta, R. A. (1982). A family study of sexual orientation. *Archives of Sexual Behavior, 11,* 511–520.

Pillard, R. C., Poumadere, J. I., & Carretta, R. A. (1986). Evidence of familial nature of male homosexuality. *Archives of General Psychiatry, 43,* 808–812.

Pillard, R. C., & Weinrich, J. D. (1986). Evidence of the familial nature of male homosexuality. *Archives of General Psychiatry, 43,* 808–812.

Plummer, K. (1981). *The making of the modern homosexual.* London: Hutchinson.

Pool, R. (1993). Evidence of homosexuality gene. *Science, 261,* 291–292.

Price, E. O., Katz, L. S., Wallach, S. J., & Zenchak, J. J. (1988). The relationship of male-male mounting to the sexual preferences of young rams. *Applied Animal Behaviour Science, 21,* 347–355.

Price, E. O., & Wallach, S. J. (1990). Sexual orientation in women: An investigation of hormonal and personality variables. *Biological Psychology, 30,* 251–264.

Rasmussen, E. W. (1955). Experimental homosexual behavior in male albino rats. *Acta Psychologica, 11,* 303–334.

Riess, B. F., & Safer, J. M. (1979). Homosexuality in females and males. In E. S. Gomberg & V. Franks (Eds.), *Gender and disordered behavior: Sex differences in psychopathology* (pp. 257–300). New York: Brunner/Mazel.

Rogers, S. M., & Turner, C. F. (1991). Male-male sexual contact in the U.S.A.: Findings from five sample surveys, 1970–1990. *The Journal of Sex Research, 28,* 491–519.

Ross, M. W. (1988). Prevalence of risk factors for AIDS infection in the Australian population. *Medical Journal of Australia, 149,* 362–365.

Ruan, F. F., & Bullough, V. L. (1992). Lesbianism in China. *Archives of Sexual Behavior, 21,* 217–226.

Ruse, M. (1988). *Homosexuality: A philosophical inquiry.* Oxford, England: Basil Blackwell.

Saba, P., Salvadorini, F., Galeone, F., & Luisi, M. (1973). Hormonal findings in male homosexuals. *IRCS Medical Science: Psychology and Psychiatry, 3,* 15.

Sachser, N., & Hendrichs, H. (1982). A longitudinal study on the social structure and its dynamics in a group of guinea pigs (*Cavia aperea f. porcellus*). *Saugetierkundliche Mitteilungen, 30,* 227–240.

Sackett, G. P. (1968). Abnormal behavior in laboratory-reared rhesus monkeys. In M. W. Fox (Ed.), *Abnormal behavior in animals* (pp. 293–331). Philadelphia: Saunders.

Saghir, M. T., & Robins, E. (1973). *Male and female homosexuality: A comprehensive investigation.* Baltimore: Williams & Wilkins.

Sanderson, S. K., & Ellis, L. (1992). Theoretical and political perspectives of American sociologists in the 1990s. *American Sociologist, 23,* 26–42.

Savin-Williams, R. C. (1987). An ethological perspective on homosexuality during adolescence. *Journal of Adolescent Research, 3,* 283–302.

Savin-Williams, R. C. (1988). Theoretical perspectives accounting for adolescent homosexuality. *Journal of Adolescent Health Care, 9,* 95–104.

Savin-Williams, R. C. (1990). *Gay and lesbian youth: Expressions of identity.* New York: Hemisphere.

Schlegel, W. W. (1962). Die konstitutionbiologischen grundagen der homosexualitat. *Menschliche Vererliche Konstitutiotnslehre, 36,* 341–364.

Schmalz, J. (1993, March 5). Poll finds an even split on homosexuality's cause. *The New York Times,* pp. 1, 11.

Schmidt, G. (1984). Allies and persecutors: Science and medicine in the homosexuality issue. *Journal of Homosexuality,* 10, 127–140.

Schneider, W., & Lewis, I. A. (1984). The straight story on homosexuality and gay rights. *Public Opinion, 7,* 16–60.

Short, R. V. (1979). Sexual differentiation of the brain of the sheep: Effects of prenatal implantation of androgen. In *Sex hormones and behavior: Ciba Foundation Symposium 62 (New Series)* (pp. 257–269). Amsterdam: Excerpta Medica.

Sigusch, V., Schorsch, E., Dannecker, M., & Schmidt, G. (1982). Official statement by the German Society for Sex Research on the research of Prof. Dr. Gunter Dorner on the subject of homosexuality. *Archives of Sexual Behavior, 2,* 445–449.

Simon, A. (1989). Promiscuity as sex difference. *Psychological Reports, 64,* 802.

Slob, A. K., & Schenek, P. E. (1986). Heterosexual experience and isosexual behavior in laboratory-housed male stump-tailed macaques (*M. arctoides*). *Archives of Sexual Behavior, 15,* 261–268.

Smitt, J. W. (1952). Homosexuality in new light. *International Journal of Sexology, 6,* 36–39.

Snortum, J. R., Gillespie, J. F., Marshall, J. P., & Mosberg, L. (1969). Family dynamics and homosexuality. *Psychological Reports, 24,* 763–770.

Socarides, C. W. (1968). A provisional theory of aetiology in male homosexuality. *International Journal of Psycho-Analysis, 49,* 27–37.

Storms, M. (1980). Theories of sexual orientation. *Journal of Personality and Social Psychology, 38,* 783–792.

Storms, M. D. (1981). A theory of erotic orientation development. *Psychological Review, 88,* 340–353.

Storr, A. (1964). *Sexual deviation.* Baltimore: Penguin.

Thompson, N. L., Jr., Schwartz, D. M., McCandless, B. R., & Edwards, D. (1973). Parent-child relations and sexual identity in male and female homosexuals and heterosexuals. *Journal of Consulting and Clinical Psychology, 41,* 120–127.

Thompson-Handler, N., Malenky, R. K., & Badrian, N. (1984). Sexual behavior of *Pan paniscus* under natural conditions in the Lamako Forest, Equateur Zaire. In R. L. Susman (Ed.), *The pygmy chimpanzee.* New York: Plenum Press.

Tourney, G. (1980). Hormones and homosexuality. In J. Marmor (Ed.), *Homosexual behavior* (pp. 41–58). New York: Basic Books.

Turner, W. (1994). Comments on discordant monozygotic twinning in homosexuality. *Archives of Sexual Behavior, 23,* 115–119.

Tuttle, G. E., & Pillard, R. C. (1991). Sexual orientation and cognitive abilities. *Archives of Sexual Behavior, 20,* 307–318.

Van den Aardweg, G. J. M. (1984). Parents of homosexuals: Not guilty? *American Journal of Psychotherapy, 38,* 180–189.

Voeller, B. (1990). Some uses and abuses of the Kinsey Scale. In D. P. McWhirter, S. A. Sanders, & J. M. Reinisch (Eds.), *Homosexuality/heterosexuality* (pp. 32–111). New York: Oxford University Press.

Ward, I. L. (1972a). Consequences of perinatal hormone manipulation on the adult behavior of female rats. *Journal of Comparative and Physiological Psychology, 78,* 349–355.

Ward, I. L. (1972b). Female sexual behavior in male rats treated prenatally with an anti-androgen. *Physiology and Behavior, 8,* 53–56.

Ward, I. L., & Renz, F. J. (1972). Consequences of perinatal hormone manipulation on the adult sexual behavior of female rats. *Journal of Comparative and Physiological Psychology, 78,* 349–355.

Wassermann, E. B., & Storms, M. D. (1984). Factors influencing erotic orientation development in females and males. *Women and Therapy, 3,* 51–60.

Weinrich, J. D. (1987). *Sexual landscapes: Why we are what we are, why we love whom we love.* New York: Charles Schribner's Sons.

Wellings, K. J. F., Wadsworth, A. M., Johnson, R. M., & Bradshaw, S. A. (1990). Sexual lifestyles under scrutiny. *Nature, 348,* 276–278.

West, D. J. (1967). *Homosexuality.* Chicago: Aldine.

Westermarck, E. (1922). *The history of human marriage.* London: Macmillian.

Whitam, F. L., Diamond, M., & Martin, J. (1993). Homosexual orientation in twins: A report on 61 pairs and three triplet sets. *Archives of Sexual Behavior, 22,* 187–206.

Whitam, F. L., & Mathy, R. M. (1986). *Male homosexuality in four societies: Brazil, Guatemala, the Philippines, and the United States.* New York: Praeger.

Whitley, J., & Bernard, E. (1990). The relationship of heterosexuals' attribution for the cause of homosexuality to attitudes towards lesbians and gay men. *Personality and Social Psychology Bulletin, 16,* 369–377.

Wilson, G. D. (1987). Male-female differences in sexual activity, enjoyment and fantasies. *Personality and Individual Differences, 8,* 125–127.

Witschi, E., & Mengert, W. F. (1942). Endocrine studies on human hermaphrodites and their bearing on the interpretation of homosexuality. *Journal of Clinical Endocrinology, 2,* 279–286.

Young, W. C. (1961). The hormones and mating behavior. In W. C. Young (Ed.), *Sex and internal secretions* (pp. 1173–1239). Baltimore: Williams & Wilkins.

Zimbardo, P. G. (1958). The effects of early avoidance training and rearing conditions upon the sexual behavior of the male rat. *Journal of Comparative Physiology and Psychology, 51,* 764–769.

Zuger, B. (1984). Early effeminate behavior in boys: Outcome and significance for homosexuality. *Journal of Nervous and Mental Disease, 172,* 90–97.

# Chapter 2

▼

# THE ROLE OF PERINATAL FACTORS IN DETERMINING SEXUAL ORIENTATION

## Lee Ellis

*In the preceding chapter, various theories of homosexuality were presented. At least since the 1970s, scientists have increasingly focused their efforts on one theory—the perinatal hormone theory. The perinatal hormone theory has led researchers to several fascinating discoveries, including evidence that the brains of lesbians and gays and heterosexuals are different, and that certain experiences and drugs taken by expectant mothers may affect the sexual differentiation of the brains of their developing fetuses.*

*As alluded to in chapter 1, the perinatal hormone theory was largely inspired by research with laboratory animals rather than humans. This research clearly demonstrated that humans are not unique in having a sexual orientation, nor in the fact that most members are heterosexual. Studies have also shown that same-sex preferences can be experimentally induced in many species by manipulating sex hormones perinatally (reviewed by Ellis & Ames, 1987, p. 241). These lines of investigation have led many to suspect that homosexuality in humans might be caused by unintended factors that disturb the delicate balance of sex hormones during the perinatal period.*

*Several research findings, some of which are quite recent, suggest that this reasoning may be correct. Thus, without contending that all causes of homosexuality can be explained by a single theory, this chapter demonstrates that significant progress has been made in identifying at least some of the primary causes.*

## BASIC TERMINOLOGY

Before presenting a detailed description of the perinatal hormone theory, I will introduce several basic concepts. One set of concepts involves *sex hormones.* The customary practice of dividing sex hormones into "male hormones" and "female hormones" is maintained in this chapter, although doing so can be misleading to those with little background in endocrinology (Gooren, Fliers, & Courtney, 1990, p. 179). This is because all sex hormones are found in both sexes; the hormonal differences between males and females are only in degree, not in kind. Males have higher average levels of male hormones and females have higher average levels of female hormones most of the time. The differences are much greater at certain times in life than at others (Ellis, 1982; Finegan, Bartleman, & Wong, 1989; Hamilton, Parry, & Blumenthal, 1988).

The general term for "male hormones" is *androgens,* and the most common and important androgen is *testosterone.* The main "female hormones" are *progesterone* and *estrogens,* all of which are chemically related to testosterone in terms of their molecular structure (Ellis & Ames, 1987, p. 239; Tourney, 1980, p. 46).

In fact, enzymes circulating in our bodies are capable of converting certain male and female hormones into one another (Melcangi, Maggi, & Martini, 1993). *Enzymes* are small protein molecules that initiate biochemical transformations. The name of the primary female hormone to which testosterone can be converted is the estrogen known as *estradiol,* and the name of the enzyme that converts testosterone to estradiol is *aromatase.* References will be made to these chemicals shortly as the process of sexual differentiation is unraveled.

Another set of concepts describes the way in which animals are sexually differentiated (or sexed). In ordinary language, we usually describe *masculinity* and *femininity* as though they are always opposite ends of a single continuum (Whitam, Diamond, & Martin, 1993; see also Bailey, this volume). This is overly simplistic and can sometimes be misleading, especially when describing behavior. Masculinity and femininity should be considered separate traits, even though they are often inversely related to one another (Lobel, Gur, & Yerushalmi, 1989, p. 302; Marsh, Antill, & Cunningham, 1989; Tuttle & Pillard, 1991, p. 308). Research suggests that masculine and feminine sexual behavior patterns are controlled by separate areas of the brain (see Tourney, 1980, p. 54).

Conceiving of sexual differentiation simply in terms of varying degrees of masculinization coincides with one of the most basic facts about how mammals are sexed. As explained below, all mammals begin fetal development destined to become female. About one half of all mammals continue this course to its conclusion, while the remaining half are gradually diverted into becoming males. Thus, from a biological standpoint, male mammals (including humans) are fundamentally variants of the female sex. This may provide a clue about why homosexuality is so much more common in males than females.

One more important concept used to describe the way in which mammals are sexed is that of *critical periods.* These are fairly narrow windows of time (i.e., a few days, weeks, or sometimes months) during which an organ of the body is fundamentally and irreversibly changed. As described shortly, there are critical periods for sexually differentiating both the genitals and various parts of the brain.

# THE SEXUAL DIFFERENTIATING PROCESS

The process of making the sexes physically different is orchestrated by genes. Over the past quarter of a century, scientists have made great strides in deciphering the ways in which genes accomplish this process (Brown, Humm, & Fischer, 1988;  Grumbach & Conte, 1985;  Maxson & Roubertoux, 1990; Page, Mosher, & Simpson, 1987;  Schwartz, Imperato-McGinley, & Peterson, 1981; Simpson et al., 1987;  Winter, 1987). The sexual differentiation process is remarkably similar across the spectrum of mammals, although the timing of the sequence of events is much more compressed in some species than in others.

For example, the sexual differentiation of rats occurs during their 25 days of gestation plus the first 10 days following birth (Meaney, 1988, p. 55). In humans, essentially the same sequence of events takes place between the first and seventh months of gestation, with the possibility of some "fine-tuning" during the first couple of months following birth (Diaz-Granados, Greene, & Amsel, 1993, p. 1065; Dobbing & Sands, 1979). The similarities in mammalian sexual differentiation means that scientists can use species who develop rapidly, such as rats, as "fast-forward" models for sexual differentiation in humans.

## Sexing the Genitals

Making males and females different hinges on genes located on a special chromosome that only males have, called the Y chromosome. Genes on this chromosome interact with genes on other chromosomes (that *both* sexes have) to masculinize the body. The Y chromosome contains the genes that initiate the necessary modifications (Jost, Vigior, Prepin, & Perchellet, 1973; Kelley, 1986, p. 500; Von Berswordt-Wallrabe, 1983, p. 110). Genes contained on the Y chromosome essentially override more basic genetic instructions located on some of the other nonsex chromosomes. In humans, the key override instructions begin functioning during the second month of gestation. This is when a pair of glands inside the pelvis (called *gonads*) start to form into ovaries. Genes on the Y chromosome block the formation of ovaries and send chemical messages to these glands to develop into testes instead (Grumbach, 1979, p. 34). Within a few days (for rats) and a few weeks (for humans), the diversion is essentially irreversible. This sets the stage for sexing the *external* genitals (Roberts, 1988).

The two most common developmental paths for the external genitals are illustrated in Figure 2.1. As shown, during the first month of gestation, the external genitals are the same for females and males. Around the second month, cells near the surface of the groin respond to sex hormones produced by the gonads. If the gonads have begun forming into testes, they produce fairly high levels of testosterone;  if ovaries are being formed, they produce minute amounts of estrogens (Breedlove, 1994).

If the genitals are exposed to high (male-typical) levels of androgens, they follow the upper developmental path shown in Figure 2.1. In the absence of high

**Figure 2.1**
The two modal paths in sexual differentiation of the external genitals during fetal development. Adapted from Ellis & Ames, 1987: 233–258. Copyright 1994 by the authors.

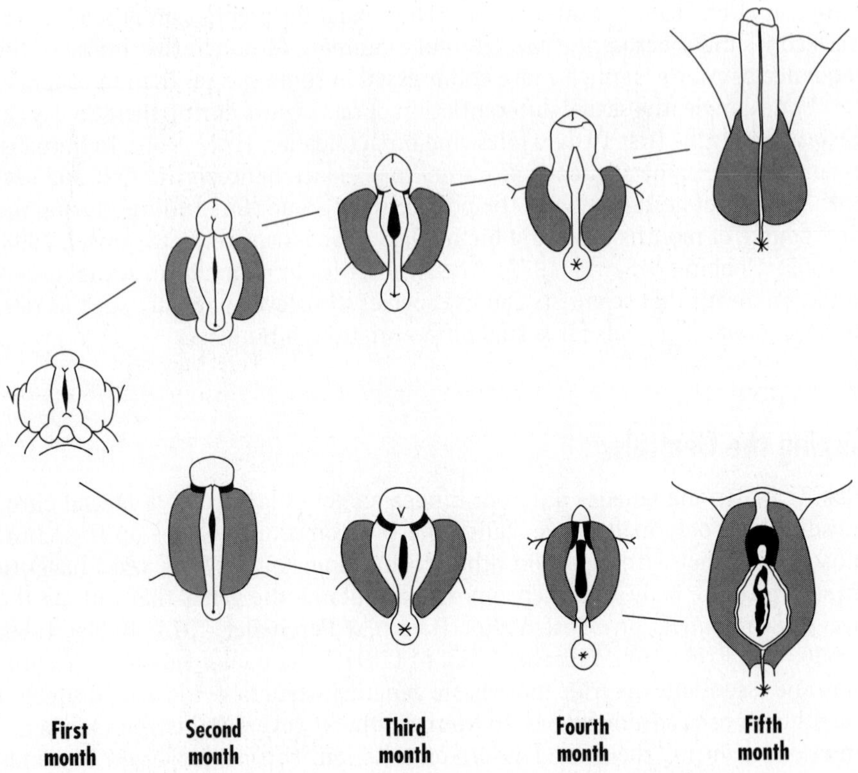

| First month | Second month | Third month | Fourth month | Fifth month |

levels of testosterone, the genitals follow the lower path. By the fifth month of gestation, sexing of the external genitals in humans is essentially finished.

Not everyone precisely follows one or the other of the two paths represented in Figure 2.1. For example, Figure 2.2 shows four human infants with sexually ambiguous genitals, which result either from "errors" in the genetic instructions or from in utero environmental factors that interfere with the biochemical unfolding of the genetic instructions (Eil, 1990, p. 918).

Among in utero factors that can interfere with sexing the genitals are drugs consumed by the mother. For example, during the 1940s and 1950s, tens of thousands of pregnant women took prescription drugs to help prevent miscarriage or otherwise maintain their pregnancy. These drugs closely resembled sex hormones, and their consumption during pregnancy resulted in an unusually high rate of partially masculinized genitals in female fetuses (reviewed by Ellis &

**Figure 2.2**
Drawings accurately rendered from actual photographs illustrate ambiguous external genitals among human infants. (Photographs from Eil 1990:918; Kuhnle et al. 1993:572; Bisat et al. 1993:142; de Bellis et al. 1994:513.)

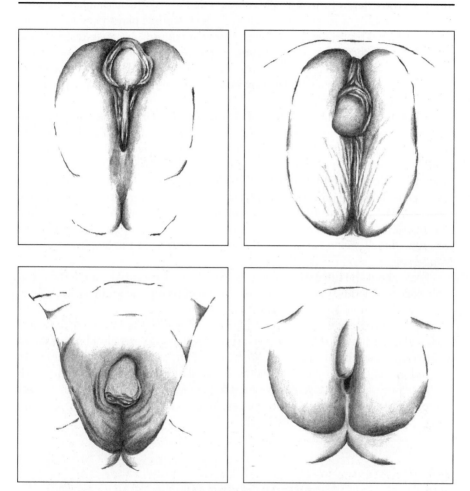

Ames, 1987, p. 247). More will be said about these drugs later because they also have been linked to unusually high rates of homosexuality.

## Sexing the Brain

The brains of human males and females are different. Some of the differences are subtle and detectable only with special instruments or when large samples are compared; other differences are easily recognizable if one knows where to look (for reviews see Booth, 1979; Gorski, 1987; Harlan, Gordon, & Gorski, 1979;

Kimura, 1992; Swaab, Gooren, & Hofman, 1992). Similar sex differences have been documented in the brains of other animals (reviewed by Breedlove, 1994; Ellis, 1982).

Most sex differences in the brain have their origins in the perinatal period, although the extent of the differences waxes and wanes throughout life (Swaab & Hofman, 1988). As is true for the genitals, testosterone plays a key role in sexing the brain. The process, however, is more intriguing because testosterone must be converted to one of the primary "female hormones" in order to have most of its masculinizing effects on the brain (Ellis, 1982; Hermans, McGivern, Chen, & Longo, 1993, p. 361). The way in which this biochemical paradox occurs is next examined.

All of the main sex hormones are chemically related and enzymes can convert one sex hormone into another. The enzyme for converting testosterone into estradiol is *aromatase*. Even though estradiol is synthesized by the ovaries rather than by the testes, it is blocked from escaping the blood system and entering the brain by a special protein in the blood, *alpha fetal protein* (AFP). AFP has a special chemical affinity for estradiol and almost no affinity for testosterone (Leger, 1992, p. 224; McEwen, Plapinger, Chaptal, Gerlach, & Wallach, 1975). When AFP and estradiol molecules unite, they form a molecule that is too large to cross through a biochemical barrier separating the brain from the bloodstream (the *blood-brain barrier*) (Ellis, 1982, p. 185).

From about the third month of gestation onward, essentially all of the estradiol produced by the ovaries is prevented from entering the brain by AFP. Much of the relatively high amounts of testosterone produced by the male testes, on the other hand, crosses the blood-brain barrier and enters the brain. Once testosterone enters the fetal brain, most of it is converted into estradiol by aromatase and masculinizes the brain (Beyer, Woznial, & Hutchinson, 1993; Silver, 1994).

In light of this complexity, it is inevitable that variations occur. It is possible that homosexuality essentially refers to persons with the genitals of one sex and part of the brain of the opposite sex. To consider this possibility, it is important to know more about the brain.

## DETAILS ON SEXING THE BRAIN

The mammalian brain consists primary of the neocortex (or cortex) and the subcortex. The human *neocortex* includes the outermost one and a half inches of the brain and the *subcortex* essentially includes everything beneath this outermost layer. In terms of functions, the neocortex specializes in "higher thought," such as reading and making sense of this paragraph.

The human subcortex is primarily responsible for regulating basic drives, such as sex, hunger, thirst, and respiration, as well as emotional attachments and repulsions. Many of the subcortical functions are "subconscious," as well as that which the neocortex would regard as irrational. In reality, the neocortex

**Figure 2.3**

A cross section of the human brain, with an enlargement of the region in and around the hypothalamus. Separating the two halves of the hypothalamus is a ventricle (called the third ventricle), which allows cerebral spinal fluid to circulate through the region. (After LeVay & Hamer, 1994) p. 46)

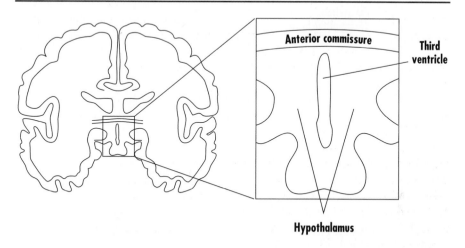

and the subcortex are interwired into an integrated system, and behavior is an expression of the response this system makes to input from the environment.

While there are sex differences in the neocortex (reviewed by Azari et al., 1992; Breedlove, 1994; Gibbons, 1991; Kimura, 1992), the best established sex differences in the human brain are located in the subcortex. In particular, certain regions in and around the hypothalamus are either larger or smaller in males than in females (Allen & Gorski, 1990; Allen, Hines, Shryne, & Gorski, 1989; Swaab & Fliers, 1985; Swaab & Hofman, 1988).

The hypothalamus and regions surrounding it constitute the main control center for sexual motivation (Gorski, 1984; Hart, 1974a, 1974b) (see Figure 2.3). Sexual motivation does not simply refer to whether an animal is ready to copulate; it also pertains to characteristics that other animals must have in order to trigger sexual arousal.

## SEXING THE BRAIN WITH REFERENCE TO SEXUAL ORIENTATION

Based on most estimates, the critical periods for sexing the genitals and the brain are shown by the solid straight lines in the upper left quadrant of Figure 2.4. Regarding the brain, there may in fact be several critical periods, with those pertaining to the subcortex generally occurring earlier than those for the neocortex.

**Figure 2.4**

Average male sex hormone levels from conception through the first twelve months following birth for both sexes (the dashed lines are explained on pages 43–44).

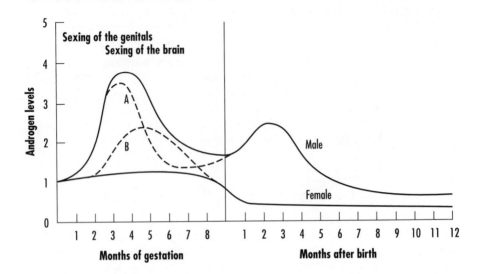

Figure 2.4 also shows the average levels of testosterone circulating in the blood system of males and females, beginning at conception and proceeding through the first year of life (Dorner, 1992; Parker, 1993; Siiteri & Wilson, 1974; Smail, Reyes, Winter, & Faiman, 1981a, 1981b; Tapanainen, Kellokumpa-Lehtinen, Pelliniemi, & Huhtaniemi, 1981). These separate male and female trends in testosterone levels are called *hormone regimens* (or *testosterone regimens*).

Both genetic and environmental factors produce differences in the typical male and female hormone regimens. For example, one of the genes responsible for sexing the genitals, and later the brain, may code for some unusual hormonal regimens. Or, as discussed later, chemicals may pass from the mother's blood supply to the fetus and sidetrack the genetic instructions.

One unexplained feature of Figure 2.4 is the rise in male testosterone levels during the first few months following birth (Corbier, Dehennin, Castanier, Mebazaa, & Roffi, 1990; Migeon & Forest, 1983; Smail et al., 1981a, 1981b; Stahl, Gotz, Poppe, Amendt, & Dorner, 1978). There is little evidence at the present time linking this postnatal rise in androgens for males with any aspect of sexual differentiation (Swaab et al., 1992, p. 209). A similar postnatal rise in testosterone, however, occurs in newborn male rats (McGivern, Handa, & Redei, 1993) and in several species of monkeys (Eisler, Tannenbaum, Mann, & Wallen, 1993; Dixson, 1993). In these species, the testosterone rise provides an important final subcritical stage for fine-tuning brain masculinization (Nordeen, Nordeen, Sengelaub, & Arnold, 1985).

As just noted, sex hormone regimens are under substantial genetic control. However, once sex hormones are produced, they in turn alter the way certain genes are expressed (Greene et al., 1986; Leger, 1992, p. 224). Genes that guide organisms through specific sequences of development by altering various biochemical substances, including hormones, are *canalization genes* (Wilson, 1978). Canalization genes are located on many chromosomes and exhibit individual variability (Bogle, Reed, & Rose, 1994; Handel, Park, & Kot, 1994).

If a canalization gene fails to activate key biochemical processes, or activates the processes earlier or later than usual, critical aspects of sexual differentiation may be affected. All four examples of partial sexual inversions in genital structures shown in Figure 2.2 (also see Bisat et al., 1993; Ellis, 1982, p. 177; Kuhnle et al., 1993; Soules, Pagon, Burns, & Matsumoto, 1993, p. 76) may be due to diversions of canalization genes. Inversions also occur in the human brain, and one result may be homosexuality. Before considering that possibility, I will further detail the perinatal hormone theory.

## Specifying the Perinatal Hormone Theory

In fairly broad terms, the perinatal hormone theory can be stated as follows: Human sexual orientation is determined during gestation and perhaps fine-tuned within the first few months after birth. Theoretically, the main determinant is the degree to which the brain is exposed to sex hormones, especially the metabolizing of testosterone to estradiol, during one or more critical periods.

If the brain is exposed to male-typical levels of testosterone (converted to estradiol) during the appropriate critical period, the individual should prefer sex partners with feminine appearances. If the sex hormone levels are in the female-typical range, the individual should prefer masculine-appearing sex partners. Presumably, this process evolved not only in humans, but throughout the animal kingdom because preferring the "correct" sex partners is a prerequisite for sexual reproduction.

Because the sexing process is fundamentally orchestrated by genes on the Y chromosome, there will normally be a fairly close correspondence between how much testosterone the external genitals are exposed to and how much testosterone enters the brain. Therefore, animals who are attracted to female-appearing sex partners will have male genitals, and those who prefer male-appearing sex partners will have female genitals. However, nothing natural is without variation, and one of these variations may be homosexuality.

More specifically, the perinatal hormonal theory of homosexuality is illustrated by the two dashed lines of Figure 2.4. Dashed line A represents the testosterone regimen of a hypothetical male who receives insufficient testosterone for male-typical brain masculinization. Nevertheless, testosterone levels would be quite adequate for fully masculinizing his genitals. According to the perinatal hormonal theory, this person would not only be attracted to other males, he would also likely exhibit other inverted sex-typical behavior patterns. This is because the unusual drop in testosterone production occurred throughout most of the critical period for brain sexing, not just the early half when the subcortical region was sexed.

Dashed line B represents a testosterone regimen that theoretically would cause lesbianism. Even though the levels of testosterone were roughly in the female range while the genitals were being sexed, there is a rise in testosterone approaching that which is typical of males when much of the brain is being sexed. This person should exhibit sexual preferences for same-sex members when she reaches puberty and display other behavior patterns that are more typical of males than of females.

## EVIDENCE SUPPORTING THE PERINATAL HORMONE THEORY

The two dashed lines in Figure 2.4 reflect hypothetical scenarios based on the perinatal hormone theory and obviously prove nothing. Four lines of evidence, however, offer support for the proposals represented by the lines. They include observed average differences between gay/lesbian and heterosexual individuals regarding brain structures, brain functioning patterns, perinatal sex hormone levels, and fingerprint patterns. Each is considered individually below.

### Brain Structures and Sexual Orientation

According to the perinatal hormone theory, differences should be found between the brains of gay/lesbian and heterosexual individuals, similar to the differences found in the brains of males and females. Most of the differences in the brains of gay males should represent demasculinization relative to the brains of male heterosexuals. Conversely, the brains of lesbians should be unusually masculinized compared to the brains of female heterosexuals. In recent years, the search for structural differences has received considerable research attention.

The first published study on physical differences between the brains of gays and heterosexuals was conducted in the Netherlands. Autopsies of the brains of 10 gay males and 22 heterosexual males revealed that a region of the hypothalamus was significantly larger in gay males than in heterosexual males (Swaab & Hofman, 1990).

Subsequently, a neurobiologist in San Diego examined the relationships between brain structures and sexual orientation. LeVay (1991) dissected the brains of 41 deceased people: 19 were gay males, 16 were heterosexual males, and 6 were heterosexual females. To reduce research bias, he remained blind as to which of the three categories each brain belonged (LeVay, 1993, p. 121). The size of one of three regions of the hypothalamus was found to be more than twice as large in heterosexual males as in gay males and heterosexual females (see Figure 2.3).

A third study was published a year later by researchers in Los Angeles (Allen & Gorski, 1992). An association between sexual orientation and a region of the brain just above the hypothalamus, the anterior commissure (see Figure 2.3), was sought. Prior research had established that the anterior commissure is generally thicker in females than in males, both in humans (Allen et al., 1989) and in rats (C. H. Kinsley, personal communication, June 1, 1994). Comparisons of the brains of 30 gay men, 30 male heterosexuals, and 30 female heterosexuals revealed a significantly thicker anterior commissure in the gay males than the heterosexual males (Allen & Gorski, 1992). In fact, the anterior commissure of gay males was even slightly thicker than that found in the average female.

Differences have also been tentatively identified in lesbians. A region of the connective tissue between the two hemispheres that is located in the neocortex was found to be significantly smaller in lesbians than in heterosexual females (Hines, 1993, p. 141).

One additional study linked the brain to sexual orientation. This study involved domestic sheep, a species in which 9% of the adult males strongly prefer other males as sex partners (Price, Katz, Wallach, & Zenchak, 1988; Zenchak & Anderson, 1980, p. 167). The amygdalae of the same-sex preferring rams contained far fewer cellular receptors for estradiol molecules than rams with opposite-sex preferences (Perkins, Fitzgerald, & Moss, in press).

At this time, all five studies must be considered preliminary and in need of replication. Nevertheless, they support those who argue that sexual orientation has a neurological foundation. The basic nature of the relationship is fairly consistent with the view that lesbians and gays have brains that are at least partly contrary to their genital sex.

## Brain Functioning and Sexual Orientation

The perinatal hormone theory not only predicts that brain structures are linked to sexual orientation, but that the brains of lesbian/gay and heterosexual individuals function differently.

A recent study investigated this hypothesis, using new technology for measuring brain wave patterns (Alexander & Sufka, 1993). Predictably, sex differences were found: When performing verbal tasks, the right hemisphere of the neocortex was more active in males than in females. Conversely, when performing spatial reasoning tasks, the left hemisphere was more active in females than in males. Regarding sexual orientation, the brain wave patterns of gay males more closely resembled those of females than the brain wave patterns of heterosexual males for both tasks (although the patterns for gay males were also somewhat distinct).

Complementing this brain wave study, other research has shown that gay males are intermediate between heterosexual males and females, usually closer to the latter than the former, in performing various cognitive tasks. For example, they more closely resemble heterosexual females than heterosexual males on tests of visual-spatial reasoning (Gladue, Beatty, Larson, & Staton, 1990; Sanders & Ross-Field, 1986a, 1986b, 1987).

Gay males are also more similar to heterosexual females than to heterosexual males regarding sleep patterns (Hall & Kimura, 1993a) and certain motor tasks (Hall & Kimura, in press-b). These findings are consistent with the view that the brains of gay males function in more demasculinized ways than is true for the brains of male heterosexuals.

## Perinatal Testosterone and Sexual Orientation

A controversial study was recently published by an East German researcher (Kaplan, 1990, p. 83) in which the amniotic fluid of fetuses was sampled during the third month of gestation. Eighteen years later, the subjects were assessed to determine their sexual orientation. Of 85 boys who had the lowest levels of testosterone in their amniotic fluid, 71% were gay at 18 years of age. Females were also studied and those with unusually high testosterone levels in their amniotic fluid during the third month of gestation also had high incidences of lesbianism at age 18 (Kaplan, 1990, p. 216).

Caution must be exercised in interpreting this study because the methodology is unprecedented. Furthermore, the normally accepted scientific protocol used to describe how amniotic fluid was sampled and how subjects were tracked nearly 20 years later was not followed (Bosinski, 1993; Diamond, personal communication, June 1, 1994).

Regardless of whether the findings from this study prove reliable, the methodology suggests a feasible procedure that could be used to critically evaluate the perinatal hormonal theory of sexual orientation (see Finegan et al., 1989). Theoretically, testosterone levels in the amniotic fluid should be significantly lower during the second trimester in male offspring who eventually become gay than for those who become heterosexual. The converse should be true for females.

## Fingerprints and Sexual Orientation

A recent comparison of dermal ridges (fingerprints) indicated that there are both sex and sexual orientation differences. Regarding sex, men have a higher total ridge count than do women (Bogle et al., 1994; Hall & Kimura, in press-a). Whereas most people have a higher ridge count on the right than on the left hand, this is especially so for males.

In regard to sexual orientation, gay males had a greater ridge count on the left than on the right hand, similar to the female pattern (Hall & Kimura, 1993b, in press-a). Dermal ridge counts are particularly interesting because they are largely determined during the second trimester (Bracha, Torrey, Gottesman, Bigelow, & Cunniff, 1992), when the neurological foundations for sexual orientation are thought to be established (Ellis & Ames, 1987).

## PERINATAL INFLUENCES ON SEXUAL ORIENTATION

Despite supportive evidence for the perinatal hormone theory, an important question remains: If the key to sexual orientation is the degree to which the brain is perinatally masculinized relative to the genitals, what would cause the brain-genital inconsistencies? In terms of Figure 2.4, what would cause males to diverge from their normal course and follow a hormone regimen similar to that represented by line A? Or, what would cause females to follow a hormone regimen represented by line B?

Four causes have been suggested: genetics, prenatal (maternal) stress, fetal exposure to various drugs, and prenatal immunological factors (Ellis & Ames, 1987). Evidence bearing on each of these factors is summarized below.

### Genetics

As noted in chapter 1, there is substantial, although not overwhelming, evidence that genes are responsible for some variation in sexual orientation. The strongest support derives from twin studies that have shown that identical twins are considerably more concordant in their sexual orientation than are fraternal twins.

There is other evidence favoring the genetic hypothesis, although it explains only a small proportion of known instances of homosexuality. Three genetically based syndromes have been linked to either homosexuality or inverted sex-typical behavior. All three of these syndromes involve enzymes that are highly influenced by genes that normally guide individuals through the process of sexual differentiation.

One of these syndromes involves the body's inability to produce an enzyme, *5-alpha-reductase*. Genetic males with this condition are unable to convert testosterone into another sex hormone, dihydrotestosterone, which masculinizes the external genitals. However, dihydrotestosterone does not masculinize the brain (Savage et al., 1980). Consequently, affected individuals, who are genetic males, have feminine-to-ambiguous-appearing genitals, although their brains are masculinized in the normal way by testosterone's conversion into estradiol (Fisher et al., 1978; Imperato-McGinley, Guerrero, Gauthier, & Peterson, 1974; Saenger et al., 1978; Savage et al., 1980). Unless diagnosed in infancy, these individuals are often reared as females. However, when they reach puberty, nearly all exhibit a preference for female, rather than male, sex partners (Delozier & Engle, 1982; Imperato-McGinley, Peterson, Gauthier, & Sturla, 1979; Rubin, Reinisch, & Haskett, 1981).

Another genetically instigated cause of sexual inversions is *androgen insensitivity*. Affected individuals are genetic males who develop testes, although the testes usually only descend slightly to form a normal scrotal sack. Although male-typical levels of testosterone are produced, one or more genes on the X chromosome (Beitel et al., 1994, p. 24; de Bellis et al., 1994, p. 521) prevent testosterone receptor sites from forming, which are needed to bind to androgen molecules in a normal way. Without these receptors, testosterone is unable to masculinize either the genitals or the brain.

Androgen insensitivity manifests itself in three clinical degrees: complete, when the external genitals are female in appearance; partial, when the genitals are ambiguous; and mild, when the genitals are male in appearance (Beitel et al., 1994). In complete androgen insensitivity, the affected individuals have the appearance of a female, both physically and behaviorally. However, they never menstruate and are infertile. Despite the fact that they are genetic males, their sexual interests are nearly always directed toward males (Ehrhardt, 1975; Ehrhardt, Evers, & Money, 1968; Money, 1969; Money, Ehrhardt, & Masica, 1968). Recently, a case of complete androgen insensitivity was reported in which the person affected preferred female sex partners (Gooren & Cohen-Kettenis, 1991). Conditions similar to androgen insensitivity have also been observed in rats and mice (von Berswordt-Wallrabe, 1983, p. 111; Meaney, Stewart, Boulin, & McEwen, 1983) and in baboons (Bielert, 1984).

A third genetically caused type of sexual inversion affects genetic females, *congenital adrenal hyperplasia* (CAH). While the main source of testosterone are the testes, small amounts are normally produced by the adrenal glands. In persons with CAH, however, an enzyme causes a high level of testosterone to be produced by the adrenal glands (Money & Dalery, 1976). Exposing the body perinatally to high testosterone levels has the same effects, regardless of which gland produces the hormone. Thus, for genetic females, CAH causes substantial, although rarely complete, masculinization of the genitals (Dittmann et al., 1990; Reinisch, 1976).

Longitudinal studies have reported that the behavior patterns of CAH females are also unusually masculine. As children, they were more likely than most females to prefer competitive sports and exhibited less interest in playing with dolls and dressing in feminine clothing (Berenbaum & Hines, 1992). In adulthood, CAH females reported fewer fantasies about romance and marriage than most women (Ehrhardt & Baker, 1974; Ehrhardt et al., 1968; Shepherd-Look, 1982; Walker & Money, 1972) and expressed a stronger interest in having careers than most girls do (Dittmann et al., 1990). At puberty, over one third of CAH females are bisexual, with the remainder more or less exclusively preferring male sex partners (Ehrhardt, 1978; Money, Schwartz, & Lewis, 1984; Money & Schwartz, 1977).

The vast majority of lesbians and gays do not exhibit any of these three clinical conditions. Nevertheless, studying them helps scientists identify some of the ways in which genes contribute to variations in sexual orientation.

Returning to Figure 2.4, variations in canalization genes may sometimes retard or delay the production of testosterone in males such that the regimen resembles the path represented by line A. Conversely, canalization genes in females may sometimes partially mimic genes on the Y chromosome that cause a rise in testosterone. If this gene begins to function around the third month, only the brain, not the genitals, will be masculinized.

# Prenatal (Maternal) Stress

When animals are exposed to stressful situations, they produce *stress hormones*. The most widely known is adrenaline; others are cortisol, corticosterone, and prolactin (Barlow, Knight, & Sullivan, 1978; Neufeld, Breen, & Hauger, 1994). The synthesis and release of stress hormones temporarily blocks the synthesis and release of sex hormones, especially testosterone (Bernstein, Gordon, & Rose, 1983; Bidzinska et al., 1993; Moore & Zoeller, 1985). Whenever stress hormone levels rise, sex hormone production tends to drop.

In pregnant females, when stress hormones are released into the blood system, the hormones pass through the placenta and enter the fetus's blood system. According to the perinatal hormone theory, if a mother experiences stress while the brain of her male fetus is being sexed, the offspring will have an increased probability of being gay. This is because, depending on the timing and severity of the stress, a mother who secretes stress hormones might prevent a male fetus she is carrying from producing sufficient testosterone to masculinize his brain. The exact effect of the same conditions on female fetuses is not clear.

Support for the prenatal stress hypothesis has come from experiments with laboratory animals. Among the methods used to induce stress in pregnant laboratory animals are exposing them to electric shock, tumbling, loud noises, bright lights, excessive heat, physical restraint, food deprivation, and badgering by cage mates (Archer & Blackman, 1971; Fitch et al., 1992).

Several studies have followed the offspring of female rats subjected to repeated episodes of stress during pregnancy. Especially in the case of male offspring, when given an opportunity to sexually interact with peers following puberty, an unusually high proportion exhibit lordosis responses to other males and show little interest in mounting females (Dahlof, Hard, & Larsson, 1977; Gotz & Dorner, 1980; Meisel, Dohanich, & Ward, 1979; Rhees & Fleming, 1981; Ward 1972b, 1974, 1977; Whitney & Herrenkohl, 1977; for a failure to replicate see Chapman & Stern, 1979).

To demonstrate that the demasculinized behavior of the prenatally stressed male offspring was due to their brains being deprived of testosterone during the critical period (which for rats occurs in the latter half of pregnancy), researchers injected stressed pregnant females with testosterone, which tends to pass to the fetus's blood supply via the placenta. This study showed that the behaviors of these male offspring were as masculine as the behavior of control offspring (Dorner, 1983).

In addition to their altered sexual orientation, unusually high proportions of prenatally stressed males were more similar to female than to male rats in other ways. They were less likely to engage in rough-and-tumble play (Ward, 1972a) and dominance-related aggression (Harvey & Chevins, 1985; Kinsley & Svare, 1986; Vom Saal, 1983) than normal males.

Another form of prenatal stress is fetal hypoxia, depriving fetuses of oxygen. When this was experimentally induced in rats, researchers found that male offspring exhibited demasculinized behavior that was similar to that caused by other forms of prenatal stress (Hermans et al., 1993). The offsprings' sexual orientations remain to be assessed.

Following the laboratory animal experiments, studies were conducted with humans to test whether prenatal stress is a cause of inverted sexual orientation and other inverted sex-typical behavior. Because these studies were not controlled experiments, they must be interpreted with considerable caution. Thus far, five studies on prenatal stress and sexual orientation in humans have been reported.

In the first study, the birth dates of several hundred gay males born in Germany between 1934 and 1953 were determined. The study revealed that a disproportionate number of the subjects were born during or within a few months immediately after the Allied blitz bombing of German cities during World War II (Dorner et al., 1980).

The second study, conducted by the same research team, asked a group of mothers of gay, bisexual, and heterosexual males to recall stressful episodes they experienced during pregnancy (e.g., deaths of close relatives, divorces, separations, traumatic financial or sexual experiences, and feelings of severe anxiety) (Dorner, Schenk, Schmiedel, & Ahrens, 1983). Consistent with the prenatal stress hypothesis, nearly two thirds of the mothers of gay males, compared to one third of the mothers of bisexuals and less than 10% of the mothers of heterosexuals, recalled such episodes.

A third study to test the prenatal stress hypothesis was carried out in the United States (Ellis, Ames, Peckham, & Burke, 1988). The mothers of gay, bisexual, and heterosexual males and lesbian and heterosexual females were asked to recall stress during each trimester of pregnancy. Mothers of gay males reported significantly more stress during pregnancy than did mothers of heterosexual males. Mothers of bisexual males and of all females were largely intermediate, although their stress levels were not significantly different from the gay or heterosexual male groups. Among the important qualifications in this study is that the differences between mothers of gay and heterosexual males were only significant in the case of mothers who recalled severe stress during the second trimester. Mild stress did not appear important.

Recently, two disconfirming studies have been published. One attempted to replicate the initial German study but failed to find a higher than normal proportion of German gay males who were born within or shortly after the bombing of German cities during the Second World War (Schmidt & Clement, 1990).

The second disconfirming study was designed to replicate the U.S. study. Bailey, Willerman, and Parks (1991) found no significant association between the sexual orientation of male offspring and their mothers' recall of stress during pregnancy. However, the researchers reported a significant link between the mothers' recall of prenatal stress and childhood effeminacy for boys.

Further evidence for the possible role of prenatal stress in sexual orientation outcome concerns the observation that stress may interact with genetics. A study found that gay males and lesbians, as well as their mothers, exhibited a deficiency in certain enzymes that normally metabolize adrenal hormones secreted during times of stress (Dorner, Poppe, & Stahl, 1991). The researchers speculated that these genetically influenced deficiencies may interfere with a male fetus's ability to produce testosterone, thereby demasculinizing his brain. Conversely, the same genes could cause the adrenal glands of female fetuses to produce unusually high amounts of male sex hormones, thereby masculinizing their brains.

In sum, evidence from animal experiments firmly supports the conclusion that mothers who are subjected to stress during pregnancy produce male offspring who have an increased probability of homosexuality as well as other inverted sex-typical behavior patterns. This is especially true if the stress is severe, uncontrollable, and persists throughout the latter half of gestation (for review see Ward, 1984). Two disconfirming studies, however, have prompted skepticism that prenatal stress is a significant cause of homosexuality in humans (LeVay, 1993, p. 125; see Small, 1993, p. 76). Until additional human studies are conducted, a final judgment regarding this issue should be suspended.

# Prenatal Drug Exposure

If sexual orientation is primarily determined perinatally, it should be possible to alter that orientation by exposing the mother to various drugs during pregnancy. Theoretically, any drug that interferes with the fetus's ability to synthesize sex hormones (especially testosterone) could affect the way the fetus's brain is sexed.

Drugs can be classified into three broad categories: recreational, therapeutic, and experimental. Through experiments with laboratory animals, drugs in all three categories have been identified that can affect sex-typical behavior, sometimes including sexual orientation. Whether similar effects occur in humans has not yet been determined with any degree of confidence.

## Recreational drugs

Recreational drugs are those that are taken to achieve pleasurable subjective sensations, rather than to treat a specific ailment. These include alcohol and nicotine, substances so widely available that some people do not consider them drugs. Also included in the category of recreational drugs are marijuana, cocaine, and the opiates.

One feature that all recreational drugs share is that they affect the brain. They can alter sex hormones in the brain and can cross the placental barrier separating the mother's and the fetus's blood supply. Thus, if these drugs are ingested by the mother during pregnancy, portions will end up in the fetus's brain.

Below is a brief summary of that which is currently known about the effects of prenatal exposure to various recreational drugs on sex-typical behavior. Most of the evidence is from experiments with laboratory animals, which may or may not resemble what happens in humans.

**Alcohol.**    It is well established that alcohol temporarily depresses the production of testosterone (Anylian, Dorn, & Swerdlow, 1978; Van Thiel & Gavaler,

1985; Ylikahri, Huttunen, & Harkonen, 1974). This appears to be caused by alcohol's tendency to inhibit the release of luteinizing hormone (LH) by the pituitary gland (Mello, Mendelson, Bree, & Skupny, 1986). LH is an important regulator of the production of testosterone.

Because alcohol readily passes through the placental barrier, prenatal exposure to alcohol is likely to temporarily interrupt testosterone production by the fetus (McGivern et al., 1993). If the mother drinks heavily during the time that the brain of a male fetus is being sexed, is it possible that the fetus's brain will fail to be masculinized?

For humans, no direct evidence is presently available. This is primarily due to the long time span between the mother's alcohol consumption and the offspring's full expression of sex-typical behavior. However, several experiments have been conducted with rats in which considerably less masculine behavior was observed in males whose mothers were exposed to alcohol-laced drinking water during pregnancy (Blanchard, Riley, & Hannigan, 1987; McGivern, Claney, Hill, & Noble, 1984; Meyer & Riley, 1986; Royalty, 1990).

In two studies, postpubertal males who were prenatally exposed to alcohol exhibited significantly greater lordosis responses toward other males than did unexposed males (Hard et al., 1984; Udani, Parker, Gavaler, & Van Thiel, 1985). Two other studies found that, relative to controls, males who were prenatally exposed to alcohol exhibited less interest in sexually receptive females and an unusually high sexual interest in other males (Dahlgren & Hard, 1991; Watabe & Endo, 1994).

An understanding of the process by which prenatal exposure to alcohol demasculinizes the behavior of male rats is still fragmentary. One study suggested that a portion of the hypothalamus, the *sexually dimorphic nucleus,* failed to enlarge as it normally does in males (Baron, Tieman, & Riley, 1988). Another study found that prenatal alcohol exposure caused male rats to develop an unusually "feminized" neocortex (Zimmerberg & Reuter, 1989).

Recent experiments with rats suggest that prenatal alcohol exposure might have demasculinizing effects through similar biochemical routes as prenatal stress and may add to one another's effect (Ward, Ward, Winn, & Bielawski, 1994). For example, both prenatal alcohol and prenatal stress may cause pregnant mothers to release corticosterone (a stress hormone) into their bloodstream, which subsequently enters the fetus's bloodstream and temporarily arrests testosterone production (Hard et al., 1984, p. 60).

**Opiates.**    Another class of drugs implicated as a cause of inversions of sex-typical behavior, including sexual orientation, is the opiates, such as heroin, morphine, and methadone. The first study to suggest a connection found that methadone administered to pregnant rats depressed testosterone levels in male fetuses (Singh, Purohit, & Ahluwalia, 1980). This study was followed by one in which pregnant female rats were injected with morphine and their offspring were followed beyond the age of puberty. Although female offspring exhibited no significant behavioral effects, the male offspring of injected mothers displayed demasculinized behavior in several respects compared to the male offspring of mothers injected with a saline solution (Ward, Orth, & Weisz, 1983).

Recently, three experiments were reported that are relevant to sexual orientation. In one, pregnant hamsters were administered morphine and a year later their offspring were compared to the offspring of control mothers. Female offspring showed no significant effects, but at puberty the male offspring of morphine-administered mothers exhibited significantly more lordosis responses toward other males than did the control males (Johnston, Payne, & Gilmore, 1992). In the other two studies, mother rats and mother hamsters were injected with endorphins, opiate-like substances naturally produced in the body. Again, the only significant effects were in the male offspring. At puberty, the male rats exhibited unusually strong lordosis responses to other males, although they also were inclined to mount females to a degree comparable to unexposed males (Kashon, Ward, Grisham, & Ward, 1992). In the hamsters, the exposed males were more sexually responsive to both males and females than unexposed males (Johnston, Payne, & Gilmore, 1994).

The research on opiates may provide a clue to the ways in which the brain is sexed. One scenario is as follows: Once the testes have formed, they produce testosterone primarily in response to luteinizing hormone (LH). LH is produced in the pituitary, an important regulator of sex hormone production which is located directly beneath the hypothalamus and is largely under its control. By acting on the hypothalamus, opiates appear to suppress the release of LH by the pituitary (Genazzani et al., 1993; Kalra & Simpkins, 1981). Without LH, the testes are inhibited from producing testosterone.

Pharmaceutical manufacturers have developed *opioid antagonists* that are capable of preventing opiates from suppressing LH release (Gooren, 1984, p. 90). The two most widely used of these drugs are *naltrexone* and *naloxone,* and they raise an intriguing possibility: If mother rats are injected not only with opiates but also with naltrexone (or naloxone), would the latter drug block the demasculinizing effects of the opiates on the behavior of male offspring? One study addressed this question, and the findings were as predicted. Unlike male offspring of pregnant rats who were only given morphine, males born to mothers given naltrexone and morphine exhibited no unusual degree of demasculinization in their behavior (Ward et al., 1983).

The same research laboratory explored another relationship, this one involving prenatal stress. Studies have shown that in addition to the release of various stress hormones, stressful experiences cause the release of endorphins (endogenous opiates) (Farabollini, Heinbroek, Facchinetti, & Van de Poll, 1991; Patel & Pohorecky, 1988; Rivier & Vale, 1988; Sanchez, Milanes, Fuente, & Laorden, 1993). As with stress in general, prenatal stress causes endorphins to rise (Ward & Weisz, 1980). Elevated endorphins could be the biochemical trigger causing the demasculinizing effects of prenatal stress on male offspring (at least in laboratory animals). If so, it should be possible to inject mothers who are experiencing stress during pregnancy with opiate antagonists, thereby preventing the brains of male offspring from being demasculinized. This deduction has been tested with rats. As expected, male offspring of stressed mothers who received naltrexone did not exhibit demasculinized behavior, while male offspring born to prenatally stressed mothers without naltrexone did (D'Amato, Castellano, Ammassari-Teule, & Oliverio, 1988; Ward et al., 1983).

**Nicotine, marijuana, and cocaine.**    Prenatal exposure to at least three other recreational drugs partially demasculinizes the behavior of male offspring in laboratory animals. These are nicotine (Lichtensteiger & Schlumpf, 1985; Segarra & Strand, 1989), marijuana (Dalterio & Bartke, 1979), and cocaine (McGivern, Raum, Sokol, & Peterson, 1989; Raum, McGivern, Shryne, & Gorski, 1990; for qualified confirmation see Vathy, Katay, & Mini, 1993). In addition, cocaine has been associated with the demasculinization of a portion of the hypothalamus (Maecker, 1993).

## Therapeutic drugs

Having reviewed evidence that prenatal exposure to various recreational drugs may sometimes cause inversions of sex-typical behavior, at least in laboratory animals, I now turn to drugs that are taken therapeutically.

One type of therapeutic drug that may cause sexual inversions is known as *progestin,* synthetic progesterone (Perone, 1994). Progestins, under various brand names, were administered to over half a million pregnant women in Western countries throughout the 1940s, 1950s, and 1960s to prevent miscarriage (Ehrhardt, Meyer-Bahlburg, Feldman, & Ince, 1984, p. 458). By the 1970s, the use of progestins was curtailed because of doubts about their effectiveness in preventing miscarriages and because of growing evidence that a side effect was that they affected the sexual differentiation of offspring (Ehrhardt & Meyer-Bahlburg, 1980, p. 186; Sureau et al., 1983, p. 247).

Several studies suggested that females exposed to progestins in utero exhibited unusually elevated levels of masculine behavior and interests as children and adolescents (Ehrhardt, 1969; Ehrhardt & Money, 1967; Money, 1969; Reinisch, 1977, 1981). Nevertheless, postpubertal follow-ups have not revealed evidence of significant homosexuality or bisexuality among these offspring by the time they had reached adulthood (Ehrhardt & Meyer-Bahlburg, 1980, p. 184).

Another therapeutic drug that affects sexual differentiation in laboratory animals is the estrogen-like drug, *diethylstilbestrol* (DES). Similar to progestins, DES was used from the 1940s through the mid-1970s by thousands of pregnant women to help maintain pregnancy (Peress, Tsai, Mathur, & Williamson, 1982). Experiments with rats and guinea pigs have shown that prenatal exposure to DES has masculinizing effects on female behavior (Dohler et al., 1984; Hines, Alsum, Roy, Gorski, & Goy, 1987; Hines & Goy, 1985).

In humans, female offspring of mothers who took DES had an increased rate of several genital abnormalities (O'Brien, Moller, & Robboy, 1979). They also exhibited considerably higher rates of lesbianism in adulthood (Ehrhardt & Meyer-Bahlburg, 1985; Meyer-Bahlburg & Ehrhardt, 1986). The evidence has been mixed regarding sex-typical behavior. Two studies of girls whose mothers took DES found no evidence of inversions (Hines, 1981; Lish et al.,

1991);  another found evidence of subtle masculinization of sex-typical behavior (Ehrhardt, Baker, Elkin, & McEwen, 1989). In the case of human males, no evidence of higher than normal rates of homosexuality or inversions of sex-typical behavior has been found (reviewed by Gooren, 1990, p. 76).

## Other drugs

Experiments with laboratory animals have identified several other therapeutic or experimental drugs that demasculinize the behavior of males or masculinize the behavior of females. These include barbiturates (Gorski, 1974), clonidine (Jarzab, Sickmoller, Gaerlings, & Dohler, 1987), cyproterone acetate (McEwen et al., 1979), hydroxyflutamide (Warrior, Page, Koutsilieris, & Govindan, 1993), diazepam (Kellogg, Primus, & Bitran, 1991;  Nakanishi, Tonjes, Fujii, & Okinaga, 1986;  Perez-Laso et al., 1994, Segovia et al., 1991), reserpine (Dorner, Hecht, & Hinz, 1976;  Lehtinen, Hyyppa, & Lampinen, 1972), cordycepin (Ulibarri & Yahr, 1987), 2,3,7,8-tetrachlorodibenzo-$p$-dioxin (Mably, Moore, Goy, & Petersom, 1992), and tamoxifen (Hancke & Dohler, 1984).

Whether these drugs have inverting effects on human sex-typical behavior (including sexual orientation) remains to be investigated, with the exception of barbiturates. One study of women who took barbiturates during pregnancy found evidence that their male offspring exhibited significantly higher rates of demasculinized gender identity (Reinish & Sanders, 1982).

## Paradoxical effects of some prenatal influences

Most of the effects of prenatal drugs and prenatal stress include demasculinizing male behavior, rather than masculinizing female behavior. In part, this may reflect the fact noted earlier that all mammals are initially female and that the most "natural" course in the process of sexual differentiation is to remain female. Such reasoning is consistent with the voluminous evidence discussed in chapter 1 that homosexuality is much more common among males than females, in humans as well as other animals.

Despite the tendency for most manipulations of prenatal factors, such as drugs and stress, to demasculinize male behavior rather than to masculinize female behavior, there are instances of the latter effect. In several experiments with pregnant rats who were injected with opiates, female offspring exhibited unusually high masculine behavior relative to control females (Vathy, Etgen, & Barfield, 1985; Vathy & Katay, 1992). As noted earlier, several studies have shown that prenatal opiates generally demasculinize the behavior of males.

In various species of rodents, prenatal exposure to DES (reviewed by Reinisch & Sanders, 1992) and alcohol (reviewed by McGivern & Handa, 1994) masculinizes the behavior of female offspring, although both drugs appear to demasculinize the behavior of male rodents. Similarly, in humans, prenatal exposure to DES masculinizes female behavior as well as demasculinizing male behavior (Reinisch & Sanders, 1992, p. 64).

Finally, most studies reported no significant effects of prenatal stress on the sex-typical behavior of female offspring (Politch & Herrenkohl, 1984). However, at least one study of prenatal stress suggested that it had masculinizing effects on female offspring (Gorski, 1980). This is despite the fact that prenatal stress has demasculinizing effects on male fetuses, at least in rodents. One research team, in fact, has suggested that prenatal stress may cause homosexuality in both sexes (Dorner et al., 1991, p. 146).

Such paradoxical effects of prenatal drugs and prenatal stress are difficult to explain, but they have been observed too frequently to be discounted as statistical aberrations. Generalizations on this issue from studies of rats and other non-human species to humans, nonetheless, are fraught with uncertainty. Researchers are seldom able to determine the exact quantity of a drug taken in humans within precise time frames, nor are they able to completely control for numerous extraneous variables, including other drugs taken in combination with those of interest (Robins & Mills, 1993). For these reasons, science does not know the full extent to which a host of drugs affect sexual differentiation.

## Immunological Factors

Considerable evidence suggests that the brain and the immune system influence one another and that much of this influence is accomplished through hormonal channels (Steplewski & Vogel, 1986; Torres-Aleman et al., 1986). It is therefore possible that the immune system could sometimes interfere with the sexing of a fetus.

Immunity refers to the tendency of an animal's white blood cells to attack foreign substances by building antibodies to those substances. One method developed for interfering with the sexual differentiation of laboratory animals has involved making either the mother's or the offspring's immune system attack one of the biochemicals required for sexing the brain. Antibodies are known to exist for nearly all biochemicals involved in sexual differentiation (Breuer & Nieschlag, 1975).

Two studies illustrate this manipulation. In one, an immune response to testosterone in female rabbits was induced (Bidlingmaier, Knorr, & Neumann, 1977). The females were subsequently mated and impregnated. The male offspring of these mothers acquired the antibodies against testosterone, which destroyed nearly all of the testosterone in their bodies. These male offspring consequently had genital structures that were distinctly feminine in appearance, with the exception of the testes themselves, which were well formed and fully capable of producing male-typical levels of testosterone. Unfortunately, the sexual preferences of these rabbits were not determined because they were killed soon after birth so that their internal sex organs could be examined.

In the other example, newborn male rats were injected with antibodies to a hormonal precursor to luteinizing hormone (LH). At sexual maturity, these males exhibited distinct signs of bisexuality (Kalcheim, Szechtman, & Koch, 1981). They mounted females and also exhibited lordosis responses to mounting efforts by other males. (For other reports of at least partial immunity-induced sexual inversions, see Goldman & Mahesh, 1970, and Goldman, Quadagno, Shryne, & Gorski, 1972.)

Whether immunological causes of homosexuality occur outside of experimental laboratories is unknown at this time. The fact that during pregnancy the fetus constitutes a foreign body inside the mother certainly sets the stage for immune reactions (e.g., the well-known Rh-negative factors in human mothers).

# SUMMARY

This chapter explored evidence pertinent to the perinatal hormone theory of sexual orientation. For more popularized writing on the theory, see Woodman (1990), Hooper (1992), Small (1993), Pool (1993), and Nimmons (1994).

Because the perinatal hormone theory was initially inspired by research on nonhuman animals, caution must be exercised when applying it to humans. Nevertheless, humans share with other mammals most of the basic genetic and biochemical processes involved in sexual differentiation, including sexual differentiation of the brain.

According to the perinatal hormone theory, the brains of some males and females may have been exposed to levels of testosterone (converted to estradiol) that typify the opposite sex during basic development. If this occurs when the region of the brain in and around the hypothalamus is being sexed perinatally, at puberty affected individuals are likely to prefer members of the same sex, rather than the opposite sex, as sex partners.

Based on controlled experiments with numerous animal species, evidence supporting this theory is now quite strong. Specifically, same-sex preferences can be induced with regularity in laboratory experiments by manipulating perinatal hormone levels.

Similar controlled experiments with humans are not possible for ethical reasons. Several lines of nonexperimental research, however, are consistent with the theory. The strongest evidence is derived from recent comparisons of the brains of gay/lesbian and heterosexual individuals. While they need to be replicated, these studies have identified subcortical regions of the brains of gay males that are closer in size to the brains of female heterosexuals than of male heterosexuals. Research studies on cognitive reasoning and on sleep patterns have also suggested that the brains of gay/lesbian people often function more like brains of the opposite sex.

Regarding the ways in which inversions of sexual orientation occur in humans, four possibilities were discussed: genetics, prenatal stress, prenatal drug exposure, and immunological factors. Certain genetic conditions have been identified that are associated with unusually high rates of same-sex preferences, although the vast majority of gay/lesbian people do not have any of these three conditions. Additional evidence that genetic factors contribute to homosexuality by influencing perinatal hormones was reviewed in chapter 1. Studies which examine homosexuality in twins and other close relatives offer considerable although not unanimous support for a genetic hypothesis.

Prenatal stress has been used in numerous studies of laboratory animals to invert the sexual orientation of offspring, especially male offspring. Three preliminary studies of human subjects linked high rates of severe stress in pregnant mothers with an increased probability of homosexuality in male offspring. However, two subsequent attempts to replicate these initial findings failed to find a significant linkage.

Nearly all evidence thus far associating drugs, especially recreational drugs (including alcohol and nicotine), with inversions of sexual orientation have been conducted by experimentally administering these drugs to laboratory animals. These studies have clearly linked fetal exposure to alcohol and opiates with demasculinization of the brain and behavior. In some studies, this demasculinization has included same-sex preferences by male offspring. No human studies have yet been reported.

The evidence is fragmentary regarding immunological factors as a cause of homosexuality. A few animal experiments have shown that the mother's immune system can attack biochemicals needed by the fetus to carry out normal sexual differentiation.

Overall, the perinatal hormone theory of sexual orientation has inspired hundreds of studies with laboratory animals and a dozen or so with humans. Much has been learned from this research about the determination of sexual orientation. Nevertheless, *many mysteries remain* regarding how nearly all of us come to prefer one sex over the other as objects of sexual desire.

# ▼ REFERENCES ▼

Alexander, J. E., & Sufka, K. J. (1993). Cerebral lateralization in homosexual males: A preliminary EEG investigation. *International Journal of Psychophysiology, 15,* 269–274.

Allen, L. S., & Gorski, R. A. (1990). Sex difference in the bed nucleus of the stria terminalis of the human brain. *Journal of Comparative Neurology, 302,* 697–706.

Allen, L. S., & Gorski, R. A. (1992). Sexual orientation and the size of the anterior commissure in the human brain. *Proceedings of the National Academy of Science U.S.A., 89,* (No. 7199).

Allen, L. S., Hines, M., Shryne, J. E., & Gorski, R. A. (1989). Two sexually dimorphic cell groups in the human brain. *Journal of Neuroscience, 9,* 497–506.

Anylian, G. H., Dorn, J., & Swerdlow, J. (1978). The manifestations, aetiology and assessment of ethanol-induced hangover. *South African Medical Journal, 54,* 193–198.

Archer, J. E., & Blackman, D. E. (1971). Prenatal psychological stress and offspring behavior in rats and mice. *Developmental Psychobiology, 4,* 193–248.

Azari, N. P., Rapoport, S. I., Grady, C. L., DeCarli, C., Haxby, J. V., Schapiro, M. B., & Horwitz, B. (1992). Gender differences in correlations of cerebral glucose metabolic rates in young normal adults. *Brain Research, 574,* 198–208.

Bailey, J. M., Willerman, L., & Parks, C. (1991). A test of the maternal stress theory of human male homosexuality. *Archives of Sexual Behavior, 20,* 277–293.

Barlow, S. M., Knight, A., & Sullivan, F. M. (1978). Delay in postnatal growth and development of offspring produced by maternal restraint stress during pregnancy in the rat. *Teratology, 18,* 211–218.

Baron, S., Tieman, S., & Riley, B. (1988). Effects of prenatal alcohol exposure on the sexually dimorphic nucleus of the preoptic area of the hypothalamus in male and female rats. *Alcohol: Clinical Experimental Research, 12,* 59–64.

Beitel, L. K., Prior, L., Vasiliou, D. M., Gottlied, B., Kaufman, M., Lumbruso, R., Alvarado, C., McGillivray, B., Trifiro, M., & Pinsky, L. (1994). Complete androgen insensitivity due to mutations in the probable a-helical segments of the DNA-binding domain in the human androgen receptor. *Human Molecular Genetics, 3,* 21–27.

Berenbaum, S., & Hines, M. (1992). Early androgens are related to childhood sex-typed toy preferences. *Psychological Science, 3,* 203–206.

Bernstein, I. S., Gordon, T. P., & Rose, R. M. (1983). The interaction of hormones, behavior and social context in nonhuman primates. In B. B. Svare (Ed.), *Hormones and aggressive behavior* (pp. 535–561). New York: Plenum Press.

Beyer, C., Woznial, A., & Hutchinson, J. B. (1993). Sex-specific aromatization of testosterone in mouse hypothalamic neurons. *Neuroendocrinology, 58,* 673–681.

Bidlingmaier, F., Knorr, D., & Neumann, F. (1977). Inhibition of masculine differentiation in male offspring of rabbits actively immunized against testosterone before pregnancy. *Nature, 266,* 647–648.

Bidzinska, B., Petraglia, F., Angioni, S., Genazzani, A. D., Crisculolo, M., Gallineli, A., Trentini, G. P., & Genazzani, A. R. (1993). Effects of different chronic intermediate stressors and Acetyl-I-Carnitine on hypothalamic Beta-Endorphin and GnRH and on plasma testosterone levels in male rats. *Neuroendocrinology, 57,* 985–990.

Bielert, C. (1984). The social interactions of adult conspecifics with an adult XY gonadal dysgenetic chacma baboon (*Papio Ursinus*). *Hormones and Behavior, 18,* 42–55.

Bisat, T., May, K., Litwer, S., & Broecker, B. (1993). Y chromosome mosaicism in the gonads, but not in the blood, of a girl with the Turner phenotype and virilized external genitalia. *Clinical Genetics, 44,* 142–145.

Blanchard, B. A., Riley, E. P., & Hannigan, J. H. (1987). Deficits on a spatial navigation task following prenatal exposure to ethanol. *Neurotoxicology and Teratology, 9,* 253–258.

Bogle, A. C., Reed, T., & Rose, R. J. (1994). Replication of asymmetry of a-b ridge count and behavioral discordance in monozygotic twins. *Behavior Genetics, 24,* 65–72.

Booth, J. E. (Ed.). (1979). *Sexual differentiation of the brain.* Clarendon: Oxford.

Bosinski, H. A. G. (1993). Book review. *Archives of Sexual Behavior, 22,* 514–517.

Bracha, S. H., Torrey, E. F., Gottesman, I. I., Bigelow, L., & Cunniff, C. (1992). Second-trimester markers of fetal size in schizophrenia: A study of monozygotic twins. *American Journal of Psychiatry, 149,* 1355–1361.

Breedlove, S. M. (1994). Sexual differentiation of the human nervous system. *Annual Review of Psychology, 45,* 389–418.

Breuer, H., & Nieschlag, E. (Eds.). (1975). *Antibodies to hormones in endocrinology: Introductory remarks.* Amsterdam: North Holland.

Brown, P. S., Humm, R. D., & Fischer, R. B. (1988). The influence of a male's dominance status on female choice in Syrian hamsters. *Hormones and Behavior, 22,* 143–149.

Chapman, R. H., & Stern, J. M. (1979). Failure of severe maternal stress or ACTH during pregnancy to affect emotionality of male rat offspring: Implications of litter effects for prenatal studies. *Developmental Psychobiology, 12,* 255–267.

Corbier, P., Dehennin, M., Castanier, A., Mebazaa, D. A., & Roffi, J. (1990). Sex differences in serum luteinizing hormone and testosterone in the human neonate during the first few hours of life. *Journal of Clinical Endocrinology and Metabolism, 71,* 1344–1348.

Dahlgren, I. L., & Hard, E. (1991). Sexual orientation in male rats prenatally exposed to ethanol. *Neurotoxicology and Teratology, 13,* 267–269.

Dahlof, L. G., Hard, E., & Larsson, K. (1977). Influence of maternal stress on offspring sexual behavior. *Animal Behaviour, 25,* 958–963.

Dalterio, S., & Bartke, A. (1979). Perinatal exposure to cannabinoids alters male reproduction function in mice. *Science, 205,* 1420–1422.

D'Amato, F. R., Castellano, C., Ammassari-Teule, M., & Oliverio, A. (1988). Prenatal antagonism of stress by Naltrexone administration: Early and long-lasting effects on emotional behaviors of mice. *Developmental Psychobiology, 21,* 283–292.

de Bellis, A. D., Quigley, C. A., Marschke, K. B., El-Awady, M. K., Lane, M. V., Smith, E. P., Sar, M., Wilson, E. M., & French, F. S. (1994). Characterization of mutant androgen receptors causing partial androgen insensitivity syndrome. *Journal of Clinical Endocrinology and Metabolism, 78,* 513–522.

Delozier, C. D., & Engle, E. (1982). Sexual differentiation as a model for genetic and environmental interaction affecting physical and psychological development. In W. R. Gove & G. R. Carpenter (Eds.), *The fundamental connection between nature and nurture* (pp. 117–136). Toronto: Lexington Books.

Diaz-Granados, J. L., Greene, P. L., & Amsel, A. (1993). Mitigating effects of combined prenatal and postnatal exposure to ethanol on learned persistence in the weanling rat: A replication under high-peak conditions. *Behavioral Neuroscience, 107,* 1059–1066.

Dittman, R. W., Kappes, M. H., Kappes, M. E., Borger, D., Stegner, H., Willig, R. H., & Wallis, H. (1990). Congenital adrenal hyperplasia I: Gender-related behavior and attitudes in female patients and sisters. *Psychoneuroendocrinology, 15,* 401–420.

Dixson, A. F. (1993). Observations on effects of neonatal castration upon sexual and aggressive behavior in the male common Marmoset (*Callithrix jacchus*). *American Journal of Primatology, 31,* 1–10.

Dobbing, J., & Sands, J. (1979). Comparative aspects of the brain growth spurt. *Early Human Development, 3,* 79–83.

Dohler, K. D., Coquelin, A., Davis, F., Hines, M., Shryne, J. E., & Gorski, R. A. (1984). Pre- and postnatal influence of testosterone propionate and diethylstilbestrol on differentiation of the sexually dimorphic nucleus of the preoptic area in male and female rats. *Brain Research, 302,* 291–295.

Dorner, G. (Ed.). (1983). *Prevention of impaired brain development by hormones and drugs.* New York: Karger.

Dorner, G. (1992). Sex hormone dependent brain organization, sexual behavior and ovarian function. *New Developments in Biosciences, 6,* 67–76.

Dorner, G., Greier, T., Ahrens, L., Krell, L., Munx, G., Sieler, H., Kittner, E., & Muller, H. (1980). Prenatal stress and possible aetiogenic factor homosexuality in human males. *Endokrinologie, 75,* 365–368.

Dorner, G., Hecht, K., & Hinz, G. (1976). Teratopsychogenetic effects apparently produced by nonphysiological neurotransmitter concentrations during brain differentiation. *Endokrinologie, 68,* 1–5.

Dorner, G., Poppe, I., & Stahl, F. (1991). Gene and environment-dependent neuroendocrine etiogenesis of homosexuality and transsexualism. *Experimental and Clinical Endocrinology, 98,* 141–150.

Dorner, G., Schenk, B., Schmiedel, B., & Ahrens, L. (1983). Stressful events in prenatal life and bi- and homosexual men. *Experimental and Clinical Endocrinology, 81,* 83–87.

Ehrhardt, A. A. (1969). *Zur Wirkung Foetaler Hormone auf Intelligenz und geschlechtsspezifisches Verhalter* [Concerning the effects of fetal hormones upon intelligence and gender-specific behavior].

Unpublished doctoral dissertation, University of Dusseldorf, West Germany.

Ehrhardt, A. A. (1975). Prenatal hormonal exposure and psychosexual differentiation. In E. Sachar (Ed.), *Topics in psychoendocrinology* (pp. 1307–1308). New York: Grune & Stratton.

Ehrhardt, A. A. (1978). Behavioral sequelae of prenatal hormonal exposure in animals and man. In M. A. Lipton, A. DiMascio, & K. F. Killam (Eds.), *Psychopharmacology: A generation of progress* (pp. 531–539). New York: Raven Press.

Ehrhardt, A. A., & Baker, S. W. (1974). Fetal androgens human central nervous system differentiation and behavior sex differences. In R. C. Friedman, R. M. Richart, & R. L. Vande Wiele (Eds.), *Sex differences in behavior* (pp. 33–51). New York: Wiley.

Ehrhardt, A. A., Baker, S. W., Elkin, E. J., & McEwen, B. S. (1989). The development of gender-related behavior in females following prenatal exposure to diethylstilbestrol (DES). *Archives of Sexual Behavior, 23,* 526–541.

Ehrhardt, A. A., Evers, K., & Money, J. (1968). Influence of androgens and some aspects of sexually dimorphic behavior in women with the late-treated adrenogenital syndrome. *Johns Hopkins Medical Journal, 122,* 115–122.

Ehrhardt, A. A., & Meyer-Bahlburg, H. F. L. (1980). Prenatal sex hormones and the developing brain: Effects on psychosexual differentiation and cognitive function. In S. Chess & A. Thomas (Eds.), *Annual progress in child psychiatry and child development* (pp. 177–191). New York: Brunner-Mazel.

Ehrhardt, A. A., & Meyer-Bahlburg, H. F. L. (1985). Sexual orientation after prenatal exposure to exogenous estrogen. *Archives of Sexual Behavior, 14,* 57–77.

Ehrhardt, A. A., Meyer-Bahlburg, H. F. L., Feldman, J. F., & Ince, S. E. (1984). Sex-dimorphic behavior in childhood subsequent to prenatal exposure to exogenous progestogen and estrogens. *Archives of Sexual Behavior, 13,* 457–477.

Ehrhardt, A. A. & Money, J. (1967). Progestin induced hermaphroditism: I.Q. and psychosexual identity in a study of ten girls. *The Journal of Sex Research, 3,* 83–100.

Eil, C. (1990). Differential diagnosis. *New England Journal of Medicine, 322,* 917–922.

Eisler, J. A., Tannenbaum, P. L., Mann, D. R., & Wallen, K. (1993). Neonatal testicular suppression with GnRH agonist in rhesus monkeys: Effects on adult endocrine function and behavior. *Hormones and Behavior, 27,* 551–567.

Ellis, L. (1982). Developmental androgen fluctuations and the five dimensions of mammalian sex (with emphasis upon the behavioral dimension and the human species). *Ethology and Sociobiology, 3,* 171–197.

Ellis, L., & Ames, M. A. (1987). Neurohormonal functioning and sexual orientation: A theory of homosexuality-heterosexuality. *Psychological Bulletin, 101,* 233–258.

Ellis, L., Ames, M. A., Peckham, W., & Burke, D. (1988). Sexual orientation of human offspring may be altered by severe maternal stress during pregnancy. *The Journal of Sex Research, 25,* 152–157.

Farabollini, F., Heinbroek, R. P., Facchinetti, F., & Van de Poll, N. E. (1991). Pituitary and brain beta-endorphin in male and female rats: Effects of shock and cues associated with shock. *Pharmacology, Biochemistry, and Behavior, 38,* 795–799.

Finegan, J. A., Bartleman, B., & Wong, P. Y. (1989). A window for the study of prenatal sex hormone influence on postnatal development. *Journal of Genetic Psychology, 150,* 101–112.

Fisher, L. K., Kogut, M. D., Moore, R. J., Goebelsmann, U., Weitzmann, J. J., Issacs, H., Griffin, J. E., & Wilson, J. D. (1978). Clinical, endocrinological and enzymatic characterization of two patients with 5-*a*-reductase deficiency: Evidence that a single enzyme is responsible for the 5 alpha-reduction of cortisol and testos-terone. *Journal of Clinical Endocrinology and Metabolism, 47,* 653–664.

Fitch, R. H., McGivern, R. F., Redei, E., Schrott, L. M., Cowell, P. E., & Denenberg, V. H. (1992). Neonatal ovariectomy and pituitary adrenal responsiveness in the adult rat. *Acta Endocrinologica, 126,* 44–48.

Gadpaille, W. J. (1980). Biological factors in the development of human sexual identity. *Psychiatric Clinics of North America, 3,* 3–20.

Genazzani, A. R., Genazzani, A. D., Volpongni, C., Pianazzi, G. A. L., Surico, N., & Petraglia, F. (1993). Opioid control of gonadotrophin secretion in humans. *Human Reproduction, 8,* 151–153.

Gibbons, A. (1991). The brain as "sex organ." *Science, 253,* 957–959.

Gladue, B. A., Beatty, W. W., Larson, J., & Staton, R. D. (1990). Sexual orientation and spatial ability in men and women. *Psychobiology, 18,* 101–108.

Goldman, B. D., & Mahesh, V. V. (1970). Induction of fertility in male rats by treatment with gonadotropin antiserum during neonatal life. *Biology of Reproduction, 2,* 444–451.

Goldman, B. D., Quadagno, D. M., Shryne, J., & Gorski, R. A. (1972). Modification of phallus development and sexual behavior in rats treated with gonadotropin antiserum neonatally. *Endocrinology, 90,* 1025–1031.

Gooren, L. (1984). The naloxone-induced LH release in male-to-female transsexuals. *Neuroendocrinological Letter, 6,* 89–93.

Gooren, L. (1990). Biomedical theories of sexual orientation: A critical examination. In D. P. McWhirter, S. A. Sanders, & J. M. Reinisch (Eds.), *Homosexuality/heterosexuality: Concepts of sexual orientation* (pp. 71–87). New York: Oxford.

Gooren, L., & Cohen-Kettenis, P. T. (1991). Development of male gender identity/role and a sexual orientation towards women in a 46,XY subject with an incomplete form of the androgen insensitivity syndrome. *Archives of Sexual Behavior, 20,* 459–470.

Gooren, L., Fliers, E., & Courtney, K. (1990). Biological determinants of sexual orientation. *Annual Review of Sex Research, 1,* 175–196.

Gorski, R. A. (1974). Barbiturates and sexual differentiation of the brain. In E. Zimmerman & R. George (Eds.), *Narcotics and the hypothalamus* (pp. 197–211). New York: John Wiley & Sons.

Gorski, R. A. (Ed.). (1980). *Sexual differentiation of the brain.* Sunderland, MA: Sinauer.

Gorski, R. A. (1984). Critical role for the medical preoptic area in the sexual differentiation of the brain. *Progress in Brain Research, 61,* 129–146.

Gorski, R. A. (Ed.). (1987). *Sex differences in the rodent brain: Their nature and origins.* New York: Oxford University Press.

Gotz, F., & Dorner, G. (1980). Homosexual behavior in prenatally stressed male rats after castration and oestrogen treatment in adulthood. *Endokrinologie, 76,* 115–117.

Greene, G. L., Gilna, P., Waterfield, M., Baker, A., Hort, Y., & Shine, J. (1986). Sequence and expression of human estrogen receptor complimentary DNA. *Science, 231,* 1150–1154.

Grumbach, M. (1979). Genetic mechanisms of sexual development. In H. L. Vallet & I. H. Porter (Eds.), *Genetic mechanisms of sexual development* (pp. 33–71). New York: Academic Press.

Grumbach, M. M., & Conte, F. A. (1985). Disorders of sexual differentiation. In J. D. Wilson & D. W. Foster (Eds.), *Williams textbook of endocrinology* (pp. 312–401). Philadelphia, PA: W. B. Saunders.

Hall, J. A., & Kimura, D. (1993a). Homosexuality and circadian rhythms. *Neuropsychopharmacology Supplement Abstracts, 19,* 1265.

Hall, J. A., & Kimura, D. (1993b). Morphological and functional asymmetry in homosexual males. *Society for Neuroscience Abstracts, 19,* 561.

Hall, J., & Kimura, D. (in press-a). Dermatoglyphic asymmetry and sexual orientation in males. *Behavioral Neuroscience.*

Hall, J., & Kimura, D. (in press-b). Performance by homosexual males and females on sexually-dimorphic motor tasks. *Archives of Sexual Behavior.*

Hamilton, J. A., Parry, B. L., & Blumenthal, S. J. (1988). The menstrual cycle in context, II: Human gonadal steroid hormone variability. *Journal of Clinical Psychiatry, 39,* 480–484.

Hancke, J. L., & Dohler, K. D. (1984). Sexual differentiation of female brain function is prevented by postnatal treatment of rats with the estrogen antagonist tamoxifen. *Neuroendocrinological Letter, 6,* 201–206.

Handel, M. A., Park, C., & Kot, M. (1994). Genetic control of sex-chromosome inactivation during male meiosis. *Cytogenetics and Cell Genetics, 66,* 83–88.

Hard, E., Dahlgren, I. L., Engel, J., Larrson, K., Liljequist, S., Lindh, A. S., & Musi, B. (1984). Impairment of reproductive behavior in prenatally ethanol-exposed rats. *Drug and Alcohol Dependence, 14,* 51–61.

Harding, C. F. (1981). Social modulation of circulating hormone levels in the male. *American Zoology, 213,* 223–231.

Harlan, R. E., Gordon, J. H., & Gorski, R. A. (1979). Sexual differentiation of the brain: Implications for neuroscience. *Reviews of Neuroscience, 4,* 31–71.

Hart, B. L. (1974a). Gonadal androgen and sociosexual behavior of male mammals: A comparative analysis. *Psychological Bulletin, 81,* 383–400.

Hart, B. L. (1974b). Medial preoptic-anterior hypothalamic area and sociosexual behavior of male dogs: A comparative neuropsychological analysis. *Journal of Comparative and Physiological Psychology, 386,* 328–349.

Harvey, P. W., & Chevins, P. F. D. (1985). Crowding pregnant mice affects attack and threat behavior of male offspring. *Hormonal Behavior, 19,* 86–97.

Hermans, R. H. M., McGivern, R. F., Chen, W., & Longo, L. (1993). Altered adult sexual behavior in male rats following chronic prenatal hypoxia. *Neurotoxicology and Teratology, 15,* 353–363.

Hines, M. (1981). *Prenatal diethylstilbestrol (DES) exposure, human sexually dimorphic behavior and cerebral lateralization.* Ann Arbor, MI: University Microfilms International.

Hines, M. (1993). Hormonal and neural correlates of sex-typed behavioral development in human beings. In M. Haug (Ed.), *The development of sex differences and similarities in behavior* (pp. 131–149). Netherlands: Kluwer Academic.

Hines, M., Alsum, P., Roy, M., Gorski, R. A., & Goy, R. W. (1987). Estrogenic contributions to sexual differentiation in the female guinea pig: Influences of diethylstilbestrol and tamoxifen on neural, behavioral and ovarian development. *Hormones and Behavior, 21,* 402–417.

Hines, M., & Goy, R. W. (1985). Estrogens before birth and development of sex-related reproductive traits in the female guinea pig. *Hormones and Behavior, 19,* 331–347.

Hooper, C. (1992). Biology, brain architecture, and human sexuality. *The Journal of NIH Research, 4,* 53–59.

Imperato-McGinley, J., Guerrero, L., Gauthier, T., & Peterson, R. E. (1974). Steroid 5 alpha-reductase deficiency in man: An inherited form of male pseudohermaphroditism. *Science, 186,* 1212–1215.

Imperato-McGinley, J., Peterson, R. E., Gauthier, T., & Sturla, E. (1979). Androgens and the evolution of male-gender identity among male pseudohermaphrodites with 5 alpha-reductase deficiency. *New England Journal of Medicine, 300,* 1233–1239.

Jarzab, B., Sickmoller, P. M., Gaerlings, H., & Dohler, K. D. (1987). Postnatal treatment of rats with Adrenergic receptor agonists or antagonists influences differentiation of sexual behavior. *Hormones and Behavior, 21,* 478–492.

Johnston, H. M., Payne, A. P., & Gilmore, D. P. (1992). Perinatal exposure to morphine affects adult sexual behavior of the male golden hamster. *Pharmacology, Biochemistry, and Behavior, 42,* 41–44.

Johnston, H. M., Payne, A. P., & Gilmore, D. P. (1994). Effect of exposure to morphine throughout gestation on feminine and masculine adult sexual behaviour in golden hamsters. *Journal of Reproduction and Fertility, 100,* 173–176.

Jost, A., Vigior, B., Prepin, J., & Perchellet, J. P. (1973). Studies on sex differentiation in mammals. *Recent Progress in Hormone Research, 29,* 1–41.

Kalcheim, C., Szechtman, H., & Koch, Y. (1981). Bisexual behavior in male rats treated neonatally with antibodies to luteinizing hormone-releasing hormones. *Journal of Comparative and Physiological Psychology, 95,* 36–44.

Kalra, S. P., & Simpkins, J. W. (1981). Evidence for noradrenegic mediation of opioid effects on luteinizing hormone secretions. *Endocrinology, 109,* 776–782.

Kaplan, L. (1990). *Das Mona Lisa Syndrom, die wie Frauen, furhlen.* Dusseldorf: ECON Verlag.

Kashon, M. L., Ward, O. B., Grisham, W., & Ward, I. L. (1992). Prenatal beta-endorphin can modulate some aspects of sexual differentiation in rats. *Behavioral Neuroscience, 106,* 555–562.

Kelley, D. B. (1986). The genesis of male and female brains. *Trends in Neuro Science, 9,* 499–502.

Kellogg, C. K., Primus, R. J., & Bitran, D. (1991). Sexual dimorphic influence of prenatal exposure to Diazepam on behavioral responses to environmental challenge and on y-Aminobutyric Acid (GABA)-stimulated Chloride uptake in the brain. *Pharmacology and Experimental Therapeutics, 256,* 259–265.

Kimura, D. (1992, September). Sex differences in the brain. *Scientific American, 267,* 119–125.

Kinsley, C. H., & Bridges, R. S. (1987). Prenatal stress reduces estradiol-induced prolactin release in male and female rats. *Physiology and Behavior, 40,* 647–653.

Kinsley, C., & Svare, B. (1986). Prenatal stress reduces intermale aggression in mice. *Physiology and Behavior, 36,* 783–786.

Kuhnle, U., Schwarz, H. P., Lohrs, U., Stengel-Ruthkowski, S., Cleve, H., & Braun, A. (1993). Familial true hermaphroditism: Paternal and maternal transmission of true hermaphroditism (46,XX) and XX maleness in the absence of Y-chromosomal sequences. *Human Genetics, 92,* 571–576.

Leger, D. W. (1992). *Biological foundations of behavior: An integrated approach.* New York: Harper Collins.

Lehtinen, P., Hyyppa, M., & Lampinen, P. (1972). Sexual behavior of adult rats after a single neonatal injection of reserpine. *Psychopharmacologia, 23,* 171–179.

LeVay, S. (1991). A difference in hypothalamic structure between heterosexual and homosexual men. *Science, 253,* 1034–1037.

LeVay, S. (1993). *The sexual brain.* Cambridge, MA: Massachusetts Institute of Technology Press.

LeVay, S., & Hamer, D. H. (1994, May). Evidence for a biological influence in male homosexuality. *Scientific American, 270,* 44–49.

Lichtensteiger, W., & Schlumpf, M. (1985). Prenatal nicotine affects fetal testosterone and sexual dimorphism of saccharin preference. *Pharmacology, Biochemistry, and Behavior, 23,* 439–444.

Lish, J. D., Ehrhardt, A. A., Meyer-Bahlburg, H. F. L., Rosen, L. R., Gruen, R. S., & Veridiano, N. P. (1991). Gender-related behavior development in females exposed to Diethylstilbestrol (DES) in utero: An attempted replication. *Journal of American Academy of Child and Adolescence Psychiatry, 30,* 29–37.

Lobel, T. E., Gur, S., & Yerushalmi, H. (1989). Cheating behavior of sex-type and androgynous children in sex-stereotyped and non-sex-stereotyped tasks. *Journal of Research in Personality, 23,* 302–312.

Mably, T. A., Moore, R. W., Goy, R. W., & Petersom, R. E. (1992). In utero and lactational exposure of male rats to 2,3,7,8-tetrachlorodibenzo-p-dioxin. *Toxicology and Applied Pharmacology, 114,* 108–117.

Maecker, H. L. (1993). Perinatal cocaine exposure inhibits the development of the male SDN. *Developmental Brain Research, 76,* 288–292.

Marsh, H. W., Antill, J. K., & Cunningham, J. D. (1989). Masculinity and femininity: A bipolar construct and independent constructs. *Journal of Personality, 57,* 625–661.

Maxson, S. C., & Roubertoux, P. (1990). The mammalian Y chromosome. *Behavior Genetics, 20,* 105–108.

McEwen, B., Liebergurg, I., Chaptal, C., Davis, P., Krey, L., MacLusky, N., & Roy, E. (1979). Attenuating the defeminization of the neonatal rat brain: Mechanisms of action of cyproterone acetate, 1, 4, 6-Androstatriene-3,17 -dione and a synthetic progestin, R5020. *Hormones and Behavior, 13,* 269–281.

McEwen, B. S., Plapinger, L., Chaptal, C., Gerlach, J., & Wallach, G. (1975). Role of fetoneonatal estrogen binding proteins in the association of estrogen with neonatal brain cell nuclear receptors. *Brain Research, 96,* 400–406.

McGivern, R. F., Claney, A. N., Hill, M. A., & Noble, E. P. (1984). Prenatal alcohol exposure alters adult expression of sexually dimorphic behaviors in the rat. *Science, 224,* 896–898.

McGivern, R. F., & Handa, R. J. (1994). *Prenatal exposure to drugs of abuse: Methodological considerations and effects on sexual differentiation.* Bethesda, MD: National Institute on Drug Abuse.

McGivern, R. F., Handa, R. J., & Redei, E. (1993). Decreased postnatal testosterone surge in male rats exposed to ethanol during the last week of gestation. *Alcoholism: Clinical and Experimental Research, 17,* 1215–1222.

McGivern, R. F., Raum, W. J., Sokol, R. Z., & Peterson, R. (1989). Long-term behavioral and endocrine effects of prenatal cocaine exposure in male rats. *Clinical Research, 36,* A125.

Meaney, M. J. (1988). The sexual differentiation of social play. *Trends in Neuroscience, 11,* 54–58.

Meaney, M. J., Stewart, J., Boulin, P., & McEwen, P. S. (1983). Sexual differentiation of social play in rat pups is mediated by the neonatal androgen-receptor system. *Neuroendocrinology, 37,* 85–90.

Meisel, R. L., Dohanich, G. P., & Ward, I. L. (1979). Effects of prenatal stress on avoidance acquisition, open-field performance and lordotic behavior in male rats. *Physiology and Behavior, 22,* 527–530.

Melcangi, R. C., Maggi, R., & Martini, L. (1993). Testosterone and progesterone metabolism in the human neuroblastoma cell line SH-SY5Y. *Journal of Steroid Biochemistry, 46,* 811–818.

Mello, N. K., Mendelson, J. H., Bree, M. P., & Skupny, A. S. T. (1986). Alcohol effects in luteinizing hormone-releasing hormone-stimulated luteinizing hormone and pollices-stimulating hormone in female Rhesus monkeys. *Pharmacology and Experimental Therapeutics, 236,* 590–595.

Meyer, L. S., & Riley, E. P. (1986). Social play in juvenile rats prenatally exposed to alcohol. *Teratology, 34,* 1–7.

Meyer-Bahlburg, H., & Ehrhardt, A. A. (1986). Prenatal diethylstilbestrol exposure: Behavioral consequences in humans. In G. Dorner, S. McCann, & L. Martini (Eds.), *Systematic hormones, neurotransmitter and brain development* (pp. 90–95). Karger: Basel.

Migeon, C. J., & Forest, M. G. (Eds.). (1983). *Androgens in biological fluids* (2nd ed.). Philadelphia: Lippincott.

Money, J. (1969). Sexually dimorphic behavior, normal and abnormal. In N. Kretchmer & D. N. Walcher (Eds.), *Environmental influences on genetic expression* (pp. 201–212). Washington, DC: U.S. Government Printing Office.

Money, J., & Dalery, J. (1976). Iatrogenic homosexuality: Gender identity in seven 46,XX chromosomal females with hyperadrenocortical hermaphroditism born with a penis, three reared as boys, four reared as girls. *Journal of Homosexuality, 1,* 357–371.

Money, J., Ehrhardt, A. A., & Masica, D. N. (1968). Fetal feminization induced by androgen insensitivity in the testicular feminization syndrome: Effects on marriage and maternalism. *Johns Hopkins Medical Journal, 123,* 105–114.

Money, J. & Schwartz, M. (1977). Dating, romantic and nonromantic friendships, and sexuality in 17 early-treated adrenogenital females, aged 16–25. In P. A. Lee (Ed.), *Congenital adrenal hyperplasia* (pp. 419–431). Baltimore: University Park Press.

Money, J., Schwartz, M., & Lewis, V. G. (1984). Adult erotosexual status and fetal hormonal masculinization and demasculinization: 46,XX congenital virilizing adrenal hyperplasia and 46,XY androgen-insensitivity syndrome compared. *Psychoneuroendocrinology, 9,* 405–414.

Moore, F. L., & Zoeller, R. T. (1985). Stress-induced inhibition of reproduction: Evidence of suppressed secretion of LH-RH in amphibians. *General and Comparative Endocrinology, 60,* 252–258.

Nakanishi, H., Tonjes, R., Fujii, T., & Okinaga, S. (1986). Effects of neuroleptics administered to lactating rats on the behavioral development of offspring. *Experimental Clinical Endocrinology, 88,* 13–24.

Neufeld, J. H., Breen, L., & Hauger, R. (1994). Extreme posture elevates corticosterone in a forced ambulation model of chronic stress in rats. *Pharmacology, Biochemistry, and Behavior, 47,* 233–240.

Nimmons, D. (1994, March). Sex and the brain. *Discover,* pp. 64–71.

Nordeen, E. J., Nordeen, K. W., Sengelaub, P. R., & Arnold, A. P. (1985). Androgens prevent normally occurring cell death in a sexually dimorphic spinal nucleus. *Science, 229,* 671–673.

O'Brien, P. C., Moller, K. L., & Robboy, S. J. (1979). Vaginal epithelial changes in young women enrolled in the National Cooperative Diethylstilbestrol Adenosis (DESAD) Project. *Obstetrics and Gynecology, 53,* 309–317.

Page, D. C., Mosher, R., & Simpson, E. M. (1987). The sex-determining region of the human Y chromosome encodes a finger protein. *Cell, 51,* 1091–1104.

Parker, C. R. (1993). The endocrinology of pregnancy. In B. R. Carr & R. E. Blackwell (Eds.), *Textbook of reproductive medicine* (pp. 17–40). Norwalk, CT: Appleton & Lange.

Patel, V. A., & Pohorecky, L. A. (1988). Interaction of stress and ethanol: Effect on beta-endorphin and catecholamines. *Alcoholism: Clinical and Experimental Research, 161,* 122–133.

Peress, M. R., Tsai, C. C., Mathur, R. S., & Williamson, H. O. (1982). Hirsutism and menstrual patterns in women exposed to diethylstilbestrol in utero. *American Journal of Obstetrics and Gynecology, 144,* 135–140.

Perez-Laso, C., Valencia, A., Rodriguez-Zafra, M., Calas, J. M., Guillamon, A., & Segovia, S. (1994). Perinatal administration of diazepam alters sexual dimorphism in the rat accessary olfactory bulb. *Brain Research, 634,* 1–6.

Perkins, A., Fitzgerald, J. A., & Moss, G. (in press). A comparison of LH secretion and brain estradiol receptors in heterosexual and homosexual rams and female sheep. In R. Goy (Ed.), *Hormones and behavior.*

Perone, N. (1994). The progestins. In J. W. Goldzieher (Ed.), *Pharmacology of the contraceptive steroids* (pp. 5–19). New York: Raven Press.

Politch, J. A., & Herrenkohl, L. R. (1984). Effects of prenatal stress on reproduction in male and female mice. *Physiology and Behavior, 32,* 95–99.

Pool, R. (1993). Evidence of homosexuality gene. *Science, 261,* 291–292.

Price, E. O., Katz, L. S., Wallach, S. J., & Zenchak, J. J. (1988). The relationship of male-male mounting to the sexual preferences of young rams. *Applied Animal Behaviour Science, 21,* 347–355.

Raum, W. J., McGivern, R. F., Shryne, J. H., & Gorski, R. A. (1990). Prenatal inhibition of hypothalamic sex steroid uptake by cocaine: Effects on neurobehavioral sexual differentiation in male rats. *Developmental Brain Research, 53,* 230–236.

Reinisch, J. M. (1976). Effects of prenatal hormone exposure on physical and psychological development in humans and animals: With a note on the state of the field. In E. S. Sachar (Ed.), *Hormone, behavior and psychopathology* (pp. 69–94). New York: Raven Press.

Reinisch, J. M. (1977). Prenatal exposure of human foetuses to synthetic progestin and estrogen affects personality. *Nature, 266,* 561–562.

Reinisch, J. M. (1981). Prenatal exposure to synthetic progestin increases potential for aggression in humans. *Science, 211,* 1171–1173.

Reinisch, J. M., & Sanders, S. A. (1982). Early barbiturate exposure: The brain, sexually dimorphic behavior and learning. *Neuroscience Review, 6,* 311–319.

Reinisch, J. M., & Sanders, S. A. (1992). Effects of prenatal exposure to Diethylstilbestrol (DES) on hemispheric laterality and spatial ability in human males. *Hormones and Behavior, 26,* 62–75.

Rhees, R. W., & Fleming, D. E. (1981). Effects of malnutrition, maternal stress, or ACTH injections during pregnancy on sexual behavior of male offspring. *Physiology and Behavior, 27,* 879–882.

Rivier, C., & Vale, W. (1988). Interaction between ethanol and stress on ACTH and beta-endorphin secretion. *Alcoholism:*

*Clinical and Experimental Research, 12,* 206–210.

Roberts, L. (1988). Zeroing in on the sex switch. *Science, 239,* 21–22.

Robins, L. N., & Mills, J. L. (1993). Effects of in utero exposure to street drugs. *American Journal of Public Health, 83,* 1–32.

Royalty, J. (1990). Effects on prenatal ethanol exposure on juvenile play-fighting and postpubertal aggression in rats. *Psychological Reports, 66,* 87–93.

Rubin, R. T., Reinisch, J. M., & Haskett, R. F. (1981). Postnatal gonadal steroid effects on human behavior. *Science, 211,* 1318–1324.

Saenger, P., Goldman, A. S., Levine, L. S., Korthschutz, D., Muecke, C., Katsuma, M., Doberre, Y., & New, M. I. (1978). Prepubertal diagnosis of steroid 5-*a*-reductase deficiency. *Journal of Clinical Endocrinology and Metabolism, 46,* 627–634.

Sanchez, M. D., Milanes, M. V., Fuente, T., & Laorden, M. L. (1993). The B-endorphin response to prenatal stress during postnatal development in the rat. *Developmental Brain Research, 74,* 142–145.

Sanders, G., & Ross-Field, L. (1986a). Sexual orientation, cognitive abilities and cerebral asymmetry: A review and hypothesis tested. *Monitore Zoologico Italiano, 20,* 459–470.

Sanders, G., & Ross-Field, L. (1986b). Sexual orientation and visuo-spatial ability. *Brain and Cognition, 5,* 280–290.

Sanders, G., & Ross-Field, L. (1987). Neuropsychological development of cognitive abilities: A new research strategy and some preliminary evidence for a sexual orientation model. *International Journal of Neuroscience, 36,* 1–16.

Savage, M. O., Preece, M. A., Jeffcoat, S. L., Ransley, P. G., Rumsby, G., Mansfield, M. D., & Williams, D. I. (1980). Familial male pseudo-hermaphroditism due to deficiency of 5-*a*-reductase. *Clinical Endocrinology, 12,* 397–406.

Schmidt, G., & Clement, U. (1990). Does peace prevent homosexuality. *Archives of Sexual Behavior, 19,* 183–187.

Schwartz, M., Imperato-McGinley, J., & Peterson, R. E. (1981). Male pseudo-hermaphroditism secondary to an abnormality in Leydig cell differentiation. *Journal of Clinical Endocrinology and Metabolism, 53,* 123–127.

Segarra, A. C., & Strand, F. L. (1989). Prenatal administration of nicotine alters subsequent sexual behavior and testosterone levels in male rats. *Brain Research, 480,* 151–159.

Segovia, S., Perez-Laso, C., Rodriguez-Zafra, M., Cales, J. M., Del Abril, A., De Blas, M. R., Collado, P., Valencia, A., & Guillamon, A. (1991). Early postnatal diazepam exposure alters sex differences in the rat brain. *Brain Research Bulletin, 26,* 899–907.

Shepherd-Look, D. L. (1982). Sex differentiation and the development of sex roles. In B. B. Walman (Ed.), *Handbook of developmental psychology* (pp. 403–433). Englewood Cliffs, NJ: Prentice-Hall.

Siiteri, P. K., & Wilson, J. D. (1974). Testosterone formation and metabolism during male sexual differentiation in the human embryo. *Journal of Clinical Endocrinology and Metabolism, 38,* 113–125.

Silver, L. M. (1994). The acquisition of sex. *Science, 264,* 116.

Simpson, E., Chandler, P., Goulmy, E., Disteche, C. M., Ferguson-Smith, M. A., & Page, D. C. (1987). Separation of the genetic loci for the H-Y antigen and for testis dermination on human Y chromosome. *Nature, 326,* 876–878.

Singh, H. H., Purohit, V., & Ahluwalia, B. S. (1980). Effects of methadone treatment during pregnancy on the fetal testes and hypothalamus in rats. *Biological Reproduction, 22,* 480–485.

Smail, P. J., Reyes, F. I., Winter, J. S. D., & Faiman, C. (1981a). The fetal hormone environment and its effects on the morphogenesis of the genital system. In S. J. Kogan & E. S. E. Hafez (Eds.), *Pediatric andrology* (pp. 9–19). The Hague: Martinus Nijhoff.

Smail, S., Reyes, F. I., Winter, S. D., & Faiman, C. (Eds.). (1981b). *The fetal gonadal environment and its effects on the morphogenesis of the genital system.* The Hague: Martinus Nijhoff.

Small, M. F. (1993). The gay debate: Is homosexuality a matter of choice or chance? *American Health, 12,* 70–76.

Soules, M. R., Pagon, R. A., Burns, M. W., & Matsumoto, A. M. (1993). Normal and abnormal sexual development. In B. R. Carr & R. E. Blackwell (Eds.), *Textbook of reproductive medicine* (pp. 67–88). Norwalk, CT: Appleton & Lange.

Stahl, F., Gotz, F., Poppe, I., Amendt, P., & Dorner, G. (1978). Pre- and early postnatal testosterone levels in rats and humans. In G. Dorner & M. Kawakami (Eds.), *Hormones and brain development* (pp. 99–109). Amsterdam: Elsevier.

Steplewski, Z., & Vogel, W. H. (1986). Total leukocytes, T cell subpopulation and natural killer (NK) cell activity in rats exposed to restraint stress. *Life Sciences, 38,* 2419–2427.

Sureau, C., Germain, G., Ferre, F., Breat, G., Goujard, J., Uzan, M., & Cedard, L. (1983). Therapeutic use of progesterone during the last two trimesters of pregnancy. In C. W. Bardin, E. Milgrom, & P. Mauvais-Jarvis (Eds.), *Progesterone and progestins* (pp. 247–258). New York: Raven Press.

Swaab, D. F., & Fliers, E. (1985). A sexually dimorphic nucleus in the human brain. *Science, 228,* 1112–1114.

Swaab, D. F., Gooren, L. J. G., & Hofman, M. A. (1992). The human hypothalamus in relation to gender and sexual orientation. *Progress in Brain Research, 93,* 205–219.

Swaab, D. F., & Hofman, M. A. (1988). Sexual differentiation of the human hypothalamus: Ontogeny of the sexually dimorphic nucleus of the preoptic area. *Developmental Brain Research, 44,* 314–318.

Swaab, D. F., & Hofman, M. A. (1990). An enlarged suprachiasmatic nucleus in homosexual men. *Brain Research, 537,* 141.

Tapanainen, J., Kellokumpa-Lehtinen, O., Pelliniemi, L., & Huhtaniemi, I. (1981). Age-related changes in endogenous steroids of human fetal testes during early and midpregnancy. *Journal of Clinical Endocrinology and Metabolism, 52,* 98–102.

Torres-Aleman, I., Rejas, M. T., Barasoania, I., Borrell, J., & Guaza, C. (1986). Corticosterone-releasing activity of immune mediators. *Life Sciences, 40,* 929–934.

Tourney, G. (1980). Hormones and homosexuality. In J. Marmor (Ed.), *Homosexual behavior* (pp. 41–58). New York: Basic Books.

Tuttle, G. E., & Pillard, R. C. (1991). Sexual orientation and cognitive abilities. *Archives of Sexual Behavior, 20,* 307–318.

Udani, M., Parker, S., Gavaler, J., & van Thiel, D. H. (1985). Effects on in utero exposure to alcohol upon male rats. *Alcoholism: Clinical and Experimental Research, 9,* 355–359.

Ulibarri, C., & Yahr, P. (1987). Poly-A+ mRNA and defeminization of sexual behavior and gonadotropin secretion in rats. *Physiology and Behavior, 39,* 767–774.

Van Thiel, D. H., & Gavaler, J. S. (1985). Endocrine effects of chronic alcohol abuse: Hypothalamic-pituitary-gonadal axis. In R. E. Tater & D. S. Van Thiel (Eds.), *Alcohol and the brain* (pp. 69–80). New York: Plenum Press.

Vathy, I., Etgen, A. M., & Barfield, R. J. (1985). Effects of prenatal exposure to morphine in the development of sexual behavior in rats. *Pharmacology, Biochemistry and Behavior, 22,* 227–232.

Vathy, I., & Katay, L. (1992). Effects of prenatal morphine on adult sexual behavior and brain catecholamines. *Developmental Brain Research, 68,* 125–131.

Vathy, I., Katay, L., & Mini, K. N. (1993). Sexually dimorphic effects of prenatal cocaine on adult sexual behavior and brain catecholamines. *Developmental Brain Research, 73,* 115–122.

Vom Saal, F. S. (1983). Variations in infanticide and parental behavior in male mice due to prior intrauterine proximity to female fetuses: Elimination by prenatal stress. *Physiology and Behavior, 30,* 675–681.

Von Berswordt-Wallrabe, R. (1983). Antiandrogenic actions of progestins. In C. W. Bardin, E. Milgrom, & P. Mauvais-Jarvis (Eds.), *Progesterone and progestins* (pp. 109–119). New York: Raven Press.

Walker, P. A., & Money, J. (1972). Prenatal androgenization of females. *Hormones, 3,* 119–128.

Ward, B., Jr., Roth, J. M., & Weisz, J. (1983). A possible role of opiates in modifying sexual differentiation. In M. Schlumpf & W. Lichtensteiger (Eds.), *Drugs and hormones in brain development* (pp. 194–200). New York: Karger.

Ward, I. L. (1972a). Female sexual behavior in male rats treated prenatally with an anti-androgen. *Physiology and Behavior, 8,* 53–56.

Ward, I. L. (1972b). Prenatal stress feminizes and demasculinizes the behavior of males. *Science, 175,* 82–84.

Ward, I. L. (1974). Sexual behavior differentiation: Prenatal hormonal and environmental control. In R. C. Friedman, R. M. Richart, & R. L. Vande Wiele (Eds.), *Sex differences in behavior* (pp. 3–17). New York: Wiley.

Ward, I. L. (1977). Exogenous androgen activates female behavior in noncopulating, prenatally stressed male rats. *Journal of Comparative and Physiological Psychology, 91,* 465–471.

Ward, I. L. (1984). The prenatal stress syndrome: Current status. *Psychoneuroendocrinology, 9,* 3–11.

Ward, I. L., Ward, O. B., Winn, R. J., & Bielawski, D. (1994). Male and female sexual behavior potential of male rats prenatally exposed to the influence of alcohol, stress, or both factors. *Behavioral Neuroscience, 108,* 1188–1195.

Ward, I. L., & Weisz, J. (1980). Maternal stress alters plasma testosterone in fetal males. *Science, 207,* 328–329.

Warriar, N., Page, N., Koutsilieris, M., & Govindan, M. (1993). Interaction of antiandrogens-androgen receptor complexes with DNA and transcription activation. *Journal of Steroid Biochemistry and Molecular Biology, 46,* 699–711.

Watabe, T., & Endo, A. (1994). Sexual orientation of male mouse offspring prenatally exposed to ethanol. *Neurotoxicology and Teratology, 16,* 25–29.

Whitam, F. L., Diamond, M., & Martin, J. (1993). Homosexual orientation in twins: A report on 61 pairs and three triplet sets. *Archives of Sexual Behavior, 22,* 187–206.

Whitney, J. B., & Herrenkohl, L. R. (1977). Effects of anterior hypothalamic lesions on the feminized sexual behavior of prenatally-stressed male rats. *Physiology and Behavior, 19,* 167–169.

Wilson, R. S. (1978). Synchronies in mental development: An epigenetic perspective. *Science, 202,* 939–948.

Winter, J. S. D. (1987). Sexual differentiation. In P. Felig, J. D. Baxter, A. D. Broadus, & L. A. Frohman (Eds.), *Endocrinology and metabolism* (pp. 983–1039). New York: McGraw Hill.

Woodman, S. (1990, November). Will your child be straight or gay? *Child,* pp. 104–107, 113–115.

Ylikahri, R., Huttunen, M., & Harkonen, M. (1974). Hangovers and testosterone. *Preventive Medicine Journal, 2,* 445.

Zenchak, J. J. & Anderson, G. C. (1980). Sexual performance levels of rams (ovis aries) as affected by social experiences during rearing. *Journal of Animal Science, 50,* 167–174.

Zimmerberg, B., & Reuter, J. M. (1989). Sexually dimorphic behavioral and brain asymmetries in neonatal rats: Effects of prenatal alcohol exposure. *Development Brain Research, 46,* 281–290.

*Chapter 3*

▼

# GENDER IDENTITY

## J. Michael Bailey

The stereotypical gay man is feminine in a number of respects. He has feminine interests such as decorating and gardening. He works in an occupation such as hairstyling or clothing design. He has feminine mannerisms. He is uninterested in sports. He is the opposite of macho, and nearly the opposite of the stereotypical lesbian. She has short hair, often wears flannel shirts, always wears pants, and never wears jewelry or makeup. She is an army captain or perhaps an athletic coach, and is a member of several women's athletic teams. She has a masculine comportment and is not deferential to others.

*Like all stereotypes, these portrayals fail to adequately characterize the diversity that exists within the gay male and lesbian worlds. Virtually anyone who knows even a few gay men or lesbians has met someone who defies the stereotypes. In the public arena, David Kopay (Kopay & Young, 1977) has written an autobiography about his life as a gay professional football player, and Marlene Dietrich, the glamorous heterosexual sex symbol, was apparently sexually involved with several women (Spoto, 1992).*

*Obviously, the stereotypes do not apply to all gay men and lesbians, but the question remains whether they are valid at all. That is, are gay men and lesbians more likely than their heterosexual counterparts to fit them? It is worth noting that these stereotypes are held by some gay men and lesbians as well. For example, gay men have a variety of words (e.g., "nelly," "swish," "blasé;" Tripp, 1975) to label feminine behavior in gay men. Some lesbians classify each other as either "butch" or "femme" (Rosenzweig & Lebow, 1992). Though suggestive, these observations are insufficient to establish the validity of the stereotypes because even the targets of invalid stereotypes are capable of believing them.*

*Considerable empirical research has focused on the relation of sexual orientation to various gender-related characteristics. Indeed, more is known about the ways in which gay and lesbian people are masculine or feminine than about the causes of sexual orientation. Before reviewing this literature, it is important to define several concepts and terms.*

## BACKGROUND AND DEFINITIONS

When we describe a man as "feminine" or a woman as "masculine," what do we mean? Presumably, we mean that the individual we are describing has some attributes more typical of the opposite sex. But many traits are more characteristic of one sex or the other, from genital shape to preference for certain television programs. Which traits, if any, are most important in our judgments of someone as "masculine" or "feminine"?

The answer to this question is complicated and controversial. People can be masculine in certain respects and feminine in others. Gay men, for instance, are feminine in their sexual orientation but masculine in their physical characteristics. Some psychologists have argued that both males and females can be arrayed along two independent dimensions of masculinity and femininity. That is, an individual can be both highly masculine and highly feminine; knowing how masculine she or he is tells us nothing about how feminine she or he is (Bem, 1974). Other psychologists have argued that there are many more than two independent dimensions of masculinity and femininity (Spence, 1984). The "structure" of masculinity and femininity remains an important, unresolved issue.

There appears to be a group of associated behaviors and feelings that is closely related to that which most people mean when they describe others as masculine or feminine. Scholars have introduced two important terms. *Gender roles* refers to those behaviors, attitudes, and personality traits that a society designates as masculine or feminine, that is, more "appropriate" for or typical of the male or female social role. In young children, the measurement of gender role behavior includes several easily observable phenomena, including preference for same- versus opposite-sex friends and interest in rough-and-tumble play, fantasy roles, toy interests, and dress-up play (see Zucker, 1985). In adults, gender roles include occupational and recreational interests, and traits such as aggressiveness and nurturance. A closely related term, *gender identity* refers to one's subjective sense of being either male or female. Some men feel very masculine and others feel somewhat feminine; they differ in their gender identity. Transsexuals are deeply convinced that they were born the wrong biological sex. Transsexualism is precisely a discordance between gender identity and anatomical sex.

Money (1987) argued that gender identity and gender roles are two sides of the same coin; gender roles express one's gender identity. Although the association between gender identity and gender roles is undoubtedly imperfect, Money's position is generally correct. Individuals with atypical gender identity, such as transsexual persons, on average, tend to have atypical gender roles as well; the converse is also true. Thus, in order to simplify terminology, I use the term *gender identity* to encompass both gender identity and gender roles in their original meanings.

# CHILDHOOD GENDER IDENTITY AND SEXUAL ORIENTATION

Typical boys behave differently than typical girls, and this difference becomes prominent by three years of age (Maccoby & Jacklin, 1974). However, some boys behave somewhat like girls, and are derogatorily called "sissies." Some girls behave somewhat like boys and are called, less derogatorily, "tomboys" (Martin, 1990). What is known about psychosexual development of boys and girls with atypical gender identity? Research has shown that most very feminine boys become gay or bisexual men. The available research on masculine girls, less definitive than that for feminine boys, suggests that they have a higher than average chance of becoming lesbians, though most will develop heterosexually.

## Feminine Boys to Gay Men?

Two moderately sized prospective studies, one by Green (1987) and one by Zuger (1984), have provided the most important evidence concerning psychosexual development of children with atypical gender identity. Both studies focused exclusively on boys, which is unfortunate for our knowledge of female development. Their results were quite consistent with each other and together provide definitive evidence concerning the relation between childhood gender identity and adult sexual orientation.

### Green's study

Green (1987) asked mental health professionals to refer to him very feminine boys. By this method and word of mouth, he recruited 66 such boys. He also obtained a control group of 56 nonfeminine boys through newspaper advertisements. The boys were first seen at about 7 years of age, with a range from 4 to 12 years, and were interviewed periodically until the final follow-up.

The feminine boys exhibited a variety of stereotypically feminine behaviors. They were much more likely than control boys to

1. Cross-dress: nearly 70% did this frequently compared to none of the controls.
2. Play with dolls: over 50% did this frequently, compared to fewer than 5% of the controls.
3. Take female roles in games such as playing house: nearly 60% took the female role versus none of the controls.
4. Relate better to girls rather than boys as peers: about 80% did so compared to fewer than 5% of the controls.
5. Wish to be girls: over 80% stated such a wish occasionally, compared to fewer than 10% of controls.

6. Have below average interest in rough-and-tumble play and sports participation: nearly 80% had below-average interest, compared to 20% of controls.

Clearly the feminine boys were atypical when compared with other boys their age.

Parents reported that the feminine behaviors emerged quite early. For instance, three quarters of parents whose son cross-dressed said that this began before their son turned four, and virtually all boys began before age six. When the cross-gender behaviors emerged, some parents reacted neutrally or even favorably. Parents presented Green with photographs of their son's cross-dressing, wearing high-heeled shoes and dresses. Presumably these were taken by parents who found the sight amusing. Other parents were horrified and intolerant of the behavior, as demonstrated by the following transcript of an interview with a mother:

**GREEN:**    Initially, how did you feel about the behavior?
**MOTHER:**    Very upset.
**GREEN:**    Even at the beginning?
**MOTHER:**    Even at the beginning. It was transitory upset at first, and then when it continued on a steady basis, it began to be much more of a long-term fear that set in.
**GREEN:**    Did you convey at first your concern about the dressing up to him?
**MOTHER:**    Yes. I reacted, overreacted is more the word, with sharp words mainly. (p. 67)

Green found evidence for a small effect of parents' reactions on their son's subsequent behavior. Among the feminine group, sons whose parents discouraged feminine behavior displayed slightly less of it over time. Perhaps the most impressive aspect of Green's data on parents is the diversity of stories they told. Given their son's highly unusual behavior, it is striking that no factor clearly differentiated the parents of the feminine boys from other parents. Although it is possible that Green failed to assess a crucial variable, his study provides no unambiguous support for the notion that feminine boys are a product of the parental psychosocial environment.

The most important overall finding of Green's study concerns the adult outcomes of the feminine boys. He reinterviewed 44 of the feminine boys and 35 of the control subjects when the average age was 18.9 years, with a range from 14 to 24 years. Some boys could not be located and others did not wish to participate; attrition is inevitable in longitudinal research.

Green initially became interested in feminine boys through his research with transsexual men, whose adult gender identities are so feminine that they often elect to undergo drastic and expensive surgeries to change their anatomical sex. Nearly all transsexual men reported that they were very feminine boys. Only one of Green's subjects became a transsexual man, a boy from the feminine group who at follow-up intended to obtain sex-change surgery. A rate of even 1 in 60 boys is much higher than would be expected by chance—the rate of male trans-sexualism in the general population appears to be approximately 1 in 12,000 (Bakker, van Kesteren, Gooren, & Bezemer, in press). On the other hand, feminine boys are clearly not very likely to become transsexual men.

Green's data provide a much clearer answer to the question of whether feminine boys become gay men. Based on interview information, he assigned two relevant numbers to each subject: a Kinsey fantasy score and a Kinsey behavior score (Kinsey, Pomeroy, & Martin, 1948). The Kinsey scale ranges from 0, indicating absolute heterosexuality, to 6, indicating absolute homosexuality. Scores 0 and 1 are typically considered to represent heterosexuality, 2 through 4, bisexuality, and 5 and 6, homosexuality. Several of Green's subjects had not yet had a sexual relationship and thus could not be rated with respect to their sexual behavior. For them, and indeed perhaps for all subjects, the Kinsey fantasy score was most relevant because it is the purest measure of psychological preference. Three quarters (33 of 44) of the feminine boys who provided follow-up data had bisexual or homosexual fantasy scores (i.e., Kinsey ratings from 2–6); none of the 35 control boys did. Of the boys who had had interpersonal sexual experience, 80% (24 of 30) had bisexual or homosexual scores, compared to 4% (1 of 25) of the control group. It is important to emphasize that these figures are based on self-report, and thus may underestimate the true rates of homosexuality in both groups due, for example, to fears of accepting or revealing homosexual feelings or experiences. Regardless, feminine boys were much more likely than controls to become gay or bisexual men.

### Zuger's study

Zuger (1984) conducted a similar prospective study of 55 feminine boys. Unlike Green, Zuger had no control group of typical boys. This is not a substantial problem, however, because population surveys provide estimates of the expected rate of homosexuality (Watson, 1993). Also different from Green's study, Zuger's study included 16 boys between the ages of 12 and 16. Parents confirmed that their son's feminine behavior began quite early, with only two mothers dating its onset after the age of 6. Overall, the boys were first seen at an average age of 9 years. At follow-up, 48 of the subjects were seen at an average age of 19.7 years. Sexual orientation was rated either by self-report or by confirmation from other sources, for example, a parent's knowledge of the son's sexuality.

Zuger's findings were remarkably similar to Green's results. Of the subjects who were successfully followed, 73% (35 of 48) were judged to have homosexual/bisexual orientations, 6% (3 of 48) to have heterosexual orientations, and 21% (10 of 48) could not be determined due to insufficient information. Although Zuger had no control group, the rate of homosexuality that he found in his sample was much higher than even the 10% rate often cited as the rate of homosexuality in the general population. (That figure, based on Kinsey et al.'s [1948] work, is now thought to substantially overestimate the true rate [Watson, 1993].)

### How conclusive is the evidence?

A determined skeptic might object that although suggestive, available studies included a rather small number of subjects. Are they sufficient to establish a link between childhood gender identity and adult male sexual orientation? Zucker (1990) reviewed prospective studies of feminine boys, including Green's and Zuger's study and several smaller reports. There were a total of 99 such boys followed to adulthood. He excluded cases first assessed in adolescence because of the possibility that parents of these boys sought treatment precisely because the boys were already gay. At follow-up, 59 of the subjects had a homosexual or bisexual orientation, 26 had a heterosexual orientation, and 14 could not be determined with information available to the researchers.

Let us assume, conservatively, that all 14 boys who could not be rated were heterosexual and that the population rate of adult male homosexuality is 10%. If in reality there were no association between childhood gender identity and adult sexual orientation, how likely is it that 59 of a sample of 99 boys would become homosexual merely by chance? The odds against this are greater than 10,000,000,000,000,000,000,000,000,000,000,000,000,000,000,000,000,000 to 1. Excluding the 14 boys of uncertain orientation and taking the more reasonable population rate of 4% suggested by Gebhard (1972), the odds against this increase to 1,000,000,000,000,000,000,000,000,000,000,000,000,000,000,000, 000,000,000,000,000,000,000,000,000,000,000,000,000,000,000,000,000,000, 000,000,000,000,000,000,000,000,000,000,000,000,000,000,000,000,000,000, 000,000,000,000,000,000,000,000,000,000,000,000,000,000,000,000 to 1. In other words, the odds against these findings occurring due to chance are astronomically high. Most theories in the social and behavioral sciences rest on findings considerably less firmly established than these. Indeed, the magnitude of this effect can scarcely be overstated. Furthermore, to my knowledge no other childhood behavior is as predictive of an adult characteristic as atypical childhood gender identity is of male homosexuality.

## Were Most Gay Men Feminine Boys?

Although very feminine boys are quite likely to become gay men, it does not necessarily follow that all or even most gay men were feminine boys. Although no one knows with certainty, it appears likely that boys with the degree of femininity studied by Green and Zuger are rarer than gay men. If so, then some gay men were not extremely feminine boys. Moreover, as noted earlier, some gay men are stereotypically masculine. Perhaps there are different developmental routes to male homosexuality. Assuming that this is the case, how common is the route through feminine childhood gender identity?

With Zucker, I reviewed 32 studies in which both gay men and heterosexual men were asked retrospectively about behaviors related to childhood gender identity (Bailey & Zucker, 1995). Typically, interviews or scales included items concerning cross-dressing, interest in rough play or sports, preference for male or female peers, interest in feminine or masculine activities and toys, and the wish to be a girl. In all studies, gay men recalled significantly more feminine behavior than did heterosexual men, on at least some measures. On no measure in any study were heterosexual men significantly more feminine.

How large were the differences? Using a statistical technique called meta-analysis (Smith, Glass, & Miller, 1980), one can calculate an "effect size" that reflects the average size of a difference between two groups, across different studies. We obtained an effect size of approximately 1.3 for the comparison of gay and heterosexual men. In order to comprehend the magnitude of this difference, it is noteworthy that Cohen (1988) proposed (somewhat arbitrarily) that an effect size of at least .80 is large. This effect size is one of the largest that has been reported in the psychological literature. Another useful way of considering the difference concerns the degree of overlap between the gay and heterosexual distributions. Almost 90% of gay men exceeded the typical heterosexual man (i.e., someone at the heterosexual median) on scores of feminine childhood gender identity, and only 2% of heterosexual men scored above the typical gay man.

These analyses suggest that many, but not all, gay men were somewhat feminine as boys. However, retrospective studies have serious methodological limitations. Memory is imperfect, especially for events that occurred years ago. Even more problematic, gay men could be more likely to remember feminine childhood behaviors, whether or not they occurred. Similarly, heterosexual men may be more likely to deny or forget such behaviors. This might be especially likely if, as some have suggested (e.g., Ross, 1980), men believe stereotypes that gay men are feminine regardless of the validity of such stereotypes. On the other hand, Zuger (1984) found that some of his feminine boys had forgotten their atypical behavior at follow-up. That is consistent with informal observations I have made in my research. Gay men I have interviewed about childhood gender identity have occasionally acknowledged feminine childhood behavior and simultaneously told me that they had not thought about this in years. Thus, it is unclear whether the methodological flaws of retrospective studies have exaggerated or reduced the true difference between gay and heterosexual men. Despite the possibility of methodological biases, retrospective and prospective studies converge to suggest two conclusions. First, feminine boys become gay men at much higher rates than expected. Second, a substantial percentage of gay men were somewhat feminine boys. It is also important to emphasize that the data support the likelihood of alternative developmental routes to adult male homosexuality, with some typically masculine boys becoming gay men.

## Tomboys to Lesbians?

Tomboys are the female equivalent of feminine boys. Do tomboys tend to become lesbians? Unfortunately, there is no certain answer. We simply do not know what becomes of tomboys because no prospective study has followed tomboys into adulthood. Indeed, there has been little research of any kind done on tomboys.

One study by Green and colleagues (Green, Williams, & Goodman, 1982) compared 49 tomboys to 50 "traditionally sex-typed" girls. The tomboys were quite different with respect to their preferred toys, the gender of their peer group, sports participation, roles taken in playing house, and the stated wish to be a boy. These findings are not very surprising because, with the possible exception of wishing to be a boy, these behaviors are part of the definition of tomboy. A prospective study of tomboys would be an important contribution to developmental psychology and sexology.

Although prospective studies are necessary to establish a link between childhood gender identity and adult sexual orientation in females, retrospective studies support the likelihood that an association exists. In our meta-analysis of retrospective studies (Bailey & Zucker, 1995), we found 16 studies of women. Relevant items were quite similar to those for males. Similar to male results, all studies found that lesbian and bisexual women recalled significantly more childhood masculinity on at least some measures, and no study reported higher scores for heterosexual women on a masculinity measure. The effect size separating heterosexual women from lesbians was nearly 1.0, which while large, was significantly smaller than for men. The female distribution indicated that 81% of lesbians exceeded the typical heterosexual woman and that only 12% of heterosexual women exceeded the typical lesbian on measures of childhood gender atypicality.

Thus, the retrospective studies suggest that, on average, lesbians were more tomboyish children than were heterosexual women. On the other hand, research suggests that masculine childhood gender identity is less predictive of homosexuality in women than is feminine childhood gender identity in men. Although to my knowledge no epidemiological study has confirmed this, tomboyism is probably more common in girls than feminine behavior is in boys. In contrast, female homosexuality appears to be less common than male homosexuality (Gebhard, 1972). If these assumptions are true, there must necessarily be more tomboys who become heterosexual women than feminine boys who become heterosexual men. Using results from our meta-analysis, we estimated that of girls as masculine as the typical prelesbian, only 6% will become lesbians. In contrast, the analogous estimate for feminine boys becoming gay men was 51%. Although these estimates are very rough, they demonstrate that cross-gender identity is substantially less predictive of homosexuality for females than males.

## ADULT GENDER IDENTITY

### Are Gay Men Feminine? Are Lesbians Masculine?

Perhaps surprisingly, research on the adult gender identity of gay men and lesbians has been less abundant and is more difficult to characterize than research on their childhood gender identity. This is surprising because stereotypes about gay men and lesbians focus on their adult, as opposed to childhood, behavior, and because it should be easier to gather information about present than past behavior.

One possible reason why childhood gender identity has been more thoroughly investigated is that differences in gender identity between heterosexual and homosexual individuals may be less pronounced in adulthood than childhood. Whitam (1977) observed that most gay men are not markedly feminine despite evidence that many were feminine boys. He speculated that a defeminization process occurred between early childhood and adulthood, most likely due to parental and peer pressures to behave in a conventional manner. Harry (1983) investigated Whitam's hypothesis by asking gay men to recall cross-gender characteristics for several age periods. Consistent with the defeminization hypothesis, he found that cross-gender identity diminished from childhood to adolescence to adulthood. One limitation of the study concerned the equivalence of items across the different time periods. For example, "Did you play with girls?" is much less appropriate when asked about adolescence or adulthood than about childhood.

### One- and two-factor scales of masculinity-femininity

This limitation of Harry's (1983) study exemplifies a second reason why the issue of gender identity differences is less clear for adults. The measurement of gender identity is presently less satisfactory for adults than for children. A number of empirically derived scales have been devised to measure a putative dimension of "masculinity-femininity." These scales were typically constructed by selecting from a large pool of items those that discriminated between men and women. Perhaps the most frequently used scale in research on sexual orientation has been the Minnesota Multiphasic Personality Inventory M-F subscale, which unfortunately includes one item ("I am very strongly attracted to members of my own sex") that directly measures sexual orientation. Pillard (1991) reviewed studies containing measures of masculinity-femininity and found that in 26 of 27 studies, gay men were significantly more feminine. Lesbians were more masculine in three of four studies. Thus, the evidence overwhelmingly supports the notion that homosexual adults are somewhat gender atypical. Unfortunately, none of the masculinity-femininity tests are based on coherent theory—much less established theory—and so it is unclear precisely what the findings mean. All that can safely be concluded is that, for example, gay men respond to some test items somewhat as women do.

For the past 20 years or so, most research on adult gender identity (in the general sense that I am using in this chapter) has employed either the Bem Sex Role Inventory (BSRI; Bem, 1974) or the Personal Attributes Questionnaire (PAQ; Spence & Helmreich, 1978). Both instruments were conceptually premised on the notion mentioned earlier, that psychological masculinity and psychological femininity are two independent factors. This two-factor theory of masculinity-femininity is highly problematic for several reasons (see Brown, 1986, chapter 9; Spence, 1984). One primary objection is that the masculinity and femininity factors measured by these scales are more appropriately conceptualized as measuring two general personality factors that differ between the sexes: desirable instrumental traits such as "active," "competitive," or "assertive," and desirable expressive traits such as "affectionate," "gentle," or "compassionate." This is not to deny the utility of these measures, but only to dispute the claim that they measure "masculinity" and "femininity" per se. Pillard (1991) found that in studies using either the BSRI or PAQ, gay men tended to be higher on the femininity—or more accurately, expressiveness—subscale and lesbians on the masculinity—instrumentality—subscale. However, gay men tended to be as high as heterosexual men on the masculinity subscale and lesbians as high as heterosexual women on the femininity subscale. These findings are intriguing, though perhaps not as important as they would be if the subscales measured core masculinity and femininity rather than sexually dimorphic personality traits.

One unfortunate consequence of the dominance of the two-factor model of masculinity-femininity has been a lack of research on alternative models and measures related to adult gender identity. In particular, it would be desirable to construct measures directly analogous to those used to assess gender identity in childhood. One difference between the two kinds of measures has been the behavioral focus of the childhood measures compared to the psychological trait focus of the adult measures. Ideally, both kinds of measures should assess both behaviors and psychological characteristics.

## Other sexually dimorphic traits

Perhaps it is unrealistic to expect simple answers to questions such as, "Are gay men feminine and lesbians masculine?" It may be more reasonable to ask, "In what ways are gay men and lesbians similar to heterosexual individuals of the same sex, and in what ways are they somewhat similar to those of the opposite sex?" The latter question implies that an answer will be multidimensional and thus complicated and that research cannot provide an answer using one or two measures. The research program required to answer it would involve many studies, of different sexually dimorphic psychological and behavioral traits.

This research program is in its infancy. However, I briefly discuss two aspects of sexually dimorphic behavior that have been examined for associations with sexual orientation: sexual behavior and aggressiveness. Some of the largest sex differences concern sexual behavior (Oliver & Hyde, 1993). With colleagues, I examined the relation of some aspects of sexually dimorphic sexual psychology to sexual orientation in both men and women: interest in visual sexual stimuli, sexual versus emotional jealousy, interest in uncommitted sex, and importance of a partner's physical attractiveness, status, and youth (Bailey, Gaulin, Agyei, & Gladue, 1994). For the most part, gay men responded similarly to heterosexual men, and lesbians similarly to heterosexual women. For example, gay and heterosexual men were equally interested in casual sex, and lesbians and heterosexual women were, relatively speaking, equally disinterested. This supports Symons's (1979) speculation that gay men's relatively high average number of sexual partners compared to heterosexual men reflects their increased opportunities, because both partners are interested in casual sex, rather than increased interest. Gay men and lesbians were also similar to same-sex heterosexual subjects in the emphasis they placed on a partner's physical attractiveness, with men emphasizing looks more than women.

We found interesting exceptions, however. For example, similar to gay and heterosexual men, lesbians appeared more interested than heterosexual women in visual sexual stimuli such as erotica—though their interest was intermediate between that of men and heterosexual women. Lesbians were also similar to men in placing relatively low emphasis on a partner's status. Gay men were similar to women in their greater concern with emotional than with sexual infidelity and were intermediate between women and heterosexual men in the emphasis they placed on a partner's youth, with heterosexual men desiring the youngest partners. The interpretations and specific implications of these findings are beyond the scope of this chapter. Nonetheless, they obviously support the general view that neither gay men nor lesbians are generally masculine or feminine. Rather, their degree of masculinity or femininity depends on the sexually dimorphic characteristic.

Consistent sex differences have also been found for aggressiveness, with men more verbally and physically aggressive (Eagly & Steffen, 1986; Hyde, 1984) and competitive (Gladue & Siemens, 1993) than women. Gay men, however, recall being relatively physically unaggressive as boys (Blanchard, McConkey, Roper, & Steiner, 1985). Two studies have focused on adult aggressiveness and sexual orientation. Gladue (1991) administered an aggressiveness questionnaire previously demonstrated to yield moderate to large sex differences in both homosexual and heterosexual subjects of both sexes. Aggressiveness was unrelated to sexual orientation among men. Among women, lesbians reported less physical aggressiveness than did heterosexual women. The sample sizes in this study were rather small (16 to 21 per group), and thus the negative findings for men should be regarded cautiously.

Gladue and Bailey (1994) administered aggressiveness and competitiveness questionnaires to a much larger sample of gay men, lesbians, and heterosexual men and women (68 to 82 per group). They found, as expected, that men were more physically and verbally aggressive and more competitive than women. The only association with sexual orientation was higher physical aggressiveness in heterosexual than gay men. This was true even though the various kinds of aggressiveness were moderately intercorrelated, again suggesting that sexual orientation is quite selectively associated with other sexually dimorphic characteristics.

### Occupations and careers

One component of gender identity concerns occupational interests. Do gay men and lesbians have gender-atypical careers? Stereotypes suggest that they do. However, for obvious reasons, it is difficult to gather accurate data about the incidence of homosexuality in different occupations. Because gay men and lesbians continue to face discrimination in the workplace, they may be hesitant to participate in such research. Gay men and lesbians who are in the least tolerant occupations may be the most likely to remain closeted and therefore the least likely to be recruited for scientific studies of homosexuality.

Nevertheless, there has been research on the career choices of gay men, but less so with lesbians. Gay men are underrepresented in blue-collar occupations and overrepresented in service occupations compared to heterosexual men, perhaps because the latter occupations are more consistent with their gender identities (Harry & DeVall, 1978). Although there are no hard data, many people believe that gay men are overrepresented among artists, dancers, and fashion designers, and that lesbians are overrepresented among soldiers and professional athletes. A methodologically rigorous study of these possibilities would be fascinating.

# OTHER SCIENTIFIC ISSUES

## What Is the Nature of the Association Between Gender Identity and Sexual Orientation?

Why is there an association between gender identity and sexual orientation? Two general approaches to this question have been explored, one primarily biological and the other psychosocial.

### Biological interpretations

The most prominent biological hypothesis is that sexual orientation is a function of the degree of masculinization relevant brain structures due to the effects of early androgens (or male hormones) influencing the brain (LeVay, 1993; Meyer-Bahlburg, 1984; see also Ellis, "The Role of Perinatal Factors," this volume for a review). The relevant findings could account for the association between gender identity and sexual orientation in at least two ways. First, brain structures that affect sexual orientation might be the same structures that affect gender identity. The hypothalamus has been the most frequently mentioned brain area hypothesized to affect sexual orientation. The first biological explanation for the association between gender identity and sexual orientation, then, would also require that the hypothalamus influence other sex-dimorphic behaviors. A second possible explanation is that the processes that masculinize the brain structures affecting sexual orientation also have more general effects. Thus, for example, the hypothalamus may affect sexual orientation while a separate area, subject to similar influences during sexual differentiation, affects gender identity. The plausibility of this explanation is somewhat supported by findings of LeVay (1991) and Allen and Gorski (1992), who demonstrated associations with male sexual orientation for two different areas of the brain.

The general hypothesis that gender identity and sexual orientation are both hormonally influenced has received empirical support from studies of girls and women with congenital adrenal hyperplasia (CAH), which is the result of prenatal and early postnatal exposure to high levels of androgens. Girls and women with CAH are somewhat masculine with regard to several components of gender identity, such as interests and career ambitions (Berenbaum & Hines, 1992; Ehrhardt & Baker, 1974). Adult women with CAH also appear to have increased rates of bisexuality and homosexuality (Dittmann, Kappes, & Kappes, 1992; Money, Schwartz, & Lewis, 1984; Zucker et al., 1992; for counterevidence, see Mulaikal, Migeon, & Rock, 1987).

### Psychosocial interpretations

Some psychoanalysts have stressed the importance of children's relative identification with the same-sex or opposite-sex parent in determining eventual sexual orientation (e.g., Bieber et al., 1962). Male homosexuality was hypothesized to result from the combination of an excessively close mother-son relationship and a distant, if not antagonistic, father-son relationship. Female homosexuality has received much less psychoanalytic attention. This pattern allegedly led to the son's identification with the mother instead of the father, as was thought to occur for heterosexual males, and the first manifestation of this process was hypothesized to be atypical childhood gender identity. Although retrospective studies have usually found gay men to recall feeling more distance from their fathers and more closeness to their mothers during childhood (for reviews, see Freund & Blanchard, 1983; Friedman, 1988), the differences have been modest (e.g., Bell, Weinberg, & Hammersmith, 1981). More importantly, the interpretation of the findings is ambiguous. Because fathers are relatively intolerant of feminine behavior in their sons (e.g., Langlois & Downs, 1980), fathers may behave in a more distant or rejecting manner toward prehomosexual sons precisely because those sons are more likely to exhibit feminine behavior. By this account, childhood cross-sex-typed behavior is a cause rather than a consequence of "father distance." Available data cannot definitively resolve which, if either, of these two possibilities explains the associations among childhood gender identity, father distance, and male sexual orientation. Biological theories of sexual orientation are more consistent with the possibility that childhood sex-typed behavior and sexual orientation have common influences that precede and, hence, are more likely to affect than be influenced by family relationships. Because we know little about the causes of either sexual orientation or gender identity, the nature of their association remains uncertain.

## Within-Orientation Differences in Gender Identity

Even the strong association between childhood gender identity and male sexual orientation is imperfect. Some feminine boys become heterosexual men, and some gay men were typically masculine boys. Some gay men and heterosexual women are very masculine; some lesbians and heterosexual men are very feminine. What can such individuals tell us about the development of sex differences, especially sexual orientation?

Writers have speculated that there may be more than one cause of homosexuality—and necessarily, heterosexuality—each with different developmental routes and associated behavior. For example, Meyer-Bahlburg (1993) speculated that hormonal theories of sexual orientation may be most relevant to lesbians and gay men who were atypical in their childhood gender identity. Similarly, Bell et al. (1981) suggested that gay men and lesbians who were gender-typical as children may have been influenced primarily by psychosocial factors in their sexual development.

Evaluating such hypotheses requires that studies about the causes of sexual orientation also include measures of gender identity. Then one can assess whether results depend on whether gay men or lesbians are typical or atypical in their gender identity. There have been preliminary efforts to examine such possibilities. For example, genetic studies of male (Bailey & Pillard, 1991) and female (Bailey, Pillard, Neale, & Agyei, 1993) sexual orientations have explored whether homosexuality associated with atypical gender identity is especially genetic compared to other kinds of homosexuality. Neither study found evidence that the degree of genetic influence was related to gender identity. Intriguingly, both studies reported that when identical twins were concordant for homosexuality (i.e., were either both gay or both lesbian), they recalled very similar childhood gender identities. This suggests that genetic factors influencing sexual orientation also affect the degree of atypical gender identity. The study of within-orientation differences in gender identity remains a potentially important and underexplored area.

## Bisexuality

Most research on sexual orientation either excludes bisexual subjects or includes them with gay or lesbian subjects. However, several studies have examined gender identity in bisexual subjects. The primary justification for studying bisexual subjects has been the possibility that they may be intermediate between homosexual and heterosexual subjects in their gender identity. Phillips and Over (1992) studied childhood gender identity in a sample of gay and bisexual men. They reported that for each of 10 items regarding childhood gender identity, bisexual men were intermediate between heterosexual and gay men. A similar analysis by Bailey (1989) and Bell et al. (1981), however, failed to find such a relationship within nonheterosexual men. Regarding nonheterosexual women, Bell et al. (1981) found that bisexual women reported less "childhood gender nonconformity" than homosexual women. Thus, the literature concerning bisexual subjects is both mixed and scanty.

## Transvestism and Transsexualism

There has historically been considerable confusion regarding the relationship among homosexuality, transvestism, and transsexualism. Most people understand "transvestite" to mean an individual who dresses in the clothing of the opposite

sex. One frequently hears the assertion that the majority of transvestites are heterosexual men. On the other hand, a visit to a gay neighborhood on Halloween
night or to a "drag" show may make one skeptical that transvestism is primarily
a heterosexual activity. The film *Paris is Burning* depicts gay African American
men who devote a considerable amount of time, money, and energy trying to look
like beautiful women. One of the men in that film described how he had considered but decided against a sex-change operation. Another man intended to obtain
the operation when he could afford it. Are the subjects of that film gay men, transvestites, or transsexuals, or do they fit more than one category?

Recently, researchers have made considerable progress in elucidating the
differences and similarities among transvestism, transsexualism, and homosexuality (Blanchard, 1989; Blanchard, 1991; Blanchard, Clemmensen, & Steiner,
1987). They can be usefully distinguished on two dimensions: development and
motivation. Most contemporary sexologists reserve the term *transvestism* to
refer to those who derive sexual gratification from cross-dressing. A transvestite typically experiences a compulsion to cross-dress, often in private. The large
majority of transvestites in this sense are heterosexual men who had masculine
gender identity as children. Most are married and have children (Talamini, 1982).
A tiny proportion of transvestites in this sense are women.

Transsexuals are individuals who want their physical anatomy to match their
gender identity—that of the opposite sex. As noted earlier, transsexualism is a
problem of gender identity in the original specific sense of gender identity as
subjective comfort with one's biological sex. The classic transsexual is a woman
or man who has felt, as long as she or he can remember, that nature played a
cruel trick by assigning her or him the wrong body. As a child, a male-to-female
transsexual was a very feminine boy; a female-to-male transsexual was a very
masculine girl. Transsexuals frequently cross-dress as well and attempt to pass
as a member of the opposite sex. They typically come to gender-reassignment
clinics in their early twenties. Some researchers refer to classic transsexuals as
"homosexual transsexuals" because they invariably have a homosexual orientation with respect to their original anatomical sex (Blanchard, 1990). Classic
transsexuals are very rare in the general population and are about as likely to be
male-to-female as female-to-male.

The picture is complicated by the existence of a second kind of transsexual.
These individuals have a very different developmental history than the classic
transsexual, and the nature of their condition is fundamentally different. Compared to others of their anatomical sex, they were not unusual in their childhood gender identities. The onset of their wish to change sexes occurred much
later, typically in their thirties (Blanchard et al., 1987). They are heterosexual.
These men—for they are nearly always male—have a history of fetishistic cross-
dressing, or transvestism in its technical sense, and can become aroused by
cross-dressing and by the idea of having a woman's body. After Blanchard (1991),
I refer to these individuals as autogynephilic transsexuals.

We know little about the causes of either classic or autogynephilic transsexualism. Nevertheless, their characteristic development and phenomenology

are distinct and regular enough to suggest general hypotheses. Classic transsexualism is probably caused by an irregularity of sexual differentiation. That is, some biological and/or social process that causes men to differ from women functions atypically in the classic transsexual. In contrast, autogynephilic transsexualism probably involves an atypical influence in the learning or conditioning of sexual stimuli, the same system that functions atypically in the development of fetishes. Interestingly, similar to autogynephilic transsexualism, fetishes are much more common in men than in women.

Developmentally and theoretically, homosexuality is more similar to classic transsexualism than to either autogynephilic transsexualism or transvestism. Both homosexuality and classic transsexualism are associated with atypical childhood gender identity, and gay men, lesbians, and classic transsexuals have homosexual orientations with respect to their anatomical sex. Some of the men in *Paris Is Burning* are probably very feminine gay men while others may be classic transsexuals. Others may be near a rather fuzzy dividing line between feminine homosexuality and classic male-to-female transsexualism. There is some indication that classic male-to-female transsexualism is becoming significantly less common, comprising a much smaller proportion of cases seen at gender-identity clinics during the last few years (Blanchard, personal communication). One possibility, admittedly speculative, is that contemporary society allows men who, in the past, would have been transsexuals to live more comfortably as very feminine gay men.

## Cross-cultural Research

Most of the research that has been reviewed was conducted in the United States during the last 25 years. It is reasonable to question the extent to which the findings are applicable to other times and places.

Historical constancies and variations in sexuality have recently received a considerable amount of scholarly attention (e.g., Boswell, 1980; Faderman, 1991; Halperin, 1990; Stein, 1990). I am personally skeptical that fundamental questions about human nature can be answered using the historical record because it is too incomplete. It is sufficiently difficult to learn about sexuality in contemporary society, even with live subjects and sophisticated data-collection techniques. I do not mean to deny the worth of historical investigations. They are a potentially rich source of fascinating hypotheses. But hypothesis testing probably requires more rigorous controls than the historical record allows.

The exploration of other cultures is generally more promising. Despite obvious barriers of language and customs, researchers can approach cultures with specific hypotheses and the methodological rigor of modern science. For example, Whitam and Mathy (1986, 1991) interviewed gay men, lesbians, and heterosexual men and women in five countries whose cultures differed appreciably in their attitudes toward homosexuality: Brazil, Guatemala, Peru, the Philippines, and the United States. They found that gay men and lesbians in all these cultures were more likely to recall cross-gender identity and behavior during childhood. Observer-rated adult gender identity was also atypical. These findings suggest that the association between sexual orientation and gender identity is not greatly affected by cultural variation.

# NORMATIVE ISSUES

## Different Identities or Identity Disorders?

Homosexuality has not been classified as a mental disorder since 1973 in the United States. In contrast, gender identity disorder of childhood and transsexualism remain as categories in the *Diagnostic and Statistical Manual of Mental Disorders-III-R* (American Psychiatric Association, 1987) and are slated for inclusion in DSM-IV as well (Bradley et al., 1991). Most people probably have little compunction considering transsexualism a mental problem. The transsexual person suffers greatly, so much that she or he is willing to endure painful, dangerous, and expensive operations that drastically alter her or his life. A few have found living with their given anatomy so distressing that they have taken matters into their own hands and mutilated their genitals (Green, 1966). By this argument, the postoperative transsexual who no longer suffers is no longer ill.

Gender identity disorder of childhood raises especially difficult questions. Prospective studies show that the vast majority of boys with this diagnosis will grow up to be (probably feminine) gay men rather than transsexuals. Despite the absence of female prospective studies, there is no reason to think that girls with the diagnosis are at any greater risk for a transsexual outcome. If such children typically adjust and lead nonpathological lives, should they be considered mentally ill?

One argument for considering children with atypical childhood gender identity to be disordered is that such children are greatly distressed and thus should receive treatment. They suffer for two general reasons. First, by definition (i.e., current diagnostic criteria) they are unhappy with their biological sex. Second, they are likely to be mistreated by their peers and have strained relations with their parents. Specialists attempt to treat both problems. They try to improve both peer and parental relations by teaching such children how to reduce their cross-gender behavior. Gender dysphoria is typically treated psychodynamically, that is, by examining inner conflicts. Controlled studies demonstrating the efficacy of such treatment remain to be conducted.

An argument against considering such children "disordered" is that the primary obstacle to their happiness is a society that is intolerant of cross-gender behavior. Moreover, unlike other behavior that society stigmatizes, such as criminality and cruelty, cross-gender behavior harms no one. Thus, labeling children with atypical gender identity as "sick" shifts the blame from society, where it belongs. This argument will become even more powerful if in the DSM-IV, the diagnostic criterion of subjective distress about one's biological sex is removed, as has been recommended (Bradley et al., 1991). The diagnostic status of gender identity disorder of childhood deserves serious debate.

## Ambivalence and Femiphobia

My primary research interest has been the causes of sexual orientation. The degree to which sexual orientation is innate or learned is immensely controversial. Yet I have been surprised to find when speaking to audiences of gay men and lesbians that the most controversial topic has not been the genetics of sexual orientation; rather, it has been the association between sexual orientation and gender identity. Controversy has taken the form of intense skepticism and even hostility.

This is particularly striking because no other interesting finding about gay and lesbian people has been better established empirically than the link between childhood gender identity and adult homosexuality. Gay and lesbian communities are deeply ambivalent about the fact that, on average, gay and lesbian people are atypical in their gender identities. This ambivalence is especially keen among gay men, so much so that I have coined a term, "femiphobia," to describe it. I have tried in vain to find discussions of this phenomenon in the scientific literature, though colleagues conducting research in the area have shared my observations. What is behind the ambivalence, and why should it be especially strong among gay men? Because this topic has not been broached, to my knowledge, no one knows the answers to these questions. I offer the following speculations, in the hopes that research and discussion will ensue.

First, gay men and lesbians have successfully used the argument that they are fundamentally no different from heterosexual people for political and social gain, and they may believe that the gender identity findings threaten this argument. One of the milestones of gay and lesbian liberation was Hooker's (1957) study that showed that gay men could not be distinguished on the basis of psychopathological test performance. Many other studies have shown that negative stereotypes about gay men and lesbians are generally untrue (see Bayer, 1981; Herek, 1990). But surely it cannot be helpful to claim something that is contradicted by empirical evidence, that is, that there are absolutely no differences between gay and lesbian people and heterosexuals. A more reasonable alternative, in my opinion, is to argue that gay men and lesbians are no different from heterosexual individuals in any respect that would justify their mistreatment. There is nothing wrong with feminine men or masculine women.

Second, similar to all people, gay men and lesbians dislike being pigeonholed into a stereotype that is not always accurate. Many gay men and lesbians are typical in their gender identities.

Two reasons for ambivalence apply more to gay men than to lesbians. First, and most importantly, in many cultures feminine boys and men are often treated badly, generally worse than masculine girls and women (Martin, 1990). If, as seems likely, many gay men were feminine boys, they probably endured harsh treatment by peers and, in some cases, parental rejection. Even merely discussing atypical gender identity may evoke memories that some gay men would prefer to be left untouched.

Second, many gay men find feminine men to be sexually unattractive. Personal classified ads in gay publications frequently request "straight-acting" partners. Few if any gay men advertise feminine traits. Jaye Davidson, the actor who played the beautiful, gay, cross-dressing man in *The Crying Game* explained: "My looks are not attractive to the gay community. To be homosexual is to like the ideal of sex. Homosexual men love very masculine men. And I'm not a very masculine person" (Giles, 1993). Thus, some gay men may not want to consider the possibility that they are feminine because it threatens their sexual self-esteem. Lesbian personal advertisements are about as likely to request "butch" as "femme" partners. I do not know why women are different in this respect.

I have suggested that gay men and lesbians are ambivalent about atypical gender identity. Ambivalence implies mixed feelings rather than unmitigated hostility. My observation has been that although they are wary about scientific evidence linking homosexuality and atypical gender identity, gay men and lesbians frequently embrace, or even delight in, gender atypicality. I recently saw the play *La Cage aux Folles,* a comedy about a gay male couple in which one member of the couple, Albin, is a cross-dressing entertainer. The play also has a touching storyline about Albin's pain at being rejected (temporarily) by the son "she" raised. The audience was disproportionately lesbians and gay men, and they, especially, appeared to revel in Albin's talent and humor. They were moved by Albin's struggle for acceptance. Both the play and the audience exemplified the commendable hope that mere difference in the mixture of masculine and feminine characteristics need not be grounds for rejection. Indeed, in some people it is cause for celebration.

## ▼   REFERENCES   ▼

Allen, L. S., & Gorski, R. A. (1992). Sexual orientation and the size of the anterior commissure of the human brain. *Proceedings of the National Academy of Sciences, 89,* 7199–7202.

American Psychiatric Association (1987). *Diagnostic and statistical manual of mental disorders* (3rd ed.). Washington, DC: Author.

Bailey, J. M. (1989). *A test of the maternal stress hypothesis for human male homosexuality.* Unpublished doctoral dissertation, University of Texas, Austin.

Bailey, J. M., Gaulin, S., Agyei, Y., & Gladue, B. A. (1994). Effects of gender and sexual orientation on evolutionarily relevant aspects of human mating psychology. *Journal of Personality and Social Psychology, 66,* 1081–1093.

Bailey, J. M., & Pillard, R. C. (1991). A genetic study of male sexual orientation. *Archives of General Psychiatry, 48,* 1089–1096.

Bailey, J. M., Pillard, R. C., Neale, M. C., & Agyei, Y. (1993). Heritable factors influences sexual orientation in women. *Archives of General Psychiatry, 50,* 217–223.

Bailey, J. M., & Zucker, K. J. (1995). Childhood sex-typed behavior and sexual orientation: A conceptual analysis and quantitative review. *Developmental Psychology, 31,* 43–55.

Bakker, A., van Kesteren, P., Gooren, L. J. G., & Bezemer, P. D. (in press). The prevalence of transsexualism in the Netherlands. *Acta Psychiatrica Scandinavica.*

Bayer, R. (1981). *Homosexuality and American psychiatry.* New York: Basic Books.

Bell, A. P., Weinberg, M. S., & Hammersmith, S. K. (1981). *Sexual preference: Its development in men and women.* Bloomington, IN: Indiana University Press.

Bem, S. L. (1974). The measurement of psychological androgyny. *Journal of Consulting and Clinical Psychology, 42,* 155–162.

Berenbaum, S. A., & Hines, M. (1992). Early androgens are related to childhood sex-typed toy preferences. *Psychological Science, 3,* 203–206.

Bieber, I., Dain, H. J., Dince, P. R., Drellich, M. G., Grand, H. G., Gundlach, R. H., Kremer, M. W., Rifkin, A. H., Wilbur, C. B., & Bieber, T. B. (1962). *Homosexuality: A psychoanalytic study.* New York: Basic Books.

Blanchard, R. (1989). The classification and labeling of nonhomosexual gender dysphorias. *Archives of Sexual Behavior, 18,* 315–334.

Blanchard, R. (1990). Gender identity disorders in adult men. In R. Blanchard & B. W. Steiner (Eds.), *Clinical management of gender identity disorders in children and adults* (pp. 47–76). Washington, DC: American Psychiatric Press.

Blanchard, R. (1991). Clinical observations and systematic study of autogynephilia. *Journal of Sex and Marital Therapy, 17,* 235–251.

Blanchard, R., Clemmensen, L. H., & Steiner, B. W. (1987). Heterosexual and homosexual gender dysphoria. *Archives of Sexual Behavior, 16,* 139–152.

Blanchard, R., McConkey, J. G., Roper, V., & Steiner, B. (1985). Measuring physical aggressiveness in heterosexual, homosexual, and transsexual males. *Archives of Sexual Behavior, 12,* 511–524.

Boswell, J. (1980). *Christianity, social tolerance and homosexuality: Gay people in Western Europe from the beginning of the Christian era to the fourteenth century.* Chicago: University of Chicago Press.

Bradley, S. J., Blanchard, R., Coates, S., Green, R., Levine, S. B., Meyer-Bahlburg, H. F. L., Pauly, I. B., & Zucker, K. J. (1991). Interim report of the DSM-IV subcommittee for gender identity disorders. *Archives of Sexual Behavior, 20,* 333–343.

Brown, R. (1986). *Social psychology: The second edition.* New York: Free Press.

Cohen, J. (1988). *Statistical power analysis for the social sciences* (2nd ed.). Hillsdale, NJ: Erlbaum.

Dittmann, R. W., Kappes, M. E., & Kappes, M. H. (1992). Sexual behavior in adolescent and adult females with congenital adrenal hyperplasia. *Psychoneuroendocrinology, 17,* 153–170.

Eagly, A. H., & Steffen, V. J. (1986). Gender and aggressive behavior: A meta-analytic review of the social psychological literature. *Psychological Bulletin, 100,* 309–330.

Ehrhardt, A. A., & Baker, S. W. (1974). Fetal androgens, human central nervous system differentiation and behavior sex differences. In R. C. Friedman, R. M. Richart, & R. L. Vande Wiele (Eds.), *Sex differences in behavior* (pp. 33–52). New York: Wiley.

Faderman, L. (1991). *Odd girls and twilight lovers.* New York: Columbia University Press.

Freund, K., & Blanchard, R. (1983). Is the distant relationship of fathers and homosexual sons related to the sons' erotic preference for male partners, or to the sons' atypical gender identity, or to both? *Journal of Homosexuality, 9,* 7–25.

Friedman, R. C. (1988). *Male homosexuality: A contemporary psychoanalytic perspective.* New Haven, CT: Yale University Press.

Gebhard, P. H. (1972). Incidence of overt homosexuality in the United States and Western Europe. In J. J. Livingood (Ed.), *NIMH Task Force on Homosexuality: Final report and background papers* (DHEW publication No. HSM 72-9116, pp. 22–29). Rockville, MD: National Institute of Mental Health.

Giles, J. (1993, April 1). [Interview with Jaye Davidson]. *Rolling Stone,* pp. 39, 59, 65.

Gladue, B. A. (1991). Aggressive behavioral characteristics, hormones, and sexual orientation in men and women. *Aggressive Behavior, 17,* 313–326.

Gladue, B. A., & Bailey, J. M. (1994). *Aggressiveness, competitiveness, and human sexual orientation.* Unpublished manuscript, Northwestern University.

Gladue, B. A., & Siemens, N. (1993, October). *Hormones and interpersonal competitiveness in men and women.* Paper presented at Annual meeting of the North Dakota Psychological Association, Fargo, ND.

Green, R. (1966). Mythological, historical, and cross-cultural aspects of transsexualism. In H. Benjamin (Ed.), *The transsexual phenomenon* (pp. 173–186). New York: Julian Press.

Green, R. (1987). *The "sissy boy syndrome" and the development of homosexuality.* New Haven: Yale University Press.

Green, R., Williams, K., & Goodman, M. (1982). Ninety-nine "tomboys" and "non-tomboys": Behavioral contrasts and demographic similarities. *Archives of Sexual Behavior, 11,* 247–266.

Halperin, D. M. (1990). *One hundred years of homosexuality and other essays on Greek love.* New York: Routledge.

Harry, J. (1983). Defeminization and adult psychological well-being among male homosexuals. *Archives of Sexual Behavior, 12,* 1–19.

Harry, J., & DeVall, W. B. (1978). *The social organization of gay males.* New York: Praeger.

Herek, G. M. (1990). Gay people and government security clearances: A social perspective. *American Psychologist, 44,* 948–955.

Hooker, E. (1957). The adjustment of the male overt homosexual. *Journal of Projective Techniques, 21,* 18–31.

Hyde, J. S. (1984). How large are gender differences in aggression? A developmental meta-analysis. *Developmental Psychology, 20,* 722–736.

Kinsey, A. C., Pomeroy, W. B., & Martin, C. E. (1948). *Sexual behavior in the human male*. Philadelphia: W. B. Saunders.

Kopay, D., & Young, P. D. (1977). *The Dave Kopay story*. New York: Arbor House.

Langlois, J. H., & Downs, A. C. (1980). Mothers, fathers, and peers as socialization agents of sex-typed play behaviors in young children. *Child Development, 51,* 1237–1247.

LeVay, S. (1991). A difference in hypothalamic structure between heterosexual and homosexual men. *Science, 253,* 1034–1037.

LeVay, S. (1993). *The sexual brain*. Cambridge, MA: MIT Press.

Maccoby, E. E., & Jacklin, C. N. (1974). *The psychology of sex differences*. Palo Alto, CA: Stanford University Press.

Martin, C. L. (1990). Attitudes and expectations about children with nontraditional and traditional gender roles. *Sex Roles, 22,* 151–165.

Meyer-Bahlburg, H. F. L. (1984). Psychoendocrine research on sexual orientation. Current status and future options. *Progress in Brain Research, 61,* 375–398.

Meyer-Bahlburg, H. F. L. (1993). Psychobiologic research on homosexuality. *Child and Adolescent Psychiatric Clinics of North America, 2,* 489–500.

Money, J. (1987). Sin, sickness, or status? Homosexual gender identity and psychoneuroendocrinology. *American Psychologist, 42,* 384–399.

Money J., Schwartz M., & Lewis V. G. (1984). Adult erotosexual status and fetal hormonal masculinization and demasculinization: 46,XX congenital virilizing adrenal hyperplasia and 46,XY androgen-insensitivity syndrome compared. *Psychoneuroendocrinology, 9,* 405–414.

Mulaikal, R. M., Migeon, C. J., & Rock, J. A. (1987). Fertility rates in female patients with congenital adrenal hyperplasia due to 21-hydroxylase deficiency. *New England Journal of Medicine, 316,* 178–182.

Oliver, M. B., & Hyde, J. S. (1993). Gender differences in sexuality: A meta-analysis. *Psychological Bulletin, 114,* 29–51.

Phillips, G., & Over, R. (1992). Adult sexual orientation in relation to memories of childhood gender conforming and gender nonconforming behaviors. *Archives of Sexual Behavior, 21,* 543–558.

Pillard, R. C. (1991). Masculinity and femininity in homosexuality: "Inversion" revisited. In J. C. Gonsiorek & J. D. Weinrich (Eds.), *Homosexuality: Research implications for public policy* (pp. 32–43). Newbury Park, CA: Sage.

Rosenzweig, J. M., & Lebow, W. C. (1992). Femme on the streets, butch in the sheets? Lesbian sex-roles, dyadic adjustment and sexual satisfaction. *Journal of Homosexuality, 23,* 1–20.

Ross, M. W. (1980). Retrospective distortion in homosexual research. *Archives of Sexual Behavior, 9,* 523–531.

Smith, M. L., Glass, G. V., & Miller, T. I. (1980). *The benefits of psychotherapy*. Baltimore: Johns Hopkins University Press.

Spence, J. T. (1984). Masculinity, femininity, and gender-related traits: A conceptual analysis and critique of current research. *Progress in Experimental Personality Research, 13,* 1–97.

Spence, J. T., & Helmreich, R. L. (1978). *Masculinity and femininity*. Austin: University of Texas Press.

Spoto, D. (1992). *The blue angel*. New York: Doubleday.

Stein, E. (1990). *Forms of desire: Sexual orientation and the social constructionist controversy*. New York: Garland Press.

Symons, D. (1979). *The evolution of human sexuality*. New York: Oxford University Press.

Talamini, J. T. (1982). *Boys will be girls: The hidden world of the heterosexual male transvestite*. Washington, DC: University Press of America.

Tripp, C. A. (1975). *The homosexual matrix*. New York: McGraw-Hill.

Watson, T. (1993). Sex surveys come out of the closet. *Science, 20,* 615–616.

Whitam, F. L. (1977). Childhood indicators of male homosexuality. *Archives of Sexual Behavior, 6,* 89–96.

Whitam, F. L., & Mathy, R. M. (1986). *Male homosexuality in four societies: Brazil, Guatemala, the Philippines, and the United States.* New York: Praeger.

Whitam, F. L., & Mathy, R. M. (1991). Childhood cross-gender behavior of homosexual females in Brazil, Peru, the Philippines, and the United States. *Archives of Sexual Behavior, 20,* 151–170.

Zucker, K. J. (1985). Cross-gender-identified children. In B. W. Steiner (Ed.), *Gender dysphoria: Development, research, management* (pp. 75–174). New York: Plenum Press.

Zucker, K. J. (1990). Gender identity disorders in children: Clinical descriptions and natural history. In R. Blanchard & B. W. Steiner (Eds.), *Clinical management of gender identity disorders in children and adults* (pp. 1–23). Washington, DC: American Psychiatric Press.

Zucker, K. J., Bradley, S. J., Oliver, G., Hood, J. E., Blake, J., & Fleming, S. (1992, July). *Psychosexual assessment of women with congenital adrenal hyperplasia: Preliminary analyses.* Poster presented at the meeting of the International Academy of Sex Research, Prague, Czechoslovakia.

Zuger, B. (1984). Early effeminate behavior in boys: Outcome and significance for homosexuality. *Journal of Nervous and Mental Disease, 172,* 90–97.

## Chapter 4

▼

# MEMORIES OF CHILDHOOD AND EARLY ADOLESCENT SEXUAL FEELINGS AMONG GAY AND BISEXUAL BOYS: A NARRATIVE APPROACH

## Ritch C. Savin-Williams[1]

*Frequently missing from scientific research on gay, bisexual, and lesbian youths is a sense of the ways in which the events occurring during their childhood and adolescence influence later development. As parents, educators, researchers, and clinicians we seldom ask our children, the students in our classrooms, or the youths in our research protocols or clinics to recall the earliest memories they have of their sexuality. Perhaps we believe that they are without early sexual memories or that it is inappropriate or ill-mannered to pursue such matters. We may want to honor their privacy or may simply be too embarrassed to talk about early childhood sexuality.*

*As a consequence, relatively little is known regarding several very important issues in pediatric sexology: the existence and content of sexual fantasies, thoughts, and feelings among children and early adolescents; the sexual activities of youths; and the meaning that children and early adolescents ascribe to their sexual desires. Gay and bisexual male youths I interviewed for a forthcoming book provided such information. Their sexual recollections often originate from first memories of infancy, are exceedingly vivid and saturated with emotionality, and are subsequently interpreted to have had profound significance for the future derivations of their sexual behavior and identity. These youths were permitted to do that which many only dream of—uninhibited self-disclosure.*

*A gay or bisexual youth may long to reminisce about his early sexual feelings but fear that his personal "story" will have little correspondence with the stories of other men and that he will consequently be ridiculed or rejected. Nevertheless, he may believe that his story has meaning for himself and that the meaning will be clarified by its recall. Because the recounting necessitates shar-ing with others aspects of an often hidden inner being, telling one's story can be both threatening and self-validating. The latter may be especially true if the youth discovers that others share facets of his unique story and will not reject or think poorly of him because of his early fantasies and sexual activities.*

*In this chapter, the uniqueness that characterizes the developmental his-tory of 44 gay and bisexual youths is portrayed intact through the narration of individual life stories. Similarities across stories are highlighted, however, to identify broad themes that reveal patterns of childhood and early adolescent memories of sexuality. The overall goal of the retrospective study that provided the data for this chapter was to understand developmental issues that are cen-tral to the well-being and resiliency of gay and bisexual male youths.*

# THE STUDY

## Research Procedures

The youths who agreed to tell their stories heard about the study through class-room lectures and word of mouth, primarily from those who had previously vol-unteered for the study. After interviewing each youth, I asked for the name of one or two other individuals who might be interested in participating.

I interviewed one half of the youths at their house or apartment and the rest at my office or a public place of their choosing, such as a café, park, or car. Tape recorders were too intrusive for the material requested so I wrote elaborate notes. The youths understood my method and were careful to pause in order that I could catch up when I fell behind. There were many long pauses and hes-itations, which also made it easier to record notes verbatim. The youths' stories cited in this chapter were derived from my notes.[2]

I introduced the study by emphasizing the critical importance of each per-sonal story:

> We all lead unique lives and have unique histories in terms of how we got to where we are today. I am interested in *your* story. In some ways your life has probably been like many others and in other ways different. If there are any questions you do not wish to answer, that is fine. Just say "pass" and I'll go to another question.

The interview consisted of initial questions regarding age, education, race, religion, community reared in, occupation of parents, and parents' marital sta-tus. The youths rated themselves on Kinsey's Sexual Orientation Scale and the extent to which they are open to others about their homosexuality. They reported when they first recollected having homoerotic attractions, the number of males and females with whom they have had sex, their age when puberty began and how they reacted to it, and the age at which they first had a wet dream. Questions regarding sexual activities focused on sexual outlets and frequency of orgasms during the junior and senior high school years, especially in terms of the ways in which orgasms were achieved: heterosexual contact, homosexual contact, masturbation, wet dreams, and bestiality. Circumstances of first orgasm and first infatuation were probed.

Each youth then recounted his personal history of the ways in which he experienced his sexual identity during childhood and adolescence. This process usually included questions that focused on thoughts and feelings at particular ages, such as: "At age 12 did you view yourself as gay, bisexual, or straight?" and "If someone had asked what you were at high school graduation, how would you have answered, both to the other person and to yourself?" Some youths remembered exact markers while others recounted that their realization of being gay or bisexual was a gradual process. It became apparent that the key to eliciting information was to encourage the youths to remember specific events or times. The details in the stories add both interest to the interview data and credibility to the stories.

Each youth then recalled his first interpersonal sexual encounter, defined as some variety of genital contact for one or both partners. After this memory was elicited, probes included: "Where did you meet?", "Who initiated the interaction?", "Who was this person to you?", "What happened sexually?", "How did you feel afterward?", "How did this affect your sense of being gay?", and "Were there further contacts?" I then elicited similar information about all individuals with whom the youth had had sexual activity prior to high school graduation.

There is no guarantee, of course, that the memories recorded in the pages that follow are accurate, but the detail and the commitment to honesty that many of the youths provided is impressive. I generally concluded each interview feeling that the story told was an authentic one and that the specific life history was shared for the first time with another. In only a few cases did the memories appear rehearsed, perhaps the consequence of having shared the story with several others. On many occasions the stories were so emotionally laden that it was difficult to hear them; at times the desire to respond was exceptionally tempting. I frequently added some measure of support, which often elicited further reflections and encouraged in-depth pursuit of the past.

I believe for the most part that the youths felt safe during the interview. All reported afterward that they had enjoyed the experience and several volunteered to be interviewed again if I ever needed them. Their readiness to refer friends to the study further illustrates their feelings of safety and comfort. I felt honored and privileged by their willingness to share some of the most memorable and painful aspects of their lives. In this chapter, I focus on the youths' accounts of early same-sex attractions and feelings.

## Characteristics of the Youths

The youths range in age from 17 to 23 years with a mean of almost 21 years. At the time of the interview, three of the youths were seniors in high school. Of the other ten not in college, five graduated from college, four dropped out of college after less than two years, and one never went to college. Twenty-one of the 44 youths were Cornell University students; eight were in other four-year colleges and two in a local community college.

All but four are White, and there is an even split in religious affiliation among "none," Jewish, Protestant, and Catholic. Almost three quarters of the youths grew up in a home in which at least one parent held a high-level professional position, such as lawyer, physician, engineer, or business manager. The vast majority of the mothers worked outside the home, frequently as a schoolteacher, salesperson, or clerical worker. Two thirds of the youths' parents had remained married to each other; one third were divorced or separated. Most of the youths' families lived in small- and medium-sized towns and suburbs.

These youths are not presented as "representative" of the population of gay and bisexual youth. For example, few youths of color or those who are closeted to themselves or to others are included; neither are those of various educational, socioeconomic, and geographical backgrounds adequately sampled. Nonverbally oriented and shy youths probably did not participate in the interview study.

## EARLY CHILDHOOD MEMORIES OF SAME-SEX ATTRACTIONS

### Natural but Wrong

Two thirds of the gay and bisexual youths reported that their same-sex attractions were deeply embodied in their "natural self." By this they implied that their homoerotic attractions were not a matter of choice but were of early, perhaps genetic, origins. Without hesitation they graphically recalled same-sex attractions that emanated from their earliest childhood memories. Early homoerotic attractions visited them without great fanfare, with no clashing of cymbals, and with no abiding shock. They remembered feeling that their attractions to other males had always been present and they frequently identified concrete, distinct memories prior to first grade. Later homoerotic attractions were felt to be contiguous with these feelings.

Same-sex attractions were often first experienced as an obsession of always wanting to be near masculinity. The males who monopolized their attention were occasionally same-age peers, but were more often older teenagers and adults— male teachers, coaches, cousins, or friends of the family.

Mickey, an 18-year-old youth, reported in his interview a lifelong fascination with older males. He grew up in an impoverished small town that included many extended family members and friends. They stopped by his home in the evenings and on weekends to visit his parents and older brothers and sisters.

I can remember wanting the men who visited us to hug me when I was real little, maybe three or four. I've always wanted to touch and be touched by guys, and I was a lot. Guys loved to manhandle me. They would throw me up in the air and I'd touch the ceiling and I'd scream and would love it and would do anything to make it happen more and more. It never was enough and I'd tire them out or I'd go to someone else who would toss me. Sometimes I would be teased for the "little points" [erections] in my pants, but no one, including myself, made much of it.

I guess I was pretty touchable—and I still am based on what guys I know or am with tell me. I didn't understand why because I thought all kids liked it. Others have told me that they liked it too, but somehow I think I liked it more. I craved and adored it and my day would not be a good one unless I had this contact. Only later did I find out why I liked being touched by guys.

At eight I fell in love with Neal, this guy who rode my bus. He was so cool, so big, but I guess he was fourteen or fifteen but he seemed like an adult. He wore these great clothes and was always in fashion and smelled so nice. I always wanted to sit with him or be next to him. But I never could because others always fought to sit next to him. I'd do anything for him and longed just for a look or a nudge. I'd fall down in front of him so he'd help me up or just that he'd notice or respond to me. He quit riding the bus one day and I never knew why but I was sad.

I think I spent my childhood fantasizing about men, not sexually of course, but just being close to them and having them hold me or hug me. I'd feel safe and warm. My dad gave me this and my older brother Mitchell gave me this but all of this was never enough. With the other men I'd feel flushed, almost hot. Maybe those were hot flashes like what women get! Those were good days.

Several youths recognized at the time that these undeniable, lifelong homoerotic attractions were not typical of other boys. Other youths simply assumed, based on the egocentric principle that their thoughts and feelings were shared by others, that all boys must feel as they do but were simply not talking about it. Eventually, however, all youths recognized that these desires were the wrong ones to have and that they should hide their attractions from others. Remarks made by peers, prohibitions taught by parents, and the silence imposed by religious leaders and schoolteachers all contributed to this recognition. Thus, although early same-sex attractions were felt to be instinctive, most of the gay and bisexual youths acknowledged from an early age that their impulses were somehow "wrong," but not necessarily "bad."

As the societal wrongness of their intuitive sexual desires became increasingly apparent, many hoped that their attractions were a phase they would outgrow or that their feelings would eventually make sense in some distant future. Very few grasped the possibility that these feelings could have meaning for their sexual identity.

Jeff, a graduate student who grew up in a wealthy suburb of New York City, complete with father, mother, younger sister, and pet dog, exemplified this early developmental awareness.

As a child I knew I was attracted to males. I was caught by my mother looking at nude photographs of men in her magazines and I heard my father say to her that, "He'll grow out of it," and so I thought and hoped I would. But until then I just settled back and enjoyed my keen curiosity to see male bodies.

You see, it did not feel threatening because (a) it felt great, and (b) father said I would grow out of it, and he was always right. So why not enjoy it until it went away?

So when I started fooling around with some of the neighborhood boys I felt different than they did about it. More comfortable than them because although I felt it was wrong I did not feel that it was bad. The wrong was because the sexual feeling s, which represented childishness in my mind, had not gone away yet. It was not bad because it felt so natural.

I knew I was attracted to boys but that did not say I had to be gay. I just felt everyone was attracted like I was but just no one talked about it because no one wanted to admit that they were immature. It was a phase that all of us would grow out of. But until then it felt important to keep it a secret, especially from my family because I wanted them to think highly of me because I was the oldest boy and all. But I still sat back and enjoyed it and waited for nature to do its self-correction.

Many youths recalled being punished or verbally threatened by their parents if they continued their sexual activities. These repercussions served as a powerful reason for feeling that same-sex desires and behaviors were wrong, but they did not prevent the youths from recognizing their same-sex attractions at an early age. These desires were not to be shared with others and acting on them was thought to be wrong because if caught, punishment would likely ensue. Balancing desire and fear became a significant dilemma.

A very extroverted child, Randy was the life of his neighborhood in a small city near a large urban center. His family was very socially active and thus Randy was allowed to spend considerable time with his many friends.

I can recall being very interested in sex several years before my friends, around age six or seven. What I wanted most at that point was to have sex with other boys as frequently as possible and, of course, at that point I was. I considered myself normal and that this behavior that I was doing with Buddy was just a fun thing to do, even though I realized that it was a taboo thing to do. I feared that at some point we might get caught by our parents. We were almost caught several times, but of course we were at it again as soon as we were alone in his basement and he was ready to initiate it; I was always too frightened to tell him I was interested or that I really wanted it.

Before puberty I didn't feel that this behavior made me anything other than what I was. I was aware we needed to keep it a secret, yet one time for a reason I can't remember I told my mom and she handled it very well. She told me, "Don't put it in your rears or hurt yourself." Buddy's mom found out and she just seemed to sort of blow it off as well.

Same-sex attractions for these youths were not foreign but natural, a lifelong intrigue with men's bodies. Eventually, many of the youths recognized that others rarely shared or understood their same-sex desires. They did not consider the meaning that their attractions had, either for the moment or for their future. Only later, with the onset of puberty, were these attractions fully linked with sexuality.

## Natural but Different: Gender Nonconformity

Another much smaller group of gay and bisexual youths recognized as well that their same-sex desires were a natural aspect of themselves. Nevertheless, they understood their homoerotic attractions as consistent with their self-perception that they were more similar to girls than boys. They were intrigued and mystified by male bodies; males were enigmatic and unapproachable. They viewed themselves as somehow "different" from their male peers, and this sense of differentness permeated all spheres of their lives. Although they were also drawn to the masculinity of boys and men, they felt more comfortable in the company of girls and women than the other gay and bisexual youths.

Compared to the majority of their male peers, these gay and bisexual youths were at odds in their attitudes, feelings, and behaviors. They felt ill at ease with typical male sports; they especially loathed team sports such as baseball and football. They may have been forced by a father or coach to participate in sports—as a right fielder, a defensive back, or a benchwarmer—and they deeply resented such coercion and their inevitable failure in sports. Stronger preferences were fervently expressed for books, make-believe games, and artistic endeavors. The gay and bisexual youths spent more time during childhood with girls, primarily because the youths had more culturally defined feminine than masculine interests.

Richard, age 19, grew up in a farming area in northern Pennsylvania. His father worked in a nearby grain mill. An only child who maintained a very close relationship with his mother, Richard interpreted his hesitation, and perhaps his inability, to conform to the "masculine jock" image as a consequence of "just being my own self."

> I have always been gay, although I did not know what that meant at the time. But I knew that I always felt queer, out of place in my hometown. I did not play basketball or wrestle, and I was not a farmer nor a slob nor did I shovel cow shit like my classmates. Girl, they would come in smelling like they looked, and you can be sure it was not a number Chanel ever heard of! There was no way that I was going to let this be a part of what I wanted for my life.
>
> I took part in dance, ballet, singing, and had good manners. I liked Broadway musicals, Barbra, Bette, Joan, Liz, Judy, and Greta. I wore stylish clothes and was my own individual self. My teachers appreciated this but not the slobs. Because of this a lot of them said that I was gay, and so I thought I must be, although I did not know what this meant except that it meant I would not be shoveling cow shit!

During recess in grade school, Richard was regularly called "fag" and "sissy." He did not, however, equate these names with having sex with other boys. It simply meant that he was different from the farm boys and was being true to his own self.

> As far back as I can remember, I was always teased about being gay or at least being not very masculine. In first and second grades, I was called a "sissy" and a "fairy" and got pushed around. I became fairly introverted during those years, with only a couple of friends.
>
> Later, in junior high school, a couple of girls and this other guy who played in the band and me would hang out and laugh at the morons. I knew I was afraid of them, but I did not want to give them the satisfaction of knowing this. I knew I was different, but I did not know what that meant. I was repulsed by these boys, but I also found them fascinating and this split was hard to understand. It just felt like there had to be more to it than just feeling like an outsider.

Another youth, Ben, age 21, remembered what it was like to live on the outside of male childhood. Ben grew up in a more suburban setting than did Richard, but his reactions to being gender nonconforming were nearly identical.

I had mostly friends who were girls and I can remember playing jump rope, dolls, and hopscotch with them, and I can remember being very interested in hairstyling and practicing on dolls. But my major activity during childhood was drawing, and I was sort of known as "the Artist," even as early as third and fourth grades. Today I can see some very gay themes in my drawings!

I detested gym and sports, even though I guess I was capable in some of them, like track, but I was just not aggressive enough to excel. I really hated football and thought that it was very crude and brutal.

Within myself I acknowledged my attractions to males, but I always denied it outwardly. I was ashamed of it, in an intense way. I felt different through all my life, even in kindergarten when I thought boys were idiots. I liked girls because they were more intelligent and interesting and did things that I thought were more human and refined. They also did the things that I liked doing.

Unfortunately for youths such as Richard and Ben, the consequences of being true to their nature was that other boys viewed them as undesirable playmates and as "weird" because they did not think or act like other boys. Labeled sissy or effeminate, they were rejected by boys and, equally important, they had little desire to fraternize with their male peers. Because other boys did not constitute an enjoyable or safe context for play or socializing, the Richards and Bens turned to girls for activities and consolation. They preferred to dance rather than shovel shit, to sing rather than yell "hike," and to draw rather than bash heads. Thus, childhood and early adolescence were usually portrayed as traumatizing times by these youths if they were subjected to the taunts of their male peers and did not have the support of girls.

Although these gay and bisexual youths may have become isolated and withdrawn from others, the fortunate ones sought and found girls for solace and support. Girls became their saviors, offering sources of emotional sustenance as the male world of childhood became increasingly distasteful. It was to these girls that many gay and bisexual youths subsequently disclosed their sexual affiliations during middle or late adolescence.

## Sexless and Masculine

In contrast to the previous two groups of youths, who felt that their same-sex attractions were natural and originated from early childhood, were those relatively few youths I interviewed who claimed that their first memory of homoerotic attractions came after childhood. Sexually explicit childhood feelings, desires, or attractions that they would now label as sexual in nature were unknown to them. Unsure of how they "became gay," the youths characterized their life before puberty as "sexless," with few memories of sexuality, and as deeply invested in masculine activities, especially sports.

With the onset of physical maturation, thoughts and feelings associated with sexuality were evoked in these gay and bisexual youths. During childhood they chased girls, but this was more of a game that they joined with other boys than a statement about their sexuality or their true sexual interests. There was little indication in their stories that they pursued girls as sex objects.

Jack, a 22-year-old, grew up in western Long Island among wealthy surrounds. His parents owned and operated a real estate firm; his older sister worked as a secretary for the family business. Jack was excused from the family business because of his involvement in sports and his pursuit of well-developed musculature and a tanned body.

> I was really into sports. In the summer I played baseball and in the fall I did track, just before the football season started. I wanted to swim, but I had to give that up if I wanted to play football. In the spring was spring track and spring training for baseball. I practiced some sport every day throughout my four years of high school.
>
> I was good but not great, best at track in long-distance running. In football I was a seldom-used receiver and sometimes safety. In baseball I started in left field. I lettered in all three, but only in track was it for all four years.
>
> Maybe I just did not have time, but I was not into sex. I would have to say that I was sexless because I cannot remember any sexual thoughts. I was not interested in girls even though I had several girlfriends. In general I felt left out of what my teammates said they were going through.

When asked during the interview to elaborate on any aspect of his sexuality during childhood, Jack drew a blank. He had many stories of athletic, but not sexual, exploits. After pubertal onset, he discovered his sexuality and expressed wonderment regarding the location of his sexual desires during childhood.

## Puberty and Its Effects

Regardless of their activities, feelings, and attractions during childhood, the elusive same-sex attractions of the gay and bisexual youths were demystified with the onset of puberty. The critical instigator may have been the biologically induced increase in sexual libido that arrives with pubertal onset. The youths reported that their sexuality now intruded into every thought, feeling, and behavior; at times this frightened them, and at other times it energized them. The ways in which they responded to the onset of puberty and the accompanying increase in sexual libido were quite diverse.

Although their growing cognizance of same-sex attractions was often electrifying, it could also create immense complications and obstacles for the gay and bisexual youths. In either case, it raised the stakes for their sense of personal identity. The intensity of the sexual feelings that emanated from puberty and the sense of "naughtiness" that some youths reported were often exhilarating. They were the beginning of an intelligibility of previously misunderstood feelings. In this they were a source of great relief. For only a few youths, however, did puberty and its accompanying effects induce clarity regarding the meaning of strongly felt sexual lusts and desires.

## Natural but Wrong

For the two thirds of the gay and bisexual youths who recalled feeling same-sex attractions early in life as a natural part of who they are, pubescence usually elicited an awareness of the link between these early attractions and the youths' sexuality. That is, it intensified the sexual component of their feelings and, for the first time, raised the possibility that this sexuality had long-term repercussions. Although many youths originally expressed hope that the sexual implications would evaporate in time, as puberty progressed they had lingering but persistent doubts that they were similar to other boys in their sexual attractions.

Mickey was fortunate because he had a lesbian aunt who was open about her sexuality. She provided a model for him that gave meaning to his same-sex desires.

> It finally began to creep into my consciousness that I might not be straight. This was in the seventh grade just about the time that I began to masturbate and my erections became a little bit more noticeable. I was proud that I was getting so big that guys didn't want to throw me around but depressed because no one did.
>
> I figured at first that it was a phase, the one I had heard about. But somehow I knew better, and I think this was because I knew what homosexuality was because I have a lesbian aunt, and she, although thought a bit eccentric, is well liked by my family. She was very open about it, although we never talked about her or me. But I knew and I think she came to know about me. I just decided to go on leading my life. I mean, what choice did I really have? If I was, I was, and there was nothing I could do about it.

Randy claimed that "massive confusion" hit him during junior high school. He discovered that several of his older friends were gay and that they had begun to wonder about him. This shocked him into self-analysis; his initial defense was to assume the liberal stance that his sexual attractions depended on the person and not the gender. He was attracted to some girls and to some boys. More important than genitalia were the person's character and personality.

Over time, however, Randy realized that he fantasized only about boys. This was thrilling to him, as long as he did not have to think about it too much. Later he sexually experimented with boys and realized that these experiences were qualitatively more erotic than his sexual experiences with girls had been during the previous two years.

Although puberty could be a freeing time, the accompanying sexual feelings were more often experienced as threatening and frightening. They threatened a childhood homeostasis and frightened their recipients with the meanings and repercussions they carried for the future. Gay and bisexual youths seldom had the experience or language to make sense of that which they were feeling. Their desires were not discussed in school or at home, except in a denigrating fashion.

If they were to accept or even articulate their same-sex attractions, they often feared that they would be committing social or emotional suicide.

## Natural but Different: Gender Nonconformity

These same fears were often expressed by the small number of youths who reported early same-sex attractions, exhibited gender nonconformity, and experienced a sense of differentness. Although the onset of puberty clarified many aspects of their lives, there was always a cost involved with the growing understanding.

For Sam, a 20-year-old from a small town in upstate New York, adolescence was a difficult period. As the middle child of five, Sam frequently felt isolated, invisible, and unable to share with others that which was most important in his life.

> When I was thirteen I grew hair in places I never did before, and I began to know that all of this meant I was attracted to males, but I dared not say this to anyone, including myself out loud. I knew that no one was interested in what interested me—other guys—and I knew enough to say nothing because no one would listen. I knew it would not be a good situation. But I knew what I liked, and I liked boys.

Another youth expressed similar feelings:

> I felt upset, not cool, not quite right, in angst and confusion. I first centered on certain people who were available as sexual objects, not because I was attracted to them as people. The physical feelings became emotional feelings with emotional situations. And that scared the shit out of me because I did not know what it could mean beyond sex but whatever it was was real. Well, maybe I did know what it was, but I did not have the words for it.
>
> As I moved into eighth grade, it became more and more clear to me what it was all about, and it was sex, but with a twist, romance.

This realization was seldom positive or uplifting for the gender-nonconforming gay and bisexual youths. Many of them began to realize that their homoerotic sexual feelings, which they knew to be wrong or which were condemned by others, were not disappearing. In addition, most had experienced extensive familial and peer rejection when they were children for these attractions or for their effeminate behavior. As early adolescents, they feared that their long history of failing to conform with social definitions of masculinity would only be prolonged. Sex was one more way in which they would be ostracized and harassed by their peers.

Richard attempted to deny the sexual aspect of his attractions, for personal as well as for interpersonal reasons. Consistent with his childhood pattern, his gender-nonconforming behavior faced an onslaught of ridicule from peers.

> In grade seven, God, I was suddenly bombarded with the reality of being attracted to men's bodies, which really floored me. I felt it had to be normal because the feelings were so intense. Although I

now know these were sexual and emotional, at the time I tried not to link it with sexuality, just with being different. I was okay with it in the seventh grade because it was me.

But I was also ostracized by the farm boys as a faggot because I was effeminate and hung out with the girls. I just did not like homosexuality because I was hit over the head with it. I never asked for it. It was never cool. I never labeled liking men as gay because it just seemed a part of me. Only later could I consciously link it with sexuality.

Similar to Richard, Ben's response to the growing self-understanding that accompanied puberty was to deny the sexual aspect of his life until a later age: "I didn't talk to anyone about it. I put the feelings in the background. I definitely knew what was going on, but I decided to deny it and that I was going to be that way for the rest of my life."

## Sexless and Masculine

The "blank slate" that many of the masculine, sexless youths described as existing prior to pubescence was disrupted with the onset of puberty. At that time, they reported first sexual impulses and homoerotic attractions. Many believed that they did not have control over either the onset or the content of these attractions. Their potential meaning threatened an established equilibrium. The youths' responses were consistent with their past defense against sexuality: suppress, resist, or deny these unwanted feelings.

Awareness for these masculine youths came later and more gradually, often in spurts of recognition. Same-sex desires were clearly present, but there was a profound obstruction that required considerable "data" or a traumatic event to overcome. The defenses were usually effective, at least for the short term. This was true for Jack.

I am not sure I was aware of what homosexuality was about at thirteen. I began to grow and develop and that was good for my athletic performance. My identification just was not in the sexual domain. I did not label myself, other than an "it." I would not have said that I was gay because I did not fit the stereotype of being gay. I was very busy and into a lot of things. Besides sports, I was a social butterfly.

I never looked really inward until college. I did everything in groups. I belonged to several jock groups, and we would go and do things on Friday and Saturday nights. We drank a lot and went out on the town—you know, just drive around. I had a lot of good friends who were girls, but most friendships were actually with other guys. I had "girlfriends" of course, but I felt feeling about them sexually would dirty our relationship.

I can recall vague signs of awareness. Like the time my family went to Fort Lauderdale. I saw all of the guys holding hands and I felt an excitement. I was thirteen or fourteen. Then I saw a Bloomingdale ad for Calvin Klein underwear that I could not take my eyes off of. Then another fleeting moment was when there was this guy, a runner, I fell over.

Gee, I guess I must have been pretty gay, huh? But somehow I blocked the meaning of these things from my mind. And the time when I was sixteen and saw two senior football teammates going at it in the second-floor school bathroom. I had not remembered that for a long time!

Girlfriends were often critical components of the charade, used to protect a youth from self-awareness and to screen him from the accusatory eyes of male peers. Girlfriends were material, not sexual, objects.

Peter, a 17-year-old high school senior, was seldom home while growing up. His parents always encouraged him to "be involved" and Peter readily acceded. This was not difficult because of his penchant for always saying and doing the right thing. Though he was voted "most popular" student during his junior year in high school, there was one part of himself which Peter feared would destroy his popularity. This secret part he felt needed to remain hidden.

> I had crushes in early adolescence. One girl and two guys. Before seventh [grade] I had no homosexuality. I wanted to go out with this one girl, but she was hard to get because she was with this other boy and very pretty. I was at the time struggling with being slightly overweight.
>
> By eighth [grade] I began to recognize feelings for male classmates, but I didn't see myself as gay because I liked girls. By ninth [grade] the homosexuality grew stronger. Like, why was I thinking these things?
>
> My first doubt about myself came last year when I was sixteen and I saw on a TV talk show male strippers, models, and dancers. I had feelings toward them I wanted to explore, but I was afraid. I kept it inside. Girlfriends I used as scapegoats, to hide from others—and maybe myself—and to protect me. It was a gradual realization. I was seventy-five percent sure I was gay, but I still kept up the hope I wasn't.
>
> So, by eleventh [grade] I saw myself as bisexual and I still do, but I lean toward homosexuality.

A growing consciousness of same-sex attractions was particularly difficult for youths who reported feeling sexless during childhood and who actively participated in masculine sports and activities with other boys. Similar to Jack and Peter, most attempted to suppress the onslaught of their homoerotic libido shortly after pubertal onset. Progress toward a gay or bisexual identity was gradual; for some it may become a lifelong process.

## Conclusion

The data provided by the 44 gay and bisexual youths support the thesis that although there were common routes to the development of an adult gay or bisexual identity, there was considerable diversity in the particulars. From an early age, the vast majority of the youths believed that they were "different" from other boys their age and that regardless of the source of this feeling, it was a natural aspect of themselves. Same-sex attractions and affections emerged early and were given sexual meaning with the onset of puberty.

Three broad patterns characterized the youths' awareness, interpretation, and affective response to childhood and early adolescent sexual attractions. The most common, shared by two thirds of the youths, consisted of same-sex attractions, which were identified as originating from earliest childhood memories. These attractions felt natural, instinctual, and omnipresent. Many of these youths stated that they "always felt gay." During childhood most recognized that these feelings were not typical of other boys and that it would be wrong to express them because of family and peer prohibitions toward such feelings. Others simply assumed that all boys felt as they did.

These boys were neither particularly masculine nor feminine in their behavior, except for their sexual attractions. They could not understand why other boys were not as preoccupied as they were with homoerotic desires. In this regard, they felt unmasculine, but they did not thus construe themselves as feminine.

A second group was composed of gay and bisexual youths who shared this natural, early disposition of same-sex attractions but who were dominated by an overwhelming sense that their differentness could be attributed to their failure to duplicate typical masculine characteristics. In many respects, these youths typified the stereotype that many gay and nongay people have of gay males: cross-gendered in behavior, personality, and interests. The feminized youths detested cultural definitions of masculinity and felt at odds with other boys because they did not share their interests in participating in team sports (especially football and baseball), competition, and aggressive pursuits. Because of their gender nonconformity, they were frequently ostracized by male peers.

To avoid becoming ostracized, they elicited friendships from girls, perhaps because of common interests, including attractions to boys. They were familiar with the arts, creativity, clothing, gentleness, and other features our culture deems feminine. They felt more comfortable and greater camaraderie with girls and their activities than with boys. Few wanted to change either their genitalia or their behavior; they did not view themselves as women in disguise—they were simply repulsed by the "grossness" of masculinity and attracted to the sensitivities of femininity. They were often outcasts in the world of their male peers, an outcome they felt was unfair and unnecessary, but inevitable.

By contrast was the relatively infrequent third pattern, masculinized gay and bisexual youths. By disposition they looked and acted like other boys their age. Their participation in typical masculine pursuits "fooled" peers into believing that they were not gay. The youths were often perceived to be social butterflies, and they actively engaged in male-male competitive sports. Their male friendships were critical to maintain. They wanted to be members of the "male crowd"; they enjoyed being with boys, seeing boys, and smelling boys. They craved the male touch and would do anything to receive it, particularly through participation in sports.

These youths denied that they had sexual feelings or attractions during childhood, perhaps because the direction of their sexual attractions was too threatening to allow into their consciousness. Their pursuit of girlfriends granted them a facade of heterosexuality and a postponement of coming out to self and others. From all appearances each of these youths was "one of the guys" and thus heavily invested in concealing his secret, which, if exposed, would threaten that status.

Similar to the other gay and bisexual boys, homoerotic attractions became too difficult to ignore with the onset of puberty. They tried to shield this information from others because of their overwhelming fear that peers would ostracize them. If teammates discovered the true nature of the youth's sexual desires and lusts, they would be shocked and, according to the interviewee, rejecting. Because of their masculinity, many of these youths masked their homosexuality for many years, appearing to be prototypical, all-American boys. The prize was heterosexual male privilege, such as leadership positions, peer acceptance, popularity, and after-school jobs; the cost, denial of their sexuality, constant fear of losing their masculinity in the eyes of others and themselves, and a life of lies and unfulfilled potential.

Unknown is the etiology of these patterns and their long-term effects on other aspects of the youths' development, including sexual identity and psychological health. Although several of the youths interviewed experienced same-sex attractions as arising abruptly and "unexpectedly," for the vast majority these feelings emerged as gradual, inevitable, and not particularly surprising. The incorporation of these patterns may be less a matter of choice than an experienced "naturalness" that is derived both from one's biological heritage and from socialization processes that began at an early age. One youth reflected on his emerging sexuality: "It was like being visited by an old friend." There was little indication that these patterns changed during the course of childhood and adolescence among the interviewed youths.

The most pervasive finding was that puberty eroticized these early same-sex affectional attractions, converting them to sexual desires. Puberty brought an acute awareness that same-sex attractions have a sexual component to them. Regardless of their pattern of awareness and interpretation, most of the youths did not immediately embrace their homosexuality and come out to themselves and others with the onset of puberty. Relatively few responded in a positive way to their same-sex desires immediately after pubertal onset. Many youths suppressed from consciousness their homoerotic attractions, allowing them to surface only gradually over an extended period of time. They paid their homoerotic feelings little heed, postponing the consequences for identity until the future. After all, they reasoned, this might be just a phase.

Because few youths believed that they could control their sexual feelings and desires, they ultimately felt that they did not choose their sexual orientation or sexual attractions. Awareness of homoeroticism may have emerged early or late, prior to puberty or thereafter, surfaced gradually or arrived impetuously and instantaneously, felt normal or wrong, or motivated sexual activity or abstinence—yet, it was one aspect of the self that was present without invitation. The development from same-sex attractions to a gay or bisexual identity was simply an unfolding of that which was already present, with puberty playing a crucial role in clarifying that homosensuality had a sexual component. The eventual incorporation of a gay or bisexual identity involved a recognition of that which the homoerotic attractions and sexual behavior meant.

For youths who were consciously aware of their same-sex lust, the sense that this information was not to be shared with others was pervasive. Although homoerotic desires may have felt natural, the youths were told by parents, friends, religious leaders, teachers, and dogma that these attractions were evil and sinful. Many knew that their homosexuality was ill-advised but did not think that it was therefore sick or immoral.

The exploration of these issues is an important endeavor because educators, researchers, and clinicians know little regarding how sexual identity is formed among sexual minorities. For example, it is not known if all patterns are equally healthy or if these patterns are lifelong characteristics. Unquestioned, however, is that from these same-sex attractions emerge first sexual encounters, which can occur during the earliest years of childhood or wait until young adulthood. Similar to initial sexual attractions, they too are interpreted in diverse ways, and these interpretations must be explored.

## ▼ ENDNOTES ▼

1. This chapter is based on data that appear in my manuscript, currently in preparation and tentatively titled, *Sex and Sexual Identity Among Gay and Bisexual Male Youths.*

2. The stories are usually a very close approximation to that which was reported. I also took the liberty of adding grammatical details and punctuation to aid understanding.

# - Part Two -

# ADOLESCENCE

## Chapter 5

▼

# Developmental Perspectives on Coming Out to Self and Others

---

### Kenneth M. Cohen
### &
### Ritch C. Savin-Williams[1]

*Many youths have few options other than to conceal their same-sex attractions from self and others. They live in an atmosphere of secrecy and myths that hinder disclosure of homoerotic sexuality. The image of the secretive and closeted gay has been perpetuated by social institutions unwilling to challenge the values of the majority culture, to come "forth on their own to declare a moratorium on social and legal discrimination, to counter cultural stereotypes, and to overturn moral condemnation" (Savin-Williams, 1990, p. 29). It has taken the collective strength of the gay/lesbian movement during the last 45 years to correct many of the erroneous beliefs that individuals and society have embraced.*

*Despite advances and society's ever increasing tolerance toward sexual minorities, many individuals with homoerotic attractions remain fearful of disclosing their sexuality. Consequently, sexual-minority youths often hide their identity from others or disclose only to a select few. McDonald (1982) noted that the process of revelation to self and others is*

> . . . a developmental process through which gay persons become aware of their affectional and sexual preferences and choose to integrate this knowledge into their personal and social lives, [thus,] coming out involves adopting a nontraditional identity, restructuring one's self-concept, reorganizing one's personal sense of history, and altering one's relations with others and with society . . . all of which reflects a complex series of cognitive and affective transformations as well as changes in behavior. (p. 47)

*In this chapter we review the various ways in which "coming out" has been conceptualized and defined. The developmental processes through which youths come to recognize their homoerotic affections and disclose their sexual feelings to others are explored. The psychological repercussions of self-recognition and defenses commonly used to ensure psychological integrity are examined. Because coming out to parents is considered by many lesbian, gay, and bisexual youths to be the most important, yet frightening, disclosure, this issue is explored in detail. Finally, self-esteem and its relationship to coming out are reviewed and suggestions for enhancing positive self-concept among adolescents, particularly through role models and the media, are considered.*

## DEFINITIONS

Despite a growing body of scientific literature on homosexuality in general, little is known about the coming-out process and its impact on an individual. Indeed, there is considerable discrepancy among researchers and clinicians regarding that which constitutes coming out. In this chapter, *coming out* is regarded as two distinct, though related, tasks: *coming out to self* and *coming out to others*. The former is a process during which a number of milestone events occur whereby an individual moves from nonrecognition of his or her homosexuality, with perhaps a degree of sensitization to being somehow different from others, to self-recognition that he or she is indeed lesbian, gay, or bisexual. The latter refers to the self-disclosure of homoerotic desires and/or experiences to others, including peers, family, and society at large. Historian D'Emilio (1992) wrote about a time when disclosure had a different meaning than it does today: "Before Stonewall,[2] the phrase had signified the acknowledgement of one's sexuality to others in the gay world; after Stonewall, it meant the public affirmation of homosexual identity" (p. 244).

In several early studies, coming out was portrayed as a protracted process that occurs before an ever-expanding "series of audiences" (Ponse, 1980) and influences an individual's social, psychological, and sexual functioning (Weinberg & Williams, 1974). Emphasizing the sociocultural aspects of coming out, Herdt and Boxer (1993) viewed coming out as a rite of passage that is achieved through rituals: ". . . coming out refers both to self-transformation and a new claim to social rights" (p. 167). In general, conceptualizations of coming out incorporated the tripartite dimensions proposed by D'Emilio (1983): recognition of same-sex desires, ensuing efforts to act on those desires and preferences, and acknowledgment of one's sexual orientation to others of the same persuasion.

Davies (1992) noted that some scholars conceptualize coming out as a single moment of recognition involving a gestalt shift in which one suddenly realizes one is gay; others view it as "a series of realignments in perception, evaluation, and commitment, driven by the affirmation 'I am gay'" (p. 75). He proposed that the latter is more popular and realistic but that there are probably multiple pathways to coming out. Davies distinguished between "individuation," whereby an individual arrives at the conclusion that he or she is gay, and "disclosure," the process through which others learn about the individual's homoerotic attractions. He suggested that individuation and disclosure interact in a reciprocal relationship. That is, "they exist in a dialectic relationship: coming out to others constantly redefines one's notion of self and the development of a self-identity drives the process of disclosure" (p. 76). Kahn (1991) empirically supported this position: Lesbians who expected a positive and supportive response to their disclosure were more likely to self-disclose to others.

Believing that coming out is a developmental process, several theoreticians have proposed stagelike models that describe the movement from first recognition to full disclosure. A dissenting voice is represented by Harry (1993), who argued against stage model conceptualizations; coming out to others is not the final step of a developmental process but the product of certain income levels, occupations, places of habitation, and sexual orientations of friends. He concluded, "people adapt their degree of self-disclosure to the circumstances in which they live" (p. 38). "Coming-out models" are examined in this chapter because we believe that they will assist the reader in appreciating the variety of ways in which coming out has been conceptualized and has developed over the last 20 years.

## Coming-Out Models

For many lesbian, gay, and bisexual individuals, the coming-out process is a gradual though continuous endeavor laden with setbacks and surprises. McDonald (1982) suggested that coming out is an "arduous developmental process" that begins in adolescence and continues well into adulthood.

Most coming-out models propose an orderly or linear series of stages based on a particular theoretical perspective (e.g., Erikson, Freud, Piaget, or Goffman). Initially, nonheterosexual individuals are described as feeling "different," something which distinguishes them from their peers. Over time, especially during puberty, these feelings of "differentness" take on an air of sexuality and sexual attraction (see Savin-Williams, "Memories of Childhood," this volume). The next step is self-recognition of the meaning of these feelings for one's sexual identity. Once homoerotic feelings have been initially accepted and integrated, the individual must confront the next developmental task, disclosure to others (Coleman, 1981/1982).

Sophie (1985/1986) reviewed six theories of gay identity development to determine their internal consistency and applicability for her exploratory study of 14 women. She distinguished four essential stages of identity development:

1. First awareness
   - Initial cognitive and emotional realization that one is "different" and that homosexuality may be the relevant issue
   - No disclosure to others
   - A feeling of alienation from oneself and others
2. Test and exploration
   - Testing must precede acceptance of one's homosexuality
   - Initial but limited contact with gay and lesbian communities or with individual gays and lesbians
   - Alienation from heterosexuality

3. Identity acceptance
   - Preference for social interactions with other gays and lesbians
   - Negative identity gives way to a positive identity
   - Initial disclosure to heterosexuals
4. Identity integration
   - View self as gay or lesbian with accompanying anger and pride
   - Publicly coming out to many others
   - Identity stability; individual is unwilling to change

Although her data fit the broad outlines of these stages, Sophie discovered that there were many intrastage variations.

Generally speaking, coming-out models can be divided into three types, based on whether the primary emphasis is on internal processes, usually termed "identity"; external manifestations—disclosure or overtness; or a combination of these two. Each is reviewed below. It should be noted that although the majority of research on coming out has been conducted with men, there is evidence that the coming-out process is highly similar for males and females. Because an increasing number of women scholars are publishing in this area (e.g., Kahn, 1991; Schneider, 1989), the assumption of no gender differences can now be more fully explored.

## Coming Out to Self

Models that focus on the internal personal identity aspects of coming out often emphasize the importance of self-recognition and acceptance. These constructs have seldom been substantiated empirically because it is difficult to delineate, measure, and validate identity components of development (Smith, 1983). Although theorists generally recognize that disclosure to others is important, some maintain that the essence of coming out involves self-recognition. For example, Benitez (1983) examined the ways in which an individual comes to define the self as gay or lesbian over time; Brady (1985), how an individual progresses through the identity stages of tolerance, acceptance, pride, and synthesis. One popular theoretical model proposes that the acquisition of a sexual identity is a significant aspect of the self-concept of gay and lesbian persons (Cass, 1979, 1984).

The sociological analogue to identity in the coming-out process is the concept "homosexual role." Identifying the self as lesbian or gay refers not so much to the psychologist's notion of identity as an internal condition but to an individual's acceptance of membership in a socially defined class labeled "homosexual" (McIntosh, 1968).[3] An individual could thus act as a gay or lesbian person but not identify himself or herself with the socially constructed phenomenon of homosexuality (see Manalansan, this volume, for examples among people of color and ethnic/racial differences). Similarly, Dank (1971) noted the significance of coming out within a social context. His definition distinguished identifying oneself as "homosexual," which necessitates new cognitive categories of sexual identity and self-acceptance, from the disclosure of that information to others. The public expression of coming out, according to Dank, signifies to the individual the end of the identity search. Thus, sociologists often separate the notions of acceptance of the homosexual role and the public expression of the homosexual role.

## Coming Out to Others

It is not uncommon for coming out to be defined strictly in behavioral terms, such as the quantity and status of persons to whom a lesbian, gay, or bisexual individual has disclosed her or his sexual identity. Hooker (1965), one of the first to define coming out in this manner, likened the coming-out process to a "debut": a time when an individual identifies the self publicly for the first time in the presence of other gay people. In contrast, Plummer's (1975) definition of coming out emphasized the decision to allow oneself to be identified as gay in the heterosexual world, which most coming-out models would place conceptually as a later developmental event than acknowledging oneself to other gays and lesbians.

Myrick (1974a) identified four categories of "outness": covert-covert (no one knows and individual tries to conceal), overt-covert (no attempt to conceal but no one knows), covert-overt (in general terms, a few friends know), and overt-overt (all know). He (1974b) estimated self-disclosure by considering the number of groups (e.g., family, employer, close heterosexual friends) that have been informed.

Variations on these themes have emerged, focusing primarily on out-to-whom issues. Many have comparable checklists that include various categories (Elliot, 1982; Fitzpatrick, 1983; Hencken, 1985; McKirnan & Peterson, 1986; Nemeyer, 1980; O'Carolan, 1982), whereas others focus on specific categories, such as family members (Cramer & Roach, 1988; Grabert, 1985) or sexual partners (Braaten & Darling, 1965; Ferguson & Finkler, 1978). Ferguson and Finkler (1978) distinguished personal outness, which they defined as involvement with another lesbian or telling a few others, from overtness, a public declaration such as joining a lesbian organization. Similarly, Lee (1977) noted stages of signification (self-label), coming out (disclose to others), and going public. His focus was primarily on the latter, which involved the absence of concealment from others.

## Coming Out to Self and Others

Sohier (1985/1986) noted the difficulty endemic to defining coming out, manifested among social scientists as well as gays and lesbians:

> For some, it is intrapersonal and means the moment they realized that they were homosexual. For others, it denotes the time between the realization and an open or public acknowledgement of the fact. And for yet others, it is a composite of the two and includes the most painful moment: Disclosure to parents and family. (p. 31)

Harry and DeVall's (1978) solution was to split the two components. "Self-definition" was defined as the age one first defined the self as gay or lesbian and "behavioral coming out" as the age one first disclosed one's sexuality to others. Although they found significant overlap between them (correlation was .65), they did not address the nature of the relationship between identity and disclosure. Clearly, self-definition as gay, lesbian, or bisexual did not occur during the same year as disclosure of that information to others for all individuals.

McDonald (1984) also found overlap but not perfect congruency between the two concepts. Those open in social situations and not attempting to pass as heterosexual had the highest level of identity congruency—an integration of sexual behaviors, feelings, fantasies, and self-image—and were most "totally homosexual."

Others have combined the internal and external processes to divide subjects into various categories. For example, Miller (1978) grouped his "homosexual" husbands into four classifications based on self-recognition and public disclosure: trade (engages in homosexual behavior but no self-recognition as homosexual), homosexual (self-recognition but no public identity), gay (self-recognition with limited public knowledge), and faggot (self-recognition with public identity).

As best exemplified by the theoretical model of Cass (1979, 1984), the most usual solution to the discrepancies in definitions is to include elements of both self-recognition and disclosure to others in the coming-out process. For example, de Monteflores and Schultz (1978) defined coming out as:

> . . . the developmental process through which gay people recognize their sexual preferences and choose to integrate this knowledge into their personal and social lives. A number of experiences are critical in this process: The awareness of same-sex attractions, first homosexual experience, coming out in the gay world, labeling oneself as gay or homosexual, coming out to friends, family, and coworkers, and coming out publicly. (p. 59)

It is questionable whether self-recognition always precedes disclosure to others. An individual can be known or highly suspected of being gay before she or he arrives at that same realization. T. Weinberg (1978) noted that most men are "doing" before "being"; that is, they engage in same-sex behavior before defining the self as gay. Examples include an adolescent caught sexually playing with a same-sex cousin, an individual who denies to self and others that she or he is lesbian or gay but engages in same-sex encounters with others, and an immigrant who has no concept of homosexuality or bisexuality but nevertheless has same-sex encounters with others. Thus, individuals may indirectly or nonverbally disclose their homosexuality or bisexuality to another, usually a sexual partner, before the identity process has progressed very far. In some Latino, Black, and Asian communities, same-sex encounters do not necessarily lead to self-identification as gay (see Manalansan, this volume; Savin-Williams, "Ethnic," this volume).

Some individuals recognize their homoerotic desires but never disclose this information to others. This is most likely to occur during repressive times (such as during the formative years of our parents or grandparents) and in some social institutions (e.g., convents and seminaries). Some, perhaps many, adolescents resolve that concealing their homoerotic affections will be their solution to their "homosexual crisis." This may be a short-term resolution, "until college," or a lifelong pattern.

To fully appreciate the complexities inherent in the coming-out process, the psychosocial factors that contribute to and result from coming out are examined within a personal context. We tackle this in a more-or-less chronological order.

# COMING OUT TO SELF

## Feeling Different

Long before many individuals with homoerotic attractions recognize that they are gay, lesbian, or bisexual, they experience distinct feelings of being different (Newman & Muzzonigro, 1993; Savin-Williams, "Memories of Childhood," this volume; Telljohann & Price, 1993). Isay (1989, p. 23) described this in boys: "They saw themselves as more sensitive than other boys; they cried more easily, had their feelings more readily hurt, had more aesthetic interests, enjoyed nature, art, and music, and were drawn to other 'sensitive' boys, girls, and adults." D'Emilio (1983, p. 20) observed that "initially their sexuality created a profound, even disturbing, sense of difference from family, community, and society." These feelings may not initially be perceived as sexual but as a strongly felt affection for someone of the same sex (Savin-Williams, 1995).

Sanders and De Koning (cited in Straver, 1976) delineated a phase of sexual identity development that they labeled as "feeling different." It lasted a number of years but first reached consciousness during the first half of puberty between 12 and 15 years of age. Intrapsychic tensions increase when youths doubt their ability to meet heterosexual obligations. Although some may be aware of their same-sex erotic attractions, others "only know that they are uninterested in intimate relationships with members of the opposite sex in their own age group, although they cannot indicate exactly what it is that they *do* want" (Sanders, 1980, p. 282). This feeling of being in a "vacuum" may have profound repercussions for issues of self-acceptance and self-rejection that evolve during later adolescence. A year or more usually elapses before the labeling of these attractions is discussed with anyone, usually first with a same-age friend (Straver & Moerings, in Straver, 1976).

Many gay men and lesbians report feeling different at a very early age, long before puberty (see Savin-Williams, "Memories of Childhood," this volume). This is congruent with that which is reported in the first five chapters of this book. Because sexual orientation is probably present in some rudimentary form before the ability to reflect and label sexual feelings and attractions, the vague, impressionistic sense of being different and isolated from peers is characteristic of many preadolescent gays and lesbians. In retrospect, without knowing why, they

**Table 5.1**

Mean Age of Developmental Milestones[1]

|  | Dank (1971) N=180 | Kooden et al. (1979) N=138 | Troiden (1979) N=150 | McDonald (1982) N=199 | Rodriguez (1988) N=251 |
|---|---|---|---|---|---|
| First same-sex attractions | 13.5 | 12.8 |  | 13 | 11.1 |
| First same-sex erotic fantasies |  |  |  |  | 13.9 |
| First homosexual sex |  | 14.9 | 14.9 | 15 | 16.9[2] |
| Label feelings but not self as homosexual |  |  | 19.7 |  | 16.2 |
| Label self gay/lesbian | 19.3 | 21.1 | 21.3 | 19 | 20.6 |
| First disclosure to other |  | 28[3] |  | 23[3] | 23.6[3] |
| First relationship |  | 21.9 | 23.9 | 21 | 22.8 |

[1] Exact wording of milestones vary somewhat across studies. All subjects are male unless otherwise specified.
[2] To orgasm.
[3] To significant nongay other.

feel that somehow this difference is important (MacDonald, 1983; Robertson, 1981). These feelings and the accompanying process of self-searching are characteristic of the early stages of many theoretical coming-out models.

Table 5.1 graphically displays the findings of ten studies that examined the ages at which various developmental milestones were achieved. Unfortunately, most of these studies have been conducted only with males. As illustrated in Table 5.1, without exception, first same-sex attractions occurred before first same-sex encounter. Thus, for many gay youths, early same-sex "experimentation" is not capricious, as it may be for heterosexual youths who experiment in sex play, perhaps out of curiosity or desperation for sexual release. Rather, it is driven by very early homoeroticism/affection. It should be noted that Table 5.1 presents age averages. Many youths reported having first attractions several years before the means. For example, in a recent study of 202 racially diverse gay, lesbian, and bisexual Chicago youths, Herdt and Boxer (1993) found that some youths reported having felt different as early as age five. Plummer (1989) reported that many youths recalled having had same-sex attractions prior to puberty, sometimes as young as age six, which were subsequently recognized during or after puberty as homoerotic in nature. In Remafedi's (1987) sample of

| | D'Augelli (1991) N=61 | Sears (1991) N=36 | | Herdt & Boxer (1993) N=202 | | Newman & Muzzonigro (1993) N=27 | D'Augelli (1994) N=200 male/female |
|---|---|---|---|---|---|---|---|
| | | male | female | male | female | | |
| First same-sex attractions | 10.8 | 9.2 | 10.2 | 9.6 | 10.1 | 12.7 | 10 |
| First same-sex erotic fantasies | | | | 11.2 | 11.9 | | |
| First homosexual sex | 15.6 | 13.6 | 17.1 | 13.1 | 15.2 | | |
| Label feelings but not self as homosexual | | | | | | | |
| Label self gay/lesbian | 17 | 16.9 | 17.4 | | | 12.5[4] | 15 |
| First disclosure to other | 19 | 19.7 | 19.4 | 16.0 | 16.0 | 16 | 16 |
| First relationship | 18.8 | | | | | | 17 |

[4] "First realized that they were gay."

gay and bisexual male youths, nearly one third recalled attractions to men that began from first memories in early childhood. For the rest, first awareness began in early to middle adolescence, ages 11 to 16 years.

Troiden (1979) quoted a gay student, who noted a sense of apartness during preadolescence: "I never felt as if I fit in. I don't know why for sure. I felt different. I thought it was because I was more sensitive" (p. 363). In Troiden's sample, 72% of males experienced this sense of being different. In an adult population (Bell, Weinberg, & Hammersmith, 1981a), considerably more gays and lesbians than heterosexuals reported that they felt sexually different while growing up: Eighty-four percent of the adult men and 74% of the adult women, compared to 11% and 10% of nongay males and females, respectively. Reasons provided for feeling different included lack of interest in members of the other sex, a desire to engage in activities or sports usually not attributed to one's sex, and possessing either feminine (for males) or masculine (for females) traits.

Teacher, writer, and gay activist Rofes (1993) recalled:

> I knew I was queer when I was a small child. My voice was gentle and sweet. I avoided sports and all roughness. I played with the girls.

I did not fit in to the world around me. I knew the meaning of "heresy" before I entered kindergarten. Heresy was a boy who cried a lot when he got hurt. Heresy was a boy who couldn't throw a baseball. Heresy was a boy putting on girl-clothing. Heresy was me. (p. 3)

## Puberty

The growing realization that being different may mean being gay, lesbian, or bisexual usually appears with the onset of puberty and thereafter increases exponentially, primarily from 10 to 18 years of age (Coleman, 1981/1982; Kooden et al., 1979; Remafedi, 1987; Riddle & Morin, 1978; Robertson, 1981; Troiden, 1979). It is as if, for some, puberty *stamps in* their homosexuality, providing clarity and a label to heretofore poorly understood feelings. A 23-year-old gay man recalled the night he first realized that the label "gay" applied to him:

I think that I was around 14 years old when I first said to myself that I have a gay side to my personality. I said it to myself when I was 14, but I know that I clearly knew it before then, I just didn't admit it to myself. I can recall that evening very well: I was lying in bed and began having an anxiety attack. I was sweating profusely and was very nervous when I realized what my impulses and desires implied. I think that at that point most of my masturbation fantasies had involved males and this became very difficult for me. I said [to myself] that I was gay. I was frightened and hated this part of myself. I said to myself, "I can't be." I couldn't accept it.

I think that what brought on this realization and the anxiety was that about one or two years earlier I had decided to stop having sex with a neighbor, and regretted it a lot thereafter. A year later, when I was about 14, I tried to get him involved in a game that we used to play and that involved sexual activity but he declined. At this point, he didn't want to do it and I began to realize that what I wanted to do was abnormal or certainly not right. This also implied that I was different from him and from my other peers. (Savin-Williams, 1995)

A 16-year-old male recollected his reaction to learning that he was gay when he was 12: "It was a shock to discover that my impassioned, if inarticulated, love affairs with fellow schoolboys which had held so much poignant beauty carried that weighty word *homosexual*" (Heron, 1983, p. 104). Eighteen-year-old Joanne remembered when she first realized that she was a lesbian

. . . like a bolt of lightening, I realized that I was gay. . . . [S]uddenly all the feelings of attraction I had been having for women, and the isolated feelings about myself due to my lack of "femininity" came together and pointed to the label, *Lesbian*. As a result, I walked around like a shell shock victim for days. (Heron, 1983, pp. 9–10)

The application of a sexual identity label not only provides an explanation for formerly vague and misunderstood feelings, but affords a context in which future thoughts and emotions can be understood.

Table 5.1 summarizes the ages at which gays, lesbians, and bisexuals first labeled their feelings as gay or lesbian (but not their identity), first labeled themselves as lesbian or gay, first revealed their sexual orientation to another,[4] and had their first relationship. Early on, lesbian, gay, and bisexual youths recognize that they have homoerotic feelings but consider them to be a part of their greater *heterosexual* whole. On average, one and a half to four years later they label themselves gay or lesbian. Not until they have done so do they disclose their sexual orientation to others (usually about two years later) and enter a serious relationship (also two years postlabeling). It is most striking that the time from which gay and lesbian youths first experience same-sex attractions to the time they disclose this to others is often eight or more years. This reflects the protracted nature of coming out and the time that is required to undo social conditioning. Savin-Williams (1995) and Herdt and Boxer (1993) found that prior sexual experience is not necessary for self-definition as gay or lesbian. For example, Herdt and Boxer noted that almost 10% of the youths had not had a same-sex experience, yet they were certain that they were lesbian, gay, or bisexual.

The inconsistencies among the studies may be due to variations in the questions asked (first feelings of attraction, labeling the feelings as gay or lesbian, self-acknowledgment, etc.), cohort effects, characteristics of the sample (e.g., gender, religion, rural/urban, social class, etc.), and perhaps other variables. Herdt (1989) noted that gays, lesbians, and bisexuals are coming out to themselves at increasingly younger ages (cohort effect), largely because of the increased visibility of homosexuality in the media and the social reality of homosexuality presented by gay and lesbian culture to adolescents. Thus, young homoerotically inclined adolescents have available to them a construct and role models of homosexuality, which increase the likelihood of recognizing and labeling their same-sex attractions.

Studies have reported that lesbians come out at a slightly older age than gays, perhaps because it takes them longer to connect "feeling different" with same-sex erotic feelings and behaviors. Bisexuality may be more of an option for women than it is for men (Golden, this volume), thus reducing the number of lesbians in the population or prolonging the coming-out process ("I know I am attracted to men so I can't be a lesbian") (Bell et al., 1981a). Others suggested that because it is easier for women to pass as heterosexual, there is little need for them to come out as lesbian (Gagnon & Simon, 1973). Indeed, two women can publicly express affection without arousing suspicion because their behavior is more likely to be interpreted as feminine than sexual.

## Clinical Concerns of Coming Out to Self

Sexual-minority adults surveyed almost 20 years ago recalled that as adolescents they were often social isolates, loners, and outcasts. Compared to heterosexuals, they ranked low on social involvement, number of friends, dating, and participation in same-sex games (Bell et al., 1981a, 1981b). It is not clear if this was a self-imposed isolation because they feared being verbally and physically abused, rejected, or shamed or if it was in response to abuse and rejection they had actually received.

It is also debatable whether today's lesbian, gay, and bisexual youths face a comparable experience growing up in a society that has, on the surface, made strides in reducing the invisibility of homosexuality. Of issue here are the *difficulties* youths face after labeling their attractions and desires as lesbian, gay, or bisexual but before disclosing this information to others. These difficulties may be imagined or realistic, but in either case they are hypothesized to negatively affect youths and their development.

While growing up, many youths internalize society's condemnation of same-sex behavior. As a result, "most teenagers describe themselves as heterosexual unless there is compelling evidence to the contrary; and predominantly homosexual adolescents often waffle between heterosexual, homosexual, and bisexual labels" (Coleman & Remafedi, 1989, p. 37). The conflict of trying to reconcile both internalized homophobia and homoerotic attractions poses a formidable developmental task. Feelings of guilt about homoerotic attractions cause some adolescents to delay achieving a positive lesbian, gay, or bisexual identity for many years, perhaps until after becoming a part of the lesbian or gay subculture (Harry & DeVall, 1978). Initially, a self-defeating identity may be adopted, with an accompanying sexual moratorium (an inhibition of sexuality) (Cass, 1979).

At a time when most youths are gradually building self-esteem and establishing an identity, some sexual-minority adolescents are learning from peers and adults that they are amongst the most hated in society. One lesbian adolescent reported, "Society told me that as a lesbian I was expendable" (Maguen, 1991, p. 46). For those who choose to hide their sexual orientation, interactions with friends, parents, teachers, and others are often based on lies and half-truths, thus undermining the development of a positive self-image.

Unacceptable desires may lead to doubts about one's normality and thereby affect self-esteem. How can a youth consider himself or herself respectable when society maintains that a central aspect of that which he or she defines as self is considered bad? Brandon, a 17-year-old teenager, recalled, "When I realized I was homosexual, the first thing I did was sit down and cry. I wept for myself, but mostly I cried because I didn't conform. I couldn't be this way, because it 'just wasn't right'" (Heron, 1983, p. 15).

Myths such as gay people hate members of the other sex, are pedophiles, suffer from developmental arrest, cause AIDS, and are a danger to the family and Western civilization may be articulated by clergy, teachers, peers, and family members. If accepted without question they may contribute to feelings of self-hatred and inferiority (Martin, 1982; Martin & Hetrick, 1988). One woman expressed this:

> Most of my life I repressed my homosexuality. This involved a lot of guilt feelings of unworthiness to the point of suicide and not wanting to live. Whether a person responds to their homosexuality or not, they still know it is there and they still know that our society thinks so little of a homosexual that he can be beat up, robbed, or murdered, and the law will not worry about it much. We have been considered lower than murderers and rapists; and many of us are law-abiding citizens who contribute to our society. (Jay & Young, 1979, p. 708)

Support for the importance of societal beliefs and values in shaping self-concept was provided by Ross (1989) in his study of four societies. Gay youths who most internalized societal stigmatization of homosexuality, who embraced negative myths about gays, and who experienced psychological "problems" came from the more conservative and antihomosexual (Australia, Ireland), as opposed to liberal (Sweden, Finland), societies.

If adolescents do not reject their sexuality, they may have concerns about their physical safety and psychological normality. For some lesbian, gay, and bisexual youths, fear and anxiety are constant companions. These teens perpetually anticipate the malevolent reactions of others if their sexual orientation were to be discovered. In some cases, these fears are not groundless because discovery may invite a hostile response. One teen who attended the Harvey Milk School, an alternative public secondary school for sexual-minority adolescents in New York City, expressed his generalized anxiety during a radio interview:

> I was concerned about my parents finding out, you know? Whether I was going to have a home to live at, you know, if they found out? Whether I was going to be able to go to college or, you know, whether I was going to be physically attacked. (Hansen, 1990)

Those who fear the pathogenic etiology of their desires may attempt to alter their sexual orientation. They may pray, date the other sex, or deny that they are sexual beings. For most, these defenses constitute a futile effort doomed to fail.

Another concern is loneliness. Growing up lesbian or gay can be an exceedingly isolating experience (Hetrick & Martin, 1987; Martin & Hetrick, 1988; Sears, 1991). Nineteen-year-old Aaron Fricke[5] recalled this isolation:

> I became withdrawn. I had no means of expression. My school grades dropped and I retreated into a life of non-stop eating and listening to the radio. In seventh grade I weighed 140 pounds; by eleventh grade, I weighed 217½ and spent eleven hours a day listening to the radio. I had trouble dealing with the outside world. And every day I lived in fear that there was nothing else, that I would never know anyone who could understand me and my feelings. (Heron, 1983, p. 39)

Feelings of isolation and loneliness are not uncommon for youths raised in small rural towns in which exposure to and acceptance of diversity are limited.[6] For example, Sears (1991) reported that 70% of his sample of Southern-raised gay and lesbian youths felt isolated. Brown (1976) noted that the small town is an environment in which there is little hope for fulfilling homoerotic needs or for obtaining social acceptance of those needs. Youths who attempt to establish a same-sex relationship in a small town may fear detection, blackmail, and verbal or physical assault. Discovery of such a relationship would inevitably result in community-wide ostracism.

## Defenses Against External and Internalized Homophobia

When confronted with homoerotic desires, many individuals use psychological defenses to ward off anxiety and depression. Tripp (1975) suggested that "heterosexual" men who yield to their need for homoerotic stimulation often use three systems of denial: assume the masculine role in same-sex encounters; claim innocence because of drunkenness, drugs, or sleep; and excuse it as no more than a "special friendship." Other classic defenses include: "It's just a phase," "I've heard all guys do it once," "He gave me head; I didn't touch him," "Hey, I got $20 for it," and "I was just curious" (Savin-Williams & Rodriguez, 1993).

Martin (1982) noted that for some gay adolescents, homoerotic desires must remain hidden from peers and, frequently, from the self. To fulfill same-sex attractions, male adolescents may resort to casual, one-time sexual encounters. Although this may satisfy sexual needs, allowing them to drop their facade for a short time, it also compartmentalizes this aspect of themselves from the rest of their lives. Because sex is casual, there is insufficient time for an emotional connection to develop (see Savin-Williams, "Dating," this volume). In its absence, these adolescents may rationalize that they engaged in the act solely for sexual gratification, rather than for a "love" of the same gender. This allows them to maintain, "I may have homosexual sex, but I'm not a homosexual." This defense may lessen the extent to which adolescents think of themselves as gay.

*Passing* as heterosexual is probably the most common adolescent adjustment to the fear of disclosure and its attendant feelings of guilt and anxiety (Dank, 1971; Lee, 1977; Martin, 1982; Sears, 1991). Goffman (1963, p. 42) referred to passing as the concealment of "information about one's real social identity, receiving and accepting treatment based on false suppositions concerning the self." Two youths illustrate this means of coping with their homosexuality:

**Youth A:** I feared not being liked and being alienated. I was president of various school clubs and once I beat up a guy for being a faggot. I was adamant that fags should be booted out of my organizations. Other kids asked me why I was so rough on them. I did not say. No one suspected me because I did sports and had a girlfriend.

**Youth B:** Still, I try, even now, to cover up myself. I'm very conscious of my masculine appearance. I won't cross my legs or limp my wrists in public. I'm always monitoring myself, my clothing, and jewelry. I'd like not to let others know I'm gay unless I decide it. I want control. I'm androgynous and proud of it. (Savin-Williams, 1995)

Sears (1991) reported that two thirds of his sample of lesbian and gay Southern youths tried to pass as heterosexual. Only 19% objected to gay-related jokes by peers, and almost 90% dated opposite-sex peers. In another study, 85% of adolescents pretended to be heterosexual some of the time (Newman & Muzzonigro, 1993). To facilitate passing, D'Augelli (1991) found that approximately one half of his sample of gay youths changed the pronoun of their dating partner and/or pretended to date women. Two thirds "introduced a partner or lover as a friend," and three quarters "avoided discussing their personal lives."

Passing, however, may lead to feelings of depression, awkwardness, and shame in interpersonal relations. Several humanistic clinical psychologists (Jourard, 1971; Maslow, 1954) proposed that healthy personality development requires significant and substantial self-disclosure to others. A person establishes contact with the real self when the public self is made congruent with it. Personal authenticity brings self-validation as a person of self-worth. To forgo this, as in passing, engenders feelings of hypocrisy and self-alienation (Lee, 1977; Martin, 1982).

Some lesbians, gays, and bisexuals have so internalized society's condemnation of same-sex love that they do not permit themselves to engage in same-sex activity or to recognize their same-sex attractions. Malyon (1981) outlined three of the most frequent responses to the dilemma, from least to most satisfactory adaptation. The first is *repression* of same-sex desires, the prevention of threatening desires from entering consciousness. Eventually, of course, the impulses must emerge and may elicit panic or cause a major disruption of established coping strategies. During this mode, a youth has little opportunity to integrate homoerotic desires with his or her identity. The second adaptation mode, the conscious *suppression* of same-sex impulses, often results in a temporary developmental moratorium. Identity formation is truncated because an adolescent attempts to pass as heterosexual, possibly leading to underachievement in school, unhappy heterosexual relations, chronic psychological disequilibrium, and a biphasic or secondary adolescence during the third or fourth decades of life when he or she finally comes out. Malyon noted, "The suppression of homosexual impulses during primary adolescence results in an interruption and mitigation of the process of identity formation. The coming-out experience prompts another phase of psychological growth, similar to that which has primacy during age-appropriate adolescence" (1981, p. 329). The third option is *disclosure* to self and others. But even here hurdles must be overcome. For example, an individual must decide whether to remain a part of heterosexual communities and perhaps feel estranged and confused, or move to lesbian or gay communities and risk conflict with parents. The process of "slowly surrendering" to the deviant identity entails weighing the costs to one's psychic self and one's relationship with others, especially family and friends (Coleman, 1981/1982; MacDonald, 1983). Some youths strategically wait until they are in college and thus less financially and emotionally dependent on the family to begin the process of coming to terms with their homoerotic attractions:

> I had feelings I wanted to explore but I was afraid. I kept it securely inside, afraid of my peers and afraid of what it would do to my family in the community. I did not want to be ostracized or let my family down. . . . It wasn't until I was in college and broke up with my last girlfriend that I was ready to tell anyone. Figured it was time to stop fooling myself and others and to face the music. (Savin-Williams, 1995)

Several authors have described defensive strategies used by adolescents to help them cope with homoerotic feelings. They are summarized as follows:

- *Rationalization* (Cass, 1979; Plummer, 1981; Troiden, 1979): "Something I'll outgrow," "I did it because I was lonely," "Just a means to earn money," or "I was drunk/high."

- *Relegation to insignificance* (Cass, 1979; Reiche & Dannecker, 1977; Troiden, 1979): "It is just sexual experimentation or curiosity that is natural at my age," or "Did it only as a favor for a friend."
- *Compartmentalization of sexual desire* (de Monteflores & Schultz, 1978; Malyon, 1981; Martin, 1982): "I mess around with other boys/girls but that does not make me a faggot/dyke," or "I just love her and not all women."
- *Withdrawal from provocative situations to remain celibate or asexual* (Cass, 1979; Lee, 1977; Sanders, 1980): "I'm saving myself for the right girl/boy."
- *Denial, frequently engaging in heterosexual dating or sexual behavior* (Bell et al., 1981a; Cass, 1979; Martin, 1982; Reiche & Dannecker, 1977; Sanders, 1980): "I can't be gay, I've had a girlfriend/boyfriend for years and I like her/him."
- *Redirection of energies to other efforts, such as intellectual or work pursuits* (Sanders, 1980).

It is frequently difficult to offer clinical or counseling assistance to an adolescent who denies homoerotic impulses because she or he cannot ask for or accept help for a problem that is believed not to exist.

## COMING OUT TO OTHERS

Although the process of coming out to others can be arduous and protracted, requiring continual decisions about when and where to come out and to whom, it is perceived by many academicians, clinicians, and mental health professionals to be a positive act. Without denying that coming out to others invites negative reactions that may compromise one's physical safety and psychological integrity, there are many advantages to proclaiming one's sexuality. Coming out to others leads to identity synthesis and integration (Cass, 1979; Coleman, 1981/1982); healthy psychological adjustment (Hammersmith & Weinberg, 1973; Gonsiorek & Rudolph, 1991); decreased feelings of loneliness and guilt (Dank, 1973); a deeper commitment to homosexuality through the fusing of gay sexuality and emotionality in a love relationship (Warren, 1974) or by viewing homosexuality as a preferred way of life (Troiden, 1989); integration through redefining and maintaining both separation and attachment (Colgan, 1987); and a positive gay identity (McDonald, 1982). Fitzpatrick (1983) found that positive consequences of disclosing sexual identity included a sense of freedom, of being oneself, of not living a lie, and of experiencing genuine acceptance. In a sample of over 300 lesbian, bisexual, and gay youths, Savin-Williams (1990) found that self-esteem was positively correlated with general openness about sexual orientation.

Many youths nonetheless choose to conceal their homosexuality from others because they fear negative reprisals or believe that their attractions are wrong. Those who are out to themselves but not to others frequently report that they choose to remain closeted because they are fearful of the unknown, wish not to hurt or disappoint a loved one, and want to avoid being rejected by parents and peers (Rector, 1982). In a sample of adult lesbians, Fitzpatrick (1983) found that the predominant reasons for not disclosing were the desire not to hurt or disappoint family members, fear of job loss, and fear of rejection. Davies (1992) noted that some gay men choose partial disclosure. That is, they compartmentalize their lives by developing two distinct groups of friends: those who know (and are likely gay) and those who do not know.

Although for many youths it is most difficult and yet most important for their identity development to come out to family members (Nemeyer, 1980), they first come out to same-sex and same-orientation friends, especially intimate friends (Hencken, 1985). Herdt and Boxer (1993) recently reported that although youths prefer to come out first to friends of the same gender, the friends' sexual orientations were not a significant factor. For two thirds of their sample, the recipient of self-disclosure was supportive, suggesting that youths may carefully consider to whom they will come out. D'Augelli (1991) found that more than half his sample of gay youths considered gay friends the most important people in their lives, compared to 15% who similarly regarded family.

Thus, it is critical to distinguish among (a) who is told earliest, (b) who is most difficult to come out to, and (c) who is most important to tell. These are likely to vary within and across individuals depending on developmental issues; that which is most critical in life at a particular moment; and personal characteristics, such as social class, religious values, and temperament.

The following sections examine several factors that are important in determining whether a lesbian, gay, or bisexual individual will come out to others.

## Predictors of Coming Out

The extent to which gays, lesbians, and bisexuals are overt about their sexual orientation is influenced by several factors, some characteristic of the individuals and others related to aspects of the environments in which they live (Harry & DeVall, 1978). The process is, of course, reciprocal in nature: As the coming-out process is experienced, perceptions of the self and the external world may undergo gradual or radical transformation. Perhaps it is safest to conclude that the acquisition of a sexual identity is accompanied by changes in behaviors and attitudes.

This section of the chapter focuses on the extent to which the coming-out process is related to sociodemographic characteristics, gay-related activities, support received from family and friends, love affairs, and self-perceptions. These have only been sporadically addressed by empirical investigations.

### Sociodemographic variables

Investigators have examined the various factors that influence the age at which an individual comes out or the way in which the coming-out experience differs as a function of age. Table 5.1 presents the findings of several investigations. As noted earlier, while first awareness of same-sex attractions frequently coincides with the onset of puberty, disclosure to others is usually a much later event, possibly delayed until the individual is an adult. There are, however, considerable individual variations in the timing of first disclosure to others. In studies spanning a range of ages, older respondents are generally more out than younger ones, presumably because they have had a longer time in which to come out (Brady, 1985; Myrick, 1974a; Savin-Williams, 1990; Straver, 1976). A counterfinding is the research of McKirnan and Peterson (1986), who reported that with increasing age the distribution of their Chicago sample significantly shifted from "completely open" to "closeted." These findings may reflect the large-scale consensus that milestone events have been occurring at chronologically earlier ages during the last two decades (Herdt, 1989; Kimmel, 1978; McDonald, 1982; Smith, 1983). These results are critically important because Cramer (1986) demonstrated that the amount of time one is out to others is a better predictor of self-esteem than age per se.

In terms of social class, self-disclosure was more prevalent among students from upper than working class backgrounds in a Netherlands sample of 15- to 26-year-old youths (Straver, 1976) and a U.S. sample of gay youths, ages 14 to 23 years (Savin-Williams, 1990). Similarly, gay men in the United States who were in the "professional" class were furthest along in the coming-out process (Brady, 1985). Myrick's (1974a) data were in basic agreement: Covert-covert men (no one knows and individual conceals) were in the lowest occupational status categories. Unclear, however, is whether social class is independent of age; that is, those who are older may be more likely to have advanced in their career than younger individuals. Again, a counterfinding was reported by McKirnan and Peterson (1986): Those in the higher categories of income and occupation were most closeted. Occupational status was unrelated to whether one was out to those most interpersonally close (friends and family) but strongly related to whether one was out to casual friends, coworkers, and acquaintances. They felt this was due to the pressures of homophobia in higher status occupations. Harry (1993) also observed that higher income individuals were least out to others. Ferguson and Finkler (1978) suggested that lower class lesbians most overt in their sexual orientation experienced more anxiety than those who were not out. This relationship was not considered to be characteristic of higher social status lesbians.

Finally, it has been suggested that gay men and lesbians are more likely to be out in the city, where anonymity protects them from social rejection, role models are more available, and heterogeneity and differentiation encourage a supportive milieu (Bell & Weinberg, 1978; Weinberg & Williams, 1974). Gay men and lesbians who live in rural small communities in which everyone knows and interacts with everyone else and in which knowledge of one's purported deviancy, such as sexual orientation, spreads quickly throughout the community, may be less likely to openly disclose their identity to others (D'Augelli & Hart, 1987; Moses & Buckner, 1980). Thus, it seems reasonable to assume that urban youths would also be more willing to disclose their sexual orientation to others. Congruent with this hypothesis, Savin-Williams (1990) reported that adolescent and young adult lesbians, gays, and bisexuals from urban areas were most out. In general, however, researchers have not examined urban/rural rearing in their research designs on coming out.

Judging from the literature reviewed above, older youths and those reared in an urban environment should be most out. Social class data are inconsistent regarding their impact on coming out.

## Activities and attitudes

Several studies with lesbians (Elliot, 1982) and gay men (Cramer & Roach, 1988; McDonald, 1982) concluded that socialization within gay and lesbian communities was more prevalent with increasing certainty of one's homosexuality. For both lesbian and gay youths, frequent bar patrons tended to be more out to others, except those who went *only* to bars and not to other lesbian and gay activities (McKirnan & Peterson, 1987b; Savin-Williams, 1990).

The best predictor of disclosure to others among a primarily Canadian lesbian population of 305 was political awareness and involvement (Elliot, 1982). Kahn (1991) reported that lesbians who embraced a feminist attitude reported less internalized homophobia, were less concealing of their homoerotic desires, and had greater "positive expectancy regarding disclosure" (p. 67). Savin-Williams (1990) found that males who were most out were politically liberal and supportive of the feminist movement. The single best predictor among both lesbian and gay youths of self-disclosure was active involvement in political and social organizations with other gays and lesbians (Savin-Williams, 1990). These activities offer, especially within lesbian communities, support for those in the midst of coming out (Ettorre, 1980; Ponse, 1980; Richardson, 1981). The ties created are sources of friendship, romance, sexual relationships, social norms for a lesbian identification, and lesbian role models. They enhance coming out as a positive experience.

In terms of attitudes toward homosexuality from a labeling perspective, T. Weinberg (1983) maintained that coming to terms with one's sexual orientation is easier if positive views toward that orientation are held. Supporting this view, McDonald (1982, 1984) reported that males most identified as gay and out of the closet had the lowest levels of homophobic prejudice; those reticent to disclose to others felt guilt, anxiety, and shame about their homoerotic attractions. Savin-Williams (1990) found that disclosure was positively associated with feeling that same-sex attractions originated from an early age and were beyond one's control. Females who were most out did not want to relinquish their sexual orientation. Gay men and lesbians highest on self-disclosure were lowest on internalized fear of societal negative attitudes toward homosexuality and on distress over homoerotic arousal and lifestyle. They were less likely than their closeted peers to desire heterosexual arousals or lifestyles (Miranda, 1986).

Several investigations, however, have not supported this view. Essentially the same attitudes toward homosexuality existed for both those who had and had not disclosed to others, suggesting that holding positive attitudes toward homosexuality is not essential for disclosure to family members, peers, and others (Grabert, 1985; Harry & DeVall, 1978). O'Carolan (1982) discovered that locus of control, the degree to which one feels in control of life's events and rejects fate as the major determinant of events, did not differentiate self-disclosure level in a Midwest sample of lesbians.

One's placement on the homosexual-heterosexual continuum has been well documented in accounting for differences in overtness. Bell and Weinberg (1978) reported that those who rated themselves as "exclusively homosexual" were most willing to disclose their sexual identity to others. Compared with men who rated themselves as not exclusively gay, they had less need to pass as heterosexual, were less likely to engage in heterosexual behaviors and fantasies, and were more known about (McDonald, 1982; Myrick, 1974b; Weinberg & Williams, 1974).

Thus, there is fairly strong support for the view that lesbians and gays who are most involved in lesbian and gay communities and who claim to be exclusively lesbian or gay are most likely to be publicly out of the closet. Results on the relationship between disclosure and attitudes toward homosexuality are mixed, with studies supporting both a lack of consistent trends and a positive co-occurrence.

### Support from family and friends

Coming out may be a positive event that bolsters an individual's self-esteem if, in the coming-out process, support from family, coworkers, friends, and lesbian and gay communities is gained (Nungesser, 1983). In a sample of Netherlands gay men, those most out had positive relations with heterosexuals and an integrated friendship network of both heterosexuals and gays (Straver, 1976). Savin-Williams (1990) found that the second strongest predictor of outness among bisexual, lesbian, and gay youths was having family members and friends accept one's sexual orientation. Another study (de Koning & Blom van Rens, cited in Straver, 1976) of gay youths reported that the number of friends or the amount of time spent socializing with them was not as crucial as having people with whom to discuss problems as one progressed through different phases of development. The research of McKirnan and Peterson (1987b) concurred: Lesbians and gay men who were most out had many confidants, individuals with whom they could intimately talk and turn to for help.

### Love affairs

Coming out was significantly correlated with "experienced gay crushes" and "interests in other males during adolescence" in Harry and DeVall's (1978) study of gay men. In addition, defining oneself as gay at an early age and coming out to others were positively correlated with engagement in teenage gay sex and desire for establishing a long-term romantic relationship with another male and negatively correlated with heterosexual dating, crushes, and interests. In terms of actually having a romantic relationship and coming-out status, McKirnan and Peterson found no relationship between coupledness and outness among 739 lesbians; among 2,625 gay men there was a slight tendency for those most out to be in a romantic relationship (Peterson, personal communication, 1988). Savin-Williams (1990) found that female youths who experienced primarily lesbian love affairs, including their first love affair, and had few sexual relations with males had the most numerous same-sex encounters and were most self-disclosing about their sexual orientation.

### Self-descriptions

Relatively few studies of coming out have investigated its relationship with personality characteristics. In general, disclosure appears to be positively related to Bem's notion of femininity for both gay and lesbian college students (Bender, Davis, Glover, & Stapp, 1976). Rector (1982) found little relationship between the development of homoerotic feelings and behaviors and psychological androgyny among adolescents with same-sex attractions. Savin-Williams (1990) reported that gays who were most out described themselves as accomplished and self-sufficient, but not as competitive-forceful or affectionate-compassionate. In addition, material possessions and good looks were not important to their sense of self-worth, but friends, career, and academics were. None of the self-descriptors predicted coming out among the lesbian youths.

### Summary

Thus far several factors have been examined that influence the coming-out process. The empirical research suggests that exclusively gay, politically liberal and/or feminist older individuals raised in an urban environment who are heavily involved in lesbian and gay communities and have supportive and accepting family and friends are most likely to be overt about their sexual orientation. In addition, those who feel that they are not in control of their sexuality and do not want to relinquish their sexual orientation are most likely to disclose their homoerotic preferences to others. It remains less clear the degree to which internalized homophobia, attitudes toward homosexuality, and social class contribute to self-disclosure.

Perhaps no single coming-out event evokes more fear and anxiety from gay, lesbian, and bisexual individuals than coming out to parents. Notwithstanding, many sexual-minority individuals report never fully feeling comfortable or out until they have disclosed their sexual orientation to their parents. Because coming out to parents is such a significant event, the following section is devoted to this issue.

# COMING OUT TO PARENTS

## Importance of Parents

For many gay and lesbian youths, the most difficult decision to make after recognizing their nontraditional sexual orientation is whether to reveal to their parents that they will not be fulfilling the parents' heterosexual dreams. Coming-out advice books strongly emphasize the critical importance of parents in the coming-out process (e.g., Borhek, 1993). However, some youths never come out to their parents, becoming, according to MacDonald (1983),

> . . . half-members of the family unit, afraid and alienated, unable ever to be totally open and spontaneous, to trust or be trusted, to develop a fully socialized sense of self-affirmation. This sad stunting of human potential breeds stress for gay people and their families alike—stress characterized by secrecy, ignorance, helplessness, and distance. (p. 1)

Under such conditions, youths may respond by running away from home or by becoming involved in prostitution or other crimes (see Savin-Williams & Cohen, this volume). They may feel that they are unable to cope with the obligatory deception, isolation, and alienation (Martin, 1982). Plummer (1989) noted the "paradox of secrecy": The stigma associated with homosexuality leads youths to conceal their same-sex attractions. But by so doing, they remain invisible and thus powerless to incite social change.

Given the historical condemnation of homosexuality and the tendency for most parents to consider their children to be extensions of themselves, telling parents may be the final exit out of the closet. Fairchild and Hayward's (1989) classic book entitled, *Now That You Know: What Every Parent Should Know About Homosexuality,* as well as others (Berzon & Leighton, 1979; Borhek, 1993; Clark, 1987; Griffin, Wirth, & Wirth, 1986; Silverstein, 1977; Woodman & Lenna, 1980), suggest strategies for parents who need help in coping with the seemingly earth-shattering news of their child's homosexuality.[7]

The most accurate generalization that can be made, however, is that the reaction of parents to the news appears "unpredictable," although most writers believe that a positive prior relationship with the parents is a good omen for a healthy resolution. Having elderly parents may be a bad omen. They may have difficulty accepting their child's homosexuality because of the sociopolitical climate of their child-rearing years (e.g., the McCarthy era), when homosexuality was viewed as an unspeakable moral sin or a deep psychological pathology (Borhek, 1993).

The advice literature is less clearly unanimous on the effects that coming out to parents have on the self-evaluations of gay and lesbian youths. Borhek (1993) believes that if the consequences are affirming and supportive, telling will enhance self-esteem.

## Theoretical and Empirical Literature on Coming Out

In contrast to this high priority of the parent-child relationship during the youth's revelatory process, the theoretical and empirical coming-out literature largely ignores or deemphasizes the issue. Troiden (1989) noted that an accepting family is one of several facilitating factors in the coming-out process; Cass (1979) treated parents as one aspect of a category that included peers, church group, and heterosexuals in general as a determining factor for whether an individual will pass as heterosexual or come out. Coleman (1981/1982) noted the significance of telling parents, but stated that one should first gauge whether the parents will be accepting.

Gays and lesbians usually reveal their sexual orientation first to close friends (Hencken, 1985; Herdt & Boxer, 1993; Savin-Williams, 1990). The nuclear family is generally told some time thereafter, although there is relatively little empirical research on the factors that determine whether adolescents will reveal their homosexuality to parents or on the effects that coming out to parents has on youths' self-esteem. An exception is a study by Newman and Muzzonigro (1993). Adolescents who grew up in families in which "traditional family values" (emphasis on religion, marriage, children, and maintaining a non-English mother tongue) were embraced were more likely to perceive their parents as being disappointed about their homosexuality. However, they were not less likely to come out to their parents or to come out at a later age than those not from families in which traditional values were held. Cramer and Roach (1988) found that gays who reported that their mothers had traditional sex role attitudes and fathers were high in religious orthodoxy perceived that their parents were more accepting of them than nontraditional parents. They speculated that perhaps these parents' emphasis on family unity resulted in an enhanced ability to come to terms with a family crisis.

In general, youths are more likely to come out to mother than to father and other family members (Cohen-Ross, 1985; Cramer & Roach, 1988; D'Augelli, 1991; Grabert, 1985; Herdt & Boxer, 1993; Remafedi, 1987; Savin-Williams, 1990), perhaps because children tend to have more distant relationships with their father than with their mother (Fitzpatrick, 1983). More mothers than fathers are told directly rather than indirectly (Cramer & Roach, 1988) because mothers are more likely to respond in an affirming manner (D'Augelli, 1991). For example, in Remafedi's (1987) sample of bisexual and gay male teenagers, over 60% were out to their mother but only one third were out to father. Over 90% had told a friend. Mothers were more likely than fathers to respond positively (21% versus 10%) to the news; negative reactions to the revelation were the norm, however, for both parents. D'Augelli (1991) reported that 9% of mothers were rejecting compared to 22% of fathers. Contrary to other reports, Cramer and Roach (1988) found that the initial reactions of mothers to their gay sons were more negative than those of the fathers, and the sons' relations with their father improved more than they did with their mother. Perhaps most revealing, nondisclosers feared more the reactions of their father than mother.

Even well-educated, liberal parents initially react somewhat negatively when informed about their child's same-sex attractions (Robinson, Walters, & Skeen, 1989). Herdt and Boxer (1993) reported that regardless of mothers' initial responses to learning about their child's same-sex attractions, the general quality of their relationship was preserved. For fathers, however, a gender effect was observed: Significantly more daughters than sons reported negative changes in their relationship with their father. Cramer and Roach (1988) noted that the relationship between fathers and their gay son may be so impaired prior to the revelation that any improvement in honesty, communication, and trust is considered a positive development for their relationship.

Many never come out to their parents, even as adults, because of fear that such disclosure would have negative implications for their relationship with their parents or their status within the family. Most youths, however, want to share this aspect of themselves with their parents (Herdt & Boxer, 1993). Cramer and Roach (1988) reported the reasons most often cited by sons for coming out to their parents:

> . . . a desire to share one's personal life, being tired of concealing one's sexuality, a desire for more freedom, and a desire for more intimacy with one's parents. These reasons indicate that most gay sons take the initiative in disclosing because they want a closer relationship with their parents. (p. 87)

Although the parent-son relationship often deteriorated immediately after disclosure, it usually improved considerably thereafter—sometimes to a level more positive than prior to disclosure.

## Coming Out and the Importance of Parental Acceptance

With a sample of 317 youths between the ages of 14 and 23 years, who completed an anonymous questionnaire, Savin-Williams (1990) found that the average lesbian adolescent/young adult felt most comfortable with her sexual orientation if she also reported that her parents accepted or would accept (if they knew) her sexual orientation. Lesbians who maintained that they had satisfying relationships with their parents and who had relatively young parents were most likely to be out to them. This is consistent with the coming-out advice literature. Congruent with these findings, Kahn (1991) reported that lesbians who felt intimidated by their parents experienced greater homophobia and less openness. She concluded that "family, fear, and intolerance may have a stronger influence in the suppression of development than a healthy environment has in the encouragement of openness" (p. 68).

Among males (Savin-Williams, 1990), parental acceptance was related to feeling comfortable being gay if the youths also reported that the parents were important for their sense of self-worth. Gay youths who were out to their mother and who had a satisfying but infrequent relationship with their father were most likely to report high self-esteem.

Because the aforementioned studies are cross-sectional and nonexperimental, issues of causation are tenuous at best. Positive self-esteem could just as easily be a precursor to and thus a cause of an individual coming out as the reverse assumption—that coming out influences self-esteem level. For example, it is not clear whether a satisfying parental relationship encourages a lesbian to come out to her parents or the relationship is satisfying because the lesbian youth has come out to them. The coming-out literature is not particularly help-ful in sorting relationships because it suggests that both are true.

The theoretical and empirical coming-out literature largely ignores the role of the parents for the adolescent and thus sheds relatively little light on various causal pathways. There is sufficient reason to believe, however, that parents are a significant factor in their child's developing sense of self-worth and sexual identity, especially in terms of a youth feeling comfortable with her or his ho-mosexuality and of a youth disclosing that information to others.

## Coming Out to Parents: A Clinical Case

Many adolescents choose to conceal their sexuality until late adolescence or early adulthood when they are less emotionally and financially dependent on their parents or are living out of the home. For some youths, parents are among the last to learn about their homoerotic attractions. Although the decision to delay this aspect of coming out may initially protect lesbian and gay youths from feared parental reactions, it may create a fissure in the parent-child relationship. Ac-cording to Rotheram-Borus, Rosario, and Koopman (1991), it is more stressful for many adolescents to hide their sexual orientation than it is to come out to parents and friends.

An adolescent who chooses to share with parents the truth about her or his sexuality is often subjected to questions, castigations, and attempts to "cure" her or his homoerotic desires before acceptance, or at least resignation, is achieved. While a child may have spent years coming to terms with same-sex at-tractions, parents may be caught off guard by the suddenness of the revelation. To illustrate several of the common reactions of parents who learn of their child's homoerotic attractions, the following vignette of a mother's attempt to under-stand her bisexual son's sexual orientation is offered.[8] Although Mrs. Collins was eventually supportive of her son Michael and his life partner, the shock of her son's self-disclosure initially sent her in pursuit of rationalizations for why he could not truly be bisexual. She began:

> I think that you are bisexual because you have a strong need for love and affection. You've always been that way and therefore you need so much that you believe that you need it from both sexes.

Mrs. Collins attempted to persuade Michael that he could easily "choose" to lead a straight life—if only he would "try hard enough."

> If you are bisexual, then you can avoid the abnormal and lead a normal, satisfying life. If you can be bi, then you can be normal. Why confuse your life? Concentrate on the norm; you *must* follow the normal path. . . . Program your mind and then the emotions and physical attractions will follow.

When Michael explained to his mother that his feelings and attractions went be-yond "mere choice" and were deeply rooted in his self-concept and self-esteem, the mother asserted:

You can never be happy [living a gay lifestyle] so just accept this as a momentary thing. . . . It is of this world, this physicality, and don't make a big issue out of [your bisexuality]. . . . Just put the other out of your head. Maybe you just have not had the kind of relationship with a girl that would be a real test. . . . You have not sampled the real thing. . . . Don't allow yourself to become preoccupied with this garbage. It doesn't allow you to find a girl. You are not allowing yourself the choice and to know how good it can be.

Mrs. Collins concluded:

It is sex, pure and simple, just physical. . . . Don't allow yourself to get involved; it's sick; you'll die [from AIDS]. We did not raise you to see you die, to come to this [homosexuality].

Such interactions are not uncommon following a child's disclosure of ho-moerotic, particularly bisexual, attractions. These words reflect a parent's an-guish about losing the heterosexual dreams for her son. Parents' words have profound implications for their child's self-concept and self-esteem—at least temporarily. A detailed analysis of the messages conveyed by Mrs. Collins and Michael's reactions clarifies the dynamics through which this is sometimes achieved.

Mrs. Collins's refusal to accept her bisexual son's homoerotic attractions and her insistence that it is a passing phase—the result of previously unsatis-factory heterosexual relationships and a desire for "sex, pure and simple"—negate Michael's feelings. Furthermore, they communicate the messages that "gay is bad" and "mother knows best." Such reactions often alienate the child from the parent and block future communications.

Mrs. Collins's explanation of the etiology of her son's sexual orientation sug-gests that it was the result of an abnormally strong need for love—of any kind—and recommends that he overcome this malady by "programming" his mind. Here Michael is told that he is weak because he needs love so desperately that he will go to any extreme to obtain it. The mother's insistence that he stop think-ing about such matters clearly indicates *her* unwillingness to discuss her son's sexuality.

Following this interchange between Michael and his mother, Michael re-ported to the interviewer that the conversation left him feeling rejected and abandoned by his mother's conditional love; misunderstood, frustrated, angry, and hurt by her blatant disregard for his feelings; uncertain about her ability to meet his future emotional needs; scolded for having "chosen" to love mem-bers of the same gender; insulted by her recipe-like recommendations for over-coming this affliction and by her implication that he did not know what he liked or who he was; and frightened by her assertion that he would never live a happy life.

Without support from those whose acceptance and love is most desired, it is difficult to develop a positive sense of self. If a child believes that his or her par-ents are disgusted with him or her, the child will likely be disgusted with him-self or herself.

On the other hand, some parents react positively when they learn that their child is lesbian, bisexual, or gay. Barbara recalled her mother's reaction when she came out to her at the age of 12.

> I was very close to my mother. . . . I went home and told my mother and my mother treated it moderately lightly—that is, she said that since I was very young, that I was much too young for such an announcement, that I should probably wait a few months at least before deciding that this was an absolute fact. But if it turned out, indeed, that I was a Lesbian, then that was fine. . . . [It was expected of me that] I was to be an honorable person in every way all of my life, and if I were honorable all of my life nothing but good would come to me. (Grier, 1980, p. 236)

Another woman remembered the solidarity and unconditional support shown by her mother when she first came out:

> When I wrote and told my mother I was bisexual, she replied: "Yes, we all are, aren't we?" That blew me away—she was taking it much more calmly than I was! My transition to Lesbianism did not surprise or unduly bother her. . . . Of course she has had to do some fast growing and information-gathering on the subject, but she has never hesitated in her support and love for me. . . . [My father] too was very accepting. . . . (Anonymous, 1980, p. 77)

Mothers who are aware that they have raised a "gender atypical" child may marshall to their child's defense. Recalled a male youth:

> I think my mother knew, certainly she was aware of the grief I got at school. We talked but never said the word "gay." She wanted me to be in therapy since 7 or 8, not to change me but so that I could be happy and sure of my homosexuality. (Savin-Williams, 1995)

Robinson, Walters, and Skeen (1989) reported that parents progress through stages similar to those Kubler-Ross (1969) described: shock, denial, guilt, anger, and acceptance. DeVine (1984) named these subliminal awareness, impact, adjustment, resolution, and integration. Parental reactions will depend on the priority given to maintaining face and to solving their own problems. Some parents initially mourn their child as if she or he had died. Most of the parents Robinson et al. (1989) studied, however, arrived at acceptance, though some were fixated at earlier stages or occasionally regressed temporarily to previous stages. Strommen (1989) found that it is not uncommon for parents to initially feel that their child is a stranger—someone whom they do not know. He suggested that acceptance depends on

> (a) the values concerning homosexuality currently held by the family members disclosed to, (b) the effects these values are perceived to have on the relationship between the disclosing family member and other family members, and (c) the conflict resolution mechanisms available to the family members. (p. 50)

The closer a lesbian, gay, or bisexual youth is to the person being confided in, the greater the latter person's reaction will impact the youth. Thus, youths are at increased risk of experiencing psychological compromises such as lowered self-esteem when they are rejected by parents and close friends.

# THE RELATIONSHIP BETWEEN COMING OUT AND SELF-ESTEEM

Coming out has the potential to affect many dimensions of an adolescent's life, including emotional and psychological well-being, self-concept, identity, and relations with family, friends, and work colleagues (Nemeyer, 1980). This section focuses on the relationship between labeling oneself as gay, bisexual, or lesbian and disclosing one's sexual orientation to others, and how these affect one dimension of self-concept—self-esteem.

Malyon (1981) traced the process of coming out primarily through changes in self-concept. The new self-awareness associated with labeling one's same-sex attractions may temporarily create anxiety, leading to feelings of self-contempt, before an individual rejects the social stereotype of lesbians and gays as lonely and depressed. With a direct increase in self-esteem, the individual shares "the secret" with an increasing number of persons. Self-concept may be quite vulnerable at this point, needing the support of friends, family, and perhaps a therapist. Eventually, an integrated identity, intimacy, and fulfilling relationships signify self-acceptance and positive self-esteem.

For many adolescents, anxiety and fear are at their apex just prior to coming out. A growing body of research indicates that coming out to others is frequently used to reduce these feelings and reestablish equilibrium. Weinberg and Williams (1974) noted that it is not passing as heterosexual per se that leads to poor self-regard, but the fear and anxiety of exposure and anticipated discrimination that result in psychological problems. They concluded: "Compared with less known-about homosexuals, the more known about are not found to have greater psychological problems, as many would expect. Thus, being known about is not the 'end of the world,' as many homosexuals fear" (p. 260). This finding was supported by research with college students who sought psychological services from a university clinic. "Gay men," those in the beginning stages of self-recognition (experienced homoerotic impulses, fantasies, and dreams but had not yet engaged in many overt same-sex behaviors) displayed more intrapsychic tensions, psychosocial problems, and social introversion than did "overt" gay students, those with many same-sex encounters (Braaten & Darling, 1965).

Indeed, a number of empirical studies document the positive association between coming out and self-esteem. A survey of 3,400 Chicago area gay men and lesbians (McKirnan & Peterson, 1986, 1987a, 1987b, 1987c) demonstrated the close link between psychological well-being and disclosure. Respondents were asked if they were out to each of nine groups (e.g., close friends, parents, coworkers). Those most closeted had the highest levels of social conflict (experienced stress with being gay or lesbian in social settings, such as work), personal conflict ("within myself" conflict), alienation, depression, and negative self-esteem.

Self-esteem was a positive, but low-order, correlate of self-disclosure in another study (Miranda, 1986). One respondent in Friend's (1980) study said, "Coming out is something everyone should go through, because if they can handle that, they can handle anything" (p. 242). The correlation between self-esteem and coming out was positive and significant.

In addition to these seminal works, a number of dissertations, including research with lesbians, have addressed the relationship between coming out and self-esteem. They are essentially of one voice: Coming out *to the self* is related to positive and not negative self-esteem. The relationship between *disclosure to others* and positive self-regard, however, is mixed.

The findings among lesbians are fairly consistent. For example, Elliot (1982) and O'Carolan (1982) found a positive correlation between self-esteem and feelings about being a lesbian; self-esteem was not, however, a significant predictor of disclosure to others (Elliot, 1982). In a qualitative study of lesbians, self-disclosure (including aspects of coming out to self and to others) was a "critical factor" influencing self-acceptance (Nemeyer, 1980).

Dissertation studies of gay men report that those most out to self are the best adjusted psychologically (Benitez, 1983). Psychological well-being (happiness, psychological health, sexual satisfaction, etc.) corresponded to movement beyond the initial tolerance stage of coming out to the later stages of acceptance, pride, and synthesis (Brady, 1985). McDonald (1984) reported that those most identified as gay and out of the closet had the optimal level of identity congruency. He concluded that the best adjusted men integrated and managed their personal identity, a process which entailed being "totally homosexual." More complex are the findings of Cramer (1986). Self-esteem was significantly higher for those who had disclosed to parents than for those who were closeted and did *not* want out. However, those who were closeted and *wanted out* had essentially the same self-esteem as those who were out to their parents. Thus, congruent with other dissertation research, Cramer's findings suggest that the primary issue is more related to internal integration and reconciliation of homoerotic feelings than the overt expression of those attractions. However, he also reported that the longer one had been out to others, the higher the self-esteem level. Generally, the literature is fairly consistent regarding the positive relationship between self-esteem and coming out to self. Less clear is the relationship between self-esteem and disclosure to others.

Two primary questions arise when considering issues of disclosure and psychological well-being: Are the two related, and if so, what is their cause-effect relationship? The empirical literature converges on the conclusion that whereas the psychological aspects of coming out (i.e., self-recognition and self-acceptance) are positively related to self-esteem, disclosure to others is less frequently a significant predictor of self-worth variables. Psychologists (e.g., Malyon, 1981) tend to view a positive sense of self as leading to progressive coming-out developments, whereas sociologists (e.g., Weinberg & Williams, 1974) view the process in reverse: By coming out to others, gays, lesbians, and bisexuals are more likely to accept themselves and their sexual orientation.

Few of the studies cited in this section addressed these issues with youths. Malyon (1981) believed that although disclosure of one's homosexuality is generally a positive developmental asset during adolescence, enhancing crisis competence, self-respect, and ego integrity, "for the individual who opts for a homosexual identity during adolescence, many problems complicate and interfere with a desirable outcome to the developmental process. Social attitudes militate against feelings of self-acceptance" (p. 328). In his review of three English studies, Plummer (1989) found that many gay and lesbian youths and those suspected of being gay or lesbian were subjected to mockery, physical violence, parental rejection, job loss, psychiatric treatment, and imprisonment—experiences which would be expected to negatively impact self-esteem. However, Savin-Williams (1990) found that males who were most out to others reported the highest levels of self-esteem.[9] Apparently, when gay youths evaluated themselves as positive and worthwhile persons it was not dependent on the hostile social world in which they live. If they had experienced the ongoing negative attitudes of others toward homosexuality, they either did not internalize them as a statement about the self or they had the necessary coping resources to overcome the negativity. These findings, however, leave unaddressed the issue of causation—whether psychological health led to disclosure to others, or whether higher levels of self-esteem ensued by disclosing to others.

## Increasing Visibility to Facilitate Coming Out and Enhance Self-Esteem: Role Models and the Media

Because of an absence of visible gay, lesbian, and bisexual role models, many adolescents erroneously believe that they are one of very few with homoerotic attractions. Unbeknownst to them, their culture and peer world are saturated with homosexually and bisexually oriented individuals, many of whom also choose to conceal their sexual orientation. This is particularly true for adults who are reluctant to come out to youths for fear that they may be accused of pedophilia or contributing to the corruption of minors.

Without healthy, visible, and functioning role models, teenagers often turn to the only gay, lesbian, and bisexual persons visible—those portrayed in the media. Desiring explanations and guidance, yet often too embarrassed to borrow books about homosexuality from the library (if there are any) or too frightened to confront friends or family with questions, adolescents frequently use the media for information. Until recently, this message was that lesbians, bisexuals, and gay men are sick, behave in gender inappropriate ways, and are doomed to destruction—usually by their own hands. One youth related, "I always thought of homosexuals as old men who walked poodles on rhinestone leashes and wore make-up. I never thought, dreamed or realized that there were, or ever had been, homosexuals who were my age" (Heron, 1983, p. 30). Unfortunately, media representations are often stereotypic and convey the message that "homosexuals" are eccentric but harmless at best, and pathological pedophiles at worst. Eighteen-year-old Deborah related her initial conceptions:

At first the word "lesbian" sounded negative to me. It was used as a put down by my peers and family. . . . I used to think that I *had* to wear guy's clothing, but now I know that that was only a stereotype. I realize that it doesn't mean I have to look or dress any particular way. (Heron, 1983, p. 102)

The visual media, particularly television and movies, frequently perpetuate stereotypes that are harmful and incite hatred. In *The Celluloid Closet,* Russo (1987) examined the manner in which gay men and lesbians have been portrayed in movies. They are frequently used for comic relief, are killed, or commit suicide: "Once homosexuality had become literally speakable in the early 1960s, gays dropped like flies, usually by their own hand, while continuing to perform their classically comic function in lesser and more ambiguous roles" (p. 52). Between the years 1962 and 1978, 22 of 28 films that contained gay themes had a central gay character die either by suicide or some other violent means. In 1991, three prominent Hollywood films—*The Silence of the Lambs, JFK,* and *Basic Instinct*—depicted lesbians, gay men, and bisexuals as either gender atypical, cross-dressers, hypersexual, asexual, man-hating killers, or psychopathic killers. The *New York Times* writer Weir (1992) observed:

In *The Silence of the Lambs,* the murders that set the plot in motion are traced to a man who is a cross-dresser, a disco dancer, a misogynist, a poodle owner and someone trapped in a man's body—quite a combination of cliches about gay men. (p. H17)

Weir concluded that certain types of movies require a villain and a hero: "Since the death of Communism, homosexual villains are fast gaining on drug dealers and investors from Japan as the new bad guys" (p. H17). This is a powerful message that movie-going adolescents are likely to internalize regarding that which their life will be or should be like.

Fear of negative repercussions keeps many public figures closeted. Although the arts are imbued with bisexuals, lesbians, and gay men whom adolescents idolize, this is often unknown by youths. It would prove reassuring for adolescents to learn that many of their heroes are lesbian or gay. Too few public figures, including sports heroes, have come forth to proudly proclaim their homosexuality or bisexuality, to report having had same-sex experiences, or to explicitly declare their homoerotic attractions. More typically, they are only widely "suspected" of being lesbian, bisexual, or gay.

In high school, students regularly study works by Oscar Wilde, Langston Hughes, Gertrude Stein, Emily Dickinson, Tennessee Williams, Walt Whitman, Audre Lorde, Virginia Woolf, Allen Ginsberg, James Baldwin, and Margaret Mead and learn about historical figures such as Socrates, Plato, Leonardo Da Vinci, Michelangelo, and Julius Caesar without ever being told that all of these admired individuals were involved in one or more same-sex relationships. Gay, lesbian, and bisexual youths need to know that they are not alone and that healthy, respectable people have homoerotic attractions. By positively representing gay people in the media, youths learn that their sexual needs are acceptable.

*13*

---

*31*

# CONCLUSION

Coming out is not a universal or fixed event. For example, some lesbian, gay, and bisexual individuals report that they have no memory of a coming-out process. They always knew that they were gay and thus were never "in the closet." Consequently, there was never the need to come out, certainly not to the self and usually not to others. Others report that they have never experienced particular events, such as the sudden revelation of homosexuality, that are purported by some theoreticians to characterize the coming-out process. There are also considerable individual differences in the timing and sequencing of the process, including the ages at which developmental milestones are achieved and the ordering of the alleged universal stages of coming out. It is important, however, to detail the coming-out process, even if it is not a rigid universal evolution, because it facilitates understanding and appreciation of the conditions faced by lesbian, gay, and bisexual youths.

Troiden (1989) cataloged various "facilitating factors" that ease the transition to a nonheterosexual identity: education, supportive friends and family, young age, no heterosexual but some same-sex experiences, and gender atypicality. Few of these have been systematically investigated. However, research has demonstrated that coming out is occurring earlier with each new cohort of gay and lesbian youths, especially in urban, media-saturated, and collegiate communities. Research is needed to assess whether coming out is also becoming increasingly more compact, lasting a shorter period of time from start to finish. For example, it is no longer extremely rare for the coming-out process to begin shortly after pubertal onset and to be essentially completed—out to friends, family, and the public—by the end of adolescence.

Most noteworthy, the psychologically and sociologically best time to come out to oneself and to others is an issue few have addressed. Apparently, coming out to oneself at a relatively early age but revealing that identity only to select others when the environment is positive and supportive (usually after high school) is best. Such individuals avoid the negative repercussions of being known as gay or lesbian in junior and senior high school settings. They take their time, disclosing their sexual identity to "safe" people, who provide social and psychological support. In the process, they learn crisis competence and develop an internal sense of self-respect and ego integrity that prepares them to face the cruelty of a homophobic society (Coleman, 1981/1982; Kimmel, 1978; Malyon, 1981). However, this conclusion may need to be reevaluated as an increasing number of lesbian, gay, and bisexual youths attend support groups in schools and local communities (e.g., the Hetrick-Martin Institute in New York City, Horizons in Chicago, the Minnesota Task Force on Gay and Lesbian Youth in Minneapolis, Project 10 in Los Angeles, and Affirmations in Detroit).

There is also clearly a need for support services for those to whom gay, lesbian, and bisexual youths come out, such as parents, who sometimes feel adversely affected. To this end, there is a growing body of coming-out advice literature and support groups for the youths' loved ones (e.g., National Federation of Parents, Families, and Friends of Lesbians and Gays).

These developments can be attributed in large part to the recent visibility of lesbian and gay issues. The "unspeakable love" has appeared on television and in movies, on athletic fields and in legislatures, on bookshelves and in medical literature, and in teen-oriented magazines. Books devoted primarily to revelatory stories (e.g., Curtis, 1988; Fricke, 1981; Heron, 1983, 1994; Stanley & Wolfe, 1980) document the pain, indecision, and occasionally violence, isolation, and alienation that accompany the coming-out process. For many others, however, the process is not particularly noteworthy or painful, certainly not the kind of revelation that inspires made-for-television, crisis-of-the-week movies.

We conclude this chapter with an excerpt from an article on the significance of coming out written by Mel Wilson (1987) for the Chicago *Windy City Times:*

> There is no agreement on the exact meaning of the words "coming out" but in all our conversations we seem able to put dates on the "event." By some sort of tacit consensus we never challenge the meaning of the term. "Coming out" is the common, shared bonding experience of gay men and lesbians, and yet for each of us it is a totally unique and singular experience . . . an experience that, once begun, never ends.
>
> It is because "coming out" is not easy that it forms a central marker in our lives: a dividing line of the "before" and "after." Gay men and lesbians "come out" for a lot of reasons—by force, for political objectives, for pride (or spite)—but there is only one "good" way to "come out" and that is to come out for ourselves. When we do, our lives become irretrievably altered—so altered, in fact, that we can't stop telling everyone we can find about it. . . .
>
> For every individual, "coming out" is a singular experience: a choice between the lady and the tiger, a choice to abandon deception and deceit, a watershed in life. "Coming out" is a choice that is personal, sometimes public, and always political. It is not a point in time, but is instead a continuum. It is a beginning to making the world whole. It is the first step in claiming our place. (p. 8)

## ▼ ENDNOTES ▼

1. Portions of this chapter previously appeared in Savin-Williams, 1990.

2. Stonewall refers to the first display of violent resistance against police by gays, lesbians, and bisexuals at the Stonewall Inn, New York City, in 1969. For a history of the events which led up to the riots, the reader is referred to the movie *Before Stonewall.*

3. Whitam (1977) refuted the contention that homosexuality is a role: "While a role, as it is ordinarily understood, may be ascribed or achieved, children are neither socialized into the 'homosexual role' nor do they rationally choose

it" (p. 1). Homosexuality, to Whitam, is a sexual orientation and thus neither a condition nor a role.

4. Kooden et al. (1979), McDonald (1982), and Rodriguez (1988) defined this as disclosure to a significant nongay other. Thus the age at which they may have disclosed to someone who was known as gay or suspected of being gay is not known.

5. See Fricke's (1981) *Reflections of a Rock Lobster* for an engaging recollection of an adolescent's coming to terms with his homosexuality and struggle to take a male date to his high school prom.

6. See personal stories in Sears's (1991) *Growing up Gay in the South.*

7. Support and information can be obtained from local chapters of Parents, Families, and Friends of Lesbians and Gays (P-FLAG) or through the national office (202-638-4200; PFLAGTL@aol.com; 1012 14th St. NW, Ste. 700, Washington, DC, 20005).

8. The following excerpt of a conversation took place in the winter of 1992 and was taped and transcribed. A mother and son were invited to discuss the son's recent disclosure to his mother of his sexuality. Names have been changed to ensure anonymity.

9. In contrast, disclosure to others did not significantly predict self-esteem level among the lesbian youths surveyed by Savin-Williams (1990). This finding is consistent with the results of other studies (Elliot, 1982; Sanders, 1980).

## ▼ REFERENCES ▼

Anonymous. (1980). My coming out herstory. In J. P. Stanley & S. J. Wolfe (Eds.), *The coming out stories* (pp. 70–78). Watertown, MA: Persephone Press.

Bell, A. P., & Weinberg, M. S. (1978). *Homosexualities: A study of diversity among men and women.* New York: Simon & Schuster.

Bell, A. P., Weinberg, M. S., & Hammersmith, S. K. (1981a). *Sexual preference: Its development in men and women.* Bloomington, IN: Indiana University Press.

Bell, A. P., Weinberg, M. S., & Hammersmith, S. K. (1981b). *Sexual preference: Its development in men and women (statistical appendix).* Bloomington, IN: Indiana University Press.

Bender, V. I., Davis, Y., Glover, O., & Stapp, J. (1976). Patterns of self-disclosure in homosexual and heterosexual college students. *Sex Roles, 2,* 149–160.

Benitez, J. C. (1983). The effect of gay identity acquisition on the psychological adjustment of male homosexuals. *Dissertation Abstracts International, 43,* 3350B.

Berzon, B., & Leighton, R. (Eds.). (1979). *Positively gay.* Millbrae, CA: Celestial Arts.

Borhek, M. V. (1993). *Coming out to parents: A two-way survival guide for lesbians and gay men and their parents* (2nd ed.). Cleveland, OH: Pilgrim.

Braaten, L. J., & Darling, C. D. (1965). Overt and covert homosexual problems among male college students. *Genetic Psychology Monograph, 71,* 269–310.

Brady, S. M. (1985). The relationship between differences in stages of homosexual identity formation and background characteristics, psychological well-being and homosexual adjustment. *Dissertation Abstracts International, 45,* 3328B.

Brown, H. (1976). *Familiar faces hidden lives: The story of homosexual men in America today.* New York: Harcourt Brace Jovanovich.

Cass, V. (1979). Homosexual identity formation: A theoretical model. *Journal of Homosexuality, 4,* 219–235.

Cass, V. (1984). Homosexual identity formation: Testing a theoretical model. *The Journal of Sex Research, 20,* 143–167.

Clark, D. K. (1987). *The new loving someone gay.* Berkeley, CA: Celestial Arts.

Cohen-Ross, J. L. (1985). An exploratory study of the retrospective role of significant others in homosexual identity development. *Dissertation Abstracts International, 46,* 628B.

Coleman, E. (1981/1982). Developmental stages of the coming out process. *Journal of Homosexuality, 7,* 31–43.

Coleman, E., & Remafedi, G. (1989). Gay, lesbian, and bisexual adolescents: A critical challenge to counselors. *Journal of Counseling and Development, 68,* 36–40.

Colgan, P. (1987). Treatment of identity and intimacy issues in gay males. *Journal of Homosexuality, 14,* 101–123.

Cramer, D. W. (1986). Coming out to the family: An exploration of the role of selected aspects of family functioning in the disclosure decision and outcome. *Dissertation Abstracts International, 46,* 2967A.

Cramer, D. W., & Roach, A. J. (1988). Coming out to mom and dad: A study of gay males and their relationships with their parents. *Journal of Homosexuality, 15,* 79–91.

Curtis, W. (Ed.). (1988). *Revelations: A collection of gay male coming out stories.* Boston: Alyson.

Dank, B. M. (1971). Coming out in the gay world. *Psychiatry, 34,* 180–197.

Dank, B. M. (1973). The homosexual. In D. Spiegel & P. Keith-Spiegel (Eds.), *Outsiders USA* (pp. 269–297). San Francisco: Rinehart.

D'Augelli, A. R. (1991). Gay men in college: Identity processes and adaptations.

*Journal of College Student Development, 32,* 140–146.

D'Augelli, A. R. (1994, January). Attending to the needs of our youth. *Division 44 Newsletter,* pp. 16–18.

D'Augelli, A. R., & Hart, M. M. (1987). Gay women, men, and families in rural settings: Toward the development of helping communities. *American Journal of Community Psychology, 15,* 79–93.

Davies, P. (1992). The role of disclosure in coming out among gay men. In K. Plummer (Ed.), *Modern homosexualities: Fragments of lesbian and gay experience* (pp. 75–83). London: Routledge.

de Monteflores, C., & Schultz, S. J. (1978). Coming out: Similarities and differences for lesbians and gay men. *Journal of Social Issues, 34,* 59–72.

D'Emilio, J. (1983). *Sexual politics, sexual communities.* Chicago: University of Chicago Press.

D'Emilio, J. (1992). *Making trouble: Essays on gay history, politics, and the university.* New York: Routledge.

DeVine, J. L. (1984). A systemic inspection of affectional preference orientation and the family of origin. *Journal of Social Work and Human Sexuality, 2,* 9–17.

Elliot, P. E. (1982). Lesbian identity and self disclosure. *Dissertation Abstracts International, 42,* 3494B.

Ettorre, E. M. (1980). *Lesbians, women and society.* London: Routledge & Kegan Paul.

Fairchild, B., & Hayward, N. (1989). *Now that you know: What every parent should know about homosexuality* (Updated Ed.). San Diego, CA: Harcourt Brace Jovanovich.

Ferguson, K. D., & Finkler, D. C. (1978). An involvement and overtness measure for lesbians: Its development and relation to anxiety and social zeitgeist. *Archives of Sexual Behavior, 7,* 211–227.

Fitzpatrick, G. (1983). Self-disclosure of lesbianism as related to self-actualization and self-stigmatization. *Dissertation Abstracts International, 43,* 4143B.

Fricke, A. (1981). *Reflections of a rock lobster: A story about growing up gay.* Boston: Alyson.

Friend, R. A. (1980). Gayging: Adjustment and the older gay male. *Alternative Lifestyles, 3,* 231–248.

Gagnon, J. H., & Simon, S. (1973). *Sexual conduct: The social sources of human sexuality.* Chicago: Aldine.

Goffman, I. (1963). *Stigma.* Englewood Cliffs, NJ: Prentice-Hall.

Gonsiorek, J. C., & Rudolph, J. R. (1991). Homosexual identity: Coming out and other developmental events. In J. C. Gonsiorek & J. D. Weinrich (Eds.), *Homosexuality: Research implications for public policy* (pp. 161–176). Newbury Park, CA: Sage.

Grabert, J. C. (1985). Homosexual men and their parents: A study of self-disclosure, personality traits and attitudes toward homosexuality. *Dissertation Abstracts International, 46,* 1336B.

Grier, B. (1980). The garden variety lesbian. In J. P. Stanley & S. J. Wolfe (Eds.), *The coming out stories* (pp. 235–240). Watertown, MA: Persephone Press.

Griffin, C. W., Wirth, M. J., & Wirth, A. G. (1986). *Beyond acceptance: Parents of lesbians and gays talk about their experiences.* New York: St. Martin's Press.

Hammersmith, S. K., & Weinberg, M, S. (1973). Homosexual identity: Commitment, adjustment, and significant others. *Sociometry, 36,* 56–79.

Hansen, L. (1990, March 11). Interview with gay and lesbian teens. Broadcast by National Public Radio.

Harry, J. (1993). Being out: A general model. *Journal of Homosexuality, 26,* 25–39.

Harry, J., & DeVall, W. B. (1978). *The social organization of gay males.* New York: Praeger.

Hencken, J. D. (1985). Sexual-orientation self-disclosure. *Dissertation Abstracts International, 45,* 2310B.

Herdt, G. (Ed.). (1989). *Gay and lesbian youth*. New York: Harrington Park Press.

Herdt, G., & Boxer, A. M. (1993). *Children of Horizons: How gay and lesbian teens are leading a new way out of the closet*. Boston: Beacon Press.

Heron, A. (Ed.). (1983). *One teenager in ten*. Boston: Alyson.

Heron, A. (Ed.). (1994). *2 teenagers in 20*. Boston: Alyson.

Hetrick, E. S., & Martin, A. D. (1987). Developmental issues and their resolution for gay and lesbian adolescents. *Journal of Homosexuality, 14*, 25–44.

Hooker, E. A. (1965). Male homosexuals and their worlds. In J. Marmor (Ed.), *Sexual inversion: The multiple roots of homosexuality* (pp. 83–107). New York: Basic Books.

Isay, R. A. (1989). *Being homosexual: Gay men and their development*. New York: Farrar Straus Giroux.

Jay, K., & Young, A. (1979). *The gay report: Lesbians and gay men speak out about sexual experiences and lifestyles*. New York: Summit.

Jourard, S. M. (1971). *The transparent self* (2nd edition). New York: Van Nostrand.

Kahn, M. J. (1991). Factors affecting the coming out process for lesbians. *Journal of Homosexuality, 21*, 47–70.

Kimmel, D. (1978). Adult development and aging: A gay perspective. *Journal of Social Issues, 34*, 113–130.

Kooden, H., Morin, S., Riddle, D., Rogers, M., Sang, B., & Strassburger, F. (1979). *Removing the stigma. Final report. Task force on the status of lesbian and gay male psychologists*. Washington, DC: American Psychological Association.

Kubler-Ross, E. (1969). *On death and dying*. New York: MacMillan.

Lee, J. A. (1977). Going public: A study in the sociology of homosexual liberation. *Journal of Homosexuality, 3*, 47–78.

MacDonald, G. B. (1983, December). Exploring sexual identity: Gay people and their families. *Sex Education Coalition News, 5*, pp. 1, 4.

Maguen, S. (1991, September 24). Teen suicide: The government's cover-up and America's lost children. *The Advocate*, pp. 40–47.

Malyon, A. K. (1981). The homosexual adolescent: Developmental issues and social bias. *Child Welfare, 60*, 321–330.

Martin, A. D. (1982). Learning to hide: The socialization of the gay adolescent. *Adolescent Psychiatry, 10*, 52–65.

Martin, A. D., & Hetrick, E. S. (1988). The stigmatization of the gay and lesbian adolescent. *Journal of Homosexuality, 15*, 163–183.

Maslow, A. H. (1954). *Motivation and personality*. New York: Harper.

McDonald, G. J. (1982). Individual differences in the coming out process for gay men: Implications for theoretical models. *Journal of Homosexuality, 8*, 47–60.

McDonald, G. J. (1984). Identity congruency and identity management among gay men. *Dissertation Abstracts International, 45*, 1322B.

McIntosh, M. (1968). The homosexual role. *Social Problems, 16*, 182–192.

McKirnan, D. J., & Peterson, P. L. (1986, October 2). Preliminary social issues survey results. *Windy City Times*, pp. 2, 8.

McKirnan, D. J., & Peterson, P. L. (1987a, March 12). Chicago survey documents anti-gay bias. *Windy City Times*, pp. 1, 2, 12.

McKirnan, D. J., & Peterson, P. L. (1987b, April 30). Social support and coping resources. *Windy City Times*, pp. 1, 8, 9.

McKirnan, D. J., & Peterson, P. L. (1987c, June 25). A profile of older gay males: A perspective from the social issues survey. *Windy City Times*, pp. 20, 22.

Miller, B. (1978). Adult sexual resocialization. *Alternative Lifestyles, 1*, 207–234.

Miranda, J. (1986, August). *Evaluation of DSM-III ego-dystonic homosexuality*. Paper presented at the annual meeting of the American Psychological Association, Washington, DC.

Moses, A. E., & Buckner, J. A. (1980). The special problems of rural gay clients. *Human Services in the Rural Environment, 5,* 22–27.

Myrick, F. L. (1974a). Homosexual types: An empirical investigation. *The Journal of Sex Research, 10,* 226–237.

Myrick, F. L. (1974b). Attitudinal differences between heterosexually and homosexually oriented males and between covert and overt male homosexuals. *Journal of Abnormal Psychology, 83,* 81–86

Nemeyer, L. (1980). Coming out: Identity congruence and the attainment of adult female sexuality. *Dissertation Abstracts International, 41,* 1924B.

Newman, B. S., & Muzzonigro, P. G. (1993). The effects of traditional family values on the coming out process of gay male adolescents. *Adolescence, 28,* 213–226

Nungesser, L. G. (1983). *Homosexual acts, actors, and identities.* New York: Praeger.

O'Carolan, R. J. (1982). An investigation of the relationship of self-disclosure of sexual preference to self-esteem, feminism, and locus of control in lesbians. *Dissertation Abstracts International, 43,* 915B.

Plummer, K. (1975). *Sexual stigma: An interactionist account.* Boston: Routledge & Kegan Paul.

Plummer, K. (1981). *The making of the modern homosexual,* London: Hutchison.

Plummer, K. (1989). Lesbian and gay youth in England. In G. Herdt (Ed.), *Gay and lesbian youth* (pp. 195–223). Binghamton, NY: Harrington Park Press.

Ponse, B. (1980). Lesbians and their worlds. In J. Marmor (Ed.), *Homosexual behavior: A modern reappraisal* (pp. 157–175). New York: Basic Books.

Rector, P. K. (1982). The acceptance of a homosexual identity in adolescence: A phenomenological study. *Dissertation Abstracts International, 43,* 883B.

Reiche, R., & Dannecker, M. (1977). Male homosexuality in West Germany—A sociological investigation. *The Journal of Sex Research, 13,* 35–53.

Remafedi, G. (1987). Male homosexuality: The adolescent's perspective. *Pediatrics, 79,* 326–330.

Richardson, D. (1981). Lesbian identities. In J. Hart & D. Richardson (Eds.), *The theory and practice of homosexuality* (pp. 111–124). London: Routledge & Kegan Paul.

Riddle, D. I., & Morin, S. F. (Eds.). (1978). Psychology and the gay community. *Journal of Social Issues, 34,* 1–138.

Robertson, R. (1981). Young gays. In J. Hart & D. Richardson (Eds.), *The theory and practice of homosexuality* (pp. 170–176). London: Routledge & Kegan Paul.

Robinson, B. E., Walters, L. H., & Skeen, P. (1989). Response of parents to learning that their child is homosexual and concern over AIDS: A national study. *Journal of Homosexuality, 18,* 59–80.

Rodriguez, R. A. (1988, August). *Significant events in gay identity development: Gay men in Utah.* Paper presented at the Ninety-sixth Annual Convention of the American Psychological Association, Atlanta, GA.

Rofes, E. E. (1993, July). *Roots of "horizontal hostility" in the lesbian and gay community.* Paper presented at the Fifteenth National Lesbian and Gay Health Conference, Houston, TX.

Ross, M. W. (1989). Gay youth in four cultures: A comparative study. In G. Herdt (Ed.), *Gay and lesbian youth* (pp. 299–314). Binghamton, NY: Harrington Park Press.

Rotheram-Borus, M.J., Rosario, M., & Koopman, C. (1991). Minority youths at high risk: Gay males and runaways. In M. E. Colten & S. Gore (Eds.), *Adolescent stress: Causes and consequences* (pp. 181–200). New York: Aldine DeGruyter.

Russo, V. (1987). *The celluloid closet.* New York: Harper & Row.

Sanders, G. (1980). Homosexualities in the Netherlands. *Alternative Lifestyles, 3,* 278–311.

Savin-Williams, R. C. (1990). *Gay and lesbian youth: Expressions of identity.* New York: Hemisphere.

Savin-Williams, R. C. (1995). *Sex and sexual identity among gay and bisexual males.* Unpublished manuscript, Cornell University, Ithaca, NY.

Savin-Williams, R. C., & Rodriguez, R. G. (1993). A developmental, clinical perspective on lesbian, gay male, and bisexual youths. In T. P. Gullotta, G. R. Adams, & R. Montemayor (Eds.), *Adolescent sexuality* (pp. 77–101). Newbury Park, CA: Sage.

Schneider, M. (1989). Sappho was a right-on adolescent: Growing up lesbian. In G. Herdt (Ed.), *Gay and lesbian youth* (pp. 111–130). Binghamton, NY: Harrington Park Press.

Sears, J. T. (1991). *Growing up gay in the South: Race, gender, and journeys of the spirit.* New York: Harrington Park Press.

Silverstein, C. (1977). *A family matter: A parents' guide to homosexuality.* New York: McGraw-Hill.

Smith, T. A. (1983). Sexual identity and reproductive motivations. *Dissertation Abstracts International, 44,* 1979B.

Sohier, R. (1985/1986). Homosexual mutuality: Variation on a theme by Erik Erikson. *Journal of Homosexuality, 12,* 25–38.

Sophie, J. (1985/1986). A critical examination of stage theories of lesbian identity development. *Journal of Homosexuality, 12,* 39–51.

Stanley, J. P., & Wolfe, S. J. (Eds.). (1980). *The coming out stories.* Watertown, MA: Persephone Press.

Straver, C. J. (1976). Research on homosexuality in the Netherlands. *The Netherlands' Journal of Sociology, 12,* 121–137.

Strommen, E. F. (1989). "You're a what?": Family member reactions to the disclosure of homosexuality. *Journal of Homosexuality, 18,* 37–58.

Telljohann, S. K., & Price, J. P. (1993). A qualitative examination of adolescent homosexuals' life experiences: Ramifications for secondary school personnel. *Journal of Homosexuality, 26,* 41–56.

Tripp, C. A. (1975). *The homosexual matrix.* New York: McGraw-Hill.

Troiden, R. R. (1979). Becoming homosexual: A model of gay identity acquisition. *Psychiatry, 42,* 362–373.

Troiden, R. R. (1989). The formation of homosexual identities. *Journal of Homosexuality, 17,* 43–73.

Warren, C. (1974). *Identity and community in the gay world.* New York: John Wiley.

Weinberg, M. S., & Williams, C. J. (1974). *Male homosexuals: Their problems and adaptations.* New York: Penguin.

Weinberg, T. S. (1978). On "doing" and "being" gay: Sexual behavior and homosexual male self-identity. *Journal of Homosexuality, 4,* 143–156.

Weinberg, T. S. (1983). *Gay men, gay selves.* New York: Irvington.

Weir, J. (1992, March 29). Gay-bashing, villainy and the Oscars. *The New York Times,* pp. H17, H22–23.

Whitam, F. L. (1977). The homosexual role: A reconsideration. *Journal of Sex Research, 13,* 1–11.

Wilson, M. (1987, April 16). Frontlines: Coming out to new perspectives. *Windy City Times,* p. 8.

Woodman, N. J., & Lenna, H. R. (1980). *Counseling with gay men and women.* San Francisco: Jossey-Bass.

# Chapter 6

▼

# ETHNIC- AND SEXUAL-MINORITY YOUTH

## Ritch C. Savin-Williams[1]

*Regardless of ethnic or sexual identification, individuals experience major life changes during the period of adolescence. One task that is central to both ethnic- and sexual-minority youth is the consolidation of a reference group orientation (Cross, 1991). According to Cross, reference group orientation (RGO) includes aspects of self-concept "that are culture, class, and gender specific. . . . It seeks to discover differences in values, perspectives, group identities, lifestyles, and world views" (p. 45). Reference group identity refers not to how one feels in general, "but how one orients oneself or how one feels regarding specific values, preferences, or symbols" (p. 46). In combination, personal and group identity compose the essential features of one's self-concept (Cross, 1991).*

*Espin (1987) noted that for ethnic group members, healthy development includes the "acceptance of an external reality that can rarely be changed (e.g., being Black, Puerto Rican, Jewish, or Vietnamese), but also an intrapsychic 'embracing' of that reality as a positive component of one's self" (p. 35). This aspect of self-concept may be more or less salient to individuals depending on the centrality of a particular reference group in their lives. Living as a minority group member in Anglo North American society often creates a sense of group distinctiveness and community.*

*Ethnic-minority adolescents with same-sex attractions must negotiate an additional formidable task in the development of a mature self-concept. They must integrate personal identity and reference group orientation within the context of two, at times competing and antagonistic, group identities: being lesbian, gay, or bisexual and an ethnic minority (Icard, 1986; Johnson, 1981; Tremble, Schneider, & Appathurai, 1989). Espin (1987) noted further complexities faced by female ethnic-/sexual-minorities:*

> By definition in the context of a heterosexist, racist, and sexist society, the process of identity development for Latina lesbian women entails the embracing of "stigmatized" or "negative" identities. Coming out to self and others in the context of a sexist and heterosexist American society is compounded by coming out in the context of a heterosexist and sexist Latin culture immersed in racist society. (p. 35)

*Hence, three tasks that ethnic-minority lesbian, bisexual, and gay youth face are: developing and defining a sexual and an ethnic identity; resolving potential conflicts in allegiance within both reference groups or communities; and negotiating homophobia and racism.*

## ISSUES CONFRONTING ETHNIC LESBIAN, GAY, AND BISEXUAL YOUTH

Being an ethnic minority and a sexual minority within a White, heterosexual social world can tax even the strongest of youths. Espin (1987) noted that Latina lesbians fear stigmatization and loss of support from both Hispanic and gay and lesbian communities. They often feel that they must choose which of two groups will be their primary identification. Coupled with conflicting pressures from peers and the mass media to assimilate by acting White and heterosexual, youths from ethnic communities who are gay, bisexual, or lesbian struggle between who they are and that which they feel they must be in order to avoid a stigmatizing identity. The progress toward a healthy and positive gay identity is not an easy transition for these youths.

A sexual- and ethnic-minority youth may want to identify closely with both communities but feel that the two place demands that are inherently oppositional. Each community may present an adolescent with conflicting information about "appropriate" sexual or ethnic behavior and the importance of choosing one identity over the other. A youth may thus feel that it is impossible to be both a sexual and an ethnic minority.

Johnson (1981) documented this conflict among Black gay men. In his research, 60% of the men primarily identified themselves according to their race/ethnic community ("Black identified"). The rest affirmed their gay reference group identity ("gay identified"). Both groups had comparable levels of mental health—self-acceptance, happiness, loneliness, and depression—but differed on social behavioral measures. The Black-identified gay men were more likely to have Black lovers and friends, live in and celebrate the Black community, and prefer traditional, subtle modes of expressing affection among gay men. The gay-identified Black men were more likely to have White lovers, live in the gay community, and favor public displays of affection among gay men. Each felt estranged from a central aspect of who he is—from the gay or Black community (Johnson, 1981).

At an Asian Lesbian Conference in Bangkok, Thailand (Historic Meet, 1991), many participants noted the problems of dual identities. "The feeling of isolation, invisibility, ostracism by society, the pain of having to lead double lives, problems of coming out to the family were common to all despite some cultural differences" (p. 5). Many felt that their invisibility handicapped their ability to network with each other. The absence of community support and the opportunity to explore and assert their sexuality within the historic Asian context of forced marriages and strong family ties prevented them from creating their own identity.

Unfortunately, because inadequate research has been conducted with ethnic-minority lesbian, bisexual, and gay youth, little is known about the ways in which the formation of a self-concept is compounded by status within an ethnic group and the racism often inherent in lesbian and gay communities. Thus, much must be extrapolated from information derived from research conducted with lesbian, bisexual, and gay ethnic adults. Several of these issues are also discussed in recent reviews by Manalansan (this volume) and Greene (1994).

Both authors warned their readers of the dangers of inferring that all nationalities within an ethnic group are identical. Greene (1994) noted that "African Americans are a diverse group of people with cultural origins in the tribes of Western Africa, with some Indian and European racial admixture" (p. 245). Thus, "gross descriptions of cultural practices may never be applied with uniformity to all members of an ethnic group" (p. 244). Mindful of this warning, which Manalansan discusses at length in a later chapter, the present review emphasizes the common dilemmas shared by lesbian, bisexual, and gay youths from various ethnic communities. These include racism in gay and lesbian communities, homophobia in ethnic communities, unique problems of coming out to family, limitations imposed by sex role expectations, and cultural shifts in levels of support for ethnic/sexual minority youths. Only within the last several years has the ultimate reference group network formed: ethnic communities for sexual-minority individuals.

## RACISM IN GAY AND LESBIAN COMMUNITIES

Many of the difficulties experienced by lesbian, gay, and bisexual youth of color emanate from the social prejudice and institutional discrimination that are inherent in White society. Racist attitudes and beliefs permeate even liberal lesbian and gay communities. Consequently, ethnic-minority individuals with same-sex attractions may be rejected when among other lesbians and gays because of their minority status or may be expected to place their sexual identity and allegiance foremost in their lives.

In a survey of Third World gays and lesbians in San Francisco, Morales and Eversley (cited in Morales, 1983) reported that 85% perceived themselves as having been discriminated against by both heterosexual and lesbian and gay communities. As a group, ethnic gays and lesbians ranked discrimination as one of the most persistent problems in gay and lesbian communities. More recently, one African American lesbian noted:

> In the gay community, I feel that the majority of the White women are prejudiced just as much as they are in the straight world. So I don't care to deal with them, really, you know, unless I feel that they are really, really sincere in what they are saying and that it doesn't make a difference the color that

I'm Black and she's White. Otherwise, I just deal with my own people. (Mays, Cochran, & Rhue, 1993, pp. 9-10)

The racism experienced by this woman was often subtle, such as the failure of White lesbians to recognize cultural differences between them and Black lesbians.

Two other examples of racism are attitudes sometimes held about Jews and Asians. Rofes (1989) observed that anti-Semitic insensitivities are common among many gay men and lesbians who are ignorant or callous about Jewish issues, such as the Holocaust. Rofes noted that a speaker at a gay political event commented that gay men should not go to their deaths from AIDS without protest, "like six million Jews did in the Holocaust" (p. 201). Although Rofes reported feeling "stunned, unable to move," and deeply hurt, he sat in silence unwilling to protest. Many Jews feel that they are supposed to assimilate into lesbian and gay communities, hiding their unique Jewish characteristics and sensitivities. As a result, the World Congress of Gay and Lesbian Jewish Organizations was founded 15 years ago (Cooper, 1989/1990).

The Japanese American gay men in Wooden, Kawasaki, and Mayeda's (1983) sample described stereotypes of Asians in gay male communities. One said, "They see us as fitting the 'Madame Butterfly' role and that of the 'good oriental'" (p. 240). Another reported, "They believe we are passive, docile, faithful, and responsible for more 'housewifey' jobs" (p. 240). Other stereotypes listed included: feminine, small genitals, youthful, easy pickups, polite, and secretive. One man concluded, "Their view is that Japanese only like Caucasian men sexually, and they associate femininity with being oriental" (p. 240).

Too frequently lesbian and gay communities do not acknowledge the presence of non-Anglo members. When acknowledgment is offered, all too often the majority culture members assume that their unique ways of conceptualizing, understanding, and enacting lesbian and gay issues are applicable for *all* ethnic group members simply because they share homoerotic attractions and identities. Thus, for ethnic-minority adolescents, a very important aspect of their identity is not recognized (Chan, 1989; Pamela H., 1989).

For example, the pressure applied by Anglo gay men and lesbians on Latino/a gays and lesbians to be activists negates an essential feature of their ethnic heritage. Hidalgo and Hidalgo-Christensen (1976/1977) argued that Puerto Rican lesbians are not visible in activist networks because they do not want to disgrace their families through public disclosure of their homosexuality. Within many Latino/a cultures, the significance of the family extends beyond the immediate biological family to include distant kin. To be publicly out affects many generations and carries a heavy cultural burden.

A gay Chinese adolescent best summarized the feelings of many ethnic-/sexual-minority youths: "I am a double minority. Caucasian gays don't like gay Chinese, and the Chinese don't like the gays. It would be easier to be white. It would be easier to be straight. It's hard to be both" (Tremble et al., 1989, p. 263).

# HOMOPHOBIA IN ETHNIC COMMUNITIES

An ethnic community seldom provides a youth refuge from homophobic prejudice because negative views toward homosexuality may, in fact, be more pervasive in such communities than in mainstream White culture (Clarke, 1983; Espin, 1987; Icard, 1986; Morales, 1983; Poussaint, 1990). In the African American community, Gates (1993) labeled this "blacklash." One African American lesbian (Mays et al., 1993) noted her dilemma:

> Instead of accepting me for the person I am, they look at me as being a lesbian and look at me as being with another woman, and they see that as being very sinful and very bad. I told them to not judge me because I am gay, to look at me for who I am inside and not just judge me on . . . what they've heard on the news or what they've heard from other people or what they've read in books. (p. 6)

Homophobia may be derivative of attitudes that exist in an ethnic-minority member's native culture. For example, gay life in Cuba must exist primarily in prostitution and the underworld (Arguelles & Rich, 1989) because there is considerable repression and animosity against gays and lesbians (for personal, vivid accounts see Arenas, 1993, and Ramos, 1994). Within Judaism, homosexuality is often considered unnatural and undesirable; there are no traditional celebrations of same-sex committed relationships or instruction for lesbians and gays to become rabbis or cantors. These points were dramatically illustrated by Raphael (1990) in his collection of short stories, *Dancing on Tisha B'av,* and by Marder, a rabbi who led a gay shul. Marder noted:

> The message conveyed to my congregants by the community to which they belong is clear: you are welcome as long as you are invisible. We will tolerate your homosexuality, but we will certainly not hold you up as role models to be admired and emulated. (1989, p. 216)

Homosexuality may be more tolerated in other groups than in one's own ethnic group. Although liberal attitudes may be expressed toward lesbians and gays in general, the "live and let live" attitude seldom extends to homosexuality within one's own community (Wooden et al., 1983). The reasons for this ethnic-group homophobia are complex and beyond the scope of this chapter, but they likely reside in the unique religious values and cultural beliefs carried over from the "homeland" as well as the tribulations that ethnic minorities have experienced surviving in the dominant Anglo culture of North America (for elaboration see Gates, 1993; Greene, 1994; Manalansan, this volume). For example, Gates (1993) noted that an antihomosexual ideology has been characteristic of the Black nationalist movement in the U.S. He quoted Professor Asante of Temple University as saying:

> "Homosexuality is a deviation from Afrocentric thought, because it makes the person evaluate his own physical needs above the teachings of national consciousness. . . . [W]e can no longer allow our social lives to be controlled by European decadence." (p. 44)

Not uncommonly, homosexuality is considered to be a "White disease," a reflection of the "younger generation" becoming too assimilated and losing touch with their heritage (Pamela H., 1989). After a Korean daughter came out to her parents, they admonished her: "Being gay is a white disease. We're Korean; Korean people aren't gay" (Pamela H., 1989, p. 284). Tremble et al. (1989) noted that many find it "inconceivable" that anyone in their ethnic community could be "homosexual":

> Being black, Muslim, Greek, and so forth, and being homosexual, are perceived to be mutually exclusive. . . . To resolve the dissonance created by a gay or lesbian child, ethnic parents may blame the dominant culture. A 20-year-old Pakistani-Canadian male explains, "My parents are hurt. They see homosexuality as being against the Muslim faith. They think of it as a white people's thing. Being gay is something I picked up from my white friends." (p. 260)

Parents often blame a decadent, urban society; homosexuality is the price some pay for the privilege of living in North America. In their state of vulnerability, the children have been seduced by Anglo-American culture (Carrier, Nguyen, & Su, 1992). Homosexuality may also be considered by parents to be a manifestation of adolescent rebellion against traditional culture.

When their family holds such views, ethnic-minority youths experience increased fear and anxiety about their same-sex attractions and coming out to others. They may anticipate that parents will not believe them if they disclose their sexual orientation. Consequently, according to Morales (1983), youths experience inordinate pain: "To live as a minority within a minority leads to heightened feelings of isolation, depression and anger centered around the fear of being separated from all support systems including the family" (p. 2).

Many ethnic-minority youths must contend with maintaining the family honor, fulfilling expectations of marriage, and satisfying cultural definitions of masculinity and femininity. Yet, increasingly, these cultural expectations are shifting, easing pressure on ethnic-minority youth and thus allowing them to celebrate their unique sexual status.

# THE FAMILY

Morales (1983) argued that the primary difference between traditional American and ethnic family constellations

> . . . centers around the integration of the extended family within its support system. The ethnic family support system resembles more of a tribe with multiple family groups rather than a nuclear family structure consisting solely of parents and children. For the ethnic person the family constitutes a symbol of their basic roots and the focal point of their ethnic identity. (p. 9)

Thus, coming out to the family may be a very onerous experience for ethnic youths who normally rely on the family as the primary support system during "the arduous times of experiencing discrimination, slander and inferior treatment" (Morales, 1983, p. 9). To alienate the family jeopardizes a youth's intrafamily relationships, associations with other ethnic-group members, and progress toward a healthy sense of self.

## The Significance of the Family

For ethnic-minority youths to successfully negotiate the development of a positive lesbian, gay, or bisexual identity, it is often paramount to come out to the family. However, this is seldom an easy task. One of Wooden et al.'s (1983) subjects noted, "Japanese are taught humility and being gay is often associated with shame. You tend to keep it quiet so you don't bring shame to your family" (p. 241).

In ethnic communities, family is defined more broadly than nuclear family members. Extended family members, including grandparents, aunts, uncles, and cousins, provide child care, advice, role models, support, and other specialized roles. The significance of the extended family in the lives of youths has been persistently documented in Asian families. If an Asian youth disgraces herself or himself, shame is brought not only to the immediate family but to all past generations, living and dead (Carrier et al., 1992; Chan, 1989; Pamela H., 1989; Morales, 1983; Tsui, 1985). The family's honor is tarnished; it is not the children who have failed but the parents.

This view has been noted as well in other ethnic communities (Espin, 1987; Medina, 1987; Yeskel, 1989). Yeskel (1989), a Jewish lesbian, recalled that when she came out she felt "as if I was throwing a huge wrench into the parental plan. I thought about killing myself just about every day. How could I destroy my parents' happiness?" (p. 43). African American, Asian American, Jewish, and Latino/a families strongly emphasize loyalty, honoring parents, and extended family ties.

Given the importance and centrality of the extended family, some youths feel that they are forced to choose between their ethnic affiliation and a gay or lesbian identity. Tremble et al. (1989) noted that minority youths often "excluded themselves from cultural activities in order to avoid shaming the family in front of friends" (p. 261). This may be particularly acute among Asian women, some of whom feel they must leave their ethnic community to be a lesbian, thus forfeiting the support of family and extended kin (Pamela H., 1989). Many decide to participate in lesbian rather than Asian activities because they fear rejection more from ethnic than lesbian communities.

## Coming Out to the Family

A youth may thus feel that he or she can never come out publicly for fear of humiliating that which is most important in his or her life: the close-knit family that extends beyond immediate members to include multiple generations. Chicana poet Torres (1980) expressed this sentiment in response to pressure from lesbians to come out to her parents:

> Somehow it would be disrespectful to say to them, "Look, I'm a lesbian, and you're going to have to deal with it." I don't have the right to do that. They've been through so much in their lives about being Chicanos and living in this society. They've just taken so much shit that I won't do that to them until I feel like it can be said. (p. 244)

In a state of near desperation, one Latina lesbian, Rodriguez (1980), came out to her mother in the twelfth grade:

I told my mother, "Look, I'm freaking out. Do you know why I'm freaking out? It's not because I'm on dope; it's not because I listen to acid rock; it's because I'm a lesbian. And if I get your understanding, then I'll be able to clean my life up. I can take this cover off."

She told me, "I always knew you were. If you're going to be a lesbian, be a good lesbian." And then she started crying. At first she was so glad that I wasn't freaking out because of her or dope, it was like, "Phew." Then it hit her, "Oh! A lesbian! That's just as bad. Aaaaaaaah!" She cried and cried. (p. 110)

As Rodriguez illustrated, parents who suspect that their child is lesbian or gay may be hesitant to publicly raise the issue for fear of embarrassing relatives and their community. Thus, a wall of silence is likely to form around a family with a lesbian daughter, gay son, or bisexual child. Even if a youth advances to the point of self-recognition of her or his sexual status, the inhibitions against stating this publicly may block further self-development.

Part of this can be accounted for by the fact that sex is often a taboo topic in Asian and Latino communities. Sexual issues in general are considered to be a highly sensitive and delicate subject, open at best to awkward discussion (Pamela H., 1989; Ratti, 1993; Tsui, 1985; Wooden et al., 1983). Without a tradition of talking about sexuality, it is very difficult for an ethnic-/sexual-minority youth to discuss sexual identity, beliefs, and practices with family members.

Japanese don't seem to discuss sex or personal things with their children, although the family unit tends to be closely knit. Coming out was difficult, because I felt I was odd. I also felt that it was wrong and I would be a disgrace to the family. (Wooden et al., 1983, p. 240)

In fact, many ethnic-minority youths delay self-disclosure or never come out to their parents. Several investigations have reported that siblings, usually sisters, are told before, and perhaps in lieu of, parents. For example, Chan's (1989) sample of Chinese, Japanese, and Korean young adults found that almost 80% had come out to a family member, usually a sister; only one quarter had come out to parents. Similar results were found with samples of Puerto Ricans (Hidalgo & Hidalgo-Christensen, 1976/1977) and Japanese Americans (Wooden et al., 1983). A primary reason for coming out to nonparent family members was noted in the former study: They can become confidants and invaluable sources of support. A reason for not coming out was offered by an individual in the latter study: "They would never understand and I would be disowned and denied seeing my younger sister" (p. 239).

There is a strong expectation in many ethnic communities that children will marry and have children. Girls are expected to play the roles of wife and mother and to be dutiful, loyal, and obedient; boys, father and procreator of heirs (Chan, 1989; Pamela H., 1989; Icard, 1986; Medina, 1987; Ratti, 1993; Tsui, 1985). Homosexuality is considered detrimental to the fulfillment of these expectations. To neglect these obligations indicates that a youth is selfish, having only his or her own pleasure in mind rather than the community good.

## CULTURAL EXPECTATIONS OF APPROPRIATE
## SEX ROLE BEHAVIOR

Ethnic communities frequently have traditional expectations regarding appropriate masculine and feminine roles. For lesbian, gay, and bisexual youths who cannot meet these expectations, this may well be another way in which their ethnic and sexual identities are incongruent. For example, a traditional virtue common in Latino communities is that Latino males should appear defiantly heterosexual—embracing and enacting the social construct of "machismo" (Carrier, 1989; Parker, 1989). Males are expected to personify traditional masculine sex roles, such as aggressiveness, dominance, power, courage, and invulnerability (Carrier, 1989).

In Hispanic culture, *same-sex behavior* per se is not sufficient to be labeled gay (Magana & Carrier, 1991). Rather, male homosexuality is equated with effeminacy and assuming the passive (receiver) role in sexual relations. If, for example, a Mexican (Magana & Carrier, 1991) or Cuban (Young, 1981) male assumes the inserter role in anal intercourse, he will not likely be considered deviant or gay. Because he embraces traditional masculine macho behavior, it is also unlikely that he will consider himself to be gay.

Carrier (1989) suggested that Mexican males who are feminine in behavior and who never think of themselves as heterosexual may experience an easier time self-identifying as gay in adulthood. Males who behave in a masculine manner may find it easier to rationalize that they are heterosexuals who occasionally enjoy insertive anal intercourse with other males. If and when they eventually self-identify as gay, they may experience a much more difficult time accepting and embracing their new identity. Bisexuality, particularly the assumption of the dominant (inserter) position, is more acceptable (Carrier, 1989).

*Etiqueta,* the proper sex role for Latina females, prescribes patience, nurturance, passivity, and subservience. Women are showpieces to be adorned. They are virgins until married, docile, inferior, and faithful. Not surprisingly, traditional Hispanic views of lesbians are negative. Latina lesbians are likely to be considered man-haters—acting macho and trying to overthrow men and masculine cultural heritage. They are perceived to engage in foreign ways and to be headstrong and independent. Sexually, lesbians are thought to be promiscuous, unchaste, and selfish (Hidalgo & Hidalgo-Christensen, 1976/1977; Ramos, 1994; Romo-Carmona, 1994). One Latina lesbian (Romo-Carmona, 1994) noted several cultural expectations:

> As Latinas, we are supposed to grow up submissive, virtuous, respectful of elders and helpful to our mothers, long suffering, deferring to men, industrious and devoted. We also know that any deviation from these expectations constitutes an act of rebellion, and there is great pressure to conform. Independence is discouraged, and we learn early that women who think for themselves are branded "putas" or "marimachas" [sluts or butches].
>
> Being a lesbian is by definition an act of treason against our cultural values. (p. xxvi)

In some Asian communities, a discrepancy between behavior sanctioned in the homeland and its subsequent interpretation following immigration to the U.S. is not uncommon. For example, in Vietnam, homosexuality is equated with femininity and being half male, half female. Nonetheless, some adolescent males engage in same-sex behavior such as mutual masturbation and fellatio. Close physical contact, holding hands, and sleeping together in the same bed are considered normal and socially sanctioned, suggesting that little is implied about future sexual identification (Carrier et al., 1992). In North America, however, a "masculine" Vietnamese adolescent male who engaged in these otherwise "normal" same-sex activities would raise considerable concern among peers and family.

In Mexico, male youths who display gender atypical or nontraditional behavior at a young age "are eventually, if not from the beginning, pushed toward exclusive homosexual behavior" (Carrier, 1989, p. 227). The ethnic-minority youths interviewed by Tremble et al. (1989) were preoccupied with reconciling homoerotic desires with their sex role behavior.

> Often these youngsters are victimized by the stereotypes within their own culture. They believe that being gay or lesbian means being gender role reversal. They go through a phase of extreme cross-gender behavior, which distresses or alienates their parents, or may leave them open to harassment or victimization. (p. 263)

These pressures can undermine psychological integrity and identity formation and sabotage the maturation of a healthy self-concept. However, there are indications of cultural shifts regarding expectations and acceptance within some ethnic-minority communities.

## Cultural Shifts

Attitudes toward homosexuality can alter. The increasing visibility and diversity of lesbian and gay life may well be changing the rigid stereotypes of gays and lesbians preserved in some ethnic communities. Tremble et al. (1989) suggested that

> . . . cultural sanctions are not fixed values. They are perceived and interpreted by individuals, families, communities, and are modified in application by the perceived characteristics of the individual involved. . . . Herein, lies the flexibility to come to terms with homosexuality. (p. 257)

Changes in cultural perspectives are not a recent phenomenon but the consequence of gradual shifts over many years. Arora (1980) noted this increasing liberalization 15 years ago:

> Today the potential for a gay person to declare his sexuality is much wider—there seems to be a more "liberal" atmosphere. No child or teenager grows up without knowing—reading—hearing the word "gay." But for a person who is homosexual, the trauma of facing social derision and alienation is by no means less. (p. 23)

Newman and Muzzonigro (1993) suggested that more important than ethnicity in the coming-out process are traditional values such as an emphasis on religion, marriage, and bearing children. Even those "traditional values," however, are mutating. Although the Catholic church has traditionally been one of the bulwarks of traditional values, change is slowly occurring. One Latina lesbian noted:

> When I was thirteen, I confessed to a priest that I was a lesbian. I thought it was a sin so I should confess it, but he said that it was alright and that he was gay. He said, "God isn't going to condemn you. God is all good. How can he condemn something that he's made?" (Gonzalez, 1980, p. 184)

One Japanese American linked changes in attitudes to generational differences:

> I feel this can be categorized into two classifications—attitudes of the first and second generations, and those of the third and fourth generations. I think those of the first and second generations are more rigid and non-accepting. They feel we are perverts and child-molesters. Those of the third and fourth are more accepting. Attitudes are changing. (Wooden et al., 1983, p. 240)

Ethnic roots, religion, social class, and date immigrated are factors that appear to matter most in predicting a liberal attitude toward homosexuality among Vietnamese (Carrier et al., 1992).

Tremble et al. (1989) found that parents from Asian, Portuguese, Greek, Italian, and Indo-Pakistani cultural backgrounds who adjusted best to their offspring's homosexuality prioritized and reinterpreted their values, maintaining, "You are my child and I love you no matter what" (p. 259). Preserving family unity was given first priority. Other parents who accepted their gay or lesbian children found precedents for homosexuality among lesbian and gay friends and family members. A third mechanism for acceptance was less satisfactory:

> Attributing homosexuality to an external source does not make parents any happier, nor could these rationales be called a real understanding, but they do seem to remove responsibility from themselves and their child. The child can be accepted as part of the family, albeit uneasily at times. (p. 261)

Cultural shifts in ethnic communities toward a more liberal attitude can be life affirming for youths striving to accept homoerotic attractions without rejecting their family and ethnic community.

## CONCLUSION

It is important to understand the dual identities, multiple roles, emotional conflicts, and psychological adjustments that result from the complex situations in which lesbian, bisexual, and gay ethnic-minority youths find themselves. Such youths endure two stigmas, being an ethnic minority and being bisexual, gay, or lesbian. Consequently, they encounter racism in gay and lesbian communities and homophobia in their cultural communities. It is a risky venture with profound repercussions for a healthy integration of personal and group identities.

Ideally these adolescents should have the opportunity to acquire information and social support from two distinct and rich sources. They should receive support from lesbian and gay communities that their cultural community would otherwise be unable to provide, including affirmation of sexuality and sexual identity; a place in which to relax and talk openly about same-sex relationships; and information about social organizations and networks that cater to other sexual-minority individuals. Similarly, familial, racial, ethnic, and cultural ties should reinforce a cultural identification, offer a deep sense of heritage and values, and provide a sense of self (Morales, 1983).

A version of this ideal reality is occurring as an increasing number of ethnic-minority youths are finding support and encouragement from non-Anglo gay and lesbian communities. Almost every major ethnic-/sexual-minority group in North America sponsors, at least in large urban areas, various support and political organizations for its community. Also available are newsletters and magazines.[2]

Forming an integrated multiple self-identification that includes ethnic and sexual identities is a protracted developmental process. Learning the skills to integrate and manage one aspect of a dissonant group identity, such as an ethnic-minority status, may facilitate the subsequent integration and management of a second dissonant group identity, such as sexual-minority status. Rofes (1989) noted that growing up Jewish, an "outsider" in a Gentile world, proved "indispensable to me as a gay man living in a world that often prefers that I not exist" (p. 198). Being targeted as a Jew was "useful preparation for later experiences of being much more overtly targeted as gay" (p. 199). Having experienced the difficulties of being ethnically "different," ethnic-/sexual-minority youths may develop coping skills that assist them to manage being sexually "different."

## ▼  ENDNOTES  ▼

1. My deepest gratitude is expressed to several Cornell students who, through their course papers, sensitized me to ethnic-minority issues and provided resources for many of the issues discussed in this chapter: Raymond Chan, "Queer-N-Asian: The Hidden Double Minority"; Andres Garcia, "Que Siga La Tradicion: Lesbians and Gay Men in Cuban Society"; Maria Larino, "Against All Odds: Latina Lesbians in the United States"; Seema Patel, "South Asian Lesbians, Bisexuals, and Gays"; and Gary Wetstein, "The Star of David and the Pink Triangle: Growing Up Jewish and Gay."

2. These include the following: *Black/Out: The Magazine of the National Coalition of Black Lesbians and Gays; Bulletin* (Comite Homosexual Latinoamericano); *Gay Asian Support Group (GASG) Newsletter; Lavender Godzilla: Voices of the Gay Asian Pacific Alliance; Men of All Colors Together Chicago; Moja = Gay & Black; National Association of Black and White Men Together Newsletter;* and *Unidad* (Gay and Lesbian Latinos Unidos).

## ▼ REFERENCES ▼

Arenas, R. (1993). *Before night falls.* New York: Penguin.

Arguelles, L., & Rich, B. R. (1989). Homosexuality, homophobia, and revolution: Notes toward an understanding of the Cuban lesbian and gay male experience. In M. B. Duberman, M. Vicinus, & G. Chauncey, Jr. (Eds.), *Hidden from history: Reclaiming the gay and lesbian past* (pp. 441–455). New York: Penguin.

Arora, D. (1980, August). When "gay" is not happy! *Society,* pp. 20–23.

Carrier, J. M. (1989). Gay liberation and coming out in Mexico. *Journal of Homosexuality, 17,* 225–252.

Carrier, J., Nguyen, B., & Su, S. (1992). Vietnamese American sexual behaviors and HIV infection. *The Journal of Sex Research, 29,* 547–560.

Chan, C. S. (1989). Issues of identity development among Asian-American lesbians and gay men. *Journal of Counseling and Development, 68,* 16–20.

Clarke, C. (1983). The failure to transform: Homophobia in the Black community. In B. Smith (Ed.), *Home girls: A Black feminist anthology* (pp. 197–208). New York: Kitchen Table Press.

Cooper, A. (1989/1990). No longer invisible: Gay and lesbian Jews build a movement. *Journal of Homosexuality, 18,* 83–94.

Cross, W. E. (1991). *Shades of Black: Diversity in African-American identity.* Philadelphia: Temple University Press.

Espin, O. M. (1987). Issues of identity in the psychology of Latina lesbians. In Boston Lesbian Psychologies Collective (Eds.), *Lesbian psychologies: Explorations and challenges* (pp. 35–55). Urbana, IL: University of Illinois Press.

Gates, H. L., Jr. (1993, May 17). Blacklash? *The New Yorker,* pp. 42–44.

Gonzalez, M. (1980). Maria Gonzalez. In R. Baetz (Ed.), *Lesbian crossroads* (p. 184). New York: William Morrow.

Greene, B. (1994). Ethnic-minority lesbians and gay men: Mental health and treatment issues. *Journal of Consulting and Clinical Psychology, 62,* 243–251.

H., Pamela. (1989). Asian American lesbians: An emerging voice in the Asian American community. In Asian Women United of California (Eds.), *Making waves: An anthology of writing by and about Asian American women* (pp. 282–290). Boston: Beacon Press.

Hidalgo, H. A., & Hidalgo-Christensen, E. (1976/1977). The Puerto Rican lesbian and the Puerto Rican community. *Journal of Homosexuality, 2,* 109–121.

Historic Meet. (1991). *Bombay Dost, 1,* 5–6.

Icard, L. (1986). Black gay men and conflicting social identities: Sexual orientation versus racial identity. *Journal of Social Work and Human Sexuality, 4,* 83–93.

Johnson, J. M. (1981). Influences of assimilation on the psychosocial adjustment of Black homosexual men (Doctoral dissertation, California School of Professional Psychology, Berkeley, 1981). *Dissertation Abstract International, 42* (11B), 4620.

Magana, J. R., & Carrier, J. M. (1991). Mexican and Mexican American male sexual behavior and spread of AIDS in California. *The Journal of Sex Research, 28,* 425–441.

Marder, J. R. (1989). Getting to know the gay and lesbian shul: A rabbi moves from tolerance to acceptance. In C. Balka & A. Rose (Eds.), *Twice blessed: On being lesbian, gay, and Jewish* (pp. 209–217). Boston: Beacon Press.

Mays, V. M., Cochran, S. D., & Rhue, S. (1993). The impact of perceived discrimination on the intimate relationships of Black lesbians. *Journal of Homosexuality, 25,* 1–14.

Medina, C. (1987, January/February). Latino culture and sex education. *SIECUS, 15,* 3.

Morales, E. S. (1983, August). Third World gays and lesbians: A process of multiple identities. Paper presented at the 91st Annual Convention of the American Psychological Association, Anaheim, CA.

Newman, B. S., & Muzzonigro, P. G. (1993). The effects of traditional family values on the coming out process of gay male adolescents. *Adolescence, 28,* 213–226.

Parker, R. (1989). Youth, identity, and homosexuality: The changing shape of sexual life in contemporary Brazil. *Journal of Homosexuality, 17,* 269–289.

Poussaint, A. (1990, September). An honest look at Black gays and lesbians. *Ebony,* pp. 124, 126, 130–131.

Ramos, J. (1994). *Companeras: Latina lesbians.* New York: Routledge.

Raphael, L. (1990). *Dancing on Tisha B'av.* New York: St. Martin's Press.

Ratti, R. (Ed.). (1993). *A lotus of another color: An unfolding of the South Asian gay and lesbian experience.* Boston: Alyson.

Rodriguez, D. (1980). Dolores Rodriguez. In R. Baetz (Ed.), *Lesbian crossroads* (pp. 110–112). New York: William Morrow.

Rofes, E. E. (1989). Living as all of who I am: Being Jewish in the lesbian/gay community. In C. Balka & A. Rose (Eds.), *Twice blessed: On being lesbian, gay, and Jewish* (pp. 198–204). Boston: Beacon Press.

Romo-Carmona, M. (1994). Introduction. In J. Ramos (Ed.), *Companeras: Latina lesbians* (pp. xx–xxix). New York: Routledge.

Torres, A. (1980). Ana Torres. In R. Baetz (Ed.), *Lesbian crossroads* (pp. 240–244). New York: William Morrow.

Tremble, B., Schneider, M., & Appathurai, C. (1989). Growing up gay or lesbian in a multicultural context. *Journal of Homosexuality, 17,* 253–267.

Tsui, A. M. (1985). Psychotherapeutic considerations in sexual counseling for Asian immigrants. *Psychotherapy, 22,* 357–362.

Wooden, W. S., Kawasaki, H., & Mayeda, R. (1983). Lifestyles and identity maintenance among gay Japanese-American males. *Alternative Lifestyles, 5,* 236–243.

Yeskel, F. (1989). You didn't talk about these things: Growing up Jewish, lesbian, and working class. In C. Balka & A. Rose (Eds.), *Twice blessed: On being lesbian, gay, and Jewish* (pp. 40–47). Boston: Beacon Press.

Young, A. (1981). *Gays under the Cuban revolution.* San Francisco: Grey Fox Press.

# Chapter 7

▼

# DATING AND ROMANTIC RELATIONSHIPS AMONG GAY, LESBIAN, AND BISEXUAL YOUTHS

## Ritch C. Savin-Williams[1]

*The erotic, sexual attraction that draws two adolescents together often includes a yearning for intimacy. Through dating, adolescents learn how to relate to each other within a personal context and experiment in associating intimacy needs with sexuality. Romantic relationships help youths clarify who they are and what they desire. These opportunities for intimacy, however, have been denied to many lesbian and gay youths who have not had the opportunity to date or form intimate relationships with those to whom they feel most erotically attracted. Thus, from a developmental perspective, they are deprived of an important adolescent experience.*

## THE IMPORTANCE OF DATING AND ROMANCE

According to Scarf (1987), the developmental significance of an intimate relationship is to help us "contact archaic, dimly perceived and yet powerfully meaningful aspects of our inner selves" (p. 79). We desire closeness within the context of a trusting, intimate relationship. Attachment theory posits that humans are prewired for loving and developing strongly felt emotional attachments (Bowlby, 1973). When established, we experience safety, security, and nurturance. Early attachments, including those in infancy, are thought to circumscribe an internal blueprint that profoundly affects future relationships, such as the establishment of intimate friendships and romances in adolescence and adulthood (Hazan & Shaver, 1987).

Developmentally, dating is a means by which romantic relationships are practiced, pursued, and established. It serves a number of important functions, such as entertainment, recreation, and socialization, that assist participants in developing appropriate means of interacting. It also enhances peer group status and facilitates the selection of a mate (Skipper & Nass, 1966). Adolescents who are most confident in their dating abilities begin dating during early adolescence, date frequently, are satisfied with their dating, and are most likely to become involved in a "committed" dating relationship (Herold, 1979).

The establishment of romantic relationships is important for youths regardless of sexual orientation. Isay (1989) noted that falling in love was a critical factor in helping his gay clients feel comfortable with their gay identity and that "the self-affirming value of a mutual relationship over time cannot be overemphasized" (p. 50). Clinician Browning (1987) regarded lesbian love relationships as an opportunity to enhance

> . . . the development of the individual's adult identity by validating her personhood, reinforcing that she deserves to receive and give love. A relationship can also be a source of tremendous emotional support as the woman explores her goals, values, and relationship to the world. (p. 51)

Because dating experience increases the likelihood that an intimate romantic relationship will evolve, the absence of this opportunity may have long-term repercussions. Malyon (1981) noted some of the reverberations:

> For example, their most charged sexual desires are usually seen as perverted, and their deepest feelings of psychological attachment are regarded as unacceptable. This social disapproval interferes with the preintimacy involvement that fosters the evolution of maturity and self-respect in the domain of object relations. (p. 326)

## CULTURE'S DEVALUATION OF SAME-SEX RELATIONSHIPS

Relatively speaking, our culture is far more willing to turn a blind eye to sexual than to romantic relationships among same-sex adolescent partners. Same-sex activity may appear "temporary," an experiment, a phase, or a perverted source of fun. But falling in love with someone of the same gender and maintaining a sustained emotional involvement with that person implies an irreversible deviancy at worst and a bad decision at best. In our homes, schools, religious institutions, and media, we teach that intense relationships after early adolescence among members of the same sex "should" raise the concern of good parents, good friends, and good teachers. One result is that youths of all sexual orientations may become frightened of developing close friendships with same-sex peers. They fear that these friendships will be viewed as sexually intimate.

It is hardly surprising that a sexual-minority adolescent can easily become "the loneliest person . . . in the typical high school of today" (Norton, 1976, p. 376).

> For the homosexual-identified student, high school is often a lonely place where, from every vantage point, there are couples: couples holding hands as they enter school; couples dissolving into an endless wet kiss between school bells; couples exchanging rings with ephemeral vows of devotion and love. (Sears, 1991, pp. 326–327)

The separation of a youth's homoerotic passion from the socially sanctioned act of heterosexual dating can generate self-doubt, anger, and resentment, and can ultimately retard or distort the development of interpersonal intimacy during the adolescent years. Thus, many youths never consider same-sex dating to be a reasonable option, except in their fantasies. Scientific and clinical writings that ignore same-sex romance and dating among youth contribute to this conspiracy of silence. Sexual-minority youth struggle with issues of identity and intimacy because important impediments rooted in our cultural values and attitudes deter them from dating those they love and instead mandate that they date those they cannot love.

## EMPIRICAL STUDIES OF SAME-SEX ROMANTIC RELATIONSHIPS AMONG YOUTH

Until the last several years same-sex relationships among sexual-minority youths were seldom recognized in the empirical, scientific literature. With the recent visibility of gay, bisexual, and lesbian youths in the culture at large, social and behavioral scientists are beginning to conduct research focusing on various developmental processes of such youths, including their sexuality and intimacy.

Bisexual, lesbian, and gay youths, whether in Detroit, Minneapolis, Pennsylvania, New York, or the Netherlands, report that they desire to have long-lasting, committed same-sex romantic relationships in their future (D'Augelli, 1991; Harry & DeVall, 1978; Remafedi, 1987a; Sanders, 1980; Savin-Williams, 1990). According to Silverstein (1981), establishing a romantic relationship with a same-sex partner helps one to feel "chosen," to resolve issues of sexual identity, and to feel more complete. Indeed, those who are in a long-term love relationship generally have high levels of self-esteem and self-acceptance.[2]

Although there are few published studies of teens that focus primarily on their same-sex dating or romantic relationships, there are suggestive data that debunk the myth in our culture that gays, lesbians, and bisexuals neither want nor maintain steady, loving same-sex relationships. In two studies of gay and bisexual male youths, same-sex relationships are regarded as highly desirable. Among 29 Minnesota youths, 10 had a steady male partner at the time of the interview, 11 had been in a same-sex relationship, and, most tellingly, all but 2 hoped for a steady male partner in their future (Remafedi, 1987a, 1987b). For these youths, many of whom were living independently with friends or on the street, being in a long-term relationship was considered to be an ideal state. With a college-age sample of 61 males, D'Augelli (1991) reported similar results. One half of his sample was "partnered," and their most troubling mental health concern was termination of a close relationship, ranking just ahead of telling parents about their homosexuality.

The difficulty, however, is to maintain a visible same-sex romance in high school. Sears (1991) interviewed 36 Southern late adolescent and young adult lesbians, gays, and bisexuals. He discovered that although nearly everyone had heterosexually dated in high school, very few dated a member of the same sex during that time. Because of concerns about secrecy and the lack of social support, most same-sex romances involved little emotional commitment and were of short duration. None were overt.

Research with over 300 gay, bisexual, and lesbian youths between the ages of 14 and 23 years (Savin-Williams, 1990) supports the finding that sexual-minority youths have romantic relationships during adolescence and young adulthood. Almost 90% of the females and two thirds of the males reported that they have had a romantic relationship. Of the total number of romances listed, 60% were with same-sex partners. The male youths were slightly more likely than lesbian and bisexual female youths to begin their romantic career with a same-sex, rather than an opposite-sex, partner.

In the same study, the lesbians and bisexual females who had a high proportion of same-sex romances were most likely to be "out" to others. However, their self-esteem level was essentially the same as those who had a high percentage of heterosexual relationships. If she began same-sex dating early, during adolescence, then a lesbian or bisexual female also tended to be in a current relationship and to experience long-lasting romances. Gay and bisexual male youths who had a large percentage of adolescent romantic relationships with boys had high self-esteem. They were more likely to be publicly "out" to friends and family if they had had a large number of romances. Boys who initiated same-sex romances at an early age were more likely to report that they have had long-term and multiple same-sex relationships.

The findings from these studies are admittedly sparse and do not provide the depth and insight that are needed to help us better understand the experience of being in a same-sex romantic relationship. They do illustrate that youths have same-sex romances while in high school. Where there is desire, some youths will find a way. Sexually active same-sex friendships may evolve into romantic relationships (Savin-Williams, 1995), and those most publicly out are most likely to have had adolescent same-sex romances. Certainly, most lesbian, gay, and bisexual youths value the importance of a same-sex, lifelong, committed relationship in their adult years.

Perhaps the primary issue is not the absence of same-sex romances during adolescence, but the hidden nature of the romances. They are seldom recognized and rarely supported or celebrated. The research data offer little information regarding the psychological impact of not being involved in a same-sex romantic relationship or of having to hide such a relationship when it exists. For this, one must turn to stories of the personal struggles of adolescents.

## PERSONAL STRUGGLES

Youths who have same-sex romances during their adolescence face a severe struggle to have these relationships acknowledged and supported. Gibson (1989) noted the troubling contradictions:

> The first romantic involvements of lesbian and gay male youth are a source of great joy to them in affirming their sexual identity, providing them with support, and assuring them that they too can experience love. However, society places extreme hardships on these relationships that make them difficult to establish and maintain. (pp. 3-130)

The 11-year-old male narrator in Picano's (1985) novel, *Ambidextrous,* had his first sexual encounter with the Flaherty sisters. It was sex, acceptability, and enjoyment, but it was not love. Love and sex, romance and friendship would come into his life when he was 14 years old—not with a girl but with Ricky.

> I joined him and we began kissing sitting up, then wrapped our arms around each other and slowly floated down to the bedspread in a kiss that seemed to last forever and to merge us completely into each other so that we were pilot and co-pilot zooming lightning swift through the lower atmosphere, high as a meteorite. (Picano, 1985, p. 88)

He and Ricky wanted to live together, but they were torn apart by their parents and life circumstances, plunging them "into an instant and near total grief that all Ricky's soothing words and kisses couldn't completely assuage" (p. 98). The narrator's romance with Ricky was perceived by family and friends as merely an adolescent chumship. The intensity of the sex, the affectionate feelings, and the emotional arousal clearly label this as a romantic relationship, a critical marker in the narrator's young life.

A significant number of youths, perhaps those feeling most insecure regarding their sexual identity, may fantasize about being sexually intimate with a same-sex partner but have little hope that it could in fact become a reality. One youth, Lawrence, reported this feeling in his coming-out story.

> While growing up, love was something I watched other people experience and enjoy. . . . The countless men I secretly loved and fantasized about were only in private, empty dreams in which love was never returned. I seemed to be the only person in the world with no need for love and companionship. . . . Throughout high school and college I had no way to meet people of the same sex and sexual orientation. These were more years of isolation and secrecy. I saw what other guys my age did, listened to what they said and how they felt. I was expected to be part of a world with which I had nothing in common. (Curtis, 1988, pp. 109–110)

A young lesbian, Diane, recalled that "love of women was never a possibility that I even realized could be. You loved your mother and your aunts, and you had girl-friends for a while. Someday, though, you would always meet a man" (Stanley & Wolfe, 1980, p. 47). Girls dated boys and not other girls. Because she did not want to date boys, she did not date.

Another youth knew he had homoerotic attractions, but he never fathomed that they could be expressed to the boy that he most admired, his high school soccer teammate. It took alcohol and the right situation.

> I knew I was checking out the guys in the shower after soccer practice. This scared the shit out of me. Like everyone else I was lookin' through *Playboys* only I was searchin' for the pricks beside the naked women. I thought of myself as hetero who had the urge for males. I fought it, said it was a phase. And then it happened.

> Derek was my best friend. After soccer practice the fall of our junior year we celebrated both mak-
> ing the "A" team by getting really drunk. We were just fooling around and suddenly our pants were
> off and our pricks were in the hands of the other. I was so scared I stayed out of school for three days
> but we kept being friends and nothing was said until a year later when I came out to everyone and he
> came up to me with these tears and asked if he made me homosexual. (Savin-Williams, 1995)

It is never easy for youths to directly confront the mores of peers whose values and attitudes are routinely supported by the culture. Nearly all youths know
implicitly the rules of socially appropriate behavior and the consequences of nonconformity. This single, most influential barrier to same-sex dating, the threat
posed by peers, can have severe repercussions. The penalty for crossing the line
of "normalcy" can result in emotional and physical pain.

## PEER HARASSMENT AS A BARRIER TO DATING

In a paper addressed to school personnel concerning high school students' attitudes toward homosexuality, Price (1982) concluded, "Adolescents can be very
cruel to others who are different, who do not conform to the expectations of the
peer group" (p. 472). Very little has changed in the last decade. For example, 17-
year-old actor Ryan Phillippe worried about the consequences on his family and
friends if he played a gay teen on ABC's soap opera "One Life to Live" (Gable,
1992, p. 3D). David Ruffin, 19, of Ferndale, Michigan, explained why he boy-
cotted his high school senior prom: "The kids could tell I was different from
them, and I think I was different because I was gay. And when you're dealing
with young people, different means not cool" (Bruni, 1992, p. 10A).

Unlike heterosexual dating, little social advantage, such as peer popularity
or acceptance, is gained by holding hands and kissing a same-sex peer in school
hallways, shopping malls, or synagogues. Lies are spun to protect secrets and to
avoid peer harassment. One lesbian youth, Kim, felt that she had to be an actress
around her friends. She lied to friends by creating "Andrew" when she was dating "Andrea" over the weekend (Bruni, 1992).

To avoid harassment, sexual minority adolescents may monitor their interpersonal interactions. They may wonder, "Am I standing too close?" or "Do I appear too happy to see him(her)?" (Anderson, 1987). Hetrick and Martin (1987)
found that youths are often apprehensive to show "friendship for a friend of the
same sex for fear of being misunderstood or giving away their secretly held sexual
orientation" (p. 31). If erotic desires become aroused and threaten expression,
youths may seek to terminate same-sex friendships rather than risk revealing
their secret. For many adolescents, especially bisexual youths, relationships with
the other sex may be easier to develop. The appeal of such relationships is that
the youths will be viewed by peers as heterosexual, thus peer acceptance will be
enhanced and the threat of harassment and rejection will be reduced. The result
is that some sexual-minority youths feel inherently "fake" and they therefore

retreat from becoming intimate with others. Although they may meet the implicit and explicit demands of their culture, it is at a cost—their sense of authenticity.

## FAKING IT: HETEROSEXUAL SEX AND DATING

Retrospective data from gay, bisexual, and lesbian adults reveal the extent to which heterosexual dating and sex are commonplace during the adolescent and young adult years (see Bell & Weinberg, 1978; Gundlach & Riess, 1968; Saghir & Robins, 1973; Schafer, 1976; Spada, 1979; Troiden & Goode, 1980; Weinberg & Williams, 1974). These might be one-night stands, brief romances, or long-term relationships. Across various studies, nearly two thirds of gay men and three quarters of lesbians report having had heterosexual sex in their past. Motivations include fun, curiosity, denial of homoerotic feelings, and pressure to conform to society's insistence on heterosexual norms and behaviors. Even though heterosexual sex often results in a low level of sexual gratification, it is deemed a necessary sacrifice to meet the expectations of peers and, by extension, receive their approval. Only later, as adults, when they have the opportunity to compare these heterosexual relationships with same-sex ones do they fully realize that which they had missed during their younger years.

Several studies with lesbian, bisexual, and gay adolescents document the extent to which they are sexually involved with opposite-sex partners. In five samples of gay and bisexual male youths, over one half reported that they have had heterosexual experiences (Herdt & Boxer, 1993; Remafedi, 1987a, 1987b; Roesler & Deisher, 1972; Savin-Williams, 1990; Sears, 1991). Few, however, had *extensive* sexual contact with females, even among those who began heterosexual sex at an early age. Sex with one or two girls was usually considered "quite enough." Not infrequently these girls were best friends who expressed a romantic or sexual interest in the gay boys. The male youths liked the girls, but they preferred friendships rather than sexual relations. One youth expressed this dilemma:

> She was a year older and we had been friends for a long time before beginning dating. It was a date with the full thing: dinner, theater, alcohol, making out, sex. At her house and I think we both came during intercourse. I was disappointed because it was such hard work—not physically I mean but emotionally. Later on in my masturbation my fantasies were never of her. We did it once more in high school and then once more when we were in college. I labeled it love but not sexual love. I really wanted them to occur together. It all ended when I labeled myself gay. (Savin-Williams, 1995)

An even greater percentage of lesbian and bisexual female adolescents engaged in heterosexual sexual experiences—2 of every 3 in one study (Herdt & Boxer, 1993), 3 of every 4 in a second (Sears, 1991), and 8 of 10 in a third (Savin-Williams, 1990). Heterosexual activity began as early as second grade and as late as senior year in high school. Few of these girls, however, had extensive sex with boys—usually with two or three boys within the context of dating. Eighteen-year-old Kimba noted that she went through a heterosexual stage,

. . . trying to figure out what was so great about guys sexually. I still don't understand. I guess that, for straights, it is like it is for me when I am with a woman. . . . I experimented in whatever ways I thought would make a difference, but it was no go. My closest friends are guys; there is caring and closeness between us. (Heron, 1983, p. 82)

Georgina also tried to follow a heterosexual script:

In sixth and seventh grades you start wearing makeup, you start getting your hair cut, you start liking boys—you start thinking about letting them 'French kiss' you. I did all those major things. But, I still didn't feel very satisfied with myself. I remember I never really wanted to be intimate with any guy. I always wanted to be their best friend. (Sears, 1991, p. 327)

One young lesbian, Lisa, found herself "having sex with boys to prove I wasn't gay. Maybe I was even trying to prove it to myself! I didn't enjoy having sex with boys" (Heron, 1983, p. 76). These three lesbian youths forfeited a sense of authenticity, intimacy, and love because they were taught that emotional intimacy can only be achieved with members of the other sex.

The reasons sexual-minority adolescents gave in research studies as to why they engaged in heterosexual sex were similar to those reported in retrospective studies by adults. The youths needed to test whether their heterosexual attractions were as strong as their homoerotic ones—thus attempting to disconfirm their homosexuality—and to mask their homosexuality so as to win peer- and self-acceptance and to avoid peer rejection. Many youths in these studies believed that they could not really know whether they were lesbian, gay, bisexual, or heterosexual without first experiencing heterosexual sex. For many, however, heterosexual activities consisted of sex without feelings that they tried to enjoy without much success (Herdt & Boxer, 1993). Heterosexual sex felt unnatural because it lacked the desired emotional intensity.

One young gay youth reported:

We'd been dating for three months. I was 15 and she, a year or so older. We had petted previously and so she planned this event. We attempted intercourse in her barn, but I was too nervous and I think she was on the rag. I didn't feel good afterwards because it was not successful. We did it every week for a month or so. It was fun but it wasn't a big deal. But then I did not have a great lust or drive. Just comfortable. This was just normal I guess. It gave me something to do to tell the other guys who were always bragging. (Savin-Williams, 1995)

Similarly, Kimberly always had a steady heterosexual relationship: "It was like I was just going through the motions. It was expected of me, so I did it. I'd kiss him or embrace him but it was like I was just there. He was probably enjoying it, but I wasn't" (Sears, 1991, p. 327).

Jacob, an African American adolescent (Sears, 1991), dated the prettiest girls in his school in order to maintain his image: "It was more like President Reagan entertaining heads of state. It's expected of you when you're in a certain position" (pp. 126–127). Another Southern male youth, Grant, used "group dates" to reinforce his heterosexual image. Rumors that he was gay were squelched because his jock friends came to his defense: "He's not a fag. He has a girlfriend" (Sears, 1991, p. 328).

These and other personal stories of youths vividly recount the use of heterosexual sex and dating as a cover for an emerging same-sex or bisexual identity. Dating provides opportunities to temporarily "pass" as straight until the meaning of homoerotic feelings are resolved or youths find a safe haven to be lesbian or gay. Heterosexual sex and dating may be less pleasurable than same-sex encounters, but many sexual-minority youths feel that the former are the only safe, acceptable options.

## IMPEDIMENTS AND CONSEQUENCES

The difficulties inherent in dating same-sex partners during adolescence are monumental. First is the fundamental difficulty of finding a suitable partner. The vast majority of lesbian, bisexual, and gay youths are closeted, not out to themselves, let alone to others. A second barrier, reviewed earlier in this chapter, is the consequences of same-sex dating, such as verbal and physical harassment from peers. A third impediment is the lack of public recognition or "celebration" of those who are romantically involved with a member of the same gender. Thus, same-sex dating remains hidden and mysterious, something that is either ridiculed, condemned, or ignored.

The consequences of an exclusively heterosexually oriented atmosphere in the peer social world can be severe and enduring. An adolescent may feel isolated and socially excluded from the world of peers. Sex with others of the same gender may be associated exclusively with anonymous, guilt-ridden encounters, handicapping the ability to develop healthy intimate relationships in adulthood. Denied the opportunity for romantic involvement with someone of the same sex, a youth may suffer impaired self-esteem that reinforces the belief that one is unworthy of love, affection, and intimacy. One youth, Rick, even doubted his ability to love:

> When I started my senior year, I was still unclear about my sexuality. I had dated women with increasing frequency, but never felt love for any of them. I discovered that I could perform sexually with a woman, but heterosexual experiences were not satisfying emotionally. I felt neither love nor emotional oneness with women. Indeed, I had concluded that I was incapable of human love. (Heron, 1983, pp. 95–96)

If youths are to take advantage of opportunities to explore their erotic sexuality, it is sometimes, at least for males, confined to clandestine sexual encounters, void of romance, affection, and intimacy but replete with misgivings, anonymity, and guilt.

> Ted was 21 and me, 16. It was New Year's Eve and it was a swimming pool party at my rich friend's house. Not sure why Ted was there but he really came on to me, even putting his arm around me in front of everyone. He'd been drinking. I wasn't ready for that but I liked it. Real nervous. New Year's

Day, every time Ted looked at me I looked away because I thought it was obvious that we had had sex. I know I was an asshole and probably hurt him. It did clarify things for me. It didn't feel like I was cheating on [my girlfriend] Beth because the sex felt so different, so right. (Savin-Williams, 1995)

A gay youth may have genital contact with another boy without ever kissing him because to do so would be too meaningful. Remafedi (1990) found this escape from intimacy to be very damaging: "Without appropriate opportunities for peer dating and socialization, gay youth frequently eschew intimacy altogether and resort to transient and anonymous sexual encounters with adults" (p. 1173). One consequence is the increased risk for contracting sexually transmitted diseases, including HIV. This is particularly risky for youths who turn to prostitution to meet their intimacy needs (Coleman, 1989).

When youths eventually match their erotic and intimacy needs, they may be surprised with the results. This was Jacob's experience (Sears, 1991) when he fell in love with Warren, an African American senior who also sang in the choir. Sex quickly evolved into "an emotional thing." Jacob explained: "He got to the point of telling me he loved me. That was the first time anybody ever said anything like that. It was kind of hard to believe that *even after sex* there are really feelings" (p. 127).

Equally common, however, especially among closeted youths, is that lesbian, bisexual, and gay teens may experience a poverty of intimacy in their lives and considerable social and emotional isolation. One youth, Grant, enjoyed occasional sex with a star football player, but he was devastated by the subsequent exclusion the athlete meted out to him: "We would see each other and barely speak but after school we'd see each other a lot. He had his image that he had to keep up and, since it was rumored that I was gay, he didn't want to get a close identity with me" (Sears, 1991, p. 330).

Largely because of negative peer prohibitions and the lack of social support and recognition, same-sex romances that are initiated have difficulty flourishing. Irwin met Benji in the eighth grade and was immediately attracted to him (Sears, 1991). They shared interests in music and academics and enjoyed long conversations, playing music, and riding in the countryside. Eventually, their attractions for each other were expressed and a romantic, sexual relationship began. Although Irwin was in love with Benji, their relationship soon ended because it was no match for the social pressures and personal goals that conflicted with Irwin being in a same-sex relationship.

Georgina's relationship with Kay began dramatically with intense feelings that were at times ambivalent for both of them. At one point she overheard Kay praying, "Dear Lord, forgive me for the way I am" (Sears, 1991, p. 333). Georgina's parents demanded that she end her "friendship" with Kay. Georgina told classmates they were just "good friends" and began dating boys as a cover. Despite her love for Kay, the relationship ended when Georgina's boyfriend told her that no one liked her because she hung around "that dyke, Kay." In retrospect, Georgina wished: "If everybody would have accepted everybody, I would have stayed with Kay" (p. 334).

Given this situation, lesbian, bisexual, and gay youths in same-sex relationships may place unreasonable and ultimately destructive demands on each other. For example, they may expect that the relationship will resolve all fears of loneliness and isolation and validate all aspects of their personal identity (Browning, 1987).

# A Success Story

A vivid account of how a same-sex romantic relationship can empower a youth is depicted in the seminal autobiography of Aaron Fricke (1981), *Reflections of a Rock Lobster*. He fell in love with a classmate, Paul.

> With Paul's help, I started to challenge all the prejudice I had encountered during 16 ½ years of life. Sure, it was scary to think that half my classmates might hate me if they knew my secret, but from Paul's example I knew it was possible to one day be strong and face them without apprehension. (p. 44)

Through Paul, Aaron became more resilient and self-confident.

> His strengths were my strengths. . . . I realized that my feelings for him were unlike anything I had felt before. The sense of camaraderie was familiar from other friendships; the deep spiritual love I felt for Paul was new. So was the openness, the sense of communication with another. (p. 45)

Life gained significance. He wrote poems. He planned a future. He learned to express both kindness and strength. Aaron was in love, with another boy.
    But no guidelines or models existed on how best to express these feelings.

> Heterosexuals learn early in life what behavior is expected of them. They get practice in their early teens having crushes, talking to their friends about their feelings, going on first dates and to chaperoned parties, and figuring out their feelings. Paul and I hadn't gotten all that practice; our relationship was formed without much of a model to base it on. It was the first time either of us had been in love like this and we spent much of our time just figuring out what that meant for us. (p. 46)

Eventually, after a court case that received national attention, Aaron won the right to take Paul to the senior prom as his date. This victory was relatively minor compared to the self-respect, authenticity, and pride in being gay that their relationship won for each of them.

# Final Reflections

As a clinical and developmental psychologist, I find it disheartening to observe our culture ignoring and condemning sexual-minority youth. One consequence is that myths and stereotypes are perpetuated that interfere with or prevent youths from developing intimate same-sex relationships with those to whom they are erotically and emotionally attracted. Separating passion from affection, engaging in sex with strangers in impersonal and sometimes unsafe places, and finding alienation rather than intimacy in those relationships are not conducive to psychological health. In one study the most common reason given for initial suicide attempts by lesbians and gay men was relationship problems (Bell & Weinberg, 1978).

A youth's limited ability to meet other bisexual, lesbian, and gay adolescents compounds a sense of isolation and alienation. Crushes may develop on "unknowing friends, teachers, and peers. These are often cases of unrequited love with the youth never revealing their true feelings" (Gibson, 1989, pp. 3–131).

Sexual-minority youths need the validation of those around them as they attempt to develop a personal integrity and to discover those similar to themselves. How long can gay, bisexual, and lesbian adolescents maintain their charades before they encounter difficulty separating the pretensions from the realities? Many "use" heterosexual dating to blind themselves and others. By so doing they attempt to disconfirm to themselves the growing encroachment of their homoerotic attractions while escaping derogatory name calling and gaining peer status and prestige. The incidence of heterosexual sex and relationships in the adolescence of gay men and lesbians attests to these desires.

Future generations of adolescents will no doubt find it easier to establish same-sex relationships. This is due in part to the dramatic increase in the visibility that adult same-sex relationships have received during the last few years. Domestic partnership ordinances in several cities and counties, victories for spousal equivalency rights in businesses, court cases addressing adoption by lesbian couples and challenges to marriage laws by several male couples, the dramatic story of the life partnership of Karen Thompson and Sharon Kowalski, and the "marriage" of former Mr. Universe Bob Paris to male Supermodel Rod Jackson raise public awareness of same-sex romantic relationships. Even Ann Landers (1992) is spreading the word. In a recent column, an 18-year-old gay teen from Santa Barbara requested that girls quit hitting on him because, as he explained, "I have a very special friend who is a student at the local university . . . and [we] are very happy with each other" (p. 2B).

A decade after Aaron Fricke fought for and won the right to take his boyfriend to the prom, a dozen lesbian, gay, and bisexual youths in the Detroit-Ann Arbor area arranged to have their own prom. Most felt excluded from the traditional high school prom, which they considered "a final, bitter postscript to painful years of feeling left out" (Bruni, 1992, p. 10A). Seventeen-year-old Brenda said, "I want to feel rich for one moment. I want to feel all glamorous, just for one night" (Bruni, 1992, p. 10A). Going to the "Fantasy" prom was a celebration that created a sense of pride, a connection with other sexual-minority teens, and a chance to dance—"two girls together, unguarded and unashamed, in the middle of a room filled with teenagers just like them" (Bruni, 1992, p. 10A). One year later, I attended this prom with my life partner and the number of youths in attendance had increased sixfold.

We need to listen to youths such as Aaron, Diane, Sadie, Georgina, and Picano's narrator, to hear their concerns, insights, and solutions. Most of all, we need to end the invisibility of same-sex romantic relationships. It is easily within our power to enhance the well-being of millions of youths, including "Billy Joe," a character in a famous Bobbie Gentry song. If Billy Joe had seen an option to a heterosexual life style, he might have considered an alternative to ending his life by jumping off the Tallahatchie Bridge.

## ▼ ENDNOTES ▼

1. Portions of this chapter were previously presented in Savin-Williams (1994).

2. The causal pathway, however, is unclear (Savin-Williams, 1990). That is, being in a same-sex romance may build positive self-regard, but it may also be true that those with high self-esteem are more likely to form love relationships and to stay in them.

## ▼ REFERENCES ▼

Anderson, D. (1987). Family and peer relations of gay adolescents. In S. C. Geinstein (Ed.), *Adolescent psychiatry: Developmental and clinical studies: Vol. 14* (pp. 162–178). Chicago: The University of Chicago Press.

Bell, A. P., & Weinberg, M. S. (1978). *Homosexualities: A study of diversity among men and women.* New York: Simon & Schuster.

Bowlby, J. (1973). *Attachment and loss: Vol. 2. Separation.* New York: Basic Books.

Browning, C. (1987). Therapeutic issues and intervention strategies with young adult lesbian clients: A developmental approach. *Journal of Homosexuality, 14,* 45–52.

Bruni, F. (1992, May 22). A prom night of their own to dance, laugh, reminisce. *Detroit Free Press,* pp. 1A, 10A.

Coleman, E. (1989). The development of male prostitution activity among gay and bisexual adolescents. *Journal of Homosexuality, 17,* 131–149.

Curtis, W. (Ed.). (1988). *Revelations: A collection of gay male coming out stories.* Boston: Alyson.

D'Augelli, A. R. (1991). Gay men in college: Identity processes and adaptations. *Journal of College Student Development, 32,* 140–146.

Fricke, A. (1981). *Reflections of a rock lobster: A story about growing up gay.* Boston: Alyson.

Gable, D. (1992, June 2). "Life" story looks at roots of homophobia. *USA Today,* p. 3D.

Gibson, P. (1989). Gay male and lesbian youth suicide. In M. R. Feinleib (Ed.), *Report of the secretary's task force on youth suicide, Vol. 3: Prevention and interventions in youth suicide (3-110–3-142).* Rockville, MD: U.S. Department of Health and Human Services.

Gundlach, R. H., & Riess, B. F. (1968). Self and sexual identity in the female: A study of female homosexuals. In B. F. Riess (Ed.), *New directions in mental health* (pp. 205–231). New York: Grunet Stratton.

Harry, J., & DeVall, W. B. (1978). *The social organization of gay males.* New York: Praeger.

Hazan, C., & Shaver, P. (1987). Romantic love conceptualized as an attachment process. *Journal of Personality and Social Psychology, 52,* 511–524.

Herdt, G., & Boxer, A. (1993). *Children of horizons: How gay and lesbian teens are leading a new way out of the closet.* Boston: Beacon.

Herold, E. S. (1979). Variables influencing the dating adjustment of university students. *Journal of Youth and Adolescence, 8,* 73–79.

Heron, A. (Ed.). (1983). *One teenager in ten.* Boston: Alyson.

Hetrick, E. S., & Martin, A. D. (1987). Developmental issues and their resolution for gay and lesbian adolescents. *Journal of Homosexuality, 14,* 25–44.

Isay, R. A. (1989). *Being homosexual: Gay men and their development.* New York: Avon.

Landers, A. (1992, May 26). Gay teen tired of advances from sexually aggressive girls. *Detroit Free Press,* p. 2B.

Malyon, A. K. (1981). The homosexual adolescent: Developmental issues and social bias. *Child Welfare, 60,* 321–330.

Norton, J. L. (1976). The homosexual and counseling. *Personnel and Guidance Journal, 54,* 374–377.

Picano, F. (1985). *Ambidextrous.* New York: Penguin.

Price, J. H. (1982). High school students' attitudes toward homosexuality. *Journal of School Health, 52,* 469–474.

Remafedi, G. (1987a). Adolescent homosexuality: Psychosocial and medical implications. *Pediatrics, 79,* 331–337.

Remafedi, G. (1987b). Male homosexuality: The adolescent's perspective. *Pediatrics, 79,* 326–330.

Remafedi, G. (1990). Fundamental issues in the care of homosexual youth. *Adolescent Medicine, 74,* 1169–1179.

Roesler, T., & Deisher, R. (1972). Youthful male homosexuality. *Journal of the American Medical Association, 219,* 1018–1023.

Saghir, M. T., & Robins, E. (1973). *Male and female homosexuality.* Baltimore: Williams & Wilkins.

Sanders, G. (1980). Homosexualities in the Netherlands. *Alternative Lifestyles, 3,* 278–311.

Savin-Williams, R. C. (1990). *Gay and lesbian youth: Expressions of identity.* New York: Hemisphere.

Savin-Williams, R. C. (1994). Dating those you can't love and loving those you can't date. In R. Montemayor, G. R. Adams, & T. P. Gullotta (Eds.), *Personal relationships during adolescence: Vol. 6. Advances in adolescent development* (pp. 196–215). Newbury Park, CA: Sage.

Savin-Williams, R. C. (1995). *Sex and sexual identity among gay and bisexual males.* Manuscript in preparation, Cornell University, Ithaca, NY.

Scarf, M. (1987). *Intimate partners: Patterns in love and marriage.* New York: Random House.

Schafer, S. (1976). Sexual and social problems of lesbians. *Journal of Sex Research, 12,* 50–69.

Sears, J. T. (1991). *Growing up gay in the South: Race, gender, and journeys of the spirit.* New York: Harrington Park Press.

Silverstein, C. (1981). *Man to man: Gay couples in America.* New York: William Morrow.

Skipper, J. K., Jr., & Nass, G. (1966). Dating behavior: A framework for analysis and an illustration. *Journal of Marriage and the Family, 27,* 412–420.

Spada, J. (1979). *The Spada report: The newest survey of gay male sexuality.* New York: New American Library.

Stanley, J. P., & Wolfe, S. J. (Eds.). (1980). *The coming out stories.* New York: Persephone.

Troiden, R. R., & Goode, E. (1980). Variables related to the acquisition of a gay identity. *Journal of Homosexuality, 5,* 383–392.

Weinberg, M., & Williams, C. J. (1974). *Male homosexuals: Their problems and adaptations.* New York: Penguin.

*Chapter 8*

▼

# PSYCHOSOCIAL OUTCOMES OF VERBAL AND PHYSICAL ABUSE AMONG LESBIAN, GAY, AND BISEXUAL YOUTHS

---

Ritch C. Savin-Williams
&
Kenneth M. Cohen[1]

*Despite the increasing visibility of lesbian, gay, and bisexual individuals in North American culture, the predominant assumption among clinicians, educators, and policy makers is that same-sex attractions are the province solely of adulthood and not of childhood and adolescence. This erroneous understanding is particularly consequential because gay, bisexual, and lesbian youths are disproportionately at risk for stressors that are injurious to themselves and others. In some cases, the threat for youths is not merely their mental health but their very lives.*

## STRESSORS IN THE LIVES OF LESBIAN, BISEXUAL, AND GAY YOUTHS

A "fact sheet" published by the Center for Population Options (1992) summarized the difficulties faced by bisexual, gay, and lesbian youths:

> Lesbian, gay and bisexual adolescents face tremendous challenges to growing up physically and mentally healthy in a culture that is almost uniformly anti-homosexual. Often, these youth face an increased risk of medical and psychosocial problems, caused not by their sexual orientation, but by society's extremely negative reaction to it. Gay, lesbian and bisexual youth face rejection, isolation, verbal harassment and physical violence at home, in school and in religious institutions. Responding to these pressures, many lesbian, gay and bisexual young people engage in an array of risky behaviors. (p. 1)

Martin and Hetrick (1988) reviewed the primary stressors in the lives of sexual-minority youths who sought the services of the Hetrick-Martin Institute (HMI) in New York City.[2] The youths, most of whom are African American or Latino/a, often felt discounted and isolated from family members, peers, and religious, educational, and social institutions. A recurring theme was the belief that they must remain hidden and invisible; their lives should be compartmentalized into public and private domains. Many youths feared that family and friends would discover their homosexuality and that they would consequently be expelled from their home or become the victims of violence.

Gay, lesbian, and bisexual youths experience unique burdens in their lives that are directly related to their sexual behavior and identity. Several early studies illustrated this point. For example, Roesler and Deisher (1972) found that the major problems reported by 60 gay and bisexual male youths were their perceived need to keep their homosexuality a secret and their belief that they were rejected by society because of their sexuality. According to Rotheram-Borus, Rosario, and Koopman (1991), gay and bisexual male youths often feel vulnerable due to "issues of disclosing or being discovered by family or friends, reactions by others to their homosexuality, and chronic stress associated with their homosexuality" (p. 191). Their investigation, conducted with HMI African American and Hispanic youths, reported that the most stressful events the youths faced were coming out to others, having their sexual orientation discovered by others, and being ridiculed because of their homosexuality. The youths felt that they had little control over the reactions of others: Would they be rejected or neglected? Ridiculed or assaulted? Raped or sexually abused? Research that addresses verbal and physical abuse and associated psychosocial outcomes among gay, lesbian, and bisexual youths is reviewed in the present chapter.

Several methodological flaws in the studies reviewed warrant consideration before a full immersion into the topic is begun. For example, all investigations include research samples that are not representative of bisexual, gay, and lesbian youth. This is an unfortunate by-product of conducting research with a population of individuals who are hidden, in denial, or as yet unaware of the meaning of their same-sex attractions. The vast majority of youths who will *eventually* identify as lesbian, bisexual, or gay seldom embrace these socially ostracized labels during adolescence and thus would never agree to participate in scientific research. Those who do are often in an urban youth-serving agency, come into contact with the legal system, or are members of college campus organizations. Consequently, the studies reported in this chapter are composed of a nonrepresentative (e.g., urban, help seeking, or college activists) fraction of the gay, bisexual, and lesbian youth population.

Lesbian, gay, and bisexual youths who are most willing to participate in research studies are often those who are suffering most from physical, psychological, and social stressors. As such, mental health providers, educators, and researchers may improperly regard all such youths as weak, vulnerable adolescents who are running away from home, prostituting themselves, abusing drugs, and attempting suicide. In reality, the vast majority of sexual-minority youths cope well with their daily, chronic stressors and develop into healthy individuals who make significant contributions to their culture.[3]

Research conducted to date explores the lives and stressors of gays and bisexual males, and not of lesbians and bisexual females. Similar to many other areas of our culture, this literature reflects the male bias of scientific research. In addition, research indicates that gay and bisexual male youths are more likely than lesbian and bisexual female teenagers to externalize their stress, thus increasing their visibility, and that female teenagers generally face their nontraditional sexual identity options later in life, usually after adolescence (see Savin-Williams, 1990). The latter finding may account for the apparent greater difficulty researchers report in recruiting lesbian adolescents for research purposes; in adolescence there are fewer lesbian youths who have identified their sexual identity to themselves and/or to others.

One common theme frequently identified in research and clinical accounts is the chronic stress that is often created by peers and family members through their verbal and physical abuse of lesbian, bisexual, and gay adolescents. In the following sections, the harassment and abuse that threaten a lesbian, bisexual, or gay youth's well-being are reviewed. Although this abuse is often associated with a number of problematic psychosocial outcomes, such as school-related problems, running away from home, conflict with the law, substance abuse, prostitution, and suicide, social scientists have not yet established the causal link between these stressors and outcomes.

## VERBAL AND PHYSICAL ABUSE

A significant number of sexual-minority youths report that they have been verbally and physically assaulted, robbed, raped, or sexually abused by family members and peers (DeStefano, 1988; Martin & Hetrick, 1988; National Gay and Lesbian Task Force, 1982; Remafedi, 1987a, 1987b; Rotheram-Borus et al., 1991). D'Augelli (1992) noted the prevalence of violence inflicted on gay men and lesbians on college campuses. One half to three quarters of those questioned reported that they had been the victim of verbal or physical abuse. The most frequent abusers were fellow students and roommates. Surprisingly, close to one third of reported incidents involved abusers who were faculty, staff, or administrators.

In studies conducted with ethnic-minority youths seeking the services of the Hetrick-Martin Institute, one half reported that they had been teased and humiliated because of their homosexuality (Rosario, Rotheram-Borus, & Reid, 1992) and slightly less than one half had experienced violent physical attacks because of their sexual identity (Hunter & Schaecher, 1990). A survey of the Los Angeles County school system found that the high incidence of antigay abuse perpetrated by classmates on bisexual, lesbian, and gay youths was apparently premeditated, rather than a chance event, and was increasing dramatically (Peterson, 1989). The most frequent abusers were fellow teenagers. These findings parallel the growing antigay violence occurring on college campuses (D'Augelli, 1992).

## Peer Harassment

There are several studies of lesbian, gay, and bisexual youths that have documented the importance of peers in their lives. For example, more than one half of gay and bisexual male college students reported that the most important person in their life was a gay or lesbian friend (D'Augelli, 1991); the remainder reported parents and "straight" friends. In a study of over 300 lesbian, bisexual, and gay youths between the ages of 14 and 23 years old (Savin-Williams, 1990), the most important aspect of their sense of self-worth was having friends of the same gender.

Peer relations can, however, be a source of great dissatisfaction and distress. One of the most difficult issues reported by HMI youths was social isolation (Martin & Hetrick, 1988). Over 95% of the teenagers disclosed that they frequently felt separated and emotionally isolated from their peers because of their feelings of differentness. Over one half of the gay and bisexual male adolescents had been ridiculed because of their sexuality, usually by peers (Rotheram-Borus et al., 1991).

Those most abused were youths who failed to comply with cultural standards of gender-appropriate behaviors and roles.

> Males experience intense peer pressure to be "tough" and "macho," and females to be passive and compliant. Although social sex roles are not intrinsically related to sexual orientation, the distinction is poorly understood by most adolescents, as well as by most adults. Adolescents are frequently intolerant of differentness in others and may castigate or ostracize peers, particularly if the perceived differentness is in the arena of sexuality or sex roles. (Gonsiorek, 1988, p. 116)

The rules of socially sanctioned behavior and the consequences of nonconformity are known implicitly by most youths.

School often becomes the locale for enforcement of appropriate behavior. Failure to conform results in dire consequences. One African American male recalled the abuse he received while riding the school bus:

> Every day I was called "fag" and "nigger." People would pick fights with me. They would throw things at me like rocks and shoes. I would never go to the back of the bus. I would sit at the front in a seat by myself because nobody wanted to sit next to me. (Sears, 1991, p. 51)

One third of Remafedi's (1987b) gay and bisexual male youths were victims of physical assaults, one half of which occurred on school property. The majority reported regular verbal abuse from classmates and almost 40% had lost a friend because of their homosexuality. In Sears's (1991) study, 97% of the lesbian, bisexual, and gay Southern youths remembered negative attitudes by classmates regarding homosexuality. The majority interviewed feared being harassed, especially if they came out in high school. Only 2 of 36 youths found a group of friends who were supportive of lesbian and gay people. To protect themselves, most chose to pass as heterosexual until they graduated from high school.

This strategy is not unique to youths growing up in the South. D'Augelli's (1992) review of the empirical literature on violence against gays, bisexuals, and lesbians on college campuses revealed that 70% to 80% of such college students chose to remain hidden in order to avoid anticipated or actual harassment. Few reported these incidences to authorities, and nearly all expected to be harassed in the future. In a more detailed study, D'Augelli (1991) reported that the recognition that publicly owning homoerotic feelings places one at substantial risk for verbal and physical abuse prompted many White male college students in a conservative community to be significantly less open about their homosexuality than they wished to be. Those who were less open had more fears, and those who dreaded physical harassment experienced lower life satisfaction.

## Adult Harassment

Violence against sexual-minority youths also takes place in the home, perpetrated by adults, including family members. Martin and Hetrick (1988) found that problems within the family was the second most commonly presented complaint of the HMI youths they interviewed, ranging "from feelings of isolation and alienation that result from fear that the family will discover the adolescent's homosexuality, to actual violence and expulsion from the home" (p. 174). Nearly one half who had suffered violence because of their sexuality reported that it was enacted by someone in their family. Others were abused in institutions such as foster homes, detention centers, and churches.

After coming out to their family or being discovered as lesbian, bisexual, or gay, many youths are "rejected, mistreated, or become the focus of the family's dysfunction" (Gonsiorek, 1988, p. 116). They more frequently fear retribution from fathers than from mothers (D'Augelli, 1991), in part because their relations with their mother are significantly better than those with their father (Boxer, Cook, & Herdt, 1991). As a result, youths reveal their sexual orientation earlier and more often to mothers than to fathers (see Savin-Williams, 1990); they intensely dread their father's reactions to their sexual identity. This may not be unfounded, for nearly 10% who disclosed their homoerotic desires to their father were kicked out of their home (Boxer et al., 1991).

Harassment from parents may be more harmful than verbal abuse and may become physically assaultive, including sexual abuse and rape. In a survey of 500 primarily male Black or Latino HMI youths, Hunter (1990) reported that 40% experienced violent physical attacks from adults or peers. Of those that were gay-related, the majority occurred in the family. Data from studies of male prostitutes, runaways, and homeless youths, discussed later in this chapter, confirm this home-based violence.

Physical violence in the home may also include sexual abuse. One in five youths reported being the victim of sexual abuse in Martin and Hetrick's study (1988). Similar to the pattern observed among female heterosexuals, most cases of sexual abuse of lesbian and bisexual female youths occurred in the home. Among the male youths, sexual abuse was also most likely to occur in the home, usually by an uncle or older brother, but sometimes by a father. Two of Remafedi's (1987a) 29 male subjects were victims of incest, one was abused by an older brother and the other by his stepfather and eight uncles. Heterosexually oriented sexual abuse occurs more frequently to lesbians than to gay males (Pratch, Boxer, & Herdt, 1991). Not infrequently, youths blamed themselves for the mistreatment because they felt that they must have seduced the adult or did not say "no" convincingly enough.

## Summary

Although definitive data suggesting that bisexual, lesbian, and gay youths are more frequently ridiculed and abused by peers and family members than are other subpopulations of adolescents are not available, it is clear that these youths face unique harassment because of their sexual behavior and identity. There is sufficient evidence, however, to suggest that the physical and verbal abuse that lesbian, gay, and bisexual adolescents receive can be a source of great stress to them and thus injurious to their mental health.

There are many potential consequences of peer and family harassment. Although research has not yet addressed the cause-and-effect relationship between harassment and negative outcomes, the two are clearly associated. In the following sections, we discuss some of the negative psychosocial outcomes that researchers and clinicians have associated with the verbal and physical abuse that lesbian, gay, and bisexual youths experience.

## OUTCOMES ASSOCIATED WITH PEER AND ADULT HARASSMENT

### School-Related Problems

Many of the school-related problems experienced by sexual-minority students are in response to the verbal and physical abuse they receive from peers. One adult recalled:

> In high school I was harassed to the point where it affected my studies and I was so afraid that I would do almost anything not to have to go to school. This went on in classes as well as between classes for almost four years. Some of the teachers knew about it and allowed it. Sometimes I was slapped or pushed or hit but the verbal harassment was worse than anything else. (Jay & Young, 1979, p. 701)

Forms of violence range from name-calling to "gay bashing" (physical attacks). Because much of this violence occurs in schools, school is too punishing and dangerous for many gay, lesbian, and bisexual youths to tolerate. Hunter and Schaecher (1990) noted that the consequences of peer harassment include poor school performance, truancy, and dropping out of school. Fricke (1981) recalled:

> School was merely a routine chore. I made no effort to pass any classes. My grades dropped as my weight increased. I had no friends, hardly even any acquaintances. I had hit the bottom of the ocean and I was sinking in the mud. (p. 35)

The problems described by Fricke have also been noted by counselors in mainstream schools (Price & Telljohann, 1991; Sears, 1988).

Most of the lesbian, gay, and bisexual students who attend the gay-sensitive Harvey Milk School in New York City have dropped out of other public schools, largely because of peer harassment (Martin & Hetrick, 1988). Over two thirds of the gay and bisexual male youths in another study (Remafedi, 1987a, 1987b) reported they had experienced school-related problems: Nearly 40% were truant, and 28% dropped out of school. These problems were evident in another study, in which over one half of the gay and bisexual male youths failed a grade (Rotheram-Borus et al., 1991).

Rofes (1989) and Newton and Risch (1981) observed that schools frequently fail to meet the needs of sexual-minority youths or to stop harassment because they fear the repercussions, lack the knowledge or resources, or are simply unaware. Some of the teachers and staff may be bisexual, lesbian, or gay but refuse to offer assistance because they fear they will be accused of recruiting or converting youth.

It is thus not surprising that Telljohann and Price (1993) found that relatively few (25%) youths in their sample of 120 lesbians and gays ages 14 to 21 years old claimed that they were able to talk with school counselors about their sexual identity. Telljohann and Price further discovered that less than one in five youths could even identify a person in their school who had been supportive of them. When questioned about that which would improve the quality of their school life, the youths suggested open discussion of homosexuality in classes, the availability of lesbian and gay support groups, and greater response by teachers and administrators to verbal and physical harassment.

## Runaway and Homeless Youths

There is little reliable empirical verification regarding the percentage of runaways who identify themselves as a sexual minority or the number of lesbian, gay, and bisexual youths who run away from home. The National Network of Runaway and Youth Services (1991) reported that 6% of all runaways identified themselves as gay or lesbian. Among African American and Hispanic teenage male runaways in New York City, 6% considered themselves gay or bisexual (Rotheram-Borus, Meyer-Bahlburg, et al., 1992). According to the U.S. General

Accounting Office (1989), 2% to 3% of homeless and runaway youths who sought services or assistance were reported by shelter staff to be gay, lesbian, or bisexual. Street youths, who make money from prostitution, were not counted in this percentage. As noted below, many of these youths are likely to be gay, lesbian, and bisexual teenagers.

These percentages are probably a gross underestimation because many youths are frightened to reveal their sexual identity to authorities. Indeed, investigations of runaways in specific locales have revealed that a much larger percentage of runaway and homeless youths are gay, lesbian, or bisexual (Robertson, 1989; Yates, MacKenzie, Pennbridge, & Cohen, 1988). For example, 40% of street youths in Seattle (Orion Center, 1986) and 25% to 35% of the runaway youths in Los Angeles (Kruks, 1991) identified themselves as gay, lesbian, or bisexual.

When the directionality of the question is reversed and lesbian, bisexual, and gay youths are asked if they have ever run away from home, the percentages are considerably higher. For example, nearly one half of bisexual and gay youths in one study (Remafedi, 1987a) had run away at least once; many, repeatedly. Many of the youths seeking the assistance of the Los Angeles Gay and Lesbian Community Services Center are runaways and "throwaways" (youths thrown out of the home by parents) who have had arguments and fights with their parents (Brownworth, 1992). Nearly one quarter are HIV positive. These are vulnerable youths, who frequently have good reason to run; by leaving they avoid abuse and maintain the family secret (Burnison, 1986), but they also face a world that is ready to exploit them.

> If you leave home because you've been kicked out for being gay or because you can't cope with the homophobia of your surroundings and you go to a totally different city, you are alone, isolated, on the streets, and very, very vulnerable. (Kruks, as cited in Brownworth, 1992, p. 41)

If these youths do not find programs that meet their needs within two weeks of their arrival on the street, drugs, prostitution, pregnancy, criminal activity, and HIV are likely to take them (Coleman, 1989; Peterson, 1989; Rotheram-Borus et al., 1991). For example, the National Coalition for the Homeless (1990) estimated that 12% to 20% of all homeless youths are HIV positive. Runaway youths are at very high risk because of the "overwhelming concerns about day-to-day survival [that] can overshadow interest in illness prevention" (Remafedi, 1988, p. 141).

## Conflict With the Law and Substance Abuse

Research indicates that gay, lesbian, and bisexual youths are at high risk for conflict with the law and abusing substances. One quarter to one half of gay and bisexual at-risk, urban male youths encountered trouble with the law, largely because of substance abuse, prostitution, truancy, and running away (Remafedi, 1987a; Rotheram-Borus et al., 1991). In the latter study, one in four encountered trouble with the police and one in seven had been jailed. Rosario, Hunter, and Rotheram-Borus (1992) found that these male youths reported an average of 3 conduct problems out of 13 listed in the Diagnostic and Statistical Manual of Mental Disorders (American Psychiatric Association, DSM-III-R, 3rd ed., rev., 1987), sufficient for a diagnosis of conduct disorder. Ninety-two percent of their sample had participated in at least 1 of the 13 behaviors; this prevalence rate was considerably higher than for comparable surveys of (assumed) heterosexual ethnic-minority youth.

Remafedi (1987a) reported that most of the bisexual and gay male youths he questioned had used illegal drugs, especially alcohol and marijuana; tobacco and nitrate inhalants were used by almost one half of the youths. Nearly 60% were currently abusing substances and met psychiatric criteria for substance abuse. Seventeen percent had been in a chemical dependency treatment program.

These data correspond to the number of African American and Hispanic lesbian, gay, and bisexual youths who had a drug or alcohol problem in New York City (Rosario, Hunter, & Rotheram-Borus, 1992; Rotheram-Borus et al., 1991; Rotheram-Borus, Rosario, et al., 1992). In one study of urban teenage lesbians, all had consumed alcohol and three quarters had used drugs, including almost one third who reported cocaine or crack use (Rosario, Rotheram-Borus, et al., 1992). In a sample of HMI gay and bisexual male youths, three quarters drank alcohol, over 40% smoked marijuana, one quarter used cocaine or crack, and 15% took hallucinogens during their lifetime (Rotheram-Borus, Rosario, et al., 1992). The authors noted that substance use was considerably higher for their sample than among national surveys: "the lifetime prevalence rates for our youths are 50% higher for alcohol, three times higher for marijuana and eight times higher for cocaine/crack" (1991, p. 17). Inflated substance abuse by lesbian, gay, and bisexual youths may be indicative of the high stress they experience because of their sexual orientation, minority status, and poverty. It may also reflect the reality that for many youths of both sexes, the bar subculture, with its emphasis on alcohol, has been a main entry into adult lesbian and gay communities.

Although there is little documentation regarding the reasons bisexual, lesbian, and gay youths use illegal substances and engage in criminal activity, they abuse drugs and commit crimes for many of the same reasons as do heterosexual youths (e.g., peer pressure and hedonism), as well as for reasons specific to their sexual identity. The latter include attempts to fog an increasing awareness that they are not heterosexual, to defend against the painful realization that being lesbian or gay means a difficult life lies ahead, and to take revenge against parents and society for rejecting them (Hammond, 1986).

## Prostitution

Coleman's (1989) extensive review of the empirical and clinical literature on prostitution among male adolescents revealed that the vast majority (at least two thirds) of male prostitutes are gay or bisexual. Some boys are situational prostitutes while others make a living from prostitution. The professional "call boys" and "kept boys" frequently work gay urban areas and are the most gay-identified, usually with a well-integrated sense of their sexual identity. These youths are often from a middle-class background and are sufficiently physically attractive to support their prostitution business. Below them in status are "street hustlers," "bar boys," and "prison punks," most of whom come from lower socioeconomic backgrounds and are conflicted about their sexual identification.

According to Coleman, many of those who sell their bodies begin doing so in their early teenage years. Among HMI gay and bisexual male youths in New York City, almost one third reported that they had exchanged money or drugs for sex at some point in their lives (Rotheram-Borus, Rosario, et al., 1992). Eventually, most drop out of school, use drugs and alcohol, and run away from home or are thrown out by their family because of their sexual orientation. Many of their parents are heavy alcohol and drug users. Consistent with their family pattern, 20% to 40% of prostitutes also abuse drugs (including heroin) and alcohol. They run away from home to escape a family situation that is frequently chaotic and intolerable and where they feel misunderstood, unwanted, and rejected. One in two youths who sell their body stated that they had been physically abused or raped. Most said they had been coerced into having unwanted sex at some point in their lives. One half had been treated for at least one sexually transmitted disease, and most were at high risk for HIV infection.

Those who become street hustlers face a burdensome life. In Minneapolis, 75% of male street hustler youths are gay, with a history of dropping out of school, substance abuse, homelessness, and running away from home (Freiberg, 1985). They view themselves as "sluts and whores," have low self-esteem, and want to discontinue hustling but see no other option. In dire need of money, they believe that they have no alternative except to mug others or prostitute themselves. Most left home because they were thrown out by their parents; however, by leaving home they did not, thereby, escape violence, sexual abuse, and drugs.

Many male street hustlers are victims of rape and exploitation (Groth & Birnbaum, 1979). They face the trauma of male-male rape and are seldom taken seriously by authorities. Thus, they infrequently report the crime, often feel "less of a man," and experience physical, emotional, and psychological problems.

Data on adolescent female-female rape and young lesbian prostitution are seldom reported, although similar to many heterosexual women, young lesbians are sexually abused and raped by men (Rothblum, 1990). Rosario, Rotheram-Borus, et al. (1992) reported that 5 of 20 Hispanic and African American New York City lesbian adolescents had exchanged sex for drugs or money. The rate of prostitution among other samples of lesbian adolescents is unknown.

Many youths report that they became prostitutes in order to survive and to escape physical, sexual, and emotional abuse in their homes and schools. The money helped them become independent from their families; for some, prostitution was a source of excitement and adventure in an otherwise dreary life. On closer examination, it is also clear that many youths turned to prostitution to meet non-sexual needs, such as to be taken care of or to receive affection and, for others, to help them cope with their homosexuality. Among their fellow prostitutes, they found camaraderie and kinship that substituted for the neglect or rejection they received from their biological family and peers.

## SUICIDE: A SPECIAL CASE

The suicide of a gay person—any gay person—is ultimately no different than the murder of a gay person. . . . A society that forces a gay person into suicide by making life unbearable and ugly, by attempting to show to us that we are sick and evil and unworthy of life, and conspires to eliminate all of us from the world—by our own hands if necessary—is a society that engages in mass coercive murder. Suicide in the gay community is not a personal isolated action. It is the most pernicious strategy yet developed to achieve a genocidal end. (Rofes, 1983, p. 148)

## Empirical Studies of Gay and Lesbian Suicide

In response to the growing realization that adolescents are at high risk for suicide, the U.S. Department of Health and Human Services (1989) commissioned the *Report of the Secretary's Task Force on Youth Suicide.* A review of the limited empirical literature led one of the Report's authors, Gibson (1989), to conclude that gay and lesbian youth represent 30% of all adolescent suicides and are two to three times more likely to make a suicide attempt than their heterosexual peers. Gibson reported that suicide is the number one cause of death among lesbian, gay, and bisexual youths and that one of the primary culprits "is a society that discriminates against and stigmatizes homosexuals while failing to recognize that a substantial number of its youth has a gay or lesbian orientation" (1989, pp. 3–110).

A controversy emerged following the publication of the report and the speedy repudiation of it by the administration of George Bush in response to conservative and religious opposition (Maguen, 1991). It has long been recognized, however, that adult gay men and lesbians are at considerable risk for suicide. Although early studies seldom included youth, some of these investigations are reviewed below because they established that individuals who experience homoerotic attractions are at high risk for suicide. For example, Saghir and Robins (1973) found that about 10% of gay men (compared to none of the heterosexual men) and lesbians (compared to 5% of heterosexual women) had made a suicide attempt. Other research supported these findings (e.g., Climent, Ervin, Rollins, Plutchik, & Batinelli, 1977).

Bell and Weinberg (1978) observed that between 24% and 41% of Black and White gay men and lesbians had seriously considered or attempted suicide. Almost one half of those who attempted suicide reported that their despair was related to the difficulty they had accepting their homosexuality and interacting with others because of their sexuality.

Jay and Young (1979) depicted the irrefutable pain and desperation engendered in growing up gay or lesbian. They found nearly 40% of lesbians and gay men had seriously considered or attempted suicide. Of these, one third of the lesbians and one half of the gay men stated that the cause was associated with their homosexuality. One woman wrote:

During my first years of coming out I considered suicide often enough not to be frightened by it. I knew how I would do it. There were times that acknowledging my homosexuality was so painful that suicide seemed an alternative. (p. 729)

It is not our intent to consider the adult suicide research in depth but to illustrate the substantial extent to which suicide and suicidal ideation have been present in lesbian and gay communities. The percentages are remarkably consistent across studies: Between 25% and 40% of individuals with homoerotic attractions have seriously considered or attempted suicide.

Only recently have researchers begun to acknowledge the risk of suicide among lesbian and gay youth. The results are not discrepant from those of the adult investigations. While there are isolated studies dating to the early 1970s that demonstrate that sexual-minority adolescents are at high risk for suicide, they have largely been ignored by mainstream academia. For example, Roesler and Deisher (1972) found that one third of their sample of gay male youths had made a "significant" suicide attempt. Recent studies of lesbian, gay, and bisexual youths reported suicide attempts in the 20% to 40% range (Remafedi, 1987a; Remafedi, Farrow, & Deisher, 1991; Rotheram-Borus, Hunter, & Rosario, 1992; Schneider, Farberow, & Kruks, 1989). These attempted suicide rates increase for special populations of sexual-minority youth: girls and boys who report being violently assaulted have rates of 41% and 34%, respectively (Hunter, 1990); homeless and street youths average 53% (Kruks, 1991); and those seeking assistance at service agencies have a 41% rate (National Gay and Lesbian Task Force, 1982). Adolescents particularly sensitive to feeling rejected by others have rates that exceed the 20% to 40% range, as well (Schneider et al., 1989).

Remafedi and colleagues (1987a, 1991) examined the prevalence and etiology of suicidal thoughts and behaviors in populations of gay and bisexual male adolescents. One in three of such youths committed at least one intentional self-destructive act; one half of these youths made multiple attempts. Their suicide attempts frequently followed sexual milestones, such as labeling of self as gay or bisexual, or coming out to others. Remafedi et al. (1991) noted that many who had not previously attempted suicide indicated that it would be a viable option in their future. The most cited reason for attempting suicide was family problems. Summarizing their psychosocial data predicting suicide attempts, Remafedi et al. concluded: "Compared with non-attempters, attempters had more feminine gender roles and adopted a bisexual or homosexual identity at younger ages. Attempters were more likely than peers to report sexual abuse, drug abuse, and arrests for misconduct" (p. 869). The attempters came from dysfunctional families, used drugs (85% reported illicit drug use), and acted out through other antisocial behaviors (more than one half had been arrested).

Martin and Hunter, reported in Hunter and Schaecher (1990), found that one in three African American and Hispanic New York City adolescents seeking help from the Hetrick-Martin Institute had considered or attempted suicide. Nearly one half of youths who requested help from the Institute had also been subjected to violence. Of those, almost one half indicated having experienced recent suicidal ideation and about one third had attempted suicide at least once.

Schneider et al.'s (1989) study of Los Angeles White and Latino gay college men (ages 16 to 24 years old) found that over one half of the youths reported that they periodically had suicidal ideations, considered suicidal action, devised a suicide plan, or made a suicide attempt. This group was characterized as having alcoholism in the family, physical abuse from family members, no religious affiliation, and a perception that those who usually supported them rejected their homosexuality. Twenty percent of the total sample reported that they had made at least one suicide attempt; almost 1 in 10 made multiple attempts (2 to 14 times). The youngest attempt was at age 12, and one half of the youths received no treatment after their first attempt. At the time of first attempt, the youths felt hopeless, worthless, alienated, lonely, and helpless. Compared with nonsuicidal gay youths, attempters were significantly younger when they first became aware of their homoerotic attractions (8 versus 11 years old), first labeled their feelings but not themselves as gay (12 versus 14 years old), and first became involved in a same-sex romantic relationship (16 versus 18 years old). Although most attempters were aware of their same-sex attractions prior to their first suicide attempt, few had reached the point of identifying themselves as gay, felt positive about their sexual orientation, or had told others about their sexual orientation. Attempts were most likely to occur when an individual was questioning his heterosexual identity or after same-sex sexual activities. Schneider et al. concluded that "suicidal behavior in gay youths may be the product both of familial factors that predispose youths to suicidal behavior, and of social and intrapersonal stressors involved in coming to terms with an emerging homosexual identity" (p. 381).

A group of younger (aged 14 to 19 years old) and more ethnically diverse gay and bisexual male youths from New York City were studied by Rotheram-Borus, Hunter, and Rosario (1992). Almost 40% had attempted suicide; of those, one half made multiple attempts. An additional one third of the 139 youths had thought about suicide every day for at least one week. Nearly 60% reported suicidal ideation during the week prior to data collection. The attempters did not differ from nonattempters in stressful life events, but they experienced more gay-related stressors, including coming out to parents, being discovered as gay by parents or other family members, and being ridiculed for their sexual identity.

Psychiatrists who specialize in therapy with adolescent patients have speculated that the most frequent causes of suicide and suicide attempts among lesbian, bisexual, and gay adolescents are feelings of disenfranchisement, social isolation, rejection from family or peers, and self-revulsion (Kourany, 1987). The high risk among sexual-minority youth for suicidal ideation, attempts, and completions has been brought to the attention of psychiatrists (Kourany, 1987), social workers (Hunter & Schaecher, 1987), health educators (Remafedi, 1985), and therapists (Coleman & Remafedi, 1989; Rothblum, 1990). Unfortunately and tragically, few have listened.

## CONCLUSION

Youths who are known to be lesbian, gay, or bisexual receive considerable verbal and physical abuse from peers and, all too frequently, from parents and other adults. This verbal abuse and threats of physical harm are sources of great stress to them, are detrimental to their mental health, and often correlate with negative outcomes such as school-related problems, running away from home, criminal activity, substance abuse, prostitution, and suicide.

We cannot generalize these findings to all gay, bisexual, and lesbian youths, primarily because most of these youths are not "out" to themselves or to others. Thus, the youths studied to date are not a representative subset of the gay, bisexual, and lesbian youth population. Rotheram-Borus, Rosario, et al. (1992) noted: "These youths are atypical in that they have publicly disclosed their sexual preferences by seeking services at a social service agency serving homosexual youths" (p. 15). They may also be "unusual" because those most abused are frequently youths who are "cross-gendered"—they do not or cannot abide by cultural definitions of acceptable feminine and masculine behavior and, thus, do not meet cultural ideals of gender-appropriate behaviors and roles. Deviating from acceptable sex roles is particularly problematic during adolescence. Peer rejection may not be expressed directly, but it is recognized nevertheless by targeted youths.

Although research has not addressed the causal pathway between harassment and negative psychosocial outcomes, the two are clearly associated with each other. Rosario, Hunter, and Rotheram-Borus (1992) explored the linkages among emotional distress, conduct problems, alcohol and drug use, and risky sexual acts among gay and bisexual ethnic-minority male youths. In their sample, as might be expected, an increase in conduct problems was associated with increased levels of alcohol and drug usage and emotional distress. However, an increase in conduct problems was associated with a decrease in reported gay-related stress (negative reactions to coming out to others, being discovered as gay, and ridicule from others), suggesting that the youths may have desensitized themselves to these stresses by their acting-out behavior. Counter to findings with heterosexual youths, the authors did not identify a single factor that accounted for multiple problem behavior; thus, it may not be possible to simply generalize research results from heterosexual to sexual-minority youths. Little is known about "normal" developmental pathways among bisexual, lesbian, and gay youths and the ways in which they are similar and divergent from heterosexual youths (Savin-Williams, 1990). What is known is that the issue of sexual identity status is not an insignificant factor in the lives of adolescents. Rosario, Hunter, and

Rotheram-Borus (1992) noted, "The experience of being gay or bisexual in our society overwhelms any potential differences in social categories involving age, ethnicity, race, social class or geographical region of the country" (p. 19).

The variety of problematic behaviors described in this review may very well end the lives of many bisexual, lesbian, and gay youths. Running away from home, engaging in high risk sexual behavior, prostituting oneself, and abusing substances all place youths at high risk for suicide or for becoming the victim of homicide. Those who survive will face the effects of growing up in a homophobic culture throughout their lives. If their social and interpersonal worlds are replete with verbal abuse and the threat of physical harm, youths in North American culture may find it difficult to totally expunge "internalized homophobia," a term Gonsiorek (1988) used to describe lesbian, gay, and bisexual individuals' incorporation of biases against homosexuality that are prevalent in the social world. This self-hatred "presents [itself] in persons who consciously accuse themselves of being evil, second class, or inferior because of their homosexuality. They may abuse substances or engage in other self-destructive or abusive behaviors" (Gonsiorek, 1988, p. 117).

The effects of peer and family harassment may be more severe for lesbian, gay, and bisexual youths who are early adolescents or ethnic minorities because they may find it more difficult to recognize and accept their homosexuality than would older youths or White youths. Early adolescents, according to Remafedi (1987a), face several conflicts that hinder their ability to cope with being lesbian, gay, or bisexual: "emotional and physical immaturity, unfulfilled developmental needs for identification with a peer group, lack of experience, and their dependence upon parents who may be unwilling or unable to provide emotional support around the issue of homosexuality" (p. 336).

Ethnic-minority youths who are gay, lesbian, or bisexual may also be at increased risk for the detrimental effects of homosexually oriented verbal and physical abuse. Savin-Williams and Rodriguez (1993) noted three unique tasks that these youths face: (a) developing and defining both a strong gay identity and a strong ethnic identity; (b) resolving potential conflicts in allegiance, such as reference group identity within one's gay and ethnic community; and (c) reconciling both homophobia and racism (p. 94). The African American and Hispanic sexual-minority youths at the Harvey Milk School had many signs of emotional isolation, vulnerability, and depression, including:

> pervasive loss of pleasure, feelings of sadness, change of appetite, sleep disturbance, slowing of thought, lowered self-esteem with increased self-criticism and self-blame, and strongly expressed feelings of guilt and failure. Again, they repeatedly report they feel they are alone in the world, that no one else is like them, and that they have no one with whom they can confide or talk freely. (Martin & Hetrick, 1988, p. 172)

The dilemma for clinicians and other health care professionals is how best to assist sexual-minority youths. Few youths are willing to seek health care providers because they fear disclosure, humiliation, and discrimination. This may be for good reason. Gonsiorek (1988) noted that rather than the client's actual problem (e.g., feelings of rejection), his or her sexual orientation may become the focus of treatment for the clinician or agency. Because of their prejudices, staff may permit, or even encourage, discrimination and name-calling. Even if they are tolerant, they often lack the knowledge or resources to be of assistance to lesbian, bisexual, and gay youths.

Guidelines are available to assist health care providers to overcome these shortcomings (e.g., Bergstrom & Cruz, 1983; Kus, 1990; Rofes, 1989; Savin-Williams & Lenhart, 1990; Silverstein, 1991). Clinicians and researchers should support the well-being of gay, lesbian, and bisexual youths by conducting research, enacting policies, and encouraging behaviors that will help minimize the internalized homophobia, self-destructive behaviors, and homicide of our youths.

## ▼   ENDNOTES   ▼

1. An earlier version of this paper (1994) was prepared for the American Psychological Association ad hoc Subcommittee on Lesbian and Gay Youth in Schools and appeared in the *Journal of Consulting and Clinical Psychology, 62,* pp. 261–269. We thank the committee members for their comments on an earlier draft.

2. The Hetrick-Martin Institute is a New York City community agency that provides educational and social services to sexual-minority youths ages 12 to 21 years old. The Institute, which became a full social service agency in 1983, also helped found and staff the Harvey Milk School, a public alternative school for New York City youth.

3. In other publications, Savin-Williams (1990, 1995) elaborates on these points, illustrating the ways in which gay, lesbian, and bisexual youths negotiate their lives to become healthy adults.

## ▼ References ▼

American Psychiatric Association. (1987). *Diagnostic and statistical manual of mental disorders* (3rd ed., rev.). Washington, DC: Author.

Bell, A. P., & Weinberg, M. S. (1978). *Homosexualities: A study of diversity among men and women.* New York: Simon & Schuster.

Bergstrom, S., & Cruz, L. (1983). *Counseling lesbian and gay male youth: Their special lives/special needs.* Washington, DC: National Network of Runaway and Youth Services.

Boxer, A. M., Cook, J. A., & Herdt, G. (1991). Double jeopardy: Identity transitions and parent-child relations among gay and lesbian youth. In K. Pillemer & K. McCartney (Eds.), *Parent-child relations throughout life* (pp. 59–92). Hillsdale, NJ: Erlbaum.

Brownworth, V. A. (1992, March 24). America's worst-kept secret: AIDS is devastating the nation's teenagers, and gay kids are dying by the thousands. *The Advocate,* pp. 38–46.

Burnison, M. (1986, May). *Runaway youth: Lesbian and gay issues.* Paper presented at the Symposium on Gay and Lesbian Adolescents, Minneapolis, MN.

Center for Population Options. (1992). *Lesbian, gay and bisexual youth: At risk and underserved.* Washington, DC: Author.

Climent, C. E., Ervin, F. R., Rollins, A., Plutchik, R., & Batinelli, C. J. (1977). Epidemiological studies of female prisoners: IV. Homosexual behavior. *The Journal of Nervous and Mental Disease, 164,* 25–29.

Coleman, E. (1989). The development of male prostitution activity among gay and bisexual adolescents. *Journal of Homosexuality, 17,* 131–149.

Coleman, E., & Remafedi, G. (1989). Gay, lesbian, and bisexual adolescents: A critical challenge to counselors. *Journal of Counseling and Development, 68,* 36–40.

D'Augelli, A. R. (1991). Gay men in college: Identity processes and adaptations. *Journal of College Student Development, 32,* 140–146.

D'Augelli, A. R. (1992). Lesbian and gay male undergraduates' experiences of harassment and fear on campus. *Journal of Interpersonal Violence, 7,* 383–395.

DeStefano, A. M. (1988, October 7). New York teens antigay, poll finds. *Newsday,* pp. 7, 21.

Freiberg, P. (1985, November 12). Minneapolis: Help for hustlers. *The Advocate,* pp. 12–13.

Fricke, A. (1981). *Reflections of a rock lobster: A story about growing up gay.* Boston: Alyson.

Gibson, P. (1989). Gay male and lesbian youth suicide. In M. R. Feinleib (Ed.), *Report of the secretary's task force on youth suicide, Vol. 3: Prevention and interventions in youth suicide (3-110–3-142).* Rockville, MD: U.S. Department of Health and Human Services.

Gonsiorek, J. C. (1988). Mental health issues of gay and lesbian adolescents. *Journal of Adolescent Health Care, 9,* 114–122.

Groth, A. N., & Birnbaum, H. J. (1979). *Men who rape: The psychology of the offender.* New York: Plenum.

Hammond, N. (1986, May). *Chemical abuse in lesbian and gay adolescents.* Paper presented at the Symposium on Gay and Lesbian Adolescents, Minneapolis, MN.

Hunter, J. (1990). Violence against lesbian and gay male youths. *Journal of Interpersonal Violence, 5,* 295–300.

Hunter, J., & Schaecher, R. (1987). Stresses on lesbian and gay adolescents in schools. *Social Work in Education, 9,* 180–189.

Hunter, J., & Schaecher, R. (1990). Lesbian and gay youth. In M. J. Rotheram-Borus, J. Bradley, & N. Obolensky (Eds.), *Planning to live: Evaluating and treating suicidal teens in community settings* (pp. 297–316). Tulsa: University of Oklahoma Press.

Jay, K., & Young, A. (1979). *The gay report: Lesbians and gay men speak out about sexual experiences and lifestyles.* New York: Summit.

Kourany, R. F. C. (1987). Suicide among homosexual adolescents. *Journal of Homosexuality, 13,* 111–117.

Kruks, G. (1991). Gay and lesbian homeless/street youth: Special issues and concerns. *Journal of Adolescent Health Care, 12,* 515–518.

Kus, R. J. (Ed.). (1990). *Keys to caring: Assisting your gay and lesbian clients.* Boston: Alyson.

Maguen, S. (1991, September 24). Teen suicide: The government's cover-up and America's lost children. *The Advocate,* pp. 40–47.

Martin, A. D., & Hetrick, E.S. (1988). The stigmatization of the gay and lesbian adolescent. *Journal of Homosexuality, 15,* 163–183.

National Coalition for the Homeless. (1990). *Fighting to live: Homeless people with AIDS.* Washington, DC: Author.

National Gay and Lesbian Task Force. (1982). *Gay rights in the United States and Canada.* New York: Author.

National Network of Runaway and Youth Services. (1991). *To whom do they belong? Runaway, homeless and other youth in high-risk situations in the 1990s.* Washington, DC: Author.

Newton, D. E., & Risch, S. J. (1981). Homosexuality and education: A review of the issue. *The High School Journal, 64,* 191–202.

Orion Center. (1986). *Survey of street youth.* Seattle, WA: Author.

Peterson, J. W. (1989, April 11). In harm's way: Gay runaways are in more danger than ever, and gay adults won't help. *The Advocate,* pp. 8–10.

Pratch, L., Boxer, A. M., & Herdt, G. (1991). *First sexual experiences among gay and lesbian youth: Person, age, and context.* Manuscript in preparation, Northwestern University Medical School, Chicago, IL.

Price, J. H., & Telljohann, S. K. (1991). School counselors' perceptions of adolescent homosexuals. *Journal of School Health, 61,* 433–438.

Remafedi, G. J. (1985). Adolescent homosexuality: Issues for pediatricians. *Clinical Pediatrics, 24,* 481–485.

Remafedi, G. (1987a). Adolescent homosexuality: Psychosocial and medical implications. *Pediatrics, 79,* 331–337.

Remafedi, G. (1987b). Male homosexuality: The adolescent's perspective. *Pediatrics, 79,* 326–330.

Remafedi, G. J. (1988). Preventing the sexual transmission of AIDS during adolescence. *Journal of Adolescent Health Care, 9,* 139–143.

Remafedi, G., Farrow, J. A., & Deisher, R.W. (1991). Risk factors for attempted suicide in gay and bisexual youth. *Pediatrics, 87,* 869–875.

Robertson, M. J. (1989). *Homeless youth in Hollywood: Patterns of alcohol use.* Berkeley, CA: Alcohol Research Group.

Roesler, T., & Deisher, R. (1972). Youthful male homosexuality: Homosexual experience and the process of developing homosexual identity in males aged 16 to 22 years. *Journal of the American Medical Association, 219,* 1018–1023.

Rofes, E. E. (1983). *"I thought people like that killed themselves": Lesbians, gay men and suicide.* San Francisco, CA: Grey Fox.

Rofes, E. (1989). Opening up the classroom closet: Responding to the educational needs of gay and lesbian youth. *Harvard Educational Review, 59,* 444–453.

Rosario, M., Hunter, J., & Rotheram-Borus, M. J. (1992). *HIV risk acts of lesbian adolescents.* Unpublished manuscript, Columbia University.

Rosario, M., Rotheram-Borus, M. J., & Reid, H. (1992). *Personal resources, gay-related stress, and multiple problem* behaviors among gay and bisexual male adolescents. Unpublished manuscript, Columbia University.

Rothblum, E. D. (1990). Depression among lesbians: An invisible and unresearched phenomenon. *Journal of Gay & Lesbian Psychotherapy, 1,* 67–87.

Rotheram-Borus, M. J., Hunter, J., & Rosario, M. (1992). *Suicidal behavior and gay-related stress among gay and bisexual male adolescents.* Unpublished manuscript, Columbia University.

Rotheram-Borus, M. J., Meyer-Bahlburg, H. F. L., Rosario, M., Koopman, C., Haignere, C. S., Exner, T. M., Matthieu, M., Henderson, R., & Gruen, R. S. (1992). Lifetime sexual behaviors among predominantly minority male runaways and gay/bisexual adolescents in New York City. *AIDS Education and Prevention, Supplement,* 34–42.

Rotheram-Borus, M. J., Rosario, M., & Koopman, C. (1991). Minority youths at high risk: Gay males and runaways. In M. E. Colten & S. Gore (Eds.), *Adolescent stress: Causes and consequences* (pp. 181–200). New York: Aldine.

Rotheram-Borus, M. J., Rosario, M., Meyer-Bahlburg, H. F. L., Koopman, C., Dopkins, S. C., & Davies, M. (1992). *Sexual and substance use behaviors among homosexual and bisexual male adolescents in New York City.* Unpublished manuscript, Columbia University, New York.

Saghir, M. T., & Robins, E. (1973). *Male and female homosexuality.* Baltimore, MD: Williams & Wilkins.

Savin-Williams, R. C. (1990). *Gay and lesbian youths: Expressions of identity.* New York: Hemisphere.

Savin-Williams, R. C. (1994). Verbal and physical abuse as stressors in the lives of lesbian, gay male, and bisexual youths: Associations with school problems, running away, substance abuse, prostitution, and suicide. *Journal of Consulting and Clinical Psychology, 62,* 261–269.

Savin-Williams, R. C. (1995). *Sex and sexual identity among gay and bisexual males.* Unpublished manuscript, Cornell University, Ithaca, NY.

Savin-Williams, R. C., & Lenhart, R. E. (1990). AIDS prevention among gay and lesbian youth: Psychosocial stress and health care intervention guidelines. In D. G. Ostrow (Ed.), *Behavioral aspects of AIDS and other sexually transmitted diseases* (pp. 75–99). New York: Plenum.

Savin-Williams, R. C., & Rodriguez, R. G. (1993). A developmental, clinical perspective on lesbian, gay male, and bisexual youths. In T. P. Gullotta, G. R. Adams, & R. Montemayor (Eds.), *Adolescent sexuality. Advances in adolescent development, Vol. 5* (pp. 77–101). Newbury Park, CA: Sage.

Schneider, S. G., Farberow, N. L., & Kruks, G. N. (1989). Suicidal behavior in adolescent and young adult gay men. *Suicide and Life-Threatening Behavior, 19,* 381–394.

Sears, J. T. (1988, April). *Attitudes, experiences, and feelings of guidance counselors in working with homosexual students: A report on the quality of school life for Southern gay and lesbian students.* Paper presented at the American Educational Research Association Meeting, New Orleans, LA.

Sears, J. T. (1991). *Growing up gay in the South: Race, gender, and journeys of the spirit.* New York: Harrington Park Press.

Silverstein, C. (Ed.). (1991). *Gays, lesbians, and their therapists: Studies in psychotherapy.* New York: Norton.

Telljohann, S. K., & Price, J. H. (1993). A qualitative examination of adolescent homosexuals' life experiences: Ramifications for secondary school personnel. *Journal of Homosexuality, 26,* 41–56.

U.S. Department of Health and Human Services. (1989). *Report of the*

*Secretary's Task Force on Youth Suicide.* Rockville, MD: Author.

U.S. General Accounting Office. (1989). *Homelessness: Homeless and runaway youth receiving services at federally funded shelters.* Washington, DC: Author.

Yates, G., MacKenzie, R., Pennbridge, J., & Cohen, E. (1988). A risk profile comparison of runaway and non-runaway youth. *American Journal of Public Health, 78,* 820–821.

*Chapter 9*

▼

# LESBIANS, GAY MEN, AND BISEXUAL PEOPLE IN COLLEGE

## Nancy J. Evans
## &
## Anthony R. D'Augelli

*Attending college is a major life transition for lesbian, gay, and bisexual youth. While most such youths acknowledge their sexual orientation to themselves during adolescence, few have "come out" prior to enrolling in college (D'Augelli, 1991a). Typically the process of disclosing one's lesbian, gay, or bisexual identity to others starts during the college years for traditionally aged students. Older lesbian, gay, and bisexual students may also find that their experiences in college change the way they view themselves and how they choose to present themselves to others. Leaving behind a culturally defined heterosexual identity and developing a new lesbian, gay, or bisexual identity are major challenges. These processes can complicate other developmental tasks faced by college students such as career decision making, the development of satisfying interpersonal relationships, and the establishment of a personal value system. For example, Levine and Bahr (1989) found that students who were beginning to develop a strong gay or lesbian self-image but were struggling with coming out had not progressed as far as other students in developing autonomy, purpose, and mature interpersonal relationships.*

*In addition to the developmental tasks faced by all college students and the challenges related to coming to terms with their sexual orientation, lesbian, gay, and bisexual students face unique challenges that result from living in a heterosexist and homophobic society. Some of these are personal, such as maintaining self-esteem and coping with being "different"; some are interpersonal, such as establishing same-sex romantic relationships and deciding whether to come out to family; and, some are environmental, such as facing harassment, violence, and discrimination. These challenges become more difficult as soon as the young adult decides to become known as lesbian, gay, or bisexual—that is, when she or he comes out to others on campus. While campus climates vary, few present a welcoming environment for lesbian, gay, and bisexual students. Homophobia among heterosexual college students is well documented (Astin, 1993; D'Augelli & Rose, 1990).*

*While addressing diversity has become a popular issue on many college campuses, the inclusion of lesbian, gay, and bisexual people in these efforts has been slow. A recent newsletter of the National Association of Student Personnel Administrators' Network on Lesbian, Gay, and Bisexual Concerns (1993) identified only 19 institutions with task forces or offices addressing lesbian, gay, and bisexual issues (von Destinon, 1993). Negative attitudes toward lesbian, gay, and bisexual individuals have been documented among student affairs staff, including resident assistant candidates (D'Augelli, 1989b), Greek organization advisors (Hughes, 1991), and psychologists (Garnets, Hancock, Cochran, Goodchilds, & Peplau, 1991). In addition, lesbians and gay men are, for the most part, invisible in the curriculum (D'Augelli, 1991b). Only recently has sexual orientation been included on a limited basis in some campus nondiscrimination policies (Bendet, 1986).*

*This chapter examines the college years as experienced by lesbian, gay, and bisexual students. Unfortunately, little empirical research has been conducted with this population. Most of the existing research is based on samples of self-identified gay, and to a lesser extent, lesbian adults. Several studies of gay and lesbian youth have included college students in their samples, but have not emphasized the role of campus life in their adjustment (e.g., Herdt & Boxer, 1993; Savin-Williams, 1990). We discuss the personal and interpersonal issues that lesbian, gay, and bisexual students face in college, as well as the challenges they experience as a result of campus climate. We also recommend implementation of specific student service, curricular, and policy interventions to meet the needs of this student population. In addition to creating a more inclusive environment for all students, these suggestions can help prevent mental health problems for lesbian, gay, and bisexual students (D'Augelli, 1993).*

## DEVELOPMENTAL ISSUES: PERSONAL ISSUES

All college students face a number of developmental tasks precipitated by the internal processes of maturation and the environmental challenges offered by their experiences in college. According to Chickering and Reisser (1993), these "vectors of development" include developing competence, managing emotions, moving through autonomy toward interdependence, developing mature interpersonal relationships, establishing identity, developing purpose, and developing integrity. Students generally experience developmental crises related to these tasks at some point during their college years, become preoccupied with an issue, resolve it, and move to another issue. Individuals can recycle tasks, become stuck, or delay addressing tasks depending on their experiences and the cultural and environmental situations in which they find themselves. For lesbian, gay, and bisexual students, dilemmas related to sexual identity often take precedence over all other developmental tasks.

Sexual identity development is a process that evolves over time rather than a decision one makes at a particular point in time (D'Augelli, 1994). The way in which one views oneself as a sexual being and chooses to present oneself may change significantly over the lifespan, particularly for individuals who identify as lesbian, gay, or bisexual. Individuals born in this society are presumed to be heterosexual, learning the norms and expectations related to heterosexuality. Thus, developing an alternative identity requires two processes: letting go of an ingrained heterosexual identity and learning what it means to be lesbian, gay, or bisexual. Given the heterosexist and homophobic society in which we live, neither process is easy. Because the relative anonymity of the college environment presents an opportunity to redefine oneself away from family monitoring, the two tasks of exiting heterosexuality and developing a new identity become real possibilities for the first time in college.

## Identity Development

### Exiting heterosexual identity

Although many individuals are aware of their same-gender sexual orientation prior to college, it is often during their college years that they surrender their assumed heterosexual identity and identify as lesbian, gay, or bisexual (Cohen & Savin-Williams, "Coming Out," this volume; D'Augelli, 1991a; Sohier, 1985/1986; Troiden, 1989; Troiden & Goode, 1980). Lesbian, gay, and bisexual individuals go through several stages in the process of relinquishing their heterosexual identity (Levine & Evans, 1991). The first is an awareness of attraction to individuals of the same gender. This usually occurs prior to college, especially for males. Eventually, most individuals move to the next stage, which involves self-labeling as gay, lesbian, or bisexual. At this time, individuals make some tentative contacts with lesbian, gay, or bisexual communities. Often these steps are taken during the college years when students are away from families, high school peers, and home communities. The success or failure of these early efforts determines if the individual moves to other stages in which he or she becomes more comfortable identifying as a nonheterosexual person and disclosing his or her sexual orientation to others. Because of the pervasiveness of heterosexist assumptions in our society, coming out (i.e., revealing one's sexual orientation to others) is a lifelong process.

### Developing a lesbian, gay, or bisexual identity

In addition to letting go of a heterosexual identity by acknowledging to self and others one's homoeroticism, the lesbian, gay, or bisexual person must also determine what it means to assume a new sexual identity. Because visible lesbian, gay, and bisexual role models are rare and cultural stereotypes are overwhelmingly negative, this can be a difficult process. It is often in the context of lesbian, gay, and bisexual communities found on college campuses that this new self-definition takes place. Internalized myths about lesbian, gay, and bisexual people must be unlearned, and an individualized identity must be created. Other aspects of the self, including values, beliefs, interests, and skills, must be examined in light of this new identity. Thus, the final stage of development, identity integration, involves incorporating a lesbian, gay, or bisexual identity into a total sense of self. This self-definition evolves over time and may be differentially revealed in various settings and circumstances.

Differences have been found in the identity development processes of lesbians and gay men. Most reflect the distinct socialization experiences of women and men in our society. Lesbians exhibit more variability than gay men in the age at which they first experience attractions to other women, whereas gay men become aware of their attractions, act on them, and disclose their orientation to others earlier than do lesbians (Garnets & Kimmel, 1991). To explain these findings, Henderson (1984) suggested that women's sexual orientation may be more variable than men's and its expression may be more tied to particular relationships; alternatively, women may be more influenced by gender role expectations and find it more difficult to relinquish their heterosexual identities. (See further discussion in Golden, this volume.) Because of these differences, gay men are more likely to be further along in their process of identity development and more likely to be visible on college campuses.

Bisexual women and men have been generally ignored by researchers (Fox, 1995; Paul, this volume). Some have suggested that bisexuality is the result of confusion about sexual orientation (Zinik, 1985). Others have observed that adolescents who are lesbian or gay more readily label themselves bisexual to avoid stigma and harassment. Because bisexually identified people are treated with ambivalence by both the heterosexual and the gay and lesbian communities, they often have a more difficult time acknowledging and disclosing their sexual orientation than do lesbians and gay men. Although bisexual identity development seems to occur in stages similar to those experienced by gay men and lesbians, wide variation exists in the timing and ordering of sexual experiences resulting in a bisexual identification (Shuster, 1987). Bisexual students are often ignored when issues concerning sexual orientation are raised. As a result of these factors, bisexual students have a particularly difficult time establishing their identity and finding support on college campuses.

## Mental Health Issues

Comprehensive reviews of the research indicate that emotional adjustment and mental illness are not related to sexual orientation (Gonsiorek, 1991, this volume). Nonetheless, the oppression, stigmatization, hostility, and rejection experienced by lesbians, gay men, and bisexuals can cause mental health problems and can exacerbate other psychological problems they may have. These problems often become especially acute during the college years. Some of the more critical mental health issues are reviewed below (for others, see Savin-Williams & Cohen, "Psychosocial Outcomes," this volume).

## Suicide

Suicide and self-destructive behaviors are serious problems among sexual-minority college students. Gibson's (1989) review suggested that lesbian and gay youth are two to three times more likely than heterosexual youth to attempt suicide and that 30% of all youth suicides may be committed by gays or lesbians. A survey of 1,900 lesbians between the ages of 17 and 24 revealed that 59% were at risk for suicide (National Lesbian and Gay Health Foundation, 1987). In another study, 19% of gay college students had made suicide attempts (Schneider, Farberow, & Kruks, 1989). The students reported feeling hopelessness, worthlessness, alienation, and pain at the time of their suicide attempts. Many attempts were related to conflict about sexual orientation.

## Substance abuse

Substance abuse is also common among lesbian and gay youth. Remafedi (1987) found that over 80% of the gay and bisexual youths aged 15 to 19 he studied used drugs, and almost 60% of them met the criteria to be classified as abusers. Among young lesbians, 8% reported that alcohol use was a problem, and 6% noted problems with drug use (National Lesbian and Gay Health Foundation, 1987). As many as 30% of the lesbian, gay, and bisexual population are estimated to be alcoholic compared to 10% of the heterosexual population (Nardi, 1982).

## AIDS

Another issue that has greatly affected lesbian and gay communities is the impact of the HIV epidemic. In D'Augelli's (1991a) study of the mental health problems of gay college men, 92% reported being worried about AIDS. Although young gay men currently in college have fewer sexual partners and engage in safer sex practices more consistently than older cohorts, they nonetheless face difficult issues of discussing safer sex with potential partners, deciding about HIV testing, and maintaining safer sex patterns over time. Young gay men particularly struggle with whether to be tested for the HIV virus, fearing that they will be unable to cope with the knowledge that they are HIV positive. Although seroprevalence rates among college students are relatively low, fear of HIV infection and its related stresses are powerful factors in the lives of young gay and bisexual men (D'Augelli, 1991a). Members of lesbian and gay communities must also cope with the impact of seeing friends and acquaintances become ill and die. Grief and depression are common reactions to this reality (Martin, 1989).

### Depression and anxiety

Young lesbians and gay men report high levels of emotional distress. Emotional problems led 72% of the gay and bisexual teenagers in Remafedi's (1987) study to seek help from a psychologist or psychiatrist. In D'Augelli's (1991a) study of gay college men, over 60% reported having trouble with their emotions and experiencing depression, and 77% noted that they felt anxious. Lesbians surveyed by the National Lesbian and Gay Health Foundation (1987) reported similar concerns, though the prevalence rate was considerably lower.

Several researchers have found evidence that positive psychological adjustment and self-esteem are associated with high levels of sexual identity development. Miranda and Storms (1989) reported that self-labeling and self-disclosure as lesbian, gay, or bisexual were related to emotional well-being. In a study of gay men and lesbians between the ages of 18 and 46, Walters and Simoni (1993) also found that acceptance of one's gay or lesbian identity was positively associated with self-esteem. Schneider and colleagues (1989) reported that only 2 of 21 gay young adults who reported serious suicide attempts indicated feeling good about being gay before the attempt, and only 4 of the men had disclosed their sexual orientation to a significant person in their life.

### Differentness

Recognizing the stressors associated with identity formation, D'Augelli (1993) noted, "It is not surprising that the most common phenomenological experience of being a young lesbian or gay man is a profound sense of difference" (p. 250). Lesbian, gay, and bisexual students are immersed in heterosexually oriented college environments. Activities, social functions, and educational programs are nearly exclusively geared to a heterosexual audience, while the issues and needs of lesbian, gay, and bisexual students are ignored. Isolation resulting from a lack of role models, difficulty in finding a peer group, and nonacceptance by the heterosexual community contribute significantly to the challenges lesbian and gay college students experience in developing a positive identity.

## Other Aspects of Development

Similar to other college students, lesbian, gay, and bisexual youths experience developmental challenges that come with establishing one's place in the adult world. Key among these are lifestyle and career decisions as well as establishing a value and belief system. For lesbian, gay, and bisexual students, however, the decisions made are influenced by their sexual orientation.

### Career issues

Many factors complicate the career decision-making of lesbian, gay, and bisexual students. Hetherington (1991) suggested that the stage of lesbian, gay, or bisexual identity development in which students find themselves affects their thinking about future careers. Students who are in the initial stages of self-identifying and coming out to others are so immersed in this process that they may not be able to focus on choosing an appropriate career. Students who have come out but have not yet fully explored their sexual identity may have a narrow view of their career options. Only when students have reached the integration stage and are comfortable with their sexual orientation can they truly begin to define the role that they want their career to play in their lives. Because many students do not reach this stage while in college, career decision-making is often incomplete or inadequate. Etringer, Hillerbrand, and Hetherington (1990) found that gay men expressed a high degree of uncertainty and dissatisfaction with their career choice. Lesbians, on the other hand, were more certain about their choices and more satisfied with them. Hetherington (1991) suggested that this finding may reflect lesbians' knowledge that they will have to be self-supporting.

The dearth of role models is a significant problem for lesbian and gay youth in choosing careers. Pope, Ehlen, and Mueller (1985) referred to lesbians, gay men, and bisexuals as the invisible minority in the world of work. When students do not see sexual-minority individuals in a wide variety of professions, they are very likely to assume that particular professions are not open to them. Botkin and Daly (1987) asked 120 college students to list jobs most interesting to lesbians and gay men as well as to heterosexual women and men. Photographer, interior decorator, and nurse were identified as being of most interest to gay men, while auto mechanic, plumber, and truck driver were suggested for lesbians. Even scholarly articles (e.g., Jones, 1978) suggest that careers in the decorative arts, fashion design, fine arts, and entertainment are most welcoming for gay men. Gay and lesbian students may limit their career choices to occupations in which they believe they will be accepted.

Geographical considerations also play a role in vocational and job selection. Living in a location with lesbian, gay, or bisexual communities is often important to nonheterosexual students. Usually, this means selecting a career that will allow the individual to live in an urban environment. This decision may be at odds with other values, such as enjoying the solitude of rural settings. Value conflicts exist for all students but may be more complicated for lesbians, gay men, and bisexual persons.

How much to disclose to potential employers during interviews must also be considered. If one intends to be open about one's sexual orientation in the workplace, being open during an employment interview would seem to make sense. However, it might be easier to secure the job first and then come out to colleagues and/or supervisor. Making this decision is not an easy task for sexual-minority youth.

### Values and beliefs

The college years are a time during which many students reevaluate the values and beliefs they have learned from their parents, peer group, and community. Deciding the role that religion will play in their lives is one aspect of this process. Because most traditional religions do not accept lesbian, gay, or bisexual identities as valid or desirable, nonheterosexual youths often struggle with their religious convictions, particularly if they were raised in a religious family (Clark, Brown, & Hochstein, 1990).

Several options are available if they wish to remain in a traditional synagogue or church: keep their sexual orientation hidden and cope with the disparity between religious teachings and their lives; acknowledge their sexuality but remain celibate, as expected by most religions; or deny their orientation and attempt to live a heterosexual life. Some denominations have lesbian and gay organizations—such as Affirmation, a group affiliated with the United Methodist Church—which provide a haven for nonheterosexual members. Other lesbian, gay, and bisexual individuals join the Universal Fellowship of Metropolitan Community Churches, the largest organization in the world designed to serve lesbian and gay individuals (Ritter & O'Neill, 1989). Because of religious doctrine and the less than welcoming stance of most churches and synagogues, many lesbian, gay, and bisexual youths forsake religious institutions altogether. The loss of a religious community and a spiritual life is often a traumatic experience for these students.

## Dual Minority Status

Students of color who are also lesbian, gay, or bisexual face even greater challenges than nonheterosexuals who are White. Being members of two or more oppressed groups presents many dilemmas for lesbian, gay, and bisexual students: not knowing who they are; not knowing what part of themselves is more important; not knowing how to cope with one part of themselves oppressing another part; not having anyone with whom to talk about the conflict they feel among the different components; and feeling misunderstood by each group of which they are a member (Wall & Washington, 1991).

Defining one's racial identity is a process similar to defining one's identity as a lesbian, gay, or bisexual person. Both begin with embracing a stigmatized identity and move to acceptance of a new, positive identity after periods of confusion and exploration (Espin, 1987). The manner in which the two processes intersect for nonheterosexual individuals of color has not yet been carefully examined.

The culture in which one grows up and its values influence how one understands oneself as a gay, lesbian, or bisexual person (see Manalansan, this volume; Savin-Williams, "Ethnic-Minority Youth," this volume). For example, heterosexism and homophobia often are justified on the basis of religious beliefs (Icard, 1986). In the African American community, religion plays a very important role. Although the Christian church is an institution from which most African Americans draw strength, it may also be a place of condemnation for the lesbian, gay, or bisexual African American. Feelings of guilt and self-hatred based on religious beliefs are also experienced by Hispanic lesbians and gay men (Carballo-Dieguez, 1989) because the rigidly defined gender roles often found in Hispanic cultures are strong barriers to acceptance. Asian American communities often deny the existence of lesbians and gays in their communities, viewing homosexuality as a "White issue" (Chan, 1989, 1995; Wooden, Kawasaki, & Mayeda, 1983).

Family plays a central role in the lives of most racial- and ethnic-minority individuals. Fear of being ostracized or bringing shame to one's family leads many lesbians, gay men, and bisexuals of color to hide their affectional orientation from their families, perhaps to an even greater extent than do nonheterosexual Whites. While little research data exist to verify the extent of homophobia among various non-Anglo racial groups, some evidence suggests that it may be even greater than among Whites (Chan, 1989; Loiacano, 1989).

On most predominately White college campuses, identifying students of color who are also sexual minorities can be extremely difficult. Thus, the level of isolation experienced by these students is compounded. Anecdotal evidence suggests that most lesbians, gay men, and bisexuals of color choose not to come out during the college years because they fear rejection from other students of color, who often serve as their primary support group.

## DEVELOPMENTAL ISSUES: INTERPERSONAL ISSUES

In addition to the complex personal issues involved in acknowledging a non-heterosexual sexual identity, a lesbian, gay, or bisexual college student faces several difficult interpersonal challenges. These entail sharing personal identity with family, such as parents, grandparents, siblings, and extended family members, and friends—both from high school and college. The challenges also include establishing new relationships, such as friendships with other lesbians, gay men, and bisexuals, and initiating same-sex intimate and romantic relationships.

The developmental tasks that gay, lesbian, and bisexual students must address include disavowing a heterosexual identity in family and peer relationships and asserting a lesbian, gay, or bisexual identity in those and other new relationships. Because a sense of self is derived in part from social relationships and because a complex set of social relationships has evolved by this time in their lives, the interpersonal challenges for lesbian, gay, or bisexual college students may feel overwhelming. Indeed, they *should* feel overwhelming: The person is redefining the parameters by which social relationships will be constructed in the future. The social negotiations involved—who to tell, what to tell, when to tell—can create high levels of stress.

There is greater turmoil for young adults who are uncertain about their sexuality than for those who are relatively clear. Youths who have acknowledged their feelings since early puberty may be generally less agitated than those who have just "put the pieces together." The successful resolution of these social challenges can pave the way to a satisfying adulthood. Those who are unable to reorient their social networks to affirm their sexual identity face considerable conflict because they are forced to deny or hide from others important aspects of their lives.

## Family Relationships

The sharing of sexual orientation status with family members is the most difficult disclosure most lesbians, gay men, and bisexuals face (Borhek, 1988). Family members have known each other for a very long time and thus presume that they know each person very well, especially by the time "children" have reached college age. When family members discover that one of their young adult members is not heterosexual, they are often shocked. It is, in part, because of family reactions that many lesbian, gay, and bisexual youths first tell a friend about their sexuality. In a recent study (D'Augelli & Hershberger, 1993), only 7% of a sample of young people 21 years old or younger had first told their mothers, and only 1% first told their fathers; three quarters first told a trusted friend. In the same study, only 11% of parents reacted positively to their offspring's disclosure. A study of college gay men found that fewer than one half had told someone in their family about their sexual orientation (D'Augelli, 1991a). Because this study surveyed openly gay men who were members of a student organization, it likely overestimates the number of gay and bisexual male college students *in general* who have told family members. Furthermore, it does not address how many youths have told everyone in their family—parents, siblings, grandparents, and extended family members. Very few lesbian, gay, or bisexual young adults are totally "out" in this way.

At college, geographical distance from family and new social, emotional, and sexual opportunities encourage a freer exploration of sexual orientation than was possible during high school. College students' relationships with parents and siblings may become strained during this time for reasons that family members do not understand. Psychologically, the young person is creating "space" to explore his or her "new" sexuality. This distancing can be very upsetting for very close families. Families that are more accustomed to encouraging independence in their members and those that are generally more accepting of differences and unconventionality are more likely to be earlier recipients of the news that their son, daughter, brother, sister, or grandchild is gay, lesbian, or bisexual.

For the college student who lives with his or her parents or whose campus is close to home, there are added burdens. These students are less free to separate from their families to establish independent lives. Their actions are under closer scrutiny, and their sense of responsibility to their parents is often greater. Regardless of the individual's particular circumstances, a negotiation of the relationship with family is usually orchestrated by the person in the beginning stages of coming out.

Disclosure to individual family members is often postponed until the person is on campus, away from home. This serves to insulate him or her from negative family reactions. As young lesbians, gay men, and bisexuals negotiate their place in the family, friends on campus who know their sexual orientation become important sources of support. These friends—and the distance from home—provide a buffer, diminishing negative feelings (e.g., shame, guilt, anger) that might be exchanged if the student resided at home.

Although emotional and physical distance helps to buffer, it also prevents open communication and sharing. If parents cannot or will not provide support, the college student's need for support must be met by an ever increasing number of friends who are accepting of her or his disclosed sexual identity. This underscores the importance of "families of creation," networks of important people who know and affirm the sexual orientation of lesbian, gay, and bisexual individuals. These "families" provide lifelong support and can be crucial if families of origin are unsupportive (Weston, 1991). As increasing numbers of parents are educated about sexual orientation and as the stigma surrounding homosexuality diminishes, more families will become affirmative with their offspring. But for most college students, such unconditional acceptance is currently beyond their reach.

## Friendships

Although the first person told about a lesbian, gay, or bisexual orientation is occasionally a parent, most often it is a close friend (D'Augelli & Hershberger, 1993). From the initial utterance, "I'm gay/lesbian/bisexual," emerges the first social unit in the creation of a new identity. The person's identity changes from this initial disclosure and increasingly more people are added to the list of "knowledgeables." As with family, there are some friends who have no idea, others who are suspicious, and others who have always known about the youth's sexual orientation even though nothing may have been said by either party. Some gay, lesbian, and bisexual college students lose friends when they disclose their sexual orientation. These friends apparently cannot realign their views of their friend from heterosexual to lesbian, gay, or bisexual. They typically hold stereotyped views about sexual orientation and are unable to overcome their discomfort and rigidity. For the young lesbian, gay, or bisexual, the closer the prior friendship, the more important the disclosure.

Often, gay, lesbian, and bisexual college students refrain from telling their best high school friend until supportive others are available. Part of the problem with telling high school friends is tactical, based on a realistic worry that one's sexual orientation will become widely known in one's hometown. For the young adult who wants to conceal her or his sexuality from family and old friends, a particularly awkward circumstance occurs when high school friends attend the same college or university as the newly emerging young lesbian, gay, or bisexual person. When this happens, the gay or lesbian youth may elect to maintain two identities—the heterosexual one that parents and friends from home relate to and the new lesbian, gay, or bisexual identity that is being shaped. Many college students, especially freshmen and sophomores, remain closeted because they are unsure of the way in which to handle this conflict. For many, a time comes when they are sufficiently secure in their new identity that they are less worried about former friends' reactions. Until then, however, the two worlds are kept distinct.

Typically, the person's psychological energies are increasingly devoted to his or her new identity because it feels more "real," more authentic. There is the exhilaration of "being oneself," instead of playing a role in a script that does not feel right. The excitement of coming out is reinforced and nourished over time by contacts with lesbian, gay, and bisexual communities. These contacts provide new friendships with people from the "forbidden" group. These new friendships may also be erotic. For the young bisexual, lesbian, or gay man, this may be the first time that erotic feelings are reciprocated. To participate in these new friendships, the college student often becomes strategically unavailable to former friends, especially those who are homophobic.

Those who come out publicly often rapidly increase their friendship network, especially if they become involved with gay, lesbian, or bisexual campus organizations or local groups. These friendships are exceedingly important because they anchor the youth's identity in a social matrix that teaches the youth about what it means to be lesbian, gay, or bisexual in a particular setting, and they provide support when high school or college friends or parents are ambivalent or rejecting. Because of their psychological importance, these friendships may be very intense. The amount of dependence on a particular friendship is generally related to the number of lesbian, gay, and bisexual friendships the person has gathered: The fewer friends, the more valuable particular friendships are. Until they find their footing in local lesbian, gay, or bisexual communities, many young people experiment with friendships.

## Romantic Relationships

Disclosing one's sexual orientation to family and friends and creating a supportive social network are preliminaries to developing intimate relationships with people of the same sex. Some lesbian, gay, and bisexual teens have had attachments, both physical and emotional, prior to college—but their numbers are few (see Savin-Williams, "Romantic Relationships," this volume). After arriving on campus and coming out to others, students may begin to date those of the same sex. Meeting others similar to themselves, of course, is difficult unless they are willing to enter lesbian- or gay-identified settings such as lesbian, gay, and bisexual student organizations. For women, socializing can be realized through feminist social and political groups, which are usually safe places for lesbian and bisexual women.

Historically, young gay men first related to other men sexually, and then emotionally. Young lesbians essentially followed the reverse order in relating to other women. These gender-typed scenarios remain in place to a considerable degree because of the strong gender role socialization still prominent in our culture. Some young gay men, however, hesitate to initiate physical intimacy as a result of fears of HIV infection, spending more time instead in nonsexual dating. Having had so little experience in the exploratory phases of relationship building, many lesbian, gay, and bisexual college students find their new romantic relationships exhilarating. These young adults are charting new ground in dating, but they are several years behind their heterosexual counterparts in actual dating experience. Despite the relative openness of most campuses compared to high schools, these same-sex relationships develop under strained conditions. For instance, few heterosexual couples fear for their physical safety on campus;

few would hesitate to hold hands in public or tell their families and friends about an important relationship.

Because of heterosexism, homophobia, and the relative inexperience these young adults have with relationships, first relationships tend to be volatile. For example, D'Augelli (1991a) found that the termination of a close relationship was considered extremely troubling for nearly one half of his sample of college gay men. The fewer prior relationships a lesbian or gay person has had, the greater attachment he or she may have for his or her first same-sex partner, although this may be less so if the initial relationship is primarily physical. As well, the more closeted the couple is, the greater their interdependence will be; closeted couples with few if any connections to others have essentially developed a two-person closet. Another related complication arises from the relative "outness" of each member of a dyad. If one is very out (e.g., is an officer of a student organization, or has told all friends and family) and the other is very closeted, the relationship may be difficult to sustain. In these situations, however, there is always the possibility that the closeted person may become increasingly more open and secure by modeling his or her dating partner. Relationships may be difficult as well if there are few open students on campus. This creates competition and jealousy for dating partners and provides little social support for a long-term involvement.

Although there is no research that directly compares heterosexual with lesbian, gay, or bisexual college dating patterns, creating and sustaining close relationships is much more complicated for lesbian, gay, and bisexual students. If nothing else, they have few, if any, visible role models of successful same-sex couples to observe and from whom to learn. Many factors conspire to intensify and ultimately destabilize the relationships they create. However, many lesbian, gay, and bisexual college students adopt heterosexual cultural ideals for their futures: They assume they will be involved in a monogamous lifelong relationship. With increasing social recognition of same-sex domestic partnerships, more lesbian, gay, and bisexual college students may presume they are headed toward such a partnership. The way in which this will affect their dating in college remains to be seen, but surely campuses will become increasingly supportive of these relationships.

## DEVELOPMENTAL ISSUES: ENVIRONMENTAL ISSUES

The campus environment is a powerful force in the lives of lesbian, gay, and bisexual students, perhaps playing a more important role in their daily lives than it does for heterosexual students. Sexuality issues have a prominent role on all campuses and the increased focus on diversity topics has often inspired discussions about sexual orientation. Campus climate is especially important for lesbian, gay, and bisexual students due to the crucial formative identity processes of these years, processes that have been delayed by several years.

Many steps taken—telling friends, being increasingly open with others, and seeking support from others on campus—are intrinsically risky. These risks are amplified if the campus is perceived as hostile, and they are lessened if the campus is viewed as hospitable and supportive. Contrary to occasional sensational news reports, there are few campuses that are lesbian, gay, and bisexual nirvanas; harassment occurs even in the most progressive environments. Evidence points to the unfortunate conclusion that most campuses are hostile environments (D'Augelli, 1992; Herek, 1993). This conclusion is based on the combined impact of frequent victimization on campuses paired with colleges' and universities' general indifference to the needs of lesbian, gay, and bisexual students. The impact of victimization is often direct; the indifference, such as the lack of services designed for these students and their absence from the academic curriculum, has an indirect impact on their development.

## Victimization

Having been very cautious in high school, the young lesbian, gay, or bisexual might presume that a college campus would be a more accepting environment. They are likely to be surprised and disappointed. Most heterosexual students enter college having little, if any, personal knowledge of lesbians and gay men and are attempting to consolidate their own sexuality while trying to fit into social groups in which homophobic remarks are expected. These conditions create classmates of lesbian, gay, and bisexual students who are likely to be homophobic to varying degrees. This is most pronounced for freshmen and males' attitudes, especially toward gay males.

Research on victimization of lesbian, gay, and bisexual students has accumulated since the first systematic survey was conducted by Herek at Yale University in 1986 (Herek, 1993). Results from surveys at different colleges and universities reach similar conclusions. First, harassment is prevalent. Berrill (1990) noted that 1,329 harassing incidents were reported by 40 lesbian, gay, and bisexual campus organizations in 1989 alone. In a comprehensive review of data from three universities, Comstock (1991) summarized the percentages of campus respondents who experienced violence because of their sexual orientation. He found that 22% of lesbian or gay people had been chased or followed; 15% had objects thrown at them; 11% were the victims of vandalism or arson; 4% had been punched, hit, kicked, or beaten; 3% were spit at; and 1% were assaulted with a weapon. Comstock concluded that lesbians and gay men are victimized at a far higher rate than others on campus, perhaps as much as four times more often than the general student population.

The studies reviewed by Comstock present only a partial picture of the campus climate experienced by lesbian, bisexual, and gay students because these studies focus only on actual victimization. Managing sexual identity also involves active avoidance of threatening situations and people. In Comstock's review, neither cases of victimization that were successfully avoided nor cases of victimization that were unreported are included. Thus, his figures and those of other campus research are likely to underreport the actual victimization of lesbian and gay students. In addition, actual incidents of direct harassment and violence against particular people are surely less common than hostile comments about lesbians and gay men in general. Although this may be changing, homophobic comments are common on most campuses.

The range of problematic campus circumstances faced by lesbians and gay men is illustrated by several studies conducted at a large state university (see D'Augelli, 1989a, for a description of the university and its community). In one study, openly lesbian and gay undergraduate students were asked about their experiences with discrimination and violence (D'Augelli, 1992). The results of the study were as follows:

1. 75% had experienced verbal harassment.
2. 25% had been threatened with physical violence at least once; 22% were chased or followed; 5% were spit upon.
3. 17% had property damaged.
4. Gay men were more frequently the objects of verbal insults and threats of violence than lesbians.
5. Nearly all expected the "average" lesbian or gay man to be harassed on campus.
6. Most hid their sexual orientation from roommates and other students.
7. Nearly half made specific life changes to avoid harassment.
8. 64% feared for their personal safety on campus. This fear was associated with having been threatened or verbally abused, having had property destroyed, or having been chased.

Other studies assessed homophobia among students planning to work in campus housing as resident assistants (D'Augelli, 1989a) and first-year students' attitudes about lesbians and gay men (D'Augelli & Rose, 1990). In the first of these two studies the results were as follows:

1. Men had significantly more homophobic attitudes than women.
2. Attitudes about lesbians, while negative, were less negative than attitudes about gay men.
3. Personal knowledge of lesbians and gay men was related to less homophobic views.
4. Everybody had heard antigay/antilesbian remarks. Most of the participants (67%) had made remarks themselves. Men made more homophobic comments than women.
5. Everybody thought that harassment of lesbians and gay men on campus was likely.

The study of heterosexual first-year students' attitudes revealed the following results:

1. 29% felt that the university would be a better place without lesbians and gay men.
2. Nearly half called same-gender behavior "wrong" and gay men "disgusting" or were indifferent to the problems of lesbians and gay men.
3. Men had more homophobic attitudes; attitudes toward gay men were more negative than attitudes toward lesbians. Men were more negative about gay men than about lesbians.
4. Students from conservative families were more homophobic about gay men than students from liberal or moderate families.
5. Personal knowledge of lesbians and gay men was related to less homophobic views.
6. Few students expressed interest in learning more about lesbians or gay men. Only 3% were very interested and 85% said they would not attend an educational program on the subject. Those least interested in learning were most homophobic.
7. Nearly all had heard antilesbian or antigay comments; over 80% had made such comments themselves. Men made such comments more often.
8. Nearly all (91%) felt that harassment was likely for the average lesbian or gay man.

These results provide overwhelming evidence of a hostile climate for lesbians and gay men. It is worth noting that openness about sexual orientation is not required to be victimized. While this climate causes persistent anxiety in lesbians and gay men who are open, it also influences closeted students who observe the consequences of openness. Much verbal harassment occurs in campus housing, and males are the most frequently attacked. Living in close quarters with gay men is apparently highly threatening for some heterosexual men. Whether the verbal attacks reflect a repudiation of their own homoerotic feelings or an effort to gain others' acceptance is unclear. What is clear is the pervasiveness of these verbal comments. Because greater personal contact is associated with less homophobic views (Herek & Glunt, 1993), perhaps the freshmen's relative lack of exposure in knowing someone who is gay, bisexual, or lesbian is partly responsible for their homophobia. Also, heterosexual students are often simply carrying into college the attitudes they held in high school. For example, in a recent study of 15- to 19-year-old males, only 12% felt sure they could be a friend of a gay person, and most (89%) described sex between men as "disgusting" (Marsiglio, 1993). In D'Augelli and Rose's (1990) study of freshmen, 75% of the males agreed with the statement "male homosexuals are disgusting."

One crucial psychological task that a young lesbian, gay, or bisexual person should accomplish on campus is to ascertain the climate—the views of students, faculty, staff, and opinion leaders, particularly the administration. How peers react to homophobic jokes, how resident assistants handle verbal harassment, and how the administration responds to an act of homophobic violence are crucial to determining the extent to which youths will and should be open about their orientation. Because aspects of these students' lives have likely been delayed because of the oppressive circumstances of their hometowns, families, and high schools, further messages of rejection can be quite debilitating. Most college students who hide their orientation live in fear of rejection, harassment, or violence. Unable to reach out to peers, their development may once again be placed "on hold."

Young lesbian, gay, and bisexual people enter colleges and universities with a tremendous sense of the future. They hope that they can place the despair of the past behind them; meet others like themselves; and find support, acceptance, and emotional and physical intimacy. Many are disappointed because they must spend considerable psychological energy developing yet another set of coping responses to avoid oppression. Open lesbian, gay, and bisexual people learn that they must change their behavior to avoid attacks. These changes often involve avoiding certain locations and people known to be gay or lesbian and presenting themselves as heterosexual at times (e.g., inventing opposite-sex dating scenarios). Sadly, some also avoid the lesbian, gay, and bisexual student organizations, where they could receive support and validation. Fear of harassment greatly complicates the lives of open students. It nails the closet more tightly for the many more who are still hiding.

## Lack of Services

Despite the mental health problems, life stresses, and victimization experienced by lesbian, gay, and bisexual students, few campuses provide adequate services for them. In a recent survey of 239 Midwest colleges and universities regarding the ways in which they address sexual orientation issues, only 75 schools responded (Dake, 1993). Of those responding, 46 reported that sexual orientation was included in their nondiscrimination policies and that there was one or more active student organization for lesbian, gay, and bisexual students. Fifty-two schools indicated that there was some form of training for students and/or staff on lesbian, gay, and bisexual issues. Only 12 schools had a lesbian/gay/bisexual task force in place. Assuming that schools that responded to the survey were more likely to be addressing these issues than schools that did not respond, these results are disheartening.

In a survey conducted at an Eastern university generally recognized for its attention to diversity issues, lesbian, gay, and bisexual students indicated that they found many services inadequate, including the campus police, programs for new students, placement, health education, academic advising, career counseling, legal services, financial aid, and the counseling center (Yeskel, 1985). In another study at a West Coast university, lesbian, gay, and bisexual students reported having trouble obtaining appropriate counseling or finding a safe place to socialize with others similar to themselves (Stoller, 1992). Additionally, several writers have commented that even when universities have established antiharassment policies that include sexual orientation, these policies are seldom enforced (Dake, 1993; Stoller, 1992). Clearly, universities are not responding to the needs of lesbian, gay, and bisexual students.

## Curriculum Issues

Another important part of the campus environment is its academic life. This climate is expressed in the courses students take, the nature of discussions they have with each other and with faculty, and the general value placed on different kinds of intellectual and scholarly discourse. If most lesbians, gay men, and bisexual people are physically invisible on campuses, they are even more invisible in the academic life of most institutions (D'Augelli, 1991b). The most obvious example occurs in the content of courses. Seldom, if ever, is material about lesbians and gay men included in classes, even if it is relevant. For example, few classes in developmental psychology cover lesbian and gay development; in social psychology, the nature of homophobia; in counseling, the psychological needs of this population. The problem, however, is much broader. Homosexuality is seldom covered in the social sciences, education, the humanities, or the arts.

This situation is slowly changing with the rapid advances in lesbian and gay studies, especially in the humanities. Generally, however, lesbian, gay, and bisexual life and culture are neglected in academic analysis and discussion. This omission perpetuates the stereotypes that provide the foundation for victimization. Considerable indirect impact on campus climate can be effected if faculty initiate efforts to include discussions of sexual orientation in their courses. Such efforts not only help the many lesbian, gay, and bisexual students in these classes (who, perhaps for the first time, find their lives addressed), but they also educate heterosexually identified students so that they can consider and modify their heterosexist assumptions and acts. For heterosexual students, the accurate information and personal contact with others erode stereotypes. For nonheterosexual students, the effect is empowerment (D'Augelli, 1991b). As more universities strive to address issues of diversity and multicultural education, it is crucial that sexual orientation issues be included.

## CREATING A SUPPORTIVE ENVIRONMENT FOR LESBIAN, GAY, AND BISEXUAL STUDENTS

Creating a supportive environment for lesbian, gay, and bisexual students must address all components of an academic community. Leadership for this effort must be shown by the college or university president, the academic vice president or provost, the director of student services, and other key administrators. Specific services must be developed, and sensitivity and awareness must permeate all student services. Efforts must be geared toward combating homophobia in the academic community as well as providing direct support for lesbian, gay, and bisexual students. These efforts must start at the level of policy and include training and awareness building, programming, and staffing.

## Services

Given the hostile environment found on college campuses, lesbian, gay, and bisexual students must be provided support services to help them address the problems they face. Ideally, an advocacy office or program should be established to focus on lesbian, gay, and bisexual issues. Such an office should assist students in filing harassment charges, provide counseling, work with students who are having trouble negotiating the system, and offer a safe place for students to gather and find support. In addition, the office should advocate for appropriate policies, educational efforts, and programming to combat homophobia and heterosexism in the university community.

One, or ideally several, lesbian, gay, and bisexual student organizations should exist on campus. They serve as support groups for students to explore their sexual orientation; meet other lesbian, gay, and bisexual students; plan social and educational activities; and, engage in advocacy for lesbian, gay, and bisexual rights. Hot lines for students coping with issues related to their identity also serve an important support function, particularly for students in crisis.

All existing student services should include programming specifically targeted for lesbian, gay, and bisexual students. Examples include programs on coming out and identity development, establishing positive relationships, safer sex awareness, AIDS education, internalized homophobia, substance abuse, and spirituality. Handbooks, promotional materials, and other media should delete heterosexist statements and language.

Each student service should also examine its specific programs to ensure that the needs of lesbian, gay, and bisexual students are being met. Health services should provide anonymous HIV testing; train staff on the health issues of lesbian, gay, and bisexual individuals; and conduct workshops for students. If possible, lesbian, gay, and bisexual staff should be employed to serve this population. Counseling services need to affirm lesbian, gay, and bisexual lives. Because research findings indicate that many lesbians and gay men prefer lesbian and gay counselors (McDermott, Tyndall, & Lichtenberg, 1989), efforts should be made to provide them. Career centers should have materials about companies that include sexual orientation in their affirmative action statements; information about coming out in the workplace; and other resources for lesbian, gay, and bisexual students.

Because much victimization occurs in residence halls, residential life personnel are a crucial frontline resource for combating homophobia. Staff must be carefully screened and trained to effectively address these issues. Nonheterosexist social programming should also be offered. Campus activities staff must be sure that programming is inclusive and that lesbian, gay, and bisexual students have opportunities to participate in all aspects of student life. They also should be responsible for assuring that lesbian, gay, and bisexual student organizations are treated fairly and funded equitably. Campus security officers must receive training to respond appropriately to incidents of harassment and violence against sexual-minority students. Obear (1991) recommended that an advocate be designated for victims of homophobic violence.

## Policy

All colleges and universities should include sexual orientation in their nondiscrimination policies. These policies should be comprehensive, covering admission, financial aid, treatment in classes, residence halls, student organizations, employment on campus, and other matters affecting enrolled students as well as university employees. In addition, strong stands should be taken by publicly visible officials of the university, starting with the president, to combat discrimination against lesbians, gay men, and bisexuals. Most importantly, nondiscrimination policies should be enforced and violators sanctioned. Harassment policies should also be extended to cover harassment based on sexual orientation as well as racial and sexual harassment. Again, enforcement of such policies is crucial to creating a safer environment for all students.

Ending benefits discrimination for university employees who are gay or lesbian, while not directly affecting students, sends a clear message that a university is sensitive and responsive to the needs of this community.

A campuswide task force to address lesbian, gay, and bisexual issues on campus is an excellent means to focus attention on the concerns of this population. It is important, however, that the task force be visible, appropriately funded and staffed, and empowered to address important issues. Too often task forces are appointed to take the heat off administrators who prefer not to act on these issues, and thus task force recommendations are frequently ignored.

## Training and Awareness Building

A number of studies have demonstrated that educational workshops and training sessions can change the attitudes of heterosexual students toward lesbian, gay, and bisexual individuals and raise awareness concerning their needs (Rudolph, 1989; Schneider & Tremble, 1986). Speaker panels that include lesbians, gay men, and bisexuals who share their stories with an audience and respond to their questions can be particularly effective in sensitizing heterosexuals to issues facing nonheterosexuals (Croteau & Kusek, 1992).

Workshops should include information about sexual orientation; lesbian, gay, and bisexual identity development; and issues facing nonheterosexual people, such as harassment and discrimination. Sensitivity-building activities should be incorporated to help participants explore myths, stereotypes, and biases concerning lesbians, gay men, and bisexuals and ways of overcoming them. Skill-building activities to help individuals learn how to confront homophobia on personal, interpersonal, and community levels should be included. Finally, workshops should provide action-planning to assist participants in developing specific interventions to address homophobia and to support sexual-minority students on campus.

To be truly effective, such training must be a universitywide effort involving administrators, faculty, student affairs staff, support staff, and students. The support and involvement of top-level administrators is crucial to the success of such an effort.

## Programming

Another type of awareness-building activity is programming that recognizes and affirms lesbian, gay, and bisexual lives. This might include a lecture series on lesbian, gay, and bisexual scholarship; lesbian, gay, and bisexual artists and entertainers in a campus cultural series; films with lesbian or gay themes or characters; and presentations of lesbian- or gay-themed theater productions. These events should be preceded or followed by opportunities to discuss the presentations or meet with the performers or speakers. Such activities help to combat the isolation and sense of difference experienced by lesbian, gay, and bisexual students and to educate the heterosexual campus community.

## Staffing

All students deserve to be treated fairly and with respect. Hiring staff, faculty, and administrators who believe in equity and care about all students, regardless of their sexual orientation, is the key to accomplishing this goal with regard to lesbian, gay, and bisexual students. In interviews, candidates for any position on campus, from a residence hall assistant to the college president, should be questioned concerning their commitment to diversity and their attitudes toward sexual-minority students. Efforts should be made to determine if individuals have truly supported such students in their previous positions.

Visible lesbian, gay, and bisexual staff and faculty can serve as important role models for students by combating stereotypes held by heterosexual students. Yet most campus environments are not perceived by sexual-minority faculty and professionals as safe places to be "out." If the efforts we recommend above are effectively implemented, this perception will inevitably change. Colleges and universities could also do more to recruit openly lesbian, gay, or bisexual staff and faculty by including nondiscrimination clauses in position announcements and discussing the climate for lesbian, gay, and bisexual individuals during interviews.

# Conclusion

Lesbian, gay, and bisexual students face many challenges in achieving personal identity in the homophobic and heterosexist society in which we live. As is true for all students, the college years are a time during which significant personal development occurs. Establishing an identity as a lesbian, gay, or bisexual individual takes precedence over other developmental tasks facing these students, such as career decision-making and the formation of a value system. Because of the stigmatization and harassment they face, these students may experience mental health problems, including low self-esteem, feelings of alienation, substance abuse, and self-destructive behavior. Interpersonal issues, particularly decisions about coming out to family and friends and the development of relationships with others, are particularly salient during the college years.

Unfortunately the college environment does not provide a welcoming context in which lesbian, gay, and bisexual students can develop. Victimization, ranging from verbal harassment to assault, is commonplace. Neither resources provided by student services nor academic curricula recognize their existence or meet their needs. They are thus left on their own; if they proclaim their existence, they take serious risks. If colleges and universities are to reflect the diversity of contemporary society and provide equal opportunities for development for all students, lesbian, gay, and bisexual people must be acknowledged and fully integrated into all aspects of campus life. Colleges and universities have a moral responsibility to provide a safe environment in which free expression and discussion can occur. For a group of young adults whose development has been hampered by pervasive heterosexism and homophobia, supportive campuses can be places for recovery and can provide exceedingly helpful opportunities for growth. Lesbian, gay, and bisexual college students can continue their seclusion in their closets, or they can move rapidly to confront deeply important personal, family, and social issues. We hope campuses will create opportunities for growth instead of perpetuating conditions of fear.

▼  **REFERENCES**  ▼

Astin, A. W. (1993). *The American freshman: National norms for Fall 1993.* Washington, DC: American Council on Education.

Bendet, P. (1986, August-September). Hostile eyes: A report on homophobia on American campuses. *Campus Voice,* pp. 30–37.

Berrill, K. (1990). Anti-gay violence and victimization in the United States: An overview. *Journal of Interpersonal Violence, 5,* 274–294.

Borhek, M. V. (1988). Helping gay and lesbian adolescents and their families. *Journal of Adolescent Health Care, 9,* 123–128.

Botkin, M., & Daly, J. (1987, March). *Occupational development of lesbians and gays.* Paper presented at the annual meeting of the American College Personnel Association, Chicago.

Carballo-Dieguez, A. C. (1989). Hispanic culture, gay male culture, and AIDS: Counseling implications. *Journal of Counseling and Development, 68,* 26–30.

Chan, C. S. (1989). Issues of identity development among Asian-American lesbians and gay men. *Journal of Counseling and Development, 68,* 16–20.

Chan, C. S. (1995). Issues of ethnic minority sexual identity: The case of Chinese American lesbians, gay men, and bisexual people. In A. R. D'Augelli & C. J. Patterson (Eds.), *Lesbian, gay, and bisexual identities across the life span* (pp. 87–101). New York: Oxford University Press.

Chickering, A. W., & Reisser, L. (1993). *Education and identity* (2nd. ed.). San Francisco: Jossey-Bass.

Clark, J. M., Brown, J. C., & Hochstein, L. M. (1990). Institutional religion and gay/lesbian oppression. *Journal of Homosexuality, 20,* 265–284.

Comstock, G. D. (1991). *Violence against lesbians and gay men.* New York: Columbia University Press.

Croteau, J. M., & Kusek, M. T. (1992). Gay and lesbian speaker panels: Implementation and research. *Journal of Counseling and Development, 68,* 396–401.

Dake, T. (1993, February). *Institutional self-evaluation on sexual orientation issues 1992: NASPA Region IV East.* Paper presented at the NASPA IV East Regional Conference, Des Moines, Iowa.

D'Augelli, A. R. (1989a). The development of a helping community for lesbians and gay men: A case study in community psychology. *Journal of Community Psychology, 17,* 18–29.

D'Augelli, A. R. (1989b). Homophobia in a university community: Views of prospective resident assistants. *Journal of College Student Development, 30,* 546–552.

D'Augelli, A. R. (1991a). Gay men in college: Identity processes and adaptations. *Journal of College Student Development, 32,* 140–146.

D'Augelli, A. R. (1991b). Teaching lesbian and gay development: A pedagogy of the oppressed. In W. G. Tierney (Ed.), *Culture and ideology in higher education: Advancing a critical agenda* (pp. ?13–233). New York: Praeger.

D'Augelli, A. R. (1992). Lesbian and gay male undergraduates' experiences of harassment and fear on campus. *Journal of Interpersonal Violence, 7,* 383–395.

D'Augelli, A. R. (1993). Preventing mental health problems among lesbian and gay college students. *Journal of Primary Prevention, 13,* 245–261.

D'Augelli, A. R. (1994). Identity development and sexual orientation: Toward a model of lesbian, gay, and bisexual development. In E. J. Trickett & D. Birman (Eds.), *Human diversity: Perspectives on people in context.* San Francisco: Jossey-Bass.

D'Augelli, A. R., & Hershberger, S. L. (1993). Lesbian, gay, and bisexual youth in community settings: Personal challenges and mental health problems. *American Journal of Community Psychology, 21,* 1–28.

D'Augelli, A. R., & Rose, M. L. (1990). Homophobia in a university community: Attitudes and experience of White heterosexual freshmen. *Journal of College Student Development, 31,* 484–491.

Espin, O. M. (1987). Issues of identity in the psychology of Latina lesbians. In Boston Lesbian Psychology Collective (Eds.), *Lesbian psychologies: Explorations and challenges* (pp. 31–51). Champaign, IL: University of Illinois Press.

Etringer, B. D., Hillerbrand, E., & Hetherington, C. (1990). The influence of sexual orientation on career decision-making: A research note. *Journal of Homosexuality, 19,* 103–111.

Fox, R. (1995). Bisexual identities. In A. R. D'Augelli & C. J. Patterson (Eds.), *Lesbian, gay, and bisexual identities across the lifespan* (pp. 48–86). New York: Oxford University Press.

Garnets, L., Hancock, K. A., Cochran, S. D., Goodchilds, J., & Peplau, L. A. (1991). Issues in psychotherapy with lesbians and gay men: A survey of psychologists. *American Psychologist, 46,* 964–972.

Garnets, L., & Kimmel, D. (1991). Lesbian and gay male dimensions in the psychological study of human diversity. In J. Goodchilds (Ed.), *Psychological perspectives on human diversity in America* (pp. 143–192). Washington, DC: American Psychological Association.

Gibson, P. (1989). Gay male and lesbian youth suicide. In ADAMHA, *Report of the Secretary's Task Force on Youth Suicide* (Vol. 3, pp. 110–142; DHHS Publication No. ADM 89-1623). Washington, DC: U.S. Government Printing Office.

Gonsiorek, J. C. (1991). The empirical basis for the demise of the illness model of homosexuality. In J. C. Gonsiorek & J. D. Weinrich (Eds.), *Homosexuality: Research implications for public policy* (pp. 115–136). Newbury Park, CA: Sage.

Henderson, A. F. (1984). Homosexuality in the college years: Development differences between men and women. *Journal of American College Health, 32,* 216–219.

Herdt, G. H., & Boxer, A. M. (1993). *Children of Horizons: How gay and lesbian teens are leading a new way out of the closet.* Boston: Beacon Press.

Herek, G. M. (1993). Documenting prejudice against lesbians and gay men on campus: The Yale Sexual Orientation Survey. *Journal of Homosexuality, 25,* 15–30.

Herek, G. M., & Glunt, E. K. (1993). Interpersonal contact and heterosexuals' attitudes toward gay men: Results from a national survey. *The Journal of Sex Research, 30,* 239–244.

Hetherington, C. (1991). Life planning and career counseling with gay and lesbian students. In N. J. Evans & V. A. Wall (Eds.), *Beyond tolerance: Gays, lesbians and bisexuals on campus* (pp. 131–145). Alexandria, VA: American College Personnel Association.

Hughes, M. J. (1991). Addressing gay, lesbian, and bisexual issues in fraternities and sororities. In N. J. Evans & V. A. Wall (Eds.), *Beyond tolerance: Gays, lesbians and bisexuals on campus* (pp. 97–116). Alexandria, VA: American College Personnel Association.

Icard, L. (1986). Black gay men and conflicting social identities: Sexual orientation versus racial identity. In J. Gripton & M. Valentich (Eds.), *Social work practice in sexual problems* (pp. 83–93). New York: Haworth.

Jones, G. P. (1978). Counseling gay adolescents. *Counselor Education and Supervision, 18,* 144–152.

Levine, H., & Bahr, J. (1989). *Relationship between sexual identity formation and student development.* Unpublished manuscript, Philadelphia College of Textiles and Science.

Levine, H., & Evans, N. J. (1991). The development of gay, lesbian, and bisexual identities. In N. J. Evans & V. A. Wall (Eds.), *Beyond tolerance: Gays, lesbians, and bisexuals on campus* (pp. 1–24). Alexandria, VA: American Association for Counseling and Development.

Loiacano, D. K. (1989). Gay identity issues among black Americans: Racism, homophobia, and the need for validation. *Journal of Counseling and Development, 68,* 21–25.

Marsiglio, W. (1993). Attitudes toward homosexual activity and gays as friends: A national survey of heterosexual 15- to 19-year-old males. *The Journal of Sex Research, 30,* 12–17.

Martin, D. J. (1989). Human immuno-deficiency virus infection and the gay community: Counseling and clinical issues. *Journal of Counseling and Development, 68,* 67–72.

McDermott, D., Tyndall, L., & Lichtenberg, J. W. (1989). Factors related to counselor preference among gays and lesbians. *Journal of Counseling and Development, 68,* 31–35.

Miranda, J., & Storms, M. (1989). Psychological adjustment of lesbians and gay men. *Journal of Counseling and Development, 68,* 41–45.

Nardi, P. M. (1982). Alcoholism and homosexuality: A theoretical perspective. *Journal of Homosexuality, 7,* 9–25.

National Lesbian and Gay Health Foundation (1987). *National Lesbian Health Care Survey: Mental health implications.* Atlanta: Author.

Obear, K. (1991). Homophobia. In N. J. Evans & V. A. Wall (Eds.), *Beyond tolerance: Gays, lesbians, and bisexuals on campus* (pp. 39–66). Alexandria, VA: American College Personnel Association.

Pope, R., Ehlen, K. J., & Mueller, J. A. (1985, March). *The hidden minority.* Paper presented at the annual meeting of the American College Personnel Association, Baltimore.

Remafedi, G. (1987). Adolescent homosexuality: Psychosocial and medical implications. *Pediatrics, 79,* 331–337.

Ritter, K. Y., & O'Neill, C. W. (1989). Moving through loss: The spiritual journey of gay men and lesbian women. *Journal of Counseling and Development, 68,* 9–15.

Rudolph, J. (1989). Effects of a workshop on mental health practitioners' attitudes toward homosexuality and counseling effectiveness. *Journal of Counseling and Development, 68,* 81–85.

Savin-Williams, R. C. (1990). *Gay and lesbian youth: Expressions of identity.* New York: Hemisphere.

Schneider, M. S., & Tremble, B. (1986). Training service providers to work with gay or lesbian adolescents: A workshop. *Journal of Counseling and Development, 65,* 98–99.

Schneider, S. G., Farberow, N. L., & Kruks, G. N. (1989). Suicidal behavior in adolescent and young adult gay men. *Suicide and Life-Threatening Behavior, 19,* 381–394.

Shuster, R. (1987). Sexuality as a continuum: The bisexual identity. In Boston Lesbian Psychology Collective (Eds.), *Lesbian psychologies* (pp. 56–71). Champaign, IL: University of Illinois Press.

Sohier, R. (1985/1986). Homosexual mutuality: Variation on a theme by E. Erikson. *Journal of Homosexuality, 12,* 25–38.

Stoller, N. (1992). Creating a non-homophobic atmosphere on a college campus. *Empathy, 3*(1), 32–36.

Troiden, R. R. (1989). The formation of homosexual identities. *Journal of Homosexuality, 17,* 43–74.

Troiden, R. R., & Goode, E. (1980). Variables related to the acquisition of a gay identity. *Journal of Homosexuality, 5,* 383–392.

von Destinon, M. (1993, April). Institutions with task forces or offices addressing gay, lesbian, and bisexual issues. *National Association of Student Personnel Administrators Network on Gay, Lesbian, & Bisexual Concerns Newsletter,* p. 9.

Wall, V. A., & Washington, J. (1991). Understanding gay and lesbian students of color. In N. J. Evans & V. A. Wall (Eds.), *Beyond tolerance: Gays, lesbians and bisexuals on campus* (pp. 67–78). Alexandria, VA: American College Personnel Association.

Walters, K. L., & Simoni, J. M. (1993). Lesbian and gay male group identity attitudes and self-esteem: Implications for counseling. *Journal of Counseling Psychology, 40,* 94–99.

Weston, K. (1991). *Families we choose: Lesbians, gays, and kinship.* New York: Columbia University Press.

Wooden, W. S., Kawasaki, H., & Mayeda, R. (1983). Lifestyles and identity maintenance among gay Japanese American males. *Alternative Lifestyles, 5,* 236–243.

Yeskel, F. (1985, June). *The consequences of being gay: A report on the quality of life for lesbian, gay, and bisexual students at the University of Massachusetts at Amherst.* Unpublished manuscript, University of Massachusetts at Amherst, Office of the Vice Chancellor for Student Affairs.

Zinik, G. (1985). Identity conflict or adaptive flexibility: Bisexuality reconsidered. In F. Klein & T. J. Wolf (Eds.), *Bisexualities: Theory and research* (pp. 7–19). New York: Haworth.

# Part Three

# ADULTHOOD
# AND
# AGING

*Chapter 10*

▼

# WHAT'S IN A NAME?
# SEXUAL SELF-IDENTIFICATION
# AMONG WOMEN

## Carla Golden

*Despite active and ongoing debates within feminist and lesbian communities regarding who is and is not a lesbian, most people believe that they know the answer to this apparently simple question. To them, lesbians are women who are sexually attracted to and involved with other women. Even among those who are aware that lesbians are a diverse group, same-gender sexual orientation (specifically in terms of sexual attraction and/or sexual activity) is considered to be the common thread in lesbian lives. This is true, of course, and to suggest otherwise would seem ludicrous. Yet, such a definition can serve to constrict rather than broaden an understanding of lesbians in particular and of women's sexuality in general. The view that a lesbian is "simply" a woman sexually oriented toward women can cause considerable confusion in understanding not only lesbians but bisexual women as well. The purpose of this chapter is to complicate the reader's sense of what it means to be a lesbian or bisexual woman, because by so doing, a rich, psychologically accurate perspective on women's sexuality is provided.*

*This chapter includes a review of feminist debates about sexual identity, followed by consideration of interview research that bears directly on issues raised in the debates. Several underlying questions thread through the debates, including whether it is possible to choose one's sexuality; whether sexuality is "set" at birth or early in development; and whether sexuality can change over the life course. These are questions about the nature of human sexuality. My goal is not to attempt to answer such major questions with one definitive theory or set of data, but to highlight the ways in which women who have given thought to these issues think about their sexuality. Many historians and social scientists agree that sexuality and sexual identities are socially constructed (D'Emilio, 1983; Faderman, 1991; Foucault, 1978); thus, listening to the ways in which women talk about what it means to identify as lesbian or bisexual can add significantly to our overall understanding of the social construction of women's sexuality. Presentation of interview data is followed by consideration of the ways in which these data challenge widely held conceptions regarding the stability of sexual orientation and its congruence with sexual behavior and identity. The interviews will be used to support an alternative perspective that women may experience their sexuality as both chosen and fluid over the course of their lives. Thus, the reader will better understand women who feel they are choosing their sexuality as well as those who feel they are expressing an inborn sexuality. Finally, the chapter concludes with a discussion of the implications of conceptualizing sexuality as potentially fluid.*

## FEMINIST SEXUAL IDENTITY DEBATES

Feminists consider it important to understand women's sexuality in the interest of knowing more about human sexuality and in discerning the ways in which its multiple forms of expression and repression are related to women's status in society. Since the earliest days of the second wave of the women's movement, feminists have examined sex, sexual desire, and intimate relationships, especially as they relate to gender. One issue that has received attention, particularly from lesbian feminist theorists, is the definition of lesbianism.

Rich's (1980) conception of the "lesbian continuum" highlighted the definitional controversy regarding who is and is not a lesbian. Rich noted that across history and cultures women have in a variety of ways been primarily committed to other women; she used the term lesbian continuum to refer to the range of such woman-identified experiences. Women who have had, or have consciously desired, genital sexual experience with women are but one point on the lesbian continuum. By conceiving of lesbianism in these terms, Rich suggested that many more forms of intimate connection between and among women, including emotional bonding, could be included than would be possible with a narrower definition based solely on sexual behavior. Furthermore, according to Rich's definition, a woman need not identify herself as a lesbian in order to be considered one. By defining lesbianism in terms of "primary intensity between women," she allowed for women from previous historical periods to be considered lesbians, even though at the time there may have been no such cultural conception.

Rich's formulations held that neither sexual relations nor sexual attractions among women are necessary for inclusion in the category lesbian. For example, Cook (1977) defined a lesbian as "a woman who loves women, who chooses women to nurture and support and to create a living environment in which to work creatively and independently, whether or not her relations with these women are sexual" (p. 48). More recently, Rothblum and Brehony (1993) edited a book on romantic but asexual relationships among contemporary lesbians. Definitions that have de-emphasized sexual feelings and behavior have not, however, been without controversy. Not only do they suggest that with whom one has sexual relations is not critical, but they imply that a woman who never consciously considers herself to be a lesbian may in fact be one.

Ferguson (1981) argued that defining lesbianism in this manner incorrectly downplays the importance of sexual feelings and behavior. Such a characterization "unsexes" lesbianism, making it more agreeable to some by diminishing that which is undeniably a significant issue—sex. Furthermore, Ferguson argued that it is not meaningful to refer to a woman as a lesbian if she does not consider herself one. She noted that before the twentieth century there was no cultural conception of lesbianism; therefore, one cannot and should not refer to women as lesbians if they did not consider themselves to be such. As an alternative, Ferguson offered the following definition:

> A lesbian is a woman who has sexual and erotic-emotional ties primarily with women or who sees herself as centrally involved with a community of self-identified lesbians whose sexual and erotic-emotional ties are primarily with women *and* who is herself a self-identified lesbian. (p. 162)

Without de-emphasizing the role of sexual behavior, this definition includes both celibate and bisexual women as lesbians, as long as they identify themselves as such.

Self-acknowledgement of lesbian identity is important, especially when the focus is on contemporary women for whom a definite cultural category of lesbian exists. Women who have same-gendered sexual experiences but resist identifying themselves as lesbians may be reacting to negative cultural attitudes toward lesbianism. By choosing to "pass" as heterosexuals, they may be holding on to the social approval and privileges accorded to heterosexuals, or denying their sexual feelings altogether. Women with only heterosexual experience who call themselves bisexual or lesbian may be making a political statement.

Even among women who openly adopt a lesbian label, there are distinctions. Some women consider themselves "born" or "true" lesbians as opposed to those they consider "false" or "not real" lesbians (Golden, 1987; Whisman, 1993). The difference is between women who feel that they are essentially lesbian and those who believe they have made a conscious decision to become lesbians. Hoagland and Penelope (1991) articulated the former position:

> Some of us feel that we have always been lesbians; some of us were in touch with it from our earliest memories, whereas others of us realize that we repressed it for years, or for most of our lives. We were, regardless of when we finally realized it, always lesbians. (p. 36)

To some "born" lesbians, it seems impossible that a woman could decide to be a lesbian. Challenging this view of "conceptual lesbianism," Allison (1994) argued:

> Nor do I believe that sexual orientation is something one can construct, that people can just decide to be lesbians or decide not to be—for political, religious, or philosophical reasons—no matter how powerful. I don't know if sexual preference and identity is genetic or socially constructed. I suspect it's partly both, but I do believe that there are people who are queer and people who are not. (p. 142)

Others suggested precisely this possibility, that lesbianism can be a distinct choice for some women. Members of the Boston Lesbian Psychologies Collective (1987) introduced their pioneering book on lesbian psychologies with the claim that "for some of us, the choice to live a lesbian lifestyle is an explicit choice not to live the lives of our parents, and more particularly the lives of our mothers" (p. 4). Radicalesbians (1973), a radical feminist political group, contended that not only is lesbianism a viable choice for women, but that recognition of the option, even if not acted upon, is critical to achieving women's equality: "Until women see in each other the possibility of a primal commitment which includes sexual love, they will be denying themselves the love and value they readily accord to men, thus affirming their second-class status" (p. 243).

In addition to sexual self-identification are the issues of sexual behavior and the gender of one's partners. Ferguson's (1981) definition of lesbianism included some flexibility by using the word "primarily," which included in the lesbian category women whose sexual relations are not exclusively with women. However, Hoagland and Penelope (1991) expressed their resentment of women who describe their sexual preference as a choice and who do not relate exclusively to women:

> We feel a great deal of hostility toward these women because they have the privilege to experiment with our lives, because they have betrayed us when being a lesbian became no longer fashionable (or politically correct) and they went right back to fucking men. (p. 36)

It is my observation that certain lesbian communities more readily accept celibate and sexually inexperienced women who choose to call themselves lesbians than bisexual women who choose to identify as lesbians. In these cases, it appears that the critical issue in determining the "legitimacy" of a woman's claim to a lesbian identity is not whether she is sleeping with women but whether she is sleeping with men.

Attempts to define who is a "real" lesbian are thus divisive. Zita (1981) aptly referred to the judging and weighing of who does and does not qualify for membership as the "Lesbian Olympics." Despite potential dangers, it is socially and politically important for groups to define themselves, and within the lesbian community this has been an ongoing project.

In a recent consideration of the sexual identity debates, Whisman (1993) contrasted the identities of lesbian feminists of the 1970s with those of the "new lesbians" of the 1980s and 1990s. The identity of lesbian feminists was often grounded in their politics and was reflected in the self-designated label "woman-identified women," which signified their bond with all women and emphasized their antipatriarchal stance. Younger lesbians, by contrast, often call themselves queers, a label that reflects their alliance with gay men and other so-called sexual deviants, and they tend to "write more about sex than about political theory" (p. 48). Whisman referred to a "nineties version of the Lesbian Olympics" in which the new lesbians take "other lesbians to task for being less hip, less sexual, in other words—not like gay men" (p. 57). Not only is sex central to what it means to be a lesbian, but a particular kind of bold and blatant sex is hailed. Still, Whisman described this clash as the latest in an ongoing process of self-definition within lesbian communities in which identities are constantly shifting and contingent upon context. Whisman concluded with two questions that reveal the extent to which the sexual identity debates remain alive:

> What is a lesbian? Who is a lesbian? One woman says it's her lust that makes her a lesbian, even if she admits that she likes men, too. Another says it's her choice to surround herself with a community of women. A third talks in terms of her deeply felt sense that she is different, queer. In the end, a lesbian must simply be any woman who calls herself one, understanding that we place ourselves within that category, drawing and redrawing the boundaries in ever-shifting ways. For there is no essential and timeless lesbian, but instead lesbians who, by creating our lives day by day, widen the range of possibilities. (p. 60)

There is indeed no timeless or essential lesbian, just as there is no essential sexuality independent of its social and historical context (Foucault, 1978). Thus, there is no one model or specifiable identity that fits all lesbians; what it means to be a lesbian will vary from woman to woman, even during the same historical period and within the same culture. Differences exist not only in the ways women understand what it means to be a lesbian and how they define it for themselves, but in the centrality of lesbianism for their sense of self.

These debates concerning sexual identity are not merely theoretical, nor are they of relevance only to those who actively contemplate feminist issues. Largely as a result of changes wrought by the women's movement, even girls and women who are not identified as feminists are now exposed to a variety of possibilities and choices for women (Faludi, 1991; Wolf, 1991). While cultural messages about female sexuality are contradictory and constantly shifting, women are more openly experiencing sexual desire and deciding the ways in which they want to express it. Little girls think about the shape and possibilities of their adult lives and adolescents more actively explore their sexuality, wondering what various sexual attractions and involvements mean for the ways in which they define themselves. Many adult women as well are consciously examining their lives and experiences and making informed decisions about that which they need and want. Implicit in this process of self-definition is the view that girls and women can choose how to live their lives, sexually and otherwise.

All of this is occurring at the same time that lesbian, gay, and bisexual people are becoming increasingly visible in the culture at large. One important consequence is that people of all ages are exposed to more than just a heterosexual model of adult life. The visibility of sexual minorities affords members of the dominant group (heterosexuals) the opportunity to consider a range of human sexualities and lifestyles that they might otherwise have failed to recognize. This can stimulate them to think about their sexuality; to question whether they could be attracted to people of the same sex; and to contemplate that which makes lesbians, gays, and bisexuals different from themselves.

As a teacher of college students, I am struck by the diverse ways in which exposure to lesbian and gay people and material (e.g., readings or films) can elicit such questioning in some students. Some are frightened and disgusted, while others are interested and curious; some see themselves as clearly different from lesbian and gay people, while others are not sure. Many students struggle with questions related to their own sexuality:

- "Am I a lesbian, or am I just in love with my roommate?"
- "Am I straight, or am I just trying to deny that I am a lesbian?"
- "Would it be best to deny my bisexuality and just focus on men (or women) in order to avoid confusion about what I really want?"
- "Am I lesbian or bisexual now that I have a girlfriend, while in high school I had a boyfriend?"
- "How can I be a lesbian if I'm attracted to this man?"
- "Have I always thought I was straight because I never considered that I could be anything else?"

Some young people know, with certainty, that they are lesbian, gay, bisexual, or heterosexual. Others are undecided and have many questions, which they are freer to explore in the 1990s. Sometimes they talk to parents or trusted friends who are quick to assure them that they could not possibly be gay; others may be more open-minded and are quick to assure them of the opposite—that they are definitely gay and that is okay. I am not suggesting that such uncertainty is the norm among young people, but neither is it a rare and uncommon experience. Nor do I think that such questioning is limited to college students. The gay and lesbian movement has been highly visible on many college campuses, but this visibility is not limited to institutions of higher learning. Exploring the sexual self-identification processes of lesbians and bisexual women sheds light on issues of relevance for all women.

## INTRODUCTION TO THE INTERVIEWS

Over the last decade, I have conducted in-depth interviews with more than 100 women actively engaged in the process of sexual self-definition (Golden, 1987, 1994). I expanded the research beyond lesbian college students from the northeastern United States to include nonstudent lesbians in their twenties, thirties, and forties. Subsequently, I interviewed heterosexual and bisexual women of varying ages. The interviewees were primarily White and from a range of social class backgrounds. The bisexual women were from the San Francisco Bay area, where there is a visible and active bisexual community. Interviews were open-ended and involved asking women to tell the story of how they came to know/identify themselves as lesbian, bisexual, or heterosexual. One of the most significant dichotomies that emerged in the interviews was whether women experienced their sexuality as something about which they made a conscious decision or as something beyond their control and over which they had little choice. Another issue was related to whether they saw their sexuality as fixed and unchanging, or whether they felt that it was fluid and changeable over the course of their lives.

# INTERVIEWS WITH LESBIANS

Some women who identified as lesbians felt their lesbianism was essentially beyond their conscious control, while others felt it was something they had consciously chosen. In the former group were women who from an early age, usually between 6 and 12 years, had considered themselves to be different from other girls. Most did not have a label for it; however, they experienced themselves as different because they felt sexually attracted to other girls or women. This was quite often described in terms of "crushes" that may have been independent of actual sexual experiences. In other words, regardless of past lesbian or heterosexual interactions or relationships, they felt themselves to be different because they were attracted to other females. Furthermore, this was experienced at the time as beyond their control—these women had not chosen to be attracted to women; they just were. Some offered comments to the effect that they were "born" lesbian, spontaneously contrasting themselves with women who described their lesbianism as a conscious choice. Following a distinction made by Ponse (1978) in her study of a Southern lesbian community, I characterized these women as "primary" lesbians. That is, these women from an early age had a conscious sense of difference based on sexual attraction toward members of the same sex and did not perceive this difference to be a conscious choice.

In contrast to primary lesbians were women I characterized, again following a distinction made by Ponse (1978), as "elective" lesbians. For these women a lesbian identity was perceived as consciously chosen. This is not to imply that it was strictly a political choice; the majority experienced it as an erotic choice as well. Unlike primary lesbians, these women did not have a conscious sense of being different from other girls at a young age. Similar to primary lesbians, however, their sense of identity was independent of sexual history. As girls, some elective lesbians had crushes on other girls; they may even have engaged in sexual play and exchanges with other girls. Despite such lesbian-like experiences, they did not consider themselves different. No one labeled their behavior as deviant and it had not occurred to them that others might consider it as such.

Elective lesbians usually had some adult heterosexual experience, but even when they had not, they maintained heterosexual identities. Regardless of their sexual experience, they never considered themselves to be different from the "average" female in terms of sexual orientation. Although they may never have explicitly called themselves heterosexuals, neither did they consider the possibility that they were anything else (much in the manner that White people never give much explicit thought to their race). Elective lesbians perceived their lesbianism as a conscious choice and did not have a history of thinking of themselves as different from other females in their sexual inclinations.

Among elective lesbians I found two distinct subpatterns that suggested another salient dimension of lesbian identity. Some women viewed their sexual attraction to women as a central, basic, and unchanging aspect of who they were. This was not merely a political stance but a strongly experienced subjective feeling about their essential natures. In light of this sense of themselves, their past heterosexual behavior and identity presented an inconsistency. Unwilling to accept this apparent discontinuity and given their belief in the stability and enduring quality of their sexuality, they repeatedly expressed the view that there was something "unreal" about their previous heterosexuality. This was reflected in a tendency to reinterpret their past history to suggest a continuity between past and present senses of self. One woman noted, "In high school, when I had a steady boyfriend, the real me, the lesbian, was suppressed. I just wasn't my real self back then." For other women, their less than satisfactory heterosexual experiences confirmed that they had really been lesbians all along. Still others pointed to their intense friendships with girlfriends as suggestive of their true lesbian identities. Sexual feelings and behaviors were central to the lesbian identities of these women.

Other elective lesbians did not view their lesbianism as an essential and enduring aspect of who they were. They did not reinterpret their past history and experience dissonance or contradiction in describing themselves as lesbians with heterosexual pasts. One woman said quite simply, "Then I was heterosexual, and now I'm a lesbian." These women expressed the view that there was nothing inconsistent about their present identity and the one they had assumed in the past. Some revealed that they had engaged in childhood sexual play with other girls or had strong attachments to camp counselors and teachers but had never thought of these as lesbian feelings. Although they currently identified as lesbians, they saw no reason to reconstruct their pasts so as to appear that they had always been lesbians. Unlike the elective lesbians previously described, they did not view sexual attraction to women as an essential and unchanging aspect of who they were, although they strongly believed they would continue to have their primary, if not all, relationships with women. Some women considered themselves lesbians whose sexual feelings could be most accurately characterized as bisexual, or just sexual. In other words, their sexuality felt fluid or changeable.

Interesting age differences with respect to these dimensions of sexuality were apparent. I have spoken with elective lesbians in their late twenties, thirties, and forties who described shifts in their thinking about the nature of their lesbianism. At an earlier age some had experienced their sexuality as essential, fixed, and invariantly focused on women, but later in the development of their lesbian identity had come to feel that their sexuality was in fact fluid. For a few, this shift resulted from heterosexual attractions or experiences later in life. Others who continued to have relationships only with women attributed their earlier position to their adamant lesbian feminist politics or to what they thought was a developmental phase many lesbians experience.

Alternatively, some elective lesbians felt that in their younger years, when they were engaged in sexual exploration and discovery, their sexuality was more fluid. In the context of lesbian culture and relationships, however, they had developed an explicit preference for women. These women viewed their sexuality as becoming more fixed over time. Whereas the college women with whom I spoke characterized their sexuality as either fixed or fluid, some older women had experienced shifts over the life course.

## Interviews With Heterosexual Women

Interviewing heterosexual women, I found that similar distinctions apply to the way they think about their sexuality. Among the college students, most simply assumed that they were heterosexual and that their heterosexuality was a "given" (i.e., biologically determined and fixed). They typically had not given the topic much thought and reacted with astonishment when I asked, "When did you first know that you were heterosexual?" The most common response was, "It never even occurred to me that I could be anything else!"

There were, however, other students who had previously thought about sexual preference issues, usually because their curiosity was prompted by a discussion in a women's studies class, a book that made reference to the social construction of sexuality, or an informed talk with a lesbian friend. After exposure to the concept of sexual fluidity, some heterosexual women rejected its applicability to themselves. They could not imagine themselves having anything but heterosexual attractions and relationships; that is, they viewed their sexuality as both determined and fixed. Some of these women openly acknowledged that the possibility that their sexuality might be fluid made them distinctly uncomfortable; others conveyed their discomfort nonverbally. For some women, however, the belief in the fixed nature of their sexuality did not appear defensive. These women were "primary" heterosexuals who believed in the central and enduring quality of their sexuality.

In contrast to those who maintained that their sexuality was essentially heterosexual were college women who acknowledged that while they had always considered themselves to be heterosexual, they either had been, or could imagine being, attracted to and becoming involved with a woman. I was particularly struck by how powerful the idea of sexual fluidity was to this subgroup of heterosexual women. When I asked when and how the possibility had first occurred to them, they mentioned women's studies classes; exposure to lesbians within feminist groups; and discrete events such as viewing a film or TV program, hearing a lecture, reading an article, or having a discussion with a lesbian friend. These had often prompted ongoing reflection, including reinterpretation of close female friendships and/or attachments to teachers and camp counselors as evidence of the possibility that they *had* been sexually attracted to women but had never recognized it as such until now. They acknowledged the possibility that their sexuality did in fact involve a choice that they had not previously realized. In this sense they were similar to the elective lesbians described above.

Thinking about sexuality, however, had led them to make a conscious choice *not* to explore their lesbian or bisexual potential. They said, in effect, that choosing to be lesbians would make their lives more difficult in a variety of ways, particularly with respect to telling their families. While it was a choice they realized they had, it was one they chose not to make. Thus, one could say that these women *were* choosing—to not identify or act as lesbians. Accordingly, these women can be characterized as "elective" heterosexuals who believe in the potential fluidity of their sexuality but choose not to act on it.

A different "strand" of elective heterosexuality was apparent among feminist women 28 through 45 years of age. Some women said that they had been attracted to women (or could imagine the possibility) as well as to men and were open to involvement in a lesbian relationship but that it had not yet happened. While they were currently heterosexual, they considered their sexuality to be fluid. Other women who had been involved in long-term marriages said that if anything should happen with their long-term partner (e.g., death or separation), they would prefer to be involved with women. Though most had never had previous lesbian experiences, they did not anticipate difficulty with such a switch. Many mentioned that they found women sexually attractive and almost all remarked that they preferred women as emotional partners.

Given the cultural mandate of compulsory heterosexuality (Rich, 1980), it is typical for most heterosexual women never to question their exclusive sexual attractions to men. Yet, the feminist movement has highlighted the issue of sexual identity for at least some heterosexual women and in their interviews, one can find evidence of decision-making and preference regarding the gender of their sexual partners. Women's choices about their sexuality are evident not only in their acceptance and adoption of a lesbian lifestyle and identity but in their conscious rejection of lesbianism because it might make life too difficult, and in their anticipation of different possibilities for the future.

## INTERVIEWS WITH BISEXUAL WOMEN

As with lesbians and heterosexual women, the bisexual women who were interviewed ranged in age from their early twenties to late forties and were questioned about the ways in which they had come to identify as bisexual. A clear distinction emerged between one group of women who described becoming aware of bisexuality through their sexual feelings and another group who became aware through an intellectual route. Women in the first group recognized their bisexuality through the experience of explicit sexual feelings for other females, feelings similar to those which they felt for males. For many of these women, the awareness of same-sex attractions started when they were fairly young; in other cases, the women were older and, because of a longer history of heterosexual attractions, were to varying degrees surprised by these explicit sexual feelings for women.

Many women described their sexual feelings as being distinct from emotional attachments and attractions. One woman, who had experienced crushes on girls from a young age, found herself not only sexually attracted to but in love with her best friend. She characterized herself as having "always had the [sexual] feelings that just exploded when I was 18." Critical to her sense of self as bisexual was falling in love, rather than the sexualized feelings for her friend. Another woman described a childhood and adolescence of experiencing crushes on other girls but of not falling in love with a woman until she was 30: "I was so happy about being in love with her. It gave validity to my feelings because there was an emotional as well as sexual attraction." For some, sexual feelings toward girls were described as stronger and longer standing, but for others, sexual feelings for females were new and felt similar to that which they had experienced with males. Because of similar sexual and emotional feelings for women and men, these women considered themselves bisexual.

While there was no ambiguity about their sexual attractions, sometimes the women were confused about the meaning of such feelings. One woman reported:

> I had these explicitly sexual feelings for another woman in my dance class, and they were so strong they really scared me. I tried to repress it, just wipe it out of my thoughts, but that didn't work and I decided that I really had to figure out what it meant.

This comment highlights two important points. First, sexual feelings were experienced as strong and spontaneous; they were not a choice or a result of conscious decision-making. Second, although the women in this group had explicit sexual attractions for other women, some were initially confused by these feelings because they had previously thought of themselves as heterosexual. While growing up they did not consider themselves different from other girls because they also had crushes on boys; either they did not think very much about their crushes on girls or they did not consider their feelings odd. For a girl who was sure she liked boys in the culturally prescribed way, having similar feelings for girls was difficult to interpret.

Although they eventually recognized that they were bisexual, it was not necessarily a smooth or easy arrival at this sexual identification. Some women identified as bisexual as soon as they became aware that they were sexually attracted to women and men. For others, sexual attractions and involvements with women signified to them that they must really be lesbians and thus they identified as such; with varying degrees of struggle, they eventually came to accept that they were also attracted to men. With the aid of an increasingly visible bisexual movement, they ultimately identified as bisexuals. Some of these women remembered that they had a very difficult time acknowledging their feelings for men because they feared rejection by some lesbians if they did. Others were in committed lesbian relationships and viewed themselves as having a bisexual *orientation* but choosing a lesbian *identity*. They identified themselves as bisexual lesbians.

A second group of bisexual women described their process of identifying as bisexual in very different terms. The prominent theme in their stories was that the "idea" of bisexuality presented itself first, followed by the experience of sexual attraction to women. For example, one woman reported:

> I became aware of my bisexuality in my early twenties. In some ways I tend to be an idea person and it came from my ideas. . . . I had a friend, who like me was married, and she brought up the idea that she had sexual feelings for me. I thought that sounded kind of interesting and I didn't feel scared or that it was a bad thing. And I just let myself go with it and we kind of had this passionate friendship.

Another woman related:

> The whole idea that sexuality didn't have to be gender specific probably occurred to me in high school when I discovered an anthropology book of my father's about human sexuality. Also, the women's movement, the idea of feminism, sisterhood, and coming into contact with lesbians all led me to think that maybe the only reason I had never thought about or been attracted to women had to do with cultural conditioning. As a function of all these things, I took it on as a specific goal to become closer friends with women and I was interested in this idea of bisexuality. The whole idea appealed to me intellectually.

Most of the women whose interest in bisexuality was sparked through a cognitive route eventually became sexually involved with women. Their sexual experiences were described in positive terms; often the most difficult part was not that they felt uncomfortable with their sexual interactions but that they had difficulty meeting an interested woman. Bisexuality may have started as an idea but it did not remain purely in the cognitive realm. Of course, there is no way of knowing the number of women who considered bisexuality an appealing idea but were dissatisfied with it in practice. Such women probably do not consider themselves bisexual and thus are not likely to volunteer for interviews.[1]

When asked about the role conscious choice had played in the development of her sexual identity, each of the bisexual women denied that she had in any way chosen to be bisexual. One woman reported, "It was just there—within me. There was a choice in that when I got to college I decided to deal with it rather than repress it, but I didn't decide to be sexually attracted to women." Another woman told me rather pointedly, "It's not like I read a book and said, 'Oh what a neat concept. Let me try this.'" This same woman reported that reading had been very important in her sexual explorations: "Reading interacts with my life and there is a constant feedback between the two." Another woman—who earlier in the interview had contended that "the idea [of bisexuality] appealed to me as the right way to be. I really see it as an ideal so it was easy to move in that direction"—later related, "I didn't say to myself I want to be a bisexual and make myself do this." Drawing on the same terminology used previously in descriptions of lesbian and heterosexual women, these women would be considered primary, not elective, bisexuals.

It was hardly surprising that women who had experienced sexual attraction to other females starting at a young age would not consider themselves to have chosen their bisexuality. More puzzling was the rejection of choice by women who described becoming aware of their bisexuality through the cognitive route. They had delineated a two-step process of identifying as bisexual: First, they had the *idea* of being sexually attracted to women, and then they decided to act on that idea. I found this explicit—in fact, adamant—rejection of choice perplexing until I listened more carefully to their words. By telling me that "it was easy to move in that direction" and "I didn't make myself do this," it was clear that they wanted to stress the "easy" and natural aspect of their sexual attraction to and involvement with women. This was not something in which they had to force themselves to engage. Because heterosexual attraction is never constructed as a choice, the question of whether they had chosen to be bisexual is interpreted as a question about whether they had chosen to be with *women*—not whether they had chosen to be with men. Apparently, to answer in the affirmative would be to create an asymmetry between feelings of attraction to women and men and to imply that attraction to women is somehow different and less real than the more "natural" attraction to men. Yet, these bisexual women experienced their sexual feelings for women to be as compelling as those for men, even if they came to it through the cognitive route. They appeared to resist viewing their bisexuality as a choice because to do so would have implied that their attraction to women was cognitive while their attraction to men was visceral, or "natural." As sexuality is constructed in this culture, heterosexual attraction rarely appears to be a choice, even to these bisexual women.

So emphatically did these women consider their sexuality to be beyond their conscious control that some even suggested that if they *could* choose their sexuality, they would have chosen to be lesbians because that would have made their lives "simpler" and "easier." One woman reported:

> For a long time I blocked my attractions to men. I wanted to feel more like a lesbian, really wanted to get behind it, but it never felt authentic. It just wouldn't stick. It felt very comfortable to be with a woman, but I had to deny something that was also there. I felt guilty for not being able to really be a lesbian.

Unlike primary lesbians or heterosexuals who described their sexuality as a central and enduring aspect of who they were, the primary bisexuals did not characterize their sexuality in fixed terms, nor was it a central component of their self-definition. While some women felt it was important to identify as bisexual for political reasons (to enhance the visibility of bisexual people), many rejected the term bisexual as one of their most salient defining characteristics. Repeatedly, they noted that it was a descriptive and not a defining term and that there was much more to their sexuality than the sex of their partners. One woman noted, "I might use bisexual as an adjective, but not as a noun."

Various expressions of choice and fluidity are apparent in this group of bisexual women. Unlike some lesbians and heterosexual women, these bisexual women did not believe they chose their sexuality, although they felt that their sexuality was fluid. This position is best articulated by the interviewee who told me:

> Heterosexual women usually fall in love with men; lesbians usually fall in love with women; I always fall in love with people who have the personal qualities that are really important to me in a partner. It seems silly to me that something like biological sex would be used to limit the potential pool of partners.

As with some lesbians and heterosexual women, the language of choice and preference is evident in the self-definitions of bisexual women. While they often do not consider their bisexuality to be a conscious decision, they are perhaps the least restricted in their choices of sexual and emotional partners. Rust (1992) echoed the view of the women I interviewed when she noted that bisexuals are different from heterosexual and lesbian women, who treat biological sex as a necessary condition for choosing a romantic partner. It is only after the critical criterion of sex is met (heterosexual women are looking for men; lesbians, for women) that other factors that are personally important (e.g., age, personality, and interests) are considered. Bisexuals also choose their romantic partners based on criteria that are personally relevant to them; however, neither biological sex nor gender are listed as a necessary criterion. This does not mean that biological sex is irrelevant. Rust pointed out that some bisexual women feel differently about women as partners than they do about men; some prefer sex with one gender more than the other; and relationships that develop with men may differ from those with women. Rust emphasized that biological sex is but one of a number of criteria that might be used in choosing a romantic partner:

> That bisexuals do not practice exclusion on the basis of biological sex or gender is a negative definition of bisexuality . . . it states what we do not do instead of what we do. The point is not that we choose not to practice sex/gender exclusion, but that we open ourselves up to the *possibility of consciously choosing our own criteria*. This, then, is the aspect of bisexuality which must be emphasized. (p. 299, italics added)

## Summary of the Interviews

Clearly, some women feel that choice has played a role in their sexual orientation and that their sexuality is fluid (Esterberg, 1994; Golden, 1987, 1994; Rust, 1992; Whisman, 1993). Some lesbians report actively choosing to accept and embrace a sexuality they believe to be inborn; other women choose to be lesbians because they prefer women and because the feminist movement has legitimated that choice. Some bisexual women talk about the ways in which the idea of bisexuality appealed to them and emphasize that they found it easy to move in that direction. Some heterosexual feminist women also use a language of possibility and preference. Although most never questioned their sexuality, some have considered the options and have chosen to pursue the road most traveled. Others leave open the possibility of change in the future, when the situation is right and the appropriate woman comes along.

These interviews reveal that one cannot predict simply on the basis of sexual attractions and involvements whether a woman considers herself to be lesbian, bisexual, or heterosexual. Among the interviewees were women who despite having only heterosexual experience reported that they were lesbians; women with bisexual experience who considered themselves to be either lesbian or heterosexual; women who despite having current same-gendered sexual experience reported that they were heterosexual or bisexual; and women who have had only heterosexual experience and yet considered themselves to be bisexual. Neither does sexual attraction neatly predict sexual involvement. Some interviewed women have experienced same- and/or opposite-gender attractions but have never acted on them; others have made a conscious decision to experience and pursue these attractions. Finally, these interviews reveal that the gender of those to whom women are sexually attracted may change over time, as may the gender of those with whom they become sexually involved.

Are these cases rare exceptions or do they represent common experiences among women exploring their sexuality? Similar to all interview research conducted with lesbians and bisexuals, these women are not drawn from random samples and therefore no claim is made that these women represent most or even a majority of lesbians or bisexual women. While it would be impossible to determine the precise percentages due to the difficulty of obtaining a truly random sample, numbers are less important than that which the interviews reveal about the variability and diversity among women as they engage in the process of sexual identification.

## DEFINITIONS OF SEXUAL ORIENTATION

A brief consideration of the ways in which psychologists think about sexual orientation and sexual identity serves to highlight that which is most significant about these interviews with women. Psychologists define sexual orientation in terms of whether a person's "primary affectional/erotic attractions" are to people of the same gender, the other gender, or to both (Gonsiorek & Weinrich, 1991; Greene, 1994). People are characterized as if they clearly belong to one of four discrete categories: lesbian, gay, bisexual, or heterosexual, even though many psychologists, following Kinsey, Pomeroy, and Martin (1948), acknowledge that human sexuality exists along a continuum and that dichotomous categories represent a distortion of the multiple forms human sexuality takes (DeCecco, 1982; Ellis, Burke, & Ames, 1987).

Sexual orientation is generally considered a stable characteristic that is established by adolescence, often before sexual activity has occurred. People are believed to know their orientation through a subjective awareness of whether they experience same- or opposite-gendered attractions (Bell, Weinberg, & Hammersmith, 1981; Gonsiorek & Weinrich, 1991). It is further assumed that a person's sexual orientation will be consistent with her or his sexual behavior and sexual identification. In other words, given a homosexual orientation, a person will engage in same-sex sexual activity and will come to identify as lesbian or gay through a process known as coming out (see Cohen & Savin-Williams, "Coming Out," this volume). Much of this research is based on male subjects and, as with most areas of psychological research and theorizing, may not be generalizable to women. The interview material presented here suggests that a woman's sexual orientation, as determined by attraction and arousal, may not always be consistent with her sexual behavior or the sexual identity she adopts. Similarly, the claim that sexual orientation is clearly established by adolescence and stable across the life course may not be applicable to women.

Consider for example, the manner in which sexual orientation is defined. There may be more to sexual orientation among women than "affectional/erotic attraction." Money (1988) argued that the definitive criterion for sexual orientation is falling in love; a homosexual person is one who falls in love with someone of the same sex. Money also identified other criteria, such as "being sexually attracted to" and "aroused by," assuming that these always occurred with falling in love. However, this is not the case for all women. In the interviews, some bisexual women reported sexual attractions to other females without being in love with them; some heterosexual women described themselves as in love with their girlfriends without experiencing sexual arousal; and some lesbians reported loving but asexual relationships.

Shively and DeCecco (1977) identified three critical components of sexual orientation: the sex of the people one fantasizes about, the sex of the people one has been sexually involved with, and the sex of the people one affectionally prefers. While this conceptual scheme allows for more than one contributor to sexual orientation, it fails to recognize that these factors may not always be consistent. For example, many women describe affectional or emotional preferences for women but experience sexual relationships exclusively with men. Chodorow (1978) characterized this pattern as heterosexual asymmetry.

Klein (1990) based his sexual orientation grid on four variables, including sexual attraction, social preference, self-identification, and lifestyle choice. The incorporation of self-identification and lifestyle choice as components of sexual orientation, rather than as outcomes, is important because it is inclusive of women's experience. In interview accounts of how they came to their current sexual identification, women spoke not only about sexual attraction and behavior but about conscious decisions to be sexually open to people of the same gender. Their self-identification could be significantly influenced by social and political, as well as sexual, considerations.

One way to resolve the issue of whether sexual identity is separate from sexual orientation or is a component of it, as Klein (1990) suggested, is to distinguish between sexual orientation as a "given" over which people have no choice and sexual identity as a label that people choose to apply to themselves.[2] Women may choose to call themselves lesbians or bisexuals because they prefer women emotionally or because of political considerations, but that does not mean that they actually choose their sexuality. In other words, they may choose their identity but not their orientation. Yet, women spoke *as if* they chose more than their self-label; they described themselves as deciding with whom to become sexually attracted and involved. Some might argue that these women were "really" bisexual and their openness to sexual relationships with women, after a history of sexual attractions and relationships exclusively with men, merely reflects a predetermined (bi)sexuality. However one thinks about this issue, some women undeniably experience their sexuality as fluid. Whether this is a result of an underlying bisexual orientation that was always present or a conscious choice cannot be definitively determined. Nevertheless, conceptualizing women's sexuality as potentially fluid allows for a more comprehensive understanding of the process of sexual self-identification in women.[3]

# CONCLUSION

Identities and behaviors that appear puzzling and difficult to explain become clearer when the fluidity of women's sexuality is taken into account. For example, women who have always considered themselves heterosexual may become aware in adulthood that they are attracted to women as well as men. These women may act on their sexual attractions, despite no previous experience, and develop strong identities as lesbians. Some may consider themselves bisexual and eventually act on their attractions, while others may consciously resist doing so—for diverse reasons. If sexuality is fluid, then it is understandable that some women consider themselves "bisexual lesbians," that is, they chose to be sexually involved with women and to identify as lesbians while acknowledging that they may experience sexual attractions to men. It makes clearer the experience of so-called transient lesbians, women who for a period of time identify as lesbians and are involved with women but who subsequently become involved with men. It explains so-called political lesbians, who decide based on feminist beliefs that it is preferable to be sexually involved with women and who make this an erotic as well as a political choice.

This expanded perspective on women's sexuality contributes to an understanding of bisexuality as a distinct form of sexual expression, and of bisexuals as women who recognize and act according to their sexual fluidity. Some lesbians consider bisexuals to be lesbians who are unwilling to forgo heterosexual privilege; some heterosexuals believe that bisexuals are simply confused and have not made up their minds. But if sexuality is not essential (fixed and unchanging) or dichotomous (focused exclusively on women or men), then bisexuals are neither confused, passing through a stage in the process of coming out, nor unwilling to give up heterosexual privilege.

Conceptualizing sexuality as fluid and as subject to personal choice also helps make sense of the fascination, fear, and even hatred of lesbians, gays, and bisexuals in our culture. For example, consider the virulent antihomosexual sentiment that characterizes recent efforts in Oregon, Colorado, and Georgia to deny civil rights to lesbian and gay people. If sexuality is not fixed and it is possible to choose one's sexual attractions, then exclusive heterosexuality *is* in danger. As the visibility of lesbian and gay people increases, and as individuals who are "out" and very comfortable with their sexuality are perceived as acceptable, it is more likely that people of all ages will decide that lesbian, gay, or bisexual lifestyles are as viable as any other. If deviations from the prescribed path of heterosexuality were not a real possibility, those people committed to the superiority of exclusive heterosexuality would have little to fear from the open integration and inclusion of lesbians, gays, and bisexuals into public life.

Despite the current scientific and media emphasis on the biological bases of homosexuality, there appears to be an underlying concern that homosexuality is not so biologically fixed and "natural." It seems to me that underlying the virulent resistance to the inclusion of lesbians and gays into mainstream society is the fear that young people (of undeclared sexuality) and heterosexual adults, upon exposure to a range of possibilities, could develop *ideas* that they might then *choose* to act upon. If those committed to exclusive heterosexuality truly believed that sexuality is fixed and set at birth, they would not be so threatened by visible lesbians and gays, nor so fearful of their potential for "converting" others.

If sexuality is potentially fluid and people can make choices about the gender of the people to whom they are attracted, then as teachers, parents, and friends of young people, we should be thinking very differently about the socialization of sexual development. This has particular relevance for sex education classes, one goal of which is to provide young people with a sense of the importance of making decisions about their sexual behavior. Issues of whether and when to become sexually active, the kinds of behaviors to engage in, and the use of protective devices are considered appropriate matters to discuss. When the topic of sexual preference or orientation is raised, however, it is not typically regarded as something about which a young person must decide. Contemporary discourse on sexuality holds that sexual orientation is predetermined early in development and is invariant over the course of life (see Ellis chapters, this volume). Thus, decision-making is reserved for lesbian and gay youth, who must consider whether and how to acknowledge their already determined sexual orientation and to confront the process of coming out (see Cohen & Savin-Williams, "Coming Out," this volume). Heterosexual youth are not encouraged to consider the implications of heterosexuality for their development except with regard to specific concerns such as pregnancy and sexually transmitted diseases.

Heterosexuals could benefit as much as self-identified lesbians and gays from discussions of the diversity and variability in human sexuality. Teaching directly about sexual fluidity would undoubtedly be viewed by some as an attempt to "convert" students, that is, to encourage them to engage in same-gender sexual experiences. Yet, educational materials that address marriage and traditional family life are rarely viewed as enforcing the singular standard of compulsory heterosexuality (Rich, 1980). Once the fluidity of sexuality is acknowledged, then it becomes problematic to repeatedly present the view that sexuality is fixed. Not only will this contradict the subjective experience of some people, especially women, but it may prevent individuals from investigating a varied realm of choices.

Perhaps more effective than direct teaching is exposure to the range of choices that people in the real world actually make. If lesbian, gay, and bisexual people were freer to express themselves and to be as visible in their public lives as are heterosexuals, then young people would learn that there are a variety of ways to live and act sexually and that intimate partners can be of the same or other gender. Regardless of whether it would be a good or bad outcome, there is no reason whatsoever to believe that this would lead to homosexuality on a massive scale. Yet, many homophobic people seem to be terrified of this possibility—that the visibility of lesbian, gay, and bisexual people will fundamentally change the world as they know it. This may be correct. Greater acceptance of all sexual choices and lifestyles might allow for more variability and diversity in the process of self- and sexual identification.

## ▼ ENDNOTES ▼

1. In my interviews with heterosexually identified women, some indicated that they had sexually "experimented" with other women and found the experiences less than satisfying, concluding that they were "really" heterosexual. In other cases, however, they acknowledged that there were other factors that could have contributed to the less than fully positive experience, including fear, inexperience, and internalized homophobia.

2. Money (1988) articulated this position most clearly. He asserted that the term sexual preference is incorrect because people do not choose their sexuality. Rather, it "is something that happens . . . like being tall or short, left-handed or right-handed, color-blind or color-seeing" (p. 11). According to Money, no one prefers to be homosexual rather than heterosexual, or bisexual rather than monosexual. One wonders whether Money has ever included women in his formulations.

3. The reader might wonder how this discussion of sexual fluidity applies to men and their sexuality. There is no similar interview research with gay or heterosexual men that addresses this issue, but from reading gay male literature, speaking with a small sample of gay men, and exchanging views with therapists who work with them, my sense is that gay men do not experience their sexuality in the fluid manner that some lesbians, bisexual, and heterosexual women do. I suspect that very few gay men could be characterized as elective gays. Although this observation might seem puzzling and lead one to question why the experience of sexuality would be different for women and men, it becomes more comprehensible with reference to psychoanalytic theories of mothering. Specifically, object relations theory provides a framework for understanding how the conditions of early infancy might lead women to have greater bisexual potential than men. To the extent that infants and young children are primarily nurtured by women (and depending on the importance one attaches to this experience as a contributor to later sexuality), one might expect boys to be more predisposed toward heterosexuality and girls to be more directed toward lesbianism (Chodorow, 1978, 1994; Dinnerstein, 1976). Including the cultural imperative toward heterosexuality, one might expect a greater incidence of bisexuality among women, or at least the expression of interest in the possibility.

## ▼ REFERENCES ▼

Allison, D. (1994). *Skin: Talking about sex, class, & literature*. Ithaca, NY: Firebrand Books.

Bell, A. P., Weinberg, M. S., & Hammersmith, S. K. (1981). *Sexual preference: Its development in men and women*. Bloomington, IN: Indiana University Press.

Boston Lesbian Psychologies Collective (Ed.). (1987). *Lesbian psychologies: Explorations and challenges*. Chicago: University of Illinois Press.

Chodorow, N. (1978). *The reproduction of mothering: Psychoanalysis and the sociology of gender*. Berkeley: University of California Press.

Chodorow, N. (1994). *Femininities, masculinities, sexualities: Freud and beyond*. Lexington, KY: University of Kentucky Press.

Cook, B. W. (1977). Female support networks and political activism. *Chrysalis, 3*, 43–61.

DeCecco, J. (1982). Definition and meaning of sexual orientation. *Journal of Homosexuality, 6*, 51–67.

D'Emilio, J. (1983). *Sexual politics, sexual communities: The making of a homosexual minority in the United States*. Chicago: University of Chicago Press.

D'Emilio, J., & Freedman, E. B. (1988). *Intimate matters: A history of sexuality in America*. New York: Harper & Row.

Dinnerstein, D. (1976). *The mermaid and the minotaur: Sexual arrangements and the human malaise*. New York: Harper & Row.

Ellis, L., Burke, D., & Ames, M. A. (1987). Sexual orientation as a continuous variable: A comparison between the sexes. *Archives of Sexual Behavior, 6*, 523–529.

Esterberg, K. G. (1994). Being a lesbian and being in love: Constructing identities through relationships. *Journal of Gay and Lesbian Social Services, 1*, 57–82.

Faderman, L. (1981). *Surpassing the love of men: Romantic friendships between women from the Renaissance to the present*. New York: William Morrow.

Faderman, L. (1991). *Odd girls and twilight lovers: A history of lesbian life in twentieth century America*. New York: Columbia University Press.

Faludi, S. (1991). *Backlash: The undeclared war against American women*. New York: Crown.

Ferguson, A. (1981). Compulsory heterosexuality and lesbian existence: Defining the issues. *Signs: Journal of Women in Culture and Society, 7*, 158–172.

Foucault, M. (1978). *The history of sexuality*. New York: Pantheon.

Golden, C. (1987). Diversity and variability in women's sexual identities. In Boston Lesbian Psychologies Collective (Ed.), *Lesbian psychologies: Explorations and challenges* (pp. 19–34). Urbana, IL: University of Illinois Press.

Golden, C. (1994). Our politics and choices: The feminist movement and sexual orientation. In B. Greene & G. M. Herek (Eds.), *Lesbian and gay psychology: Theory, research, and clinical applications* (pp. 54–70). Thousand Oaks, CA: Sage.

Gonsiorek, J. C., & Weinrich, J. D. (1991). The definition and scope of sexual orientation. In J. C. Gonsiorek & J. D. Weinrich (Eds.), *Homosexuality: Research implications for public policy* (pp. 1–12). Newbury Park, CA: Sage.

Greene, B. (1994). Lesbian and gay sexual orientations: Implications for clinical training, practice, and research. In B. Greene & G. M. Herek (Eds.), *Lesbian and gay psychology: Theory, research, and clinical applications* (pp. 1–24). Thousand Oaks, CA: Sage.

Hoagland, S., & Penelope, J. (1991). *For lesbians only*. London: Onlywoman Press.

Kinsey, A. C., Pomeroy, W. B., & Martin, C. E. (1948). *Sexual behavior in the human male.* Philadelphia: W. B. Saunders.

Klein, F. (1990). The need to view sexual orientation as a multivariable dynamic process: A theoretical perspective. In D. S. McWhirter, S. A. Sanders, & J. M. Reinisch (Eds.), *Homosexuality/heterosexuality: Concepts of sexual orientation* (pp. 277–282). New York: Oxford University Press.

Money, J. (1988). *Gay, straight, and in-between: The sexology of erotic orientation.* New York: Oxford University Press.

Ponse, B. (1978). *Identities in the lesbian world.* Westport, CT: Greenwood.

Radicalesbians (1973). Woman-identified woman. In A. Koedt, E. LeVine, & A. Rapone (Eds.), *Radical feminism* (pp. 240–245). New York: Quadrangle Books.

Rich, A. (1980). Compulsory heterosexuality and lesbian existence. *Signs: Journal of Women in Culture and Society, 5,* 631–660.

Rothblum, E. D., & Brehony, K. (1993). *Boston marriages: Romantic but asexual relationships among contemporary lesbians.* Amherst, MA: University of Massachusetts Press.

Rust, P. C. (1992). Who are we and where do we go from here? Conceptualizing bisexuality. In E. R. Weise (Ed.), *Closer to home: Bisexuality and feminism* (pp. 281–310). Seattle, WA: The Seal Press.

Shively, M. G., & DeCecco, J. P. (1977). Components of sexual identity. *Journal of Homosexuality, 3,* 41–48.

Whisman, V. (1993). Identity crises: Who is a lesbian, anyway? In A. Stein (Ed.), *Sisters, sexperts, queers: Beyond the lesbian nation.* New York: Penguin.

Wolf, N. (1991). *The beauty myth: How images of beauty are used against women.* New York: William Morrow.

Zita, J. (1981). Compulsory heterosexuality and lesbian existence: Defining the issues. *Signs: Journal of Women in Culture and Society, 7,* 172–187.

# Chapter 11

▼

# GAY AND LESBIAN RELATIONSHIPS

Letitia Anne Peplau
Rosemary C. Veniegas
&
Susan Miller Campbell[1]

*Few heterosexual Americans have a close friend who is gay or lesbian, and fewer still invite gay or lesbian couples to their homes. In a recent national survey, only one person in three indicated that any of their female or male friends, relatives, or close acquaintances were lesbian or gay (Herek, 1994). Many heterosexuals who believe that they do not know any lesbians or gay men are mistaken—they are simply unaware of the sexual orientation of their friends, coworkers, or acquaintances. Fearing social rejection, discrimination, and harassment, many lesbians and gay men conceal their sexual orientation. This point is illustrated in a study of 275 lesbian couples, most of whom had been together for more than five years and currently lived with each other (Eldridge & Gilbert, 1990). Several couples (15%) were raising children. Despite their strong commitment to the relationship, more than three quarters of these couples concealed their lesbianism and the true nature of their relationship from their neighbors, two thirds had not disclosed to their employers, more than one half had not told their fathers, and more than one third kept the true nature of their relationship a secret from their mothers. As a result of such concealment, gay and lesbian couples remain largely invisible to heterosexual society.*

*Lacking personal contact with lesbian and gay couples, many heterosexuals' attitudes about same-sex relationships are based on stereotypes, media images, and hearsay—sources that are often negative and of questionable accuracy. Many Americans do not view lesbians and gay men as real people, but rather as abstract symbols who challenge conventional roles for women and men and who threaten traditional religious and family values. More than half of all Americans consider the "homosexual lifestyle" unacceptable (Turque, 1992), and a common belief is that same-sex couples have transient and troubled relationships.*

*Social science research on lesbian and gay relationships challenges prevailing stereotypes. In this chapter we summarize the growing body of scientific research about the love relationships of lesbians and gay men. We consider the quality of same-sex partnerships, the dynamics of power and the division of labor, problems and conflicts, the ending of relationships through breakups and death, and new forms of couples counseling. Research findings highlight the diversity among same-sex partnerships and reveal many basic commonalities among human love relationships regardless of sexual orientation.*

## LOVE AND COMMITMENT

*The engraved invitation read, "After 20 years of love and life together, Emalee and Sarah would like to renew the vows they made to one another. You are invited to share in the joy of the 20th anniversary of their commitment ceremony. A reception and dinner at their home will follow the ceremony."*

Love and companionship are important ingredients for a happy life. A national survey of Americans found that most people, regardless of sexual identity, consider love to be extremely important for their overall happiness (Freedman, 1978). Ample research documents that intimate relationships are a key factor in psychological health and happiness. In a recent review, Myers (1992) concluded, "Whether young or old, male or female, rich or poor, people in stable, loving relationships do enjoy greater well-being" (p. 156).

Many gay men and lesbians desire an enduring love relationship (Bell & Weinberg, 1978) and are successful in achieving this goal. Empirical surveys about intimate relationships report that 40% to 60% of gay men and 45% to 80% of lesbians are currently in a romantic relationship (Peplau & Cochran, 1990). These figures may underestimate the true proportions because most studies survey relatively young individuals, who may be less likely to have settled into a committed relationship. Studies that include older adults report that many lesbians and gay men establish lifelong partnerships (Blumstein & Schwartz, 1983; McWhirter & Mattison, 1984). For example, a study of lesbians over the age of 60 found relationships lasting 30 years and longer (Kehoe, 1989).

## Love and Satisfaction

Many people believe that gay and lesbian relationships are unhappy. For example, one study found that heterosexual college students expected gay and lesbian relationships to be less satisfying and more prone to discord than heterosexual relationships, and they believed gay and lesbian couples to be "less in love" than heterosexual partners (Testa, Kinder, & Ironson, 1987). However, available research provides no evidence that same-sex couples are typically troubled or less successful than heterosexual couples.

Several studies have compared gay, lesbian, and heterosexual couples in order to investigate differences in the partners' love for each other and their satisfaction with the relationship. These studies often matched same-sex and heterosexual couples on age, income, and other background characteristics that might otherwise bias the results. In an illustrative study, Peplau and Cochran (1980) selected matched samples of 50 lesbians, 50 gay men, 50 heterosexual women, and 50 heterosexual men who were currently in a romantic/sexual relationship. Among this sample of young adults, about 60% said they were in love with their partner, and most of the rest said they were "uncertain" about whether they were in love. On Rubin's standardized Love and Liking Scales, the lesbians and gay men generally reported very positive feelings for their partners and rated their current relationships as highly satisfying and close. No significant differences were found among lesbians, gay men, and heterosexuals on any measure of relationship quality. Other studies using standardized measures of satisfaction, love, and adjustment have found the same pattern—no significant differences among couples based on sexual orientation. Gay men and lesbians report as much satisfaction with their relationships as do heterosexuals (Cardell, Finn, & Marecek, 1981; Dailey, 1979; Duffy & Rusbult, 1986; Kurdek & Schmitt, 1986a, 1986b, 1987; Peplau & Cochran, 1980; Peplau, Padesky, & Hamilton, 1982). Thus, contrary to prevailing stereotypes, research indicates that most gay and lesbian couples are happy.

These findings do not imply that all gay men and lesbians have problem-free relationships. As reported later in this chapter, there are sources of conflict in same-sex relationships, just as there are in heterosexual relationships. Rather, the point is that lesbians and gay men are no more likely than heterosexuals to have dysfunctional relationships.

In the last decade, researchers have begun to identify factors that enhance satisfaction in same-sex relationships. Social exchange theory predicts that satisfaction is high when a person perceives that a relationship provides many rewards, such as a partner's intelligence, interesting personality, sense of humor, or sex appeal. Satisfaction is also high when a relationship entails relatively few costs, for instance, when conflict is low and a partner has few irritating behaviors. Several studies have found that perceived rewards and costs are significant predictors of happiness in lesbians' and gay men's relationships (Kurdek, 1991a; Kurdek & Schmitt, 1986a). For example, Duffy and Rusbult (1986) compared the relationships of lesbians, gay men, and heterosexuals. In all three groups, greater satisfaction was significantly associated with the experience of relatively more personal rewards and fewer personal costs. In a study of lesbian relationships, Peplau et al. (1982) found support for another exchange theory prediction, that satisfaction is higher when partners are equally involved in or committed to a relationship.

Other correlates of satisfaction in gay and lesbian relationships have been investigated as well. For example, partners' values about relationships can make a difference. Individuals vary in the degree to which they value "dyadic attachment" (Peplau, Cochran, Rook, & Padesky, 1978). A person is high in attachment to the extent that he or she emphasizes the importance of shared activities, spending time together, long-term commitment, and sexual exclusivity in a relationship.

Lesbians and gay men who strongly value togetherness and security in a relationship report significantly higher satisfaction, closeness, and love for their partner than do individuals who score lower on attachment values (Eldridge & Gilbert, 1990; Peplau et al., 1978; Peplau & Cochran, 1981). Individuals can also differ in the degree to which they value personal autonomy, defined as wanting to have separate friends and activities apart from their primary relationship. Although some studies have found that lesbians and gay men who place strong emphasis on autonomy report significantly lower love and satisfaction than individuals who score lower on autonomy values (Eldridge & Gilbert, 1990; Kurdek, 1989), other studies have not (Peplau et al., 1978; Peplau & Cochran, 1981).

There may also be links between the balance of power in a relationship and partners' satisfaction. Several studies of lesbians and gay men have found that satisfaction is higher when partners believe they share relatively equally in power and decision-making (Eldridge & Gilbert, 1990; Harry, 1984; Kurdek, 1989; Kurdek & Schmitt, 1986a; Peplau et al., 1982). Finally, a recent study suggests that happy and unhappy couples may differ in their approach to problem-solving (Kurdek, 1991a). In both lesbian and gay relationships, satisfied partners were more likely than unhappy partners to use positive problem-solving approaches, such as focusing on the specific problem at hand. Partners in happy couples were less likely than other couples to use such negative approaches as launching a personal attack, growing defensive, or withdrawing from the interaction.

## Commitment

It is estimated that roughly one in every two recent heterosexual marriages will end in divorce (Martin & Bumpass, 1989). These figures are a forceful reminder that romantic relationships do not necessarily last "until death do us part" or even for a very long time. How do lesbians and gay men fare in their efforts to maintain enduring intimate relationships? Those interested in heterosexual relationships can use official marriage records and census reports to chart the length of relationships, but comparable data are not available for gay men and lesbians.

One of the few large-scale studies of lesbian, gay, and heterosexual couples (Blumstein & Schwartz, 1983) assessed the stability of relationships over an 18-month period. For couples who had already been together for at least 10 years, the breakup rate was quite low: Only 6% of lesbian couples, 4% of gay couples, and 4% of married couples separated during the 18-month period. Among couples together for 2 years or less, some differences in the breakup rates were found: 22% for lesbian couples, 16% for gay couples, 17% for heterosexual cohabiting couples, and 4% for married couples. It is noteworthy that the largest difference among these short-term couples was not between heterosexual and same-sex couples, but rather between legally married couples and unmarried couples, regardless of sexual orientation.

Relationship researchers have identified several factors that affect the longevity of intimate relationships and that help to explain the greater duration of legally married couples (e.g., Levinger, 1979). A first factor concerns positive attraction forces that make one want to stay with a partner, such as love and satisfaction with the relationship. As we noted earlier, research shows that same-sex and male-female couples typically report comparable levels of happiness in their relationships.

Second, the duration of a relationship is also affected by barriers that make it difficult for a person to leave a relationship. Barriers include anything that increases the psychological, emotional, or financial costs of ending a relationship. Heterosexual marriage can create many barriers to separation, such as the cost of divorce, investments in joint property, concerns about children, and one partner's financial dependence on the other. These obstacles may encourage married couples to work toward improving a deteriorating relationship, rather than ending it. In contrast, gay and lesbian couples are less likely to experience comparable barriers to the ending of a relationship—they cannot marry legally, they are less likely to co-own property, their relatives may prefer that they end their relationship, they are less likely to have children in common, and so on.

Kurdek and Schmitt (1986a) systematically compared the attractions and barriers experienced by partners in gay, lesbian, and heterosexual cohabiting couples and in married couples. They found no differences across the four groups in attractions; all groups reported comparable feelings of love and satisfaction. However, barriers, assessed by statements such as "many things would prevent me from leaving my partner even if I were unhappy," differed. Married couples reported significantly more barriers than either gay men or lesbians, and cohabiting heterosexual couples reported the fewest barriers of all. Similarly, in their study of lesbian, gay, and heterosexual couples, Blumstein and Schwartz (1983) found that couples who pooled some or all of their financial assets together were less likely to break up. Not surprisingly, married heterosexuals were the couples most likely to have joint finances. In a recent longitudinal study of cohabiting lesbian and gay couples followed over a four-year period, Kurdek (1992) also found that couples who pooled their finances were less likely to break up.

A third factor affecting the longevity of a relationship is the availability of alternatives to the present relationship. To the extent that people want to be involved in an intimate relationship, having fewer potential partners available may encourage partners to work out their problems. In contrast, a person who believes that many attractive partners are readily available or who would be just as happy single may be quicker to end a relationship. Only two studies have compared the perception of available alternatives among gay, lesbian, and heterosexual couples, and they differ in their findings. One study found that lesbians and married couples reported significantly fewer alternatives than did gay men and heterosexual cohabitants (Kurdek & Schmitt, 1986a). In contrast, a second study found no significant differences among lesbians, gay men, and heterosexuals—all of whom reported having moderately poor alternatives (Duffy & Rusbult, 1986).

In summary, research finds that gay and lesbian couples can and do have committed, enduring relationships. On average, heterosexual and same-sex couples report similar high levels of attraction toward their partner and satisfaction with their relationship. Couples differ, however, in the obstacles that make it difficult to end a relationship. Here, the legal and social context of marriage creates barriers to breaking up that do not typically exist for same-sex partners or for cohabiting heterosexuals. The relative lack of barriers may make it less likely that lesbians and gay men will be trapped in hopelessly miserable and deteriorating relationships. However, weaker barriers may also allow partners to end relationships that might have improved if given more time and effort. As lesbians and gay men gain greater recognition as "domestic partners," the barriers for gay and lesbian relationships may become more similar to those of heterosexuals. Currently, for example, several large companies have extended health benefits to same-sex domestic partners and increasing numbers of lesbian couples are raising children jointly (see Patterson, this volume). The impact of such trends on the stability of same-sex relationships is an important topic for further investigation.

## POWER AND THE DIVISION OF LABOR

*Jim is deeply in love with Tom, and the two have been together for almost a year. When Jim suggested that they move in together, Tom gave excuses. Jim wonders just how much Tom cares for him and tries hard to make their relationship work. When they disagree about something, Jim usually gives in and lets Tom have his way, rather than risking an argument.*

## Power

Who has more say in a relationship? Does one partner dominate the other? Researchers have studied the balance of power, that is, the general way in which power is distributed in a relationship. Today, many Americans endorse power equality as an ideal for love relationships, and this emphasis on egalitarianism is especially strong among young adults. For example, Peplau and Cochran (1980) compared the relationship values of matched samples of young lesbians, gay men, and heterosexuals. All groups rated "having an egalitarian (equal power) relationship" as quite important. When asked what the ideal balance of power should be in their current relationship, 92% of gay men and 97% of lesbians said it should be "exactly equal." Not everyone, however, was successful in attaining this egalitarian ideal. Only 59% of lesbians, 38% of gay men, 48% of heterosexual women, and 40% of heterosexual men reported that their current relationship was "exactly equal." The percentage of people who describe their relationship as equal in power has varied across studies. For instance, equal power was reported by 59% of the 140 lesbians studied by Reilly and Lynch (1990) and by 60% of the 243 gay men studied by Harry and DeVall (1978).

Several factors can tip the balance of power away from equality. Social exchange theory predicts that greater power accrues to the partner who has relatively greater personal resources, such as education, money, or social standing. Several studies have provided empirical support for this hypothesis. In two separate studies of gay men, Harry found that unequal decision-making was associated with partner differences in age and income; men who were older and wealthier tended to have more power than their partner (Harry, 1984; Harry & DeVall, 1978). Similarly, in their large-scale study of couples, Blumstein and Schwartz (1983) concluded that "in gay male couples, income is an extremely important force in determining which partner will be dominant" (p. 59). For lesbians, research findings on personal resources and power are less clear-cut. A study of 77 young adult lesbians in Los Angeles found that differences in income and education were significantly related to power (Caldwell & Peplau, 1984). Another study reported that perceptions of which partner had "more say" were unrelated to education or age but were associated with large differences between the income of the two women (Reilly & Lynch, 1990). In contrast, Blumstein and Schwartz (1983) concluded, "Lesbians do not use income to establish dominance in their relationship. They use it to avoid having one woman dependent on the other" (p. 60). Further research on the balance of power among lesbian couples is needed to clarify these inconsistent results.

A second prediction from social exchange theory is that when one person in a relationship is relatively more dependent or involved than the other, the dependent person will be at a power disadvantage. This has been called the "principle of least interest" because the less interested person tends to have more power. Studies of heterosexuals have clearly demonstrated that lopsided dependencies are linked to imbalances of power (e.g., Peplau & Campbell, 1989). To date, only one study has tested this hypothesis with same-sex couples. Among the young lesbians studied by Caldwell and Peplau (1984), there was a strong association between unequal involvement and unequal power, with the less involved person having more power.

Another approach to understanding power in relationships focuses on the specific tactics that partners use to influence each other. For example, Falbo and Peplau (1980) asked lesbians, gay men, and heterosexuals to describe how they influence their romantic partner to do what they want. These open-ended descriptions were reliably categorized into several influence strategies. The results led to two major conclusions. First, gender affected power tactics, but only among heterosexuals. Whereas heterosexual women were more likely to withdraw or express negative emotions, heterosexual men were more likely to use bargaining or reasoning. But this sex difference did not emerge in comparisons of lesbians and gay men influencing their same-sex partner. Second, regardless of gender or sexual orientation, individuals who perceived themselves as relatively more powerful in the relationship tended to use persuasion and bargaining. In contrast, partners low in power tended to use withdrawal and emotion.

Another study comparing the intimate relationships of lesbians, gay men, and heterosexuals also found that an individual's use of influence tactics depended on his or her relative power in the relationship (Howard, Blumstein, & Schwartz, 1986). Regardless of sexual orientation, a partner with relatively less power tended to use "weak" strategies such as supplication and manipulation.

Those in positions of strength were more likely to use autocratic and bullying tactics, both "strong" strategies. Further, individuals with male partners (i.e., heterosexual women and gay men) were more likely to use supplication and manipulation. Similarly, Kollock, Blumstein, and Schwartz (1985) found that signs of conversational dominance, such as interrupting a partner in the middle of a sentence, were linked to the balance of power. Although interruption has sometimes been viewed as a male behavior, it was actually used more often by the dominant person in the relationship, regardless of that person's gender or sexual orientation. Taken together, the results suggest that although some influence strategies have been stereotyped as masculine or feminine, they may more correctly be viewed as a reflection of power rather than gender.

## Division of Labor

All couples face decisions about who will do what in their life together. For a dating couple these decisions range from who will do the driving to who will take the lead in initiating sexual intimacy. When a couple decides to live together, new questions arise about responsibilities for housework, finances, and entertaining guests. Traditional sex roles have provided ready-made answers to these questions for heterosexuals—the man is the leader and breadwinner and the woman is the follower and homemaker. Heterosexuals who reject traditional roles may find that it takes considerable effort to forge new patterns of relating.

How do gay and lesbian couples organize their lives together? Tripp noted, "When people who are not familiar with homosexual relationships try to picture one, they almost invariably resort to a heterosexual frame of reference, raising questions about which partner is 'the man' and which 'the woman'" (1975, p. 152). Historical accounts of gay life in the United States before the advent of gay rights organizations and the modern feminist movement suggest that masculine-feminine roles were fairly common (see Jacobson & Grossman, this volume). For example, Wolf (1980) described lesbian experiences in the 1950s in these terms:

> The old gay world divided up into "butch" and "femme." . . . Butches were tough, presented themselves as being as masculine as possible . . . and they assumed the traditional male role of taking care of their partners, even fighting over them if necessary. . . . Femmes, by contrast, were protected, ladylike. . . . They cooked, cleaned house, and took care of their "butch." (p. 40)

Today, most lesbians and gay men actively reject traditional husband-wife or masculine-feminine roles as a model for enduring relationships (Blumstein & Schwartz, 1983; Harry, 1983, 1984; McWhirter & Mattison, 1984; Peplau & Gordon, 1983).

Most lesbians and gay men are in dual-worker relationships, so that neither partner is the exclusive breadwinner and each partner has some measure of economic independence. The most common division of labor involves flexibility, with partners sharing domestic activities or dividing tasks according to personal preferences. For example, in Bell and Weinberg's (1978) study nearly 60% of lesbians and gay men said that housework was shared equally. Asked if one partner consistently does all the "feminine tasks" or all the "masculine tasks," about 90% of lesbians and gay men said "no." Indeed, some gay men and lesbians report that one of the things they appreciate about same-sex relationships is being able to avoid traditional roles: "Role playing seems to me by nature to involve dominance and control," one gay man explained, "both of which make me feel uncomfortable" (Jay & Young, 1977, p. 369). A lesbian explained that she and her partner joke about butch-femme roles. "She will say, 'Well, I guess I'm the femme today,' but we really aren't into role playing at all. . . . If we see couples into butch-femme relationships, we go, 'Oh, yick!'" (Blumstein & Schwartz, 1983, p. 451).

Several researchers have suggested that today many lesbians and gay men base their relationships on a friendship model (Harry, 1983, Peplau, 1991). In best friendships, partners are often of relatively similar age and share common interests, skills, and resources. Unlike traditional marriages, best friendships are usually similar in status and power.

Additional research about the division of labor in same-sex relationships is needed. One particularly valuable direction for inquiry is the examination of the ways in which same-sex couples juggle the various responsibilities they have to their partner, job, children, aging parents, and community activities (e.g. Shachar & Gilbert, 1983). When both spouses in a heterosexual marriage have full-time jobs, women shoulder the majority of housework and child care, creating a substantial imbalance in workload (Crosby, 1991). Perhaps an understanding of the more egalitarian division of labor in same-sex relationships will provide clues about how all couples can arrive at a more equitable sharing of responsibilities.

## PROBLEMS AND CONFLICT

*Joan and Kate have lived together for six years. Joan's career as an attorney frequently takes her out of town and Kate's work as a librarian at a local college is also very demanding. Increasingly Joan and Kate have little time to spend with each other. They often argue out of frustration and fear that their relationship is headed for a breakup. Both women are unwilling to compromise their careers but do not want to lose the relationship.*

Disagreements and conflicts occur in all intimate relationships. A study of heterosexual newlyweds identified 85 different types of conflicts (Gottman, 1979). Among lesbian and gay couples, the range of possible conflicts is probably equally large. Because most of the available information about problems in lesbian and gay relationships comes from reports by therapists about their clients, the full range of problems encountered in same-sex partnerships may not be represented. Issues described in the literature include differences in background or values, concerns about finances or work, sexual problems, jealousy or possessiveness, and problems with family members (Berger, 1990; Berzon, 1988; Browning, Reynolds, & Dworkin, 1991; George & Behrendt, 1988). In short, many problems in same-sex relationships are similar to those in heterosexual relationships. There are, however, problems specific to same-sex couples. We consider two problems that arise from gender socialization and from homophobia.

## Merger and Competition

Some authors have speculated that the gender socialization of men and women may create unique problems for same-sex couples that are not encountered by heterosexuals. For example, it has been suggested that lesbians are at special risk of becoming overly involved and identified with each other, in part because our society teaches women to value intimacy and emotional closeness. Evidence for this point comes from clinicians who work with lesbian couples in therapy and have described a problem called "merger," "fusion," or "enmeshment" (Falco, 1991; Krestan & Bepko, 1980; Roth, 1984; Smalley, 1987). *Merger* has been defined as "the difficulty of maintaining separate identities within the relationship, and a tendency for merging in thoughts, actions, or feelings" (Browning et al., 1991, p. 185). In therapy, merger is inferred when partners seem to be too emotionally close, or when partners appear confused about their individual feelings, opinions, or personal identity. Burch (1986) provided the following illustration of a merger problem:

> Judith and Maria both complained that they did not follow their own desires because that would disturb the other. Maria said, "She makes me feel guilty when I go out with my friends without her, so I can't do it." Judith said, "I can't tell Maria when I'm unhappy because she takes it so personally." (p. 60)

Burch noted that merger can occur in all types of relationships but suggested that lesbians have a greater tendency toward enmeshment because of their psychological development as women and because the larger society does not recognize or value lesbian relationships. These clinical reports illustrate that merger can be a problem for some lesbian couples. However, in the absence of systematic research comparing the frequency of merger problems among lesbians and among heterosexual couples, the claim that this problem is more common among lesbians remains untested.

It has been suggested that gay couples are vulnerable to unique problems that result from men's traditional socialization. For instance, Hawkins (1992) linked male socialization for achievement, competitiveness, sex, and aggression to problems commonly reported by therapists who work with gay couples, including conflicts over finances or jobs, anger and violence, jealousy, and sexual difficulties. Hawkins also commented on gay men's communication skills, asserting that male socialization "leaves men ill-equipped to deal with relationships. . . . When two men then try to build a relationship, the problem is compounded because both are lacking in the interpersonal skills needed" (p. 82). Other clinicians have also emphasized that gay couples have problems because of adherence to stereotypic male roles (e. g., George & Behrendt, 1987; Shannon & Woods, 1991).

Although these speculations and clinical observations about problems in gay couples are intuitively plausible, counterevidence is also available. For instance, in interviews with 156 gay couples not in therapy, McWhirter and Mattison (1982) found no pervasive lack of verbal expressiveness. "In fact gay men have a tendency to over-communicate with each other. At times they process their feelings and behaviors 'to death,' causing relationship fatigue and distress" (p. 88). Systematic research is needed to test the accuracy, prevalence, and generalizability of clinical beliefs about gender-linked problems in gay and lesbian couples.

## Coming Out and Being Out

*Bill and Roger have lived together for a year. Bill is active in a local gay political organization and regularly asks Roger to attend organization events with him. Roger refuses because he fears that his boss or family might find out that he is gay. When Roger's parents visit, he asks Bill to spend the week with friends. The couple had a major fight about Roger's decision not to come out to his family, and Bill stomped out of the apartment without packing any of his things.*

Society's negative attitudes toward homosexuality create problems for gay and lesbian couples. A common dilemma for lesbians and gay men concerns whether to reveal their sexual orientation to friends, family, coworkers, and others in their social network. Decisions about whether to "come out" or "be out" about their relationship can be a source of conflict for gay and lesbian couples.

Reports by therapists have identified ways in which disclosure about one's sexual orientation can affect relationships. In some couples, partners disagree about how much they want to reveal about themselves and their relationship. For example, Roger prefers to keep his relationship hidden, fearing harassment at work or rejection by his parents. Bill prefers a more open approach. Disagreements of this sort can be particularly stressful; the less open partner may feel pressured into more disclosure than is comfortable, and the more open partner may interpret the other's fear of disclosure as a lack of commitment to the relationship (Murphy, 1992; Shannon & Woods, 1991). As an illustration, Decker (1984) explained that if one member of a couple wants to give a party for coworkers at home and expects the other to pretend that he or she is "just a roommate," confusion, anger, and depression may result.

Even when partners agree about the extent to which they will be open, problems can arise because of negative reactions from family, friends, or coworkers. Murphy (1989) found that the anticipation of negative reactions from parents created stress in lesbian relationships. Writing about a woman whose father disapproves of her lesbianism, Murphy (1989) reported, "She and her lover felt so much conflict about seeing her father that they would fight with each other 'over any stupid thing' before visiting him" (p. 48). Many therapists believe that resolving issues about "outness" is central to a successful same-sex relationship (e.g., George & Behrendt, 1988; Murphy, 1992; Shannon & Woods, 1991).

Belonging to an ethnic-minority group can make coming out even more difficult (see Manalansan, this volume). Two small studies have suggested that gay and lesbian Asian Americans may experience considerable stress concerning coming out (Chan, 1989; Wooden, Kawasaki, & Mayeda, 1983). On the one hand, Asian Americans place great importance on family and community relationships and so being cut off from these ties is a serious threat. On the other hand, Asian American culture is extremely negative about homosexuality, and individuals who identify openly as gay or lesbian risk bringing shame not only on themselves but also on their family and community. As one Asian American explained, "I wish I could tell my parents—they are the only ones who do not know about my gay identity, but I am sure they would reject me. There is no frame of reference to understand homosexuality in Asian American culture" (Chan, 1989, p. 19). Thus, the common fears of lesbians and gay men that coming out may lead to rejection and stigmatization may be heightened for Asian Americans and members of other ethnic groups that emphasize strong family ties and have strong antigay attitudes.

## Violence and Partner Abuse

*"The fighting began with intense arguments that were devastating. . . . When she was angry it was like being stabbed in the chest. She was the source of that pain; she was also the only source of comfort, understanding and affirmation of love. . . . One day we had an argument, and she hit me. We were on my motorcycle, I was driving, and all I could think was what an insane thing it was—to hit my arm and risk our lives." (Lisa, 1986, p. 38)*

In some relationships conflicts escalate into psychological abuse and physical violence. Estimates of battering and prolonged physical abuse in heterosexual relationships range from 25% to 33% (Herbert, Silver, & Ellard, 1991; Koss, 1990). Adequate information about the frequency of abuse in gay and lesbian relationships is not currently available. Understandably, some lesbians and gay men have been reluctant to discuss violence in same-sex couples for fear of contributing to negative attitudes toward homosexuality. In a book about violence in lesbian relationships, Hart (1986) explained, "We recognized how threatening the reality of lesbian battering was to our dream of lesbian utopia—a nonviolent, fairly androgynous . . . community struggling for social justice" (p. 13). Nonetheless, there is growing evidence that violence is a problem for some lesbian and gay couples (e.g., Kanuha, 1990; Lobel, 1986; Morrow & Hawxhurst, 1989; Renzetti, 1992; Waterman, Dawson, & Bologna, 1989).

As in heterosexual relationships, abuse in same-sex couples can take many forms, including verbal abuse (e.g., demeaning the partner in front of others), negative actions (e.g., destroying partners' property), sexual coercion, and physical violence. Many of the same factors that contribute to heterosexual partner abuse appear to affect violence in gay and lesbian couples. For example, the misuse of alcohol or drugs is a common precursor to violence. Jealousy, dependency, and dominance may also contribute to abuse (Renzetti, 1992; Schilit, Lie, & Montagne, 1990). Individuals who stay in an abusive relationship often report that they are socially isolated and have no one to turn to for help. In addition, homophobia may create unique problems for lesbians and gay men who face violence in a relationship. For example, Renzetti (1982) reported that many of the abused lesbians she studied did not turn to their family for help. In some cases, the family did not know that the woman had a lesbian partner. In other cases, the family knew that a woman was lesbian but the woman nonetheless chose not to seek help from relatives because she feared that knowledge of the battering would reinforce their negative, homophobic attitudes.

More research is needed to clarify the magnitude of the problem of abuse in gay and lesbian couples and to understand the factors that contribute to this violence. To date, most published studies of violence in same-sex relationships have investigated lesbian relationships. Even less is known about abuse in gay relationships. Also needed are better community services to help lesbians and gay men who are victims of abuse. Currently, social service agencies lack adequate information and resources to address gay and lesbian battering (Hammond, 1988). Indeed, existing shelters for battered women are often hesitant to extend services to lesbians (Lobel, 1986; Renzetti, 1992). Although public discussion of battering in same-sex couples is relatively new, it is already apparent that violence is a significant problem.

## WHEN RELATIONSHIPS END

*Jennifer and Michelle lived together for two years. Their relationship was always stormy, but both women tried to work out their problems. Finally deciding that the relationship would never get any better, Jennifer moved out last weekend. Jennifer feels guilty about ending the relationship but is relieved that their stressful fights are over. Michelle was very surprised by Jennifer's decision and feels deeply hurt and depressed.*

Couples who have dated casually may break up after a few months. More enduring relationships may end as partners grow apart or discover incompatibilities. Sadly, relationships of any length can end tragically when a partner dies. During the current AIDS epidemic, bereavement has become an all too familiar experience for many gay couples. In this section, we examine research about the experience of breaking up and bereavement in gay and lesbian couples.

## Breaking Up

Relationships end for diverse reasons, many of which have been considered in our discussion of the problems and conflicts experienced in gay and lesbian relationships. Two studies have specifically addressed the reasons lesbian and gay partners give for a breakup. In one study, 50 lesbians rated the extent to which each of 17 possible factors had contributed to the ending of a past relationship (Peplau et al., 1983). Among this sample of young lesbians (median age 26), who may not have been ready for a permanent commitment, issues of independence were the most important factor cited. One half of the women rated their desire to be independent as a major factor, and nearly one third indicated that their partner's desire to be independent was a major factor. A second theme concerned differences between the partners in interests (36%), attitudes about sex (24%), background (17%), intelligence (10%), and/or political views (7%). These findings highlight the potential importance of similarity for relationship satisfaction among lesbians, a point amply documented among heterosexuals (Brehm, 1992). Perhaps surprising in light of society's hostility toward homosexuality, issues about being lesbian were not commonly cited as reasons for a breakup. Less than 20% of women cited as a major factor their feelings about being a lesbian, 14% cited "societal attitudes toward lesbian relationships," and only 2% cited pressure from their parents.

In a longitudinal study of cohabiting couples, Kurdek (1991b) investigated factors contributing to the breakup of lesbian and gay relationships. Although only 12 gay men and 14 lesbians were included in this breakup sample, the results offer preliminary evidence about the reasons for dissolution. In open-ended descriptions of reasons for the breakup, the most common themes were nonresponsiveness (e.g., "There was no communication between us and little support"), partner problems (e.g., "He had a big drug and alcohol problem"), and sexual issues (e.g., "She had an affair"). Participants also rated the importance of 11 specific issues that might have contributed to their separation. Highest ratings were given for the partner's frequent absence, sexual incompatibility, mental cruelty, and lack of love. Kurdek noted that these diverse explanations for separation are similar to those reported in studies of heterosexuals.

A final source of information about factors leading to breakups is a large-scale study of lesbian and gay couples conducted by Blumstein and Schwartz (1983). They followed a sample of 493 gay and 335 lesbian couples for an 18-month period and compared those who ended their relationship to those who stayed together. Money mattered: Couples who argued about money, fought about their level of income, and did not pool their finances were more likely to break up than other couples. The partners' commitment to their jobs was also a factor. Couples who said that work intruded into their relationship were more likely to break up, and partners who were more ambitious and spent more time at work were more likely to leave the relationship. In contrast, couples who spent a lot of time together were more likely to survive the test of time. Sexual satisfaction also contributed to the longevity of a relationship.

The ending of an important relationship is usually an emotion-laden experience. In the Kurdek study (1991b), participants rated their emotions following separation. The most common negative emotional reactions were loneliness, confusion, anger, guilt, and helplessness. Common positive emotions included personal growth, relief from conflict, increased happiness, and independence.

Research with heterosexual dating couples found similar emotional reactions (Hill, Rubin, & Peplau, 1976). This study also showed that the kind of emotional reactions experienced depend on the part that each person played in the breakup: Individuals who had initiated the breakup were more likely to feel guilty, free, and happy, whereas partners who wanted to continue the relationship but were left behind felt lonelier and more depressed.

The severity of emotional reactions to a breakup depends on many factors. Kurdek (1991b) found that lesbians and gay men who placed great emphasis on attachment to a partner had more difficult emotional reactions than did individuals who gave less emphasis to attachment (see also Peplau & Cochran, 1981). In addition, individuals had a more difficult emotional adjustment when their relationship had been of longer duration, when the couple had pooled their finances, and when they had felt greater love for their partner.

## The Death of a Partner

One of the most stressful events in life is the death of a spouse (Holmes & Rahe, 1967). Much is known about the psychological reactions of heterosexuals to bereavement and about the sources of social support usually available to a grieving spouse. When a heterosexual partner dies, a period of public grieving is commonly allowed. In addition to the support of friends and family, widows and widowers can turn to religious institutions and to self-help groups for the widowed. There is no reason to believe that the emotional anguish of bereavement is different for lesbians and gay men who lose a beloved partner. After the death of her partner of 15 years, one older lesbian reacted the following way:

> I became a hermit. For at least a year I wept when I looked at anyone—this I hid—but I still became depressed. For several years I frequently visited the mausoleum and talked to her (No one else around). My work is my savior. (Kehoe, 1989, p. 49)

Although the personal pain of loss may be similar for people regardless of their sexual orientation, the social circumstances of bereavement often differ considerably.

Same-sex partners who have been closeted about their relationship may receive little social support. They may be unable to talk about the nature of their loss or the meaning that it has for them. According to mental health professionals, their grief may never be adequately expressed and so the period of mourning may be prolonged (McDonald & Steinhorn, 1990). Even when lesbian and gay partners have been open about their relationship, a surviving partner may encounter difficulties. For example, they may not be granted bereavement leave from work. Without legal documents such as wills or joint insurance policies, widowed partners may not have rights to their joint property (see Rubenstein, this volume). Even when partners take legal precautions, problems can still arise. An older woman who had been named the beneficiary of her lover's part in the house and business they owned together explained:

Her will is being contested by her family and the property we had in joint ownership is in litigation. Even the burial plans were overruled by them, and they finally made the medical decision to remove her life support systems. (Kehoe, 1989, p. 49)

A gay man described the problems created by the family of his lover:

Not two months after he died they were accusing me of stealing from him and demanding a complete accounting for the money spent during the time he was sick. . . . Right after the funeral, . . . they wanted to get into the apartment . . . as if it was his house, not mine. . . . I really wonder, do straight people go through this, or is there more respect? (Shelby, 1992, p. 146)

Currently, information on the bereavement process for lesbians and gay men remains sparse. Clinicians are only beginning to develop therapeutic approaches to help lesbians and gay men who have lost their partners (Saunders, 1990; Siegal & Hoefer, 1981).

## Losing a Partner to AIDS

Gary's partner Miguel recently died from AIDS. Gary had cared for Miguel through the night sweats, delusions, and pain. As he watched over Miguel every night, Gary asked himself why he had not gotten the virus. He felt guilty for being the healthy one and sometimes wished that he also had AIDS.

Because the AIDS epidemic struck first in the United States in gay communities, many gay men have lost a loved partner to this disease. The difficulties of bereavement are heightened when AIDS is the cause of death, both because victims tend to die at an untimely young age and because of the social stigma of AIDS (Stulberg & Smith, 1988). Before the AIDS crisis, it would have been unusual for a young adult to confront the death of many friends to disease. But in many gay communities, attendance at funerals has become a familiar part of life. A study of 745 gay men in New York City found that nearly one third had suffered the loss of a lover or close friend to AIDS. Some had experienced multiple losses. The more people an individual knew who had died of AIDS, the greater the person's risk of experiencing serious psychological distress, including anxiety, depression, sleep problems, and increased use of recreational drugs and sedatives (Martin, 1988).

An additional problem experienced by some surviving partners and friends has been termed "survivor guilt" (Wayment, Silver, & Kemeny, 1994). Men who have engaged in risky sexual behavior but do not test positive for HIV may believe that they "should" be HIV positive and have been spared by chance. As one man explained:

As a surviving partner, one whose number of living friends has dwindled steadily from 1983 to 'mostly deceased by 1989,' I'm here to tell you that the stress and anxiety are real. It's very difficult to figure out why some of us are left and others are not, especially when we all did the same things. (p. 21)

Experts acknowledge that professional services to assist people whose partners have died from AIDS are inadequate (Kubler-Ross, 1987).

# COUPLES COUNSELING

Lesbians and gay men seek counseling for many of the same relationship problems as do heterosexuals. Yet their experiences in therapy can be quite different because gay men and lesbians often confront antihomosexual bias from therapists. Only recently have clinicians begun to acknowledge this problem and to create gay and lesbian affirmative approaches to therapy. Another recent trend has been the development of couples counseling for same-sex partners.

## Bias in Psychotherapy

*Karen began seeing a psychotherapist because she was having problems in her relationship with Amy. The therapist, believing that homosexuality reflects psychological immaturity, encouraged Karen to break up with Amy. The therapist told Karen that her affair with Amy was just a "phase" she would outgrow and advised Karen to start dating men.*

The process of psychotherapy is inevitably influenced by the values and biases of the therapist (Murray & Abramson, 1983). A large-scale survey of members of the American Psychological Association identified many ways in which therapists sometimes provide biased and inadequate care to lesbian and gay clients (Garnets, Hancock, Cochran, Goodchilds, & Peplau, 1991). For instance, therapists may view a client's homosexuality as a sign of psychological disorder, trivialize or demean gay and lesbian lifestyles, or be poorly informed about lesbian and gay identity development and the societal context of antihomosexual prejudice. When relationship problems are the reason for entering therapy, lesbians and gay men may encounter additional types of bias (DeCrescenzo 1983/1984; Falco, 1991; Ussher, 1991). A therapist may underestimate the importance of intimate relationships for gay men and lesbians or regard same-sex partnerships as unhealthy or transient. A therapist may be insensitive to the nature and diversity of lesbian and gay relationships, perhaps relying on inaccurate stereotypes about masculine and feminine roles in same-sex couples (Eldridge, 1987). In addition, a therapist may fail to consider couples counseling when it might be more appropriate than individual psychotherapy. Therapists who are themselves gay or lesbian are not necessarily invulnerable to these biases (Anthony, 1981/1982; Stein, 1988).

## Affirmative Therapies for Lesbian and Gay Couples

*Peter started seeing a therapist because of increasing conflicts with his lover, Sean. They argued a lot about money, housework, and sexual values. The therapist suggested that Sean and Peter consider couples counseling so they could work together to solve their problems.*

Some therapists believe that it is not enough to provide unbiased therapy for lesbians and gay men. Rather, clinicians should go further by developing approaches to therapy that affirm the value and legitimacy of gay and lesbian lifestyles. Gay and lesbian affirmative psychotherapies place importance on the development of a positive gay or lesbian identity in the context of loving and healthy relationships with same-sex others (DeCrescenzo, 1983/1984; Malyon, 1981/1982). Affirmative therapists are especially sensitive to the psychological consequences of societal prejudice and homophobia, including the possibility that lesbians and gay men may have internalized negative attitudes and beliefs about homosexuality (Gonsiorek, 1988).

Within the framework of affirmative psychotherapy, clinicians are now creating therapeutic approaches specifically for lesbian and gay couples. For some relationship problems, a couples approach may be preferable to seeing one or both partners individually. In a discussion of therapy with gay couples, Shannon and Woods (1991) noted that all couples in healthy relationships, regardless of sexual orientation, share such characteristics as commitment, respect for each other, the expression of feelings, and the ability to resolve conflicts. Based on their knowledge of gay men's experiences, Shannon and Woods highlighted additional issues that are often important for gay couples. These include each partner being able to accept and value his homosexuality and giving up rigid male stereotypic roles that can detract from a successful same-sex relationship. In a discussion of affirmative therapy for lesbians, Browning and colleagues (1991) noted the potential value of feminist therapy in helping lesbian clients understand the influences of both sexism and homophobia in their lives. Currently, therapists are developing treatment models for specific relationship issues that can affect gay and lesbian couples, including sexual problems (Hall, 1988; Reece, 1988), alcohol abuse (Glaus, 1988/1989; Kus, 1990), and physical abuse (Hammond, 1988; Morrow & Hawxhurst, 1989).

Affirmative therapies emphasize the role of therapists as advocates for social change as well as service providers (Brown, 1989; Browning et al., 1991; Shannon & Woods, 1991). Although many gay affirmative therapists are themselves gay men or lesbians, an affirmative approach can be used by therapists regardless of their sexual orientation. The key is drawing on knowledge about the personal and relationship experiences of lesbians and gay men, being sensitive to the diversity of lesbians and gay men, and developing expertise in effective treatment approaches (Fassinger, 1991).

## CONCLUSION

We have reviewed a growing body of scientific research on gay and lesbian relationships. Although many gaps remain in our knowledge, much has been learned about same-sex couples in the past 20 years. Public interest in same-sex couples appears to be increasing, perhaps spurred by the recent efforts of lesbians and gay men to secure legal rights in such arenas as health benefits for domestic partners, child custody, marriage rights, and service in the armed forces.

Research has demonstrated that most lesbians and gay men desire intimate relationships and are successful in creating them. Many same-sex couples want an equal-power relationship, although not all couples attain this ideal. Many times, differences between partners in personal resources and psychological dependency on the relationship set the stage for power inequalities. However, same-sex couples do not typically adopt "husband" and "wife" roles in their relationships. Instead, most lesbian and gay couples have a flexible division of labor, sharing housework and other chores. Contrary to stereotypical beliefs, same-sex partnerships are no more vulnerable to conflicts and dissatisfactions than their heterosexual counterparts. The loss of a close relationship through breakup or death is always a painful emotional experience. Because of the AIDS epidemic, many gay men have confronted the untimely loss of friends and lovers. In recent years, therapists have developed new gay affirmative approaches to helping lesbian and gay couples cope effectively with problems that occur in their relationships.

Many similarities have emerged in the relationship experiences of lesbians, gay men, and heterosexuals, suggesting that there is much commonality in the issues affecting all contemporary couples. That which most clearly distinguishes same-sex from heterosexual couples is the social context of their lives. Whereas heterosexuals enjoy many social and institutional supports for their relationships, gay and lesbian couples are the object of prejudice and discrimination. Drawing on their clinical observations, therapists have begun to analyze the impact of social rejection on the adjustment of gay and lesbian couples. However, additional research is needed to understand more fully how traditional social institutions and hostile attitudes affect all facets of gay and lesbian relationships.

Scholars are increasingly emphasizing the rich diversity that exists among gay and lesbian couples. Gender differences between the relationships of lesbians and gay men have received the most attention (e.g., Peplau, 1991). Additional studies are needed, however, to understand the varieties of same-sex partnerships and how such factors as culture and ethnicity influence lesbian and gay couples. Virtually all studies discussed in this chapter examined the relationships of White, educated, middle-class people. The few studies that considered ethnic-minority lesbians or gay men typically focused on issues such as identity development or AIDS (e.g., Chan, 1989; Espin, 1987; Loiacano, 1989; Wooden et al., 1983), not on relationships. Additional research on ethnic-minority couples will help to clarify issues that are especially prominent among ethnic-minority lesbians and gay men. These issues include how relationships are shaped by racial or ethnic identity, how conflicting loyalties to families and to love relationships are balanced, how couples react to potential homophobia in their ethnic communities and to racism or other prejudice in gay and lesbian communities, and how different forms of spirituality affect couples' lives.

## ▼ ENDNOTES ▼

1. We are grateful for the advice of Linda Garnets, Ph.D., and for the assistance of Talia Barag.

▼    **REFERENCES**    ▼

Anthony, B. D. (1981/1982). Lesbian client-lesbian therapist: Opportunities and challenges in working together. *Journal of Homosexuality, 7,* 45–57.

Bell, A. P., & Weinberg, M. A. (1978). *Homosexualities: A study of diversity among men and women.* New York: Simon & Schuster.

Berger, R. M. (1990). Men together: Understanding the gay couple. *Journal of Homosexuality, 19,* 31–49.

Berzon, B. (1988). *Permanent partners: Building gay and lesbian relationships that last.* New York: Dutton.

Blumstein, P., & Schwartz, P. (1983). *American couples: Money, work, sex.* New York: Morrow.

Brehm, S. S. (1992). *Intimate relationships,* (2nd ed.). New York: McGraw-Hill.

Brown, L. S. (1989). Toward a lesbian/gay paradigm in psychology. *Psychology of Women Quarterly, 13,* 445–458.

Browning, C., Reynolds, A. L., & Dworkin, S. H. (1991). Affirmative psychotherapy for lesbian women. *Counseling Psychologist, 19,* 177–196.

Burch, L. (1986). Psychotherapy and the dynamics of merger in lesbian couples. In T. S. Stein & C. J. Cohen (Eds.), *Contemporary perspectives on psychotherapy with lesbians and gay men* (pp. 57–71). New York: Plenum.

Caldwell, M. A., & Peplau, L. A. (1984). The balance of power in lesbian relationships. *Sex Roles, 10,* 587–599.

Cardell, M., Finn, S., & Marecek, J. (1981). Sex-role identity, sex-role behavior, and satisfaction in heterosexual, lesbian, and gay male couples. *Psychology of Women Quarterly, 5,* 488–494.

Chan, C. S. (1989). Issues of identity development among Asian-American lesbians and gay men. *Journal of Counseling and Development, 68,* 16–20.

Crosby, F. (1991). *Juggling.* New York: Free Press.

Dailey, D. M. (1979). Adjustment of heterosexual and homosexual couples in pairing relationships: An exploratory study. *Journal of Sex Research, 15,* 143–157.

DeCrescenzo, T. A. (1983/1984). Homophobia: A study of the attitudes of mental health professionals toward homosexuality. *Journal of Social Work and Human Sexuality, 2,* 115–135.

Decker, B. (1984). Counseling gay and lesbian couples. *Journal of Social Work and Human Sexuality, 2,* 39–53.

Duffy, S. M., & Rusbult, C. E. (1986). Satisfaction and commitment in homosexual and heterosexual relationships. *Journal of Homosexuality, 12,* 1–24.

Eldridge, N. S. (1987). Gender issues in counseling same-sex couples. *Professional Psychology: Research and Practice, 18,* 567–572.

Eldridge, N. S., & Gilbert, L. A. (1990). Correlates of relationship satisfaction in lesbian couples. *Psychology of Women Quarterly, 14,* 43–62.

Espin, O. (1987). Issues of identity in the psychology of Latina lesbians. In Boston Lesbians Psychologies Collective (Ed.), *Lesbian psychologies* (pp. 35–51). Urbana, IL: University of Illinois Press.

Falbo, T., & Peplau, L. A. (1980). Power strategies in intimate relationships. *Journal of Personality and Social Psychology, 38,* 618–628.

Falco, K. L. (1991). *Psychotherapy with lesbian clients.* New York: Brunner/Mazel.

Fassinger, R. E. (1991). The hidden minority: Issues and challenges in working with lesbian women and gay men. *Counseling Psychologist, 19,* 157–176.

Freedman, J. (1978). *Happy people.* New York: Harcourt Brace Jovanovich.

Garnets, L., Hancock, K. A., Cochran, S. D., Goodchilds, J., & Peplau, L. A. (1991). Issues in psychotherapy with lesbians and gay men. *American Psychologist, 46,* 964–972.

George, K. D., & Behrendt, A. E. (1988). Therapy for male couples experiencing relationship problems and sexual problems. In E. Coleman (Ed.), *Psychotherapy with homosexual men and women: Integrated identity approaches for clinical practice* (pp. 77–88). New York: Haworth Press.

Glaus, K. H. (1988/1989). Alcoholism, chemical dependency and the lesbian client. *Women and Therapy, 8,* 131–144.

Gonsiorek, J. C. (1988). Current and future directions in gay/lesbian affirmative mental health practice. In M. Shernoff & W. A. Scott (Eds.), *The source book on lesbian and gay healthcare* (2nd ed.) (pp. 107–113). Washington, DC: National Gay and Lesbian Health Foundation.

Gottman, J. M. (1979). *Marital interaction: Experimental investigations.* New York: Academic Press.

Hall, M. (1988). Sex therapy with lesbian couples: A four stage approach. In E. Coleman (Ed.), *Psychotherapy with homosexual men and women: Integrated identity approaches for clinical practice* (pp. 137–156). New York: Haworth Press.

Hammond, N. (1988). Lesbian victims of relationship violence. *Women and Therapy, 8,* 89–105.

Harry, J. (1983). Gay male and lesbian relationships. In E. Macklin & R. Rubin (Eds.), *Contemporary families and alternate lifestyles: Handbook on research and theory* (pp. 216–234). Beverly Hills, CA: Sage.

Harry, J. (1984). *Gay couples.* New York: Praeger.

Harry, J., & DeVall, W. B. (1978). *The social organization of gay males.* New York: Praeger.

Hart, B. (1986). Preface. In K. Lobel (Ed.), *Naming the violence: Speaking out about lesbian battering* (pp. 9–16). Seattle, WA: Seal Press.

Hawkins, R. L. (1992). Therapy with male couples. In S. Dworkin & F. Guiterrez (Eds.), *Counseling gay men and lesbians* (pp. 81–94). Alexandria, VA: American Association for Counseling and Development.

Herbert, T. B., Silver, R. C., & Ellard, J. H. (1991). Coping with an abusive relationship: How and why do women stay? *Journal of Marriage and the Family, 53,* 311–325.

Herek, G. M. (1994). Assessing heterosexuals' attitudes toward lesbians and gay men: A review of empirical research with the ATLG Scale. In B. Greene & G. M. Herek (Eds.), *Lesbian and gay psychology: Theory, research, and clinical applications* (pp. 206–228). Thousand Oaks, CA: Sage.

Hill, C. T., Rubin, Z., & Peplau, L. A. (1976). Breakups before marriage: The end of 103 affairs. *Journal of Social Issues, 32,* 147–168.

Holmes, T. H., & Rahe, R. H. (1967). The social readjustment rating scale. *Journal of Psychosomatic Research, 11,* 213–218.

Howard, J. A., Blumstein, P., & Schwartz, P. (1986). Sex, power, and influence tactics in intimate relationships. *Journal of Personality and Social Psychology, 51,* 102–109.

Jay, K., & Young, A. (1977). *The gay report: Lesbians and gay men speak out about sexual experiences and lifestyles.* New York: Summit Books.

Kanuha, V. (1990). Compounding the triple jeopardy: Battering in lesbian of color relationships. *Women and Therapy, 9,* 169–184.

Kehoe, M. (1989). *Lesbians over 60 speak for themselves.* New York: Haworth Press.

Kollock, P., Blumstein, P., & Schwartz, P. (1985). Sex and power in interaction: Conversational privileges and duties. *American Sociological Review, 50,* 34–46.

Koss, M. P. (1990). The women's mental health research agenda: Violence against women. *American Psychologist, 45,* 374–380.

Krestan, J., & Bepko, C. (1980). The problem of fusion in the lesbian relationship. *Family Process, 19,* 277–289.

Kubler-Ross, E. (1987). *AIDS: The ultimate challenge.* New York: Macmillan.

Kurdek, L. A. (1989). Relationship quality in gay and lesbian cohabiting couples: A 1-year follow-up study. *Journal of Social and Personal Relationships, 6,* 39–59.

Kurdek, L. A. (1991a). Correlates of relationship satisfaction in cohabiting gay and lesbian couples: Integration of contextual, investment, and problem-solving models. *Journal of Personality and Social Psychology, 61,* 910–922.

Kurdek, L. A. (1991b). The dissolution of gay and lesbian couples. *Journal of Social and Personal Relationships, 8,* 265–278.

Kurdek, L. A. (1992). Relationship stability and relationship satisfaction in cohabiting gay and lesbian couples: A prospective longitudinal test of the contextual and interdependence models. *Journal of Social and Personal Relationships, 9,* 125–142.

Kurdek, L. A., & Schmitt, J. P. (1986a). Relationship quality of partners in heterosexual married, heterosexual cohabiting, and gay and lesbian relationships. *Journal of Personality and Social Psychology, 51,* 711–720.

Kurdek, L. A., & Schmitt, J. P. (1986b). Relationships of gay men in closed or open relationships. *Journal of Homosexuality, 12,* 85–99.

Kurdek, L. A., & Schmitt, J. P. (1987). Partner homogamy in married, heterosexual cohabiting, gay, and lesbian couples. *Journal of Sex Research, 23,* 212–232.

Kus, R. J. (1990). Alcoholism in the gay and lesbian communities. In R. J. Kus (Ed.), *Keys to caring: Assisting your gay and lesbian clients* (pp. 66–81). Boston: Alyson.

Levinger, G. (1979). A social psychological perspective on marital dissolution. In G. Levinger & O. C. Moles (Eds.), *Divorce and separation* (pp. 37–63). New York: Basic Books.

Lisa. (1986). In K. Lobel (Ed.), *Naming the violence: Speaking out about lesbian battering* (pp. 37–40). Seattle, WA: Seal Press.

Lobel, K. (Ed.). (1986). *Naming the violence: Speaking out about lesbian battering.* Seattle, WA: Seal Press.

Loiacano, D. K. (1989). Gay identity issues among Black Americans: Racism, homophobia, and the need for validation. *Journal of Counseling and Development, 68,* 21–25.

Malyon, A. (1981/1982). Psychotherapeutic implications of internalized homophobia in gay men. *Journal of Homosexuality, 7,* 59–69.

Martin, J. L. (1988). Psychological consequences of AIDS-related bereavement among gay men. *Journal of Consulting and Clinical Psychology, 56,* 856–862.

Martin, T. C., & Bumpass, L. L. (1989). Recent trends in marital disruption. *Demography, 6,* 37.

McDonald, H. B., & Steinhorn, A. I. (1990). *Homosexuality: A practical guide to counseling lesbians, gay men and their families.* New York: Continuum.

McWhirter, D. P., & Mattison, A. M. (1982). Psychotherapy for gay male couples. *Journal of Homosexuality, 7,* 79–91.

McWhirter, D. P., & Mattison, A. M. (1984). *The male couple.* Englewood Cliffs, NJ: Prentice-Hall.

Morrow, S. L., & Hawxhurst, D. M. (1989). Lesbian partner abuse: Implications for therapists. *Journal of Counseling and Development, 68,* 58–62.

Murphy, B. C. (1989). Lesbian couples and their parents: The effects of perceived parental attitudes on the couple. *Journal of Counseling and Development, 68,* 46–51.

Murphy, B. C. (1992). Counseling lesbian couples: Sexism, heterosexism and homophobia. In S. Dworkin & F. Guiterrez (Eds.), *Counseling gay men and lesbians* (pp. 63–79). Alexandria, VA: American Association for Counseling and Development.

Murray, J., & Abramson, P. R. (1983). *Bias in psychotherapy.* New York: Praeger.

Myers, D. G. (1992). *The pursuit of happiness.* New York: Avon.

Peplau, L. A. (1991). Lesbian and gay relationships. In J. C. Gonsiorek & J. D. Weinrich (Eds.), *Homosexuality: Research findings for public policy* (pp. 177–196). Newbury Park, CA: Sage.

Peplau, L. A., & Campbell, S. M. (1989). The balance of power in dating and marriage. In J. Freeman (Ed.), *Women: A feminist perspective* (4th ed.) (pp. 121–137). Mountain View, CA: Mayfield.

Peplau, L. A., & Cochran, S. D. (1980, September). *Sex differences in values concerning love relationships.* Paper presented at the annual meeting of the American Psychological Association, Montreal, Canada.

Peplau, L. A., & Cochran, S. D. (1981). Value orientations in the intimate relationships of gay men. *Journal of Homosexuality, 6,* 1–19.

Peplau, L. A., & Cochran, S. D. (1990). A relationship perspective on homosexuality. In D. P. McWhirter, S. A. Sanders, & J. M. Reinisch (Eds.), *Homosexuality/heterosexuality: Concepts of sexual orientation* (pp. 321–349). New York: Oxford University Press.

Peplau, L. A., Cochran, S., Rook, K., & Padesky, C. (1978). Women in love: Attachment and autonomy in lesbian relationships. *Journal of Social Issues, 34,* 7–27.

Peplau, L. A., & Gordon, S. L. (1983). The intimate relationships of lesbians and gay men. In E. R. Allgeier & N. B. McCormick (Eds.), *Gender roles and sexual behavior: The changing boundaries* (pp. 226–244). Palo Alto, CA: Mayfield.

Peplau, L. A., Padesky, C., & Hamilton, M. (1982). Satisfaction in lesbian relationships. *Journal of Homosexuality, 8,* 23–35.

Reece, R. (1988). Causes and treatments of sexual desire discrepancies in male couples. In E. Coleman (Ed.), *Psychotherapy with homosexual men and women: Integrated identity approaches for clinical practice* (pp. 157–172). New York: Haworth Press.

Reilly, M. E., & Lynch, J. M. (1990). Power-sharing in lesbian partnerships. *Journal of Homosexuality, 19,* 1–30.

Renzetti, C. M. (1992). *Violent betrayal: Partner abuse in lesbian relationships.* Newbury Park, CA: Sage.

Roth, S. (1984). Psychotherapy with lesbian couples: The interrelationships of individual issues, female socialization, and the social context. In E. S. Hetrick & T. S. Stein (Eds.), *Innovations in psychotherapy with homosexuals* (pp. 89–114). Washington, DC: American Psychiatric Association.

Saunders, J. M. (1990). Gay and lesbian widowhood. In R. J. Kus (Ed.), *Keys to caring: Assisting your gay and lesbian clients* (pp. 224–243). Boston: Alyson.

Schilit, R., Lie, G., & Montagne, M. (1990). Substance abuse as a correlate of violence in intimate lesbian relationships. *Journal of Homosexuality, 19,* 51–65.

Shachar, S. A., & Gilbert, L. A. (1983). Working lesbians: Role conflicts and coping strategies. *Psychology of Women Quarterly, 7,* 244–256.

Shannon, J. W., & Woods, W. J. (1991). Affirmative psychotherapy for gay men. *Counseling Psychologist, 19,* 197–215.

Shelby, R. D. (1992). *If a partner has AIDS: Guide to clinical intervention for relationships in crisis.* New York: Haworth Press.

Siegal, R. L., & Hoefer, D. D. (1981). Bereavement counseling for gay individuals. *American Journal of Psychotherapy, 35,* 517–525.

Smalley, S. (1987). Dependency issues in lesbian relationships. *Journal of Homosexuality, 14,* 125–135.

Stein, T. S. (1988). Theoretical considerations in psychotherapy with gay men and lesbians. *Journal of Homosexuality, 15,* 75–95.

Stulberg, I., & Smith, M. (1988). Psychosocial impact of the AIDS epidemic on the lives of gay men. *Social Work, 33,* 277–281.

Testa, R. J., Kinder, B. N., & Ironson, G. (1987). Heterosexual bias in the perception of loving relationships of gay males and lesbians. *Journal of Sex Research, 23,* 163–172.

Tripp, C. A. (1975). *The homosexual matrix.* New York: Signet.

Turque, B. (1992, September 14). Gays under fire. *Newsweek,* pp. 35–40.

Ussher, J. M. (1991). Family and couples therapy with gay and lesbian clients: Acknowledging the forgotten minority. *Journal of Family Therapy, 13,* 131–148.

Waterman, C. K., Dawson, L. J., & Bologna, M. J. (1989). Sexual coercion among gay male and lesbian relationships. *Journal of Sex Research, 26,* 118–124.

Wayment, H. A., Silver, R. C., & Kemeny, M. E. (1994). *Spared at random: Survivor reactions in the gay community.* Unpublished manuscript, Department of Psychology, University of California, Los Angeles.

Wolf, D. G. (1980). *The lesbian community.* Berkeley: University of California Press.

Wooden, W. S., Kawasaki, H., & Mayeda, R. (1983). Lifestyles and identity maintenance among gay Japanese-American males. *Alternative Lifestyles, 5,* 236–243.

# Chapter 12

▼

# LESBIAN AND GAY
# PARENTS AND THEIR CHILDREN

## Charlotte J. Patterson[1]

Heather lives in a little house with a big apple tree in the front yard. . . . Heather's favorite number is two. She has two arms, two legs, two eyes, two ears, two hands and two feet. Heather has two pets: a ginger colored cat named Gingersnap and a black dog named Midnight. Heather also has two mommies: Mama Jane and Mama Kate. (Newman, 1989, pp. 1–3)

*Heather, the fictional child in* Newman's *story, is growing up in a lesbian family. A storybook intended for children,* Heather Has Two Mommies *has ignited acrimonious controversies in school districts across the country (Henry, 1993). The very presence of this book in school libraries has raised questions among educators about whether children should be allowed to read stories about other children who are growing up in lesbian or gay families. Some parents have asked that the book be removed from school libraries, and some school board members have suggested that youngsters ought to be protected from even the idea that lesbian families exist. Recently, when the Superintendent of Schools for New York City supported implementation of a "Rainbow Curriculum" that, among other things, suggested the use of* Heather Has Two Mommies *in elementary school classrooms, the move was widely viewed as contributing to his dismissal (Barbanel, 1993; Dillon, 1993). On the other hand, many teachers, parents, and school administrators across the country wholeheartedly support the use of books such as this one (Henry, 1993).*

*What is it that makes a fictional story about a girl like Heather so controversial? In this chapter, I outline three interrelated reasons. First, while Heather is a fictional character, the growing phenomenon of lesbian and gay parenting that she represents is very real. Second, although widespread prejudice suggests that lesbian and gay parents are maladjusted or that children raised by lesbian or gay parents suffer irreparable harm, the reality as illuminated by research to date is quite different. Third, if children raised by lesbian and gay parents develop in normal ways, the challenge to deeply held ideas about families and child development is undoubtedly significant. Thus, when considering whether families such as Heather's are acceptable and legitimate, the stakes are very high.*

*In this chapter, I first review information about the prevalence and diversity of lesbian and gay parenting, as well as the legal context in which lesbian and gay families currently live. I then describe the results of research on lesbian and gay families and discuss implications of the research findings for theories of psychological development and for the politics of family life. Finally, I describe services that have been developed specifically for lesbian and gay families. The chapter concludes with a discussion of future directions for research, service, and advocacy relevant to the needs of lesbian mothers, gay fathers, and their children.*

## GAY AND LESBIAN PARENTING TODAY

How many lesbian and gay families with children are there in the United States today? What are the important sources of diversity among them? What is the nature of the legal context within which lesbian and gay families are living? In this section, I address each of these questions.

### Prevalence of Gay and Lesbian Families With Children

No accurate count of lesbian and gay families with children is available, in large part because the number of lesbian and gay adults in the United States today cannot be estimated with confidence. Many take pains to ensure their sexual orientation is not revealed because of fear of discrimination. (Blumenfeld & Raymond, 1988). Fearing that they would lose child custody and/or visitation rights if their sexual orientation were to be known, many lesbian and gay parents attempt to conceal their gay or lesbian identities (Pagelow, 1980)—sometimes even from their own children (Dunne, 1987).

Despite these difficulties, estimates of gay and lesbian families with children in the United States have been offered. The number of lesbian mothers is estimated to range from 1 to 5 million and gay fathers, from 1 to 3 million (Gottman, 1990). Estimates of the number of children of gay or lesbian parents range from 6 million to 14 million (Editors of the Harvard Law Review, 1990).

One approach to making estimates of this kind is to extrapolate from that which is known or believed about base rates in the population. For example, there are just over 250 million people in the United States today (U.S. Bureau of the Census, 1991). Kinsey, Pomeroy, and Martin (1948) are often quoted as estimating that approximately 10% of the population can be considered gay or lesbian. Using these figures, one can estimate that there are currently about 25 million gay men and lesbians in the United States. According to several large-scale survey studies (e.g., Bell & Weinberg, 1978), about 10% of gay men and 20% of lesbians are parents, most of whom have children from a heterosexual marriage that ended in divorce. Calculations using these figures suggest that there may be 3 to 4 million gay or lesbian parents in the United States today. If, on average, each parent has two children, that would place the number of children of lesbians and gay men at 6 to 8 million. The accuracy of such estimates is, of course, no better than that of the figures on which they are based, and there are questions about almost all of the figures involved in such estimates. It does, however, seem clear that a substantial number of people are involved.

In addition to lesbians and gay men who became parents in the context of heterosexual marriages before coming out, growing numbers of lesbians and gay men are becoming parents after coming out. One recent estimate suggests that 5,000 to 10,000 lesbians have borne children after coming out (Seligmann, 1990). The number of lesbians who are bearing children is also believed to be increasing (Patterson, 1994a). Additional avenues to parenthood, such as foster care, adoption, coparenting, and multiple parenting are also being explored increasingly both by lesbians and gay men (Patterson, 1994b; Ricketts, 1991). Estimates such as those presented above may therefore minimize the actual figures.

## Diversity Among Lesbian Mothers, Gay Fathers, and Their Children

One important distinction among lesbian and gay families with children concerns the sexual identity of parents at the time of a child's birth or adoption. Probably the largest group of children with lesbian and gay parents today is that of children who were born in the context of heterosexual relationships between the biological parents and whose parent or parents subsequently identified as gay or lesbian. These include families in which the parents divorce when the husband comes out as gay, the wife comes out as lesbian, or both parents come out, as well as when one or both of the parents comes out and the parents decide not to divorce. Gay or lesbian parents may be single, or they may have same-sex partners. A gay or lesbian parent's same-sex partner may or may not assume stepparenting relationships with the children. If the partner also has children, the youngsters may assume step-sibling relationships with one another. In short, gay and lesbian families with children born in the context of heterosexual relationships are themselves a relatively diverse group.

In addition to children born in the context of heterosexual relationships between parents, lesbians and gay men are believed to be increasingly choosing parenthood (Martin, 1993; Patterson, 1994a, 1994b; Pies, 1985, 1990). The majority of such children are conceived by means of donor insemination (DI). Lesbians who wish to bear children may choose a friend, relative, or acquaintance to be the sperm donor, or they may choose to use sperm from an unknown donor. When sperm donors are known, they may take parental or avuncular roles relative to children conceived via DI, or they may not (Martin, 1993; Patterson, 1994a, 1994b; Pies, 1985, 1990). Gay men may also become biological parents of children whom they intend to parent, whether with a single woman (who may be lesbian or heterosexual), with a lesbian couple, or with a gay partner. Options pursued by gay men and lesbians also include both adoption and foster care (Ricketts, 1991). Thus, children are today being brought up in a diverse array of lesbian and gay families.

In addition to differences in parents' sexual identities at the time of a child's birth, another distinction among lesbian and gay parents is the extent to which family members are related biologically to one another (Pollack & Vaughn, 1987; Riley, 1988; Weston, 1991). Although as heterosexual stepfamilies proliferate, biological relatedness of family members is probably less often taken for granted than it once was, it is often even more prominent as an issue in lesbian and gay families with children. When children are born via DI into lesbian families, they are generally related biologically only to the birth mother, not to her partner. Similarly, when children are born via surrogacy to a gay couple, only the father who served as a sperm donor is biologically related to the child. In adoption and foster care, of course, the child will probably have no biological relation to the adoptive or foster parent.

Another distinction of particular importance for lesbian and gay families concerns custodial arrangements for minor children. As in heterosexual families, children live with one or both biological parents, or they spend part of their time in one parent's household and part of their time in another's home. Many lesbian mothers and gay fathers have, however, lost custody of their children to heterosexual spouses following divorce, and the threat of custody litigation almost certainly looms larger in the lives of most divorced lesbian mothers than it does in the lives of divorced heterosexual ones (Lyons, 1983; Pagelow, 1980). Although no authoritative figures are available, it seems likely that a greater proportion of gay and lesbian parents than heterosexual parents lose custody of children against their will. Probably for this reason, more lesbians and gay men are noncustodial parents (i.e., do not have legal custody of their children) and nonresidential parents (i.e., do not live in the same household with their children) than might otherwise be expected.

Beyond these basic distinctions, a number of others can also be considered. Other important ways in which lesbian and gay families with children may differ from one another include income, education, ethnicity, gender, and culture. Difficulties and ambiguities in the definition of sexual orientation should also be considered. Although such variability undoubtedly contributes to differences in the qualities of life, little research has yet been directed to understanding such differences among lesbian and gay families.

## Legal and Public Policy Issues

When considering the environment within which lesbian and gay parenting takes place, it is important to acknowledge that the legal system in the United States has long been hostile to lesbians and gay men who are or who wish to become parents

(Editors of the Harvard Law Review, 1990; Falk, 1989; Polikoff, 1990; Rivera, 1991). Lesbian mothers and gay fathers have often been denied custody and/or visitation with their children following divorce. Although some states now have laws stipulating that parental sexual orientation as such cannot be a factor in determining child custody following divorce, in other states gay or lesbian parents are presumed to be unfit as parents. Regulations governing foster care and adoption in many states have also made it difficult for lesbians or gay men to adopt or to serve as foster parents (Ricketts, 1991; Ricketts & Achtenberg, 1990).

One of the central issues underlying judicial decision-making in custody litigation and in public policies governing foster care and adoption involves concern about the fitness of lesbians and gay men to be parents. Specifically, policies have sometimes been constructed and judicial decisions have often been made on the assumptions that gay men and lesbians are mentally ill and hence not fit to be parents, that lesbians are less maternal than heterosexual women and hence do not make good mothers, and that lesbians' and gay men's relationships with sexual partners leave little time for ongoing parent-child interactions (Editors of the Harvard Law Review, 1990; Falk, 1989). Because these assumptions have been frequently used to limit gay and lesbian parental rights, and because they are open to empirical evaluation, they have guided much of the research on lesbian and gay parents that is discussed below.

In addition to judicial concerns about gay and lesbian parents, three principal fears regarding the effects of such parenting on children have also been reflected in judicial decision-making about child custody and in public policies such as regulations governing foster care and adoption (Patterson, 1992). One concern is that the development of sexual identity among children of lesbian and gay parents will be impaired. For instance, some judges fear that children will grow up to be gay or lesbian, an outcome that they generally view as negative. Another is that gay and lesbian parents will have adverse effects on other aspects of their children's personal development. For example, some judges fear that children in the custody of gay or lesbian parents will be more vulnerable to behavior problems or to mental breakdown. A third concern is that these children will have difficulties in social relationships. For example, judges may worry that children will be teased or stigmatized by peers because of the sexual orientation of their parents. Because such concerns have often been explicit in judicial determinations when lesbian or gay parents' custody or visitation rights have been denied or curtailed and because these assumptions are open to empirical test, they have provided an important impetus to research.

## RESEARCH ON LESBIAN MOTHERS AND GAY FATHERS

Systematic research on lesbian mothers, gay fathers, and their children is a phenomenon of the last 20 years. Despite the diversity of lesbian and gay parenting communities, research to date has with few exceptions been restricted to relatively homogeneous groups of participants. Samples of parents have generally been composed of White, middle- or upper-middle-class, well-educated individuals living in major urban centers, generally in the United States. In this chapter, studies that are exceptions to this trend are specifically noted. In this section, research on those who became parents in the context of heterosexual relationships, before coming out as lesbian or gay, is presented first. I then describe studies of lesbians who became parents after coming out. For more detailed reviews of research on lesbian and gay parents, see Patterson (in press, 1995).

## Lesbians and Gay Men Who Became Parents in the Context of Heterosexual Relationships

As discussed above, one important impetus for research in this area has come from extrinsic sources, such as judicial concerns about the psychological health and well-being of lesbian as compared with heterosexual mothers. Other empirical work resulted from concerns that are more intrinsic to the families themselves, such as what and when children should be told about their parents' sexual orientation. In this section, I review first the research arising from extrinsic concerns, then the work stemming from intrinsic concerns. Although some of these parents may not have been married to the heterosexual partner with whom they had children, it is likely that most of the research participants were married. To avoid the use of more cumbersome labels, then, I refer to divorced lesbian mothers and to divorced gay fathers.

### Divorced lesbian mothers

Because it has often been raised as an issue by judges presiding over custody disputes (Falk, 1989), a number of studies have assessed the overall mental health of lesbian as compared to heterosexual mothers. Consistent with data on the mental health of lesbians in general (Gonsiorek, 1991), divorced lesbian mothers score at least as high as divorced heterosexual mothers on assessments of psychological health. For instance, studies have found no differences between lesbian and heterosexual mothers on self-concept, happiness, overall adjustment, or psychiatric status (Falk, 1989).

Another area of judicial concern has focused on maternal sex role behavior and its potential impact on child development (Patterson, 1995). Stereotypes cited by the courts suggest that lesbians might be overly masculine and/or that they might interact inappropriately with their children. In contrast to expectations based on the stereotypes, however, neither lesbian mothers' reports about their sex role behavior nor their self-described interests in child-rearing have been found to differ from those of heterosexual mothers. Reports about responses to child behavior and ratings of warmth toward children have not differed significantly between lesbian and heterosexual mothers.

However, some differences between lesbian and heterosexual mothers have been reported. Among the most straightforward are the reports by Lyons (1983) and Pagelow (1980) that divorced lesbian mothers had more fears about loss of child custody than did divorced heterosexual mothers. Similarly, Green, Mandel, Hotvedt, Gray, and Smith (1986) reported that lesbian mothers were more likely than heterosexual mothers to be active in feminist organizations. Given the environments in which these lesbian mothers were living, findings such as these are not surprising.

A few other scattered differences are more difficult to interpret. For instance, Miller, Jacobsen, and Bigner (1981) reported that lesbian mothers were more child-centered than heterosexual mothers in their discipline techniques. In a sample of African American lesbian and heterosexual mothers, Hill (1987) found that lesbian mothers reported being more flexible about rules, more relaxed about sex play and modesty, and more likely to have nontraditional expectations for their daughters. Pending confirmation and replication, these findings are best viewed as suggestive.

Several studies have also examined the social circumstances and relationships of lesbian mothers. Divorced lesbian mothers have consistently been reported to be more likely than divorced heterosexual mothers to be living with a romantic partner (Harris & Turner, 1985/1986; Kirkpatrick, Smith, & Roy, 1981; Pagelow, 1980). Whether this represents a difference between lesbian and heterosexual mother-headed families, on the one hand, or reflects nothing more than sampling biases of the research, on the other, cannot be determined on the basis of information in the published reports. Information is sparse about the impact of such relationships in lesbian mother families, but what has been published suggests that, similar to heterosexual stepparents, co-resident lesbian partners of divorced lesbian mothers can be important sources of conflict as well as support in the family.

Relationships with the fathers of children in lesbian mother homes have also been a topic of study. Few differences in the likelihood of paternal financial support have been reported for lesbian and heterosexual families with children. Kirkpatrick and her colleagues (1981) reported, for example, that only about one half of heterosexual and about one half of lesbian mothers in their sample received financial support from the fathers of their children. Findings regarding frequency of contact with the fathers are mixed, with some (e.g., Kirkpatrick et al., 1981) reporting no differences as a function of maternal sexual orientation and others (e.g., Golombok, Spencer, & Rutter, 1983) reporting more contact among lesbian mothers.

Although most research to date has involved assessment of possible differences between lesbian and heterosexual mothers, several studies have reported other comparisons. For instance, in a study of divorced lesbian mothers and divorced gay fathers, Harris and Turner (1985/1986) found that gay fathers were likely to report higher incomes and that they encouraged more sex-typed toy play among their children, whereas lesbian mothers were more likely to see benefits for their children (e.g., increased empathy and tolerance for differences) as a result of having lesbian or gay parents. In comparisons of relationship satisfaction among lesbian couples who did or did not have children, Koepke, Hare, and Moran (1992) reported that couples with children scored higher on overall measures of relationship satisfaction and the quality of their sexual relationship. These findings are intriguing, but more research is needed before their interpretation is clear.

Another important set of issues, as yet little studied, concerns the conditions under which lesbian mothers experience enhanced feelings of well-being, support, and ability to care for their children. Rand, Graham, and Rawlings (1982) reported that the psychological health of lesbian mothers was associated with the mothers' openness about their sexual orientation with their employer, ex-husband, children, and friends, and with their degree of feminist activism. Kirkpatrick (1987) found that lesbian mothers living with partners and children had greater economic and emotional resources than those living alone with their children. Much remains to be learned about determinants of individual differences in psychological well-being among lesbian mothers.

Many other issues concerning families headed by divorced lesbian mothers are also in need of study. For instance, when a mother is in the process of coming out as a lesbian to herself and to others, at what point in that process should she address the topic with her child and in what ways should she do so—if at all? And what influence ought the child's age and circumstances have in such a decision? Reports from research and clinical practice suggest that early adolescence may be a particularly difficult time for parents to initiate such conversations and that disclosure may be less stressful at earlier or later points in a child's development (Patterson, 1992, 1995), but systematic research on these issues is just beginning. Similarly, many issues remain to be addressed regarding stepfamily and blended family relationships that may emerge as a lesbian mother's household seeks new equilibrium following her separation or divorce from the child's father.

### Divorced gay fathers

Although considerable research has focused on the overall psychological adjustment of lesbian mothers compared to heterosexual mothers, no published studies of gay fathers make such comparisons with heterosexual fathers. This may be attributable to the greater role of judicial decision-making as an impetus for research on lesbian mothers. In jurisdictions in which the law provides for biases in custody proceedings, these are likely to favor female and heterosexual parents. Perhaps because, other things being equal, gay fathers are unlikely to win custody battles over their children after divorce, fewer such cases have reached the courts. Consistent with this view, only a minority of gay fathers have been reported to live in the same households as their children (Bigner & Bozett, 1990; Bozett, 1980, 1989).

Research on the parenting attitudes of gay versus heterosexual divorced fathers has, however, been reported. Bigner and Jacobsen (1989a, 1989b) compared gay and heterosexual fathers, each of whom had at least two children. Their results revealed that, with one exception, there were no significant differences between gay and heterosexual fathers in their motives for parenthood. The single exception concerned the greater likelihood of gay fathers to cite the higher status accorded to parents in the dominant culture as a motivation for parenthood (Bigner & Jacobsen, 1989b).

Bigner and Jacobsen (1989a) also asked gay and heterosexual fathers to report on their behavior when interacting with their children. Although no differences emerged in the fathers' reports of involvement or intimacy, gay fathers reported that their behavior was characterized by greater responsiveness, more reasoning, and more limit-setting. These reports by gay fathers of greater warmth and responsiveness, on the one hand, and greater control and limit-setting, on the other, are strongly reminiscent of findings from research with heterosexual families and would seem to raise the possibility that gay fathers are more likely than their heterosexual counterparts to exhibit authoritative patterns of parenting behavior such as those described by Baumrind (1967; Baumrind & Black, 1967). Caution must be exercised, however, in the interpretation of results which stem entirely from paternal reports about their behavior.

In addition to research comparing gay and heterosexual fathers, a handful of studies have made other comparisons. For instance, Robinson and Skeen (1982) compared sex role orientations of gay fathers with those of gay men who were not fathers and found no differences. Similarly, Skeen and Robinson (1985) found no evidence to suggest that gay men's retrospective reports about relationships with their own parents varied as a function of whether they were parents themselves. As noted above, Harris and Turner (1985/1986) compared gay fathers and lesbian mothers, reporting that while gay fathers had higher incomes and were more likely to report encouraging their children to play with sex-typed toys, lesbian mothers were more likely to believe that their children received positive benefits, such as increased tolerance for diversity, from having lesbian or gay parents. Studies such as these suggest a number of issues for research on gender, sexual orientation, and parenting behavior, and it is clear that there are many valuable directions that future work in this area could take.

Considerable research in this area has also arisen from concerns about the gay father's identity and its transformations over time. Thus, work by Miller (1978, 1979) and Bozett (1980, 1981a, 1981b, 1987) sought to provide a conceptualization of the processes through which a man who considers himself to be a heterosexual father may come to identify himself, both in public and private, as a gay father. Based on extensive interviews with gay fathers in the United States and Canada, these studies emphasized the pivotal nature of identity disclosure and of the reactions to disclosure by significant people in a man's life. Miller (1978) suggested that while a number of factors, such as the extent of occupational autonomy and amount of access to gay communities, may affect how rapidly a gay man discloses his identity to others, the most important of these is likely to be the experience of falling in love with another man. It is this experience, more than any other, Miller argued, that leads a man to integrate the otherwise compartmentalized parts of his identity as a gay father. This hypothesis is, of course, open to empirical evaluation, but such research has not yet been reported.

# Lesbians and Gay Men Choosing to Become Parents

Although for many years lesbian mothers and gay fathers were generally assumed to have become parents in the context of previous heterosexual relationships, both men and women are believed increasingly to be undertaking parenthood in the context of pre-existing lesbian and gay identities (Crawford, 1987; Patterson, 1994a, 1994b). Although a substantial body of research addresses the transition to parenthood among heterosexuals, little research has explored the transition to parenthood for gay men or lesbians. While many issues that arise for heterosexuals also face lesbians and gay men (e.g., concerns with how children will affect couple relationships, economic concerns with supporting children), lesbians and gay men must also cope with many additional issues because they are members of stigmatized minorities. These issues are best understood by viewing them against the backdrop of pervasive heterosexism and antigay prejudice.

Antigay prejudice is evident in institutions involved with health care, education, and employment that often fail to support and, in many cases, are openly hostile to lesbian and gay families (Casper & Schultz, this volume; Pollack & Vaughn, 1987). Lesbian and gay parents may encounter antigay prejudice and bigotry even from their families of origin. Many if not most of the special concerns of lesbian and gay parents and prospective parents stem from problems created by such hostility.

Several interrelated issues are often faced by lesbians and gay men who wish to become parents (Crawford, 1987; Patterson, 1994b). One of the first needs among this group is for accurate, up-to-date information about how lesbians and gay men can become parents, how their children are likely to develop, and what supports are available to assist them. In addition to these educational needs, lesbians and gay men who are seeking biological parenthood are also likely to encounter various health concerns, ranging from medical screening of prospective birth parents to assistance with DI techniques, prenatal care, and preparation for birth. As matters progress, a number of legal concerns about the rights and responsibilities of all parties are likely to emerge. Associated with all of these will generally be financial issues; in addition to the support of a child, auxiliary costs of medical and legal assistance may be considerable. Finally, social and emotional concerns of many kinds are also likely to emerge (Pies, 1985, 1990; Patterson, 1994b; Pollack & Vaughn, 1987; Rohrbaugh, 1988).

As this brief outline of issues suggests, numerous questions are posed by the emergence of prospective lesbian and gay parents. What are the factors that influence lesbians' and gay men's inclinations to make parenthood a part of their lives and through what processes do they exert their influence? What effects does parenting have on lesbians or gay men who undertake it, and how do these effects compare with those experienced by heterosexuals? How effectively do special services, such as support groups, serve the needs of lesbian and gay parents and prospective parents for whom they were designed? What are the elements of a social climate that is supportive for gay and lesbian parents and their children? As yet, little research has addressed such questions.

The earliest studies of childbearing among lesbian couples were reported by McCandlish (1987) and Steckel (1987). Both investigators reported research based on small samples of lesbian couples who had given birth to children by means of DI. Their focus was primarily on the children in such families, and neither investigator provided much in the way of systematic assessment of mothers. McCandlish (1987), however, highlighted events and issues that were significant among families. For instance, she noted that, regardless of their interest in parenting prior to the birth of the first child, nonbiological mothers in each couple unanimously reported an "unexpected and immediate attachment" to the child (McCandlish, 1987, p. 28). Although both mothers took part in parenting, they reported shifting patterns of caretaking responsibilities over time, with the biological mother taking primary responsibility during the earliest months and the nonbiological mother's role increasing in importance after the first year. Couples also reported changes in their relationships following the birth of the child, notably a reduction or cessation in sexual intimacy. Though the best interpretation of results from these pioneering studies is by no means clear, the work raises important issues and questions.

A recent study by Hand (1991) examined the ways in which 17 lesbian and 17 heterosexual couples with children under two years of age shared child care, household duties, and occupational roles. Her principal finding was that lesbian couples shared parenting more equally than did heterosexual couples. Lesbian nonbiological mothers were significantly more involved in child care and regarded their parental role as significantly more salient than did heterosexual fathers. Lesbian biological mothers viewed their maternal role as more salient than did any of the other mothers. Fathers viewed their occupational roles as more salient than did any of the mothers, whether lesbian or heterosexual. Hand's major result was, however, that lesbian couples were more likely than heterosexual couples to share child care relatively evenly.

Another recent study (Osterweil, 1991) involved 30 lesbian couples with at least one child between 18 and 36 months of age. Consistent with Hand's results for parents of young children, Osterweil reported that biological mothers viewed their maternal role as more salient than did nonbiological mothers. In addition, although household maintenance activities were shared about equally, biological mothers reported somewhat more influence in family decisions and somewhat more involvement in child care. Osterweil (1991) also reported that the couples in her study scored at about the mean for normative samples of heterosexual couples in overall relationship satisfaction. Taken together, results of the Hand and Osterweil studies suggest that lesbian couples who have chosen to bear children are likely to share household and child care duties to a somewhat greater degree than do heterosexual couples, and that lesbians are relatively satisfied with their couple relationships.

As this brief discussion has revealed, studies on lesbians who have chosen to become parents are still sparse. Most research has been conducted on a relatively small scale and many important issues have yet to be addressed. Studies of gay men who have chosen to become parents are not yet available. Much remains to be learned about the determinants of lesbian and gay parenting and about its impact on lesbian and gay parents themselves.

## RESEARCH ON CHILDREN OF LESBIAN AND GAY PARENTS

Research on children in lesbian and gay families has, with few exceptions, been conducted with relatively homogeneous groups of White, well-educated, middle-class, largely professional families living in or around urban centers in the United States or in other Western countries. Unless otherwise specifically noted, these characteristics apply to the research described in this section. Research on children born in the context of heterosexual relationships is presented first, followed by a description of work with children born to or adopted by lesbian or gay parents.

## Research on Children Born in the Context of Heterosexual Relationships

As with research on lesbian mothers, much of the impetus for research in this area has come from judicial concerns with the welfare of children residing with gay or lesbian parents. Research in each of three main areas of judicial concern—namely, children's sexual identity, other aspects of children's personal development, and children's social relationships—is summarized here. For other recent reviews of this material, see Gibbs (1988), Green and Bozett (1991), Patterson (1992), and Tasker and Golombok (1991).

Reflecting issues relevant in the largest number of custody disputes, most of the research compares development of children with custodial lesbian mothers to that of children with custodial heterosexual mothers. Because many children living in lesbian mother-headed households have undergone the experience of parental divorce and separation, it has been widely believed that children living in families headed by divorced but heterosexual mothers provide the best comparison group. Although some studies focus exclusively on children of gay men or lesbians, most compare children in divorced lesbian mother-headed families with children in divorced heterosexual mother-headed families.

### Sexual identity

Following Money and Ehrhardt (1972), I consider research on three aspects of sexual identity. Gender identity concerns a person's self-identification as male or female. Gender role behavior concerns the extent to which a person's activities and occupations are regarded by the culture as masculine, feminine, or both. Sexual orientation refers to a person's choice of sexual partners—for example, heterosexual, homosexual, or bisexual. To examine the possibility that children in the custody of lesbian mothers experience disruptions of sexual identity, I describe research findings relevant to each of these three areas of concern.

Research on gender identity has failed to reveal any differences in the development of children as a function of their parents' sexual orientation. For example, Kirkpatrick and her colleagues (1981) compared development among 20 children of lesbian mothers with that among 20 same-aged children of heterosexual mothers. In projective testing, most children in both groups drew a same-sex figure first, a finding that fell within expected norms. Of those who drew an opposite-sex figure first, only three (one with a lesbian mother, and two with heterosexual mothers) showed concern with gender issues in clinical interviews. Similar findings have been reported in projective testing by other investigators (e.g., Green et al., 1986), and studies using direct methods of assessment (e.g., Golombok et al., 1983) have yielded similar results.

Research on gender role behavior has also failed to reveal difficulties in the development of children with lesbian mothers. For instance, Green (1978) reported that 20 of 21 children of lesbian mothers in his sample named a favorite toy consistent with conventional sex-typed toy preferences, and that all reported vocational choices that fell within typical limits for conventional sex roles. Results consistent with those described by Green have also been reported by other investigators. In interviews with 56 children of lesbians and 48 children of heterosexual mothers, Green and his colleagues (1986) found no differences with respect to favorite television programs, television characters, games, or toys. These investigators reported that daughters of lesbian mothers were more likely to be described as taking part in rough-and-tumble play or as playing with "masculine" toys, such as trucks or guns, but found no comparable differences for sons. In all studies, the behavior of lesbian mothers' children was seen as falling within normal limits.

Rees (1979) administered the Bem Sex Role Inventory to 12 young adolescent offspring of lesbian mothers and 12 same-aged youngsters of heterosexual mothers. Although children of lesbian and heterosexual mothers did not differ on masculinity or androgyny, adolescent offspring of lesbian mothers reported greater psychological femininity than did their same-aged peers with heterosexual mothers. This result runs counter to expectations based on stereotypes of lesbians as lacking in femininity. Although provocative, it should be interpreted cautiously pending replication. Overall, research has failed to reveal any notable difficulties in the development of sex role behavior among children of lesbian mothers.

A number of investigators have also studied sexual orientation, the third component of sexual identity. For instance, Huggins (1989) interviewed 36 teenagers, half of whom were the offspring of lesbian mothers and half of heterosexual mothers. No child of a lesbian mother identified as lesbian or gay, but one child of a heterosexual mother did. Generally similar results have been reported by other investigators (e.g., Gottman, 1990). Studies of the offspring of gay fathers have yielded similar results (Bozett, 1987). Based on the results of these studies, there is no reason to believe that the offspring of lesbian or gay parents are any more likely than those of heterosexual parents to become lesbian or gay themselves.

As clear as these results are, it should be recognized that research on the development of sexual identity among the offspring of lesbian and gay parents has been criticized from a number of perspectives. For instance, many lesbian women do not self-identify as lesbians until adulthood (see Brown, 1995); for this reason, studies of sexual orientation among adolescents may count as heterosexual some individuals who will identify as lesbian later in life. Concern has also been voiced that in many studies that compare children of divorced heterosexual mothers with children of divorced lesbian mothers, the lesbian mothers were more likely to be living with a romantic partner; in these cases, maternal sexual orientation and relationship status have been confounded. While these and other methodological issues await resolution, it remains true that no significant problems in the development of sexual identity among children of lesbian mothers have yet been identified.

## Other aspects of personal development

Studies of other aspects of personal development among children of gay and lesbian parents have assessed a broad array of characteristics. Among these have been psychiatric evaluations and assessments of behavior problems, personality, self-concept, locus of control, moral judgment, and intelligence. Concerns about possible difficulties in personal development among children of lesbian and gay parents have not been sustained by the results of research (Patterson, 1992). As was true for sexual identity, studies of other aspects of personal development have revealed no significant differences between children of lesbian or gay parents and children of heterosexual parents. On the basis of existing evidence, fears that children of gay and lesbian parents suffer deficits in personal development appear to be without empirical foundation.

## Social relationships

Studies assessing potential differences between children of gay and lesbian versus heterosexual parents have sometimes included assessments of children's social relationships. Because of concerns voiced by the courts that children of lesbian and gay parents might encounter difficulties among their peers, the most common focus of attention has been on peer relations. Studies in this area have consistently found that children of lesbian mothers report normal peer relations and that adult observers agree with this judgment (Patterson, 1992). Anecdotal and first-person accounts describe children's worries about being stigmatized as a result of their parents' sexual orientation (e.g., Pollack & Vaughn, 1987), but research findings to date provide no evidence for the proposition that children of lesbian mothers have difficulties in peer relations. Further work would be especially welcome in this area.

Research has also been directed toward description of children's relationships with adults, especially fathers. For instance, Golombok and her colleagues (1983) found that children of lesbian mothers were more likely than children of heterosexual mothers to have contact with their fathers. Most children of lesbian mothers had some contact with their fathers during the year preceding the study, but most children of heterosexual mothers had not; indeed, almost a third of the children of lesbian mothers reported at least weekly contact with their fathers, whereas only 1 in 20 of the children of heterosexual mothers reported this. Kirkpatrick and her colleagues (1981) also reported that lesbian mothers in their sample were more concerned than heterosexual mothers that their children have opportunities for good relationships with adult men, including fathers. Lesbian mothers' social networks have been found to include both men and women, and their offspring as a result have contact with adults of both sexes. Overall, results of research to date suggest that children of lesbian parents have satisfactory relationships with adults of both sexes.

Concerns that children of lesbian or gay parents are more likely than children of heterosexual parents to be sexually abused have also been voiced by judges in the context of child custody disputes (Patterson, 1992). Results of research in this area show that the great majority of adults who perpetrate sexual abuse are male; sexual abuse of children by adult women is extremely rare. Lesbian mothers are thus extremely unlikely to abuse their children. Existing research findings suggest that gay men are no more likely than heterosexual men to perpetrate child sexual abuse. Fears that children in custody of gay or lesbian parents might be at heightened risk for sexual abuse are thus without empirical foundation (Patterson, 1992, 1995).

## Diversity Among Children With Divorced Lesbian or Gay Parents

Despite the great diversity evident within gay and lesbian communities (Blumenfeld & Raymond, 1988), research on differences among children of lesbian and gay parents is as yet very limited. Here I focus on the impact of parental psychological and relationship status as well as on the influence of other stresses and supports.

One important dimension of difference among gay and lesbian families concerns whether the custodial parent is involved in a romantic relationship, and if so the implications this may have for children. Pagelow (1980), Kirkpatrick et al. (1981), and Golombok et al. (1983) reported that divorced lesbian mothers were more likely than divorced heterosexual mothers to be living with a romantic partner. Huggins (1989) reported that self-esteem among daughters of lesbian mothers whose lesbian partners lived with them was higher than that among daughters of lesbian mothers who did not live with a partner. This finding might be interpreted to mean that mothers who have high self-esteem are more likely to be involved in romantic relationships and to have daughters who also have high self-esteem, but many other interpretations are also possible. In view of the small sample size and absence of conventional statistical tests, Huggins's (1989) finding should be interpreted with great caution. Particularly in view of the judicial attention that lesbian mothers' romantic relationships have received during custody proceedings (Falk, 1989), it is surprising that more research has not examined the impact of this variable on children.

Rand, Graham, and Rawlings (1982) found that lesbian mothers' sense of psychological well-being was related to the extent to which they were open about their lesbian identity with employers, ex-husbands, and children. In their sample, a mother who felt more able to disclose her lesbian identity was also more likely to express a positive sense of well-being. In light of the consistent finding that, in heterosexual families, children's adjustment is often related to indexes of maternal mental health (Sameroff & Chandler, 1975), one might expect factors that enhance mental health among lesbian mothers to also benefit the children of these women, but this possibility has not yet been studied.

Another area of great diversity among families with a gay or lesbian parent concerns the degree to which a parent's sexual identity is accepted by other significant people in children's lives. Huggins (1989) found a tendency for children whose fathers were rejecting of maternal lesbianism to report lower self-esteem than those whose fathers were neutral or positive. Due to small sample size and absence of conventional statistical tests, this finding should be seen as suggestive rather than definitive. Huggins's results raise questions, however, about the extent to which reactions of important adults in a child's environment influence responses to discovery of a parent's gay or lesbian identity.

Effects of the age at which children learn of parents' gay or lesbian identities have also been a topic of study. Paul (1986) reported that those who were told either in childhood or in late adolescence found the news easier to cope with than did those who first learned of it during adolescence. Huggins (1989) reported that those who learned of maternal lesbianism in childhood had higher self-esteem than did those who were not informed of it until they were adolescents. From a clinical standpoint, many writers agree that early adolescence is a particularly difficult time for children to learn of their parents' lesbian or gay identities (Patterson, 1992).

As this brief review reveals, research on diversity among families with gay and lesbian parents is only beginning. Existing data favor early disclosure of identity to children, good maternal mental health, and a supportive milieu, but the available data are still very limited. No information is yet available on differences attributable to race or ethnicity, family economic circumstances, cultural environments, or related variables. Because none of the published work has employed observational measures or longitudinal designs, little is known about the details of actual behavior in these families or about any changes over time. It is clear that much remains to be learned about differences among gay and lesbian families and about the impact of such differences on children growing up in these homes.

## Research on Children Born to or Adopted by Lesbian Mothers

Many writers have recently noted an increase in childbearing among lesbians, but research with these families is as yet very new (Patterson, 1992, 1994a). In this section, I summarize the research to date on children born to or adopted by lesbian mothers. Although some gay men are also undertaking to become parents after coming out, no research has yet been reported on these families.

In one of the first systematic studies of children born to lesbians, Steckel (1985, 1987) compared the progress of separation-individuation among preschool children born via DI to lesbian couples with that among same-aged children of heterosexual couples. Using parent interviews, parent and teacher Q sorts, and structured doll play techniques, Steckel compared independence, ego functions, and object relations among children in the two types of families. Her main results documented impressive similarity in development among children in the two groups. Similar findings, based on extensive interviews with five lesbian-mother families, were also reported by McCandlish (1987).

Steckel (1985, 1987), however, reported suggestive differences between the two groups. Children of heterosexual parents saw themselves as somewhat more aggressive than did children of lesbians, and they were viewed by both parents and teachers as more bossy, domineering, and negativistic. Children of lesbian parents, on the other hand, saw themselves as more lovable and were portrayed by parents and teachers as more affectionate, responsive, and protective toward younger children. In view of the small sample size and the large number of statistical tests performed, these results must be interpreted with caution. Steckel's (1985, 1987) work was, however, the first to make systematic comparisons of development among children born to lesbian and to heterosexual couples.

The first study to examine psychosocial development among preschool- and school-aged children born to or adopted by lesbian mothers was conducted by Patterson (1994a). Thirty-seven four- to nine-year-old children were studied, using a variety of standardized measures. The Achenbach and Edelbrock Child Behavior Checklist and an open-ended interview were used to assess children's social competence, behavior problems, self-concepts, and preferences associated with sex role behavior. In this way, the study sought to provide an overview of the children's development.

Results showed that children scored in the normal range for all measures. On the Child Behavior Checklist, for example, the scores for children of lesbian mothers on social competence, internalizing behavior problems, and externalizing behavior problems did not differ from the scores for a large normative sample of American children. Likewise, children of lesbian mothers reported sex role preferences within the expected normal range for children of this age. On most subscales of the self-concept measure, answers given by children of lesbian mothers did not differ from those given by same-aged children of heterosexual mothers studied in a standardization sample.

On two subscales of the self-concept measure, however, Patterson (1994a) noted that children of lesbian mothers reported feeling more reactions to stress (e.g., feeling angry, scared, or upset) but a greater sense of well-being (e.g., feeling joyful, content, and comfortable with themselves) than did the same-aged children of heterosexual mothers in the standardization sample. One possible interpretation of this result is that children of lesbian mothers reported greater reactivity to stress because, in fact, they experienced greater stress in their daily lives than did other children. Another possibility is that, regardless of actual stress levels, children of lesbian mothers were better able to acknowledge both positive and negative aspects of their emotional experience. Although this latter interpretation is perhaps more consistent with the differences in both stress reactions and well-being, clarification of these and other potential interpretations must await the results of further research.

## IMPLICATIONS OF RESEARCH FINDINGS

Research on lesbian and gay families with children, though relatively new and subject to criticism on a number of grounds, has nevertheless yielded results that are worthy of attention. In this section, I summarize limitations of research to date, consider major findings in light of these limitations, and discuss implications of the research for theories of psychosocial development and for the politics of family life.

Without denying the consistency of major research findings to date, it is important to acknowledge that the research is subject to various criticisms. For instance, most research has involved small samples of families that are predominantly White, well-educated, relatively affluent, and living in urban areas of the United States; the degree to which results would hold with other populations is thus difficult or impossible to evaluate at this time. It would also be desirable to have data based on observational methods and collected within longitudinal designs, but studies of this kind have not yet been reported. Other issues could also be raised (see Patterson, 1992).

Despite shortcomings, however, central results of existing research on lesbian and gay families with children are exceptionally clear. First, research to date has succeeded in bringing to light the fact that lesbian and gay families with children exist. Given the relative invisibility of lesbian mothers, gay fathers, and their children, this achievement is significant in itself and should not be overlooked.

Beyond their witness to the sheer existence of lesbian and gay parents and their children, the existing studies, taken together, also yield a picture of a thriving family life. Certainly, they provide no evidence that psychological adjustment among lesbian mothers, gay fathers, or their children is impaired in any significant respect relative to heterosexual parents or their children. Indeed, the available evidence suggests that home environments provided by lesbian and gay parents are as likely as those provided by heterosexual parents to support and enable psychosocial growth among family members.

As discussed above, existing research has focused primarily on comparisons between lesbian and gay families, on the one hand, and heterosexual families, on the other. This approach reflects the concern of researchers to address prejudices and negative stereotypes that have been influential in judicial decision-making and in public policies relevant to children and families in the United States. Now that results of research have begun to converge so clearly on answers to questions posed in this way, it would appear that the time has come to address a broader range of issues in this area.

Many important research questions arise from a focus on the interests of lesbian and gay families themselves. For instance, many lesbian and gay couples with children are interested in distinctions between the experiences of biological and nonbiological parents. How important, they ask, is the biological link in influencing experiences of parenthood? Similarly, both lesbian and gay families can benefit from more information about diversity among lesbian and gay families with children, and from a better understanding of their sources. It would seem likely that, in the future, scholarship will increasingly concern itself with the study of sources of strength and resilience in lesbian and gay families with children.

In the meantime, however, the central results of research to date have important implications. If psychosocial development among children born to lesbian mothers is, as research suggests (Patterson, 1994a; Steckel, 1987), essentially normal, then traditional theoretical emphases on the importance of parental heterosexuality need to be reconsidered. Although many possible approaches to such a task are possible (Patterson, 1992), one promising approach is to focus on the significance of family process rather than structure. Thus, structural variables such as parental sexual orientation may ultimately be seen as less important in mediating children's developmental outcomes than qualities of family interactions, relationships, and processes. By including variables of both types, future research will facilitate such comparisons.

Results of research with lesbian and gay parents and their children also have implications for the politics of family life. If, as would appear to be the case, neither parents nor children in lesbian and gay families have any special risk of maladjustment or other psychosocial problems, then a good rationale for prejudice and discrimination is more difficult to provide. Without such a rationale, many legal precedents and public policies relevant to lesbian and gay families would require reconsideration. Ultimately, lesbian and gay families with children might come to be viewed as normal, and policies might be designed to protect their legitimate interests. Until that happens, however, lesbian and gay families will have a broad range of special needs.

## SERVICES FOR LESBIAN AND GAY FAMILIES

In response to the special concerns of lesbian and gay families with children, a variety of services and programs have been created. In this section, examples of programs and services that have arisen in three different contexts are described:

parent groups, health care centers, and legal advocacy groups. For more detailed discussion of these issues, see Patterson (1994b).

## Parent Groups

Lesbian and gay parents have recently formed groups throughout the country. Such groups include informal children's play groups arranged by friends; regional associations that sponsor picnics, carnivals, and other community events; and international organizations that publish newsletters and sponsor conferences. In addition to filling the needs of existing families, many groups also provide services and programs for lesbians and gay men who are considering parenthood.

The largest group in North America is the Gay and Lesbian Parents' Coalition International (GLPCI). The GLPCI newsletter lists more than 40 chapters in cities around the world, is published quarterly, and sent to readers in 55 countries. It contains news of national and chapter activities, interviews with gay and lesbian parents, reports of current legal issues, and notices about other matters of interest for lesbian and gay parents and prospective parents. The group also sponsors "Just for Us," an organization for the children of gay and lesbian parents.

Through its central office and local chapters, GLPCI sponsors numerous activities for parents and prospective parents, including an annual convention. The national Alternative Parenting Resources project collects information regarding the policies of adoption agencies, sperm banks, and fertility programs; researches state laws as they pertain to adoption by openly lesbian families; creates lists of supportive gynecologists and fertility specialists in every state; and disseminates this information. The GLPCI central office has also compiled a lengthy bibliography on gay fathers, lesbian mothers, and their families.

Much of the support that GLPCI provides to prospective parents is made available through the efforts of local chapters that sponsor workshops and support groups for gay men and lesbians who are interested in parenthood. For example, at least one chapter sponsors a support group for individuals and couples who are in various stages of adoption and/or surrogacy arrangements. Through such activities, prospective gay and lesbian parents can learn more about local parenting opportunities, legal issues, and medical resources, as well as meet others in lesbian and gay communities who are interested in becoming parents (Patterson, 1994b).

## Health Care Centers

Some medical clinics that focus on the health care needs of gay and lesbian communities also provide services for parents and prospective parents. Such clinics have generally not been formally affiliated with hospitals or medical schools but have been established as freestanding primary care centers for urban lesbian and gay communities. Two well-known examples are the Lyon-Martin Women's Health Services in San Francisco and the Whitman-Walker Clinic in Washington, D.C.

Lyon-Martin Women's Health Services, founded in 1978, is a primary care community clinic specifically for women, with a primary focus on health care for lesbians and bisexual women. The clinic provides an array of medical and health-related services, including preventive and primary health care, HIV services, support services for mothers, and programs for sexual-minority youth. It also sponsors the Lyon-Martin Lesbian/Gay Parenting Services (LGPS), which provides services for current and prospective lesbian and gay parents.

Over the last several years, the LGPS has offered a broad array of programs for lesbian and gay families with children. These include an information and referral service; support groups for prospective parents; and workshops, forums, and special events for lesbian and gay families. Support groups are led by professional health educators and range from eight-week groups for lesbians considering parenthood to six-week childbirth education classes. Many informational meetings and workshops, such as "Considering Parenthood," "Legal Issues," "Adoption," "Choices in Pregnancy and Birth," and "Lesbians and Gay Men Parenting Together," are also offered by the Lyon-Martin LGPS. Panel participants include professionals in health care, social services, and the law, all from a lesbian- and gay-affirmative perspective.

In addition to educational programming, LGPS also sponsors a number of special events that are primarily social and recreational in character. Examples include a lesbian and gay family picnic, opportunities for children to use colorful special equipment for climbing and jumping, and a parenting fair with access to information on a range of local parenting resources in a festive atmosphere. These community events provide valuable information, support, and recreational opportunities for lesbian and gay families, and help to counter feelings of isolation among lesbian and gay parents and their children.

Under the auspices of its Lesbian Choosing Children Project (LCCP), the Whitman-Walker Clinic provides services for lesbian and gay parents and prospective parents. The LCCP was a cosponsor with GLPCI of Metropolitan Washington, D.C., of a workshop on creating alternative families (described above). In addition, the LCCP has sponsored "Maybe Baby" groups for lesbians considering parenthood, and workshops on special topics such as "Options and Issues for Non-Biological Mothers." Similar programs are available in other urban areas.

## Legal Advocacy Groups

Legal advocacy groups within lesbian and gay communities also provide services to current and prospective lesbian and gay parents. Especially prominent among such groups are the Lambda Legal Defense and Education Fund and the National Center for Lesbian Rights.

Lambda Legal Defense and Education Fund (LLDEF), founded in 1973 and based in New York City, works to advance the rights of sexual minorities through litigation and to provide education to the public, the legal profession, and the government about discrimination based on sexual orientation. The work of LLDEF covers a broad spectrum of issues, including "discrimination in employment, in housing, in immigration, and in the military; AIDS and HIV-related issues; parenting and relationship issues; domestic partner benefits; and constitutional rights" (Perkins, 1992, p. 2). LLDEF filed amicus briefs in cases involving the rights of lesbian nonbiological parents in New Mexico, Minnesota, and Wisconsin (Perkins, 1992; Perkins & Romo-Carmona, 1991). For instance, an attorney for LLDEF represented the plaintiff in *Alison D. v. Virginia M.,* a well-known New York case in which a nonbiological mother sought visitation rights following the breakup of her relationship with her child's biological mother (Rubenstein, 1991). Work by LLDEF in this and related cases has been influential in legal advocacy for causes that are critical to gay and lesbian families with children.

The National Center for Lesbian Rights (NCLR), founded in 1977 and based in San Francisco, promotes awareness, respect, and recognition of lesbians and their rights (Chasnoff, 1992). The NCLR offers legal representation, amicus work, and technical assistance to cooperating counsel and other attorneys around the country. For example, NCLR has filed amicus briefs in cases involving the rights of nonbiological lesbian parents following the death of a biological parent and the breakup of a relationship between biological and nonbiological parents.

The NCLR has also been a pioneer in second-parent adoptions (Chasnoff, 1992; Ricketts & Achtenberg, 1990). Second-parent adoptions enable an unmarried parent to adopt a child without another parent of the same sex giving up his or her legal rights as a parent. By securing legal recognition of the relationship between nonbiological parents and their children, the availability of second-parent adoptions is of particular importance to lesbian and gay couples who wish to parent. Over 200 second-parent adoptions have been granted to date in seven states and the District of Columbia (Chasnoff, 1992). In addition to representing nonbiological parents in second-parent adoption cases, NCLR provides technical assistance to parents and their attorneys who are seeking such adoptions, is developing a manual for use by attorneys in such cases, and provides training sessions for lawyers who handle second-parent adoption cases. NCLR has also drafted model statewide legislation in California that would change the existing stepparent adoption law to a second-parent adoption law. If enacted, this reform would streamline and simplify the process of seeking second-parent adoptions (Chasnoff, 1992).

An additional aspect of NCLR activities in support of gay and lesbian families with children is the NCLR publications program. They include a variety of materials relevant to lesbian and gay parenting, including "AIDS and Child Custody: A Guide to Advocacy," "Lesbians Choosing Motherhood: Legal Implications of Donor Insemination and Co-Parenting," and "A Lesbian and Gay Parent's Legal Guide to Child Custody." These publications can assist parents and prospective parents in their efforts to secure legal protection for their families. Thus, the publication program greatly extends the range of NCLR's service to lesbian and gay parents and their children.

## DIRECTIONS FOR RESEARCH, SERVICE, AND ADVOCACY

Although some innovative programs and services are available for lesbian and gay parents and their children, their availability is still extremely limited. In this section, I discuss directions for research, service, and advocacy relevant to lesbian and gay families with children.

### Directions for Research

One of the important directions for research in this area is to identify and explore factors that influence gay and lesbian couples' and individuals' inclinations to make parenthood a part of their lives (Crawford, 1987). Having lived so long in the shadow of antigay prejudice, many lesbians and gay men do not think of parenting as an option. What kinds of influences are important in this regard? Does the degree of an individual's or a couple's integration with different parts of the gay/lesbian and/or heterosexual communities make a difference? What role do personal, social, and economic variables play in such decisions? We need to know more about the factors that influence decisions about parenthood among lesbians and gay men.

A related direction for research is assessment of the climate for lesbian and gay parenting in various areas. What are the important criteria that should be used in such an assessment, and how do different locales measure up against them? One approach is to use state-level indicators as rough indexes. For example, a statewide gay/lesbian rights law is a positive indicator with regard to the climate for lesbian and gay parenting, as is the accomplishment of second-parent adoptions in that state. On the other side, negative indicators include the existence of sodomy laws and/or other adverse legal precedents. One might also review regulations pertaining to adoption and foster care placements. Ratings of this sort could be useful for couples and individuals seeking parenthood, parents considering relocation, and activists and advocacy groups deciding how best to direct their activities.

The climates of local communities might also be assessed with the needs of lesbian and gay parents and their children in mind. For instance, one might ask whether there are gay and lesbian parent groups in existence, whether any second-parent adoptions have been completed within this community, and whether relevant health care and medical resources are available to lesbian and gay families. Such assessments should be geared to specific locales, because communities that are located in geographical proximity to one another may vary tremendously in the climates they provide for gay and lesbian families with children.

Such efforts to examine and describe the atmosphere for lesbian and gay family life also raise questions about which aspects of a community make it an attractive place for gay and lesbian parents and their children to live. Such characteristics in some cases are similar to those for heterosexual families (e.g., safe streets, good schools), while in other cases they vary even among lesbian and gay families as a function of the family's other identities, interests, or needs. For instance, interracial or multiracial families might value especially the opportunity to live in multiracial neighborhoods.

It is also valuable to learn more about the effectiveness of existing services for lesbian and gay families. Although many new services and programs have emerged for prospective parents as well as for parents and their children, there have been few attempts to evaluate their effectiveness. How effectively do available services serve the needs that they are intended to address? What populations are targeted by existing programs and with what success do programs and services reach the communities for which they are intended? What are the essential elements of effective programs? And how can existing programs be improved? All of these are critical questions for community-oriented research on lesbian and gay parenting services.

Finally, the knowledge base relevant to gay and lesbian parenting is still very limited. Lesbians and gay men interested in parenting often want descriptive information about child and adolescent development among the offspring of lesbian and gay parents. Many lesbians and gay men considering parenthood also have questions about the ways in which parenthood can be expected to affect existing couple relationships in lesbian and gay families. Others are concerned about relationships with members of their families of origin as well as with friends, neighbors, and colleagues. Still others focus on family members' interactions with institutional contexts, such as educational, legal, and medical settings. Such topics are open to empirical study; the work has begun, but much remains to be accomplished.

## Directions for Service

There are a number of ways in which efforts to provide improved services for lesbian and gay parents might be directed. In part because services for lesbian and gay parents are so new, and in part because of widespread discrimination, expanded services are needed at all levels. At the national level, an organization such as GLPCI has the potential to develop lists of health care, legal, and other resources on a state-by-state basis, as well as to provide technical assistance to local groups. At regional and local levels, individual parent groups are mounting educational events and other programs in support of lesbian and gay parenting in their communities. Even in major urban areas, however, most such programs are in a nascent state, depend heavily on the efforts of volunteers, and reach mainly affluent, well-educated segments of lesbian and gay communities. In many smaller towns and rural areas, there are as yet no services.

One of the major needs, then, is for expansion of services. Such efforts are perhaps most needed outside of the major urban centers where services tend to be more readily available. Programs and services should be developed by and for low-income and ethnic-minority lesbian and gay individuals and couples who are parents or who may wish to become parents. Of necessity, such work would involve identification of medical, legal, and other resources that are open to members of sexual minorities as well as to ethnic minorities and low-income communities. Services should also be developed for the children of lesbian and gay parents.

In seeking to expand services for sexual-minority parenting communities, it is important not to overlook important resources outside lesbian and gay communities. For instance, building public library collections in areas relevant to lesbian and gay parenting can provide an important resource that is available to large numbers of people, regardless of sexual orientation. Educational institutions such as high schools, colleges, and universities can also provide important resources for prospective lesbian and gay parents by including accurate information in the curriculum; by providing speakers and other relevant programming; and by making available to students articles, books, and video materials that relate to parenting by individuals with sexual-minority identities (Casper & Schultz, this volume). Similarly, religious groups can provide important perspectives by providing special activities for lesbian and gay families with children, and by educating their members about lesbian and gay parenting (Kahn, 1991).

Another major aim of service to prospective lesbian and gay parents is to eliminate discrimination against lesbian and gay parents and their children. To the degree that this effort meets with success, many of the special needs of gay or lesbian parents and their children will decrease in significance. Although it is unlikely that antigay prejudice will be eliminated in the foreseeable future, work in this area is still of great importance. Prevention efforts relevant to lesbian and gay parenting should be designed to counter homophobic stereotypes of lesbians and gay men with accurate information about the realities of life in lesbian and gay families, and to provide an understanding of psychosocial processes underlying prejudice and discrimination.

## Directions for Advocacy

Among the greatest current needs of lesbian and gay families with children is for activism to promote social and political change. Gay and lesbian parents and their children have issues in common with those of many other families, but they also have unique concerns that arise from prejudice against lesbian and gay families.

The basic issues of children and families in this country are, in many cases, also the issues of lesbian and gay families with children. For instance, many families with children would benefit from enhanced neighborhood safety, better public schools, flexible working hours for parents, and better access to health care. Improved economic conditions and a more equal distribution of economic resources would benefit children in economically stressed lesbian and gay families, just as they would benefit children in other economically disadvantaged homes. In other words, a common stake is held by gay, lesbian, and heterosexual families in many issues of public policy relevant to families with children.

Even allowing for overlap with the needs of other families, lesbian and gay families with children also have a unique agenda. They need legal recognition for their family relationships; equal access to foster care and adoption; equal access to medical care; and an end to harassment, bigotry, and hate crimes. Lesbian and gay parents need to know that their sexual orientation will not be held against them as they pursue parenthood, bring up their children, or seek custody of their children after a partner's death or the breakup of an intimate relationship between parents. Similar to the offspring of heterosexual parents, children of lesbian and gay parents need to be sure that their relationships with parents will be protected by law. Accomplishment of these aims requires sustained advocacy efforts in judicial and legislative domains (Polikoff, 1990; Rubenstein, 1991).

## Conclusion

For many gay men and lesbians, as for many heterosexuals, parenthood is an important part of life. In the United States today, however, prejudicial attitudes, discriminatory practices, and institutionalized heterosexism place many unnecessary roadblocks in the path of lesbians and gay men who wish to become parents and create many obstacles to the protection of family relationships in existing lesbian and gay families with children. Gay and lesbian communities across the country have begun to address these issues, but much work remains to be done.

In the meantime, services for lesbians and gay men can assist individuals in coping with prejudice, overcoming discriminatory practices, and compensating for institutionalized heterosexism. Lesbians and gay men who wish to become parents face considerable prejudice. Although much of this prejudice springs from inaccurate assumptions about gay and lesbian parents and their children, it is nevertheless widespread. Gay and lesbian parents are likely to encounter negative reactions from family members, heterosexual friends, coworkers, and health care providers, as well as from other gay men and lesbians (Pollack & Vaughn, 1987). To counter this, lesbians and gay men need both accurate information and socioemotional support.

Lesbian and gay families with children are also likely to encounter difficulties that stem from discriminatory practices. Even in major urban centers, some health care providers refuse to assist lesbians seeking to conceive a child. Outside of major urban centers, many forms of medical assistance (e.g., for infertility testing or treatments) are entirely unavailable. Similarly, regulations in many states are unfavorable to lesbian and gay couples who wish to adopt children or to become foster parents. To persist in the face of such discriminatory practices, lesbians and gay men need socioemotional support as well as access to educational, economic, and legal resources.

Finally, gay men and lesbians who are or who want to become parents must also cope with many forms of institutionalized heterosexism. Because lesbian and gay couples cannot legally marry in the United States, an array of issues ranging from health insurance to inheritance affect the welfare of their children. Similarly, because schools and most other institutional settings with which children and parents come into contact are designed for heterosexual families, they present many issues for lesbian and gay families (see Casper & Schultz, this volume).

In this context, it is easy to understand that a book such as *Heather Has Two Mommies* could generate controversy. The possibility depicted by the book—that Heather is a happy, healthy child growing up in a loving lesbian family—is precisely at the center of debate. Even as the realities of family life shift to create more children like Heather and even as the results of research appear to support *Heather*'s central thesis, the forces of heterosexism are increasingly determined to deny these possibilities. As adults discuss the issues, however, it is easy to overlook the interests of children, for whom the book was originally intended.

Like other children, young people growing up in lesbian and gay families can benefit from access to positive images of life in families like their own. Indeed, such images can also be helpful for children from heterosexual families by enriching their appreciation of the differences among families. Books such as *Heather Has Two Mommies* make it easier for everyone to imagine, as indeed appears to be the case, that even in the face of prejudice and discrimination, it is possible for loving lesbian and gay parents to raise happy, healthy children. Because contemplation of this possibility, even in fiction, is viewed by some as alarming or controversial illustrates clearly the need for research, service, and advocacy relevant to the needs of lesbian and gay families.

▼    **ENDNOTES**    ▼

1. Parts of this chapter have appeared in Patterson (1994b), "Lesbian and Gay Couples Considering Parenthood: An Agenda for Research, Service, and Advocacy," *Journal of Gay and Lesbian Social Services,* and in Patterson (1995), "Lesbian Mothers, Gay Fathers, and Their Children" in A. R. D'Augelli & C. J. Patterson (Eds.), *Lesbian, Gay and Bisexual Identities Across the Lifespan.* New York: Oxford University Press.

## ▼ REFERENCES ▼

Barbanel, J. (1993, February 8). Political miscalculations threaten Fernandez's job. *New York Times*, sec. 1B, p. 2.

Baumrind, D. (1967). Childcare practices anteceding three patterns of preschool behavior. *Genetic Psychology Monographs, 75,* 43–88.

Baumrind, D., & Black, A. E. (1967). Socialization practices associated with dimensions of competence in preschool boys and girls. *Child Development, 38,* 291–327.

Bell, A. P., & Weinberg, M. S. (1978). *Homosexualities: A study of diversity among men and women.* New York: Simon & Schuster.

Bigner, J. J., & Bozett, F. W. (1990). Parenting by gay fathers. In F. W. Bozett & M. B. Sussman (Eds.), *Homosexuality and family relations* (pp. 155–176). New York: Harrington Park Press.

Bigner, J. J., & Jacobsen, R. B. (1989a). Parenting behaviors of homosexual and heterosexual fathers. In F. W. Bozett (Ed.), *Homosexuality and the family* (pp. 173–186). New York: Harrington Park Press.

Bigner, J. J., & Jacobsen, R. B. (1989b). The value of children to gay and heterosexual fathers. In F. W. Bozett (Ed.), *Homosexuality and the family* (pp. 163–172). New York: Harrington Park Press.

Blumenfeld, W. J., & Raymond, D. (1988). *Looking at gay and lesbian life.* Boston: Beacon Press.

Bozett, F. W. (1980). Gay fathers: How and why they disclose their homosexuality to their children. *Family Relations, 29,* 173–179.

Bozett, F. W. (1981a). Gay fathers: Evolution of the gay-father identity. *American Journal of Orthopsychiatry, 51,* 552–559.

Bozett, F. W. (1981b). Gay fathers: Identity conflict resolution through integrative sanctioning. *Alternative Lifestyles, 4,* 90–107.

Bozett, F. W. (1982). Heterogeneous couples in heterosexual marriages: Gay men and straight women. *Journal of Marital and Family Therapy, 8,* 81–89.

Bozett, F. W. (1987). Children of gay fathers. In F. W. Bozett (Ed.), *Gay and lesbian parents* (pp. 39–57). New York: Praeger.

Bozett, F. W. (1989). Gay fathers: A review of the literature. In F. W. Bozett (Ed.), *Homosexuality and the family* (pp. 137–162). New York: Harrington Park Press.

Brown, L. S. (1995). Lesbian identities: Concepts and issues. In A. G. D'Augelli & C. J. Patterson (Eds.), *Lesbian, gay and bisexual identities over the lifespan: Psychological perspectives* (pp. 3–23). New York: Oxford University Press.

Casper, V., Schultz, S., & Wickens, E. (1992). Breaking the silences: Lesbian and gay parents and the schools. *Teachers College Record, 94,* 109–137.

Chasnoff, D. (1992, Spring). *Newsletter of the National Center for Lesbian Rights.* San Francisco: National Center for Lesbian Rights.

Crawford, S. (1987). Lesbian families: Psychosocial stress and the family-building process. In Boston Lesbian Psychologies Collective (Ed.), *Lesbian psychologies: Explorations and challenges* (pp. 195–214). Urbana, IL: University of Illinois Press.

Dillon, S. (1993, February 11). Board removes Fernandez as New York schools chief after stormy 3-year term. *New York Times*, sec. 1A, p. 6.

Dunne, E. J. (1987). Helping gay fathers come out to their children. *Journal of Homosexuality, 13,* 213–222.

Editors of the Harvard Law Review (1990). *Sexual orientation and the law.* Cambridge, MA: Harvard University Press.

Falk, P. J. (1989). Lesbian mothers: Psychosocial assumptions in family law. *American Psychologist, 44,* 941–947.

Gibbs, E. D. (1988). Psychosocial development of children raised by lesbian mothers: A review of research. *Women and Therapy, 8,* 55–75.

Golombok, S., Spencer, A., & Rutter, M. (1983). Children in lesbian and single-parent households: Psychosexual and psychiatric appraisal. *Journal of Child Psychology and Psychiatry, 24,* 551–572.

Gonsiorek, J. C. (1991). The empirical basis for the demise of the illness model of homosexuality. In J. C. Gonsiorek & J. D. Weinrich (Eds.), *Homosexuality: Research implications for public policy.* Beverly Hills, CA: Sage.

Gottman, J. S. (1990). Children of gay and lesbian parents. In F. W. Bozett & M. B. Sussman (Eds.), *Homosexuality and family relations* (pp. 177–196). New York: Harrington Park Press.

Green, G. D., & Bozett, F. W. (1991). Lesbian mothers and gay fathers. In J. C. Gonsiorek & J. D. Weinrich (Eds.), *Homosexuality: Research implications for public policy* (pp. 197–214). Beverly Hills, CA: Sage.

Green, R. (1978). Sexual identity of 37 children raised by homosexual or transsexual parents. *American Journal of Psychiatry, 135,* 692–697.

Green, R., Mandel, J. B., Hotvedt, M. E., Gray, J., & Smith, L. (1986). Lesbian mothers and their children: A comparison with solo parent heterosexual mothers and their children. *Archives of Sexual Behavior, 7,* 175–181.

Hand, S. I. (1991). *The lesbian parenting couple.* Unpublished doctoral dissertation, The Professional School of Psychology, San Francisco, CA.

Harris, M. B., & Turner, P. H. (1985/1986). Gay and lesbian parents. *Journal of Homosexuality, 12,* 101–113.

Henry, T. (1993, January 12). Making gays and lesbians part of the rainbow curriculum. *USA Today,* sec. 4D, p. 1.

Hill, M. (1987). Child-rearing attitudes of black lesbian mothers. In the Boston Lesbian Psychologies Collective (Ed.), *Lesbian psychologies: Explorations and chal-*

*lenges* (pp. 215–226). Urbana, IL: University of Illinois Press.

Hitchens, D. J., & Kirkpatrick, M. J. (1985). Lesbian mothers/gay fathers. In D. H. Schetky & E. P. Benedek (Eds.), *Emerging issues in child psychiatry and the law* (pp. 115–125). New York: Brunner-Mazel.

Hoeffer, B. (1981). Children's acquisition of sex-role behavior in lesbian-mother families. *American Journal of Orthopsychiatry, 5,* 536–544.

Huggins, S. L. (1989). A comparative study of self-esteem of adolescent children of divorced lesbian mothers and divorced heterosexual mothers. In F. W. Bozett (Ed.), *Homosexuality and the family* (pp. 123–135). New York: Harrington Park Press.

Kahn, Y. H. (1991, Spring). Hannah, must you have a child? *Out/Look,* (12), pp. 39–43.

Kinsey, A. C., Pomeroy, W. B., & Martin, C. E. (1948). *Sexual behavior in the human male.* Philadelphia: W. B. Saunders.

Kirkpatrick, M. (1987). Clinical implications of lesbian mother studies. *Journal of Homosexuality, 13,* 201–211.

Kirkpatrick, M., Smith, C., & Roy, R. (1981). Lesbian mothers and their children: A comparative survey. *American Journal of Orthopsychiatry, 51,* 545–551.

Koepke, L., Hare, J., & Moran, P. B. (1992). Relationship quality in a sample of lesbian couples with children and child-free lesbian couples. *Family Relations, 41,* 224–229.

Lyons, T. A. (1983). Lesbian mothers' custody fears. *Women and Therapy, 2,* 231–240.

Martin, A. (1993). *The lesbian and gay parenting handbook.* New York: HarperCollins.

McCandlish, B. (1987). Against all odds: Lesbian mother family dynamics. In F. W. Bozett (Ed.), *Gay and lesbian parents* (pp. 23–38). New York: Praeger.

Miller, B. (1978). Adult sexual resocialization: Adjustments toward a stigmatized identity. *Alternative Lifestyles, 1,* 207–234.

Miller, B. (1979). Gay fathers and their children. *Family Coordinator, 28,* 544–552.

Miller, J. A., Jacobsen, R. B., & Bigner, J. J. (1981). The child's home environment for lesbian versus heterosexual mothers: A neglected area of research. *Journal of Homosexuality, 7,* 49–56.

Money, J., & Ehrhardt, A. A. (1972). *Man and woman, boy and girl: The differentiation and dimorphism of gender identity from conception to maturity.* Baltimore: Johns Hopkins University Press.

Newman, L. (1989). *Heather has two mommies.* Boston: Alyson Press.

Osterweil, D. A. (1991). *Correlates of relationship satisfaction in lesbian couples who are parenting their first child together.* Unpublished doctoral dissertation, California School of Professional Psychology, Berkeley, CA.

Pagelow, M. D. (1980). Heterosexual and lesbian single mothers: A comparison of problems, coping and solutions. *Journal of Homosexuality, 5,* 198–204.

Patterson, C. J. (1992). Children of lesbian and gay parents. *Child Development, 63,* 1025–1042.

Patterson, C. J. (1994a). Children of the lesbian baby boom: Behavioral adjustment, self-concepts, and sex-role identity. In B. Greene & G. Herek (Eds.), *Contemporary perspectives on lesbian and gay psychology: Theory, research, and applications* (pp. 156–175). Beverly Hills, CA: Sage.

Patterson, C. J. (1994b). Lesbian and gay couples considering parenthood: An agenda for research, service, and advocacy. *Journal of Gay and Lesbian Social Services, 1,* 33–55.

Patterson, C. J. (1995). Lesbian mothers, gay fathers, and their children. In A. R. D'Augelli & C. J. Patterson (Eds.), *Lesbian, gay and bisexual identities across* the lifespan: Psychological perspectives (pp. 262–290). New York: Oxford University Press.

Patterson, C. J. (in press). Gay and lesbian parenthood. In M. H. Bornstein (Ed.), *Handbook of parenting.* Hillsdale, NJ: Lawrence Erlbaum Associates.

Paul, J. P. (1986). *Growing up with a gay, lesbian, or bisexual parent: An exploratory study of experiences and perceptions.* Unpublished doctoral dissertation, University of California at Berkeley, Berkeley, CA.

Perkins, P. (Ed.). (1992). *The lambda update, 9*(1). New York: Lambda Legal Defense and Education Fund.

Perkins, P., & Romo-Carmona, M. (1991). *The lambda update, 8*(1). New York: Lambda Legal Defense and Education Fund.

Pies, C. (1985). *Considering parenthood.* San Francisco: Spinsters/Aunt Lute.

Pies, C. (1990). Lesbians and the choice to parent. In F. W. Bozett & M. B. Sussman (Eds.), *Homosexuality and family relations* (pp. 137–154). New York: Harrington Park Press.

Polikoff, N. (1990). This child does have two mothers: Redefining parenthood to meet the needs of children in lesbian mother and other nontraditional families. *The Georgetown Law Review, 78,* 459–575.

Pollack, S., & Vaughn, J. (1987). *Politics of the heart: A lesbian parenting anthology.* Ithaca, NY: Firebrand Books.

Rand, C., Graham, D. L. R., & Rawlings, E. I. (1982). Psychological health and factors the court seeks to control in lesbian mother custody trials. *Journal of Homosexuality, 8,* 27–39.

Rees, R. L. (1979). *A comparison of children of lesbian and single heterosexual mothers on three measures of socialization.* Unpublished doctoral dissertation, California School of Professional Psychology, Berkeley, CA.

Ricketts, W. (1991). *Lesbians and gay men as foster parents.* Portland, ME:

National Child Welfare Resource Center, University of Southern Maine.

Ricketts, W., & Achtenberg, R. (1990). Adoption and foster parenting for lesbians and gay men: Creating new traditions in family. In F. W. Bozett & M. B. Sussman (Eds.), *Homosexuality and family relations* (pp. 83–118). New York: Harrington Park Press.

Riley, C. (1988). American kinship: A lesbian account. *Feminist Issues, 8,* 75–94.

Rivera, R. (1991). Sexual orientation and the law. In J. C. Gonsiorek & J. D. Weinrich (Eds.), *Homosexuality: Research implications for public policy.* Beverly Hills, CA: Sage.

Robinson, B. E., & Skeen, P. (1982). Sex-role orientation of gay fathers versus gay nonfathers. *Perceptual and Motor Skills, 55,* 1055–1059.

Rohrbaugh, J. B. (1988). Choosing children: Psychological issues in lesbian parenting. *Women and Therapy, 8,* 51–63.

Rubenstein, W. B. (1991). We are family: A reflection on the search for legal recognition of lesbian and gay relationships. *The Journal of Law and Politics, 8,* 89–105.

Sameroff, A. J., & Chandler, M. (1975). Reproductive risk and the continuum of caretaking casualty. In F. D. Horowitz (Ed.), *Review of child development research* (Vol. 4) (pp. 187–244). Chicago: University of Chicago Press.

Seligmann, J. (1990, Winter/Spring). Variations on a theme. *Newsweek* (Special Edition: The 21st Century Family), pp. 38–46.

Skeen, P., & Robinson, B. (1985). Gay fathers' and gay nonfathers' relationships with their parents. *Journal of Sex Research, 21,* 86–91.

Steckel, A. (1985). *Separation-individuation in children of lesbian and heterosexual couples.* Unpublished doctoral dissertation, The Wright Institute Graduate School, Berkeley, CA.

Steckel, A. (1987). Psychosocial development of children of lesbian mothers. In F. W. Bozett (Ed.), *Gay and lesbian parents* (pp. 75–85). New York: Praeger.

Tasker, F. L., & Golombok, S. (1991). Children raised by lesbian mothers: The empirical evidence. *Family Law, 21,* 184–187.

United States Bureau of the Census (1991). *Statistical abstract of the United States, 1991.* Washington, DC: U.S. Department of Commerce.

Weston, K. (1991). *Families we choose: Lesbians, gays, kinship.* New York: Columbia University Press.

# Chapter 13

▼

# LESBIAN AND GAY PARENTS ENCOUNTER EDUCATORS: INITIATING CONVERSATIONS

Virginia Casper
&
Steven Schultz[1]

There is not one but many silences, and they are an integral part of the strategies that underlie and permeate discourses. (Foucault, 1978)

*Close connections between school and home are viewed by most teachers as central to their work. Yet cultural misunderstandings frequently occur between parents and educators, eroding effective communication (Derman-Sparks, 1989; Lightfoot, 1978). Responding to the challenges of antibias and multicultural education, many teachers are beginning to recognize the cultural backgrounds of the children they teach. In the process, many have further increased their awareness of the importance of school-home communication.*

*In addition to language miscommunications and divergent expectations about the responsibilities of the school and home, silences also complicate attempts to understand each others' points of view. An open dialogue between parents and teachers is a route toward understanding, but all too frequently the prevailing communication is an active but "silenced dialogue" that occurs under the surface of parent-teacher discourse.[2] Dialogue not only brings lesbian and gay parenting into the open, it allows children to experience greater congruence between their understandings of family at home and that which they experience in school.*

*We began a research project three years ago that built on our interests, past research, and the questions of our graduate students at Bank Street College regarding communication between lesbian and gay parents and their children's teachers and administrators. As we heard teachers and students grapple with issues emerging in their classrooms, we became aware that despite the increasing number and visibility of nontraditional families, there was little published research on lesbian- and gay-headed families and their interactions with schools. We wanted to learn about the concerns and questions these parents had as they enrolled their young children in school. We were equally interested in the responses and experiences of school staff to teaching children with lesbian or gay parents. Our interviews sought to determine their thoughts and feelings about lesbians and gay men and how their images of homosexuality— and children—meshed with their practice.*

*The following is primarily a descriptive account. We include excerpts from our interview transcripts because the voices of parents and teachers speak both clearly and eloquently. The commentary is meant to organize, highlight, and provide particular meaning to aspects of the narratives. We reserve our views about the broader implications of this work for the final section. It should be clear that when researchers use themselves as instruments for data collection, their experiences, values, and perspectives become a part of the work (Wilcox, 1982). This certainly is the case in our study. We do not pretend to remove all vestiges of our "biases"; therefore, it is only fair to be explicit about those aspects of our background that have most direct bearing on the work. Of the three researchers responsible for this study (Casper, Schultz, and Wickens), two of us are lesbian/gay parents and one of us is neither lesbian/gay nor a parent. We all have a history of work promoting multicultural and antibias activity with young children, and we have done this as teachers and as teacher educators. All of us hold the values and aims of progressive education close to our work, and we all have a history of engaging in progressive activities outside the classroom within the larger political arena. We see our obvious commonalities and our clear differences as important strengths in our work together. The commonalities allowed us to work together as a team. Our differences kept us honest.*

## THE CHALLENGES OF PARENTHOOD

Parenthood is currently viewed as part of the complex and transactional nature of adult development (Benedek, 1959; Erikson, 1963). Shanok (1991) defines *parenthood* as a role, and *parenting* as a relationship where "identity and intimacy together combine to form the essence of human experience: . . . the discrete self in relation to family, friends, community" (p. 2). Although deciding to become a parent is a different endeavor than becoming a parent, a process of identity change occurs nonetheless. Considerations about adoption, natural childbirth, sharing of caregiving roles, financial considerations, and fantasies about the child's place in the family begin before the infant's arrival. After the child's arrival, couples frequently redefine their priorities, social life, and even social crowd. Louis, one of our interviewees, reflected on the changes in his life:

**Louis:**   It's interesting, but . . . before I had the kids, I would go to [my parents] and all [they] would talk about was the kids. It was kind of lonely after awhile, listening about their kids. I found out that after we had ours, all we did was talk about the kids. So we fit right in with them. . . . Our single friends had very little in common with us now. . . . Now we were with our family in terms of meeting new friends who were also gay and had children. Also, the disco days were over, and I haven't been to a movie for two years. . . . What do you talk about with your mother as a single gay male? Not really much, unless you talk about a couch for the living room, or gossipy thing s about the family. My mother is now much more involved in our lives. She's a grandmother and she really enjoys it.

The birth of a child is the beginning of an exciting and turbulent time. Shadows of one's childhood return, and adults often form or re-form new relationships with their families of origin. These well-known developmental principles serve as a pivot around which to begin to understand the enormity of the issues gay and lesbian parents face. For new gay and lesbian parents, changing adult identity and the disclosure of homosexuality intersect with the usual heavily charged issues of parenthood. This confluence of factors can result in confusion and/or fears of being judged as an inadequate parent, largely because of a clear societal bias against lesbian and gay people having *any* relationship with children, much less a parental one. For some parents, the reality of raising a child shakes their self-conception; for others it may be the impetus to "come out" as gay or lesbian to their parents for the first time. This disclosure can have ramifications for the relationship, ranging from severely negative to joyously positive. Along with the usual well-meaning advice from neighbors and friends regarding the care of one's new baby, gay and lesbian parents also face the aforementioned issues. In addition, we must not forget the powerful influence that teachers and administrators can have on parents, especially when raising their firstborn child.

Research on the psychosocial effects of being raised by same-sex parents informs us that these children are just as healthy as those raised by heterosexual parents (Patterson, this volume). Although researchers are examining the ways in which family structures, including those created by the loss of a parent through divorce or death, affect child-development (e.g., Eiduson, 1981), research on lesbian-/gay-headed family structures does not usually appear in traditional research volumes on American families or in basic child development texts (Cowen & Hetherington, 1992; Michaels & Goldberg, 1988). Small-scale, in-depth studies of lesbian-/gay-headed families, however, are being published in newer research journals and books (Patterson, 1992; Schultz & Casper, 1993; Steckel, 1985). This new work is more focused on process and includes a number of publications that describe the experiences of the families in rich detail (Benkov, 1994; Clay, 1990; Lewin, 1993; Martin, 1993; Rafkin, 1990; Weston, 1991). In addition, there are now well over 20 books for both older and younger children of lesbian-/gay-headed families.[3]

## CULTURAL CONSIDERATIONS

Children who have lesbian or gay parents, especially children whose parents have been open about their sexual orientation and family structure, may discover that the dominant cultural values reflected in the school are foreign to them. Explicitly, through a noninclusive curricular study of the family, and implicitly, through the almost exclusive illustration of heterosexual-headed families in picture books and other media, family is defined in ways that are quite different from their experiences. As these children of lesbian and gay parents enter school, they come into contact with a broader social world. Although they have had a connection with this world before—at the playground, through TV, and during family activities—the school as a *social institution* provides a different contact. As representatives of the dominant culture, schools have as their stated or unstated goal the socialization of children into mainstream cultural norms (Schultz, 1988). When the school culture is viewed as embodying these norms, it can be seen as a "backdrop" that highlights children's family configurations more clearly than the playground and more personally than TV.

Young children of gay and lesbian parents who enter school for the first time and who previously held an unquestioning acceptance of the naturalness of their family are suddenly confronted with countless situations in which a totally different family configuration is the norm. These children must contend with the frequent representation and labeling of their family configuration as deviant or, perhaps most commonly, nonexistent. Clark's (1955/1970) pioneering work on the self-images of African American children demonstrated that the nonrepresentation of important aspects of one's identity can result in illegitimate feelings about oneself. Another example is the real-life experiences of young girls and women who were excluded from the literature on the school lives of children. It was only with the application of the women's movement to early childhood education that studies exposed the sex stereotyping or invisibility of women in children's literature (see Cuffaro, 1975; Harrison, 1973; Nilsen, 1977; Sprung, 1975).[4] These biases continue to persist today (Sadker & Sadker, 1994; Streitmatter, 1994). The misrepresentation and underrepresentation in early childhood curricula of children of different races, genders, and family structures have the effect of delegitimizing their present lives and limiting their possibilities for the future. To the extent that the school system embodies dominant cultural values, the lives of lesbians and gay men will not be represented.

## TALKING TO PARENTS AND SCHOOL STAFF: METHODOLOGY

Although in-depth interviews were our primary research tool, we also collected data through observations and anecdotes. We became a clearinghouse for information from colleagues and graduate students. Additional stories came from participants at conferences where we presented preliminary results from this study. This provided important, useful information.

Interviews were obtained through a structured outreach process. Using connections with Center Kids[5] and through personal and other organizational contacts (particularly organizations of African American lesbians and gay men), we assembled a highly diverse group of parents to interview. The population of 36 informants that comprise this study include gay and lesbian parents and school staff who are White, African American, and Latino/a and who are middle, working, and lower class. The primary children attend private schools, day care centers, and public schools up through the second grade—though some siblings (whose teachers or administrators were not interviewed) attended grades up to 5th. (see Table 13.1). Whenever possible, we employed a triadic structure involving interviews with the child's parent(s), teacher, and school administrator. Because a number of parents did not want the school personnel to know about their sexual orientation, we also included some parent-only interviews. In addition, we interviewed several school staff who offered valuable information based on their years of work in the schools. When follow-up was possible, interviews were conducted for three successive years. This enabled us to note educational, developmental, and parent and teacher attitudinal changes.

Due to issues of confidentiality and invisibility, gathering research participants within gay and lesbian communities has its own set of standards in terms of numbers of subjects and recruitment techniques considered sufficient for study (Morin, 1977). Although our population was not based on a random selection, we believe it represents a broad cross section of gay and lesbian parents in the greater New York–Tristate area in terms of race, class, and family structure.

We asked the interviewees open-ended questions with flexible follow-up inquiries. This technique enabled the gathering of in-depth information without locking us into a standard format that might have worked with one parent or administrator but would have been a dismal failure with another. This type of data collection helped blend the "native's point of view" with a more distanced perspective. We embrace Geertz's (1973) criteria for a good ethnography: an optimal blend of "experience-near" and "experience-far" perspectives. Near experiences permitted a closer understanding and feeling for what it is like to be a lesbian or gay parent or a teacher or an administrator of a child with lesbian or gay parents. Far experiences afforded a perspective sufficiently distant to label, categorize, and compare the information—to blend what was learned with knowledge gleaned from other research and theoretical writing.

## EXPERIENCES OF EDUCATORS

For educators, similar to any other group, age, family background, historical period, and geographical area in which one lives influence the point of view that is brought into the classroom. The educators we interviewed represent a breadth of prior experience with and points of view about gay and lesbian issues. We gleaned from the interviews how those experiences influenced them and the ways in which they have used their recollections to think about the lesbian-/gay-headed families with whom they work. Furthermore, their experiences educating children of gay and lesbian parents have changed them and helped them to further develop their values and philosophies. Some were able to identify experiences from their past that were similar to those of their students. We heard

Table 13.1
Descriptive Data of Families

| Parents | Resident | Ethnicity | Children | Yrs. in study | Grade | | | School | Out | Other Informants | |
|---|---|---|---|---|---|---|---|---|---|---|---|
| | | | | | Child 1 | Child 2 | Child 3 | | | Teachers | Admin. |
| Maritza & Sharon | Suburbs | Puerto Rican/ Caucasian | 1 | 1989–1990 1990–1991 1991–1992* | daycare kindergarten 1st grade | | | private private | no yes yes | Carla | Joan Lise |
| James & Mathew | Manh. | African American/ Caucasian | 2 | 1989–1990 1990–1991 1991–1992* | preschool kindergarten 1st grade | preschool | | private public magnate public magnate | no yes yes | Sasha Theresa asst/Pat | Joan Emory |
| Jacqueline & Nora | Suburbs | Caucasian | 1 | 1990–1991 1991–1992 | kindergarten 1st grade | | | public magnate | no/yes yes | Fred | |
| June & Shelley | Manh. | Caucasian | 2 | 1989–1990 1990–1991 | kindergarten 1st grade | 2nd grade 3rd grade | | public public | yes yes | Penny Edna | Enrico Enrico |
| Shanique | Brooklyn | African American | 1 | 1990–1991 | 1st grade | | | public | no | Saul | |
| Ricky & Maggie | Manh. | Caucasian | 1 | 1990–1991 | kindergarten/ 1st grade | | | public | yes | Cathy | Beverly |
| Esperanza | Queens | Puerto Rican | 2 | 1990–1991 | 1st grade | 4th grade | | public | no | | |
| Manuel | Brooklyn | Puerto Rican | 2 | 1990–1991 | kindergarten | 5th grade | | public & private | no | | |
| Al & Richard | Manh. | Puerto Rican/ African American | 3 | 1990–1991 | preschool | preschool | 1st grade | public | yes/no | Gerry | Lisa |
| Maureen & Naomi | Suburbs | Caucasian | 1 | 1989–1990 | 1st grade | | | public & private | yes | | |

Additional Educators:
Teachers: Fran and Leslie—private
Guidance Counselors: Eleanor—public
Administrators: Father Stephen—parochial

*Follow-up communication, not full interview.

stories from those whose views about gay and lesbian issues have changed greatly and from others who have remained consistent. Some educators clearly articulated the origins of their biases and tried to prevent them from influencing their actions. This awareness can be helpful in distinguishing between one's personal belief system and the way in which one wants to approach gay and lesbian parents and their children. From our interviews three groups of educators can be distinguished.

A first grouping consisted of several young teachers who spoke about first meeting lesbian and gay people at college, a time when, for many young adults, opportunities for new experiences arise. Interestingly, none of them remembered exactly what they formerly thought, but they had memories of experiencing "differences." One such teacher made an important distinction about the explicit or implicit manner in which a person's lesbian or gay identity is known to a "straight" person.

CATHY[6]:    There were a whole lot of people [at college] who were very open about it. I think a lot of times people will know someone who is lesbian or gay, but it's not really discussed and they don't really know if the person is lesbian or gay. Whereas at college, people were out in no uncertain terms. They were very clear about it.

I've heard this many times, that one of the biggest ways of breaking down stereotypes is actually spending time with someone who is whatever it is you have a stereotype about. So I guess *if I* had a lot of stereotypes, and I'm not really sure at this point what I did think . . . but knowing people and working with people who I knew were gay definitely encouraged me not to have them anymore.

Cathy reflected on her first experiences knowing lesbian and gay people and realized that what was particularly important was their clear acknowledgment and discussion of their sexual orientation. Cathy recognized that having known lesbian and gay students and having engaged them to discuss their issues played a large role in chipping away stereotypes that she may have initially had. Personally knowing gay and lesbian people outside of the world of education is not a prerequisite for interacting with gay and lesbian parents in schools, but for some teachers it made a difference in their comfort level, which in turn, allowed them to ask parents questions and thus become more knowledgeable about the parents' views and concerns.

A second general grouping consisted of administrators who told stories of relatives who are lesbian or gay or who challenged their attitudes about lesbian and gay people. In the following excerpt, Emory, a public school principal, related what helped him develop an inclusive philosophy in his school. By his account, inclusiveness is based on a "live and let live" point of view. His experiences with gay men and lesbians occurred after college by virtue of the neighborhood in which he lives.

EMORY:    I grew up in an area that was very White, middle class, looked like everyone was cut from the same mold. I think what has affected me the most is living [in Greenwich Village] where so many . . . I don't think you can function here unless you become a person who is very accept[ing], understanding of difference. You just can't deal with it otherwise. You're crippled, in some way, if you can't deal with this issue. As far as I'm concerned, everybody has the right to do whatever they want to do, as long as it doesn't infringe on my rights.

*I can do whatever I want to do, they can do whatever they want to do. People can live the way they want to live. I'll live the way I want to live.*

While emphasizing that living in Greenwich Village requires an openness to diversity, Emory distances his life from the lives of his lesbian and gay neighbors. There is no overlap. It is noteworthy that Emory's description was objective and cerebral compared to the rich descriptions of the personal contacts with lesbian and gay people provided by younger women teachers regarding their college experiences.

The third general grouping was composed of those who did not necessarily have direct contact with lesbian and gay people. Their sensitivity to sexual-minority issues was derived from generalizing their parallel experiences in other areas of life, such as race, gender, and class. Some educators spoke about a dichotomy between the way in which they were raised and their aspiration to be open to those different from themselves. In the following example, a young teacher grappled with her upbringing and her desire to move beyond it. She was teaching in a day care center outside the New York City metropolitan area; there had been no discussion in her center about gay and lesbian issues, although she had a child with two mothers in her group.

**CARLA:** I'm not always the most liberal person in the world, so when I meet somebody who is in some way different I know that I have my prejudices. You can't help that. I grew up in middle-class America with White people all around. . . . So all of those thing s are still there as much as you can eventually get rid of them . . . however you get rid of thing s like that. It's hard because you don't know what questions to ask. . . . How do you approach someone and ask them something personal. Where do you begin? . . . What if somebody says to me "It's none of your damn business?"

Several of our informants spontaneously raised personal memories that helped them gain an understanding of developmental issues related to the children they were teaching. Of the ten teacher informants represented in the study, there were only two male teachers, reflecting the scarcity of men in early childhood teaching (Lee & Wolinsky, 1973; Robinson, 1988). In the following exchanges, we compare the experience of these two men who, by chance, both lost their fathers in childhood and are teachers of 5-year-old boys being raised by lesbian mothers without a father living in the home.

**FRED:** My father died when I was 15. . . . You go through everything then. . . . [I had a] chip on my shoulder. But now I'm starting to look at how I acted then. It's only been in the last five years that I can sort it out, that it's become clear. That reflection, I think, comes with time. The same thing with the situation with Dan [the child in his class]. They [the child's parents] can set up as much as he can handle, but there are some thing s that you're just not going to be able to foresee . . . with the father gone, the fact that he doesn't see his father anymore. . . . It's a big break. I went through that. It causes a lot of pain, and you have to deal with it, because it's not going to change. . . . He is a bright boy . . . but he knows he's different.

Fred compared his father's death with Dan's father's absence through divorce. Through the confusion between the meaning of not living with one's father and the cause of the father's absence, it is clear that Fred had concerns about this child's long-term development, influenced, in part, by his personal experience.

Also drawing from personal experience, Saul used his father's death to illustrate an opposite point concerning the effects of father absence. Saul was angry about the assumption that a boy growing up with two mothers must, by necessity, have a male figure in his life. His experience with father loss shaped his viewpoint about children's developmental needs.

**SAUL:**    Where I'm coming from is that my father died when I was nine and a lot of the adult men really moved in to fill the gap. I appreciated it and even then I understood that my mother was alone and a lot of people were supporting us and it was important. [But] without being able to verbalize it, I understood from that age that this was really offensive. The assumption wasn't that I had lost a specific human being who could not be replaced, but that I had lost the man that has to be in a boy's life and I was offended by the whole idea of Big Brothers. So whether I was gay or straight, I would have this perspective that it's absurd to say you need a male or a female role model. You need at least one caring adult caretaker, period.

These two teachers most clearly demonstrate that apparently similar experiences, when framed against one's world views, can lead to diametrically opposed conclusions. Many of the views expressed in these vignettes are based on deep personal experiences. It is the personal examination, here afforded by the process of our interviewing, that plays a role in bringing these experiences into the foreground of an informant's consciousness and helps educators make connections between their personal experiences and how they treat families. There are myriad ways in which prior exposure to diversity can, with varying degrees of self-conscious examination, assist educators to remain open to the needs of lesbian-/gay-headed families.

## PARENTAL COMMUNICATION WITH THE SCHOOLS

Although the parents we interviewed shared a common bond of being lesbian or gay adults raising children, we found considerable diversity in their views about disclosure. They did not all believe that *they* should be the ones to communicate their family structure to the school. Shanique, an African American lesbian raising a 6-year-old son in Bedford-Stuyvesant, discussed her feelings about coming out: "No, there's no way I would come out. If you tell them, they might . . . change their attitude against you, and you gonna feel, like rejecting. So let them find out on their own."

Manuel, a Puerto Rican single gay man raising two children, had also not come out to school personnel. As a preadoptive father, he felt powerful constraints against coming out.

**MANUEL:**    And it's really sad that we can't . . . because of the repercussions. It's very unfair. . . . Because people make parents, not gay or straight. And you have some lousy heterosexual parents that I see on the street, you know. I mean, so it has nothing to do with . . . the sexuality issue. But especially when you're dealing with city agencies. All of the nonsense. All of the bureaucracy. You're not really sure of the person you're dealing with. It's not wise. It's not wise at all.

The obvious similarities between these two statements are that neither parent was ready to come out at their children's school. However, on closer examination it becomes evident that they reflect two contrasting lines of reasoning concerning disclosure. Shanique framed her rationale in terms of personal rejection; rejection is heightened when she makes clear reference to her sexuality. It exposes her to ridicule and vulnerability. By assigning responsibility to the other, Shanique placed herself in a more powerful interactional position.

By contrast, Manuel was more concerned with the power of the official social agencies who have direct links to his family. He believes that it is not *wise* to come out to city agencies because they have the power to literally take his family away from him. In fact, the removal of two foster children from the home of two gay men in Boston is a real-life case in point.[7] Given the extreme consequences of disclosure, Manuel's reservations are not only understandable, they are also eminently rational.

A third perspective was taken by parents who are militant about coming out. Two gay men raising two young children interviewed the school staff to determine their attitudes before deciding to place their older child there.

**JAMES:**    We went and spoke to the teacher and principal about it. [We asked,] "Would you have any problems?" And if they did have any problems, I was hoping they would tell me. And the issue is that I wasn't ready to slap a lawsuit on their hands. It's just that I didn't want to deal with it. . . . If they want to live and think that way, that's fine. I just don't want to be subjected to it. Let them live there, I won't send my child to that school.

James and Matthew also invited the children in their son's class to his birthday party early in the school year. At this party, their family configuration was evident to everyone.

Lesbian and gay parents are not of one accord in their beliefs, values, or behaviors. They do not all agree about the importance or consequences of disclosing their sexual orientation to their children's educators.

## The Importance of Context in Disclosure

What might account for these differences? Clearly, personal ideology is an important factor, as are individual personality characteristics and beliefs about the impact of secret-keeping on children and how disclosure influences the way in which school staff treat children. These differences may also be associated with other contextual factors, which no doubt affect many decisions of parents, regardless of whether they are straight or lesbian/gay.

Contextual influences consist of several factors, including social circumstances, such as the neighborhood in which a family lives. A homogeneous neighborhood where homosexuality is invisible is clearly a different context for lesbian and gay parents than a heterogeneous neighborhood that includes a highly visible lesbian and gay presence. Other contextual influences include cultural taboos and practices that impinge on such things as privacy and economic class. These affect the ways in which the choices available to parents are restricted or enlarged. For example, James and Matthew would rather move out of an intolerant neighborhood than keep their gay identity a secret. But Esperanza did not have that option.

Esperanza, a Puerto Rican lesbian mother of two, was working as a paraprofessional in a Queens public school near the one that her children attended. She noted that if she could be assured that there would be no repercussions in disclosing her true family structure, "I would shout it at the top of my lungs, from the highest mountain. But that's not real." Her fear was that the principal of her children's school, who is a friend of the school principal who employs her, would share this information. Esperanza had no illusions about the consequences of this: the loss of her job.

June and Shelley, parents of a school-age son and daughter, offer another example of the influence that class can have on parental decision-making about disclosure.

**JUNE:**    We've gone to all of them and said, "You know, our family structure is different from the other kids, and it may not be familiar to you and there's lots that we can tell you about it if you have questions. . . ." When we first went to the schools, we felt very strongly that we weren't going to go to a school unless we had some assurance ahead of time. . . . We spoke to the principal, and he couldn't have walked up those steps ahead of me faster.

**SHELLEY:**    I remember that we had gone on a tour of the school and we stopped to speak to him and we said, "Are you comfortable with a lesbian family?"

**JUNE:**    I think he felt assaulted by the question. . . . It was like, "Why are you discussing this with me? I don't have a problem with this, so we shouldn't talk about this 'cause there isn't any problem." . . . As long as it isn't mentioned it's okay.

White, middle-class professional women, June and Shelley were living in a part of town that included one of the most visible lesbian and gay communities in the country. Although they reported that the principal was uncomfortable with them, their confidence in their rights and abilities and their perseverance with the topic were, at least in part, contextually enhanced.

## Coming Out: Anxiety Versus the Desire to Be Open

This diversity in perspective among lesbian and gay parents was balanced by considerable similarities. Across all economic and cultural boundaries, most parents articulated feelings of stress and fear when they described how they disclosed their family configuration to the school, or when they explained why they had not done so. A gay man who had not yet informed the school about his sexual orientation described the imagined reaction of his child's teacher: "Oh my God. He's raising the child in sin!" These feelings were elaborated by June, who described herself and her partner as having good interpersonal skills and being comfortable with their sexuality. Even with these advantages, however, she said that coming out to school personnel is always difficult.

**JUNE:**    I mean, with all our practice and skills and whatever, I'd say that every time we have to do it you feel your blood pressure go up, you feel your heart pound, your palms sweat. It isn't easy. . . . We get the lowered eyes and the muffled clearing of throat and the back turn.

They not only feared the way in which teachers would respond to them, but whether teachers would use this knowledge to hurt their children. Manuel described this fear of "how they're going to treat your children . . . after you say that [the child is living in a gay household] you know, and with that you have to be real careful. Very careful. I mean there's a lot that goes on."

Teachers need to be sensitive to parental anxiety regarding disclosure. Even if a teacher provides a warm and accepting environment, some parents may still be reluctant to discuss their family arrangement with the teacher or school administrators. These issues extend beyond the boundaries of the school; thus, teachers should not feel slighted or mistrusted because parents, who are feeling unsafe, are unable to come out to them.

Regardless of how anxious parents feel about coming out, all parents expressed the desire to live openly as lesbians or gay men who have children. These opposing feelings seem in most cases to form a dynamic of anxiety and openness. James and Matthew, who waited almost two years before they disclosed their sexual orientation to their child's teacher, discussed the hazards of *not* coming out, the consequences of which have been reported elsewhere (Vermeulen, 1991).

**JAMES:**    It's also giving a very negative message that what you're doing is wrong. So how can [your children] have a clear, positive concept and understanding about what this relationship is about if someone's telling them not to tell anybody?

Research demonstrates that the recent visibility of gay and lesbian people has fostered a change of mood in the psychological and social service communities, as well as in lesbian and gay communities. Cain (1991), for example, documented the American Psychiatric Association's response to lesbian and gay social and political activism to de-medicalize and normalize homosexuality in 1973. Since then, some professionals have come to regard coming out as healthy. This change has prompted some gay men and lesbians to be open about their relationships with mental health and community agencies. Similarly, some teachers, having given the issue considerable thought, believe that the responsibility for coming out belongs to the parent(s). A preschool teacher in a private school reflected this point of view, without perhaps having fully considered the cultural context.

**FRAN:**    I think . . . that you have to have an open line of communication. . . . I mean if people chose to do this, they chose to have a child . . . then they have to be open about it. . . . I would think that if you have a gay family that comes in and they're trying to hide the fact that this is the kind of family they are, or not address it at all, then I think that this needs to be addressed to the family first of all. I guess that's not really the teacher's position to do this but maybe—if it is—saying, "Gosh, you know, we have a school psychologist." Because I think that would be detrimental to the child and the family as a whole because I think that's too key to the family's well-being if someone's saying, "Oh my God, I'm embarrassed that we're a gay family."

Fran places responsibility for coming out squarely on the parents' shoulders, and her statement contains several assumptions. She believes that harm will befall the children and the family if the parents are not open about their family structure. She also suspected that all parents, deep down, want to be open. When Fran related that a teacher might "pull a parent out" if the parent does not come out, there was an assumption (which was not supported by our findings) that a teacher can pick out lesbian and gay parents. Finally, it is important to underscore her belief that situations of disclosure might require psychological intervention. As Al highlights below, sociological explanations involve a shared responsibility that psychological explanations—and ameliorations—tend to lack.

Fran's position sharply contrasted that of Al, a Puerto Rican man who shares the fathering of three boys, two of whom have been diagnosed with AIDS, with his African American male partner. Al had not informed his oldest son's teacher in a public neighborhood school about his family structure.

**Al:**     I never volunteered anything. It makes it very difficult, because homosexuality is not accepted per se, but in the Spanish culture it is even worse. I don't want to advertise, and I don't think it is my responsibility to sit on a soapbox and tell everybody that we're gay and we have three children. Because it doesn't make any difference. If you're going to ask me, I'm going to say it. So I don't volunteer the information. I make it known in other ways. If you're smart enough, you're going to put it together. If you have a problem with it, it's your problem, it's not my problem. It's you that has to tell me, not I to tell you.

Al's version of the world is somewhat more complex than Fran's view. In his statement, he took into account cultural attitudes toward homosexuality and did not assume that lesbian or gay parents should shoulder full responsibility for communicating the family structure and its implied meaning to the school. The very act of disclosure is a *shared responsibility,* and as such he was willing to provide some information. On a very conscious, deliberate level, he was demanding that teachers join him in taking risks—in articulating their suspicions regarding the unorthodox family structure of their students and taking an active responsibility to help lesbian and gay parents disclose this information. School staff need to take risks alongside the parents and to take the responsibility to learn about lesbian and gay parenting.

## The Mechanics of Disclosure

Parents find many ways, both subtle and blatant, to communicate their family makeup to the school. At other times their sexual orientation is disclosed for them, without their choice or awareness.

Many of the parents in our study who comprised two-parent families simply allowed themselves to be visible as caring adults—as parents—of their child to the teacher and other children. By taking their child to school and picking her or him up, volunteering to help out in the classroom, and discussing child-rearing issues with the teacher, these parents chose to communicate their family configuration to the sensitive teacher. Some parents used this as a prelude to more direct communication; others simply left it at this, feeling it was a more "natural" type of communication.

Altering application forms is a common means of communicating family structure to the school. Some lesbian parents cross out "father" and write in "co-mother." Interestingly, altered applications have not always been understood by teachers. Carla, a nursery school teacher in New Jersey, described her difficulty deciphering this information.

**CARLA:** All you have is this piece of paper [the application with "father" crossed out and "co-mother" written in] and you're going to have a little boy in your class and you're looking at it and you're saying, "Well, what is this? What does this mean?" And you go to the director [and ask], "Well, when [they] filled that out, what did they mean?" [She says], "Well, I don't know." There's a lot of mystery there that could [have been] cleared up right away.

On the other hand, Cathy, a teacher of a combined kindergarten/first grade class in a public school in New York City described her assumptions that Lizzie's parents *are* lesbians.

**CATHY:** I got Lizzie's records, and I saw on the records that they had crossed out "father" and written in "co-parent." It [Ricky] was sort of a name [that] could be a man or a woman's. So I wasn't exactly sure what all that meant, although the first thing that I thought of was that they were probably lesbian parents.

As described earlier, parents occasionally interview potential school personnel prior to enrolling their child. Sometimes this is done to help the parents determine whether their child should attend the school, and other times to inform the school. Parents have also chosen to discuss their sexual orientation during the admission process or with their child's teacher during the school year. In one case, a 3-year-old child of two gay fathers who had not come out to the school came out for them; while talking to his teacher, 3-year-old Jeffery told her that "he had a good weekend because he got to sleep in the bed with Daddy and Matthew." Children disclosing their parents' sexuality probably occurs more frequently than parents realize because teachers often do not reveal this knowledge—even in conferences with the parent. Consequently, there are those who, like Jeffery's parent's, did not find out until much later that their sexual identity was known by their child's teacher.

There are also times when the child's teacher or other classroom staff simply guessed the family configuration. Al described the importance of schools reflecting the makeup of the world around them, in children, staff, and curriculum. He found this in the public day care center that his 3-year-old son attends. Al told how Gerry, the teacher, recognized that he is gay.

**AL:** They knew about it, because they're sensitive. They're open to these kinds of things. . . . Gerry is gay. You pick up that I'm gay. . . . There's a reality there, because this is how our staff is made up. There are different kinds of people and we talk about it. Gerry . . . is extremely flamboyant. . . . He's not there saying, "I'm gay, and everybody should be gay," but it's just that freedom you have to go in there and that openness to be able to say, "I disagree with you." . . . You see them as human beings in a place that's very reflective of society. . . . The day care center is Black, White, Hispanic. It's a mixture of people.

One parent described a situation in which she was inappropriately approached by the assistant teacher of her son's public school kindergarten classroom.

**JACQUELINE:**    And she ultimately just said to me point-blank one morning when I dropped him off when we were just sitting around chatting, "Well you didn't tell me about you and Nora." . . . It was not something I didn't intend to bring up and to raise. I would have set a meeting, I wanted to do it. She did it in the morning when there were parents behind me, children all around who had needs, and it was inappropriate for her to bring it up at that point and it's not as if it's something I wouldn't have discussed in all detail, in all detail within limits . . . any questions that she had to ask about I would have been *thrilled* to talk about it, but the setting really limited the focus and then it's hard to get back to it.

"Forced" disclosure often results in feelings of ambivalence for parents. Although Jacqueline and Nora later stated that they were relieved that their family makeup was out in the open, they expressed resentment because they were not able to choose the time and place in which to come out. They would have preferred to discuss their family in the privacy of a parent conference with the head teacher. Instead, their family structure was quickly, and unexpectedly, revealed by the assistant teacher during a time that the parents considered inappropriate.

Al offered a different perspective. Because his child's center encompassed informality and diversity, it did not feel inappropriate to Al when the center staff discovered his family makeup and his sexual orientation. The crucial and unusual qualities of the center included the diversity of the day care center staff and the children, both of which reflected the variability of the neighborhood. This enriched atmosphere had a powerful impact on the ease of disclosure and communication for parents such as Al because it made being a member of a gay-headed family just one aspect of many that constitute the individual in this community setting. This case illustrates the importance of the inclusion of a diverse staff and student body for promoting an atmosphere that is truly multicultural.

Disclosure emerged from our research as a key and requisite issue, but a need for broader communication between parents and school staff also exists. More open and honest communication could, for example, help parents and teachers address curricular issues or their divergent views about gender nonconformity.

## GENDER ISSUES

Most educators are aware that they cannot presume that their theories and beliefs about child development are necessarily the same as those held by the parents of the children they teach. A common difference between gay and lesbian parents and school staff starkly demonstrates this basic tenet. We have repeatedly observed that educators and parents conceptualize role models, sex role development, and gender nonconformity quite differently. There are almost as many definitions of "role model" as there are informants. This signals a need for more exact terminology.

For example, Maritza noted: "When I think of role models, I think of his teacher, about people who come to his class, people who do things with him every day. I don't think of MTV. We aren't into that. I think about history books."

The issue teachers consistently raised about children with gay and lesbian parents echoed traditional theories of same-sex identification—the availability of same-sex role models.[8] Some placed greater emphasis on the emotional tie between the child and the role model, and others framed it in a less sophisticated way by simply implying without a rationale that the physical presence of a role model is crucial. This concern was expressed by almost every teacher and was crystallized in a statement made by a preschool teacher. She assumed that men were not part of the life of a 3-year-old boy who was being raised by two mothers, and she wondered about the effects:[9]

> And I feel that in both ways, I mean with boys being raised by two women, and a girl by men. I remember when Lonnie was first at the center and he had a fear of jumping off the blue house. I remember thinking, do his parents, Diane and Val, ever get rough with him? And then I wondered, where does this fear come from? I mean Lon is a tall, lanky kid, so I could say that just physically, he wasn't ready to jump yet. But this is one of the things I thought, "If there were a man in his life, would he be less afraid?"

We found such honest comments helpful because they clearly articulate what others only hinted. However, the teacher made several assumptions based on the child's behavior and her knowledge of his family. The first assumption was that Lonnie did not have male contacts. The second was that a man would provide rough-and-tumble experiences for this child and, conversely, that a woman could not or would not provide such play. Third, the simple fact that 3-year-olds have fears was not considered. We use this example as a metaphor because of the richness of interpretation. There are many reasons why Lonnie might not have been ready to jump off the house. Within a short time he did, and with gusto. In the two years since this teacher made the statement quoted above, she has changed her thinking and now makes a point to talk with new staff about different family structures and how easy it is to make generalized assumptions. She advises them to watch, listen, wait, and learn.

Few children raised by gay and lesbian parents grow up in gender-separate worlds. Some teachers appeared mystified and surprised by this fact, perhaps because they had not given the matter much thought. This is not to imply that gender issues are not important for lesbian and gay parents. But in their interpretations of the concept, they are less concerned with models of family life in which both sexes need to be present for healthy development to occur. This viewpoint is exemplified by one lesbian mother of a 5-year-old boy.

**MARITZA:**    We feel it is important that he has role models of both sexes . . . people that we feel are good people, like the dentist is female. We feel the same thing about culture. We want him to be exposed to as many role models as possible. We think it is more important that he is around people who have the same kind of morality, ethics that we have, rather than what sex.

Parents repeatedly emphasized the all-consuming nature of heterosexual norms. Many underscored the importance of a person's *individual qualities* and stated that they want their children to know that there are many ways of being male or female. Even parents who felt that same-sex role models are valuable exhibited some ambivalence. When asked about the importance of role models in their child's life, Nora and Jacqueline responded:

**JACQUELINE:**   I don't know the answer to that question. That's the big issue of people in my family.

**NORA:**   Although interestingly enough, none of her sisters are with their husbands . . . so none of them have any role models of any consistency.

**JACQUELINE:**   If the need were communicated to me from Dan [their son] then it would be something I would pursue. I don't feel it as being real important? [said with rising intonation of a question].

When pressed to elaborate the reasons it was not important, Jacqueline continued:

**JACQUELINE:**   I don't know many men . . . much less role models for Dan. [Pauses.] That's not altogether true. I have cousins and relatives who could be role models for Dan but who don't necessarily embrace the relationship. [Pauses.] But I don't know if I would say that if he didn't have a male teacher three years in a row. I can't answer that question because I don't have any way of basing it otherwise. He spends five days a week with an extremely nurturing, loving, gifted male teacher who adores him and thinks that Dan is just, you know, the cat's meow. And I don't think he hurts from that. He spends as much time with Fred as with us. I guess I do value it.

Jacqueline's apparent ambivalence may reflect her changing views about how children develop (she had only recently left a heterosexual marriage). These newly emerging ideas are confronting powerful messages from family and society. She believes that men have an important place in her son's life, but she was grappling with the emphasis and meaning they should have. We heard other examples of ambivalence, even from informants with long-standing gay or lesbian identifications. For example, although pleased with her son's male teacher, one mother questioned what it meant that the school assigned her son to this man's class: "I wondered if the school wondered if he needed a male. Maybe that was more in our minds than their mind. I am sure there must have been other reasons to put him in Andy's class."

The majority of parents we interviewed were clear that their children should be exposed to multiple men and women. Beyond that, they wanted their children to understand that there are many ways of being male and female, gay and straight. While no teacher challenged this notion, rarely did a teacher discuss it in-depth. For lesbian and gay parents, however, it was a consistent theme throughout the interviews.

Most educators had traditional views about role models and sex-stereotyped play. When we encouraged them to discuss concerns they had about these children's developmental outcome, they persistently returned to gender issues. Emory, a principal of an urban public school, discussed role models as they pertain to all children who are missing a parent of one gender or another (not necessarily only children from lesbian and gay parents).

**EMORY:**   That's a hard one to answer. I'm not sure it can be limited to the issue of gay and lesbian parents. I feel that there were kids [at my school] who did not have a male in their lives, whose fathers might have died, who lived with two females. I think that kids who did not have—especially male children who did not have—a male in their lives were very, very close and attached to me and other male teachers in the school. [There was] a lot of hugging, holding hands, and bonding with males in the school. . . . But I do think the kids sought out that other relationship that they may not have had at home.

When asked whether he thought this behavior reflected their sense of self, Emory continued.

I don't think I can answer that question. I don't know. I just know clearly there were kids who didn't live with a male . . . boys who did not live with a male, who would run and give me a hug every time they saw me. And it was clear after a number of times that they were looking for some male figure to be able to relate [to].

Emory was saying, in effect, "I don't really know what I think about this, but I know what I see." This is the gist of many educators' statements. Father Stephen Moore, a priest at a parochial school, made similar points within a theoretical, societal view, prefacing his remarks with the well-worn "some of my best friends are homosexuals."

**FATHER STEPHEN:**   A bottom line in my dealing is that with the importance of the traditional family and the presence of the father, with that being eroded, I don't like to see or participate in things that would facilitate that erosion. . . . Then we do experience where a parent dies and a child is denied the male presence or the presence of a male father, there is an emotional effect on the child. Children need that presence of the male and the female.

Another teacher, who had been extremely responsive to the children of lesbian/gay-headed families whom she has taught, also had questions.

**PENNY:**   I just wonder about long term. I have a friend in Ireland. She is an unmarried mother and is raising a child. Her father is dead. She doesn't have contact with her brothers and there are very few men in her life. The child has no male influence in his life. I think it is something that he has mentioned and it is not good for him. Just a mom. I know that lots of children have grown up when the fathers were away at war or away for work reasons but I think there were always some males around. Like when Enrico [the principal in her school] said when he was young, his father was away at war but his uncles were around. I think that in that situation long ago when the father was away, there were other people who stepped in and acted as the father.

Stepping in and "acting like the father" is one set of behaviors and beliefs all educators should ponder. We need only to recall the words of the teacher Saul earlier in the chapter to remember how variable the meaning and impact various family structures may be to different children.

It is crucial for educators to remember that which most of us already know but often forget in practice: The road to clear, unwavering gender identity is a long one. We observed many children and heard many anecdotes of children asking simple questions about family structure. Frequently teachers could not answer them, were too stunned to answer, or answered but spoke too quickly. An example of what can be accomplished in a classroom when a child asks a hard question was provided by Cathy, a young teacher who realized that basic gender concepts form the backdrop against which children place their thoughts and feelings about gender roles and family structure. She related a conversation with a 5-year-old girl who has two mothers.

**CATHY:**  She told me there's mommy kisses and there's daddy kisses, and there's different kinds of kisses. And all she gets is mommy kisses. She doesn't get daddy kisses. And I said, "Well, how are daddy kisses different?" And she said, "Men have scratchy chins and stuff from having hair on their face." And I said, "Do you have uncles or anything?" And she said, "Yeah, I have a bunch of uncles." And I said, "Don't you get kisses from them?" And she said, "Yes." Then I said, "Then you're getting kisses that are sort of like daddy kisses." And then I asked her if there was anything else. And she was like, "No." I think she's thinking that she's missing out on something, and she doesn't know yet that in a lot of ways she isn't. I don't think she is. She has two very supportive, wonderful parents, and other supportive adults in her life as well.

This vignette is particularly important. Cathy did not presume this child was necessarily expressing loss or sadness. Through a supportive scaffolding, Cathy helped the child reach a more sophisticated level of understanding gender differences and appreciating her experience.[10] If a deeper need was being expressed, Cathy's response did not interfere by aggravating or denying it.

In another example, a day care teacher described how a 3-year-old boy used his dramatic play to bring his family constellation to life and to consider other family structures:

There were a lot of thing s when Lonnie would play with the doll people. At the beginning he never really made up the typical nuclear family, he would have two mommies and a little boy, and they did all the thing s together and that was the way his play went. After a while, he had two mommies and a daddy also, and then after more time, he got rid of one of the mommies and put the daddy there, but sometimes, he would put the daddy to the side and the other mommy would come in and I think he was, in a lot of ways, trying to figure all that out.

For such a child, the issue at hand is not *confusion* about his family structure but his attempt to actively *define* it. Over the course of that year, some of the other 3-year-olds began their versions of "playing house." First, they would play "mommy-mommy"; then another child would lead the play with "mommy-daddy." In a similar vein, when a young child with a mother and father tells a child with two fathers, "I have two daddies too" or "Why can't I have two mommies?" a teacher of 3-year-olds knows that he does not necessarily wish that his mother or father would disappear.

These issues are not discussed in early childhood programs. Although antibias and multicultural curricula are increasingly being implemented, they are interpreted differently, depending on the personal beliefs of the teacher, principal, superintendent, or school board. While the field of psychology informs us that there are many paths to growth and development, some teachers misinterpret gender nonconformist play as an early indicator of homosexuality (Cottin-Pogrebin, 1983). Although some correlation has been found between cross-gender play and boys who grow up with effeminate qualities, research has demonstrated that homosexuality is a complex transactional, developmental, and genetic process that to date has still not been teased apart (Bailey, this volume; Green, 1987).

Gender-assigned roles are deeply rooted in society. Through our discussions with two day-care teachers of infants and toddlers, it became clear that children with two fathers or mothers provided an opportunity for these professionals to question their basic assumptions about the roles of parents.

**FRAN:**  And that was a question that came up for me a lot, well, who's like the mother and who's like the father? Well, I don't know. In one case, I would have to say that Val is more like the mom, and Diane is definitely more like the father, who's busy and not as accessible and is away more. But I wouldn't say that emotionally, you know what I mean? And even with Rena and Miriam it wasn't as clear at all. But people wanted to do that.

**LESLIE:**  I remember one of the things with my staff was overcoming some stereotypes and the stereotype with Rena and Miriam, it never made much sense to anyone [assistant teachers] that Rena was the birth mother.

**FRAN:**  Because Rena seems more masculine in some ways.

**LESLIE:**  One thing I have to say that I've discovered about myself is that I [now] have a tendency to call the drop-off parent. . . . Well, the one who's most consistent. Because that was something I asked myself one day, "Who should I call?" And I remember thinking this [about] Rena and Miriam because when the father is the primary drop-off and pickup person, now I always call the person who is most involved in the child's life at the center.

This is a rich example of how change in thinking occurs. The entire center became involved in this issue and the discussion deepened the understanding for all children and families. For us, this was a poignant indicator of how our differences separate and unite us.

# CONCLUSION

Children growing up with lesbian and gay parents must have their lives acknowledged. But this alone is not enough. Young adults raised by lesbian mothers recall feelings of isolation; their families were not acknowledged in school and they did not know many other children who lived in similar families (Center Kids Panel, 1992). This silence has existed not only in heterosexual communities but among the social circles of lesbian and gay parents; there has not been sufficient discussion and support of the lives of these children within lesbian and gay communities. Fortunately, for some families living in large cities there are now network and support groups.

The issues raised in this chapter should be of concern to both parents and teachers and should be reflected in the larger arena of the school. Administrators should encourage frank discussions that support same-sex parenting by addressing such questions as: How can the administration help teachers and parents? What kinds of parent meetings can support the work of teachers in building a more inclusive curriculum? What administrative changes are necessary? How difficult would it be to alter the "mother" and "father" line on school applications to a more generic "parent" line or to simply ask for a listing of family members, or to use the single word "family" followed by a few blank lines?

Teacher preparation programs can push future educators to a deeper consideration of multiculturalism and antibias and their effect on the quality of children's lives.

Same-sex *parenting* is not the only subject that is absent from curriculum and parent work in schools. All school personnel—teachers, administrators, guidance counselors, assistants—and teacher educators must feel more comfortable saying and hearing the words "lesbian" and "gay." Teachers and parents could more easily discuss family constellations if the existence of lesbian and gay people was accepted. Older children should hear these words in discussions of James Baldwin, for example, and younger children should hear them associated with discussions about Sasha's Papi and Daddy. Teachers must be reassured that using these words will not make older children lesbian/gay and that they are not inappropriate words to use with young children. The argument that one should not talk about lesbian and gay people because it might promote homosexuality in children is itself biased because it assumes that it is not a good thing to be lesbian or gay.

Teacher preparation programs should also include this topic in course work and supervised fieldwork. If teachers engage in open discussions about the needs of lesbian and gay parents or initiate contact with lesbian and gay people in an effort to understand the ways that society constrains their lives, they may feel more comfortable when they encounter gay and lesbian parents in their classroom.

We believe that the best approach is to avoid adopting a "blind" attitude—one that denies that there are differences among people. It is more constructive to recognize one's feelings, attempt to trace their origins, and work toward changing those attitudes that are harmful to others. Of course, the first task involves discovering these feelings—many of which are hidden from us (Schultz & Casper [with Wickens], 1993).

One such hidden area is feelings regarding gender identity. Child psychology courses must move beyond traditional theories of gender identity development to include new theory and research. When teaching theories of gender identification, it is important to ask students to apply these theories in their thinking and practice. Future educators should be clear about their values and deep-seated beliefs regarding homosexuality and make an honest assessment of where theory and values intersect in their thinking. There is not just one way to be male or female, as lesbians and gay men and their children demonstrate. By including the lives of lesbians and gay men in developmental courses and by integrating anthropological and sociological data (Bruner, 1990), instructors can convey to students that which children require for healthy gender development. Outcomes other than a heterosexual orientation and the variety of routes that children can take to adulthood must be considered.

Schools can make the words *lesbian* and *gay* more visible for parents, as well. One day care center director affirmed lesbians and gay men when she opened the first curriculum night by saying, "We are proud to have children from diverse backgrounds with us this year; children from different cultural backgrounds, children with special needs, and children with lesbian and gay parents. I welcome you all." When these words become more common in our vocabularies, there will be less need for teachers and parents to use euphemisms like "nontraditional family" or "alternative families." Naming *is* important. Only when the differences of lesbian-/gay-headed families are acknowledged without negative connotations will these families truly be treated like any other family.

We do not think that it is appropriate to offer specific techniques for teachers to use to improve the quality of their communications with lesbian and gay parents. Each family and school is different, sometimes in fundamental ways. Therefore, teachers need to fashion individual approaches in order to build environments that are supportive of parental disclosure.

This chapter presents the varied, authentic, and too often silenced voices of lesbian and gay parents. Hearing these parents and their concerns can affect feelings and actions. In this respect, attitudes are important. One teacher in a day care center advises other teachers to "explore their own feelings about what it means to have a gay family." As one of our informants noted, there are plenty of people who

**FRAN:**    think that it's something that exists out there in the world that has nothing to do with them and don't really want to have anything to do with it. . . . They need to address those feelings in themselves and really work through them because they are really going to get projected on the family.

We agree. Prior experiences and present values are crucial—as are ongoing experiences. Leslie, one of the teachers we interviewed early in the study, spoke to us after we presented our findings at a conference workshop she attended: "I guess I was a little upset to hear some of the things I said. I know I said it, but that was three years ago. I've changed."

Attitudes *and* actions can change over time.

It is crucial that parents move beyond their fears and talk to teachers about their family configurations and their sexual orientation. This is a unique burden being asked of gay and lesbian parents; heterosexual parents are not asked to discuss their sexual orientation with teachers. The stresses and dangers of self-disclosure are real, testaments of an unjust society that encourages discrimination against people based on characteristics such as race, sex, class, and sexual orientation. We do not want to romanticize this, nor do we want to ignore the painfully slow process that will lead to acceptance of gay and lesbian people in our society. Change is difficult, especially when the oppressed group initiates it. But without the group's involvement, the eventual results of change will not reflect the group's needs.

In 1932, Counts called for schools to build a new social order. His call was a noble one and is still relevant in today's world. But a truly new social order cannot be built by schools alone. Social change must occur in league with teachers, parents, and community. Clear and nonbiased understandings of family, gender, and culture will require the actions of educators and other professionals, parents, and activists.

## ▼ ENDNOTES ▼

1. We gratefully acknowledge the generous support of the Paul Rapoport Foundation, New York City, and thank all parents and educators interviewed for sharing their experiences and thoughts. We also thank Elaine Wickens, who was a primary researcher on this project; Harriet K. Cuffaro and Edna K. Shapiro for their support of our work in this area at Bank Street College; and Edna K. Shapiro for her insightful critique of this article. The responsibility for the content of this article rests with us. Parts of this chapter have been published in *Teacher's College Record* (Fall 1992) under the title, "Breaking the Silence: Lesbian and Gay Parents and the Schools." Some excerpts are from our book *Tentative Trust: Enhancing Communication Between Gay and Lesbian Parents and the Schools* (1993).

2. This point about silenced dialogues as they affect White teachers and the parents and community of ethnic-minority children was made eloquently by Delpit (1988). She argued that the dialogue between teachers and parents is silenced and that it does not necessarily result in *no* communication but in a warped communication that results in devastating effects on ethnic-minority children.

3. Many of these books have difficulties. For example, they assume a didactic approach or, as one of the teachers we interviewed described, they are like "self-help books." However, there are also many wonderful and engaging books in this genre, and even those of the self-help variety are a welcome contribution to a barren area of children's literature. For a representative sample, see *Jenny Lives With Eric and Martin* (Bosche, 1983), *Asha's Mums* (Elwin & Paulse, 1990), *Heather Has Two Mommies* (Newman, 1989), *The Duke Who Outlawed Jelly Beans and Other Stories* (Valentine, 1991), and *Anna-Day and the O-Ring* (Wickens, 1994).

4. There is extensive writing on the topic of sexism in early childhood curricula, much of it published during the 1970s. These publications point to the differentiated expectations and available activities for boys and girls, as well as to the hidden curricula that showed teachers encouraging particular and differential behaviors in boys and girls. A primary ingredient in sexist curricula is the focus on boys and men and the invisibility of the lives of girls and women.

5. Center Kids is the largest organization in the New York City area of lesbian and gay parents and their children. They currently have over 1,000 families in their membership.

6. The names and other identifying characteristics of interviewees have been changed to protect their anonymity.

7. In 1985, two young children were removed by the Massachusetts Agency for Children from the preadoptive homes of two gay men who had been living together in Boston for almost 10 years. This removal led to a policy that

required the state to ask the sexual preference of foster parent applicants and to place foster children in "traditional family settings." These settings were either the homes of relatives of the child or the homes of families with married couples. Massachusetts was the first state to adopt a policy that a child could be placed in a "nontraditional home" only as a last resort and with "the prior written approval of the state's commissioner of social service" (Facts on File, 1985, pp. 403–404). At the present, these stipulations regarding nontraditional families are no longer a part of the Human Services policy.

8. As educators of teachers, we are concerned about the oversimplification and mechanistic interpretations of both psychoanalytic and social learning theories in the schools and in the world at large. In teaching child development, we believe it is helpful to emphasize the cognitive-developmental tradition begun by Kohlberg (1966) and more recent gender schema theorists such as Bem (1983).

9. This teacher taught in the room next to Lonnie's and spent time with him but was not his primary caregiver.

10. The concept of scaffolding is derived from the work of Vygotsky (1934/1962) and elaborated by Wood (1980) and Rogoff (1990). Scaffolding refers to the application of guided participation in which an adult or peer supports a child to achieve what she or he could not alone.

## ▼    References    ▼

Bem, S. (1983). Gender schema theory and its implications for child development: Raising gender-aschematic children in a gender-schematic society. *Signs: Journal of Women in Culture and Society, 8,* 498–616.

Benedek, T. (1959). Parenthood as a developmental phase: A contribution to libido theory, *Journal of the American Psychoanalytic Association, 7,* 389–417.

Benkov, L. (1994). *Gay and lesbian parents: Revolution in the family.* New York: Crown.

Bosche, S. (1983). *Jenny lives with Eric and Martin.* London: Gay Men's Press.

Bruner, J. (1990). *Acts of meaning.* Cambridge, MA: Harvard University Press.

Cain, R. (1991). Disclosure and secrecy among gay men in the United States and Canada: A shift in views. *Journal of the History of Sexuality, 2,* 25–45.

Casper, V., Schultz, S., & Wickens, E. (1992). Breaking the silences: Lesbian and gay parents and the schools. *Teachers College Record, 94,* 109–137.

Center Kids Panel (1992, January 11). *Empowering our children: How do we prepare our kids to live in and cope with the wider world?* Presentation at the Lesbian and Gay Community Center, New York City.

Clark, K. B. (1955/1970). *Prejudice and your child* (2nd ed.). Boston: Beacon.

Clay, J. (1990). Working with lesbian and gay parents and their children. *Young Children, 45,* 31–35.

Cottin-Pogrebin, L. (1983). The secret fear that keeps us from raising free children. *Interracial Books for Children Bulletin, 14,* (3 & 4).

Counts, G. S. (1932). *Dare the school build a new social order?* Carbondale, IL: University of Southern Illinois Press.

Cowen, C. P., & Hetherington, E. M. (1992). *Advances in family research.* Hillsdale, NJ: Lawrence Erlbaum.

Cuffaro, H. K. (1975). Reevaluating basic premises: Curricula free of sexism. *Young Children, 30,* 1–8.

Delpit, L. (1988). The silenced dialogue: Power and pedagogy in educating other people's children. *Harvard Educational Review, 58,* 280–298.

Derman-Sparks, L. (1989). *Anti-bias curriculum: Tools for empowering young children.* Washington, DC: NAEYC.

Eiduson, B. (1981). The child in the non-conventional family. In M. Lewis & L. Rosenblum (Eds.), *The genesis of behavior: The uncommon child.* New York: Plenum.

Elwin, R., & Paulse, M. (1990). *Asha's mums.* Toronto, Canada: Women's Press.

Erikson, E. H. (1963). *Childhood and society.* New York: W. W. Norton.

*Facts on File* (1985, May 24), *45*(2323), 403–404.

Foucault, M. (1978). *The history of sexuality, Volume 1.* New York: Pantheon.

Geertz, C. (1973). *The interpretation of culture.* New York: Basic Books.

Green, R. (1987). *The "sissy boys syndrome" and the development of homosexuality.* New Haven, CT: Yale University Press.

Harrison, B. G. (1973). *Unlearning the lies: Sexism in the school.* New York: Liveright.

Kohlberg, L. (1966). Cognitive-developmental analysis of children's sex-role concepts and attitudes. In E. E. Maccoby (Ed.), *The development of sex differences* (pp. 82–193). Stanford, CA: Stanford University Press.

Lee, P., & Wolinsky, A. (1973). Male teachers of young children: A preliminary empirical study. *Young Children, 28,* 342–352.

Lewin, E. (1993). *Lesbian mothers: Accounts of gender in American culture.* Ithaca, NY: Cornell University Press.

Lightfoot, S. L. (1978). *Worlds apart: Relationships between families and schools.* New York: Basic Books.

Martin, A. (1993). *The lesbian and gay parenting handbook: Creating and raising our families.* New York: Harper-Collins.

Michaels, G. Y., & Goldberg, A. (1988). *Transition to parenthood: Current theory and research.* Cambridge, MA: Cambridge University Press.

Morin, S. F. (1977). Heterosexual bias in psychological research on lesbianism and male homosexuality. *American Psychologist 32,* 629–637.

Newman, L. (1989). *Heather has two mommies.* Boston: Alyson.

Nilsen, A. P. (1977). Alternatives to sexist practices in the classroom. *Young Children, 32,* 53–58.

Patterson, C. J. (1992). Children of lesbian and gay parents. *Child Development, 63,* 1025–1042.

Rafkin, L. (1990). *Different mothers: Sons and daughters of lesbians talk about their lives.* Pittsburgh, PA: Cleis Press.

Robinson, B. E. (1988). Vanishing breed: Men in child care programs. *Young Children, 43,* 54–58.

Rogoff, B. (1990). *Apprenticeship in thinking.* Oxford: Oxford University Press.

Sadker, M. & Sadker, P. (1994). *Failing at fairness: How America's schools cheat girls.* New York: Scribner's.

Schultz, S. B. (1988). *The hidden curriculum: Finding mechanisms of control and resistance in the preschool.* Unpublished doctoral dissertation, Teachers College, Columbia University, New York.

Schultz, S. B., & Casper, V. (with E. Wickens) (1993). *Tentative trust: Enhancing communication between gay and lesbian parents and the schools.* Unpublished manuscript, Bank Street College of Education, New York.

Shanok, R. S. (1991). Parenthood: A process marking identity and intimacy capacities. *Zero to Three, 11*(2), 2.

Sprung, B. (1975). *Non-sexist education for young children: A practical guide.* New York: Citation Press.

Steckel, A. (1985). *Separation-individuation in children of lesbian and heterosexual couples.* Unpublished doctoral dissertation, Wright Institute Graduate School, Berkeley, California.

Streitmatter, J. (1994). *Toward gender equity in the classroom: Everyday teachers' beliefs and practices.* Albany, NY: State University of New York Press.

Valentine, J. (1991). *The Duke who outlawed jelly beans and other stories.* Boston: Alyson.

Vermeulen, K. (1991). A family comes out. *Outlook, 12,* 46–48.

Vygotsky, L. S. (1934/1962). *Thought and language* (2nd. ed.). Cambridge, MA: MIT Press.

Weston, K. (1991). *Families we choose: Lesbians, gays, kinship.* New York: Columbia University Press.

Wickens, E. (1994). *Anna-Day and the O-ring.* Boston: Alyson.

Wilcox, K. (1982). Ethnography as a methodology and its application to the study of schooling: A review. In G. Spindler (Ed.), *Doing the ethnography of schooling: Educational anthropology and action* (pp. 456–488). New York: Holt, Rinehart and Winston.

Wood, D. (1980). Teaching the young child: Some relationships between social interaction, language and thought. In D. R. Olsen (Ed.), *The social foundations of language and thought* (pp. 280–295). New York: W. W. Norton.

# Chapter 14

▼

# LESBIANS, GAY MEN, AND THE LAW

## William B. Rubenstein[1]

*The struggle for equality by lesbians and gay men moved to the center of American life at the outset of the 1990s. During the coming decade, lesbian and gay issues will form a greater part of the American political scene and public consciousness than during any other era in American history. With Bill Clinton's election and his first presidential directives, a heated debate erupted regarding the presence of lesbians and gay men in the U.S. military. Nearly every religious organization in the country is struggling with questions ranging from same-sex marriage to the ordination of openly lesbian and gay ministers. Yet, at no time in American history have sexual minorities been more visible: Lesbians and gay men battle in Congress, in the streets, and in courtrooms for civil rights; well-known figures publicly discuss their sexual orientation; and gay and lesbian characters appear regularly on prime-time television shows. Few Americans can continue to claim that they have not come into contact with gay and lesbian people.*

*At the same time, lesbians and gay men face stiffer opposition than ever before. A well-organized and well-funded religious right has pledged that gay/lesbian rights will be the "abortion" issue of the 1990s. The message is that adherents will vehemently challenge advances by lesbians and gays. Indeed, voter initiatives to repeal laws prohibiting discrimination on the basis of sexual orientation—and to bar enactment of such laws in the future—are at issue in dozens of states throughout the country. And more lesbians and gay men are attacked every year simply because of their sexual orientation: Antigay/antilesbian violence rose 31% between 1990 and 1991 in five major cities (Boston, Chicago, Minneapolis/Saint Paul, New York, and San Francisco), with more than 1,800 incidents of antigay/antilesbian violence reported in these cities alone (National Gay and Lesbian Task Force, 1992).*

*The law is a primary arena in which the struggle for lesbian and gay rights has been, and will continue to be, played out. Throughout American history, sexual relations have been a concern of the secular legal system, as well as an issue of religious morality and medical "science." American society has long maintained laws that directly dictate which combinations of individuals may have sex with one another and in what manner. For example, sex outside of marriage was traditionally proscribed by most states (Leonard, 1993), as was sex between people of different races.[2] It was not until the late 1960s that the United States Supreme Court struck down as unconstitutional laws that criminalized interracial marriages.[3] In addition to these direct prohibitions, the state has long maintained various mechanisms to indirectly channel sexual relations. For example, government jobs could be denied to individuals whose sexual practices were not approved by the state (Leonard, 1993).*

*For lesbians and gay men, state regulation of sexuality has been particularly harsh. State sodomy laws criminalize one way in which sexual minorities express their love for one another. Discrimination against lesbians and gay men exists in employment and housing, and gays and lesbians are often denied access to programs and public places solely because of their sexual orientation. No state has recognized same-sex relationships, and sexual orientation has often been used to deny gays and lesbians custody of, or visitation with, their children. Lesbians and gay men are frequently legally barred from adopting children or becoming foster parents.*

*Not only has the law typically failed to redress discrimination against sexual minorities, but such discrimination is often sanctioned by the government itself. The federal government, for example, has openly denied lesbians and gay men the opportunity to serve their country in the military; effectively denied employment to them in the FBI, CIA, and other security-related positions; and placed burdens on lesbian and gay applicants for security clearances.*

*Alongside this stark picture of the barriers faced by lesbians and gay men, however, lives another image. This portrait is of a constantly growing movement to eradicate these barriers, of lesbians and gay men and their advocates who, in the past 40 years, have made enormous strides in abolishing some of the barriers to equal participation in American society.*

*This chapter represents an effort to understand the legal situation of lesbians and gay men. It provides both a snapshot of the current state of lesbian and gay rights and a moving picture of the strides of their civil rights movement. By focusing on several areas of the law—sodomy law reform, discrimination, and family law—this chapter depicts both the struggle for liberation and equality for gay and lesbian people and the work that still needs to be accomplished.*

## Sodomy Law

In modern American society, sodomy laws serve as a legal basis for the regulation of lesbian and gay sexuality and of lesbian and gay life generally. Discrimination against lesbians and gay men is often predicated on the existence of laws prohibiting same-sex activities; sodomy laws are given as the reason, for instance, for depriving lesbians and gay men of government jobs or of custody of their children. Sodomy laws are used, with varying degrees of success, against lesbian and gay litigants in nearly every possible legal context. In addition to these legal effects, sodomy laws have serious symbolic consequences as well: Such laws brand the manner in which lesbians and gay men express love for one another as "criminal" and are commonly understood as criminalizing not merely same-sex acts but lesbians and gay men themselves.

Sodomy laws were not always understood in this way. Historically, sodomy laws were drafted in order to proscribe sexual behavior that did not lead to procreation, including oral and anal sex between people of the same or opposite genders.

The argument against sodomy laws is one of liberty and privacy—namely, that individual citizens enjoy a sphere of privacy or control over a set of personal decisions that the government is not entitled to dictate. Most simply, "liberty" means that so long as adult individuals are engaging in behavior that is consensual and does not harm others, the government cannot control it. It follows that the state cannot come into a person's bedroom and tell that individual the manner in which she or he may engage in sexual relations with another consenting adult. To do so, it is argued, violates liberty guaranteed to each adult by the Constitution.

*In 1961, every state in the United States had a sodomy law.* While these laws outlawed heterosexual as well as homosexual sodomy, every one of them criminalized the manner in which gay men and lesbians express love for one another— even if the acts took place between consenting adults in the privacy of their home.

*Today, fewer than half the states have sodomy laws.* Nearly all of the states that no longer have sodomy laws abolished their law through legislative action rather than through a court decision declaring it unconstitutional. In particular, many state legislatures in the past 30 years modernized their entire system of criminal law by adopting a version of the "Model Penal Code," a document drafted in the late 1950s by an influential institute of lawyers and law professors to modernize state criminal codes. The Model Penal Code proposed decriminalizing private, consensual, adult sexual behavior including homosexual sex. As state legislatures adopted the code throughout the 1960s and 1970s, they did away with their sodomy laws. In several states, though, the legislatures were so appalled to be without a prohibition on same-sex sodomy that they added new laws barring *only* homosexual sodomy.[4]

The other major locus for sodomy law reform has been the courts. However, despite much effort and a number of highly publicized legal challenges, in only a few states have sodomy laws been declared unconstitutional by the highest court in that state. Most importantly, in 1986, the United States Supreme Court rejected a constitutional challenge to Georgia's sodomy law in the *Bowers v. Hardwick* case.[5] Michael Hardwick was arrested for having sex with another man in his own bedroom. Although the state did not criminally prosecute him for this act, Hardwick brought a civil suit challenging the sodomy law as violating his constitutional rights. He was joined in this effort by a heterosexual couple, who complained that they feared that the Georgia law—which applied to *all* oral and anal intercourse—could be enforced against them as well. By a 5-4 vote, the Supreme Court ruled against Hardwick. Despite the Georgia law's ban on all oral and anal intercourse, the Court focused only on *homosexual* sodomy. It held that the "right to privacy" recognized under the federal Constitution did not encompass a right to engage in homosexual sodomy and, therefore, that states are free to criminalize such conduct.

The *Hardwick* decision was a major blow to the movement for lesbian and gay rights in the United States. Thus, despite the progress made in the past few decades, in nearly one half of the states in the United States, it is still illegal for lesbians and gay men to express love to one another. To lesbians and gay men, this means, as Larry Kramer wrote, "We are denied the right to love. Can you imagine being denied the right to love?" (1987, p. 178). Worse still, the U.S. Supreme Court has condoned this oppression, ruling in the *Hardwick* case that same-sex love has no place in American constitutional jurisprudence.

Despite its harsh outcome, the *Hardwick* decision has not retarded the movement for civil rights. In fact, the decision may have activated many in lesbian/gay communities and solidified support for this fight among many nongay people. Notwithstanding *Hardwick*, for example, the effort to eradicate sodomy laws has continued, based on challenges brought in state courts under *state* constitutional theories. Since *Hardwick*, sodomy laws have been declared unconstitutional by lower courts in Michigan, Tennessee, and Texas, and by the highest court in Kentucky (Rubenstein, 1993). In 1993, the state of Nevada and the District of Columbia repealed their sodomy statutes.

Nor has *Hardwick* impaired gains in other areas.

## DISCRIMINATION

While the premise for the repeal of sodomy statutes has been a claim to "privacy," privacy has been only one goal of the lesbian/gay rights movement. Beyond wanting to be left alone by the government regarding control over life's most intimate decisions, lesbians and gay men also want to be able to be open about their sexual orientation, just as heterosexuals openly discuss their lives and relationships, without fearing discrimination or worse. By contrast to sodomy's argument for privacy, the argument for civil protection for lesbians and gay men is essentially one of being guaranteed an ability equal to heterosexuals' to be open about one's life.

*In 1971, there was not a single law, ordinance, or policy prohibiting discrimination against lesbians and gay men.* No one had ever heard of, nor had any public or private entity ever adopted, a policy that prohibited discrimination on the basis of sexual orientation.

*Today, eight states, the District of Columbia, and more than 100 municipalities ban discrimination against lesbians and gay men.*[6] These laws generally ban discrimination on the basis of sexual orientation in employment, housing, and places of public accommodation. In 1981, Wisconsin became the first state to pass a lesbian/gay rights law on a statewide level, but for the next nine years no state followed. Since 1990, however, seven states have done so—Massachusetts, Hawaii, Connecticut, New Jersey, Vermont, California, and Minnesota. Interestingly, these laws are sometimes passed *before* the state repeals its sodomy law. Wisconsin passed its civil rights law in 1981 but did not repeal its sodomy law until 1983. Massachusetts enacted a gay/lesbian rights law in 1990, even though it still has a sodomy law.

Notwithstanding these advances, in 42 states it remains perfectly legal for a private-sector employer to deny employment or to refuse to serve or rent to lesbians and gay men based solely on their sexual orientation—unless one happens to be in a municipality that has a lesbian/gay rights ordinance. In 1991, a restaurant chain, Cracker Barrel, fired all of its lesbian and gay employees, announcing that it was a "family" restaurant where such employees were not welcome. Although Cracker Barrel operates in many states throughout the country, its actions only occur in areas that are not protected by lesbian/gay rights laws.

Moreover, in those areas that lesbians and gay men have gained some protection from discrimination, a powerful backlash has taken place—and is intensifying. Since the first civil rights laws banning discrimination on the basis of sexual orientation were enacted in the 1970s, these laws have faced challenge by forces of the radical right. In the 1970s, Anita Bryant, known nationally as the spokesperson for Florida orange juice, instituted a nationwide campaign to repeal local ordinances prohibiting discrimination on the basis of sexual orientation and to enact laws banning lesbians and gay men from teaching in the public schools and from being around children. A number of local ordinances were repealed in these campaigns.

Currently, in the 1990s, a new wave of antigay hysteria is sweeping the country. In 1992, in two states (Colorado and Oregon) voters were asked to amend their state constitutions so as to repeal the portions of local sexual orientation laws that banned discrimination against lesbians, gay men, and bisexuals. These constitutional amendments would also have prohibited any locality in the state from enacting such laws in the future. While the Oregon constitutional amendment was defeated (57%-43%), the Colorado constitutional amendment, known as Amendment 2, was enacted by the state's voters by a margin of 53%-47%. At the same time, voters in Tampa, Florida, repealed that municipality's recently enacted gay/lesbian rights law. A lawsuit was immediately filed in Colorado and Amendment 2 was stopped by the courts from going into effect.[7] That case will be reviewed by the United States Supreme Court in 1995.

Notwithstanding the unconstitutionality of Amendment 2, antilesbian/antigay ballot initiatives continue to be proposed by the radical right. In 1993, voters in Cincinnati, Ohio, adopted such an amendment changing the city charter, while voters in Lewistown, Maine, repealed a recently enacted law prohibiting discrimination on the basis of sexual orientation, and voters in Portsmouth, New Hampshire, registered their disapproval of such a provision. Similarly, nearly a dozen municipalities in Oregon have enacted laws barring nondiscrimination protection for lesbians and gay men. As in Colorado, the courts have barred the Cincinnati law and most of the Oregon laws from taking effect.[8]

These ballot initiatives demonstrate the tenuous nature of civil rights protection. Enacted by local legislatures to protect minorities from majoritarian prejudice, civil rights laws are then prone to repeal through ballot initiatives by the very majority that the law is designed to protect against. These initiatives—which attempt to deny the opportunity to provide an equal playing field to minorities—deprive minority citizens of the equal protection of the law and thus, not surprisingly, have met with disapproval by the courts. This dynamic—law, repeal, lawsuit—between the proponents and opponents of civil rights protection for lesbians and gays is likely to continue throughout the decade, particularly as the radical right (as noted above) has switched its primary emphasis from abortion to gay rights.

While the courts have so far crushed attempts by the populace to deprive legislatures of the chance to pass gay rights protection, the judiciary has not been as protective of other types of governmental discrimination against lesbians and gay men. In policing government actions that discriminate against gay and lesbian people—for instance, the firing of a lesbian civil servant—courts have ruled that the Constitution generally prohibits the government from firing lesbians and gay men without first articulating some nexus between the worker's sexual orientation and his or her ability to do the job. This "nexus" requirement is also a part of the federal civil service regulations protecting federal employees.[9] Yet, in practice, the nexus test has provided little protection for lesbians and gay men: The federal government has successfully prohibited lesbians and gay men from serving in the military[10] and from working for the FBI[11] and CIA,[12] and created extra burdens for lesbians and gay men who apply for security clearance.[13] State and local governments are no better: Often, they openly ban lesbians and gay men from holding jobs ranging from teaching[14] to police work.[15] Despite the nexus requirement and other constitutional standards, courts have with near and unique uniformity ruled that such government line-drawing that discriminates against lesbian and gay people does not offend the Constitution. In the cases cited above, the courts have condoned the military's bias against lesbians and gay men as well as that of the FBI, CIA, Foreign Service, Defense Department Security Clearance office, and many school boards and police departments. The Constitution has been little more than a promise to lesbians and gay men.

Thus, in most areas of the United States, lesbians and gay men are not protected from the reach of the criminal law within their homes, and they are left, in effect, legally naked if they choose to come out publicly. What is worse, in the smattering of states and municipalities with some protection against discrimination, highly visible hate campaigns are being waged to deprive lesbians and gay men of these hard-fought civil rights. With such minimal legal protection—and often confronted by employers who frown upon them—gay and lesbian people must constantly negotiate how open to be about their sexual orientation in all realms of their life.

# FAMILY RIGHTS

Lesbians and gay men form relationships with one another in much the same way as heterosexuals do. Unlike heterosexual unions, however, same-sex relationships are not recognized by law. In seeking protection for relationships, lesbians and gay men want both to guarantee the privacy and autonomy society provides for heterosexual couples—particularly in marriages—and to gain the public recognition and economic responsibilities and benefits that accompany marital status.

Additionally, lesbians and gay men have children. Some have children from a prior heterosexual marriage; some lesbians have had children through alternative insemination or with a male friend; other lesbians and gay men adopt children or become foster parents (see Patterson, this volume). Regardless of how they came to be parents, lesbians and gay men are confronted with a myriad of legal issues that arise because of society's misperceptions about the relationship between sexual orientation and parenting ability.

## Coupling

*In 1981, no public or private entity in the United States recognized same-sex relationships.* Indeed, until the early 1980s, few advocates within the lesbian and gay rights movement prioritized family issues. One exception was the many lesbian and gay parents—especially the former—who were losing their rights to their natural children in custody and visitation battles with their former (heterosexual) spouses. Another exception was a series of lawsuits brought in the early 1970s, immediately following the Stonewall Rebellion, challenging the constitutionality of marriage laws that prohibited same-sex marriages. These cases, brought in Minnesota, Washington State, and Kentucky, were each rejected by the courts in those states, without being taken seriously.[16]

The 1980s, however, witnessed an explosion of attention to relationship issues within lesbian and gay communities. Among many developments, two central events of the 1980s helped spur this family rights movement for lesbian and gay men: AIDS and the Sharon Kowalski case. AIDS has made the consequences of not having a legal relationship crushingly apparent to lesbian and gay couples. For instance, a gay man whose partner is dying may have difficulty inquiring about his condition or visiting him in the hospital because the men have no legal relationship with one another. Once the lover dies, the surviving partner will not automatically share in the estate, nor enjoy the tax benefits of so doing, and may indeed lose control of property the couple purchased together. He may also face eviction from his home. The survivor, moreover, could very well face legal challenges from his partner's biological family regarding the deceased's will or even the disposition of his lover's remains.

The situation of Sharon Kowalski and Karen Thompson has similarly focused attention within lesbian and gay communities on family rights. Kowalski

and Thompson lived together as partners for four years when, in 1983, Kowalski was in a tragic car accident that left her physically and mentally disabled.
For more than nine years after the accident, Thompson fought with Kowalski's
biological family for the right to be Kowalski's legal guardian. The plight of the
couple received considerable attention within lesbian/gay communities and
highlighted the consequences of the legal system's failure to recognize same-
sex relationships.[17]

Because of AIDS, the Kowalski case, and many similar though less publicized cases, same-sex couples have become increasingly sophisticated in prepar-
ing legal documents to secure their relationships with one another. But for many,
such second-class attempts to make a relationship resemble a marriage do not
go far enough. A number of same-sex couples around the country have filed challenges to their states' marriage statutes;[18] statutes have also been introduced in
state legislatures that would change the definition of marriage to include same-
sex couples.[19] Other activists strongly believe that marriage is not the answer.
They feel that lesbian and gay couples should not appropriate the mechanisms
of oppression—particularly of the oppression of women—in order to secure legal
recognition of their relationships (Ettelbrick, 1993). Rather than focus on marriage, many individuals in lesbian and gay communities have centered their attention on developing a new form of recognition for relationships: Entitled
"domestic partnership," this concept was invented as a basis for the recognition
of lesbian and gay familial relationships (Rubenstein, 1993).

This growing movement for legal recognition of same-sex relationships has
yielded a number of significant milestones in recent years. *As of 1994, dozens of
municipalities and many more private institutions recognize lesbian and gay relationships through "domestic partnership" programs, according different types
of benefits to these newly acknowledged unions.* Additionally, the highest court
in the state of New York recognized same-sex couples as "family" in a 1989 decision.[20] Perhaps most significantly, in 1993, Hawaii's highest court reinstated
a legal challenge to the constitutionality of Hawaii's marriage law,[21] signaling
the possibility that Hawaii might soon recognize lesbian and gay marriages.

The lower court in the Hawaii case dismissed the challenge brought by a
group of lesbian and gay couples. The state's highest court, however, held that the
trial court's dismissal was hasty, reasoning that denying same-sex couples the opportunity to marry was discrimination on the basis of *gender.* Under Hawaii state
constitutional law, gender discrimination triggers the closest review by the court.
The Hawaii Supreme Court sent the case back to the trial court with instructions
to apply this strict constitutional standard; the state of Hawaii will now have to
demonstrate that its ban on same-sex marriages is necessary to serve a compelling
state interest that cannot be achieved in any less restrictive way. It is rare for a law
to survive such strict judicial scrutiny; consequently, some believe that the Hawaii
Supreme Court will ultimately order the state to recognize same-sex marriages.

Despite significant gains over the past decade, lesbian and gay couples' legal
situation remains abysmal. Not one state recognizes same-sex relationships by
permitting gay and lesbian people to marry one another—not one. While advances

are inching ahead at the local level, the only real breakthrough—the Hawaii marriage decision—could lead to a backlash that limits the gains that have been made. If Hawaii recognizes same-sex marriages, it will likely touch off a loud nationwide debate about these relationships. Generally speaking, marriages in one state are recognized by another state, unless they violate the public policy of the second state. Courts will be called on to interpret what this means in each of the other 49 states and the District of Columbia. At the same time, state legislatures, and perhaps Congress, can be expected to step into the picture if Hawaii allows same-sex marriages, in order to limit the recognition of Hawaii marriages in their states. Regardless of the outcome of the Hawaii decision, though, it is clear that the issue of the legal recognition of lesbian/gay relationships will remain a matter of significant public debate in the coming years.

## Parenting

As noted above, lesbians and gay men are parents and have become parents through a variety of routes. In 1987, it was estimated that approximately 3 million gay men and lesbians in the United States were parents, and between 8 and 10 million children were raised in gay or lesbian households.[22]

Traditionally, lesbians and gay men could be deprived of their children solely on the basis of their sexual orientation. Many states had judicial opinions stating that sexual orientation per se was a reason to deprive a parent of custody of, or visitation with, his or her biological children. The court did not have to show that the children were somehow harmed by the parent's sexual orientation—it was presumed to be so. Such decisions were based on a series of myths about having lesbians or gay men around children, including the irrational fear that homosexuality was somehow related to child molestation; the concern that a lesbian/gay parent would raise children to be lesbian/gay; and the consideration that the children would face ridicule and stigmatization by peers (Rubenstein, 1993). Similarly, it was extremely difficult, if not impossible, for lesbians and gay men to adopt or become foster parents;[23] two states (Florida and New Hampshire) explicitly ban "homosexuals" from adopting.[24] In many places, lesbians cannot avail themselves of alternative insemination services because these are made available only to married women, a status denied lesbians.

Yet, as in the area of coupling, developments have permeated parenting law as well, with state courts less likely to consider a parent's sexual orientation as a pertinent factor in custody and visitation decisions. Most states have adopted a nexus test, according to which a parent's sexual orientation is only taken into account to the extent it can be shown to have some relationship to her or his parenting ability (Rubenstein, 1993). Moreover, courts in about half a dozen states have recognized "second-parent adoptions," permitting a lesbian/gay co-parent to adopt her or his partner's biological children.[25]

At the same time, lesbian and gay parents still face enormous deprivations. In about a dozen states, lesbians and gay men continue to be deprived custody of, or visitation with, their children solely because of their sexual orientation. For example, in 1993, a court in Virginia deprived Sharon Bottoms of her child solely because she is a lesbian; the court transferred custody of the child to Sharon's mother, the child's grandmother. While the case is on appeal, Virginia law leans toward a rule that allows lesbian and gay parents to lose their children to the child's other biological parent solely on the basis of sexual orientation.[26] Moreover, the Florida ban on gay/lesbian adoption was recently upheld by an intermediate appellate court in Florida as being constitutional;[27] that decision will now be reviewed by the state's highest court.

In sum, even as we develop new family structures with one another and with the assistance of emerging technological advances, lesbians and gay men have no legal protection for the families we form. We remain a strange anomaly to the area of family law, challenging the very structure of an edifice constructed upon the model of a mother, father, and 2.4 children.

## STRUGGLE

The gains made by lesbians and gay men in the legal arena in the past 40 years have been against great odds. Those battling for rights have been brave men and women who have risked their comfort, livelihood, families, and, in some cases, lives for justice. Lesbians and gay men have been denied the right to form social and political organizations, to meet with one another in bars and restaurants, to march for equal rights, and to speak publicly about their issues.

The First Amendment to the United States Constitution—the right to free speech and association—has generally provided the most constitutional protection for lesbian/gay people. With some notable exceptions,[28] the First Amendment has successfully protected lesbian and gay political organizations in the fight for gay and lesbian rights. For example, the First Amendment has protected the right of a male high school student to take another male to his high school prom;[29] it has safeguarded numerous lesbian and gay student groups in their quest for recognition at state universities throughout the country;[30] and it has been successfully employed to fight government censorship of lesbian and gay speech.[31]

The protections provided by the First Amendment are important because the struggle for lesbian and gay rights continues into the 1990s. As outlined above, new efforts to deprive lesbians and gay men of legal protection are keeping pace with the enactment of those protections.

The law represents a unique promise to members of our society and, at the same time, can reflect the basest desires and most repulsive instincts of human beings. Despite this tension, the struggle for *legal* rights for lesbians and gay men is, for good reason, at the heart of our revolution—because the law holds out the hope that our society is capable of treating *all* of its citizens, including lesbians and gay men, with the dignity and respect that each deserves.

## ▼ ENDNOTES ▼

1. This chapter is an adaptation of the introduction to W. B. Rubenstein's (1993) *Lesbians, Gay Men, and the Law.*
2. See *McLaughlin v. Florida,* 379 U.S. 184 (1964).
3. See *Loving v. Virginia,* 388 U.S. 1 (1967).
4. These developments are described in Rubenstein (1993). The states that currently have gay-only sodomy laws are: Arkansas, Kansas, Missouri, Montana, Tennessee, and Texas. The Texas statute has been declared unconstitutional by an intermediate appellate court, *Dallas v. England,* 846 S.W.2d 957 (Tex. App. 1993), while the Texas Supreme Court has declined to rule on the law's constitutionality—*State v. Morales,* 1994 Tex. LEXIS 17 (Jan. 12, 1994)—on the grounds that the state's civil courts lacked jurisdiction to consider the constitutionality of this criminal statute in a civil test case.
5. 478 U.S. 186 (1986).
6. For a list of the municipalities that have done so, see Rubenstein (1993).
7. See *Evans v. Romer,* 854 P.2d 1270 (Colo. 1993).
8. See, e.g., *Equality Foundation v. City of Cincinnati,* 838 F. Supp. 1235 (S.D. Ohio 1993); *Merrick v. Board of Higher Education,* 841 P.2d 646 (Ore. App. 1992).
9. See, e.g., *Norton v. Macy,* 417 F.2d 1161 (D.C. Cir. 1969).
10. See, e.g., *BenShalom v. Marsh,* 881 F.2d 454 (7th Cir. 1989), *cert. denied,* 494 U.S. 1004 (1990); *Woodward v. United States,* 871 F.2d 1068 (Fed. Cir. 1989), *cert. denied,* 494 U.S. 1003 (1990); *Rich v. Secretary of the Army,* 735 F.2d 1220 (10th Cir. 1984).
11. See, e.g., *Padula v. Webster,* 822 F.2d 97 (D.C. Cir. 1987); *Ashton v. Civiletti,* 613 F.2d 923 (D.C. Cir. 1979). The Clinton Administration settled a case alleging that the FBI discriminated against a career agent on the basis of his sexual orientation—see *Buttino v. Federal Bureau of Investigation,* 801 F. Supp. 298 (N.D. Cal. 1992)—and adopted a policy of nondiscrimination.
12. See *Doe v. Webster,* 769 F. Supp. 1 (D. D.C. 1991), *aff'd. in part and rev'd. in part,* and *Doe v. Gates,* 60 Empl. Prac. Dec. (CCH) 41949 (D.C. Cir. 1993).
13. See *High Tech Gays v. Defense Ind. Sec. Clearance Office,* 895 F.2d 563 (9th Cir. 1990).
14. See, e.g., *National Gay Task Force v. Board of Education of the City of Oklahoma City,* 470 U.S. 903 (1985).
15. See, e.g., *Childers v. Dallas Police Department,* 513 F. Supp. 134 (N.D. Tex. 1981). But see *Dallas v. England,* 846 S.W.2d 957 (Tex. App. 1993).
16. *Singer v. Hara,* 522 P. 2d 1187 (Ct. App. Wash. 1974), *review denied,* 84 Wash.2d 1008 (1974); *Baker v. Nelson,* 191 N.W.2d 185 (Minn. 1971), *appeal dismissed,* 409 U.S. 810 (1972); *Jones v. Hallahan,* 501 S.W.2d 588 (Ky. Ct. App. 1973).
17. The final decision in the *Kowalski* case, granting Thompson guardianship of Kowalski, is reported at 478 N.W. 2d 790 (Minn. Ct. App. 1991).

18. See, e.g., *Baehr v. Lewin,* 852 P.2d 44 (Haw. 1993), *clarified,* 74 Haw. 645 (1993), *on remand; Dean v. District of Columbia,* No. 90-13892 (D.C. Super. Ct. Dec. 30, 1991), *on appeal.*
19. Cal. A.B. 167 (Burton D.S.F. 1991).
20. *Braschi v. Stahl Associates, Co.,* 543 N.E.2d 49 (N.Y. 1989).
21. *Baehr v. Lewin,* 852 P.2d 44 (Haw. 1993), *clarified,* 74 Haw. 645 (1993), *on remand.*
22. *ABA Annual Meeting Provides Forum for Family Law Experts,* 13 Fam. L. Rep. (BNA) 1512, 1513 (1987).
23. See, e.g., *Appeal in Pima County Juvenile Action B-10489,* 727 P.2d 830 (Ariz. Ct. App. 1986).
24. Florida explicitly bars gay adoption; New Hampshire explicitly prohibits gay adoption and foster care. The Florida law has been declared unconstitutional by a number of Florida trial courts, see, e.g., *Seebol v. Farie,* reported in Rubenstein (1993), although a recent appellate court decision upheld the constitutionality of the law, see *State, Dep't of Health v. Cox,* 627 So.2d 1210 (Fla. App. 1993), in a case now on appeal to the Florida Supreme Court (see below). The New Hampshire Supreme Court upheld its law against a constitutional challenge, *In Re Opinion of the Justices,* 530 A.2d 21 (N.H. 1987).
25. See, e.g., *In Re The Adoption of a Child Named Evan,* 583 N.Y.S.2d 997 (N.Y. Sur. 1992).
26. See *Roe v. Roe,* 324 S.E.2d 691 (Va. 1985).
27. *State, Dep't. of Health v. Cox,* 627 So.2d 1210 (Fla. App. 1993), *on appeal.*
28. There are a number of serious internal and external limitations on the applicability of the First Amendment. First, the First Amendment is only triggered where "state action" exists, although antigay silencing is not so limited. Instances of private censorship—an encyclopedia's failure to include an entry on gay/lesbian life, for example—are not actionable. See, e.g., *Hatheway v. Gannett,* 459 N.W.2d 873 (Wisc. App. 1990) (private newspaper refused to run advertisements with the words "lesbian" and "gay"). Second, even where there is state action, the First Amendment applies only to conduct that is speech and to association that is political. Claims for gay and bisexual litigants have failed where courts have ruled that the speech at issue, such as coming out, was not "political" and thus not protected by the First Amendment. See, e.g., *Rowland v. Mad River Local School District, Montgomery County, Ohio,* 730 F.2d 444 (6th Cir. 1984), *cert. denied,* 470 U.S. 1009 (1985). Third, the First Amendment does not extend to protect speech that will cause "imminent lawless conduct"; some courts have ruled that gay and lesbian organizations will lead to outbreaks of sodomy and are therefore appropriately subjected to state regulation. See, e.g., *Gay and Lesbian Students Association v. Gohn,* 656 F. Supp. 1045 (W.D. Ark. 1987), *rev'd., Gay and Lesbian Students Ass'n v. Gohn,* 850 F.2d 361 (8th Cir. 1988). Similarly, some lesbian/gay expression is considered obscene and therefore beyond the protection of the First Amendment (see Hunter, 1992, describing prosecution of a Cincinnati art museum for display of Robert Mapplethorpe

photographs depicting, inter alia, gay sexuality). First Amendment rights are also limited in the sense that the First Amendment is not absolute— where the government has a compelling state interest in policing such rights, they can be curtailed. Moreover, where First Amendment rights clash with other First Amendment rights, someone must prevail. Lesbian and gay litigants have lost cases on these grounds as well (see *New York Times,* 1991). Finally, sometimes the First Amendment just does not work. There have been absolutely outrageous instances of courts refusing to recognize First Amendment rights. For instance, after the Ohio Secretary of State refused to permit the incorporation of Cincinnati's Gay Activist Alliance, his decision was upheld by every level of the Ohio state judiciary and certiorari was denied by the United States Supreme Court. *State ex rel. Grant v. Brown,* 313 N.E.2d 847 (Ohio 1974) *(per curiam), appeal dismissed and cert. denied sub nom. Duggan v. Brown,* 420 U.S. 916 (1975).
29. See *Fricke v. Lynch,* 491 F.Supp. 381 (D. R.I. 1980).
30. See, e.g., *Gay and Lesbian Students Ass'n v. Gohn,* 850 F.2d 361 (8th Cir. 1988); *Gay Students Services v. Texas A & M University,* 737 F.2d 1317 (5th Cir. 1984); *Gay Lib v. University of Missouri,* 558 F.2d 848 (8th Cir. 1977), *cert. denied sub nom. Ratchford v. Gay Lib,* 434 U.S. 1080 (1978); *Gay Alliance of Students v. Matthews,* 544 F.2d 161 (4th Cir. 1976); *Gay Students Organization of the Univ. of New Hampshire v. Bonner,* 509 F.2d 652 (1st Cir. 1974); *Student Coalition for Gay Rights v. Austin Peay University,* 477 F. Supp. 1267 (M.D. Tenn. 1979); *Wood v. Davison,* 351 F. Supp. 543 (N.D. Ga. 1972).
31. See, e.g., *Alaska Gay Coalition v. Sullivan,* 578 P.2d 951 (Alaska 1978) (city could not refuse to list gay group in city-sponsored organizational directory).

## ▼ REFERENCES ▼

Ettelbrick, P. (1993). Since when is marriage a path to liberation? In W. B. Rubenstein (Ed.), *Lesbians, gay men, and the law* (pp. 401–405). New York: The New Press.

Hunter, N. D. (1992). Life after Hardwick. *Harvard Civil Rights and Civil Liberties Law Review, 27*, 531–554.

Hunter, N. D., Michaelson, S. E., & Stoddard, T. B. (1992). *The rights of lesbians and gay men: The basic ACLU guide to a gay person's rights* (3rd ed.). Carbondale, IL: Southern Illinois University Press.

Kramer, L. (1987). *Reports from the holocaust: The making of an AIDS activist.* New York: St. Martin's Press.

Leonard, A. S. (1993). Fornication: A grubby little exercise in self-gratification.

In A. S. Leonard (Ed.), *Sexuality and the law: An encyclopedia of major legal cases* (vol. 3). New York: Garland.

National Gay and Lesbian Task Force. (1986). *Anti-gay violence: Causes, consequences, responses.* Washington, DC: Author.

*New York Times.* (1991, May 13). Judge rules Scouts can block gay man as a troop leader. p. B13.

Rubenstein, W. B. (Ed.). (1993). *Lesbians, gay men, and the law.* New York: The New Press.

Schmalz, J. (1993, May 7). In Hawaii, step toward legalized gay marriage. *New York Times,* p. A14.

*Chapter 15*

▼

# OLDER LESBIANS AND GAY MEN: OLD MYTHS, NEW IMAGES, AND FUTURE DIRECTIONS

Sharon Jacobson
&
Arnold H. Grossman[1]

*There is little doubt that America is "graying." Within this graying population is a diversity of men and women of varying ethnic backgrounds; chronological ages, such as the young-old, old-old, and centenarians; and lifestyle distinctions—including the homeless, the developmentally disabled, gay men, and lesbians—who remain virtually invisible in the traditional study of aging. This chapter focuses on two of these groups: The men whom Berger (1982a) referred to as the "gay and gray" and the women Kehoe (1986a) called the "triply invisible minority." They are the older lesbians and gay men in our society.*

*Gay men and lesbians face a plurality and diversity of sexual, cultural, and developmental issues across the life course. Their issues will be different at age 15 than at 55, or 75, or 95. It is important to recognize that not everyone assumes a sexual identity as a lesbian or gay man at the same age, nor are the sexual identities of these individuals static.*

*In this chapter, we describe a cohort of men and women who are all too often left at the margins of gay and lesbian agendas. We begin by providing information about the prevalence of older lesbians and gay men in society and the various paths that they have taken in forming a lesbian or gay identity. Next, we review the traditional, negative myths as well as more recent positive images of personal acceptance and celebration, and we explore the various ways that older lesbians and gay men have coped throughout their lives while living in a heterosexist society. We then review research related to older gay men and lesbians and describe the services that are currently available to meet their needs. Finally, we discuss that which still needs to be researched and suggest directions for future services and training.*

## PREVALENCE OF OLDER LESBIANS AND GAY MEN

As with other segments of the lesbian and gay population, one of the most difficult questions to answer is how many older lesbians and gay men are currently
living in the United States. Although there are no reliable estimates, recent calculations have ranged from 3.5 million over the age of 60 years (Dawson, 1982)
to 1.75 million over the age of 65 years (Berger, 1982b). In terms of lesbians only,
Poor (1982) reported that a minimum of 834,000 lesbians over the age of 65
years lived in the United States in 1977. Jacobson (in press), using Kinsey,
Pomeroy, Martin, and Gebhard's (1953) prevalence rate of 6%, predicted that a
minimum of 1,100,880 lesbians over the age of 65 years are currently living in
the United States.

The most common approach to estimating the number of lesbians and gay
men in the population regardless of age has been to multiply Kinsey, Pomeroy,
and Martin's (1948) estimate of 10% by the appropriate census data. Although
Weinberg (1993) raised concerns about this method, he recommended that it
suffices until a more accurate one is developed.

Several factors contribute to the difficulty in estimating the prevalence of
older lesbians and gay men in the United States. One is the lack of agreement on
the definition of "old" (Jacobson, in press). In a review of six studies on older
lesbians and gay men, Lucco (1987) reported that researchers used a variety
of ages ranging from 40 to 60 years. In one study, Wolf (1978) used a lower age
of 40 years because it matched the age of the youngest potential member of an
organization for older lesbians and gay men. Kehoe (1988), in a study of 100
older lesbians, used a lower age of 65 years.

A second factor is the lack of a clearly delineated definition of who is gay or
lesbian (Berger, 1984). To date, research participants have either been older individuals who were willing to self-identify or who participated in a gay or lesbian
organization (Berger, 1984; Chafetz, Sampson, Beck, & West, 1974; Galassi, 1991;
Kehoe, 1986a, 1988; Lucco, 1987; Minnigerode & Adelman, 1978; Riege-Laner,
1979; Tully, 1989).

Not all older lesbians and gay men are willing to reveal their sexual identity
(Poor, 1982). In her study of 100 lesbians over the age of 65 years, Kehoe (1988)
asked, "What word do you prefer to use to describe your emotional and/or sexual preference?" (p. 46). One woman responded, "Anything but lesbian" (p. 46).
Another woman stated, "I think I would not like to be identified by sexual preference—either a homosexual or a heterosexual [one]" (p. 47).

In considering the prevalence of older lesbians and gay men in the United
States, two points are clear. First, the number is substantial. Second, the current
methods of estimating prevalence have not been sensitive to the diversity of lesbian and gay identities.

## VARIOUS IMAGES OF OLDER LESBIANS AND GAY MEN

Older lesbians and gay men have spent much of their lives in a world that is actively hostile and oppressive toward homosexuality and sexual minorities. To survive, they have had to develop a variety of coping mechanisms to manage the stigma attached to the images of "pervert" and "sexual deviant" prevalent in their culture. For example, Dunker (1987) wrote, "The excesses of the McCarthy era with the persecution of homosexuals frightened many of [them] into keeping [their] private lives private" (p. 75). Older lesbians and gay men have likely spent an incredible amount of energy learning how to either cope and defend or to attack and challenge the expectation of compulsory heterosexuality and negative cultural attitudes (Friend, 1990; Kameny, 1990).

Friend (1989, 1990) argued that the lifelong process of resisting or internalizing heterosexist discourse and the negative cultural attitudes associated with homosexuality have resulted in a variety of images of older lesbians and gay men. His proposed model illustrates these various images along two continuums.

> One continuum represents cognitive/behavioral responses. At one endpoint of this continuum is the internalization of the pervasive heterosexist ideologies. This results in the belief that homosexuality is sick and/or otherwise negative. At the other end of the continuum is a cognitive/ behavioral response to heterosexism that involves challenging or questioning the validity of these negative messages. As a result, there is a reconstruction of what it means to be lesbian or gay into something positive and affirmative. This affirmative reconstruction is the foundation of the reverse discourse of resistance described by Foucault (1978).
>
> Associated with this cognitive behavioral continuum is a set of corresponding affective responses. For example, if one end of the cognitive/behavioral continuum is the negative evaluation of homosexuality, the corresponding emotional response to these beliefs is internalized homophobia. Feelings of self-hatred, low self-esteem, and minimal or conditional self-acceptance may result. Associated with the other end of the cognitive/behavioral continuum (a gay or lesbian identity reconstructed as positive) are the feelings of increased self-acceptance, high self-esteem, personal empowerment, and self-affirmation. (Friend, 1990, pp. 102–103)

In our review of research on older lesbians and gay men, we present information at three points on these continuums: the two poles and the midpoint. These three points represent the identity of the stereotypic, the passing, and the affirmative lesbian and gay elder.

### Stereotypic Older Lesbians and Gay Men

Friend (1989) described individuals who embrace this identity as those who conform to and are reflective of traditional, negative myths that are commonly used to describe older lesbians and gay men. These are people who have and continue to spend their lives in fear and secrecy. They grew up afraid of being discovered and institutionalized and of losing close interpersonal relationships (Friend, 1989, 1990).

As adults they placed distance between themselves and their families and friends for fear of losing support (Friend, 1989, 1990). Perhaps of greater importance were their negative perceptions of self. Their internalized homophobia often results in feelings of distress, shame, lack of self-respect, and self-loathing. Ultimately, these feelings may lead to despondency, misery, and suicide.

## Passing Older Lesbians and Gay Men

Friend (1989, 1990) characterized individuals with this identity as accepting heterosexist discourse and being conditionally comfortable with their gay or lesbian identity. They view heterosexuality as superior and invest considerable energy attempting to appear heterosexual. These older lesbians and gay men attempt to exist in at least two separate and compartmentalized worlds (Friend, 1990). They spend their lives maneuvering between their public identity as heterosexual and their private identity as a gay man or a lesbian. Gay men and lesbians who are not White must balance three spheres of identity: their private identity as a sexual minority and their public identities as members of an ethnic community and the heterosexual macroculture (Albro & Tully, 1979; Morales, 1990).

This compartmentalization of self, Friend (1990) suggested, may result in a segmented self and a lack of genuineness in heterosexual relationships as well as in gay or lesbian relationships. Furthermore, this psychological splitting can result in increased levels of anxiety and self-consciousness about being discovered. Older lesbians and gay men with this identity may also experience fewer opportunities for emotional support during times of crisis (Friend, 1990).

## Affirmative Older Lesbians and Gay Men

A third group of older lesbians and gay men has challenged heterosexist ideology and reconstructed for themselves a positive image and identity (Friend, 1989). The route that individuals take in creating this affirmative identity varies. Some may view the process of self-empowerment as a form of personal activism, while others extend the process, making it a form of personal as well as professional activism (Friend, 1989, 1990).

> While some may be engaged in resistance as an active attempt for social change, this is likely not true for all of the older lesbian and gay adults in this group. For others, self-acceptance and social integration may not be a conscious socio-political form of resistance. Rather, it may simply illustrate people living lives that comfortably reflect individualistically who they are without struggling to change dominant socio-sexual ideologies. In order to manage the conflicts that being lesbian or gay in a heterosexist environment generates, people in this group may reconstruct the meaning homosexuality has for them individually without being committed to a purposeful attempt for social change. (Friend, 1990, p. 108)

Just as there is uncertainty regarding the absolute number of older lesbians and gay men in the United States, we are not sure about the prevalence of those who cluster within each of Friend's identity groups in society. What is known is that the majority of research with older lesbians and gay men has been with those who portray an affirmative image (Friend, 1989, 1990).

## RESEARCH ISSUES WITH OLDER GAY MEN AND LESBIANS

Research on gay and lesbian aging, other than from a pathological perspective, did not begin until the mid-1970s. Since then a growing body of literature has emerged that explores the social, political, and emotional aspects of these individuals' lives.

Bias and prejudice have affected research on older lesbians and gay men. Homosexuality is not a "socially acceptable" area of study in many research settings, and homophobia has made it nearly impossible to locate truly representative samples of sexual minorities. The latter also limits reliability that is afforded by large samples and the opportunity for control groups. Compounded by ageism and myths, these serious limitations convey the message that older people neither display an interest in leading active, satisfying lives nor have the ability to do so. One of the consequences of these biases and stereotypes is that almost all research concerned with older people fails to address issues of sexuality and sexual orientation; hence, many studies of older adults do not specifically relate to the lives of older sexual minorities. If one includes racism in the research agenda, one should not be surprised to learn that studies concerning ethnic-minority older lesbians and gay men are virtually nonexistent. Consequently, the research reported in these sections is based on relatively small samples of White lesbians and gay men.

The older lesbians and gay men that have been most accessible to researchers are those who Friend (1989, 1990) described as affirmative. They are typically White, middle- or upper-middle-class, well-educated men and women who live in or near an urban area and are members of a lesbian or gay male organization.

## RESEARCH ON OLDER GAY MEN

In describing the older gay people with whom he worked in 1982 at Senior Action in a Gay Environment (SAGE), Dawson (1982) stated:

> When today's older gays were young, they faced an unrelieved hostility towards homosexuality that was far more virulent than it is today. . . . The need for secrecy caused an isolation which imperiled

their most intimate relationships. And the greatest damage was done to those gay people who *believed* what society said about them, and thus lived in corrosive shame and self-loathing. (p. 5)

Born near the beginning of the 20th century, these older adults grew up and lived the majority of their adult lives when homosexuality was characterized as a mental illness in the *Diagnostic and Statistical Manual* of the American Psychiatric Association. Many feared that their families would use homosexuality as grounds for institutionalizing them or that they would be subjected to other forms of victimization (Friend, 1989). As noted by Hooker in 1967, "The necessity of escaping the penalties of social or legal recognition [impelled] many homosexuals to lead a highly secret private life" (p. 169).

Most of the more than 100 older gay men who were interviewed between 1978 and 1984 by Vacha (1985) "knew that they were 'different' from an early age. The luckier ones were able to find others like themselves. . . . Overall, it was a world of great danger and secret liaisons" (pp. 212–213). The secrecy forced many older gay men to live in a dichotomized world. Most married and had children, socialized with heterosexual friends, and joined religious institutions that told them that they were sinful and an abomination. In hiding their sexual orientation, they kept parts of themselves from their families and friends—distancing themselves in their interpersonal relationships. Some, described as loners, may have had relatively little contact or genuine intimacy with their families of origin (Friend, 1989).

## Stereotypes

The phenomena described above led Kelly (1980) to summarize the traditional composite stereotype of the older, aging gay man.

He no longer goes to bars, having lost his physical attractiveness and thereby his sexual appeal to the young men he craves. He is oversexed, but his sex life is very unsatisfactory. He has been unable to form a lasting relationship with a sexual partner, and he is seldom sexually active anymore. When he does have sex, it is usually in a tearoom. He has disengaged himself from the gay world and his acquaintances in it. He is retreating farther and farther into the "closet"—fearful of disclosure of his "perversion." Most of his associations are increasingly with heterosexuals. In a bizarre and deviant world centered around youth, he is labeled "an old queen" and he has become quite effeminate. (pp. 182–183)

Using questionnaires, interviews, and participant observation, Kelly (1980) studied gay men in Los Angeles. Thirty men were over 65, six were over 75, and seven in the oldest group refused to divulge their age. Based on the data from these 43 individuals, Kelly formulated the following new composite:

[The] older gay man in the study group does not frequent tearooms but occasionally goes out to bars, particularly those that serve his peer group. The extent of his participation in the gay world is moderate but based largely on his individual desires. He has many gay friends and fewer heterosexual friends. His sex life is quite satisfactory and he desires sexual contact with adult men, especially those near his own age, but he is not currently involved in an exclusive relationship. He does not consider himself effeminate, nor does he like to define himself in terms of gay age-labels, but he remembers the terms that were commonly applied to "old gays" when he was younger. (p. 186)

Studies by Vacha (1985), Berger (1982a), Friend (1980), and Weinberg and Williams (1974) explored the components of societal myths about older gay men. These studies also attempted to use research to impact social attitudes toward this group. As Kimmel (1979) stated after interviewing 14 aging gay men about their life history and experiences, "The wide diversity of their patterns of aging, the presence of positive aspects of gay aging, and the high life satisfaction of many of the respondents contradict the stereotype of the lonely, isolated gay man" (p. 239).

After surveying the research conducted on older gay men, Berger (1992) concluded, "Stereotypes about them have been extreme, and the results of research on this group have dramatically defied these stereotypes" (p. 217). Research findings are presented below that addresses various themes commonly enumerated in composite stereotypic portrayals.

## Sex Lives

Researchers report that most older gay men remain sexually active and are generally satisfied with their sex lives. Berger (1982a) found that almost two thirds of his sample of 112 gay men over 40 years of age reported having sex once a week or more. Other researchers have found a decrease in the number of sexual partners and in the frequency of sexual activity among older gays, but greater sexual satisfaction (Bell & Weinberg, 1978; Bennett & Thompson, 1980; Mallett & Badlani, 1987).

## Discovery or Disclosure

Older gay men worry less about disclosure or discovery of their homosexuality than younger gay men. Older gay men are less likely to object to being seen in public with a known gay or lesbian, less likely to report that they would not like to associate with a known gay or lesbian, and more likely not to care who knows about their homosexuality (Berger 1982a). Weinberg and Williams (1974) reported that older gay men in their study were more likely to disclose their homosexuality to a greater proportion of their friends, relatives, work associates, and other gay men and women than the younger men in their study.

## Relationships

Most of the older gay men Vacha (1985) interviewed believed that gay relationships were not transient. They also reported having younger friends and found difficulty only with the flamboyance and openness of younger men. Also reported were a high degree of intergenerational relationships, which Vacha attributed not so much to the partiality of older men for those younger but to the absence of fear about entering into relationships in which there is a large age discrepancy. He suggested that the stigma against such relationships is not as strong in the gay community as in general society. Furthermore, Vacha found that older men did not exchange status, security, and financial favor for a younger man's physical beauty, in large part because the older gay men did not have these to offer.

In their groundbreaking study of gay couples, McWhirter and Mattison (1984) interviewed 312 participants between the ages of 20 and 69 years. Thirty-nine were over 50 years of age, and most of these men were categorized in "Stage Six—Renewing (Beyond Twenty Years)" of their model.[2] The primary characteristics of Stage Six couples are achieving security, shifting perspectives, restoring the partnership, and remembering. McWhirter and Mattison's (1984) model illustrates the fact that many elderly gay men are involved in a positive and loving relationship.

In their commentary on Stage Six, McWhirter and Mattison (1984) stated:

> Couples start out together by losing themselves in the blending of their individual personalities. . . . The continuation of their partnership over time depended upon their ability to separate and find themselves individually without abandoning the relationship. . . . In the later years, there is a return to the need for togetherness that gets expressed in their renewing. . . . The men describe a rejuvenation of their relationship with an emphasis on the pleasures they get from doing things together again, such as traveling, gardening, or cooking. . . . We find tenderness and playfulness, as well as feelings of contentment and satisfaction with their years together. (p. 125)

McWhirter and Mattison suggested that there may be a "surviving" stage beyond the sixth. It is the time when gay men live alone after losing a partner of many years and when the surviving partner is "struggling with solitude while comforted by the happy memories of the past" (p. 126).

## Mental Health

Research demonstrates that older gay men are as well-adjusted and more self-accepting than younger ones, are less likely to be engaged in counseling because of their homosexuality, and report high levels of life satisfaction. Weinberg (1970) found that there were no differences between younger and older gay men on measures of loneliness, unhappiness, or depression; however, older gay men achieved healthier scores on self-concept and self-acceptance and were less likely to desire psychiatric treatment. The older gay men in Friend's (1980) study also received high scores in the area of self-acceptance. Using a Life Satisfaction Index, Berger (1982a) found that older gay men scored as high or higher than other older persons in two surveys of the general population. Very few received or desired counseling for their homosexuality. Most of the older gay men in Vacha's (1985) interviews described themselves as having a greater sense of self-confidence and contentment in their later years than in their youth.

## Loneliness

The older gay man is not a loner and is not socially and emotionally isolated. Weinberg (1970) did not find differences of loneliness among the different age groups of gay men in his study. Berger (1982a) reported that none of the men in his study could be described as a loner, and most preferred to socialize with same-age peers rather than with younger men. Although his sample of gay men over 40 showed consistently lower attendance at political/social service organizations, bars, and social clubs than a group of younger men in a comparable study, they did attend bars or bathhouses about once a month or more and visited political and social organizations with similar frequency.

Francher and Henkin (cited in Berger, 1992) suggested, based on interviews with 10 older gay men, that "older gay men are well equipped to deal with loneliness because they have had to develop, early in life, skills for dealing with loneliness and alienation from the traditional male role" (p. 219). Moreover, they argued that older gay men were less likely to be isolated because they replaced traditional family-of-origin supports with support from families of choice. Vacha (1985) concluded that among those men who lived alone, "many expressed a desire for a lover yet admitted that this conflicted with their greater need for independence. They rarely expressed a sense of loneliness or dissatisfaction; for many living alone was an affirmative choice" (p. 217).

## Reacting to Aging

Gay men do not grow older before their time, despite the importance they may attach to youth. Older gay men experience less anxiety and worry about older age than younger gay men (Berger, 1982a), and they do not perceive themselves as aging sooner than heterosexual men (Minnigerode, 1976). In their survey of gay men and lesbians of all ages, Jay and Young (1979) reported a high prevalence of positive attitudes toward aging among their sample. Vacha (1985) concluded that many of the men in his study who aged well had a somewhat metaphysical or religious attitude toward life.

Kimmel (1978) suggested that the stigmatization of gay persons that occurs throughout their lifetimes because of their sexual orientation may be combined in the older years with the stigma of old age in our youth-oriented society. In contrast, Vacha (1985) argued that gay people are better able to handle the stigmatization of old age because they have been discriminated against for their sexual/affectional preference all their lives. This "mastery of stigma"

hypothesis in old age was also echoed by Berger and Kelly (1986), who indicated that gays and lesbians are more likely to learn to be self-reliant and independent and to assume greater role flexibility, taking on tasks that are necessary for day-to-day survival without concern as to whether the tasks are "womanly" or "manly."

## Supportive Networks

Most older gay men are integrated in supportive networks and have had a significant other(s) for extended periods of their lifetimes (Berger, 1982a). They have a wide range of relationships, including lovers, ex-lovers, friends, and sometimes children, all of whom compose a self-selected family (Vacha, 1985). Older gay men may especially need these relationships for support during bereavement and for assistance if physically disabled (Kimmel, 1978).

Berger (1982a) found in his sample that just under one half of gay men over 40 years lived with a lover and almost three fourths of the participants had a primary sexual relationship with another man at some time in the past. Berger (1982b) identified three types of relationships among older gay men: "committed," in which they maintained a long-term sexual relationship, either monogamous or serial, with another man and had a high level of commitment to their partner; "independent," in which gay men had close friendships and brief affairs, with most having a few close friends and/or living with other gay men; and "ambisexual," in which gay men had relationships with both men and women for substantial portions of their lives. Typically, men in the last category moved from earlier heterosexual relationships to later same-sex ones; some maintained both, continuing to lead dichotomous lives.

## Older Gay Men and AIDS

Through September 1993, the Centers for Disease Control and Prevention (1993) reported a cumulative total of 34,234 cases of AIDS in males and females over 50 years of age. This represents more than 10% of all cases since the CDC began tracking the disease. According to Kooperman (1993), the CDC expects over 1,000 new AIDS cases among people over age 50 each year.

As a result of preliminary findings of a study conducted in San Francisco, Kooperman (1993) indicated that elderly gay men pose a special problem in relation to the HIV/AIDS epidemic. First, many gay elderly men do not take safer sex practices seriously because they believe AIDS is a young gay man's disease. Second, many elderly gay men who have lived their lifetimes in the closet and are not willing to reveal their sexual orientation in their later years will not reach out to AIDS education and services organizations. Thus, prevention and intervention efforts will not be useful for such men. Third, some elderly gay men are engaging in high-risk behaviors such as having sex with strangers and hiring prostitutes.

One reason for this failure to protect self and others may be the elderly gay man's acceptance of the "dirty old man" stereotype that is frequently associated with sexually active older men (Kimmel, 1978). This stigmatization "is further reinforced by the myth that homosexuals are tragic figures whose life inevitably ends badly" (Kimmel, 1978, p. 128). If one adds AIDS to this list of stigmata, feelings of low self-worth among older gay men who grew up during a period of intense antigay stigmatization are likely to be prevalent. Furthermore, as the media and the public fail to make distinctions between identity and behavior, "gay" and "AIDS" become equated in the public's perception (Altman, 1988).

Consequently, older gay men must confront and manage potentially damaging remarks or actions regarding not only their homosexuality but also HIV/AIDS—a double stigma. If they are HIV positive, they must decide either to reveal their sexual orientation, if they have not done so, and their illness or live with the knowledge that both will be discovered after their death (Grossman, 1991).

One source of support is offered by organizations such as Senior Action in a Gay Environment (SAGE). Kochman (1993), the Executive Director, reported that SAGE's support groups for HIV-positive gay people (primarily men) have an enrollment of nearly 300. These men and women often have images that equate AIDS with dirt, sex, drugs, and shame and often believe that AIDS is their fate because they are gay or lesbian. AIDS proves to them that they are as bad as they believe they are. Kochman reported that these beliefs are especially current among those in their 60s and 70s who have been the victims of intense homophobia; believe that they are hated by society; feel invalidated; have low self-images; and are not at ease attending a church, synagogue, or other place of worship. Therefore, managing the double stigma of AIDS and homosexuality is stressful for these older gay men and lesbians and their relatives.

## Conclusion

Professionals working with gay and lesbian youth and young adults frequently report that most of these individuals do not know an older gay or lesbian person. Vacha (1985) stated, "The stereotype is that older gay men [and women] don't exist, they burn out like a candle at both ends, they die, they vanish, kaput!" (p. 213). With their invisibility comes the loss of potential role models about aging as a gay man or lesbian. This vacuum is now being filled with printed histories, such as those found in Vacha's (1985) book that contains in-depth interviews with older gay men, as well as in the oral histories of older lesbians and gay men in two books published by Hall Carpenter Archives (Hall Carpenter Archives Lesbian Oral History Group, 1989; Hall Carpenter Archives Gay Men's Oral History Group, 1989).

# RESEARCH ON OLDER LESBIANS

Considerably less is known about older lesbians than about older gay men or younger lesbians. In this section, we draw from studies on older lesbians to understand stereotypes about them. We then use these studies to create a series of new images that reflect the diversity of older lesbians and explore the personal and political ways that these older individuals affirm a positive identity.

## Stereotypes

An early discussion on gay and lesbian aging was held in 1978 in Tucson, Arizona (Wolf, 1978). One panel discussion included gay men, lesbians, and heterosexual men and women describing perceptions and images of older lesbians. The portraits that emerged ranged from total nonexistence to "bitter, role-playing, lonely bar dykes" (Wolf, 1978, p. 3). Others observe that society views older lesbians as a "social embarrassment"; as never aging; and as either "cured," committing suicide, or dying of alcoholism (Kehoe, 1986a). These images reinforce the negative stereotypes, invisibility, and devaluation of the lives of older lesbians.

Kehoe (1988) described the life that she and other lesbians experienced during the first two decades of the twentieth century:

> For most it was, at best, awkward and puzzling. Sexuality was never talked about openly, much less homosexuality. The only book we knew about homosexuality among women, *The Well of Loneliness,* was not always easy to get, even in urban areas. . . . As we passed through high school and on to college, we learned that "homosexuality," as it was called, was an illness to be cured, a "perversion," or, at best, a "phase" outgrown in adulthood. Like *The Well of Loneliness,* this was all pretty depressing news and required considerable ego satisfaction in other areas of our lives for us to maintain psychological equilibrium. Some young lesbians, in the early decades of this century, went along with the tide and adjusted to a heterosexual marriage. Others fled to the convent. Because there was much less opportunity for women to support themselves in pre–World War II America, one may surmise that the convent was sometimes a refuge for women who wished to avoid the social pressures of a conventional male/female marriage. (p. 15)

Lesbians have traditionally been a group of women who spent their lives being invisible, not necessarily because of poor self-image but from fear of losing their jobs, families, friends, and freedom. Dunker (1987) described the reasons women remain in the closet:

> For many whose relatives and close friends have never known of their secret, the risks are too great, especially the risk of exposing their deception to people who love them as they have always known them. Combined with an older person's usual resistance to change, fear of causing pain to those they love is reason enough to continue in the closet. (pp. 75–76)

Some lesbians learn to live with this silence and do not feel the need to proclaim their lesbian identity (Kehoe, 1988). Over time, some older lesbians assume the stereotypic behaviors and attitudes described by Friend (1990). Others feel the need to create and celebrate new and positive images of being both old and lesbian.

In the past, Kehoe (1988) stated, it was enough for researchers to demonstrate that lesbians and gay men were as valuable and acceptable as heterosexual women and men. They worked to maintain the dichotomous labeling while attempting to deconstruct the stereotypes. The stereotypes and labels assigned to gay men and lesbians carry with them political, psychological, and social ramifications (Glyptis, 1989). These tend to strip gay men and lesbians of the power to control and name their experience.

> There exists today a pressing personal need for us to reclaim that which is life-enhancing and lovely within the "lesbian" and "gay" community. Yet we have, I think, a simultaneous need to dive down deep, to risk, to question, to continually challenge the old terms, assumptions, and institutions, to radically remake the meaning of our lives and restructure the social organization of our bodies. (Katz, 1983, p. 173)

That which should be challenged is the stereotypical image of older lesbians as "bitter, role-playing, lonely bar dykes" (Wolf, 1978, p. 3).

## Life Satisfaction

The first aspect of the stereotype is that of embitterment. Today's older lesbians survived very difficult times; they lived through the Depression, experienced the "queer-baiting" of the McCarthy era, and learned to cope with nonsupportive families and peers in a generally homophobic environment (Kehoe, 1988). To compensate, they established families of choice who provided them with social support through rough times and partners with whom they could weather life's storms (Kehoe, 1988). Berger (1982b) suggested that coping mechanisms developed to fend against the stigma that is directed toward gay men and lesbians has aided older people in handling their life crises. Despite various stigmata, however, Kehoe (1988) reported that 80% of the lesbians in her study responded that they were either "highly satisfied" or "satisfied" with their lives.

One 69-year-old lesbian spoke about her choices and feelings:

> I lived in a little suburb for awhile outside of Buffalo. It was kind of a snobbish little place where people played bridge and golf and got married in their twenties. I might even have gotten married and had a family, when I think of it now. And in a way, I'm glad I didn't get stuck in that conventional community and turn into a bridge person, playing golf, or going to the country club and those things. I am glad in a way. If I had been "normal." . . . Am I saying "normal"? [if I had been] a heterosexual in those days, I might have fallen into the scheme of life and not known any of the diversity that I have had. (Minnigerode & Adelman, 1978, pp. 455–456)

## Butch/Femme

Another aspect of the classic stereotype is that lesbians adopt roles as either butch or femme in their love relationships and in their interactions with other lesbians. Ponse (1978) and Smith (1989) argued that the terms *butch* and *femme* carry different meanings for different people. Some lesbians view the terms as associated with a role they play; others consider them a part of their identities. Ponse (1978) reported that butch/femme role-playing was more prevalent in the past than in current society. Nevertheless, many lesbians continue to consider these roles and qualities essential aspects of their identity.

The attributes assigned to each of these roles varies. For some, butch entails being "logical (as opposed to emotional), factual, directive, capable of decision making, as well as being able to take care of tasks outside the home and to handle emergency situations" (Ponse, 1978, p. 115). Others focus on the physical appearance of the butch, describing her as virile, masculine in appearance and dress, the financial provider, and the household handyman (Wolf, 1979). Femmes, on the other hand, are often viewed as passive, docile, and nurturing (Ponse, 1978); as cute, pretty, ladylike, and attractive; and as those who wear makeup, cook, clean, and take care of their "butch" (Wolf, 1979).

For lesbians who were part of lesbian communities during the 1940s and 1950s, butch/femme roles were at the core of lesbian sexuality. They were viewed as creating an image of lesbian sexuality appropriate to the culture and climate of the time. Despite changes in women's relationships and reactions to resistance and oppression, butch/femme roles remained constant (Davis & Kennedy, 1990). In their research on lesbian bar life in Buffalo during the 1940s and 1950s, Davis and Kennedy (1990) found that not only were the roles of butch and femme the ruling code of behavior, they were also the "primary organizer for the lesbian stance toward the straight world as well as for building love relationships and for making friends" (p. 432).

In the past, some women felt pressured to choose a role (Wolf, 1979). One older lesbian who participated in Wolf's study of the lesbian community discussed how she felt pressured into selecting a role:

> It was 1960 . . . and something inside of me finally said: I want to meet them. So I went to the ballpark, the place where lesbians play softball, and I had hair clear down to my butt, and I had Levi's and a sweatshirt on and because I didn't have short hair but yet I had butch clothes on, they were very suspicious of me and I had to go to bed with one of them and then have her brag about it around to have them accept me as a lesbian. . . . Then, all of a sudden, I was a very popular butch. I was forced into the role—they decided I was butch because I was aggressive and strong and could fight and because (pause) I, too, decided I was a butch. There were only two categories available to me . . . and I knew I wasn't a femme. And I wasn't turned on when butches aggressed me, so I had to be a butch. (p. 42)

Without any other model, wife/husband roles became a common pattern for lesbian relationships in this early era, particularly for working-class lesbians (Kehoe, 1988). Presently, however, Kehoe (1988) reported that butch/femme role-playing is not supported, or even acknowledged, by most of those she surveyed.

Martin and Lyon (1984) reported similar findings in a study conducted by Almvig (1982). Although Almvig anticipated that older lesbians in her study would report ongoing involvement in butch/femme relationships, this was not so. There are, however, lesbians who continue to embrace the images and roles of butch and femme, especially those who frequently attend bars (Kehoe, 1988; Martin & Lyon, 1984).

## Loneliness

A third image of the older lesbian stereotype is that of a lonely, isolated woman. Although it is certainly true that some older lesbians have "suffered brutal repression for their sexuality" (Dawson, 1982, p. 5), only a minority have grown old in isolation. In addition, while some older lesbians have been isolated from their families of origin (Kimmel, 1992), many have formed families of choice and friendship networks from whom they receive support (Berger, 1985; Kimmel, 1992; Lipman, 1986; Raphael & Robinson, 1984, Wolf, 1978).

In describing the portrait of older, retired, academic lesbians, Kehoe (1986b) wrote:

> Nevertheless, the retired academic gynophile[3] who is alone at sixty or beyond is less likely to be lonely. She has wider solitary, scholarly interests. Although she may miss a lost partner with whom she spent many years she is often able to "live alone and like it" much more comfortably than her heterosexual, widowed contemporary. She has not been the dependent half of a couple; she can continue to manage her own affairs. Or in the framework of the new mores, she can seek out another relationship. She is not so likely to be homebound or remain isolated in suburbia. She is not so intimidated to go out alone. Solitude gives her the chance to read all the books she has never been able to enjoy because of her demanding work schedule and her need to keep up with her professional field. At long last, she has time to write. These are precious privileges circumscribed by days that are too short. (pp. 160–161)

## The Bars

A final aspect of the stereotype of older lesbians is that they are bar dykes. The women that Kehoe (1988) and Jacobson (1993) interviewed reported that they "did not, nor would they have dared, look to bars as places for socializing with other lesbians" (Kehoe, 1988, p. 19). Women from both studies reported that they were too fearful to go to bars. Police raids were a regular event, and "a woman with a respectable job risked her career by visiting them" (Kehoe, 1988, p. 19).

One 68-year-old woman felt that age and socioeconomic status had a bearing on whether one frequented the bars:

> To judge from what I saw during those "salad days" of mine, younger lesbians without or just beginning careers tended to gravitate to the bars to find sister lesbians regardless of the presence or absence of other commonalities. Later, as one grew older and filled a more responsible position in the economic structure, there was a strong tendency to frequent the bars much less and to congregate in the homes of similarly successful lesbians. (Jacobson, 1993)

An 82-year-old woman, who visited the bars about once a month during the 1940s and 1950s, noted that some bar managers exploited lesbians. "We never went on Saturdays because the manager let non-members in then, to make money off of straight people who wanted to gawk" (Jacobson, 1993).

Jacobson (1993) interviewed several lesbians over the age of 65. None reported presently going to bars. One 68-year-old woman gave the following reasons for not going to the lesbian bar in her town:

> Well, things don't get going in a lesbian bar until pretty late, 9-10 o'clock and [there's] a lot of smoke. [It] costs a lot of money, the drinks are expensive because you have to pay for protection. Well most senior women do not have a lot of money they can throw around. If you are not dead from cigarettes at that age, you probably don't want to be exposed to all that smokiness and you feel like a half ass. Probably because there are all these good-looking things around and they are making cracks about the "mummy from the third century at the bar, you know. That old one. Yeah, that old woman." What do you call it when you are prejudiced about age? Ageist, well they can be. . . . they have to find someone to look down on so they look down on the older ones. . . . Most older people, I think just want to go to bed earlier. . . . Plus you just can't handle yourself . . . if a mugger comes. (Jacobson, 1993)

While these women may have attended the bars at one point during their youth, very few attend the lesbian bars today. Only 7 of the 100 women surveyed by Kehoe and none of the 5 that responded in the pilot study conducted by Jacobson (1993) frequented the bars. Older lesbians today are finding other ways to meet women and other activities to participate in during their free time.

## Ageism

Kehoe (1986a) referred to older lesbians as the "triply invisible minority." The three forces of invisibility are age, gender, and sexual orientation. Copper (1988) wrote that "someone over the hill is metaphorically out of sight. In my youthful complacency, by using that phrase I was banishing old age from my awareness" (Copper, 1988, p. 14). One cannot talk about older lesbians without addressing the issue of ageism.

Copper (1988) and Macdonald and Rich (1983) are critical of the erroneous image of a stable and solid lesbian community that provides all-loving, all-supportive security for older lesbians. They are not alone in their conviction. Several of the women who participated in Kehoe's (1988) study shared their experiences with ageism in the lesbian community. Kehoe noted:

> One attempted to explain it by writing, "Almost all known younger lesbians feel they will become aged and do not want to face it." Others expressed their disappointment differently: "I would like to see younger women working to change negative images of old age among other young women and more effort given to older women running older women's programs"; "Younger lesbians talk a good one how bad ageism is, but *socially* they want nothing to do with older women"; "There is a degree of

ageism in the lesbian community here—a certain amount of patronizing." One woman summed it up: "The lesbian community thinks young." (p. 59)

Writing about ageism from a radical feminist perspective, Copper (1988) and Macdonald and Rich (1988) viewed ageism as a social disease that creates a binary opposition between young and old. They argued that ageism places lesbians in a stratified system of grandmothers, mothers, and daughters and that ageism perpetuates a patriarchal model that marginalizes the older woman into invisibility and servitude.

Lesbians who relate to one another as daughter/mother/grandmother have internalized a message of the patriarchal system. This message clearly states that patriarchy only needs, accepts, and allows young, productive, sexy women to become visible. An Australian feminist singer illustrated these points in a song written about what happened to women after World War II (Small & McDonald, 1984).

And after it was over, you had to learn again
To be just wives and mothers, when you'd done the work of men
So you worked to help the needy, and you never trod on toes
And the photos on the pianos struck a happy family pose
. . . And you never thought to question
You just went on with your lives
'Cause all they taught you who to be was mothers, daughters, wives
. . . And now you're getting older and in time the photos fade
And in widowhood you sit back and reflect on the parade
Of the passing of your memories as your daughters change their lives
Seeing more to our existence than just mothers, daughters, wives.

It is not just the daughters who now see more to their "existence than just mothers, daughters, wives." Growing numbers of older lesbians have also expanded the vision of their existence (Copper, 1988).

Ageist thinking isolates women from those who are older and prevents them from benefiting from the wisdom elder women possess (Macdonald & Rich, 1983). Nelson (1986) pointed out how her views on aging changed after her mother's death and with the aging of her own body.

The room fills again with Mother's presence and the memory of her saying to me, "Just wait till you're old and sick and then you'll understand." The words were a disguised way of saying, "You stupid person, you think you are so smart, but you don't understand my situation at all. However, someday you will. Someday you will be old and sick—in pain. You will be isolated from younger women who ignore you, discount your work, and you will remember me. And you will be sorry for the way you've treated me."

And she was right. I do remember her. For now it is I who am getting old and sick and disabled—and now I am surrounded by younger feminist women, lesbians, who have the same mentality toward me I had toward my mother. They do not want to hear about my pain. I feel them separate themselves from me, as though my weaknesses might contaminate them. And now I also understand how I was under the illusion that if I drove myself night and day, if I moved into the fast lane, I would prove my strength and that would prove my superiority to my mother. My strength would prove that no longer would I be prey to the traditional oppression I'd experienced as a child and young woman. (pp. 126–127)

Copper (1988) and Macdonald and Rich (1983) suggested that one way of bridging the gap between younger and older lesbians is by recognizing that older lesbians are not the mothers of the younger lesbians. Furthermore, they suggested that we reprogram the words that we hear when we see an old person. Rich shared the following:

If I carry in my head the notion that you are "young enough to be my daughter" or you are thinking "she is old enough to be my grandmother," the quality of our dialogue is instantly converted. Our roles are defined for us; the possibility for real exchange between us is radically diminished. (p. 102)

## Affirming Older Lesbians

The process of affirming one's self as an older lesbian is an individualized one. It requires the willingness to challenge assumptions that are made about one's life by heterosexist ideology and to critically examine "whether being an older lesbian or gay person necessarily means living a life described by the stereotypes" (Friend, 1989). The terms that are used to reconstruct the older lesbian's identity should be those with which an older lesbian is personally comfortable. For the majority of older lesbians, this means viewing oneself as positive and valuable (Friend, 1989, p. 252). The motivation for this transformation is sometimes intrinsic. Speaking about the process of affirming herself, one older lesbian said:

For many years, homosexuals, men and women, had to live in a heterosexual world and absorb the guilt and the shame and the stereotyping that was foisted upon us. We felt sick. We felt queer. But after a while . . . I began to dispel all that internalization and realize that I was a human being. I was a moral woman and I had raised a wonderful family. My children and my grandchildren loved me and respected me. And there must be a reason for that. Because I'm a respectable and respectful citizen, living my life the best way I could. And I developed a very strong identity of what I was—I'm a lesbian woman and I live like one. I defy anyone else to pass judgment on the way I live and my personal health. (KYW-TV, 1985, cited in Friend, 1989, p. 254)

For other women, the affirmation process is both personal and political. It serves as a means to resist societal norms and views of self that are imposed by others (Friend, 1989). It involves reconstructing a positive identity of self as a lesbian, as a woman, and as an aged person. Furthermore, this transformation provides one with the skills to critically examine other societal roles. One older lesbian spoke of the valuable contributions that she was making to her family.

I think the legacy I would like to leave as a Black lesbian mother is to have my children have loving relationships. To learn to respect each other. Learn to respect women as human beings. I feel we have a double struggle. That is to say gay men and lesbians of color, to change what society thinks we should be or shouldn't be. (Pioneer Productions, 1984)

Those who challenge the assumptions of compulsory heterosexuality face the possible loss of their family of origin. Kimmel (1978) argued that the ability to cope with potential loss will assist adjustment to losses incurred as part of the aging process. Furthermore, the process of affirmation allows one to challenge the meanings attached to family and to develop a social convoy that is based on affirming the value of the older lesbian (Kahn & Antonucci, 1980). Finally, it encourages the empowerment of the gay and lesbian microculture (Albro & Tully, 1979; Friend, 1989).

> Today as younger lesbians are beginning to consolidate their strengths and influence, the presence of old lesbians is sorely needed for role models and mentors, for a source of wisdom and courage, and by their numbers to make all of us more visible, a force to be reckoned with. Many young lesbians need assurance that they can grow into a rich and creative old age not much affected by prejudice. An older lesbian's obvious pride and pleasure in being who she is, politically active or not, can encourage younger ones to have confidence in their futures. A pair of assured, lively, contented old dykes can give the lie to much of the homophobic and ageist propaganda that young lesbians are subjected to. (Dunker, 1987, p. 72)

The affirmative older lesbian has the power to teach others, heterosexual men and women, gay men and lesbians to affirm their sexuality without devaluing that of others.

# SERVICES FOR OLDER LESBIANS AND GAY MEN

The last two decades have witnessed the emergence of an increasing number of services and organizations developed to respond to the needs of older lesbians and gay men. These organizations offer a variety of services. For example, one of the largest and most comprehensive models for delivering services to older lesbians and gay men is SAGE (Senior Action in a Gay Environment). SAGE, headquartered in New York City, was founded in 1977 to address issues of gay and lesbian aging.[4]

In this section, we discuss three types of services offered by a number of organizations: social and education activities, outreach services, and outreach education. We draw from the programs offered by SAGE and other support and advocacy organizations in discussing each type of service.[5]

## Social and Education Activities

The need for social interaction, networking with peers, and leisure is one that spans the life course. Older lesbians and gay men are no exception. Numerous groups have emerged throughout the country that provide opportunities for social, educational, and recreational interactions, including monthly potlucks, speakers, dances, trips, picnics, rap groups, workshops, brunches, and other events. In addition to fulfilling the social needs of older lesbians and gay men, many groups and organizations offer information and assistance in obtaining fair and adequate health care, legal assistance, and financial planning.

SAGE provides social and educational activities on an individual and group level. For example, SAGE furnishes complimentary theater tickets to seniors to attend theater events with their peers, and it operates an international pen pal service that facilitates friendships internationally, intergenerationally, and across living situations. On a group basis, SAGE offers a "drop-in" center every week-day afternoon and one Sunday per month, hosts parties, offers bus trips out of the city each year, and plans a monthly day trip. SAGE hosts a number of work-shops on a variety of topics, as well as monthly socials and brunches. These ac-tivities and others are planned and conducted either by or with the assistance of older lesbians and gay men who volunteer at the center.

## Outreach Services to Older Lesbians and Gay Men

Not all older lesbians and gay men are able to come to a drop-in center or to at-tend the variety of social and educational functions that are available in their communities. Some may be homebound or living in a nursing home. Others may be struggling with their identity as a gay man or lesbian and feel uncom-fortable going to a center specifically for sexual minorities. Still others are so-cially shy and withdrawn.

SAGE and other support and advocacy organizations provide a number of outreach services to meet the needs of older lesbians and gay men. For example, a number of organizations host information and referral lines that provide callers with information regarding entitlements, housing, health care, medical services, legal problems, alternative-living situations, housekeeping/homemaker services, and a wide variety of other services.

SAGE's certified social workers conduct assessments of older gays and les-bians who are homebound and provide case-management services to these indi-viduals. Some programs offer visitation programs for those who are aged and homebound, telephone reassurance lines, and transportation services for doc-tor's appointments or other essential errands.

## Outreach Education

While direct-service delivery remains an important need, it does not diminish the importance of outreach education. Efforts to educate professional commu-nities and the general public impact the lives of older lesbians and gay men as well as other lesbian and gay cohorts. In order to alter the public's attitudes about older lesbians and gay men and to advocate for a more sensitive service de-livery system, a number of support and advocacy organizations conduct profes-sional training seminars and public education programs.

SAGE and other service and advocacy programs provide educational training concerning the lives of older lesbians and gay men in a wide variety of settings and through a diverse array of media. For example, in-service training sessions are conducted at local agencies to sensitize staff to the issues and needs of older lesbians and gay men. Information is disseminated at conferences, and SAGE has a speakers' bureau that fills requests for individual speakers as well as for panel and group discussion leaders. Educational materials are included in publications, such as newspapers and magazines, and on television and radio.

## DIRECTIONS FOR RESEARCH, SERVICE, AND ADVOCACY

There is a need for continued efforts in the areas of research, service, and advocacy. Over the last 20 years, a growing body of research has emerged, services for older lesbians and gay men have continued to develop and increase in visibility, and support and advocacy organizations for older gay men and lesbians have increased in number and are more proactive in meeting the needs of its members. However, there is much work left to be done.

The research that has been completed has raised questions and offered directions for future research. Services are required that are sensitive to the needs of older lesbians and gay men in a variety of living situations. Training is necessary for service and health-care providers with whom they interact. Advocacy efforts are needed in a number of areas to ensure the rights and fair treatment of gay men and lesbians. The following represent suggested directions for future research, service, and advocacy efforts.

## Research

1. On the psychosocial, spiritual, leisure, health, and medical deficits and strengths of older lesbians/gay men who are (a) ethnic minorities (b) living in low income and/or rural communities, (c) surviving partners of long-term coupled relationships, and (d) providing care to someone who is dying.
2. On knowledge, attitudes, and skills acquired in becoming self-affirming gay men and lesbians—and their implications for aging.
3. On the impact of "passing" as heterosexual on the lives of older lesbians and gay men.

## Service

1. HIV/AIDS-prevention education designed for and specifically directed at older lesbians and gay men.

2. Referral services to gay/lesbian-affirmative professionals for health, leisure, spiritual, counseling, health, and medical assistance.
3. Create and maintain community resources for older lesbians and gay men relating to educational, social, and recreational services.
4. Create and maintain support services for older lesbians and gay men who are homebound, in hospitals, or in skilled nursing facilities.
5. Initiate educational programs to train and sensitize professional providers of services to older adults regarding the needs of gay and lesbian older adults, and train these providers to facilitate older lesbians and gay men to accept their homosexuality and to support their decisions regarding disclosure or nondisclosure of their sexual orientation.

## Advocacy

1. For gay and lesbian nondiscrimination state laws and the addition of sexual orientation to nondiscrimination policy statements of institutions.
2. For passage of domestic-partnerships benefit laws by municipalities and provision of benefits by institutions.
3. For passage of laws that provide rights regarding inheritance and legacies to surviving gay or lesbian partners.
4. For changing institutional policies so that a partner of a lesbian or gay man who has been designated by a health-care proxy to make necessary medical decisions cannot be overruled by family members.
5. For support of gay and lesbian couple relationships, especially when one person is institutionalized.

## CONCLUSION

In this chapter, we discussed the difficulty in estimating the prevalence of aging gays and lesbians in North America and illustrated the various identities of these individuals. We reported current knowledge concerning older gay men and lesbians by reviewing the limited available literature. We began by enumerating the stereotypes and the myths that exist about aging gay men and lesbians. Findings from research studies were used to combat those stereotypes and to paint a more realistic picture of what is known about gay and lesbian aging.

Unfortunately, there are far too few research studies with far too few participants to make broad generalizations about this cohort of gay men and lesbians. Research is still needed in a variety of areas. Service-delivery systems must become more accessible to aging lesbians and gay men, and advocacy efforts are still needed to obtain and protect the rights and privileges of these individuals. Work in this area has just begun.

# ▼ SERVICES AND ORGANIZATIONS FOR OLDER LESBIANS AND GAY MEN IN THE UNITED STATES[6]   ▼

**DIGNITY/USA TASK FORCE ON AGING**
William C. Mayes
235 S. 23rd Street, #3R
Philadelphia, PA 19103
(215) 732-3831

**ECOLS**
Emerald Community Outreach to
Lesbians/Gay Seniors, Inc.
c/o SALMACIS
P.O. Box 1604
Eugene, OR 97440-1604
(503) 688-4282

**G-40**
P.O. Box 6761
San Francisco, CA 94101
(415) 552-1997

**GALAXY**
Gay and Lesbian Accommodations for the
Experienced in Years
GALAXY Retirement Center Fund
3507 23rd Street
San Francisco, CA 94117
(415) 648-8678

**GLOE**
Operation Concern—Gay and Lesbian
Outreach to Elders
8153 Market Street
San Francisco, CA 94103
(415) 626-7000

**GLOW**
Gay and Lesbian Older Washingtonians
P.O. Box 75195
Washington, DC 20013
(301) 587-3966

**GLOW**
Gay and Lesbian: An Older Way
Center for Human Services
2255 Third Street
Philadelphia, PA

**LAVENDER PANTHERS**
(formerly Gay Lesbian Elder Action
Network)
1407 E. Madison, Box 6
Seattle, WA 98122

**LOAF**
Lesbians Over the Age of Forty
New York City, NY
(212) 741-2610

**NALGG**
National Association for Lesbian and Gay
Gerontology
1853 Market Street
San Francisco, CA 94103

**NATIONAL GAY AND LESBIAN TASK FORCE**
1734 14th Street, NW
Washington, DC 20009
(202) 332-6483

**OLD LESBIAN ORGANIZING COMMITTEE**
P.O. Box 14816
Chicago, IL 60657

**OPTIONS FOR WOMEN OVER 40**
The Women's Building
3543 Eighteenth Street
San Francisco, CA 94110
(415) 431-6405 or (415) 431-6944

**PROJECT RAINBOW: SOCIETY FOR SENIOR GAY AND LESBIAN CITIZENS**
Gay and Lesbian Community Service
Center
255 S. Hill Street
Room 410
Los Angeles, CA 90012
(213) 621-3180

**PROJECT RAINBOW: SOCIETY FOR SENIOR GAY AND LESBIAN CITIZENS**
Gay and Lesbian Community Service Center
1213 North Highland
Hollywood, CA 90028

**SAGE**
Senior Action in a Gay Environment
208 West 13th Street
New York, NY 10011
(212) 741-2247

**SAGE—TRAINED AFFILIATES**

**1. GEMS**
P.O. Box 22
Manchester, CT 06045
(203) 646-4772

**2. NORTH MIAMI FOUNDATION FOR SENIOR CITIZEN'S SERVICES**
620 NE 127th Street
N. Miami, FL 33161
(303) 893-1450

**3. SHIRLEY TIANO**
33 Fisher Street
Amherst, MA 01002
(413) 549-5122

**4. GLEAM (Gay & Lesbian Elders Active in Minnesota)**
P.O. Box 6515
Minneapolis, MN 55406-6515
(612) 721-8913 or
(612) 724-8021

**5. INFORMATION FOR OLDER GAY PEOPLE**
Box 22043
Lincoln, NE 68542-2043

**6. IGLAB (Ithaca Gay and Lesbian Activities Board)**
P.O. Box 6634
Ithaca, NY 14850-6634

**7. SAGE—MILWAUKEE**
Eldon E. Murray
1715 E. Irving Place
Milwaukee, WI 53202
(414) 271-1500

**8. SAGE—OTTAWA**
Anne Carswell
1 Iona Avenue, #2
Ottawa, Ontario K1L 8E7
(613) 746-7281
(613) 746-0353 (fax)

**SAGE OF CALIFORNIA, INC.**
Seniors Active in a Gay Environment
P.O. Box 4071
San Diego, CA 92104

**SHORT MOUNTAIN SANCTUARY**
P.O. Box 68
Liberty, TN 37095

**SLIGHTLY OLDER LESBIANS AND GAY MEN'S RAP GROUPS**
The Pacific Center
2712 Telegraph Avenue
Berkeley, CA 94705
(415) 548-8283

**SOL, DENVER**
Slightly Older Lesbians
Gay and Lesbian Community Center
1436 Lafayette Street
Denver, CO 80218
(303) 831-6268 or (303) 837-1598

**SOL, SANTA CRUZ**
Slightly Older Lesbians
Pat Rutherford
3060 Porter #31
Soquel, CA 95073
(408) 462-6927

**SOUTH BAY SLIGHTLY OLDER LESBIANS AND MEN'S SUPPORT GROUP, SAN JOSE**
Billy De Frank
Lesbian and Gay Community Center
86 Keyes Street
San Jose, CA 95112
(408) 293-4229

**SOUTHERN CALIFORNIA WOMEN FOR UNDERSTANDING**
9054 Santa Monica Blvd.
West Hollywood, CA 90069
(213) 274-1086

**STONEWALL UNION TASK FORCE ON LESBIAN AND GAY AGING**
P.O. Box 10814
Columbus, OH 43201-7814
(614) 299-7764

**THE CENTER 55**
Gay and Lesbian Center
2025 East 10th Street
Long Beach, CA 90804
(213) 434-3089

**VINTAGE**
Gay and Lesbian Community Center
1436 Lafayette Street
Denver, CO 80218
(303) 831-6268 or
(303) 837-1598 (Hotline)

**WEST COAST CRONES**
Operation Concern
1853 Market Street
San Francisco, CA 94131

---

## ▼  ENDNOTES  ▼

1. The authors extend their thanks to Nancy Kropf and Philip Bockman for their helpful comments on earlier drafts of this chapter.

2. The first five stages in the McWhirter and Mattison (1984) model are: One—Blending (Year One), Two—Nesting (Years Two and Three), Three—Maintaining (Years Four and Five), Four—Building (Years Six Through Ten), and Five—Releasing (Years Eleven Through Twenty).

3. Kehoe (1986b) "coined this word to express and encompass those extra dimensions of the woman-to-woman relationship which the word lesbian somehow fails to include—at least for gay women of the pre–World War II period, as well as for all those for whom intellectual and emotional compatibility is paramount and for whom genitality is not crucial" (p. 160).

4. In September 1992, SAGE held its first national conference for organizations planning SAGE-like programs in their communities. As a result of this conference, eight communities across the United States and one in Canada are hosting SAGE affiliate programs. The list of SAGE trained affiliate sites is included in the section listing services and organizations.

5. The information on the SAGE program was taken from the SAGE Annual Report for the fiscal year, 1991–1992.

6. The information in "Services and Organizations," with the exception of the SAGE affiliates, is reprinted with the permission of the National Association for Lesbian and Gay Gerontology. A copy of this guide may be obtained by writing the National Association for Lesbian and Gay Gerontology, 1853 Market Street, San Francisco, CA, 94103.

## ▼  REFERENCES  ▼

Albro, J. C., & Tully, C. T. (1979). A study of lesbian lifestyles in the homosexual micro-culture and in the heterosexual macro-culture. *Journal of Homosexuality, 4,* 331–344.

Almvig, C. (1982). *The invisible minority: Aging and lesbianism.* New York: Utica College of Syracuse University.

Altman, D. (1988). Legitimation through disaster: AIDS and the gay movement. In E. Fee & D. M. Fox (Eds.), *AIDS: The burdens of history* (pp. 301–315). Berkeley, CA: University of California Press.

Bell, A. P., & Weinberg, M. S. (1978). *Homosexualities: A study of diversity among men and women.* New York: Simon and Schuster.

Bennett, K. C., & Thompson, N. L. (1980). Social and psychological functioning of the aging male homosexual. *British Journal of Psychiatry, 137,* 361–370.

Berger, R. M. (1982a). *Gay and gray: The older homosexual man.* Urbana, IL: University of Illinois Press.

Berger, R. M. (1982b). The unseen minority: Older gays and lesbians. *Social Work, 27,* 236–242.

Berger, R. M. (1984). Realities of gay and lesbian aging. *Social Work, 29,* 57–62.

Berger, R. M. (1985). Rewriting a bad script: Older lesbians and gays. In H. Hidalgo, T. L. Peterson, & N. J. Woodman (Eds.), *Lesbian and gay issues: A resource manual for social workers* (pp. 53–59). Silver Spring, MD: National Association of Social Workers.

Berger, R. M. (1992). Research on older gay men: What we know, what we need to know. In N. J. Woodman (Ed.), *Lesbian and gay lifestyles: A guide for counseling and education* (pp. 217–234). New York: Irvington.

Berger, R. M., & Kelly, J. J. (1986). Working with homosexuals of the older population. *Social Casework: The Journal of Contemporary Social Work, 67,* 203–210.

Centers for Disease Control and Prevention (1993, October). *HIV/AIDS Surveillance Report, 5,* 11.

Chafetz, J. S., Sampson, P., Beck, P., & West, J. (1974). A study of homosexual women. *Social Work, 19,* 714–723.

Copper, B. (1988). *Over the hill: Reflections on ageism between women.* Freedom, CA: Crossing Press.

Davis, M., & Kennedy, E. L. (1990). Oral history and the study of sexuality in the lesbian community. In M. Duberman, M. Vicinus, & G. Chauncy, Jr. (Eds.), *Hidden from history: Reclaiming the gay and lesbian past* (pp. 426–440). New York: Meridian.

Dawson, K. (1982, November). Serving the gay community. *SIECUS Report,* pp. 5–6.

Dunker, B. (1987). Aging lesbians: Observations and speculations. In Boston Lesbian Psychologies Collective (Eds.), *Lesbian psychologies: Explorations and challenges* (pp. 72–82). Urbana, IL: University of Illinois Press.

Friend, R. A. (1980). Gay aging: Adjustment and the older gay male. *Alternative Lifestyles, 3,* 231–248.

Friend, R. A. (1989). Older lesbian and gay people: Responding to homophobia. *Marriage and Family Review, 14,* 241–263.

Friend, R. A. (1990). Older lesbian and gay people: A theory of successful aging. *Journal of Homosexuality, 20,* 99–118.

Galassi, F. S. (1991). A life review workshop for gay and lesbian elders. *Journal of Gerontological Social Work, 16,* 75–86.

Glyptis, S. (1989). Leisure and unemployment. In E. L. Jackson & T. L. Burton (Eds.), *Understanding leisure and recreation: Mapping the past, charting the future* (pp. 181–210). State College, PA: Venture.

Grossman, A. H. (1991). Gay men and HIV/AIDS: Understanding the double stigma. *JANAC: Journal of the Association of Nurses in AIDS Care, 2*, 28–32.

Hall Carpenter Archives Gay Men's Oral History Group. (1989). *Walking after midnight: Gay men's life stories*. London: Routledge.

Hall Carpenter Archives Lesbian Oral History Group. (1989). *Inventing ourselves: Lesbian life stories*. London: Routledge.

Hooker, E. (1967). The homosexual community. In J. H. Gagnon & W. Simon (Eds.), *Sexual deviance* (pp. 167–184). New York: Harper & Row.

Jacobson, S. A. (1993). Unpublished transcripts of interviews with lesbians over the age of 65. University of Georgia, Athens, GA.

Jacobson, S. A. (in press). Methodological issues in research on older lesbians. *Journal of Gay and Lesbian Social Services*.

Jay, K., & Young, A. (1979). *The gay report*. New York: Summit Books.

Kahn, R. L., & Antonucci, T. C. (1980). Convoys across the life course: Attachment, roles, and support. In P. B. Baltes & O. G. Brim (Eds.), *Life span development and behavior* (Vol. 3, pp. 253–286). New York: Academic Press.

Kameny, F. E. (1990). Introduction. *Journal of Homosexuality, 20*, 1–5.

Katz, J. N. (1983). *Gay/lesbian almanac: A new documentary*. New York: Harper & Row.

Kehoe, M. (1986a). Lesbians over 65: A triply invisible minority. *Journal of Homosexuality, 12*, 139–152.

Kehoe, M. (1986b). A portrait of the older lesbian. *Journal of Homosexuality, 12*, 157–161.

Kehoe, M. (1988). Lesbians over 60 speak for themselves. *Journal of Homosexuality, 16*, 1–111.

Kelly, J. (1980). Homosexuality and aging. In J. Marmor (Ed.), *Homosexual behavior: A modern reappraisal* (pp. 176–193). New York: Basic Books.

Kimmel, D. C. (1978). Adult development and aging: A gay perspective. *Journal of Social Issues, 34*, 113–130.

Kimmel, D. C. (1979). Life history interviews of aging gay men. *International Journal of Aging and Human Development, 10*, 239–248.

Kimmel, D. C. (1992). The families of older gays and lesbians. *Generations, 17*, 37–38.

Kinsey, A. C., Pomeroy, W. B., & Martin, C. R. (1948). *Sexual behavior in the human male*. Philadelphia: W. B. Saunders.

Kinsey, A. C., Pomeroy, W. B., Martin, C. R., & Gebhard, P. H. (1953). *Sexual behavior in the human female*. Philadelphia: W. B. Saunders.

Kochman, A. (Speaker). (1993). *AIDS and the elderly*. (Cassette Recording No. ASA3-691). San Francisco: American Society on Aging.

Kooperman, L. (Speaker). (1993). *AIDS and the elderly*. (Cassette Recording No. ASA3-691). San Francisco: American Society on Aging.

Lipman, A. (1986). Homosexual relationships. *Generations, 10*, 51–54.

Lucco, A. J. (1987). Planned retirement housing preferences of older homosexuals. *Journal of Homosexuality, 14*, 35–56.

Macdonald, B., & Rich, C. (1983). *Look me in the eye: Old women, aging and ageism*. San Francisco: Spinsters Ink.

Mallett, E. C., & Badlani, G. H. (1987). Sexuality in the elderly. *Seminal Urology, 5*, 141–145.

Martin, D., & Lyon, P. (1984). The older lesbian. In B. Berzon (Ed.), *Positively gay* (pp. 134–145). Los Angeles: Mediamix Associates.

McWhirter, D. P., & Mattison, A. M. (1984). *The male couple: How relationships develop*. Englewood Cliffs, NJ: Prentice Hall.

Minnigerode, F. A. (1976). Age-status labeling in homosexual men. *Journal of Homosexuality, 1,* 273–275.

Minnigerode, F. A., & Adelman, M. R. (1978). Elderly homosexual women and men: Report on a pilot study. *Family Coordinator, 27,* 451–456.

Morales, E. (1990). Ethnic minority families and minority gays and lesbians. *Marriage and Family Review, 14,* 217–239.

National Association for Lesbian and Gay Gerontology. (1993, March). *Lesbian and gay aging resource guide.* San Francisco, CA: Author. (Available from National Association for Lesbian and Gay Gerontology, 1853 Market Street, San Francisco, CA, 94103).

Nelson, M. (1986). Flowersong. In M. Adelman (Ed.), *Long time passing: Lives of older lesbians* (pp. 122–130). Boston: Alyson.

Pioneer Productions. (1984). *Silent pioneers* [Film]. New York: Pioneer Productions.

Ponse, B. (1978). *Identities in the lesbian world: The social construction of self.* Westport, CT: Greenwood.

Poor, M. (1982). The older lesbian. In M. Cruikshank (Ed.), *Lesbian studies* (pp. 165–173). Old Westbury, NY: Feminist Press.

Raphael, S., & Robinson, M. (1984). The older lesbian: Love relationships and friendship patterns. In T. Darty & S. Potter (Eds.), *Women-identified women* (pp. 67–82). Palo Alto, CA: Mayfield.

Riege-Laner, M. (1979). Growing older female: Heterosexual and homosexual. *Journal of Homosexuality, 4,* 267–275.

SAGE (1992). *SAGE Annual Report 1991–1992.* New York: Author. (Available from SAGE, 208 West 13th Street, New York, NY, 10011.)

Small, J. (Singer & Writer) & McDonald, H. (Producer). (1984). *Mothers, daughters, wives* [Record]. Oakland, CA: Redwood Records.

Smith, E. A. (1989). Butches, femmes, and feminists: The politics of lesbian sexuality. *NWSA Journal, 1,* 398–421.

Tully, C. T. (1989). Caregiving: What do midlife lesbians view as important? *Journal of Gay and Lesbian Psychotherapy, 1,* 87–103.

Vacha, K. (1985). *Quiet fire: Memoirs of older gay men.* Trumansburg, NY: Crossing Press.

Weinberg, M. S. (1970). The male homosexual: Age-related variations in social and psychological characteristics. *Social Problems, 17,* 527–537.

Weinberg, M. S. (Speaker). (1993). *Forming an agenda for gay and lesbian research* (Cassette Recording No. ASA3-122). San Francisco: American Society on Aging.

Weinberg, M. S., & Williams, C. J. (1974). *Male homosexuals: Their problems and adaptations.* New York: Oxford University Press.

Wolf, D. C. (1978, November). *Close friendship patterns of older lesbians.* Paper presented at the 30th annual convention of the Gerontological Society of America, Dallas, TX.

Wolf, D. (1979). *The lesbian community.* Berkeley, CA: University of California Press.

# - Part Four -

# CULTURAL AND MENTAL HEALTH ISSUES

# *Chapter 16*

▼

# GAY CULTURES, GAY COMMUNITIES: THE SOCIAL ORGANIZATION OF LESBIANS, GAY MEN, AND BISEXUALS

## Kristin Gay Esterberg[1]

*Academic research and popular depictions would have us believe that sexual identities are simply about sex. Much of the research literature focuses, for example, on the role of sexuality, especially its physiological components, in defining a lesbian, gay, or bisexual identity; other research is concerned with the etiology, or "causes" of homosexuality. While studies that examine lesbian, gay, and, to a much lesser extent, bisexual life[2] in a much larger context are becoming increasingly common, sexology's stamp on lesbian and gay research, which stresses the sexual aspects of lesbian and gay life, is far more apparent. Popular accounts have also assumed that lesbians, gays, and bisexuals are primarily sexual beings. Unlike heterosexuals, who are defined by their family structures, communities, occupations, or other aspects of their lives, lesbians, gay men, and bisexuals are often defined primarily by what they do in bed. Many lesbians, gay men, and bisexuals, however, view their identity as social and political as well as sexual. For this reason, it is important to study the social contexts of lesbian, gay, and bisexual lives and the communities they create.*

*The term* community *has experienced a resurgence in recent years. In common conversation, people speak of all types of communities: workplace or occupational communities, recreational communities ("the running community"), racial/ethnic communities ("the African American community," "the Italian American community"), and so forth. Lesbians, gay men, and, increasingly, bisexuals use the same language to refer to their social groupings. Unlike earlier views, contemporary notions of community do not necessarily imply a geographically bounded, physical location. Instead of an actual place, people often speak of an identification or sense of connection with a social category or group (di Leonardo, 1984; Herrell, 1992). People are members of a community—whether a lesbian or gay community, an ethnic community, or some other type of community—because they feel a sense of kinship and belonging. Geographical proximity and face-to-face interaction help community members maintain contact and develop institutions that facilitate the growth of communities, but proximity and intimacy are by no means strictly necessary for maintaining the sense of shared identity that predicates contemporary notions of community. Some speak, for example, of a national or even an international lesbian and gay community, connected by books and periodicals, national political institutions, and other signs of a cultural life that allow even isolated lesbians, gay men, and bisexuals to feel part of a much larger social grouping.*

*Lesbian and gay communities are in some respects similar to racial and ethnic communities in that both are based on a shared identity defined as "other" in relation to the majority. For both groups, community provides the terrain on which social identities are enacted. They provide shared meanings for behavior and a means for ongoing interactions of group members—whether face-to-face, long distance, or media-based (Esterberg, 1991). There are also differences between lesbian/gay and racial/ethnic communities (Epstein, 1992; Esterberg, 1994). As Herrell (1992) noted, "The difference between the gay and other American 'subcultural' communities is that, for gays and lesbians, the experience of community derives, not from parents and peers during childhood, but from adult participation in a network of institutions and from shared responses to the pervasive denial of social personality itself" (p. 248).*

*Lesbians, gay men, and bisexuals are racially and ethnically diverse. We are divided by class, gender, and all the social cleavages that characterize American life. Unlike some others, gay and lesbian communities attempt to fashion commonalities out of a much larger set of disparate experiences, and gay and lesbian communities attempt to socialize diverse adult members into a shared community life.*

*Mirroring lesbian and gay social life during the twentieth century, research on lesbian and gay communities has, by and large, been separated along gender lines. One body of research focuses on gay men's communities, often seen primarily in sexual and social terms, and the other on lesbian communities, often considered in conjunction with the feminist movement and in political terms. Despite the emphasis on separation, gay men, lesbians, and bisexuals have certainly participated in shared activities and institution building, and some participants and scholars alike refer to shared lesbian and gay men's communities, which sometimes include bisexuals.*

*I focus primarily on the two communities as distinct though certainly overlapping. In recent years, lesbian and gay communities have moved closer together. The AIDS epidemic has inexorably changed the nature of gay men's communities, and the "lesbian sex wars" of the early 1980s—in which lesbians vigorously debated the nature of lesbian sexuality and the place of woman-made pornography and other graphic representations of sexuality—have fundamentally shaken the myth of a uniform lesbian community. As gay men and lesbians alike have responded to the AIDS epidemic and the threats of the radical right in the 1980s and 1990s, they have increasingly participated in common pursuits. In the 1990s, at least for some areas of the United States, it may well make sense to begin speaking of a shared lesbian and gay community.*

*In the same way that lesbians and gay men have developed communities apart from one another and lesbian lives have often been ignored by gay men, communities and networks of ethnic-minority gay men and lesbians have, with few exceptions, been rendered largely invisible both by White lesbian and gay community participants and by researchers of lesbian and gay social life. Although there are a few outstanding works that detail the lives and social relationships of ethnic-minority gay men and lesbians, much more work needs to be done (see, for example, Anzaldúa, 1987; Beam, 1986; Garber, 1989; Hemphill, 1991; Lorde, 1982; Moraga & Anzaldúa, 1981). Similarly, although working-class men and women have long participated in an active bar culture, only recently have discussions of working-class gay and lesbian life been published (see especially Kennedy & Davis's [1993] lovingly researched oral history of Buffalo's lesbian bar community, as well as the writings of Nestle [1987, 1992]).*

## HISTORICAL PERSPECTIVES ON GAY AND LESBIAN COMMUNITIES

I didn't know any gay people when I moved here [in 1945]. As a matter of fact, I didn't even know the word *lesbian*. I knew how I felt, but I didn't know how to go about finding someone else who was like me, and there was just no way to find out in those days. . . . I don't know what brought up the subject, but one of the girls turned to me and said, "Are you gay?" and I said, "I try to be as happy as I can under the circumstances." They all laughed. Then they said, "No, no," and told me what it meant. (Lisa Ben, publisher of the first lesbian newsletter in the United States, in Marcus, 1992, pp. 6–7)

In the last few years, a number of remarkable books have chronicled the recent history of lesbian and gay communities in the United States and their movements for social change (Bérubé, 1990; D'Emilio, 1983b; Duberman, 1993; Faderman, 1991; Kennedy & Davis, 1993; Newton, 1993). These works provide extraordinary insights into the social organization of lesbians and gay men: the friendships they nurtured, the erotic relationships they celebrated, and the communities they created. As outlined by Bérubé (1990) and D'Emilio (1983a), contemporary gay and lesbian communities gained shape during and after World War II. Prior to the war, a few bars and public places existed where men found other men for erotic encounters and, much less frequently, where women found other women. The large-scale mobilization of men and women into the military and women's entrance into the wartime labor force enabled those with erotic desires for others of the same gender to find each other. At the same time, the mass movement of people into cities across the United States enabled a degree of anonymity and independent living hitherto unavailable, especially for women, many of whom had not previously lived outside of a family setting. In his book *Coming Out Under Fire*, Bérubé (1990) described the vibrant social life for gay men and women[3] that developed during World War II. Bars and other public gathering places, such as the Black Cat Cafe in San Francisco and the If Club in Los Angeles, appeared in large- and medium-sized cities to cater to gay men and, to a lesser extent, lesbians. At war's end, this gay life did not stop. Many of the returning service men and women stayed in the cities where they had begun to form networks of gay men and women. Further, many of those who were purged from the military with undesirable discharges felt they could not return to their rural homes. They migrated to the cities—such as San Francisco and New York— where they knew a gay and lesbian life existed.

Gay and lesbian life, which continued to develop after the war, flourished mainly in the bars. Public communities were slow to develop because of the stigma attached to homosexuality and the dangers of going to the bars, which were frequent targets of police raids and harassment. Openly gay men and women, many of whom were working class, were assaulted on the streets and in the bars (for an excellent fictional account of the rigors of 1950s and 1960s gay life, see Feinberg, 1993; see also Kennedy & Davis, 1993; Nestle, 1987). For working-class "butch" lesbians, who could not hide their sexual orientation, job security was certainly difficult to find. In the cold years of the McCarthy era, gays and lesbians and those suspected of homosexuality were purged in large numbers from government and military jobs. Even those willing or able to hide their sexual orientation feared losing a job; being evicted from a house or apartment; or losing the approbation of heterosexual friends, coworkers, and neighbors. These fears of public disclosure made participating in an open and public gay and lesbian community difficult. Despite these obstacles, communities grew in the bars and bathhouses; in the personal friendship networks; in a few resort communities, such as Cherry Grove on Fire Island (Newton, 1993); and in the nascent homophile movement's attempts to organize politically.

## The Homophile Movement

I don't think there was any thinking gay person who hadn't, at some time back in the 1920s or 1930s, said at a bar one night when feeling a little happy, "You know, we should have an organization. We should get together and have a gay organization." And usually you would be laughed out of the place. People would say, "You'll never get a bunch of faggots together, those dizzy queens. You'll never get them to do anything." (Chuck Rowland, cofounder, Mattachine Society, in Marcus, 1992, p. 32)

It takes courage to march around with a picket sign, yes, but try walking around with one sometime favoring civil rights for homosexuals. (Gene Damon, pseudonym of Barbara Grier, Daughters of Bilitis member and editor of The Ladder, in Morgan, 1970, p. 299)

D'Emilio (1992) argued that the history of lesbian and gay politics is intricately entwined with the history of lesbian and gay community building and social movement activity: "The structure of the community marks the terrain on which the movement can operate, and the actions of the movement are continually reshaping the life of the community" (p. 237). The 1969 Stonewall Rebellion, in which working-class gay men and lesbians fought back against police raids at the Stonewall Inn in New York City, is commonly viewed as marking the birth of the lesbian and gay liberation movement. Yet lesbian and gay historians have revealed a much longer history of organizing for social change by lesbians and gay men in the homophile movement of the 1950s and 1960s (Adam, 1987; D'Emilio, 1983b; Duberman, 1993; Marcus, 1992).[4] This earlier movement is also chronicled in the film *Before Stonewall* and in community oral history projects such as those in Boston and San Francisco.

The homophile movement, although small, signaled the beginning of continuous social movement activity on behalf of lesbians and gay men in the United States. Their goals were primarily integrationist; that is, rather than developing a self-conscious, organized "homophile" community, their aim was to integrate gay men and lesbians into the mainstream of heterosexual life. The original goals of the Daughters of Bilitis, the only homophile organization exclusively for women, were reprinted on the inside front cover of every issue of their publication, *The Ladder*. These included "education of the variant . . . to enable her to understand herself and make her adjustment to society in all its social, civic and economic implications." This was to be accomplished by, among other things, establishing a library "on the sex deviant theme" and "by advocating a mode of behavior and dress acceptable to society." Despite these accommodationist goals, a by-product of homophile organizing was to increase the visibility of lesbians and gay men and to make *more* salient, rather than less, lesbian and gay sexual identity (Esterberg, 1994).

Organizing by the homophile movement highlights several features of lesbian and gay community life. First, organizing was segregated by gender and class: The homophile movement was predominantly White and middle class. Although in their social and sexual activities gay men were more likely to mix with others of different classes and, in certain situations, different race and ethnic groups, women's bars were separated by class. In accordance with the rigid gender roles of the 1950s and early 1960s and fearful of losing their jobs, middle-class women tended not to socialize in bars. Daughters of Bilitis, in fact, originally formed as an alternative to lesbian bars; members were actively discouraged from participating in the butch-femme bar life. Instead, they were encouraged to dress "femininely" and to "adjust" to the feminine role. Other homophile organizations, such as the Mattachine Society and One, Inc., although technically open to women, were dominated by middle-class White men; after a short, more radical founding period, they too moved toward a similar integrationist stance. As a whole, homophile organizations did not encourage lesbians and gay men to develop strong and active autonomous communities. Instead, in the repressive years of the McCarthy era, homophile leaders encouraged participation in the broader heterosexual community, considering that a more secure route to acceptance. By their very efforts at building organizations, however, the homophile movement helped strengthen lesbian and gay life and paved the way for a more radical social movement in the 1970s, one which actively sought to create a distinctive lesbian and gay life.

# GAY LIBERATION

**Q:**  Do you think homosexuals are revolting?
**A:**  You bet your sweet ass we are. We're going to make a place for ourselves in the revolutionary movement. (Gay Liberation Front flyer, in Marotta, 1981, pp. 80–81)

The gay liberation movement was sparked by the increasing militancy of the homophile movement and the other radical movements for social change during the latter part of the 1960s. The precipitating event was the 1969 Stonewall Rebellion, in which working-class gay men and lesbians, including drag queens and butch lesbians, fought back when police raided the Stonewall Inn in New York City (Duberman, 1993).

Gay liberation, along with the resurgence of feminism in the 1970s, brought radical changes to gay, lesbian, and bisexual life. Gay men saw the birth of a highly commercialized sexual culture, and women saw the emergence of a "lesbian nation." The term "clone culture" has been used by some participants and observers to describe urban gay men's communities in the 1970s (Levine, 1990). Many gay men in urban areas cultivated a homogeneous style, consisting of masculine attire, such as tight jeans and leather jackets, that emphasized gay male sexuality. Some used the term "clone" to refer to those who adopted the style and participated in the vibrant social and sexual scene of urban gay men. "Lesbian nation" refers to the title of a book by Johnston (1973). Many lesbians in the 1970s focused on building autonomous, separatist lesbian communities as a response to society's pervasive sexism and heterosexism.

The life that developed in the gay meccas of New York and San Francisco and in smaller lesbian communities, such as Amherst/Northampton, Massachusetts, and Madison, Wisconsin, was not replicated uniformly across the nation. Nonetheless, gay and lesbian culture and community spread from the centers in the forms of periodicals, such as *The Advocate, Gay Community News, Lavender Tide,* and *Lesbian Connection;* books published by small presses, including Daughters, Inc., and Alyson Publications; music by "women's" music performers such as Linda Tillery, Alix Dobkin, and Holly Near; and other cultural productions, including art shows and oral history projects.

Especially among feminist lesbians in the 1970s, culture and community building were explicit aims. In their attempts to build a "lesbian nation," where lesbian life could flourish free from heterosexist and sexist oppression, many chose to separate themselves from the sexism they found in working politically and socially with gay men. But in creating these communities, their aims to be truly inclusive often fell short when confronted with the very real and persistent differences of class, race, and ethnicity among women. At the same time that lesbians were creating an explicitly antimaterialist political and cultural life, many gay men were actively creating a distinctive sexual and social life. Men developed an extensive community network, centered in bars, bathhouses, and a highly commercialized sexual culture. Although many women and men did not feel at home in the segregated lesbian and gay subcultures growing up around them and wished to create a more integrated community, the two communities could not have been more distinct.

## GAY MEN'S COMMUNITIES

After work, we go to the gym, either the Y or the Bodycenter; then we stop by One Potato or Trilogy for dinner. On Friday nights, we cruise the Eagle and Spike. On Saturday nights, we go dancing at the Saint, and on Sunday nights, we go to the baths. (Retail clerk quoted in Levine, 1992, p. 76)

I have been a full-time fag for the past five years, I realized the other day. Everyone I know is gay, all my fantasies are gay, I am what Gus called those people we used to see in the discos, bars, baths, all the time—remember? . . . I am completely, hopelessly gay! (Fictional character in Holleran, 1978, p. 17)

In a recent anthology focusing on gay men's culture in America, Herdt and Boxer (1992) made a clear distinction between early gay men's culture (which they referred to as "homosexual"), rooted in a furtive bar life, and today's contrasting "gay" culture, anchored by more positive cultural images and shared community institutions such as gay pride parades. Herdt argued, "The secret world of the gay bar and covert social networks made homosexuality an individualized sort of puberty rite into a secret oppressed society. There was no manifest gay culture at the time. Today, the political power of the gay and lesbian community suggests that coming out is more of a collective initiation rite, a public coming-of-age status-adjustment transition into the adult gay community" (Herdt, 1992, p. 31). Since the 1960s, the gay men's community has grown dramatically.

Martin Levine noted in his study of the 1970s' West Village (New York) "clone culture" that the gay liberation movement of the 1970s fundamentally altered forms of gay men's social and sexual lives. Gay liberationists and activists worked to reduce police harassment of bars and other gay institutions; at the same time, they sought to decrease the stigma of gender deviance attached to gay men. As a result, urban gay neighborhoods thrived, complete with gay-owned bars, bathhouses, shops, bookstores, professional services, and a wide variety of political, recreational, and cultural organizations. As Levine (1992) explains:

Many early gay rights activists had participated in either countercultural, antiwar, or civil rights movements and were therefore prepared to advocate libertarian values and the destigmatization of homosexuality. For example, they championed an ethic sanctioning self-expression, especially in regard to experimentation with drugs and sex. (pp. 73–74)

Certainly, coming out into the flourishing gay social and community life during the height of the 1970s was dramatically different from coming out during the 1950s. Urban men's communities saw an increased emphasis on sexual freedom and self-expression, and the "clone culture" that developed in major cities in the 1970s transformed earlier stereotypes of gay men. Replacing the image of gay male effeminacy with a hypermasculine sensibility, "butch" presentational strategies highlighting men's erotic features and sexual availability were a major feature of clone culture. In the pre-AIDS 1970s, many urban gay men's social lives centered around cruising and tricking; a wide variety of businesses and social institutions catering to gay men's erotic desires prospered. For some, the essence of gay liberation and community of the 1970s was its exuberant celebration of male sexuality.

While a highly sexualized gay male subculture flourished, gay rights activists of the 1970s also expressed frustration with the apolitical stance of the "new gay man" and his emphasis on gay sociability. As D'Emilio wryly noted:

> Reformers fought for the right to be gay, free from harassment and punishment. Since the sexual subculture had been the location where gay men most acutely experienced both their gayness and their vulnerability, the fading police presence seemed incontrovertible evidence that they were free. As far as they could tell, gay liberation had succeeded. . . . Activist harangues about the persistence of job discrimination, about media invisibility, about the role of the churches and the military in excluding homosexuals from equal participation in American life seemed like the ravings of grim politicos who just didn't know how to have fun. (1992, p. 251)

Thus, while many men made the social rounds of parties, bars, bathhouses, and restaurants, creating a sexual subculture of liberation, others worked in overtly political venues for increased freedoms for lesbians and gay men.

## Lesbian Nation

Lesbianism is one road to freedom—freedom from oppression by men. (Martha Shelley, radical lesbian activist, in Morgan, 1970, p. 306)

Out of her activism in the feminist movement, more often than not, a new kind of lesbian has emerged, a lesbian who calls herself a lesbian activist or a radical lesbian and has learned most recently the enormous power and freedom of the open assertion of who and what one is. (Abbot & Love, 1971, p. 606)

If gay men experienced their subordination primarily in terms of their sexual lives, lesbians experienced gender as at least as important in limiting their opportunities for self-determination. And if gay men set out to create communities based on sexual ties, lesbians set out to create communities based not on sex but on relationships. Although lesbians certainly participated with gay men in activist organizations and the establishment of urban gay and lesbian communities, they

worked in far greater numbers to create an autonomous lesbian-feminist move‑
ment and separate lesbian communities and cultures. Lesbian feminists were in‑
fluenced by radical critiques of gender and women's position in a male-dominated
society. Rather than understanding their oppression as rooted solely in a denial
or repression of their lesbian sexuality, lesbian feminists sought to understand
women's oppression in broader terms, rooted in the institutions of family, church,
and state. In solidarity with other women, some lesbian feminists sought to redefine lesbianism in primarily homosocial ways: as women bonding with other
women. "Feminism is the theory, lesbianism is the practice" was the slogan championed by some. Radicalesbians, for example, in a much-cited position paper,
asked: "What is a lesbian?" And they responded, "A lesbian is the rage of all women
condensed to the point of explosion. She is the woman who, often beginning at
an extremely early age, acts in accordance with her inner compulsion to be a
more complete and freer human being than her society . . . cares to allow her"
(Radicalesbians, 1970/1988, p. 17). Similarly, in a controversial essay, the poet
Adrienne Rich outlined the notion of a lesbian continuum; defined thus, lesbianism included a range of "woman-identified experience; not simply the fact
that a woman has had or consciously desired genital sexual experience with another woman" (1980/1983, p. 192). If some gay men in the 1970s were furiously
attempting to define themselves and their communities by their sexual experiences with other men, some lesbians were just as furiously attempting to de-sex
lesbian identity and community (Snitow, Stansell, & Thompson, 1983).

Lesbian feminism was never the predominant form of lesbian self-definition
(Whisman, 1991). Many women felt an allegiance to working with their gay
brothers, and others felt little connection with the primarily White and middle-
class feminist movement. Yet lesbian feminism was enormously influential in
the creation of a vibrant and visible lesbian culture and community. Throughout
the 1970s, lesbians created "women's" (lesbian) music festivals, feminist books
and bookstores, coffeehouses, support groups, and a wide variety of cultural, political, and social organizations and institutions. (For descriptions of lesbian-
feminist communities, see Faderman, 1991, chapter 9; Krieger, 1983; Wolf,
1979.) Yet lesbian-feminist communities were often narrow and intolerant of
those who diverged from community ideals, including women who had been
openly lesbian in the pre-Stonewall butch-femme bar life. Nestle (1987) recalled:

> Many of us were active in political change struggles, fed by the energy of our hidden butch-femme
> lives, which even our most liberal-left friends could not tolerate. Articulated feminism added another
> layer of analysis and understanding, a profound one, one that felt so good and made such wonder-
> ful allies that for me it was a gateway to another world—until I realized I was saying *radical femi-
> nist* when I could not say *Lesbian*. (p. 107)

Zita (1981) called the attempt to define just who "belonged" in lesbian community as the Lesbian Olympics, "where competing lesbians are ranked, categorized, accepted, and rejected" (p. 173; see also Krieger, 1983; Whisman, 1993). Yet
despite the problems involved, lesbian communities also served as the basis for
an autonomous lesbian life.

# FROM LESBIAN NATION TO LESBIAN SEX/
# FROM CLONE CULTURE TO QUEER NATION

"We're here; we're queer. Get used to it." (Queer Nation slogan)

In the 1970s, gay men and lesbians alike moved away from creating a social movement and toward creating a community and culture. Yet the cultures they created could not have been more distinct, and attempts at mixed lesbian and gay organizations were fraught with tension. The 1980s brought major changes to lesbian and gay men's communities, changes that, perhaps, moved their experiences closer to one another and may have served to re-ground lesbian and gay identity and community within a combined social movement for change.

A more openly sexual lesbian scene, with its own woman-made pornography, go-go bars, and frankly sexual style, more akin to gay men's culture than to lesbian feminism, developed in some large urban centers in the 1980s. The lesbian "sex wars" generated by the diverging styles made apparent the deep disagreements about the nature of lesbian sexuality, the place of fantasy and graphic representations of women's sexuality, and the ambiguous place of bisexual women within the "lesbian nation." Lesbian community, long painted in rosy hues by its participants, could no longer be seen as a place of harmony, where women's perceived essential sameness *as women* could override all disagreements and conflicts based on difference. As butches and femmes, working-class women and ethnic-minority women demanded a widening of the boundaries of the lesbian nation, lesbian community life changed dramatically. Lesbian feminism had been decentered, as Stein (among others) argued (1992). As a result, lesbian culture in the 1990s is far more diverse than that imagined in the 1970s.

At the same time, the AIDS epidemic has shaped gay men's sexual and social lives in ways previously unimaginable. With the spread of AIDS and HIV throughout gay men's communities, gay men, along with lesbians and bisexuals, have mobilized to stop the spread of the epidemic, to provide services to their ill and dying brothers (and sisters, though women, especially lesbians, with AIDS have yet to be fully recognized), and to change an intransigent political and medical system that treats gay men's lives as hardly worth saving. The AIDS epidemic challenged the complacency of many formerly apolitical gay men; their beliefs that full societal acceptance was at hand were badly shaken by the treatment they received by the medical and political establishment. As gay men organized to stop the spread of AIDS and to care for their ill friends and lovers, the social institutions that kept alive a vigorous sexual social life changed. Bathhouses and back rooms of bars were shut down, and social cliques and networks were torn apart by death and illness. At the same time, the number of AIDS and HIV political-action and service-providing groups grew rapidly. The diffusion of information about safer sex practices and ways to decrease transmission of HIV led to an increased emphasis on relationships, love, and dating. At the same time that some lesbians have moved closer to the frank and expressive sexuality of gay men, gay men have moved closer to the relationship ideals expressed by many lesbians. As

Gorman expressed it, "The [gay men's] community finds itself no longer in adolescence but rather increasingly taking on the roles and tasks of adulthood. This transformation is reflected politically, economically, demographically, sociologically, culturally, and with respect to gender issues" (1992, p. 103).

Perhaps it is this shift toward a middle ground by lesbians and gay men, or the resurgence of a radical right threatening the political gains made in the 1970s and early 1980s, that has sparked the beginnings of joint social-movement activity and a tentative shared community of lesbians and gay men. Many younger lesbians are more likely to embrace a queer identity in ACT UP and Queer Nation than a feminist lesbian identity. Although all is not well in those groups and some feminists (young and old) have decried their sexism, Queer Nation and ACT UP actively seek to create a combined queer community (Elliott, 1992; Whisman, 1991; see also Maggenti, 1993). Whether the future holds increased mixed-gender organizing and community building remains to be seen. At the same time, groups such as the National Latino/a Lesbian and Gay Organization, the National Coalition for Black Lesbians and Gays, and Asian Pacifica Lesbian Network have provided autonomous organizations for ethnic/sexual minorities and have highlighted the race and class divisions within lesbian and gay communities. Whether, and how, their challenges to broaden the leadership and visions of gay communities to include ethnic minorities will be met, or whether ethnic communities will remain largely autonomous, remains to be seen.

## AN EMERGING BISEXUAL COMMUNITY

Before I became sexual with women, I was worried about calling myself bisexual. Now I'm worried because it seems so imprecise. I deal with it by saying "lesbian-identified bisexual" (or, when I'm feeling perverse, "faggot-identified lesbian"), but then almost no one understands. (Queen, 1991, p. 17)

When I think of being bisexual, I am reminded of my Jewish ancestors who, kicked out of different countries, tried to find a place to call home. I, too, have wandered, in the gay and straight worlds. (Gorlin, 1991, p. 252)

Bisexual people have largely been invisible—and, when visible, maligned—within lesbian and gay communities. Stereotyped as fence-sitters or undecided, as people in transition to a "true" lesbian or gay identity, or as traitors, bisexuals have been made to feel less than welcome in lesbian and gay communities. Bisexuality calls into question the very dualistic categories we use to define sexuality; by its nature, bisexuality highlights the fluidity of sexual experience and the continuous nature of sexuality. Many have argued that underneath the categories, everyone (or almost everyone) is essentially bisexual; in fact, one of the goals of the early gay liberationists was to unleash "the homosexual in everyone" and smash rigid sexual categories. This goal has long been abandoned, however, and holding a proud and open bisexual identity is a relatively recent phenomenon (see Hutchins & Kaahumanu, 1991, and Weise, 1992, for recent anthologies).

It is only since the 1980s that bisexual groups have become active in major cities. Even in the early 1990s, many bisexuals still feel isolated. Yet bisexuals' attempts to assert an autonomous identity and to openly express attractions to both genders have been met with resistance in gay and, especially, lesbian communities. Rust (1992) recently noted that many lesbians' experience is essentially similar to the experience of bisexual women; lesbians have often had significant sexual or affectional relationships with men, but they prefer to label themselves lesbian. Lesbian-feminist singer Holly Near is one of the most famous lesbians to speak openly about her relationships with men, and she has been criticized both by lesbians, for relating to men, and by bisexuals, for not claiming a bisexual identity. Lesbian communities, Rust argued, are threatened by the emergence of a vigorous bisexual women's contingent because lesbians and bisexual women may be staking a claim to the very same territory.

Despite the arguments about bisexuality within lesbian and gay communities, many bisexual men and women have worked hard to help build the very communities from which they feel excluded. Some continue to work within lesbian and gay communities, pushing the boundaries to include an open bisexual presence. Others feel included within Queer Nation and its in-your-face politics and inclusion of all sexual minorities. Still others work to create a distinct bisexual movement and bisexual community. Where this movement will go—whether autonomous bisexual communities will flourish, or whether bisexual men and women will continue to push lesbian, gay, and heterosexual communities to expand their boundaries—remains to be seen.

## THE FUTURE OF COMMUNITY

What is the future of lesbian, gay, and bisexual community? And why does it *matter?* Why bother with creating communities? Why stress that which is different—sexual identity—when that is what serves to exclude lesbians, gay men, and bisexuals from heterosexual society? Despite the gains of the homophile movement of the 1950s and 1960s and the lesbian and gay movements of the 1970s and 1980s, lesbians, gay men, and bisexuals still have a long way to go in attaining full acceptance in a heterosexist society. The indifferent response by the American public to the AIDS epidemic galvanized many formerly apolitical gay men into action (see Shilts, 1987, for a chronicle of the early years of the AIDS epidemic). Recent attacks by the radical right, including attempts to pass state constitutional amendments that would legalize discrimination against lesbians, gay men, and bisexuals, have provided a similar impetus to coordinated activism in the 1990s.[5]

Although communities clearly provide a basis for social movement activity, they also serve other purposes. In fact, the vast majority of lesbians, gays, and bisexuals do not participate in the political aspects of community life. From a developmental perspective, communities provide a way to socialize gay, lesbian, and bisexual youth—and those who come to claim these identities in later life—into a larger community. As Herdt described in his study of a Chicago "coming out" group for adolescents, coming out is a rite of passage—"a category change of the most profound sort in self and other representations and relationships" (1992, p. 59). Communities offer a set of shared meanings for interpreting the experiences of those who desire same-sex lovers and partners and a mechanism for valuing those desires instead of denigrating them. Lesbian, gay, and bisexual communities can provide a set of positive, prideful images that offset heterosexist images of lesbians, gay men, and bisexual people as perverse and perverted, sick and sinful. For young people who are just coming into their sexual identities, for those who are isolated, communities can furnish a lifeline.

Certainly, lesbian, gay, and bisexual communities have their share of problems —of exclusion, intolerance, sexism, racism, and classism. But communities can also provide a link to other lesbians, gay men, and bisexuals and a means to assert a vivid queer presence in the world. At their very best, communities offer a model of compassion, support, and commitment, as evidenced by the way in which the AIDS crisis has brought together gay men, bisexuals, and lesbians in caring for the dying, sick, and well in our communities. As our movements and our communities shift and grow in response to changing social and historical circumstances, they help shape what it means to be a lesbian, a gay man, or a bisexual person.

## ▼ ENDNOTES ▼

1. I'm grateful to Sue Bergmeier, Jeff Longhofer, and Jerry Floersch for listening to me grumble and for carefully reading the manuscript, and to Ritch Savin-Williams and Ken Cohen for their attentive editing.

2. In the sections that follow, I speak primarily of a lesbian and gay community and *not* a bisexual community because until very recently, bisexuals have not organized around a bisexual identity (as opposed to a lesbian, gay, or heterosexual identity) or created what we might call bisexual communities. Although gay men's communities may be slightly more welcoming of bisexuals, lesbian communities have not been entirely receptive to bisexual women (see Hutchins & Kaahumanu, 1991; Weise, 1992). A more complete discussion of bisexual community is provided below.

3. In keeping with the terms commonly used by the women themselves during the World War II era, I use the phrases "gay women" and "gay community" in discussions of early lesbian and gay community life.

4. In the 1950s, the term "homophile" was sometimes used as a euphemism for "homosexual" because it stressed the emotional aspects of attraction to others of the same gender. Homophile movement leaders eventually adopted the term for the same reason.

5. These amendments attempt to overturn existing municipal legislation that prohibits discrimination on the basis of sexual orientation; the amendments also seek to prohibit future attempts to pass such protections. Colorado and Oregon faced such initiatives in 1992; approximately eight states faced them in 1994. Although later declared unconstitutional by a Colorado court, Amendment 2 was passed by a majority of Colorado voters.

# ▼ References ▼

Abbott, S., & Love, B. (1971). Is women's liberation a lesbian plot? In V. Gornick & B. K. Moran (Eds.), *Woman in sexist society: Studies in power and powerlessness* (pp. 601–621). New York: Basic Books.

Adam, B. (1987). *The rise of a gay and lesbian movement.* Boston: Twayne.

Anzaldúa, G. (1987). *La frontera/borderlands.* San Francisco: Spinster/Aunt Lute Press.

Beam, J. (1986). *In the life.* Boston: Alyson.

Bérubé, A. (1990). *Coming out under fire: The history of gay men and women in World War Two.* New York: Free Press.

D'Emilio, J. (1983a). Capitalism and gay identity. In A. Snitow, C. Stansell, & S. Thompson (Eds.), *Powers of desire: The politics of sexuality* (pp. 100–113). New York: Monthly Review Press.

D'Emilio, J. (1983b). *Sexual politics, sexual communities: The making of a homosexual minority in the United States, 1940–1970.* Chicago: University of Chicago Press.

D'Emilio, J. (1992). *Making trouble: Essays on gay history, politics, and the university.* New York: Routledge.

Di Leonardo, M. (1984). *The varieties of ethnic experience: Kinship, class, and gender among California Italian-Americans.* Ithaca, NY: Cornell University Press.

Duberman, M. (1993). *Stonewall.* New York: Dutton.

Elliott, B. (1992). Holly Near and yet so far. In E. R. Weise (Ed.), *Closer to home: Bisexuality and feminism* (pp. 233–254). Seattle: The Seal Press.

Epstein, S. (1992). Gay politics, ethnic identity: The limits of social constructionism. In E. Stein (Ed.), *Forms of desire: Sexual orientation and the social constructionist controversy* (pp. 239–293). New York: Routledge.

Esterberg, K. (1991). *Salience and solidarity: Identity, correctness, and conformity in a lesbian community.* Unpublished doctoral dissertation, Cornell University, Ithaca, NY.

Esterberg, K. (1994). From accommodation to liberation: A social movement analysis of lesbians in the homophile movement. *Gender and Society 8,* 424–443.

Faderman, L. (1991). *Odd girls and twilight lovers: A history of lesbian life in twentieth century America.* New York: Columbia.

Feinberg, L. (1993). *Stone butch blues.* Ithaca, NY: Firebrand Books.

Garber, E. (1989). A spectacle in color: The lesbian and gay subculture of jazz age Harlem. In M. Duberman, M. Vicinus, & G. Chauncey (Eds.), *Hidden from history: Reclaiming the gay and lesbian past* (pp. 318–331). New York: NAL Books.

Gorlin, R. (1991). The voice of a wandering Jewish bisexual. In L. Hutchins & L. Kaahumanu (Eds.), *Bi any other name: Bisexual people speak out* (pp. 252–253). Boston: Alyson.

Gorman, E. M. (1992). The pursuit of the wish: An anthropological perspective on gay male subculture in Los Angeles. In G. Herdt (Ed.), *Gay culture in America: Essays from the field* (pp. 87–106). Boston: Beacon Press.

Hemphill, E. (1991). *Brother to brother: New writings by black gay men.* Boston: Alyson.

Herdt, G. (1992). "Coming out" as a rite of passage: A Chicago study. In G. Herdt (Ed.), *Gay culture in America: Essays from the field* (pp. 29–67). Boston: Beacon Press.

Herdt, G., & Boxer, A. (1992). Introduction: Culture, history, and life course of gay men. In G. Herdt (Ed.), *Gay culture in America: Essays from the field* (pp. 1–28 ). Boston: Beacon Press.

Herrell, R. K. (1992). The symbolic strategies of Chicago's gay and lesbian pride day parade. In G. Herdt (Ed.), *Gay culture in America: Essays from the field* (pp. 225–252). Boston: Beacon Press.

Holleran, A. (1978). *Dancer from the dance.* New York: New American Library.

Hutchins, L., & Kaahumanu, L. (1991). *Bi any other name: Bisexual people speak out.* Boston: Alyson.

Johnston, J. (1973). *Lesbian nation.* New York: Touchstone.

Kennedy, E. L., & Davis, M. (1993). *Boots of leather, slippers of gold: The history of a lesbian community.* New York: Routledge.

Krieger, S. (1983). *The mirror dance: Identity in a women's community.* Philadelphia: Temple University Press.

Levine, M. (1992). The life and death of gay clones. In G. Herdt (Ed.), *Gay culture in America: Essays from the field* (pp. 68–86). Boston: Beacon Press.

Lorde, A. (1982). *Zami: A new spelling of my name.* Trumansburg, NY: Crossing Press.

Maggenti, M. (1993). Wandering through herland. In A. Stein (Ed.), *Sisters, sexperts, queers: Beyond the lesbian nation,* (pp. 245–255). New York: Penguin.

Marcus, E. (1992). *Making history: The struggle for gay and lesbian equal rights 1945–1990.* New York: HarperCollins.

Marotta, T. (1981). *The politics of homosexuality.* Boston: Houghton Mifflin.

Moraga, C., & Anzaldúa, G. (1981). *This bridge called my back: Writings by radical women of color.* Watertown, MA: Persephone Press.

Morgan, R. (1970). *Sisterhood is powerful: An anthology of writings from the women's liberation movement.* New York: Vintage.

Nestle, J. (1987). *A restricted country.* Ithaca, NY: Firebrand Books.

Nestle, J. (1992). *The persistent desire: A femme-butch reader.* Boston: Alyson.

Newton, E. (1993). *Cherry Grove, Fire Island.* Boston: Beacon Press.

Queen, C. (1991). The queer in me. In L. Hutchins & L. Kaahumanu (Eds.), *Bi any other name: Bisexual people speak out* (pp. 17–21). Boston: Alyson.

Radicalesbians. (1970/1988). The woman identified woman. In S. L. Hoagland & J. Penelope (Eds.), *For lesbians only: A separatist anthology* (pp. 17–22). London: Onlywomen Press.

Rich, A. (1980/1983). Compulsory heterosexuality and lesbian existence. In A. Snitow, C. Stansell, & S. Thompson (Eds.), *Powers of desire: The politics of sexuality* (pp. 177–205). New York: Monthly Review Press.

Rust, P. (1992). The politics of sexual identity: Sexual attraction and behavior among lesbian and bisexual women. *Social Problems, 39,* 366–387.

Shilts, R. (1987). *And the band played on.* New York: St. Martin's Press.

Snitow, A., Stansell, C., & Thompson, S. (1983). *Powers of desire: The politics of sexuality.* New York: Monthly Review Press.

Stein, A. (1992). Sisters and queers: The decentering of lesbian feminism. *Socialist Review, 22,* 33–55.

Weise, E. R. (1992). *Closer to home: Bisexuality and feminism.* Seattle: Seal Press.

Whisman, V. (1991). *Different from whom? Competing definitions of lesbianism.* Paper presented at the 1991 annual meeting of the American Sociological Association, Cleveland, Ohio.

Whisman, V. (1993). Identity crises: Who is a lesbian, anyway? In A. Stein (Ed.), *Sisters, sexperts, queers: Beyond the lesbian nation* (pp. 47–60). New York: Penguin.

Wolf, D. G. (1979). *The lesbian community.* Berkeley: University of California Press.

Zita, J. (1981). Historical amnesia and the lesbian continuum. *Signs, 7,* 172–187.

# Chapter 17

▼

# DOUBLE MINORITIES: LATINO, BLACK, AND ASIAN MEN WHO HAVE SEX WITH MEN

## Martin F. Manalansan IV

*This chapter delineates cultural and social issues in analyzing same-sex phenomena among Latino, Black, and Asian men. The expression "men who have sex with men" is used to demarcate the inadequacy of current popular terms such as "homosexual," "gay," and "bisexual" when referring to ethnic-minority groups. Even the phrase, men who have sex with men, is unable to capture the complex ways in which different cultures provide meanings and structures for such phenomena.*

*The term "double minority" suggests the ways in which class, education, cultural background, and racial/ethnic affiliation are inflected in the means by which men who have sex with men are culturally constructed and understood across different groups. Invisibility and powerlessness often permeate the lives of those in Latino, Black, and Asian communities. Because of the stigma and threat of violence attached to same-sex encounters and their practitioners, men who have sex with men are multiply marginalized. Despite the appellation "double minorities," the term does not adequately capture the various hierarchies and oppression that these men must face within their ethnic/racial group and in mainstream society.*

*The importance of emphasizing these aspects of sexual identity among ethnic communities is most apparent in the AIDS pandemic. Even when there is tacit agreement among behavioral scientists, social service providers, and educators about the inadequacy of sexual identifiers such as "gay" or "bisexual" in understanding the behavior of men who have sex with men, research, prevention, and education activities still adhere to a White mainstream model. For example, in a recent HIV-prevention study (U.S. Conference of Mayors, 1994) of Native American, Asian, Black, and Latino gay and bisexual men in five cities, there was an initial recognition that finding a representative sample of men would be problematic. Although the report noted the existence of men from these communities who did not identify as either gay or bisexual but who nonetheless had sex with other men and though it reiterated the importance of the relationship between cultural and sexual practices, no attempt was made to contextualize the men's reported sexual identity with their cultural, economic, and political norms and practices. For each of the racial/ethnic groups in the five cities, the report erroneously assumed the existence of a viable gay and lesbian community and recruited only self-proclaimed gay- and bisexual-identified men. Thus, they may well have missed many of those who were at risk for HIV infection through same-sex encounters.*

*This chapter attempts to fill in gaps left by uncritical analyses of the social dynamics of sexual practices and identities. I argue that it is necessary to examine specific conditions that exist in each ethnic and national group without resorting to the monolithic and biased assumption of a universal "gay identity," which is perpetuated by both mainstream and gay communities. Sexual identity, as demonstrated below, is shaped by social, political, economic, and cultural realities, all of which must be considered. Therefore, a view sensitive to the diversity or plurality of experiences is vital in understanding the dynamics of men who have sex with men in Latino, Black, and Asian groups.*

*In the first section of this chapter, the meaning, provenance, and politics of three ethnic/racial categories—Latino, Black, and Asian—are examined. This section also provides a brief profile of the three groups in terms of ethnic composition, history, and demography. Next is an analysis of the ways in which men who have sex with men are portrayed and understood in the three communities. These sections also describe and analyze intragroup differences in attitudes and ideas about these men. The final section is a discussion of themes that emerged in the three groups of men who have sex with men.*

## DEFINING THE POPULATION: ISSUES OF DIVERSITY

### Latinos

Latinos are the fastest growing minority population in the United States. By 1990, they numbered over 20 million (U.S. Department of Commerce, 1993). The Latino population increased by 34% in the 1980s, three times the rate of Blacks and six times the rate of Whites (Singer et al., 1990). Projections indicate that by the year 2020, Latinos will be the largest minority group in the United States (Davis, Haub, & Willette, 1988).

Latinos live in every state of the union, but they cluster in certain states and metropolitan areas (Davis et al., 1988). Three states have significant Latino populations. California has the largest number, with 4.5 million Latino residents; Texas has nearly 3 million, and New York has 1.7 million Latino residents (Davis et al., 1988). Seventy-three percent of the 8.7 million Mexican Americans live in Texas and California, while 61% of the 2 million Puerto Ricans live in New York and New Jersey. Fifty-nine percent of the 803,000 Cubans reside in Florida (Davis et al., 1988). Other Latinos number 3 million and include Dominicans, Colombians, Argentineans, Ecuadoreans, and refugees from Nicaragua and El Salvador.

Social science scholars have long recognized that "Latino" is essentially a plurality of cultures and races. Despite linguistic commonality, each subgroup has its own unique cultural and historical experiences. The Latino/Hispanic ethnic category, essentially an American bureaucratic creation, is contextual. It is used more in formal situations, such as answering a census questionnaire, than in informal contacts. Most Latinos, given the choice, would rather be identified according to their nationality (Moore & Pachon, 1985, p. 11). The Latino label is also part of a political consciousness, expressing the solidarity of different subgroups united in the face of American society. For example, agencies or organizations dedicated to the promotion of civil rights, provision of services, or the academic study of all subgroups are appropriately named Latino or Hispanic (e.g., Hispanic Studies Program).

This label or name has profound implications for the study of Latino communities. The undifferentiated grouping of Latinos for study has caused considerable debate, not only among the different subgroups, but among scholarly fields such as public health (Hayes-Bautista & Chapa, 1987; Trevino, 1987; Yankauer, 1987). This debate concerns not only the issue of naming ethnic categories (Latino versus Hispanic), but the implications of such names in epidemiological terms, such as counting HIV cases.

There is a tendency in the scientific literature, more specifically in works on AIDS and AIDS/HIV prevention, to gloss intragroup differences within the Latino community. There are discussions of the Latino family, the Latino church, and Latino values, as if they exist in a monolithic fashion. While there are indeed patterns of social behavior and interactions that cut across various subgroups, the generalizability of any findings on Latinos is limited because of participant biases toward particular subgroups. The geographic area in which a study is conducted will include an overrepresentation of certain Latino groups and exclude others, thereby shaping the findings. For example, while the Northeast United States has a preponderance of Puerto Ricans, the West Coast Latino community is composed primarily of Chicanos/Mexicans. The relative inclusion of a given subgroup and choice of research locale present sociocultural parameters for the interpretation and significance of research results for all Latino communities.

In this report, the term "Latino" will be used for simplicity. Examples and studies from Central or Latin American societies are used to complete this review, due to the dearth of studies available on specific Latino groups, particularly regarding attitudes toward homosexuality. This does not mean that there is a direct correspondence between the experiences of the natives of these societies and the immigrants from these countries. Examples from various countries are used merely to bolster existing observations from studies on the Latino community. The general use of terms such as "Latino culture" and "Latino attitudes" should be viewed with caution, given the divergent experiences of various Latino groups.

There are glaring differences among Latino national groups. Most of these differences are based on each national group's U.S. immigration history and political status. For example, Mexican Americans or Chicanos, because of their geographic proximity and long contact with the U.S., are the largest Latino group and have the most established political organization among Latinos. Puerto Ricans are U.S. nationals, and Puerto Rico is a commonwealth of the U.S. Puerto Ricans are also highly mobile. In fact, there is a circular migration of Puerto Ricans between the East Coast and Puerto Rico. In response to changing economic conditions, waves of Puerto Rican migration oscillate between the two areas.

## Blacks

Blacks are currently the largest minority group in the U.S. In 1990, the Black population reached over 29 million (U.S. Department of Commerce, 1993). The concentration of Blacks is in the southern and northeastern states. Among urban areas, New York City has the largest Black population in the country with almost 2 million (Farley & Allen, 1989).

The history of the Black community in the United States is, apart from Native Americans, the longest of any minority group. This history is fraught with social strife, oppression, and violence stemming from racial hatred. Although this chapter does not purport to provide a recapitulation of historical developments in Black life, the discussion that follows reflects the conditions of racial inequality that exist in America.

While many people may equate Black identity with skin color, historical and current definitions revolve around the various social meanings attributed to "being Black." Black political consciousness is not only an awareness of physical differences but of social, political, economic, and cultural disenfranchisement. The need for Black people to coalesce against such adversities has led scholars and political activists to critically examine the notion of a monolithic community.

Unlike the majority of Latinos who have come to the U.S. within the last few decades and have maintained many of the cultural traditions of their homelands, Blacks have developed their cultural traditions in this country. However, recent immigrants from the Caribbean and Africa have introduced new cultural, political and economic elements to the community. This has created a new diversity in Black cultural life. Presently, there is an awareness of the differences between foreign-born Blacks and those born here.

Honey (1988) noted the necessity of recognizing cultural diversity in the Black community, particularly in the inner city, to properly respond to the AIDS epidemic. It is necessary to recognize that this diversity implies not only differences in countries of origin but also differences in cultural practices, educational attainment, economic status, racial consciousness, and most importantly, epidemiological profiles. A case in point is Haitians, who comprise a distinct category in AIDS epidemiological reports. In the New York City Department of

Health AIDS Surveillance Unit report (1990), Haitians who do not identify as homosexual or as intravenous drug users are usually categorized as "persons from countries where risks are unclear," and in Centers for Disease Control AIDS reports, they are categorized as "person(s) born in Pattern II country." They constitute a group that has not assimilated into the racial categorization and politics (see Woldemikael, 1989).

## Asians

Asians are a fast-growing minority group in the United States. According to the U.S. Department of Commerce report (1993), Asian/Pacific Islanders almost doubled in population from 3.5 million in 1980 to over 7 million in 1990. The largest national group is the Chinese with over 1.6 million residents followed by Filipinos (1.4 million) and the Japanese (850,000).

Asian, or officially "Asian/Pacific Islander," is a recent and problematic category term that attempts to capture the range of people who are descended from the Asian continent, such as East Asia (Japan, China, Korea, Taiwan, and Mongolia), South Asia (Bangladesh, India, Nepal, Sri Lanka, and Pakistan), and Southeast Asia (Indonesia, Singapore, Philippines, Vietnam, Cambodia, Thailand, and Malaysia). This category also includes Pacific Islanders, those coming from or descendants of people from Hawaii and the countries of Micronesia, Melanesia, and Polynesia. The term "Pacific Islander" has never been clearly articulated in the literature nor is it a notable feature in scholarly and political activities among Asian Americans. In fact, the term has been used by scholars and activists only as an administrative afterthought. If it is to have any meaning, however, Pacific Islander must be used either as a separate category apart from Asian American or as a highly regarded and visible component of political organizing, community building, and academic pursuits.

In this chapter, the discussion is limited to that which has been demarcated as Asian or Asian American. In doing so, I emphasize that, unlike Latinos who have the Spanish language and other cultural features such as Catholicism as common denominators, so-called Asians have disparate histories, cultures, and languages. Asian American panethnic identity—that is, an identity that spans national groupings—has a long and torturous history. Asian American identity has traditionally been viewed as the domain of East Asians such as Japanese and Chinese. Espiritu (1992) argued that during various times and situations there emerged a panethnic identity, intragroup cooperation, and collective action. At the same time, acts of dissent against this monolithic identity have been perpetrated by such groups as South Asians and Filipinos. As a result, social cleavages within so-called Asian American communities have occurred among national groups.

The immigration history of each Asian national group belies both their political, economic, and cultural status within the ethnic group. Chinese and Japanese immigrants who immigrated to the U.S. in the late nineteenth century established themselves earlier than did other national groups. Even with the arrival of Filipinos and South Asian Indians in the early part of the century, the Chinese and Japanese groups were more numerous and politically prominent.

After the 1965 Immigration Act, which permitted the reunification of immigrant families, and with the end of the Vietnam War, there was a large increase in the number of immigrants coming from Asian countries, particularly medical professionals and Indochinese refugees. Residential clustering has been influenced in part by immigration history. The West Coast has traditionally been a predominant area of residence for Asian immigrants; the East Coast outside of New York and Boston and the Midwest outside of Chicago have seen the rise of new enclaves, particularly among Hmong and Cambodian refugees. Such differences have in fact created glaring economic disparities among national groups. The "model minority" stereotype of Asians, which assumes that all Asians are economically successful and well assimilated, disintegrates in the face of the social and economic plight of such groups as Filipinos and Indochinese refugees.

## LATINO MEN WHO HAVE SEX WITH MEN

There has been little research on Latino male homosexuality and bisexuality in America. Most research on the topic has been spurred by the AIDS crisis and is characterized by a generalized and descriptive view of a so-called homogenous Latino culture. Other, more in-depth, and particularistic studies on same-sex and bisexual phenomena examine Central and Latin American societies. These research studies emphasize the heterogeneity of Latino attitudes and beliefs about homosexuality and bisexuality. In this section, both approaches to the study of same-sex and bisexual phenomena in the Latino community are presented.

Latino cultural attitudes toward sexuality in general are founded on the private and personal nature of sex and the hierarchy of gender, notably the phenomenon of *machismo* (Marin, in press; Singer et al., 1990). Machismo is a complex cultural phenomenon. It is primarily based on the belief that men exercise authority over women (Singer et al., 1990). This belief extends to the realm of sex in that it encourages men to be sexually active and make numerous conquests. The mark of the "macho" man is his insatiable sexual appetite. This folk belief of the man as a sexual machine is important for understanding the ways in which Latinos categorize homoerotic phenomena.

Folk models of homosexuality in Central and Latin America distinguish two categories, *activo* and *pasivo* (Murray, 1987). This dichotomy is used for grouping or categorizing Latino men who have sex with other men according to the position assumed in same-sex anal intercourse. *Activos* are the inserters, the ones who penetrate, while the *pasivos* are the insertees. The active partner is considered masculine and heterosexual, and the passive partner is considered effeminate and homosexual. These concepts are very simplistic, even with the addition of the category *moderno,* or *internacional.* The *moderno/internacional* is a man who assumes either position depending on the situation. In Mexican sexual taxonomy, this category is viewed as anomalous and "foreign," "not Mexican" (Taylor, 1986). Even with this triad, these folk categories fail to adequately address the nature of homoerotic phenomena in Latino societies.

Linguistically, these folk models reflect the stigma associated with homosexuality—there is no positive or self-validating word for one who identifies himself as homosexual or "gay." In fact, self-identification as homosexual or gay is nothing short of social suicide in many Latin and Central American countries. It also means that self-identification, if it happens at all, may be based on that which constitutes being *maricón* or *pato,* that is, being effeminate and assuming the passive position in anal intercourse (see Almaguer, 1991; Alonso & Koreck, 1989; Lancaster, 1988).

Caballo-Dieguez (1990) suggested that Latino cultures associate homosexuality with effeminacy. Because Latino cultural constructions of gender give primacy to the male and all that is "masculine," the classic Latino stereotype of the homosexual is problematic for gay men because it impels the conceptualization of same-sex phenomena within a narrow band. Thus, given the *activo/pasivo* dichotomy and the machismo phenomenon, identity and practice in Latino same-sex encounters become entangled in a web of stigma, denial, and dominance.

Many Latinos consider gay identity a part of the White gay political movement rather than a lifestyle or sexual orientation (Morales, 1990). Latinos more easily see themselves as indulging in bisexual practices (not identity) than homosexual or gay ones. Amaro (1990) reported that of 284 Latino males surveyed in the Northeast who self-identified as gay, 28% reported having unsafe sex with a woman the previous year. This number did not reflect those who had safe sex with a woman. These data provide a glimpse of the problem of understanding bisexual and same-sex phenomena in the Latino community, as well as pointing to the importance of educating Latino gay men about safer heterosexual sex.

Bisexual practices in Latino culture are in part extensions of heterosexual machismo and in part closeted homosexuality. Singer et al. (1990) suggested that there is a greater preponderance of bisexual practices in Latino culture than in White culture. Carrier's (1985) unstructured interview study of 53 men in Guadalajara, Mexico, reported that two thirds disclosed having both heterosexual and same-sex encounters. Carrier noted that in Mexican bisexual practices there was no stigmatization of the active inserter role; those who played this role were considered heterosexual.

De la Vega (1990) established an informal typology of bisexual behavioral patterns in Latino cultures. First, there is "the closeted, self-identified homosexual Latino [who] is homosexual in his self-identity but bisexual in his behavior" (p. 49). Family and social concerns may prevent him from adopting an effeminate public persona. Second, there is the "closeted latent-homosexual Latino [who] may define himself as heterosexual but [who] is haunted by his own attraction to men which humiliates and angers him" (p. 49). He is a "sporadic bisexual," who identifies as heterosexual and denies a gay or bisexual identity, although he may be the passive partner in his same-sex encounters. Last, there is "the 'super-macho' heterosexual Latino [who] allows himself to have sexual intercourse with homosexuals, because he does not really consider them to be real males;" he considers them as "pseudo-females" (p. 50).

This structure of bisexual practices creates a sociosexual arena in which identities are not always congruent with behavior. Male heterosexuals and avowed and closeted gay men can have sex with each other and still be accommodated within Latino sexual ideology. Being married or courting a member of the opposite sex as well as living by cultural norms that value machismo enables these men to obscure the discrepancy between their self-identities and their sexual practices.

The stigma of homosexuality in Latino cultures is not a simple social anathema but a compendium of ambiguous, often conflicting views and attitudes. Bonilla and Porter (1990) compared attitudes of Latinos, Blacks, and Whites toward homosexuality. Results suggested that Latinos were the same as Whites and were less conservative than Blacks in their views about the morality of homosexuality. Similar to Whites, the majority of Latinos believed that being gay was morally tolerable. However, Latinos were the most conservative among the three groups regarding granting civil rights to gay people. Bonilla and Porter suggested that there is no significant disparity among Latino subgroups in their attitudes toward homosexuality.

Gayness and bisexuality must be viewed as social constructs, not universal categories. The implications of this for AIDS and HIV research, particularly prevention education in Latino communities, are wide-ranging. First, the categories gay and bisexual are not culturally appropriate; many Latino men do not use these to identify themselves. Therefore, statistics on Latino gay and bisexual men should be considered tentative (Alonso & Koreck, 1989). Second, the use of such categories in the AIDS-prevention literature excludes a significant number of Latino men who have sex with other men but who do not self-identify as either gay or bisexual. Furthermore, because they do not consider themselves gay, Latino men who assume the *activo* or penetrator role in same-sex anal sex may view their part as safe (Rogers & Williams, 1987). Latino men who do not identify as either gay or bisexual may not consider themselves at risk.

Studies among recent Latino immigrants suggest that while Western jargon such as "gay" is slowly being adopted, folk models of *pasivo/activo* still prevail. These folk models inform and shape practices, attitudes, and beliefs. This means that HIV educators should not impose their preconceived social categories of sexual orientation on Latino men with the expectation that their meaning will be shared or recognized. Educators must also be prepared to use native categories if they are to be effective in the treatment of risky behavior and practices.

The categories gay and bisexual are considered to be part of the White (gay) community. Latinos who self-identify as gay or bisexual must contend with a largely White-dominated gay subculture and the prejudices harbored toward Latino people. As in the larger society, gay/bisexual self-identified Latino men also face discrimination and prejudice harbored against people who adopt a gay identity. Within their culture, they may have to contend with cultural beliefs that associate homosexuality with effeminacy. Thus, self-identified gay Latino men encounter dual discrimination as Latinos and gay men.

Alfredo Villanueva-Collado (1989), a Puerto Rican poet, reflected on the unique dilemma faced by Latino gay and bisexual men who immigrate to America:

> Now, I submit to you there is widespread cultural resistance to any group that does not meld perfectly with WASPS. The one term I have never discussed is "anglo-american." They do not have to wear a discursive identification tag. They constitute the racial, national, cultural norms; and latinos, hispanics, spiks, neoricans, chicanos, or whatever we are called, are words designed to remind us of this fact. As a group, we are the Other—needed to preserve the great myth of an open pluralistic society. To immigrate means to accept this myth, to internalize it, and to impose it on others, exchanging one more crucial identity: that of the oppressed for that of the oppressor. (pp. 38–39)

Villanueva-Collado placed this struggle within the unique context of gay/ bisexual Latino men who face the seemingly pluralist world of the American gay community. He discussed the issue of racism within this community:

> One of the fascinating effects immigration has had on Spanish Americans has to do with race and gender: Within my own gay community, mixed couples usually have a dominant anglo and a submissive hispanic. I miss the voices of women who have married anglos; I personally know of several cases where the experience echoes that of Hispanic gays. (p. 42)

He encapsulated the core gay/bisexual Latino experience by arguing that among Latino men who have sex with men, the issue is not only of sexual preference but a struggle among the practices, norms, and ideals of two cultures, one dominant and the other subordinate. The problems of power and powerlessness, assimilation, and cultural resistance that all Latino immigrants face in American society are echoed and magnified in the experiences of gay/bisexual Latino men.

## BLACK MEN WHO HAVE SEX WITH MEN

Social science literature on Black male homosexuality and bisexuality lacks intensive analytical and descriptive accounts. The literature consists of brief descriptions of the dynamics inherent in being Black and gay and are usually experiential or phenomenological in character. However, there is a rich collection of Black gay poetry and fiction from which this chapter makes systematic yet limited extrapolations. Interpretations are made of materials that support or reinforce ideas presented in other more extensive social studies of the Black community.

Black gay men have a long-documented history in America. As early as 1646, Dutch historical manuscripts reported the existence of same-sex practices among Black men. These records revealed that these men were oppressed and punished by Dutch colonials (Katz, 1976). Later records indicated a thriving Black gay community on the East Coast, with most accounts coming from prison and psy-chiatric annals. One particular account, dated 1893, reported an "annual con-vocation of negro men called the drag dance" taking place in either Washington D.C. or New York City, in which cross-dressing and same-sex sexual contact ap-parently occurred (Katz, 1976, p. 43).

In the 1920s, cultural activities among networks of Black gay men flour-ished. With Harlem as their mecca, groups of gay men created cultural forms that reflected a period of tolerance of homosexuality within the Black commu-nity. The blues, an example of these forms, was distinctly Afro-American and re-flected tolerant attitudes toward gay men and lesbians in such songs as "Sissy Blues" and "Freakish Blues" (Garber, 1989). Private gatherings such as rent par-ties and buffet flats provided dancing, liquor, jazz music, and, most importantly, encouraged same-sex patronage. Public gatherings in places called speakeasies encouraged same-sex cruising. The most spectacular of these public gatherings were the Harlem costume balls, which Langston Hughes called "spectacles in color." At these balls most men and women cross-dressed. These gatherings, both public and private, "provided an arena for homosexual interaction" (Garber, 1989, p. 325), but they became less frequent with the Depression and the end of the Harlem Renaissance.

Despite this brief shining interlude in the 1920s, Black gay and bisexual men have long suffered humiliation and oppression at the hands of the medical and political bureaucracy. Early historical records indicated that Black men who were suspected of homoerotic practices were either executed in the sixteenth through nineteenth centuries or committed to mental asylums. Unlike other American gay and bisexual men, Black males have had to contend with issues of race as well as sexuality. James Tinney (1986) explained this dilemma:

> Black lesbians and gays have often found themselves "caught in the middle" (so to speak) since the "two-ness" of identity (to use a term of W. E. B. Du Bois) reflected in being both Black and gay was not wholly approved in either the Black or gay communities. To maintain comfortability in the Black community, particularly in those places that cultivate Black culture and Black solidarity, many have felt the need to downplay their homosexuality. . . . And in order to maintain comfortability in the gay community, others have felt the need to downplay their blackness. (p. 73)

Joseph Beam (1986b) further explained this situation in his book *In the Life:*

> Visibility is survival. . . . It is possible to read thoroughly two or three consecutive issues of the *Advocate,* the national biweekly gay newsmagazine, and never encounter, in the words or images, Black gay men. . . . We ain't family. Very clearly, gay male means: White, middle-class, youthful, nautilized, and probably butch, there is no room for Black gay men within the confines of this gay pentagon. (pp. 14-15)

This "double identity" led many researchers to question the ways in which the different identities, Black and gay, shape the lives of these men. Johnson's (1981) dissertation explored the effect of cultural assimilation on the social and psychological adjustment of 60 Black gay men as a function of the degree to which their main reference group membership was Black or gay. One's primary

reference group identity was significantly correlated with patterns of social interaction with Whites, Blacks, and other gays. Black-identified participants interacted or were greatly involved with other Blacks as sexual partners, friends,
or lover ideals. Gay-identified participants were the exact opposite. They interacted more with Whites and other gay men and maintained a strong preference
for Whites as sexual partners, best friends, and lover ideals. Black-identified gay
men were "more comfortable in all Black social settings and felt less isolated
from the general Black community than did gay-identified respondents" (p. 3).
However, few members of either reference group reported being actively involved
with the broader Black community. Black-identified respondents tended to be
more covert than gay-identified respondents about their homosexuality with
their heterosexual friends, neighbors, and members of the general public.

In an ethnographic study of the gay community in Harlem, Hawkeswood
(1990) focused on Black men who primarily identified as Black and secondarily
as gay. Hawkeswood noted that in the Black community being gay did not necessarily mean participation in the social life of the gay community. Nonetheless,
he noted:

> Gay Black men are especially concerned with their homosexuality as they perceive their sexuality as
> a distinguishing feature not only of their individual personalities, but also as a point of differentiation
> from other types of Black men in the Black community. (p. 2)

In the gay Black community, Black men who have sex with other men are categorized into two types: "sissies" and "men" (Hawkeswood, 1990). "Sissies" are effeminate men, and "men" are masculine or butch individuals. These differences
are manifested socially in a variety of expressive media, including clothing, language, nonverbal gestures, and beverages consumed. Hawkeswood determined
through an analysis of life histories that most sissies were not pejoratively regarded by the surrounding community even though they had adopted female gender role traits.

These roles or types, unlike the Latino categories of *pasivo* and *activo,* are
not based on sexual activity and do not directly shape sexual encounters. In sexual activities, the gender roles are often reversed. For example, sissies often assumed the active role in sexual encounters. Being effeminate socially did not
prevent the inversion of roles in the bedroom. In this social situation, sissies
were able to call themselves men.

Hawkeswood (1990) suggested that tolerance of gay Black men by other
Blacks is often based on "overlooking" their sexual activities or identity and focusing on what they "do" or are able to do within the Black community. Thus,
the distinction between gay Black men and other Black men in the community
is not based on sexuality alone, but on social activities. Gay Black men are viewed
by informants in the Harlem Black community as involved in responsible activities, such as buying homes, going to school, holding down good jobs, attending
church, and contributing to the well-being of the extended family. These activities reinforced the distinction between these men and those who are considered
"street corner men," that is, men who have been stereotyped as the "ne'er do

well." Compared to the latter, gay Black men were viewed as a better type of Black men by the community (Hawkeswood, 1989). In a community such as Harlem where problems of survival (food, clothing, shelter, education, etc.) are more crucial concerns than people's sexuality (Hawkeswood, 1990, p. 14), these men were viewed as responsible individuals leading socially constructive lives. Therefore, according to informants in Harlem's Black community, being a gay man neither provoked antagonism nor was seen as deviant.

However, Fullilove (1989) criticized the view that the Black community tolerated gay Black men because they were ideal consumers. Fullilove questioned the extent to which the status of relative economic privilege—having the dispensable income, education, and social background to acquire goods and services—encompasses most gay Black men. She advised scholars and community workers to reexamine the general socioeconomic conditions heretofore believed to characterize gay Black men. Furthermore, she cautioned against using observations of openly gay or gay self-identified Black males to justify the claim that the Black community is tolerant of gay men.

There are few studies of the Black community that investigated attitudes toward homosexuality. Those that did, however, reported that there are differences in tolerance of homosexuality within the Black community that follow class lines. John Soares (1979) noted:

> Black, middle-class families, notably the Black "sociable" described by Nathan Hare in *The Black Anglo-Saxons* and by E. Franklin Frazier in his classic *The Black Bourgeoisie,* are so persistently monitoring their social standing that any family member departing from their peer group norm would experience a certain degree of ostracism. But for what appears to be the majority of working-class Black people, gay lovers and steadies are accepted into the family with a lack of flag waving and statement making that has been known to surprise even their middle-class brothers. (p. 265)

Clarke (1983) underscored Soares's observations of the differential degrees of homophobia within the Black community.

> The poor and working class Black community, historically more radical and realistic than the reformist and conservative Black middle class and the atavistic "holier than thou" (bourgeois) nationalist, has often tolerated an individual's lifestyle prerogatives, even when that lifestyle was disparaged by the prevailing culture. Though lesbians and gay men were exotic subjects of curiosity, they were accepted as part of the community (neighborhood)—or at least, there were no manifestos calling for their exclusion from the community. (p. 206)

Although tolerance may exist in specific sectors of the Black community, the complexity of sexual and racial issues faced by gay Black men remains to be adequately addressed.

Fullilove (1989) noted that gay-identified Black men constitute a small subset of all Black men who have sex with other men. This was important, she argued, because sexual identity informs the various networks in which these men function. Furthermore, there appears to be a dearth of research on and cultural acknowledgement of bisexuality within Black communities. The Polaris Research and Development (n.d.) study of the San Francisco Black community indicated that "within the Black community, bisexual men are 'hidden.' They are often married and have spouses who are unaware that they have sexual relations with other men" (p. 69).

The problem of self-identification among Black men was conceptualized in terms of a public/private dichotomy in a study by the National Task Force on AIDS Prevention (n.d.), a project of the National Association of Black and White Men Together. Among 952 predominantly gay-identified Black males, 74% of the respondents reported identifying as gay/homosexual in private, as opposed to 48% who identified themselves as such in public. Eighteen percent of the men reported identifying privately as bisexual, and 13% publicly acknowledged this identity. Six percent privately acknowledged being heterosexual, and 34% publicly avowed this sexual orientation.

This phenomenon was underscored by the Polaris study when it noted:

> There is often a great distinction between how Black respondents describe their sexual identity and how they behave. Thus, we found men who identified themselves as exclusively heterosexual who then reported having sex with other men; self-identified bisexual men who indicated that all of their sexual relations had been with other men during the year prior to the study; and men who called themselves homosexual who reported sexual relations with women. (p. 64)

Loiacano (1989) interviewed three Black gay men and three Black lesbians. All six informants revealed problems in finding support for their sexual and racial identities in the gay and Black communities. All six feared that their sexual identity would jeopardize their acceptance and life within their community. Furthermore, they faced the crucial task of negotiating between these two identities.

Another source of documentation regarding the Black gay experience is found in numerous literary works, such as the anthology *In the Life* (Beam, 1986a). The book's title is a cultural expression describing "street life," that is, the lifestyle of pimps, prostitutes, and drug dealers, as well as "gay life." It succinctly portrays the rather interstitial position occupied by gay Black men within the Black community. Their experiences are notably etched with rejection and alienation from their Black community. Beam (1986a) wrote:

> I cannot go home as who I am. . . . When I speak of home, I mean not only the familial constellation from which I grew, but the entire Black community, the Black press, the Black church, Black academicians, the Black literati, and the Black left. Where is my reflection? I am most often rendered invisible, perceived as a threat to the family, or am tolerated if I am silent and inconspicuous. I cannot go home as who I am and that hurts me deeply. (p. 231)

For many gay Black men, tolerance is conferred as long as they remain silent and invisible. Homophobia within the Black community is illustrated in poems and short stories by Craig Harris (1987a, 1987b), Assoto Saint (1987), and Essex Hemphill (1987), among others. Their works document bashings, rejection by family and church, and subsequent social isolation. In addition, their writings describe how "gayness" is viewed by the Black community as an element of White mainstream culture, thus posing an ominous threat to the integrity of the Black family. For these writers, the experience of being Black and gay has both individual and sociopolitical dimensions. Beam (1986a) encapsulated this view:

> Black men loving Black men is an autonomous agenda for the eighties, which is not rooted in any particular sexual, political or class affiliation, but in our mutual survival. The ways in which we manifest the love are as myriad as the issues we must address. Unemployment, substance abuse, self-hatred, and the lack of positive images are but some of the barriers to our loving. . . . Black men loving Black men is a call to action, an acknowledgement of responsibility. We take care of our own kind when the night grows cold and silent. These days the nights are cold-blooded and the silence echoes with complicity. (p. 242)

The place of gay Black men within the community has been tenuous at best. An example is Bayard Rustin, who was an integral part of Dr. Martin Luther King's advisory group. His homosexuality led some in the upper echelons of the civil rights movement to urge him to resign as Dr. King's adviser.

Hemphill (1991) noted that some Black intellectuals who championed civil rights and Black advancement were the very individuals who portrayed Black gay men as the nemesis of the civil rights struggle. He illustrated this by analyzing the work of Frances Cress Welsing, who wrote that Black gay men were "engaged in sexual genocide [and] in treason against the race" (1991, p. 53). For Cress, homosexuality was a dysfunctional reaction to racial oppression and thus inimical to the progress of the Black community. Cress's views are still shared by many Black nationalists. This example of homophobia within the Black movement reinforces the marginal status of Black gay men within the community.

Bonilla and Porter (1990) reported that Blacks were less morally tolerant of homosexuality but were more amenable to granting civil rights to gays and lesbians than were Latinos. Blacks' moral intolerance toward homosexuality may be due in part to Black churches' conservative stance toward the issue. Blacks' willingness to grant public rights to gay men and lesbians may be due to their history of civil rights struggles.

Studies indicate that due to rather ambiguous social attitudes toward Black gay and bisexual men, self-identification of sexual orientation is complex if not problematic. Researchers, service providers, and HIV educators must find ways in which to accommodate those men who do not identify as either gay or bisexual. Social service programs or campaigns directed toward this community should take into account the problem of negotiating racial identity and consciousness with sexual orientation.

## ASIAN MEN WHO HAVE SEX WITH MEN

The literature on Asian American men who have sex with men has only begun to emerge during the past few years. Unlike studies on Black and Latino populations, issues of sexuality within Asian American scholarship have been slow to develop. At the advent of the AIDS pandemic in the early 1980s, Asians were perceived to be immune to, if not totally untouched by, the disease. This perception was based not only on epidemiological data but an "Orientalist" stereotype of Asians, particularly men, as inscrutable and sexually inactive individuals.

Studies of homoerotic phenomena in Asian societies indicate a wide range of cultural attitudes, from the relative tolerance of particular gendered forms of homosexuality in Thailand (Jackson, 1989) and in the Philippines (Hart 1968; Whitam & Mathy, 1986) to overt suppression in Singapore and Japan (Murray, 1992). These differences in attitudes are usually not referenced by research on Asian gay and bisexual men in the United States. Instead, most works suggest that all Asian communities exhibit restrictive and repressive attitudes toward gays and lesbians.

Same-sex phenomena are usually conflated with hermaphroditism and transvestism in most Asian societies. As such, there are elaborate traditions of cross-dressing men in Indonesia, Philippines, Japan, and China. These traditions as they have been understood and/or practiced by Asian men in the United States have elaborated Orientalist views of feminized Asian men.

Fung (1991) noted that these ideas and attitudes toward Asian men have also been propagated in gay pornography. Racist underpinnings of "Orientalism" extended to the production of images, practices, and institutions in gay communities. He argued:

> There is a kind of doubleness, of ambivalence, in the way that Asian men experience contemporary North American gay communities. The "ghetto," the mainstream gay movement, can be a place of freedom and sexual identity. But it is also a site of racial, cultural, and sexual alienation sometimes more pronounced than that in straight society. (p. 159)

The kind of racism experienced by Asian men is manifested in beliefs such as all Asian men are sexual bottoms, passive and subservient partners, and effeminate/feminine. Slang words such as "rice queens" (White men who desire Asian men) and "rice bar" (places that cater to Asian gay men and their admirers) are obvious examples of the predicaments in which Asian men who have sex with men find themselves.

Studies of Asian men who have sex with men are few in number and have primarily investigated the "double" experience of racial and sexual oppression within Asian and mainstream society. One example is an exploratory, qualitative study of 13 Japanese American gay men (Wooden, Kawasaki, & Mayeda, 1983), who discussed issues of coming out and homophobia in their families, the Japanese American community, gay communities, and society at large. One participant described his experience of being gay in the Japanese American community:

> I think the JA community tolerates homosexuality in other communities, but in their own community—no way! It is looked upon as being dishonorable and disgraceful. I do not feel these attitudes are changing at all. (p. 239)

Another noted that the gay community reflects the prejudices of White society: "These prejudices transcend being gay. Even in selecting gay activities, one has to consider acceptable locations and the composition of the groups to be encountered" (pp. 240–241).

Succeeding studies explored issues of identity formation among Asian gay men and lesbians, without considering the applicability of findings across Asian national groups. Gock (1994) and Chan (1989) represent subsequent research efforts to study Asian American gays and lesbians. They lumped identities into either sexual or ethnic categories without considering age, class, and cultural/national background. Differences resulting from immigration status, including place of birth and socialization, and legal personhood are issues they failed to address, even though both are central considerations when one identifies as gay or lesbian. Both works provide a model of development for ethnic/racial and gay identities but erroneously posit a monolithic Asian American identity and community. Although fraught with methodological and conceptual limitations, they are important because they laid the groundwork for studying lesbian and gay issues among Asians.

During the past five years, however, works of fiction, literary criticism, and informal essays on history and social issues in journals such as *Amerasia* and *Lavender Godzilla* have investigated intra–Asian American differences. A recently published interdisciplinary anthology (Ratti, 1993a) probes the gay and lesbian experience within the context of immigration and diaspora. The focus is on South Asians, who have long been neglected in Asian American studies and activism. Islam (1993), an author of one paper in the anthology, reflected on global ties among Asian lesbians in different parts of the world. Other essays (Ratti, 1993a; Shah, 1993) documented activist efforts of South Asians in America and elsewhere. An interview with South Asian lesbian filmmaker and theorist, Pratibha Parmar, examined issues of cultural and psychic displacement of diasporic people that complicate the predicament of gay and lesbian immigrants. An essay by ABVA (1993), an AIDS organization in India, argued for recovering a historical past in India that was accepting if not tolerant of same-sex encounters and their practitioners. However, the most important feature of this anthology is its sensitivity to the diversity among South Asians in terms of gender, national groupings, class, and immigration experience.

To address several of these issues, I began an ongoing ethnographic research project on Filipino gay men in New York City. Informants were asked to reflect on several different identities with which they are confronted in everyday life (Manalansan, 1994). The research includes the life narratives, informal interviews, and participant observations of Filipino gay men. A majority of the informants were immigrants who have lived in the U.S. for more than seven years.

In terms of ethnic/racial identities, the Filipino gay informants usually identified as Filipino or Filipino American. In official contexts, such as organization meetings or public documents, however, informants reported that they identified as Asian Pacific Islander. While all informants identified as gay, many of them noted that they were different from gay men from other ethnic groups, including other Asian gay men. There was a general consensus that they had less "angst" or issue with being gay. In fact, several of them insisted that coming out was never a problem. One informant said, "Coming out is an American issue. It is rarely a problem with us Filipinos."

Filipino gay informants seldom identified as Asian or with an Asian community. For many of them the term "Asian" was viewed in geographic terms. Animosities between Filipinos and other Asian groups were also apparent. These tensions have become evident with the creation of Filipino-specific gay and lesbian organizations, such as Barangay on the West Coast and Kambal sa Lusog in New York. Similar organizations have been established among South Asians (e.g., Trikon on the West Coast and SALGA—South Asian Lesbian and Gay Association—in New York) and Koreans.

Class and place of birth were reported to be the basic markers of intragroup differences among Filipino gay men. Informants reported that Filipino gay men who came from the lower classes in the Philippines or America usually displayed the stereotypical behavior of the *bakla,* the Tagalog term for effeminacy, transvestism, and homosexuality. Such behavior included being overtly effeminate, working as a hairdresser or female impersonator, and gossiping. Filipino gay men who were perceived as "low class" were also viewed as pursuing heterosexual men.

The dynamics of social relationships among Filipino gay informants were usually understood in class terms as well. Filipino gay men socialized with other gay men whom they perceived to be within their class or who at least acted within the decorum of a particular class. However, some informants said that because there were only a few other Filipino gay men in the area, they were forced by circumstances to associate with those outside their class in situations such as Filipino religious or national celebrations.

Some informants saw a major difference between Filipino gay men who were born and raised in the Philippines and those who were born and/or raised in America. American-born Filipino gay men were held in disdain and with suspicion by Philippine-born individuals because they apparently did not act Filipino or speak a Philippine language.

Even within the group of informants born and raised in the Philippines, there were considerable differences beyond class, such as membership in an ethnolinguistic or regional group. Therefore, in Filipino gay men peer groups, the composition usually included one or two ethnolinguistic groups. In antagonistic encounters among Filipino gay men, slurs and stereotypes about specific ethnolinguistic groups, such as "the loud Pampango" or the "miserly Ilocano," were used.

In summary, the documentation of diversity among Asian American groups regarding attitudes toward and practices of homosexuality has only recently begun. There remains considerable work to be done to delineate the various cultural articulations of same-sex encounters and practitioners. Future research should analyze the ways in which these attitudes and practices are transplanted and inflected in American society, transformed or remain constant in the immigrant context, and influence the lives of various Asian American men who have sex with men.

# CONCLUSION: GENERAL THEMES

Despite the linguistic, racial, historical, and cultural diversity among Latino, Black, and Asian American gay and bisexual communities, they share common themes. These themes contextualize the lives of men in these communities within the larger framework of American society and AIDS-prevention efforts. These themes demonstrate the ways in which the problem of AIDS prevention among Latino, Black, and Asian groups is a complex interaction of sociocultural, political, economic, and biological forces.

## Power and Minority Status

The fundamental issue that these men encounter is *powerlessness*. They are marginal members of marginal groups, hence the name "double minorities." These men must contend with their ethnicity/race and sexual orientation as sources of stigma or discrimination both within their ethnic and sexual communities and in society at large. Therefore, it is imperative to view issues of sexual identity and same-sex practices among Latinos, Blacks, and Asians as connected yet distinct from those of mainstream White populations.

Being gay or bisexual is not the same as being Latino, Black, or Asian. The relative "invisibility" of sexual orientation versus the glaring externality of race and ethnicity illustrates that being a double minority does not mean the Janus—or two-faced—predicament. Stigmata attached to either one are different. In relation to the issue of powerlessness, the forces of discrimination and prejudice may be the same for racial- and sexual-minority members, but the impact is different. Discrimination against gay and bisexual men from ethnic-minority groups is greater than it is for gay White men and for heterosexual ethnic minorities (Winnow, 1984).

Gay men, lesbians, and bisexuals from ethnic minorities may be barred access to housing, education, and social networks within their communities because of their sexual orientation. However, identities are used strategically and situationally. They are not seamless. This chapter emphasizes the *fluidity of social and sexual identities*. These identities are continually being negotiated and renegotiated in response to life events and historical/social forces. It is important to understand the interplay between identities and sociocultural context.

## Intragroup Diversity

A glaring misconception among scholars and laypeople is the overwhelming confidence in the accuracy of such categories as Latino, Hispanic, Black, African American, and Asian. The conflation of linguistic affiliations, culture, political consciousness, skin color, and ethnic/racial identities into broad categories such as Latino, Black, or Asian obscure not only the diversity that exists within and among these groups, but also the conflicts with the meanings that these categories hold for different members. A common name does not imply homogeneity or strong political and communal links.

Internal differences among Latinos, Blacks, and Asians are due in part to cultural assimilation and the differing roles each national group played in the history of American immigration. Levels of English language acquisition and co-optation into American cultural ways of life may be attributed in part to the aforementioned differences. Diversity within each grouping usually demarcates differences in attitudes, specifically tolerance and conceptualization of same-sex encounters.

## Universal Versus Particular: Cultural Categories and Practices

A central and sometimes emotional debate among scholars of cross-cultural issues concerns the applicability of universal categories such as "gay" or "homosexual" to all cultures. Although this chapter is not the proper venue for analyzing this debate, it is imperative to consider its consequences for AIDS-prevention efforts. This issue is related to the previous one of intraethnic differences. It is important for educators to understand the ways in which each national group constructs particular cultural notions of men who have sex with other men.

Researchers and service providers such as HIV/AIDS educators must note that these Western categories assume different forms and meanings. Therefore, different support systems are required for various groups and individuals who identify themselves as such. Being gay or bisexual is an issue that is resolved both individually and socially. In a multicultural society such as the United States, this issue is compounded by the often conflicting views on homosexuality held by mainstream, hegemonic culture and national/ethnic groups. Furthermore, due to assimilation, conflicts exist among divergent gay subcultures that are similar to White versus Hispanic, Asian, or Black, or more specifically, Cuban, Jamaican, Filipino, etc.

The designations of gay and bisexual should be viewed as products both of sociocultural and phenomenological perceptions of sexual practices and cultural ideals. For example, a first-generation Latino man from Venezuela who has sex with other men may view himself as heterosexual. The designation of gay or bisexual does not enter his realm of possible identities because he is married and maintains the active (inserter) position in same-sex anal intercourse. Another illustrative case is a Black man from Harlem who has sex with other men and self-identifies as gay. Because of the distinct Black gay life and community that has developed in Harlem, it is possible for this man to identify as gay and still occasionally have sex with women. His lifestyle illustrates the difficulty involved in identifying the axes of meaning, such as behavior versus identity or culture versus individual, on which sexual identity categories are constructed.

The category of bisexual is problematic. The majority of cases of bisexuality are probably undisclosed. Cultural norms rather than self-denial may explain this phenomenon for some individuals. Even within American gay communities, bisexuals are often regarded with suspicion. They are often considered to be duplicitous "fence-sitters," closet cases, sex maniacs, or, worse, political traitors to the cause of the gay and lesbian rights movement (Paul, this volume; Wofford, 1991). In some cultures, bisexual practices are mere extensions of heterosexuality. In others, bisexual practices are ways of circumventing the stigma of gay self-identification. Some scholars view bisexuality as identity conflict and as a transitional stage to homosexuality. Others conceptualize bisexuality as the integration of gay and heterosexual identities into a dual sexual orientation (Zinik, 1985). However, even as a scientific or clinical category, bisexuality still eludes precise definition and is embroiled in debates among researchers (Hansen & Evans, 1985).

Issues pertaining to cultural categories and practices are especially important to those, such as HIV educators, who provide services to racial/ethnic minority communities. Given these differences in self-identification, researchers, service providers, and educators must grapple with the viability of gay and bisexual categories in these communities. Future research needs to critically examine and document the ways in which such categories are culturally negotiated and behaviorally manifested among racial/ethnic minority communities.

▼ **REFERENCES** ▼

ABVA (AIDS Bhedbav Virodhi Andolan). (1993). Homosexuality in India: Culture and heritage. In R. Ratti (Ed.), *A lotus of another color: The unfolding of the South Asian gay and lesbian experience* (pp. 21–33). Boston: Alyson.

Almaguer, T. (1991). Chicano men: A cartography of homosexual identity and behavior. *Differences, 2,* 75–100.

Alonso, A. M., & Koreck, M. T. (1989). Silences, "Hispanics," AIDS and sexual practices. *Differences, 1,* 101–124.

Amaro, H. (1990). *AIDS/HIV related knowledge, attitudes, beliefs and behaviors among Hispanics in the Northeast and Puerto Rico.* Unpublished paper prepared for the Northeast Hispanic AIDS Consortium, Boston.

Beam, J. (1986a). Brother to brother: Words from the heart. In J. Beam (Ed.), *In the life: A Black gay anthology* (pp. 230–242). Boston: Alyson.

Beam, J. (1986b). Introduction. In J. Beam (Ed.), *In the life: A Black gay anthology* (pp. 13–18). Boston: Alyson.

Bonilla, J., & Porter, J. (1990). A comparison of Latino, Black, and non-Hispanic White attitudes toward homosexuality. *Hispanic Journal of Behavioral Sciences, 12,* 437–452.

Caballo-Dieguez, A. (1990). *Hispanic men who have sex with men. Considerations for HIV-related behavioral research.* Unpublished manuscript, HIV Center for Clinical and Behavioral Studies, New York State Psychiatric Institute and Columbia University, NY.

Carrier, J. M. (1985). Mexican male homosexuality. *Journal of Homosexuality, 11,* 75–85.

Chan, C. (1989). Issues of identity development among Asian-American lesbians and gay men. *Journal of Counseling and Development, 68,* 16–20.

Clarke, C. (1983). The failure to transform: Homophobia in the Black community. In B. Smith (Ed.), *Home girls: A Black feminist anthology* (pp. 197–208). New York: Kitchen Table.

Davis, C., Haub, C., & Willette, J. (1988). U.S. Hispanics: Changing the face of America. In E. Acosta-Belen & B. R. Sjostrom (Eds.), *The Hispanic experience in the United States: Contemporary issues and perspectives* (pp. 32–90). New York: Praeger.

De la Vega, E. (1990). Considerations for reaching the Latino population with sexuality and HIV information and education. *Siecus Report, 18,* 43–50.

Espiritu, Y. L. (1992). *Asian panethnicity.* Philadelphia: Temple University Press.

Farley, R., & Allen, W. R. (1989). *The color line and the quality of life in America.* New York: Oxford University Press.

Fullilove, M. T. (1989). Ethnic minorities, HIV disease and the growing underclass. In J. W. Dilley, C. Pies, & M. Helquist (Eds.), *Face to face: A guide to AIDS counseling. San Francisco: AIDS Health Project* (pp. 230–240). San Francisco: University of California Press AIDS Health Project.

Fung, R. (1991). Looking for my penis: The eroticized Asian in gay video porn. In Bad Object Choices (Ed.), *How do I look? Queer film and video* (pp. 145–168). Seattle, WA: Bay Press.

Garber, E. (1989). A spectacle in color: The lesbian and gay subculture of jazz age Harlem. In M. B. Duberman, M. Vicinus, & G. Chauncey (Eds.), *Hidden from history: Reclaiming the gay and lesbian past* (pp. 318–331). New York: New American Library.

Gock, T. (1994). Asian Pacific Islander identity issues: Identity integration and pride. In B. Berzon (Ed.), *Positively gay* (expanded ed.) (pp. 247–252). Los Angeles: Mediamix Association.

Hansen, C. E., & Evans, A. (1985). Bisexuality reconsidered: An idea in pursuit of a definition. *Journal of Homosexuality, 11,* 1–6.

Harris, C. (1987a). The least of my brothers. In D. Aaab-Richard, C. G. Harris, E. Hemphill, I. Jackson, & A. Saint (Eds.), *Tongues untied* (p. 38). London: Gay Men's Press.

Harris, C. (1987b). Weekend plans. In D. Aaab-Richard, C. G. Harris, E. Hemphill, I. Jackson, & A. Saint (Eds.), *Tongues untied* (pp. 38–40). London: Gay Men's Press.

Hart, D. (1968). Homosexuality and transvestism in the Philippines: The Cebuano Filipino Bayot and Lakin-on. *Behavior Science Notes, 3,* 211–248.

Hawkeswood, W. G. (1989). *Anthropology and AIDS: Issues confronting the anthropologist in the field.* Paper presented at the American Anthropological Association Annual Meeting, Washington, DC.

Hawkeswood, W. G. (1990). *"I'm a Black man who just happens to be gay." The sexuality of Black gay men.* Paper presented at the American Anthropological Association Annual Meeting, New Orleans.

Hayes-Bautista, D. E., & Chapa, J. (1987). Latino terminology: Conceptual bases for standardized terminology. *American Journal of Public Health, 77,* 61–68.

Hemphill, E. (1987). In the life. In D. Aaab-Richard, C. G. Harris, E. Hemphill, I. Jackson, & A. Saint (Eds.), *Tongues untied* (p. 53). London: Gay Men's Press.

Hemphill, E. (1991). If Freud had been a neurotic colored woman: Reading Dr. Frances Cress Welsing. *Outlook, 13,* 50–55.

Honey, E. (1988, June). AIDS and the inner city: Critical issues. *Social Casework: The Journal of Contemporary Social Work,* pp. 365–370.

Islam, S. (1993). Toward a global network of lesbians. In R. Ratti (Ed.), *A lotus of another color: The unfolding of the South Asian gay and lesbian experience* (pp. 41–46). Boston: Alyson.

Jackson, P. A. (1989). *Male homosexuality in Thailand: An interpretation of*

contemporary Thai sources. Elmhurst, NY: Global Academic Publishers.

Johnson, J. M. (1981). *Influence of assimilation on the psychosocial adjustment of Black homosexual men.* Unpublished doctoral dissertation, California School of Professional Psychology, Berkeley, CA.

Katz, J. (1976). *Gay American history: Lesbians and gay men in the U.S.A.* New York: Harper & Row.

Lancaster, R. N. (1988). Subject honor and object shame: The construction of homosexuality and stigma in Nicaragua. *Ethnology, 28,* 111–126.

Loiacano, D. K. (1989). Gay identity issues among Black Americans: Racism, homophobia, and the need for validation. *Journal of Counseling and Development, 68,* 21–25.

Manalansan, M. (1994). Searching for community: Filipino gay men in New York City. *Amerasia 20,* 59–73.

Marin, B. (in press). Hispanic culture: Implications for AIDS prevention. In J. Boswell, R. Hexter, & J. Reinisch (Eds.), *Sexuality and disease: Metaphors, perception and behavior in the AIDS era.* New York: Oxford University Press.

Moore, J., & Pachon, C. (1985). *Hispanics in the United States.* Englewood Cliffs, NJ: Prentice-Hall.

Morales, E. S. (1990). HIV infection and Hispanic gay and bisexual men. *Hispanic Journal of Behavioral Sciences, 12,* 212–222.

Murray, S. O. (Ed.). (1987). *Male homosexuality in Central and South America.* New York: Gay Academic Union.

Murray, S. O. (1992). Homosexuality in Japan since the Meiji restoration. In S. O. Murray (Ed.), *Oceanic homosexualities* (pp. 363–370). New York: Garland.

National Task Force on AIDS Prevention (n.d.). *Summary of findings: National HIV research study of Black men.* Washington, DC: Author.

New York City Department of Health AIDS Surveillance Unit. (1990). *AIDS surveillance update.* New York: Author.

Polaris Research and Development (n.d.). *A baseline survey of AIDS risk behaviors and attitudes in San Francisco Black communities.* San Francisco: Author.

Ratti, R. (1993a). Feminism and men. In R. Ratti (Ed.), *A lotus of another color: The unfolding of the South Asian gay and lesbian experience* (pp. 47–53). Boston: Alyson.

Ratti, R. (1993b). Introduction. In R. Ratti (Ed.), *A lotus of another color: The unfolding of the South Asian gay and lesbian experience* (pp. 11–17). Boston: Alyson.

Rogers, M., & Williams, W. W. (1987). AIDS in Blacks and Hispanics: Implications for prevention. *Issues in Science and Technology, 3,* 89–94.

Saint, A. (1987). Hooked for life. In D. Aaab-Richard, C. G. Harris, E. Hemphill, I. Jackson, & A. Saint (Eds.), *Tongues untied* (pp. 89–93). London: Gay Men's Press.

Shah, N. (1993). Sexuality, identity and the uses of history. In R. Ratti (Ed.), *A lotus of another color: The unfolding of the South Asian gay and lesbian experience* (pp. 113–132). Boston: Alyson.

Singer, M., Flores, C., Davison, L., Burke, G., Castillo, Z., Scanlon, K., & Rivera, M. (1990). SIDA: The economic, social, and cultural context of AIDS among Latinos. *Medical Anthropology Quarterly, 4,* 72–114.

Soares, J. V. (1979). Black and gay. In M. E. Levine (Ed.), *Gay men: The sociology of male homosexuality* (pp. 263–274). New York: Harper & Row.

Taylor, C. L. (1986). Mexican male homosexual interaction in public contexts. *Journal of Homosexuality, 11,* 117–136.

Tinney, J. S. (1986). Why a Black gay church? In J. Beam (Ed.), *In the life: A gay Black anthology* (pp. 70–86). Boston: Alyson.

Trevino, F. M. (1987). Standardized terminology for Hispanic populations. *American Journal of Public Health, 77,* 69–72.

U.S. Conference of Mayors. (1994). *Assessing the HIV-prevention needs of gay and bisexual men of color.* Washington, DC: Author.

U.S. Department of Commerce. (1993). *Statistical abstracts of the United States.* Washington, DC: Government Printing Office.

Villanueva-Collado, A. (1989). Emigration/immigration: Going home where I belong. In S. Torres-Saillane (Ed.), *Hispanic immigrant writers and the identity question* (pp. 30–50). New York: Ollantay Press.

Whitam, F., & Mathy, A. (1986). *Homosexuality in four societies.* New York: Praeger.

Winnow, J. (1984). *Investigation into employment and hiring practices of gay/lesbian businesses, specifically regarding race, color, national origins and ethnicity: Findings, recommendations and support documentation.* San Francisco: Human Rights Commission of San Francisco.

Wofford, C. (1991). The bisexual revolution: Deluded closet cases or vanguard of the movement. *Outweek, 84,* 32–70.

Woldemikael, T. (1989). A case study of race consciousness among Haitian immigrants. *Journal of Black Studies, 20,* 224–240.

Wooden, W. S., Kawasaki, H., & Mayeda, R. (1983). Lifestyles and identity maintenance among gay Japanese-American males. *Alternative Lifestyle, 5,* 236–243.

Yankauer, A. (1987). Hispanic/Latino— What's in a name? *American Journal of Public Health, 77,* 15–17.

Zinik, G. (1985). Identity conflict or adaptive flexibility? Bisexuality reconsidered. *Journal of Homosexuality, 11,* 7–20.

## Chapter 18

▼

# Two-Spirit Persons: Gender Nonconformity Among Native American and Native Hawaiian Youths

## Walter L. Williams

*One of the most common errors in the behavioral sciences is the evaluation of human behavior through the lens of only one society. This bias has had particularly tragic results in the study of same-sex eroticism, resulting in a characterization of homosexuality as "deviant" and "abnormal." Given the widespread discrimination against lesbians, bisexuals, and gay men in Euro-American culture, it is not difficult to understand the ways in which such behavior would be considered marginal and the reasons why such persons might suffer psychological problems. However, if a wider focus is taken, it becomes apparent that the majority of the world's cultures before the spread of Christianity and Western colonialism did not prohibit same-sex eroticism. In fact, many cultures, from as far as Siberia to South Africa and from Melanesia to Mesopotamia, had special respected roles for homosexually inclined people (Conner, 1993; Herdt, 1984; Murray, 1992; Williams, 1986). By considering the entire span of human history, it becomes apparent that it is not homosexuality that is abnormal but heterosexist prejudice. Prejudice and social stigma are sources of the psychological disturbances that some sexual minorities suffer, rather than same-sex orientation per se.*

*In striving to gain a wider focus, it is necessary to locate data about the social acceptance of homosexuality in other cultures. Yet, the number of anthropologists and historians who are researching this topic is pitifully small. More researchers need to conduct field and archival studies and to encourage students to do the same. Once beyond ethnocentric blinders, there is much to learn from the wisdom of ancient cultures. This chapter is based on the limited research that has been done and on fieldwork that I have been conducting during the last two decades.*

*After three years of library research on same-sex eroticism in other cultures, I began field research on this topic in the early 1980s. I first went to*

*Native American reservations of the Northern Plains, followed by trips to the Navajo Nation of the Southwest, the Mayas of Yucatán in Mexico, First Nations peoples in Canada, and the Aleuts and Yu'pik Eskimos of Alaska. In 1987 and 1988, as a Fulbright scholar, I conducted research in Southeast Asia and expanded my focus to include Indonesia (Williams, 1991), the Philippines, and Thailand (Williams, 1990). Since 1984, I have interviewed Native Hawaiians on the islands of Moloka'i, Oahu, and the Big Island of Hawai'i, as well as related Polynesians on the island of Rarotonga in the South Pacific.*

*In Polynesia, terms used for homosexually inclined individuals are* aikane *and* mahu. *Among the hundreds of Native American languages, most have words for alternative gendered same-sex oriented persons, including* nadleh *(Navajo),* winkte *(Lakota), and* achnucek *(Aleut). The common term anthropologists have used cross-culturally to describe such persons is* berdache. *This term originated from the Persian word* bardaj, *meaning an intimate friend, which was popular in France in the sixteenth through the eighteenth century to describe an effeminate male who assumed the passive role in sex with men. Today, Native American gays and lesbians prefer using the term* two-spirit person *to refer to themselves. Their emphasis on spirituality prompts a different way of thinking about the association between homoeroticism and the sacred.*

## SPIRITUALITY

Early European missionaries commented in amazement that Native Americans honored androgynous males and females as sacred persons. They were viewed as extraordinary beings, of a higher order than the average person. The missionaries, coming from a Christian tradition with rigid gender roles and a condemnation of sexual variations, could not bring themselves to a tolerant view of two-spirit persons. They could not comprehend the relationship that the Indians saw between androgyny and religion.

Spirituality is, for many Native American tribes, at the heart of two-spirit traditions (Williams, 1986). In Native North American animist religions, a multiplicity of spirits exist in the universe. All things are spiritual. Everything that exists is equally due respect because everything is part of the spiritual order of the universe. The world cannot be complete without this diversity. In these religions, there is no hierarchy of importance among the spirits of animals, plants, and other beings that populate the earth. Humans are not more spiritual than other beings. The spirit of man is not more important than the spirit of woman; each spirit is different, but these differences complement each other, leading to spiritual wholeness.

American Indian religions view androgynous persons—that is, males who are feminine or females who are masculine—as evidence that that person has been blessed with *two* spirits. Because both the masculine and the feminine are respected, a person who combines them is considered as higher than the average person, who only has one spirit. Therefore, persons who act like the other sex are not condemned as "deviant" but are blessed for their possession of a double dose of spirituality. They are not "abnormal" but "exceptional," somewhat similar to the way in which a musically or intellectually gifted person might be seen in Euro-American culture.

Because Native American religions place considerable emphasis on the belief that everything that exists comes from the spirit world, if a person varies from the average person then that implies that the spirits must have paid particular attention to making that person the way he or she is. It follows, therefore, that such a person would have an especially close connection to the spirit world. Accordingly, two-spirit persons are often viewed as sacred people, spiritually gifted individuals who can aid others with their spiritual needs. In many tribes, such persons are often shamans or sacred people who work closely with shamans (Williams, 1986, chapters 1–2).

## MAKING POSITIVE CONTRIBUTIONS TO SOCIETY

Two-spirit people are androgynous persons, who are seldom inclined toward indigenous men's or women's traditional labor roles. A gentle male might not be very effective as a warrior and hunter; a masculine female might not be content to structure her life around child care and food preparation. By recognizing their specialness and encouraging them to assume alternative gender roles, Native cultures provide such persons with a means of contributing positively to society. A Crow Indian elder told me, "We don't waste people, the way White society does. Every person has their gift, every person has their contribution to make" (Williams, 1986, p. 57).

Sometimes this contribution has life or death implications. Among the Kaska Indians of the Canadian subarctic, for example, people are heavily dependent on big-game hunting for food. In the cold climate, which is too far north to farm, a family without a hunter could starve during the long winter. Kaska women do not usually hunt because they need to remain near the home to protect, breastfeed, and nurture their small children. Only the husband and older sons hunt for big game. If a family does not have at least one or two sons to search for game, they might face disaster once the father becomes too old or infirm to hunt. In this situation, Kaska families without sufficient sons feel fortunate if they have a masculine-inclined daughter. They cannot afford to waste her potential talents.

In this situation, the parents perform a special ceremony to transform this young daughter into a son. She becomes "like a man." They tie the dried ovaries of a bear to a belt that she always wears next to her abdomen. They believe this will give her luck on the hunt, will prevent menstruation when she reaches puberty, and will protect her from becoming pregnant. From about age 5, she is trained by her father for men's tasks. According to Kaska informants, such females are said to develop "great strength" and usually become "outstanding hunters" (Honigmann, 1964, pp. 129–130).

Female hunters react violently if a male makes sexual advances toward them. Kaska people explained to an anthropologist their belief that if a female hunter engages in heterosexual sex, "her luck with game will be broken." This belief is not simply a superstition; a female who becomes pregnant and then has to breastfeed an offspring for several years simply cannot be a dependable hunter. Thus, in the Kaska view, the only sensible sexual partner for a female hunter is another female. A Kaska female hunter traditionally would be expected to marry a woman, just as a male hunter would. She and her wife choose a male to impregnate the wife, but the female hunter is considered to be the true father of the child. By this means, she can have a marriage and family, just like male hunters (Honigmann, 1964).

Many other Native American groups likewise have accepted the view that masculine females should become hunters and take a feminine woman for a wife. At least before Christian missionaries brought alien Western ideas, Native belief systems incorporated same-sex marriages into their kinship systems. The Mohaves of Arizona, for example, believe that the real father of a child is the *last* person to have sex with the mother before the birth. If a woman becomes pregnant by a male but then has sex with her female partner, the female-female marriage is recognized and the female lover is fully accepted as the child's parent (Devereux, 1969, pp. 262, 416–420).

Many other cultures, conversely, value daughters so highly that parents without a daughter hope for a feminine son who could be raised like a daughter. In my fieldwork in Hawai'i, I was told by many Native Polynesians that parents who have only sons select the most androgynous and encourage him to take on the *mahu* role. Mothers in particular are said to desire having a *mahu* son. While there has not been sufficient research to conclude whether these folk explanations are accurate, their statements are amazingly similar to the testimony of an early Spanish explorer in South America, Fernandez de Piedrahita, who reported that among the Lache Indians of Columbia,

> it was a law among them that if a woman bore five consecutive male children, without giving birth to a female, they could make a female of one of the sons when he reached the age of twelve—that is to say, they could rear him as a woman and teach him the habits of a woman, bringing him up in that wise. In their bodily form and manners they appeared so perfectly to be women that no one who beheld them could distinguish them from the others. These were known as *cusmos* and they performed womanly tasks with the strength of men, as a result of which, when they had attained the proper age, they were given in wedlock as women. And indeed the Laches preferred them to true women, whereby it follows that the abomination of sodomy was freely permitted. (translated from Requena, 1945, p. 16)

Such traditions of acceptance were quite common in many aboriginal cultures of the Western Hemisphere. In Alaska, early Russian explorers reported that the Aleuts and Kodiak Eskimos thought it especially prestigious to have an effeminate son. If parents noticed signs of gender-atypical behavior in a young son, they dressed him in feminine clothing and styled his hair like a woman's. They trained him in women's skills and in all ways raised him as an especially gifted child. When he was between 10 and 15 years of age, this son was married to a wealthy man. For an Aleut man, having a boy-wife marked a major social accomplishment, and the boy's family benefited from the association with their new wealthy in-law. Because the boy was treated with great respect by the husband and by society in general, this practice of same-sex marriage provided a no-lose situation for easy social mobility among Aleut and Kodiak families (Williams, 1986, pp. 45–46, 193–194, 254–255).

## Androgyny as an Inborn Character

While families valued two-spirit children, the reports of early European explorers should not lead us to believe that parents forcibly imposed such alternative gender roles on unwilling children. Native American children generally have wide latitude to live where they are comfortable and in a manner that is compatible with their "spirit"—that is, their inclinations or basic character. Children raised by traditionalist families can decide in which household they wish to live, and adults do not try to coerce them to choose differently. Children are allowed to live where and how they wish.

If children feel manipulated in a direction other than the one they are inclined to take, they refuse to cooperate. Refusal is interpreted as a reflection of the child's spirit. Thus, children who are reported to have been "chosen" by parents to assume an alternative gender role already have evidenced an inclination for gender-atypical behavior. For example, a Pueblo 60-year-old two-spirit person who was interviewed by White (1980, pp. 99–101) remembered that when he was 6 years old, his relatives told him they were not going to raise him as an ordinary man but as someone special. They stated this as a matter of fact based on their observation of his androgynous character. The boy accepted the two-spirit role with the same positive attitude. He valued his specialness and grew up with a secure position in his Pueblo traditional community.

Even in tribes that traditionally emphasized warfare and in which most boys were socialized for violent aggression that would make them suitable warriors, two-spirit persons were honored. While bravery was highly prized in such cultures and cowards were despised, no demands for demonstrations of bravery were placed on two-spirit boys. Among warlike tribes, such as the Navajo, Mohave, and Lakota, early documentary accounts state that androgynous males were noted as "peaceful persons" who had received their instructions from a vision. While bravery was valued, power obtained in a dream was even more highly prized. Therefore, rather than viewing such persons as seeking to "escape" masculinity, Native American explanations maintain that two-spiritedness is a reflection of the child's inborn individual character. Even today, traditionalist Indian people still follow such traditions of acceptance. This spiritual explanation means that adults will

not impose such roles on children or restrict gender-atypical children from acting out their desires.

According to an anthropologist working with the Yumas of Arizona in the
1920s, when a young girl manifested an unfeminine character, her parents sometimes tried to interest her in women's pursuits. But if she resisted, she was
viewed as having undergone a change of spirit as a result of dreams while in infancy. Growing up, such a female played and hunted with boys but had no interest in heterosexual relations with them. These females were given the name
*kwe'rhame,* defined as "women who passed for men, dressed like men and married women." They were known for bravery and skillful fighting in battle (Forde,
1931, p. 157).

While there has not been enough research on Native American sexuality and
gender to indicate on which reservations such traditions have continued into
the present, even today Indians of numerous tribes believe that two-spiritedness
is evident by early childhood. Many informants of different tribes have told me
that a two-spirit character emerges in a child by age 3 to 5. Only after a child
demonstrates gender-nonconformist behavior do adults single out that child as
special. A Hupa two-spirit male told me:

> I was real feminine as a child, from as early as I can remember. Noticing how I like to do cooking
> and cleaning, my grandmother said I would grow up as a woman. Within the family, Indians believe
> you can be whatever you choose. (personal field notes, 1985)

Although Native people refer to persons as "choosing" to be a two-spirit, this
term is used within the context that the spirits chose this role for selected individuals. This does not mean that a person can freely and rationally choose to be
of a certain character. When asked by an anthropologist if two-spirit persons
"choose" their gender nonconformity and homosexual sexuality, Zapotec Indians
in Mexico considered this as ludicrous as the notion that someone could freely
choose their eye color. They strongly defended the right of two-spirit people to
follow their different ways, saying simply, "God made them that way" (Chiñas,
1985, pp. 1–4).

The belief that two-spiritedness is inborn is held by many Native Americans.
For example, speaking about male two-spirits, a Lakota traditionalist told me:

> It is obvious from infancy that one is a *winkte.* He is a beautiful boy, and the sound of his voice is ef-
> feminate. It is inborn. The mother realizes this soon and allows the boy to do feminine things—how
> to prepare meat and other foods. They all end up being homosexual. (personal field notes, 1982)

This view is not a product of recent gay liberation influences. In the 1930s, anthropologist Margaret Mead wrote similarly about an Omaha boy who showed
"marked feminine physical traits" and who later ended up taking on the
"berdache" two-spirit role (Mead, 1935, p. 294).

Even earlier, in the 1910s, anthropologist Elsie Clews Parsons knew several
two-spirit persons at Zuni Pueblo, including a young boy whose features were
"unusually fine and delicate." Parsons observed that this boy always played in
the girls' play group (Parsons, 1916, pp. 521–522). This is similar to an 1850s'

report by a frontier trader who remarked about numerous feminine young male children among the Crows, who "cannot be brought to join in any of the work or play of the boys, but on the contrary associate entirely with the girls. . . . When arrived at the age of 12 or 14, and his habits are formed, the parents clothe him in a girl's dress" (Dening, 1961, pp. 187–188).

In 1903, an anthropologist reported meeting a Crow two-spirit male who "was decidedly effeminate in voice and manner. I was told that, when very young, these persons manifested a decided preference for things pertaining to female duties." Even if parents gently suggested that such boys assume a standard masculine role, they invariably resisted (Simms, 1903, pp. 580–581). The family adjusted to the child's basic character rather than the child conforming to standard gender norms. The consistency of reports from various Native cultures over the centuries is striking. As early as 1702, a French explorer living with the Illinois Indians noted that feminine males were notable "from their childhood, when they are seen frequently picking up the spade, the spindle, the axe [women's tools], but making no use of the bow and arrows, as all the other small boys do" (Pierre Liette, quoted in Katz, 1976, p. 228). It is the characteristic of males preferring feminine pursuits during childhood and playing in girls' play groups that is most frequently reported in the published literature.

## A Unique Childhood

In interviews with two-spirit males, I also found another pattern, one that is more individual and less stereotypically feminine. For example, a Hupa two-spirit male remembered: "I was always into something else, things that were never expected of me. I did what I wanted to do, and I liked that" (personal field notes, 1985). A Lakota *winkte* reported memories of being different from other children while growing up on the reservation:

> I was different. I never played with the boys. I played with the girls a little, or off in my own little world. There were other things I had to do besides play. I did drawings and things. I hung around my grandparents a lot. My grandfather taught me the traditions, and my grandmother taught me how to sew and cook. I was the only child there and they basically responded to my interests. I loved things like beadwork. I was mostly involved in doing artistic things. It isolated me from the other kids, so I took a liking to it. I did all the isolating things. You do beadwork and you're not bothered with other kids. (personal field notes, 1985)

Among the Yaqui Indians of northern Mexico, I also identified this pattern of uniqueness, which was expressed by a Yaqui man who characterized his male two-spirit cousin as "androgynous" rather than "feminine." This is a distinction that non-Native observers, accustomed to thinking in male/female, either/or dichotomies, are likely to miss (see Golden, this volume). By the time this Yaqui boy was 9 years old, he was considered by his relatives to be extremely noncompetitive and to have a cooperative approach to life. He also was recognized as having an unusually strong proclivity for dreaming. His family recognized that he was not typical, but rather than look down on him for his different ways, they valued and understood his uniqueness. His cousin told me:

> He has lived as if he has some higher understanding of life. He is a very wise old young man. He can draw out of people their feelings. One time we kids got down on him for not being typically masculine, but my great aunt, who is the clan matriarch, came down on us *real* strongly. She said it was part of his character and we should respect him. After that, we protected him when he was around mestizos. They were typically machismo, but we did not let anyone trouble him. I have really learned to value him. His being my cousin made me question the homophobia in society, similar to my great aunt's leadership with questioning women's roles. (personal field notes, 1985)

The tendency for a family to feel protective toward a two-spirit relative has also been observed among the Hopi by ethnographer Richard Grant. In 1978, Grant met a 15-year-old Hopi boy whom he described as "quite androgynous." In the boy's family, "everyone manifests a special kind of protective attitude toward him." Four years later, at a ceremonial dance, Grant tried to chat casually with the young man, whereupon other Hopis, as he described,

> sort of moved in around him and I had a distinct impression of threat coming from them. It was very clear that they were strongly committed to protecting him. So I backed off. . . . I was able to continue observing, and I noted that his companions continuously formed a protective ring around him while he, in his turn, was quite flagrant in his behavior (what we would call a real "queen"). He consistently uses "female talk" forms in his speech. (personal communication, 1985)

This use of women's speech patterns is often noted in the sources about male two-spirit persons.

This feminine speaking style is also evident during singing events, a popular Indian form of entertainment. A nineteenth century observer of a Navajo night singing reported that the *nadlehs* sang in falsetto (Karsch-Haack, 1911, p. 321). At a 1973 traditional Cherokee songfest I attended on the Eastern Cherokee reservation in North Carolina, a male falsetto singer was quite popular. This extremely effeminate male was without a doubt the star of the singing event. While his sexuality was never mentioned, Cherokees of all ages fawned over him to an extreme degree. On the Crow reservation in Montana, *bade'* take a leading role in social singing events and are always invited to stand with the women singers to sing in the feminine style. Crow people greatly value their singing (personal field notes, 1982).

## APPRECIATION OF DIFFERENCE

This appreciative response is quite different from the manner in which gender-nonconformist children are treated in Euro-American culture. Peer groups, parents, and teachers alike attempt to force these children to conform to gender norms; psychiatrists appear most interested in discovering a "cause" for such gender nonconformity (see Bailey, this volume). The motivating factor in this research is often to discover a way to prevent such behavior. Many other cultures, by contrast, are more interested in finding the best social role for these unique individuals. Given these social values, parents have no motive to discourage such a child. Accepting gender variation as an acknowledged reality, they provide a recognized social alternative. They simply admit that this is the way these children will be.

Today, traditionalist Native families play an important role in helping their child fit into these recognized alternative gender roles. It helps greatly when a culture has a respected and recognized alternative gender tradition. For example, a Lakota *winkte* I interviewed remembered the following from when he was about 12 years old: "My mother explained *winkte* to me and asked me if I was going to be that way. By then I had decided I was the way I was, so she never tried to change me since then" (personal field notes, 1982). I have heard similar statements from Polynesian *mahus*, who reported that their parents asked them as children if they were going to become a *mahu*. Because the parents had knowledge of an established and respected gender-variant tradition, it was easy for them to accommodate their child. Another Lakota told me:

> *Winktes* have to be born that way. People know that a person will become a *winkte* very early in his life. About age 12 parents will take him to a ceremony to communicate with past *winktes* who had power to verify if it is just a phase or a permanent thing for his lifetime. If the proper vision takes place and communication with a past *winkte* is established, then everyone accepts him as a *winkte*. (personal field notes, 1982)

The association with past *winkte* spiritual power is an important aspect of the social acceptance of two-spirit persons. Another Lakota *winkte* I interviewed related his spiritual experience:

> I have always filled a *winkte* role. I was just born this way, ever since I can remember. When I was eight I saw a vision of a person with long gray hair and with many ornaments on, standing by my bed. I asked if he was female or male, and he said "both." He said he would walk with me for the rest of my life. His spirit would always be with me. I told my grandfather, who said not to be afraid of spirits, because they have good powers. A year later, the vision appeared again, and told me he would give me great powers. He said his body was man's, but his spirit was woman's. He told me the Great Spirit made people like me to be of help to other people.
>
> I told my grandfather the name of the spirit, and grandfather said it was a highly respected *winkte* who lived long ago. He explained *winkte* to me and said, "It won't be easy growing up, because you will be different from others. But the spirit will help you, if you pray and do the sweat." The spirit has continued to contact me throughout my life. If I practice the *winkte* role seriously, then people will respect me. . . .
>
> Once I asked the spirit if my living with a man and loving him was bad. The spirit answered that it was not bad because I had a right to release my feelings and express love for another, that I was good because I was generous and provided a good home for my [adopted] children. I want to be remembered most for the two values that my people hold dearest: generosity and spirituality. If you say anything about me, say those two things. (personal field notes, 1982)

By appealing to this personal visionary experience, two-spirit traditionalists have a spiritual source of strength that provides them with psychological balance and self-esteem. Far from ignoring or covering up their difference, gender-atypical Native persons are provided with a spiritual explanation for their difference that gives them a personal sense of power.

## ACCEPTANCE OF SEXUAL DIVERSITY

Characteristics such as generosity and spirituality are upheld as ideals for such persons, but these people are not expected to deny or suppress their sexuality. In fact, alternative-gendered persons are *expected* to be same-sex oriented in their affectional inclinations. This accepting attitude toward sexual diversity in many Native American and Polynesian cultures is congruent with their larger value systems. Sex is not solely for the purpose of marriage and reproduction but is valued as a means of relaxation, entertainment, and stress reduction. Perhaps its most important social function is the creation of intimate bonds among unrelated individuals. In this context, sexual expression is not restricted to a single marriage partner. Sex is a gift from the spirit world, to be widely enjoyed and appreciated. This attitude results in a casualness regarding sexuality and a lack of cultural proscriptions repressing human sexual variations. Stigmatizing individuals because of their sexual behavior and restricting people's choices generally are not considered to be a valid function of society. Personal freedom is too highly regarded for such an approach.

The way that such a society functions is best illustrated by traditional Mohave culture. George Devereux, an anthropologist who lived with this Southwestern tribe in the 1930s, reported that the Mohave had an "easy" culture, providing "a rational, supportive, lenient and flexible upbringing" for children (Devereux, 1969, pp. viii–ix). His studies of mental illness among the Mohave found that both the incidence and the severity of mental illness were drastically lower than among Euro-Americans of the time. He concluded that the main reason for their higher rates of mental health was the Mohaves' easygoing pattern of child rearing (Devereux, 1969).

The Mohave attitude toward sexuality was consistent with their carefree attitude toward life in general. Devereux noted that "Mohave sex-life is entirely untrammeled by social restraint" (Devereux, 1937, p. 518). They viewed sex as an enjoyable and humorous sport, a gift from nature and the spirit world to be freely indulged. Devereux reported that Mohaves talked incessantly about sex and never censored their sexual talk in the presence of children. Hearing this talk and observing adults' sexual activities with no social restrictions placed on them, Mohave children grew up with an adventuresome attitude toward sex. Children did not wear clothing until puberty, and they were encouraged to explore their bodies. Urinating competitions among boys, to see who could pee the farthest, were common. Groups of males also engaged in masturbation contests to see who could reach orgasm most quickly and who could shoot their ejaculate the far-thest. Devereux reported that casual same-sex relations were frequent, from early childhood through adulthood (Devereux, 1937, pp. 498–99, 518).

Although the ease of sexual experimentation with both sexes was enjoyed in a lighthearted way, Devereux noted:

> Even the most casual coitus implied, by definition, also an involvement of the "soul": body cohabit-ing with body and soul with soul. . . . Many children cohabited with each other and even with adults long before puberty; the [nonsexual] latency period was conspicuous by its absence. Children were much loved, brought up permissively, and looked after at once generously and lackadaisically. (Dev-ereux, 1969, p. xii)

Mohave children spent their prepubertal years exploring their environment with their age mates, playing, swimming, and indulging in sexual play.

Because the culture placed a high value on kindness to children, Mohave children learned to like and trust everyone. Children interacted, sexually and otherwise, with various people of different ages. As a result, Mohaves tended not to restrict themselves to an "overintense and exclusive emotional attachment" to a single person. Devereux wrote, no doubt at least partly from his own per-sonal experience, "This explains why the adult Mohave is so highly 'available,' both sexually and for friendship" (Devereux, 1969, p. xiii). Mohave sexual pat-terns tell much about the shape of the overall culture. That is, their casual atti-tude toward sex reflected their carefree and freedom-loving attitude toward life in general (Devereux, 1969, p. xiii).

## SAME-SEX BEHAVIOR DURING CHILDHOOD

In such an atmosphere, exploratory same-sex behavior during childhood and adolescence can take place in an open and accepted manner. No other anthro-pologist has studied Mohave sex life as intensely as Devereux, so the extent to which such liberationist attitudes continue today is not known. But in my con-versations with many Native Americans of diverse tribes in the 1980s and 1990s, and also with Native Hawaiians, I have found that sexual play continues to be viewed as an important element in growing up and learning adult roles. I have been told by many Polynesian men that their first sexual experience occurred when they were quite young, often between 5 and 9 years old, and with an older male relative. This was usually a cousin or an uncle, and their sexual involvement occurred in the context of a close emotional bond. As adults, they reflected on this sexual relationship with fond memories, even if they were heterosexually oriented. The sexual activities were merely one aspect of a loving relationship and were an important part of their maturation process. Because homosexuality is not regarded by the society as dirty or sinful, they were not afflicted with nega-tive memories of "child abuse" that so commonly plague Euro-American adults who engaged in same-sex eroticism during childhood.

If Native traditionalist adults learn about the sexual activities of their children, their reaction is usually one of amusement rather than alarm. Cognizant of societal acceptance of such behavior, children who engage in consensual sexual behavior are not psychically damaged and do not suffer feelings of guilt or shame. Cross-cultural data thus suggest that current American psychological studies about the damage of same-sex child abuse can be traced mainly to societal homophobia rather than to the intrinsic harm of the sexual behavior itself. Further research on this topic is needed, especially with adults who engaged in same-sex behaviors during childhood but who do not feel that those behaviors resulted in psychic harm. Truly unbiased studies are needed to determine which factors lead some children to feel their childhood experiences were abusive and which factors lead others to opposite conclusions. Investigators should explore whether there are differences between same-sex and other-sex involvements, between boys and girls, and between the negative and neutral reactions of others if childhood sexual involvement becomes known.

Cross-cultural perspectives demonstrate that many current American suppositions about sex may be improper assumptions based solely on investigations in a single, sex-negative society. Unfortunately, little cross-cultural documentation exists regarding female-female sexual activities during childhood. However, for males worldwide, data clearly suggest that same-sex involvements have been commonly accepted in many cultures. For example, ethnographer Grant reported in the 1970s that it was commonly known within the reservation community that Hopi males up to their late twenties would often participate in same-sex activities with their friends, without social disapproval. Grant wrote:

> Everyone considers homosexual behavior normal during adolescence, and nearly all boys form special bonds, which include sexual behavior. It is expected that all will "grow out of it," however, so that in adulthood [heterosexual] marriage and the production of children will occur. (personal communication, 1985)

Among seventeenth-century Mayas, this type of same-sex relationship was institutionalized among boys and young men. In the early seventeenth century, the Franciscan Guatemalan friar Juan de Torquemada wrote about the Mayas telling him a legend of a god who came down to earth and taught the males how to have sex with each other:

> Convinced therefore that it was not a sin, the custom started among parents of giving a boy to their young son, to have him for a woman and to use him as a woman; from that also began the law that if anyone approached the boy [sexually], they were ordered to pay for it, punishing them with the same penalties as those breaking the condition of a marriage. (Quoted in Guerra, 1971, pp. 172–173)

This custom of an adolescent male having a younger boy as a "wife" negates the view of homosexuality as "abnormal." The norm for that culture was for a boy to be a boy-wife in his youth, graduate in the teenage years to being a husband of a younger boy, and then in his twenties to marry a woman. This custom did not exist in isolation among the Mayas. Though very little is known about sexual variance in most cultures, same-sex marriages among male youths have been socially accepted and honored in many areas of the world, from the Azande war-riorhoods of East Africa to the Edo courts and Buddhist monasteries of Japan (see Williams, 1986, chapter 12). The widespread existence of such customs also illustrates the inclination of many, if not most, males—in the absence of social taboos—to interact sexually with both males and females during at least part of their lifetime.

Among many cultures, such as the Zapotecs of Mexico, same-sex behavior among males is so common that same-sex eroticism is not used as a means of classifying people. Only the gender-variant *muxe*, or two-spirit, is considered different. Gender-conformist masculine boys may be sexually active with other boys or adult men and their behavior does not mark them as deviant. Though boys commonly become sexually active with men before puberty, when they reach their mid-twenties almost all marry women. This occurs primarily to en-sure the reproduction of offspring, but even after marriage a male may continue to have sex with other males without censure (Chiñas, 1985). In most Native cultures, marriage is traditionally and primarily viewed as an economic arrange-ment for securing the family's subsistence and raising the next generation. A marriage partner is not expected to fulfill all sexual desires. The emphasis of the sexual value system is to provide independence for each person in making deci-sions about her or his life.

## SAME-SEX BEHAVIOR OF ALTERNATIVELY GENDERED PERSONS

Although sexual behavior may often occur between two masculine males or two feminine females, many cultures socially encourage homosexuality between a gender conformist and an androgynous person of the same biological sex. I in-terviewed many androgynous male Polynesians and Native Americans who re-ported that other boys or men approached them for sex, beginning when they were as young as 5 or 6 years old. From that point, they were socialized to take the passive/insertee role in sex. They almost invariably enjoyed and preferred to be anally penetrated by a masculine man; others most enjoyed sucking the man's penis. Few wanted to reverse sexual roles, and indeed some did not even want their penis to be touched. They often experienced ejaculation solely from the pleasure of being anally penetrated; even when they did not ejaculate, they re-ported feeling "an internal orgasm."

The vast majority of my Native interviewees expressed pleasant memories about their childhood sexual experiences. In 1982, a Lakota *winkte* matter-of-factly said that he became sexually active when he was 8 years old, after begin-ning an affair with a 40-year-old man. "Since he was good to me and for me, it was considered by my family to be okay and my own business—no one else's" (personal field notes, 1982). Another recalled in 1985 that when he was 8 years old, his uncle, who was in his thirties, gave him body rubs in which he rubbed the boy's genitals.

> I never knew if it was right or wrong. I was too afraid to know what was happening. They'd call it molestation today, but I don't think it had any bad impact on me in the long run one way or the other. There was no harm done. It intrigued me that I could do this. And then my feelings started to awaken inside of me as I got older, and I began sexual intercourse with men. (personal field notes, 1985)

When this same person was 10 years old, two heterosexual Indian men intoxicated and raped him. He recalled,

> I knew I liked the male sex, but I didn't like it to be that intense. I didn't like the rape. But then at age 10 I began a whole string of involvements in sex, from ministers to tribal presidents to government officials. Mostly Indian, but White as well. I never was attracted to someone my age. . . . I was never connected to women, never any sexual attraction at all. (personal field notes, 1985)

His experiences over the next 6 years were ongoing sexual encounters with heterosexually married men, rather than full-time relationships. Sometimes he initiated these affairs, and he has fond memories of his promiscuous times. However, when he was 16 he met a 32-year-old unmarried, masculine construction worker with whom he moved in and began a long-term relationship. This Lakota male is now over 40 and continues to live happily in his marriage with the older man. They are financially stable, own a house, and are emotionally supportive of each other.

The only Native man I interviewed who felt traumatized by sex during childhood was a 25-year-old Blackfoot gay man. When he was 9 years old, he was forcibly raped by his alcoholic grandfather. He remembered the anal rape as physically painful and emotionally disgusting. Because this boy hated his grandfather, who had often physically beaten him and his sister, and because the man had no concern for the boy's pain, the violent rape was particularly damaging. To cope with his trauma, he turned to drugs and alcohol. Only after years of counseling with a patient therapist did he learn to cope and at last could begin to enjoy sex with his European gay male lover, with whom he now lives happily.

Without a doubt, his case constituted child abuse, and his memories stand in sharp contrast to the positive feelings expressed by other Native males who engaged in consensual and loving sexual relationships during childhood. Even the Lakota *winkte* cited above who was raped at age 10 grew up without extensive psychic harm because his previous enjoyable sexual experiences allowed him to place the rape in perspective. These cases indicate that the pleasurableness of initial sexual experiences may be extremely important in determining a person's later psychological health. Thus, if our society is truly concerned with protecting youth, it is important to ensure that young people's initial sexual encounters are pleasant and enjoyable for them. Enjoyment and positive memory, not the age at which the youth begins to be sexually active, are crucial in promoting the development of psychological health and maturity.

The above cases illustrate the extreme contrast between child-abusive societies, in which children suffer rapes and oppression, and child-loving societies, such as the Mohaves and Zapotecs, in which children are permitted to be sexually free and unrepressed. Child-loving cultures are better able to produce children with positive self-esteem and little psychosis, partly because they have evolved a formula in which sexual diversity and gender variance are recognized and accepted. Persons in those societies who are gender nonconformist and same-sex oriented are not just grudgingly tolerated, but honored as exceptional two-spirited persons having special spiritual gifts.

## Economic Contributions to the Family

Besides spirituality, the other important factor generating respect for sexual diversity in both Native American and Polynesian cultures is the strong economic contribution that androgynous people often make to their family and community. In my interviews with Native Hawaiians, I have been struck by an especially strong respect for family, which is the basis of acceptance of same-sex inclined and bisexually inclined individuals. Similar to Native Americans, Polynesians have traditionally lived in extended families with wide networks of kin dependent on each other. In this family organization, not everyone has to have children.

By contrast, in societies characterized by the nuclear family, everyone must reproduce if they are to have someone to care for them in their old age. In an extended family, however, persons who do not reproduce have nephews and nieces who will take care of them. In fact, it is an economic advantage for one or two adults not to reproduce because then there is a higher ratio of food-producing adults to food-consuming children.

Today in our geographically mobile society, it might not be possible for many people to reconstruct this emphasis on the extended family, but knowledge of the importance of a wide network of kin can serve as inspiration for developing other alternatives. In my opinion, the best potential for accomplishing this is through encouraging longstanding close-friendship networks (see Weston, 1992). As an anthropologist, one of the most striking aspects I see in contemporary American culture is the severely restricted number of persons on whom Americans depend emotionally. Current social problems suggest that the small nuclear family is not doing a very good job providing emotional support and personal financial interdependence. If emotional bondings beyond the nuclear family can be created, whether in extended families or in long-term friendship networks, a much healthier society will evolve.

In Native American extended families, two-spirit persons, being both masculine and feminine, make particularly important economic contributions because they can do both women's and men's work. They provide assistance to their siblings' children and thus advance the status of the extended family as a whole. This family role is particularly strong among the Navajo, whose word *nadleh* suggests spiritual transformation. A traditionalist Navajo woman, whose uncle was a well-respected *nadleh* healer, told me:

They are seen as very compassionate people, who care for their family a lot and help people. That's why they are healers. *Nadlehs* are also seen as being great with children, real Pied Pipers. Children love *nadlehs*, so parents are pleased if a *nadleh* takes an interest in their child. One that I know is now a principal of a school on a reservation. . . . *Nadlehs* are not seen as an abstract group, like "gay people," but as a specific person, like "my relative so-and-so." People who help their family a lot are considered valuable members of the community. (personal field notes, 1982)

Thus, it is within the context of individual family relations that much of the high status of two-spirit people must be evaluated. When family members know that one of their relatives is this type of person and when they have positive cultural reinforcements to account for such individual diversity, then tensions are not imposed on the family. Without interference from external societal and religious groups claiming that there is something wrong with parents who raise such a child, unprejudiced family love can express itself.

In this context, an individual who in Euro-American culture would be considered a misfit, an embarrassment to the family, is instead central to the family. Because other relatives do not feel threatened, family disunity and conflict are avoided. The two-spirit person is not pressured to suppress gender-atypical or same-sex behavior and thus does not develop a poor self-image or engage in self-destructive behavior. Considered to have special strengths, such persons are too strongly valued by their families to have their talents and potential contributions wasted.

Instead of being suppressed or discarded, the unique energies of two-spirit persons are channeled into productive labor that benefits the extended family. Traditionally, masculine female two-spirits are known as skilled hunters and brave warriors (see Williams, 1986, chapter 11). Androgynous male two-spirits are known as excellent cooks, skilled craftspersons, potters, beadworkers, and seamstresses and for having the best-decorated houses (see Williams, 1986, chapter 3).

This reputation reflects a strong striving for prestige by those who are different. Unlike Euro-American society, in which prestige is a reflection of material wealth, in many Native American cultures a person gains prestige by helping others. Whether helping to heal people through shamanistic abilities, teaching the young, working hard for the well-being of their family, showing their generosity, or displaying their talents in superior craftwork, the theme that unites all of these endeavors by two-spirit people is an especially strong striving for prestige.

The female two-spirit in traditional times, then, had an inclination not just to be a hunter and warrior but to be an outstanding one. Her strong personal motivation to prove to everyone that she deserved to be accepted in those roles led her to work especially hard. Likewise, the androgynous male child who did not demonstrate bravery in warfare or success in the hunt could still gain renown for spiritual, intellectual, and artistic skills. In many tribes, two-spirit persons traditionally had particular opportunities to accumulate wealth. For example, in some California groups, the two-spirits prepared the dead for burial and were entitled to keep the property that was placed with the body.

Among the Navajos, *nadlehs* participate in both women's and men's economic activities, gaining twice as much as the average man or woman. *Nadlehs* also make pottery, baskets, and woven goods. Because their crafts are associated with spiritual power, their products are always heavily in demand as trade goods. Beyond this, because they are believed to be lucky in amassing wealth, *nadlehs* usually act as the head of their extended family and have control of family property. Because their opportunities for accumulating wealth are greater than those of an ordinary person, it is easy to support the belief that *nadlehs* ensure prosperity. In 1935, an ethnographer published an interview with a *nadleh* that reflected the quiet self-confidence and centrality of a two-spirit person within the Navajo family. The *nadleh* reported:

> A family that has a *nadleh* born into it will be brought riches and success. . . . I have charge of everything that my family owns. I hope that I will be that way until I die. Riches do not just come to you; you have to pray for what you get. . . . My parents always took better care of me. . . . The family, after I grew up, always gave me the choice of whatever they had. (Hill, 1935, p. 278)

## Conclusion

This reaction of Native families to an androgynous child is opposite to that of most Euro-Americans. As the large caseload of psychiatric therapy in the United States attests, severe damage can result when children evolve a negative self-image. Gender-atypical children in North America, recognizing their difference from the norm and reminded of it by relatives and peers, easily acquire feelings of deviance or inferiority. Denying meaningful differences ("I am the same as you except for this one minor difference") is not a very effective means of reducing the prejudice directed against them. Because society considers gender and sexual differences important, making an appeal that "we're all really just the same" frequently results in prejudiced persons recoiling in terror; they fear that someone might consider them deviant as well.

My cross-cultural research suggests that the most effective means for inculcating social acceptance of androgynous persons is through cultural emphasis and appreciation for the unique gifts of such persons. Difference is transformed from "deviant" to "exceptional." The difference is emphasized, becoming a basis for respect rather than stigmatization. Native American and Polynesian cultures utilize the talents of androgynous persons precisely because these cultures offer prestige and rewards *beyond* those which are available to the average person.

Both Native American and Native Hawaiian sources often remark that androgynous males are particularly clean and tend to have the best-decorated homes. These characteristics are similar to the emphasis on personal looks, clothing style, and interior decoration in contemporary Euro-American urban gay subculture. These historic similarities cannot be explained by cultural diffusion. Rather, they are a result of gender nonconformists' individual pride for doing well in a cultural system in which they are not typical. Euro-American traditional family values allow at best only a grudging tolerance for androgynous and sexually nonconformist individuals, whereas in Native cultures family members are taught to feel especially blessed and fortunate to have a two-spirit relative.

Family and community respect for two-spirit persons was noted repeatedly by early anthropologists. For example, in the Zuni pueblo in the 1890s, Stevenson described a two-spirit *lhamana* named We'wha: "His strong character made his word law among both the men and the women with whom he associated. Though his wrath was dreaded by men as well as by women, he was beloved by all the children, to whom he was ever kind." When We'wha became ill with heart disease in 1896, Stevenson wrote that she had "never before observed such attention as every member of the family showed." Despite their efforts, within a week We'wha went into a coma and died. Stevenson reported: "Darkness and desolation entered the hearts of the mourners. . . . We'wha's death was regarded as a calamity. . . . [It was] a death which caused universal regret and distress in Zuni" (Stevenson, 1901/1902, pp. 37–38, 310–313).

An anthropologist who lived among the Navajo in the 1930s also emphasized the extremely favorable attitudes of families toward *nadleh*s:

> The family which counted a transvestite among its members or had a hermaphrodite child born to them was considered by themselves and everyone else as very fortunate. The success and wealth of such a family was believed to be assured. Special care was taken in the raising of such children and they were afforded favoritism not shown to other children of the family. As they grew older and assumed the character of *nadle* [sic], this solicitude and respect increased. . . . This respect verges almost on reverence in many cases. (Hill, 1935, p. 274)

This anthropologist quoted several Navajo informants to illustrate these attitudes:

> They know everything. They can do both the work of a man and a woman. I think when all the *nadle* are gone, that it will be the end of the Navaho.
>
> If there were no *nadle,* the country would change. They are responsible for all the wealth in the country. If there were no more left, the horses, sheep, and Navaho would all go. They are leaders just like President Roosevelt. A *nadle* around the hogan will bring good luck and riches. They have charge of all the riches. It does a great deal for the country if you have *nadle* around.
>
> You must respect a *nadle.* They are, somehow, sacred and holy. (Hill, 1935, p. 274)

Another reason two-spirit persons are respected is because they are often the person who will care for elderly relatives. Being homoerotically inclined, they seldom have children. This is also true in Hawai'i, where, according to Polynesian informants, the *mahu* is traditionally the family member who cares for the aged parents. This arrangement is advantageous for heterosexual siblings, allowing them more time to care for their children. Hawaiian traditionalists value their *mahu* relatives partly because such persons are not reproductive. Traditionalists strongly defend their *mahu* relatives and friends by asking: "How could I turn my back on them? They are my relatives. They are part of my family" (personal field notes, 1992). Ironically, it is traditional family values—Polynesian style—that are the basis for acceptance of the *mahu*. Because their families are strong, much stronger than the weak nuclear family system of the West, they dare not turn their back on relatives. These are *real* "traditional family values": unconditional love, a certainty of mutual dependence, acceptance of people the way they are, and a respect for the magic and power of human diversity.

Having this level of support and high family expectations, two-spirit people and *mahus* are often renowned for being hard workers and productive, intelligent contributors to their family. Their relatives benefit, much more so than among Euro-American families, where heterosexist prejudice often divides families and causes relatives to lose the potential contributions of talented and exceptional individuals. If families in contemporary society incorporate such loving values into raising children, the strength of true family values can be increased. This can be learned if we listen to the wisdom of Native American and Polynesian traditionalist people. An Indian from Arizona expressed the essence of this wisdom when he concluded:

> Among my people, gay is a special status. . . . The more unique someone is, the more valuable they are, the more unique their vision, the more unique their gift, their perspective, everything they can offer is something that other people can't offer. . . . The thing that's different about where I come from, is that all human beings are respected because all human beings have potential, all human beings have value. (quoted in Von Praunheim, 1980, p. 148)

# ▼ REFERENCES ▼

Chiñas, B. (1985, May). Isthmus Zapotec "berdaches." *Newsletter of the anthropological research group on homosexuality, 7,* 1–4.

Chiñas, B. (1991). *The isthmus Zapotecs.* New York: Holt, Rinehart and Winston.

Conner, R. P. (1993). *Blossom of bone: Reclaiming the connections between homoeroticism and the sacred.* San Francisco: Harper.

Dening, E. T. (1961). *Five Indian tribes of the upper Missouri,* (edited for publication by John Ewers). Norman: University of Oklahoma Press.

Devereux, G. (1937). Institutionalized homosexuality of the Mohave Indians. *Human Biology, 9,* 498–521.

Devereux, G. (1969). *Mohave ethnopsychiatry.* Washington, DC: Smithsonian Institution.

Forde, C. D. (1931). Ethnography of the Yuma Indians. *University of California Publications in American Archeology and Ethnology, 28,* 83–278.

Guerra, F. (1971). *The pre-Columbian mind.* London: Seminar Press.

Herdt, G. H. (Ed.). (1984). *Ritualized homosexuality in Melanesia.* Berkeley: University of California Press.

Hill, W. W. (1935). The status of the hermaphrodite and transvestite in Navaho culture. *American Anthropologist, 37,* 273–279.

Honigmann, J. J. (1964). *The Kaska Indians: An ethnographic reconstruction.* New Haven: Yale University Press.

Karsch-Haack, F. (1911). *Das gleichgeschlechtliche leben der naturvölker [The same-sex life of indigenous people].* Munich: Verlag von Ernst Reinhardt.

Katz, J. (1976). *Gay American history.* New York: Crowell.

Mead, M. (1935/1963). *Sex and temperament in three primitive societies* (rev. ed.). New York: Morrow Quill.

Murray, S. O. (1992). *Oceanic homosexualities.* New York: Garland.

Parsons, E. C. (1916). The Zuni la'mana. *American Anthropologist, 18,* 521–522.

Requena, A. (1945, July–September). Noticias y consideraciones sobre las anormalidades sexuales de los aborigenes americanos: sodomia. *[Notes and considerations concerning sexual abnormalities of aborigional Americans: Sodomy].* Acta Venezolana, 1, 16.

Simms, S. C. (1903). Crow Indian hermaphrodites. *American Anthropologist, 5,* 580–581.

Stevenson, M. C. (1901/1902). The Zuni Indians. *Bureau of American Ethnology Annual Report.* Washington, DC: Smithsonian Institution.

Von Praunheim, R. (1980). *Army of lovers.* London: Gay Men's Press.

Weston, K. (1992). *Families we choose: Lesbians, gays, and kinship.* New York: Columbia University Press.

White, E. (1980). *States of desire: Travels in gay America.* New York: Dutton.

Williams, W. L. (1986). *The spirit and the flesh: Sexual diversity in American Indian culture.* Boston: Beacon Press.

Williams, W. L. (1990). Male homosexuality in Thailand [Review essay]. *Journal of Homosexuality, 19,* 126–138.

Williams, W. L. (1991). *Javanese lives: Women and men in modern Indonesian society.* New Brunswick, NJ: Rutgers University Press.

*Chapter 19*

▼

# Bisexuality:

# Exploring/Exploding the Boundaries

Jay P. Paul

*Sexual labels continue to haunt and define us in contemporary Western society. In mainstream American culture, a significant aspect of one's social identity is derived from the label that purports to summarize the totality of one's sexual feelings and emotional ties to others. However, human sexuality cannot be reduced to conventional categories of "sexual orientation" without serious compromise to its variability and complexity. In conventional reductionistic thinking, discontinuities and inconsistencies in sexual experiences and relationships are typically ascribed meanings that "neutralize" them. Despite efforts to define sexual orientation as a universal, transhistorical, and "core" aspect of self, it is a construct that is deeply embedded in our cultural values and our preoccupation with gender. This is not to say that individuals do not vary in their sexual experiences, tastes, and relationships; however, our insistence on seeing these preferences as fixed or invariant, as having broad implications for self-identity and personality, and as being determined primarily by gender is primarily a cultural phenomenon. Homosexual and bisexual behavior is structured very differently in different cultures and social strata outside of the Western urban context of defined gay and lesbian communities (Adam, 1985; Callender & Kochems, 1985; Carrier, 1985; Herdt, 1981; Parker & Carballo, 1990; Williams, this volume). Nominal categories based on sexual preferences (homosexual/heterosexual/bisexual) exist, but they may say more about the individual's sociopolitical affiliations than about her or his erotic experiences and desires. Concern with AIDS prevention has spurred a new wave of research on sexual behavior, and much of it has reinforced the notion that sexual labels are not always predictive of sexual behaviors (Doll et al., 1992; Earl, 1990; Manalansan, this volume).*

*Sexual labels may be least illuminating when applied to those whose sexual experiences are complex, such as cases where attraction crosses gender divisions. There has been debate in the literature as to whether bisexuality is a "sexual orientation" (or "sexual preference") that should be viewed as a "master status trait" (Hughes, 1945) equivalent to homosexuality and heterosexuality.*

*Bisexuality blurs the boundaries between groups defined by the conventional heterosexual/homosexual dichotomy and further disturbs lay beliefs by underscoring the fact that sexual partner preferences may shift for some people over the course of their lives (Golden, this volume). This confounds both traditional psychodynamic thinking—which treats sexual orientation as a facet of gender identity, realized through identification with one parent—and scientists who continue to search for universal biological determinants of homosexuality, whether they be genetic, hormonal, or structural/anatomical differences in the brain (Ellis, this volume).*

*Despite our culture's less than ideal constructions of sexual preference and sexual identity, these formulations structure the social world in which we live. Given the limitations of our knowledge on sexuality, what suggestions can be made for the mental health professional who wishes to be prepared to work with those exploring issues germane to bisexuality? Most concerns of those who approach a professional may be summarized as falling either within the realm of personal identity or within the province of relationships and the interpersonal world of the bisexual. This chapter attempts to dispatch with several common sexual myths and to address a number of interrelated questions that may arise:*

- *How does one conceptualize and explore sexual orientation and sexual labels?*
- *What are some of the issues particular to individuals whose erotic attractions and relationships involve both men and women?*
- *What are some of the relationship issues that arise for couples in which one or both partners are bisexual?*

## DEVELOPING CONCEPTS OF SEXUALITY

### What Do We Mean by Sexual Preference?

Over the last century, paradigms of sexuality changed rapidly, with discourse shifting from the province of morality and religion (sin) to that of medicine (sickness) and, ultimately, to the social sciences (social deviance/diversity). Variations in sexual behavior became something to be explained by one's essence or nature, and science attempted to demonstrate the ways in which sexual preference was linked to various personal traits. Biological explanations of sexuality predominated, and although Freud's (1905/1953) work on psychosexual development shifted the focus of subsequent schemata to the contributions of social forces, his thinking could not free itself from the biological determinism and psychophysical parallelism of his era. Classical psychodynamic theory suggested that not only a sense of maleness or femaleness, but also sexual attraction, was determined by the resolution of the Oedipal conflict. This formulation simply incorporated cultural constructions of homosexual desire as a sign of gender inversion, and homosexuality was thus not very distinct from transvestism or transsexualism. Because bisexuality confused this simple gender-based dichotomy (evident from references to it as "psychic hermaphroditism"), it was dismissed and any ambiguous cases were carefully scrutinized to identify the "true" underlying sexual orientation. Thus, initial constructions of sexual orientation used the dichotomy of heterosexual/homosexual derived from male/female and failed to differentiate gender identity, social sex role, sexual object choice, and sexual role. These aspects of self continue to be conflated, especially by those who seek common biological mechanisms driving both gender-typed behavior/roles and sexual behavior (e.g., Pillard & Weinrich, 1987).

It has been almost half a century since Kinsey, Pomeroy, and Martin (1948) provided evidence debunking conventional notions of heterosexuality and homosexuality as mutually exclusive patterns and identities. Although the findings of Kinsey and his colleagues (1948, 1953) had a tremendous impact on subsequent research and emerging constructs of sexuality, they had much less impact among the general public in undermining the conventional formulations of sexual orientation as either heterosexual or homosexual. Nonetheless, their seven-point scale representing the continuum of gender-based sexual attraction has become not only a standard of sexological research but an additional labeling device used by some in a fashion that probably would have horrified Kinsey (e.g., identifying oneself as "a Kinsey Three"). The "Kinsey scale" was originally a unidimensional measure that combined lifetime sexual behavior and erotic attractions; it has been criticized as conceptually reductive, as there is no reason to expect an individual's sexual behavior and feelings to be synchronous. Since that time, our understanding of the construct of sexual preference has become more complex and multidimensional. By 1978, Bell and Weinberg were using separate Kinsey scale continuua to measure sexual experiences and sexual feelings. These measures of sexual preference were still very much tied to physiological response and did not consider the social context or ascribed meanings of such behavior.

Shively and De Cecco (1977) differentiated several independent components of a person's sexuality—biological sex, gender identity, social sex role, and sexual orientation—with sexual orientation further subdivided into the dimensions of physical sexual activity, erotic fantasies, and affectional preferences for one gender versus the other. Suppe (1984b) proposed a "multidimensional approach" to the measurement of "sexual identity." To the components of the Shively and De Cecco model, he added the neglected aspect of self-definition, as well as arousal cue-response patterns (described in Suppe, 1984a). This attempt to include aspects of self-concept and reference group affiliation in the measurement of sexual orientation was then extended by Klein, Sepekoff, and Wolf (1985), who considered seven distinct dimensions—sexual behavior, sexual fantasies, erotic attraction, emotional preference, social group preference, self-identification, and heterosexual/ homosexual lifestyle preference—as well as temporal changes (past versus present) and satisfaction with these dimensions, as measured by the present versus ideal ratings. In work that attempts to integrate the conceptualizations described above with the Bell and Weinberg (1978) typology of same-sex relationship styles, Coleman (1987) described a useful clinical tool for assessing sexual orientation, utilizing a pie-chart format rather than a series of continuua, which avoids the potential problem of the Kinsey categories having labeling implications. Coleman's assessment tool also expanded the focus on relationships by emphasizing not only the gender(s) of one's partner(s), but the types of relationships one has (e.g., sexually exclusive/nonexclusive; primary/nonprimary).

In summary, there has been a broadening of the construct of sexual orientation and its assessment to include variables related to the social and relational context of sexual behavior, as well as the inclusion of temporal shifts in sexual attractions and behaviors.

## How Can We Describe the Development of Sexual Preference?

Developmental shifts or discontinuities in sexual behavior patterns across the lifespan raise interesting questions about the nature of sexual orientation and pose a challenge to those who define sexual attraction as fixed or relatively invariant over the life course. If sexual behavior patterns can change, sometimes repeatedly, over an individual's lifetime, and sexual self-identification can also fluctuate within an individual over time, what determines constancy versus change? Research suggests that such alterations in sexual attractions occur and may remain at variance with self-labels (Blumstein & Schwartz, 1977; Golden, this volume; Lever, Kanouse, Rogers, Carson, & Hertz, 1992; Plummer, 1981; Ponse, 1978). Herdt (1984) pointed out that when fluidity of sexual orientation is discussed, which he noted is a frequent metaphor for bisexuality, shifts may be considered on a variety of levels. These include erotic responsiveness, culturally determined transitions in the tolerance for versus restrictions placed on particular sexual contacts across the life course, and self-concept. If gross discrepancies exist between one dimension of sexuality and another—for example, sexual fantasy and sexual behavior—it is important to understand the factors that may determine future development or shifts in sexual preference. Despite models of same-sex identity formation that presume a natural progression toward internal consistency, discrepancies across the multiple dimensions of sexual preference and identity are unlikely to be inherently contradictory or transient. Cultural values reflecting the way in which sexual experiences are structured and coded are more likely to impact the stability of such patterns of concordance or discordance and influence any transitions over the life course.

The utility of our classificatory system of sexual preference in understanding the nature and development of patterns of erotic and emotional attraction remains unclear. Those who have explored the determinants of human sexuality have often come away confused or with inconclusive findings (e.g., Bell, Weinberg, & Hammersmith, 1981), typically because research models try to verify a single causal agent or developmental sequence to sexual partner preference. Research looking for differences among those identified as homo-sexual, heterosexual, and bisexual presumes that distinctive within-group con-sistencies can be identified; yet there is tremendous intragroup variability in sexual histories, practices, and relationships (Savin-Williams, "Childhood Mem-ories," this volume). The primary fallacy may be viewing all patterns of same-sex behavior as synonymous and thus determined by the same set of factors. Research suggests that cultures ascribe a variety of meanings to sexual behav-ior based on circumstantial or contextual factors and on the demographic char-acteristics of the actors; furthermore, there is a variety of social identities or roles that are "determined" by sexual behavior. While this emphasizes the power of culture to shape behaviors and determine the social role implications for var-ious activities, it does not rule out a biological basis to sexual preference.

Despite the flurry of recent public attention to biological explanations for homosexuality (Angier, 1991a, 1991b; Crabb, 1991; Gorman, 1991; Henry, 1993; Maddox, 1991), critical scientific scrutiny has raised serious questions about methodological flaws and lack of replicability in many studies cited as substan-tiating biological theories (Gooren, Fliers, & Courteny, 1990). The debate on sex-ual orientation between social constructionists and biological determinists in the 1970s and 1980s created more acrimony than intellectual synthesis (see Esterberg, this volume). It appears likely that sexual choice is determined by a variety of factors, including biological, social, and sexual scripting determinants. In the early part of the century, Krafft-Ebing (1935) described the different de-velopmental patterns of nonexclusive same-sex interests and behavior by utiliz-ing an innate/acquired distinction, which has since been resurrected by other researchers. For example, Weinrich (1988), although not explicitly embracing this dichotomy, differentiated between forms of sexual attraction that he calls "limerence," which involves eroticizing the qualities of a particular known per-son, and "lustiness," which refers to erotic responsiveness to all persons with specific characteristics, a presumed product of imprinting or of a critical-period experience in the process of biological maturation. While this formulation re-veals some appreciation for the complexities of sexual attraction, it remains an oversimplification. The interactions among biological factors, experiential fac-tors, and culture in the development of sexual attractions and the explanation of discontinuities in sexual biographies remain unclear.

## Are Sexual Preferences Intrinsically Gender Based?

Despite the fact that human behavior has a plasticity and variability that moves sexual behavior beyond its biological roots in procreation, our constructs of sex-uality are for the most part determined by biological and, in particular, gender-specific considerations. Our culture's categories of sexuality are based on the gender(s) to whom one is sexually attracted, presuming this to be a necessary and sufficient determinant. The assumption that gender is the critical variable derives from genitally focused, deterministic models of sexuality that portray sexual attraction as primarily serving a reproductive purpose. Emotional and sexual relationships may, however, spring from a tremendous variety of sources (see Ross, 1984, for a list of possible motivations), and the relative weights of different contributing factors may vary considerably. Gender is not critical to many of these expressed needs or motivators. Suppe (1984a) distinguished four types of cues pertinent to sexual arousal: cues that inhibit sexual arousal; neutral cues, that neither inhibit nor intensify sexual arousal; cues that enhance, but are not required for sexual arousal; and paraphiliac cues, which are prerequisites for sexual arousal. Features related to biological sex and gender (e.g., primary and secondary sexual characteristics) may not necessarily be paraphiliac cues, although our categories of sexual orientation suggest that erotic attraction is determined by such partner traits.

Ross (1984) and Kaplan and Rogers (1984) explored the gender-based assumptions behind contemporary constructs of sexual attraction. Ross suggested that our focus on gender in categorizing sexual interactions (as well as the players) does not allow for the possibility that the biological sex of a partner is not necessarily a critical factor in determining sexual attraction; other preferred-partner characteristics (e.g., eyes, voice, smell, playfulness, physical fitness, sensuality, emotionality) may be more salient to the participants than their biological sex. In contrast to the arguments of Weinrich (1988), Kaplan and Rogers argued that sexual attraction and arousal are typically determined by secondary sexual characteristics, which are not purely "male" or "female." For example, a bisexual male interviewed by Fast and Wells (1975) described his new male lover as "a lot like Linda physically—slight and dark." Ross and Paul (1992) explored these ideas in an exploratory study of the salient characteristics of same-sex and other-sex partners of a small bisexual sample. They elicited the dimensions salient to respondents in differentiating among various sexual partners, nonsexual friends, and others, using the repertory grid technique. The constructs elicited from each respondent were then reduced to a minimal number of factors using principal components analysis (Slater, 1976, 1977). As the dimension of masculinity/femininity was included in all repertory grids, it was possible to evaluate the extent to which this dimension was salient to the factors extracted by the analysis. They concluded that gender did not appear to be a critical variable in sexual attraction among this group; instead, more interactive characteristics appeared to be significant. Zinik (1985) reported that many bisexuals viewed their sexuality as an attempt to integrate all of their personal relationships and to transcend gender so that sex and intimacy are potentials in relationships with both males and females. Furthermore, our emphasis on gender of sexual partner in defining sexual orientation is distinct from other cultures, where identity is derived not from with whom one has sex, but the sexual role (e.g., in Latino cultures where "true sex" involves penetration, the role of inserter or insertee) that one plays (for example, see Carrier, 1985, and Manalansan, this volume).

## The Problem of Defining "The Bisexual"

The preceding discussion fails to clarify a question that many professionals may wish to answer: How is one to "determine" sexual orientation when faced with a bisexual sexual biography? Definitions of bisexuality that are overly inclusive—that label any pattern other than lifelong heterosexual behavior or lifelong same-sex behavior as "bisexual"—are problematic. Such definitions confound sexual experience with identity. Research indicates that most women who identify as lesbian and many men who identify as gay have had some heterosexual experience (Bell & Weinberg, 1978; Rust, 1992; Saghir & Robins, 1973; Savin-Williams, "Dating and Relationships," this volume). On the other hand, overly restrictive criteria may reflect a bias against treating bisexuality as a legitimate option by disqualifying all contenders. Altschuler's (1984) criteria for a "true bisexual" include "roughly equal male and female preferences, . . . more or less . . . equivalent sex and of equal frequency with men and women," equal pleasure from such sex, and "a random pattern of activity . . . a man today and a woman tomorrow, or a week or two of one involvement and a comparable period of the other" (pp. 484–485). This definition not only excludes most who might be identified as bisexual, but suggests a person whose relationships are rather unstable, comparable to Masters and Johnson's (1979) description of the "ambisexual."

An inherent problem in the existing taxonomy is the assumption that it can be applied in an objective and meaningful fashion to describe an essential aspect of a person: his or her inherent potentiality for sexual relationships with males and/or females. Instead, this taxonomy can more appropriately be described as a labeling scheme that refers to an individual's identification with a particular sexual community—categories that are inherently culturally dependent and primarily meaningful on a social level. Sexual labels denote a special salience given to particular sexual experiences and relationships in reviewing the sum of one's sexual life but are not necessarily predictive. Thus many researchers have moved away from describing individuals simply as "bisexual" and instead are more explicit about whether people are bisexually active, self-identified bisexuals, etc. Given that which such labels can and cannot imply, this chapter next examines how one might understand and facilitate the process of self-exploration.

## EXPLORING SEXUAL PREFERENCE AND IDENTITY

### Formation of Sexual Preference Identity

Much of the research on same-sex identity formation presumes some underlying and stable core trait of "sexual orientation" that is expressed or experienced and that then leads to the formation of an identity based upon the available social categories (Cass, 1979; Coleman, 1981/1982b; Troiden, 1979). Thus, such models tend to be linear, positing a single pathway and set sequence of stages in the development of such an identity and defining a specific end objective to this process. Especially in earlier models of gay and lesbian identity formation, the progression through such stages is freighted with moralistic and social/political overtones. These models of identity development typically ignore the potential for ongoing shifts in identity across the life course and fail to critically examine cultural assumptions that underlie such developmental schemes. Thus, Warren (1974) could contend that an inescapable consequence of adopting a gay identity is a sense of distinctness, of being different or set apart from more conventional persons. Troiden (1979) viewed the final stage of same-sex development to involve some sort of commitment to that identity (differentiating from "acceptance" in terms of being reluctant to abandon the identity even if given the opportunity to do so), which seems to set a value on maintaining one's sexuality as a central aspect of one's being and which has a tone that is more suggestive of the era's aims of gay liberation than of psychological theories of identity formation.

The development of identity and the development of sexual preference may best be understood as interrelated and reciprocal rather than as independent processes. The identity that one comes to "own" can guide and direct one's emotional and erotic preferences rather than simply describe them. Weinberg, Williams, and Pryor (1994) found that short-term shifts in sexual feelings were more likely among those who identified as bisexual than those who identified as gay, lesbian, or heterosexual—leading them to suggest that a bisexual identity had less of a deterministic, "anchoring" effect on sexual feelings than those labels denoting an exclusive sexual preference. A related finding was of greater shifts and apparent fluidity in sexual feelings among the women in their sample. This gender difference has been noted by other researchers (Blumstein & Schwartz, 1977; Weinrich, 1988) and linked to differences in the context in which such sexual exploration/experimentation occurs. Women may not only find that their same-sex experiences are perceived by males as unrelated to their heterosexual responsiveness, but may have their first lesbian activity orchestrated by a male partner (Blumstein & Schwartz, 1976) or generally approved of by their male partner (J. Dixon, 1985). Cultural beliefs linking homosexuality to "flawed" gender identity and gender role are primarily attributions made about males. In contemporary Western culture, there appear to be definite gender differences in both the implications of same-sex experiences for one's masculinity or femininity and the readiness with which sexual experiences are translated into sexual identities by women as opposed to men (Paul, 1983/1984). Thus Blumstein and Schwartz (1977) reported:

> Women often felt that such [lesbian] activities were a natural extension of female affectionate behavior and did not have implications for their sexuality. Men, on the other hand, were much more preoccupied with what the experience meant for their masculinity, sometimes fearing that they might never again be able to respond erotically to a woman. (p. 43)

For some individuals trying to make sense of their heterosexual and homoerotic feelings and experiences, choosing a label may be experienced as a diminution of their potentialities as a consequence of the demands of conforming to a given category. This may be compounded by social pressures. It appears that the values of sexual-minority communities tend to enforce their own standard of behavior and relationships rather than substituting a permissive, "anything goes" attitude toward all forms of sexual expression (Silber, 1990; Weinberg et al., 1994). This reinforcement occurs on a variety of levels, including "narrowing opportunities for sexual/social/emotional expression, building attitudes that attach a fixed quality to identity and preference, reinforcing behaviors that are consistent with identity, and providing a system of rewards that encourages commitment to a particular mode of behavior" (Cass, 1990, p. 252). It can also be difficult to bridge two very different communities, each with its share of animosity and tension toward the other. Thus, there are profound pressures within society to adopt a particular identity and reference group, as well as social and intrapsychic benefits to adopting such a label. Gochros (1985) suggested that this contributes to the dissolution of some marriages of bisexually active men and that "these couples, and particularly the wives, became caught in the clash between political forces and were unable to tolerate such an ambiguous status as that of 'bisexuality'" (p. 112).

### Clinical implications

The therapist who takes an open, relativistic approach and considers sexual labels to be proximal descriptors of sexual patterns rather than unequivocal representations of one's inner nature may be best able to assist clients in reviewing the costs and benefits of assuming each of the available "identities." Some clients are more comfortable with a deterministic perspective, because it relieves them and the clinician of exploring many alternative options (Hart, 1984). I have worked with heterosexually married men who preferred to see their homoerotic desires as a previously repressed, biologically determined core trait; having emerged, the decision to end their marriages seemed an inevitability. In such cases, it is helpful for the therapist to acknowledge the client's wish for closure on the subject and the immediate benefits of such a resolution but to also point out the decisions and life-course options that this choice does not resolve or determine.

Because heterosexual, bisexual, and homosexual identities have very personal meanings—both for the individual and for the professional helping the individual to explore such issues—it is always a challenge for the professional to remain neutral and avoid subtly steering the client toward the adoption of a given label. The client must decide what the identity will mean to her or him personally and how well this identity serves her or his needs. The meanings and associations carried by sexual labels may vary tremendously, and self-labeling may serve different coping functions at different times. The mental health professional must remember that the therapeutic goal is to reduce the negative connotations and "detoxify" culturally stigmatized identities (bisexual, gay, or lesbian), thereby assisting the individual to freely select the identity option that best serves him or her for that phase in life. The value of supporting and validating the client's inner experience in the face of a society that denies its legitimacy cannot be overstated, especially when the client feels isolated from similar others.

## Questioning Sexual Preference Versus Sexual Preference "Confusion"

Those who question their sexual preference are initially confronting information about themselves that is dissonant with a presumed heterosexual identity. In some models of same-sex identity formation, this is described as "identity confusion" (Cass, 1979). Those who identify as bisexual are commonly perceived as "confused" and out of touch with their "true" sexuality. In this formulation, bisexuality is considered merely a phase, either transitional or transitory. While this may be true for some people, it fails as a generalization. Weinberg et al. (1994) found that self-identified bisexuals were no more likely to report confusion with respect to their sexual preferences than the self-identified gay and lesbian sample.

For those exploring their sexual attractions and their sexual identity, conflicts can occur along two distinct dimensions: (1) attempting to examine and clarify one's sexual desires and affiliations in a culture that severely stigmatizes and devalues many forms of sexual expression; and (2) difficulties "fitting" the variations in one's feelings, behaviors, and affiliations into the perceived available categories for summarizing one's sexual life. Weinberg and his colleagues (1994) found that confusion expressed by the gay/lesbian subgroup was primarily a consequence of external pressures, such as fear of stigmatization and other negative social reactions. Although bisexuals experienced confusion associated with these same external pressures, they had more of a struggle with defining the meaning of their amalgamation of same-sex/other-sex feelings and translating them into a lifestyle and identity, as the following quotes exemplify:

> In the past, I couldn't reconcile different desires I had. I didn't understand them. I didn't know what I was. And I ended up feeling really mixed up, unsure, and kind of frightened. (Weinberg et al., 1994, p. 27)

> I was afraid of my sexual feelings for men and . . . that if I acted on them, that would negate my sexual feelings for women. I knew absolutely no one else who had . . . sexual feelings for both men and women, and didn't realize that was an option. (Weinberg et al., 1994, p. 27)

For those exploring the meanings of bisexual experiences for their identity in our culture, where a fixed social identity and status exist only for those who indicate a sexual "preference" that excludes either their own or the other gender, confusion is not only understandable but practically unavoidable. Thus, the experience of "confusion" amongst those whose experience commingles heterosexual and homoerotic desire is less of intrapsychic origin and more a function of the inadequacy of socially validated categories of sexual/affectional attraction and of the tensions created by competing demands for loyalty from the lesbian, gay, and heterosexual communities. The following quotes describe the inadequacy or imprecision of sexual labels for many bisexuals, the problematic reactions to such a self-label, and the experienced split in social worlds:

> I want to be able to express the truths of my life, and my sexuality, in a language that does not obscure. The word choices available now restrict me. I am not tolerant of these restrictions, of a world view that consigns dissidents to limbo. I want some place to belong, a name to be called. (Queen, 1991, p. 17)

> If you're gay, people accept you once they know what you are. But being bisexual, of course, you're rather in between and they don't know how to react to you. Basically you have to play the gay, even though that's not really what you want. (Norris & Read, 1985, p. 127)

> The integration of my gay and my straight life had two confusing factors. The first was geographic. Most of my activities involving gays or bisexuals—and most of my political activism—occurred in the city. However, in suburbia, where I lived and taught, I was seen as a straight, married man. It seemed as though I led two lives. Neither community knew me as bisexual, though I was open with my married life with all my gay friends, and I was open with Sandy [his wife] about my gay life. (Matteson, 1991, p. 47)

This confusion is also a consequence of the fact that bisexual behavior and a bisexual identity may be condoned at certain developmental points as an intermediate stage, but treated with suspicion over a protracted period. Thus, the adolescent in our culture is given limited permission to "experiment" or "rebel" sexually but is expected to subsequently conform to a more conventional exclusive heterosexuality. A bisexual self-identity may also be initially accepted for those who are "coming out"—but only so long as it is a transitional role to be followed by a commitment to either a gay or lesbian identity. In this respect, the mental health professional can help by providing corrective information on human sexuality that allows the individual to integrate his or her varying affectional feelings, sexual impulses, and desires and by giving permission to the individual to choose whether to act on any of her or his sexual feelings.

## The Problem of Marginality and Social Invisibility

The individual exploring sexual feelings and relationships with both males and females must not only contend with the obstacles of the social invisibility of "the bisexual," but also with the competing demands for affiliation with the heterosexual, lesbian, or gay communities:

> I came to the Boston Bisexual Women's Network very confused and desperate. Would I ever get what I wanted? It didn't seem possible. . . . I wanted to be wild and free, with both women and men, but

the price seemed so damn high—ostracism from every community I had ever tried to make serve as home. (Terris, 1991, p. 58)

The sociological construct of marginality—describing the anomalous social position of individuals unable to find any clear group membership role due to their straddling of conventional social boundaries—provides a conceptual frame for understanding the problematic identity of the bisexual and the social forces that pressure people to identify and affiliate with either the heterosexual or lesbian/gay communities. Within those communities, bisexuals are sometimes treated as suspect—either as heterosexuals seeking an exotic sexual experience, as people who are unwilling to acknowledge their "real" same-sex orientation, or as people whose bisexuality is a transitional state and identity before identifying as lesbian or gay.

Until the late 1980s, bisexual networks and social structures were close to nonexistent. Although bisexual groups have existed since the late 1970s in San Francisco, New York, Boston, and Chicago (cities that continue to be organizing centers of bisexual activists), it is only in the last few years that there has developed both a national network (BiNET USA) and an international conference. Despite the growth of new bisexual-identified political and social organizations, these groups are still comparatively small, and those who want support for their same-sex feelings and relationships remain primarily dependent on the more extensive resources of the gay and lesbian communities. Thus, meeting other bisexually identified people is a highly significant experience for those who need the support of a sexual minority network yet who find their identity and loyalties treated with suspicion by gay and lesbian communities. The impact is described by one bisexual woman:

In college, I first met a woman who considered herself to be bisexual. I had never heard the term before, but the sense of discovery I felt was immediate and powerful. Upon hearing her description of what being bisexual meant to her, I experienced a profound sense of relief, excitement, and self-recognition. I now had a way to understand all of me. (Fox, 1991, p. 33)

Failing that, providing information on available bisexual resources, such as organizations, magazines, books, newsletters, and social groups, may help to reduce the experience of marginality (see "Selected Bisexual Resources" at the end of this chapter).

## An Example of Marginalization: Bisexual Women in the Lesbian Community

Research findings suggest that distrust and suspiciousness may be a particular problem for women who adopt a bisexual rather than a lesbian self-identity and who are part of the lesbian community. Blumstein and Schwartz (1974, 1976) first noted that bisexual women were perceived as a threat and as untrustworthy by some lesbians. This appeared to derive from the political meanings with which lesbian sexuality and self-labeling have been imbued. For some lesbians, personal identity is a political statement derived from feminist analysis. Bisexual women are thus viewed as avoiding both the commitment to the political ends of the lesbian community and as unwilling to face the loss of "heterosexual privilege" by taking on the stigmatized identity of the lesbian (Ponse, 1978). In a small exploratory study of a women's community in a Midwestern U.S. city, Silber (1990) noted:

> Sexual identity for these women is entwined with their ideological beliefs (radical feminism) as well as their reference groups or communities (lesbian feminists and heterosexuals). For these women, identifying oneself sexually is not based simply on erotic behavior or desires. Because they belonged to and identified with a politicized sexual community that was critical of heterosexuals and bisexuals, how they identified sexually became a very important marker of self. (p. 137)

The notion that the province of one's personal relationships could be the litmus test of one's political loyalties imposes serious constraints on the acknowledgment and expression of heterosexual attractions. Thus, one woman who had been known to friends as lesbian described her coming-out process as a bisexual to be difficult.

> I had to come out again as bi. While I didn't experience the psychic upset that accompanied coming out as a lesbian, I found coming out to my friends as bi much harder. I was embarrassed about it, because I live within a radical, alternative subculture where being a lesbian feminist is greatly respected and being bi [is] not understood. At first many friends, both women and men, gay and straight, were disappointed with the new bi version of my sexual orientation. I was disappointed too. My identity was no longer tidy. It felt neither hetero nor gay, but in limbo. (Woodard, 1991, p. 86)

Rust (1993) analyzed data from 346 self-administered questionnaires from self-identified lesbians. When asked about their beliefs about bisexual women (contrasting this with their stated beliefs about lesbians), Rust found that lesbians made "morally neutral" distinctions (e.g., viewing bisexuality as a transitional phase) more often than "invidious" distinctions (e.g., viewing bisexual women as denying their "true" sexuality). Nevertheless, her data indicated widespread support among lesbians for several common generalizations about bisexual women: that they are in transition to lesbianism, that bisexuals are in denial of their core homosexuality, that they have an easier time "passing" as heterosexual and more of a desire to do so, that they are more likely to desert their female friends, and that bisexuals cannot be trusted as political allies because they will abandon lesbian political struggles under pressure. These beliefs were interpreted by Rust (1993) as being part of a lesbian subcultural ideology that has "effectively contained the threat of bisexuality" (p. 226).

# Coming to Terms With Internalized Homophobia and Biphobia

Homophobia has been used to refer to the culturally-defined negative attributions and affective responses to homosexuality and those individuals perceived as gay or lesbian. Biphobia has been used to describe the parallel set of negative beliefs about and stigmatization of bisexuality and those identified as bisexual (Paul, 1988; Paul & Nichols, 1988). These attitudes are transmitted and reinforced by various cultural institutions. Biphobic and homophobic prejudicial attitudes are not particular to those who identify as heterosexual but span the sexual continuum; they are internalized by all members of our society to a greater or lesser degree.

## Clinical implications

An important task of psychotherapy with sexual-minority clients is to explore and challenge these assumptions—whether they are promulgated by the larger heterosexist society or by members of sexual-minority communities—to permit clients to integrate their sexual desires and feelings with their self-concept without diminishing their self-esteem or unnecessarily narrowing their perceived potentialities.

One of the most significant predictors of accepting attitudes toward sexual minorities is exposure to members of such groups through friendships and acquaintanceships (Herek, 1984, 1988, 1991; Schneider & Lewis, 1984). In addition, exposure to educational interventions about homosexuality and gay/lesbian people have been found to be helpful in reducing negative attitudes (Goldberg, 1982; Stevenson, 1988). As social interactions with self-identified gay men, lesbians, and bisexuals help to confront stereotypes, provide positive role models, and restructure the internalized meanings associated with such sexual identities, therapists may wish to explore the barriers that make such contacts difficult for clients. Depending on one's geographic location, there are likely to be a variety of gay and lesbian groups; it may be more difficult for individuals to gain direct contact with bisexuals. The client may also need time to work through negative attitudes before she or he is able to freely interact with others to break down stereotypes. The therapist may find it helpful to implement a series of desensitization tasks (e.g., first encouraging the client to drive or walk by a gay- or lesbian-identified bar or center; then to watch the people going in and coming out from a spot across the street from this setting; next, to walk to the door of such a setting; and finally, to enter such a setting). In addition, the therapist who is gay, lesbian or bisexual must determine the circumstances under which he or she finds it appropriate to disclose his or her sexual orientation to clients. Such a disclosure may serve the therapeutic process by helping to diminish internalized homophobia or biphobia and may provide reassurance that the therapist can understand the client's experience. In some circumstances, however, it may divert attention from the client's experience and make the client hesitate sharing negative reactions to gays, lesbians, and bisexuals.

The process of disclosure to others is also a significant part of working through internalized homophobia or biphobia. Positive responses to the act of disclosure are very important to building self-acceptance; negative reactions, on the other hand, will be stressful and may compromise self-acceptance. Thus, the process of disclosure to the therapist and the therapist's response to that information is a significant link to promote a positive self-identity. The therapist can also help clients who wish to tell their family and friends about their sexuality by aiding the assessment of potential consequences of such discussions with various members of the client's social network. In this regard, the therapist can help the client evaluate different means and circumstances under which this information could be disclosed. In addition, "damage control" or preparation for negative contingencies may be crucial.

## COUPLES AND RELATIONSHIP ISSUES

There is an inherent complexity in the relationships of those who are attracted to both women and men. Such attractions can be expressed by a tremendous diversity of coupling arrangements, both contemporaneously and sequentially. The traditional cultural model of a monogamous, cohabiting, lifelong (and heterosexual) relationship is often not readily adapted to suit the preferences or needs of bisexual men and women. Bisexually active men and women may or may not choose to marry. Some may also be married prior to any awareness of their bisexuality. For those who marry, problems that arise may be specific to the wedded couple, and others may simply be shared by all couples in which at least one partner is bisexual.

### Coming Out to Partners

Although the process of coming out to a partner is stressful for most couples, research indicates that both the immediate and long-term consequences can vary widely from couple to couple (Coleman, 1985b; Gochros, 1985). Much of the research on bisexually active spouses in heterosexual marriages has been of men (Brownfain, 1985; Coleman, 1981/1982a, 1985b; D. Dixon, 1985; Matteson, 1985; Myers, 1991; H. Ross, 1971; M. Ross, 1979; Schneider & Schneider, 1990; Wolf, 1985, 1987) or of the heterosexual wives of such men (Auerback, 1987; Gochros, 1985; Hays & Samuels, 1989). This is simply a reflection of a problematic gender bias within the larger field of research on sexual minorities. Research on bisexually active women in marriages (Coleman, 1985a; J. Dixon, 1985) suggests that there may be distinct gender differences in the process of moving from a heterosexual self-identity to a bisexual, lesbian, or gay identity. Comparing a sample of married bisexually active women to an earlier study of men (Coleman, 1981/1982a), Coleman (1985a) found that women were less likely to be aware of their homoerotic feelings prior to marriage, more likely to report sexual difficulties within the marital relationship, less likely to try to eliminate their homoerotic feelings through therapy, and more likely to terminate the marriage earlier due to marital conflicts and dissatisfaction.

Coming out is not a single event, but an ongoing series of disclosures and explorations for both partners (Cohen & Savin-Williams, "Coming Out," this volume). It is typical for the disclosure process to actually be a series of discrete divulgences. This may include acknowledging same-sex erotic attractions, expressing the desire to act on those attractions, disclosing past same-sex experiences, disclosing ongoing same-sex experiences, redefining one's sexual orientation, and talking explicitly about same-sex relationships. How each divulgence is transacted will have a considerable impact on the outcome of the process for the marital relationship. The content to be disclosed will have an impact on its reception: Acknowledging homoerotic feelings, or even occasional same-sex activity, is less threatening to a spouse than admitting to an ongoing sexual relationship in which there is some degree of emotional commitment.

### Clinical implications

The therapist can work to prepare bisexual married clients for this process in individual psychotherapy, as well as assist couples in therapy where one partner is coming out as bisexual, gay, or lesbian. Clarifying the client's expectations and hopes for the coming out process can provide clues to the likelihood of a continued marriage. Other important considerations include the values held by the couple with regard to marriage, the level of concern and emotional commitment expressed by the bisexual partner for the spouse in this process, the availability and extent of social supports, and the level of self-disclosure involved in each divulgence. The therapist can provide an arena to practice and try out different communication strategies.

## Therapeutic Tasks

Although the therapist can maintain a focus on the couple relationship in the individual therapy of a bisexual married man or woman, therapeutic work is typically more effective and less prolonged when the couple agrees to come in together for sessions. As with any couples therapy, the therapist must evaluate the overall strength and flexibility of the relationship, patterns of interaction and roles, partners' satisfaction with the relationship, communication skills, the presence of other ongoing issues or stressors, and prior history that would clarify the partners' skills and deficits in problem resolution. Other areas of inquiry should include the homophobia or biphobia of each partner, the quality of the couple's sex life, the supports available to both partners, and the degree to which the bisexual partner had acknowledged or concealed her or his bisexual attractions from the spouse.

The couples therapist may find her or his assumptions challenged, both with respect to marriage and with respect to sexual preference, when working with married gay men, lesbians, and bisexual men and women who wish to remain married. It behooves therapists with such clients to carefully examine any stereotypes, assumptions, and values that they may hold with respect to marriage and gay, lesbian, or bisexual lifestyles (Green & Clunis, 1988). For example, contrary to the beliefs of some therapists, Matteson (1985) found that more recent marriages of bisexuals were for positive reasons rather than as an escape from homosexuality. Brownfain (1985) described a range of marital relationships and resolutions to conflicts within marriages in which one spouse is bisexual. Therefore, a therapist may do a considerable disservice by failing to consider the intricacies of each individual relationship and attempting to impose a unitary or standard solution to complex situations—whether it be to view bisexuality as an unstable state and require the bisexual spouse to adopt an exclusive sexual preference (Blair, 1974) or to encourage the perception of same-sex activities as "addictive" or compulsive (Schneider & Schneider, 1990).

Support groups have become an important therapeutic tool for working with couples with a bisexual spouse. A significant problem for the bisexual spouse's partner is the absence of a formal support network or informal support group of nonjudgmental friends with whom to share her or his feelings. While the newly "out" bisexual or lesbian/gay spouse can usually find support and freedom from sexual-minority communities, the monosexual partner may increasingly feel isolated and "closeted." He or she may have feelings of shame, homophobia, biphobia, loss, mistrust, resentment, hurt, betrayal, confusion, inadequacy and powerlessness and may lack a place to ventilate feelings, especially if faced with social disapproval and ostracism from usual sources of support (Gochros, 1985; Hays & Samuels, 1989). Support groups for mixed-orientation couples are strongly advocated by Wolf (1985) and Auerback (1987). They can be therapeutic, permitting each partner to receive support from and provide support to others in similar situations, reducing isolation, self-doubt, and stigma. In addition, couples can problem-solve together, provide realistic expectations, suggest alternative relationship and sexual scripts, and model healthy conflict resolution to other members.

## Concerns With HIV and AIDS

More recently, bisexuals have frequently been described in the media as "villains," "libertines," "tortured souls," and "pariahs" (Gelman, 1987; Smilgis, 1987). With national attention focused on AIDS, bisexuality has been deemed "morally questionable" because of the risk bisexual men are viewed as posing as vectors of HIV transmission to both their female partners and the heterosexual community at large. Yet research suggests that bisexual men, although they may conceal their bisexuality from some partners, are not unmindful of the need to protect their female partners (Stokes, McKirnan, & Burzette, 1993) and are less likely than heterosexual men to engage in high-risk sexual activities (Lever et al., 1992). Research, limited by the use of a convenience sample, suggests that men who do not identify as gay or bisexual but engage in same-sex activity may be less likely to inform their wives of their sexual behavior than those who identify as gay or bisexual (Earl, 1990). In any event, AIDS has increased the value placed on sexual fidelity or monogamy and made disclosure of bisexuality more loaded and possibly less frequent (Weinberg et al., 1994).

This is a more potent issue for bisexually active men than women because the risk of HIV infection faced by bisexual men is greater and has received more attention in the press. Nonetheless, bisexually active women may feel uncomfortable disclosing their bisexuality to lesbians because they would be perceived as being at greater risk than women who have sex exclusively with women. For some married men, becoming HIV positive may force disclosure of their bisexuality; this makes the crisis even more explosive. The wife is not only faced with the simultaneous discovery of a spouse's bisexuality, marital infidelity, and potentially terminal illness—which stirs feelings of loss, betrayal, vulnerability, and uncertainty about the future—but is also confronted with the very real possibility of being HIV infected herself. Because of the powerful emotions evoked by the issues of HIV infection and transmission, therapists must be cognizant of their own countertransference and biphobia/homophobia when exploring these concerns (Myers, 1991).

## Reinventing the Relationship

The disclosure of a partner's bisexuality may not necessitate changes in the couple's relationship. Some bisexuals prefer monogamous relationships, especially given widespread concern with AIDS, and find that erotic attractions can be satisfied through fantasy and affectional needs through friendships. Upon follow-up, Weinberg et al. (1994) observed a shift toward a preference for monogamy among their bisexual sample. They attributed this to concerns with AIDS and the sense that the demands of a multiple-relationship lifestyle were too great to maintain. Nonmonogamy is certainly not for all couples. It demands a high level of flexibility, trust between partners, communication skills, awareness of individual emotional needs and the assertiveness to voice them, the capacity to handle jealousy, time-management skills, and support from outside the relationship.

For couples who attempt a sexually "open" relationship, the couple must be prepared to define a mutually satisfactory set of ground rules. Numerous books and articles have been written, primarily in the 1970s, on working out guidelines for nonmonogamous relationships (e.g., O'Neill and O'Neill's [1972] *Open Marriage: A New Lifestyle for Couples,* Watson and Whitlock's [1982] *Breaking the Bonds: The Realities of Sexually Open Relationships*)—a product of that era's exploration of open marriages. Ground rules developed by the couple should recognize the acceptable limits of both partners, be readily subject to revision and renegotiation, and provide guidelines that are as explicit as possible with regard to that which is and is not acceptable in outside relationships. Couples may find that they alternate between opening up their relationship and monogamy at different points in their relationship; this flexibility reflects a sensitivity to the needs of their primary relationship and acknowledges the primacy of that relationship.

An important issue that must be resolved is that of disclosure to others outside of the marriage. A bisexual person's disclosure to a spouse may be an early step in a process of resolution about the former's emerging sexual-minority status and public identity as a married heterosexual. Thus, he or she may be prepared to integrate these divergent aspects of social identity by sharing this information with significant others. The nonbisexual spouse, however, being more recently informed, may lag behind the bisexual spouse in accepting and resolving these issues and may grapple with confusion, homophobia, feelings of shame, and apparent inconsistencies in her or his relational world. Thus, he or she may be ill-prepared to cope with additional persons sharing this "secret." It is necessary for the couple to reach some consensus about how, when, and if others are told within their common social group.

The aforementioned issues will likely also affect the children in the marriage. Parents need to sort through their feelings and reactions and work out a mutual understanding of the implications of this information for their relationship and children. If this issue clearly divides the parents, it would be unrealistic to expect the children to react positively to its disclosure. A parent who is overwhelmed by emotions may be less in touch with that which is of primary concern to the children. In addition, the heterosexual parent may need to work through her or his biphobia, homophobia, and erroneous fears that this information will "damage" the children. In fact, research indicates that children respond well to their parents' openness and that early awareness can foster the social skills needed to problem-solve around disclosure to peers (Paul, 1986).

## Conclusion

Cultures dictate the forms by which sexual desire is expressed toward both men and women. Contemporary Western culture is distinctive in that it not only establishes expectations regarding types of sexual behavior but also reinforces a set of fixed identities, each with a distinct social status that tends to polarize one's sexual essence as either gay/lesbian or heterosexual. Given that context, there is tremendous individual variability in the manner in which people whose sexuality melds same-sex and heterosexual desire resolve their understandings of themselves and their relationships. Despite the limited number of available sexual labels, an individual's relationships and sexuality may vary considerably.

Those working in the field of human sexuality need first to rid themselves of preconceived, culturally bound notions of sexual behavior. This process will free both therapist and client to seek creative solutions to the personal and lifestyle issues that may emerge in the course of psychotherapy. Given the lack of information and misinformation provided to the general public in our society, the therapist must be able to serve as educator and to challenge sexual myths and stereotypes. Such stereotypes may not only be relevant to those exploring their bisexual potential but to many other psychotherapy clients. A history of relationships with both male and female partners may be irrelevant or it may be crucial to a client's presenting problems and to the work accomplished in psychotherapy; the therapist will only know by letting go of culturally derived assumptions and beginning with the client's frame of reference.

This chapter identifies some of the concerns that may emerge in working with those who are behaviorally bisexual or exploring the possibilities involved in expressing erotic and loving feelings toward both men and women. As such, it can only provide a rudimentary guide to such issues. It may be more important for this chapter to challenge the reader's perspective on sexual preferences, which may in turn lead to an examination of implicit assumptions in other works—both in other chapters of this book and elsewhere.

## ▼ Dedication ▼

This book chapter is dedicated to the memory of David Lourea, bisexual activist and former leader of the San Francisco Bisexual Center.

## ▼ Acknowledgments ▼

This work was supported in part by grants from the National Institute of Mental Health (MH42459—The Center for AIDS Prevention Studies) and by a grant from the National Institute of Alcohol Abuse and Alcoholism (AA08233).

## ▼ Selected Bisexual Resources ▼

Bay Area Bisexual Network (BABN)
2404 California Street, #24
San Francisco, CA 94115
[Produces magazine *Anything That Moves: Beyond the Myths of Bisexuality*]

Bisexual Network of Austin
P.O. Box 8439
Austin, TX 78713
[Produces newsletter *Bi-News*]

BiNet Oregon (The Bisexual Network of Oregon)
P.O. Box 8232
Portland, OR 97214-8232
[Produces newsletter *Northwest Bi Ways*]

BiNet USA
P.O. Box 7327
Langley Park, MD 20787
[Produces BiNet quarterly national newsletter]

Bisexual People of Color Caucus/BiPOL
584 Castro Street, #422
San Francisco, CA 94114

Bisexual Resource Center (BRC)
[formerly East Coast Bisexual Network
(ECBN)]
P.O. Box 639
Cambridge, MA 02140
[Produces *International Directory of Bisexual Groups*]

Boston Bisexual Women's Network
P. O. Box 639
Cambridge, MA 02140
[Produces newsletter *BiWomen*]

## ▼ References ▼

Abse, D. (1990). On male bisexuality and marriage. In C. Socarides & V. Volkan (Eds.), *The homosexualities: Reality, fantasy, and the arts* (pp. 47–78). Madison, CT: International Universities Press.

Adam, B. (1985). Age, structure, and sexuality: Reflections on the anthropological evidence on homosexual relations. *Journal of Homosexuality, 11,* 19–34.

Altschuler, K. (1984). On the question of bisexuality. *American Journal of Psychotherapy, 38,* 484–493.

Angier, N. (1991a, August 30). Zone of brain linked to men's sexual orientation. *New York Times,* pp. 1, 18.

Angier, N. (1991b, September 1). The biology of what it means to be gay. *New York Times,* pp. 1, 4.

Auerback, S. (1987). Groups for the wives of gay and bisexual men. *Social Work, 32,* 321–325.

Bell, A., & Weinberg, M. (1978). *Homosexualities: A study of diversity among men and women.* New York: Simon & Schuster.

Bell, A., Weinberg, M., & Hammersmith, S. (1981). *Sexual preference: Its development in men and women.* Bloomington, IN: Indiana University Press.

Blair, R. (1974). Counseling concerns and bisexual behavior. *Homosexual Counseling Journal, 1,* 26–30.

Blumstein, P., & Schwartz, P. (1974). Lesbianism and bisexuality. In E. Goode (Ed.), *Sexual deviance and sexual deviants* (pp. 278–295). New York: Morrow.

Blumstein, P., & Schwartz, P. (1976). Bisexuality in women. *Archives of Sexual Behavior, 5,* 171–181.

Blumstein, P., & Schwartz, P. (1977). Bisexuality: Some social psychological issues. *Journal of Social Issues, 33,* 30–45.

Bressler, L., & Lavender, A. (1986). Sexual fulfillment of heterosexual, bisexual and homosexual women. *Journal of Homosexuality, 12,* 109–122.

Brownfain, J. (1985). A study of the married bisexual male: Paradox and resolution. *Journal of Homosexuality, 11,* 173–188.

Callender, C., & Kochems, L. (1985). Men and not-men: Male gender-mixing statuses and homosexuality. *Journal of Homosexuality, 11,* 165–178.

Carrier, J. (1985). Mexican male bisexuality. *Journal of Homosexuality, 11,* 75–86.

Cass, V. (1979). Homosexual identity formation: A theoretical model. *Journal of Homosexuality, 4,* 219–235.

Cass, V. (1990). The implications of homosexual identity formation for the Kinsey model and scale of sexual preference. In D. McWhirter, S. Sanders, & J. Reinisch (Eds.), *Homosexuality/heterosexuality: concepts of sexual orientation. (The Kinsey Institute series, Vol. 2)* (pp. 239–266). New York: Oxford University Press.

Coleman, E. (1981/1982a). Bisexual and gay men in heterosexual marriage: Conflicts and resolutions in therapy. *Journal of Homosexuality, 7,* 93–103.

Coleman, E. (1981/1982b). Developmental stages of the coming out process. *Journal of Homosexuality, 7,* 31–43.

Coleman, E. (1985a). Bisexual women in marriages. *Journal of Homosexuality, 11,* 87–100.

Coleman, E. (1985b). Integration of male bisexuality and marriage. *Journal of Homosexuality, 11,* 189–208.

Coleman, E. (1987). Assessment of sexual orientation. *Journal of Homosexuality, 14,* 9–24.

Coleman, E. (1989). The married lesbian. *Marriage and Family Review, 14,* 119–135.

Crabb, C. (1991, September 9). Are some men born to be homosexual? *U.S. News and World Report,* p. 58.

Dixon, D. (1985). Perceived sexual satisfaction and marital happiness of bisexual and heterosexual swinging husbands. *Journal of Homosexuality, 11,* 209–222.

Dixon, J. (1985). Sexuality and relationship changes in married females following the commencement of bisexual activity. *Journal of Homosexuality, 11,* 115–134.

Doll, L., Peterson, L., White, C., Johnson, E., Ward, J., & The Blood Donor Study Group. (1992). Homosexually and nonhomosexually identified men who have sex with men: A behavioral comparison. *The Journal of Sex Research, 29,* 1–14.

Earl, W. (1990). Married men and same-sex activity: A field study on HIV risk among men who do not identify as gay or bisexual. *Journal of Sex & Marital Therapy, 16,* 251–257.

Fast, J., & Wells, H. (1975). *Bisexual living.* New York: M. Evans.

Fox, A. (1991). Development of a bisexual identity: Understanding the process. In L. Hutchins & L. Kaahumanu (Eds.), *Bi any other name: Bisexual people speak out* (pp. 29–36). Boston: Alyson.

Freud, S. (1905/1953). Three essays on the theory of sexuality. In *Standard edition of the complete psychological works of Sigmund Freud* (Vol. 7) (rev. ed.). London: Hogarth Press.

Gelman, D. (1987, July 13). Bisexuals and AIDS: A perilous double love life. *Newsweek,* pp. 44–46.

Gochros, J. (1985). Wives' reactions to learning that their husbands are bisexual. *Journal of Homosexuality, 11,* 101–115.

Goldberg, R. (1982). Attitude change among college students toward homosexuality. *Journal of American College Health, 30,* 260–268.

Gooren, L., Fliers, E., & Courtney, K. (1990). Biological determinants of sexual orientation. *Annual Review of Sex Research, 1,* 175–196.

Gorman, C. (1991, September 9). Are gay men born that way? *Time,* pp. 60–61.

Green, G., & Clunis, D. (1988). Married lesbians. *Women and Therapy, 8,* 41–49.

Hansen, C. (1985). Bisexuality reconsidered: An idea in pursuit of a definition. *Journal of Homosexuality, 11,* 1–6.

Hart, J. (1984). Therapeutic implications of viewing sexual identity in terms of essentialist and constructionist theories. *Journal of Homosexuality, 9,* 39–51.

Hays, D., & Samuels, A. (1989). Heterosexual women's perceptions of their marriages to bisexual or homosexual men. *Journal of Homosexuality, 18,* 81–100.

Henry, W. (1993, July 26). Born gay? *Time,* pp. 36–38.

Herdt, G. (1981). *Guardians of the flutes: Idioms of masculinity.* New York: McGraw-Hill.

Herdt, G. (1984). A comment on cultural attributes and fluidity of bisexuality. *Journal of Homosexuality, 10,* 53–62.

Herek, G. (1984). Beyond "homophobia": A social psychological perspective on attitudes toward lesbians and gay men. *Journal of Homosexuality, 10,* 1–21.

Herek, G. (1988). Heterosexuals' attitudes toward lesbians and gay men: Correlates and gender differences. *The Journal of Sex Research, 25,* 451–477.

Herek, G. (1991). Stigma, prejudice, and violence against lesbians and gay men. In J. Gonsiorek & J. Weinrich (Eds.), *Homosexuality: Research implications for public policy* (pp. 60–80). Newbury Park, CA: Sage Publications.

Hughes, E. (1945). Dilemmas and contradictions of status. *American Journal of Sociology, 50,* 253–259.

Kaplan, G., & Rogers, L. (1984). Breaking out of the dominant paradigm: A new look at sexual attraction. *Journal of Homosexuality, 10,* 71–76.

Kinsey, A., Pomeroy, W., & Martin, C. (1948). *Sexual behavior in the human male.* Philadelphia: W. B. Saunders.

Kinsey, A., Pomeroy, W., Martin, C., & Gebhard, P. (1953). *Sexual behavior in the human female.* Philadelphia: W. B. Saunders.

Klein, F., Sepekoff, B., & Wolf, T. (1985). Sexual orientation: A multi-variable dynamic process. *Journal of Homosexuality, 11,* 35–49.

Krafft-Ebing, R. von. (1935). *Psychopathia sexualis.* F. Rebman. (Trans.). New York: Physicians & Surgeons Book Co. [12th German edition published 1906].

LeVay, S. (1991). A difference in hypothalamic structure between heterosexual and homosexual men. *Science, 253,* 1034–1037.

Lever, J., Kanouse, D., Rogers, W., Carson, S., & Hertz, R. (1992). Behavior patterns and sexual identity of bisexual males. *The Journal of Sex Research, 29,* 141–167.

Lourea, D. (1985). Psycho-social issues related to counseling bisexuals. *Journal of Homosexuality, 11,* 51–62.

MacDonald, A. (1981). Bisexuality: Some comments on research and theory. *Journal of Homosexuality, 6,* 21–35.

Maddox, J. (1991). Is homosexuality hard-wired? *Nature, 353,* 13.

Masters, W., & Johnson, V. (1979). *Homosexuality in perspective.* Boston: Little, Brown.

Matteson, D. (1985). Bisexual men in marriage: Is a positive homosexual identity and stable marriage possible? *Journal of Homosexuality, 11,* 149–172.

Matteson, D. (1991). Bisexual feminist man. In L. Hutchins & L. Kaahumanu (Eds.), *Bi any other name: Bisexual people speak out* (pp. 43–50). Boston: Alyson Publications.

Myers, M. (1991). Marital therapy with HIV-infected men and their wives. *Psychiatric Annals, 21,* 466–470.

Nichols, M. (1988). Bisexuality in women: Myths, realities, and implications for therapy. *Women and Therapy, 7,* 235–252.

Norris, S., & Read, E. (1985). *Out in the open: People talking about being gay or bisexual.* London: Pan Books.

O'Neill, N., & O'Neill, G. (1972). *Open marriage: A new lifestyle for couples.* New York: M. Evans & Co.

Parker, R., & Carballo, M. (1990). Qualitative research on homosexual and bisexual behavior relevant to HIV/AIDS. *The Journal of Sex Research, 27,* 497–525.

Paul, J. (1983/1984). The bisexual identity: An idea without social recognition. *Journal of Homosexuality, 9,* 45–63.

Paul, J. (1985). Bisexuality: Reassessing our paradigms of sexuality. *Journal of Homosexuality, 11,* 21–34.

Paul, J. (1986). *Growing up with a gay, lesbian, or bisexual parent: An exploratory study of experiences and perceptions.* Unpublished doctoral dissertation, University of California, Berkeley, CA.

Paul, J. (1988). Counseling issues with a bisexual population. In M. Shernoff & W. Scott (Eds.), *The sourcebook on lesbian/gay health care* (pp. 142–147). Washington, DC: National Lesbian & Gay Health Foundation.

Paul, J., & Nichols, M. (1988). "Biphobia" and the construction of a bisexual identity. In M. Shernoff & W. Scott (Eds.), *The sourcebook on lesbian/gay health care* (pp. 259–264). Washington, DC: National Lesbian & Gay Health Foundation.

Pillard, R., & Weinrich, J. (1987). The periodic table model of the gender transpositions: Part I. A theory based on masculinization and defeminization of the brain. *The Journal of Sex Research, 23,* 425–454.

Plummer, K. (1981). Homosexual categories: Some research problems in the labeling perspective of homosexuality. In K. Plummer (Ed.), *The making of the modern homosexual* (pp. 53–75). Totowa, NJ: Barnes & Noble.

Ponse, B. (1978). *Identities in the lesbian world.* Westport, CT: Greenwood Press.

Queen, C. (1991). The queer in me. In L. Hutchins & L. Kaahumanu (Eds.), *Bi any other name: Bisexual people speak out* (pp. 17–21). Boston: Alyson.

Ross, H. (1971). Modes of adjustment of married homosexuals. *Social Problems, 18,* 395–393.

Ross, M. (1979). Heterosexual marriage of homosexual males: Some assorted factors. *Journal of Sex and Marital Therapy, 5,* 142–151.

Ross, M. (1984). Beyond the biological model: New directions in bisexual and homosexual research. *Journal of Homosexuality, 10,* 63–70.

Ross, M., & Paul, J. (1992). Beyond gender: The basis of sexual attraction in bisexual men and women. *Psychological Reports, 71,* 1283–1290.

Rust, P. (1992). The politics of sexual identity: Sexual attraction and behavior among lesbian and bisexual women. *Social Problems, 39,* 366–386.

Rust, P. (1993). Neutralizing the political threat of the marginal woman: Lesbians' beliefs about bisexual women. *The Journal of Sex Research, 30,* 214–228.

Saghir, M., & Robins, E. (1973). *Male and female homosexuality: A comprehensive investigation.* Baltimore: Williams & Wilkins.

Schneider, J., & Schneider, B. (1990). Marital satisfaction during recovery from self-identified sexual addiction among bisexual men and their wives. *Journal of Sex and Marital Therapy, 16,* 230–250.

Schneider, W., & Lewis, I. (1984, February/March). The straight story on homosexuality and gay rights. *Public Opinion, 7,* 16–20, 59–69.

Shively, M., & De Cecco, J. (1977). Components of sexual identity. *Journal of Homosexuality, 3,* 41–48.

Silber, L. (1990). Negotiating sexual identity: Non-lesbians in a lesbian feminist community. *The Journal of Sex Research, 27,* 131–140.

Simon, W., & Gagnon, J. (1986). Sexual scripts: Permanence and change. *Archives of Sexual Behavior, 15,* 97–120.

Slater, P. (1976). *The measurement of interpersonal space by grid technique. Vol. 1.* London: Wiley.

Slater, P. (1977). *The measurement of interpersonal space by grid technique. Vol. 2.* London: Wiley.

Smilgis, M. (1987, February 16). The big chill: Fear of AIDS. *Time,* pp. 52–53.

Sprague, G. (1984). Male homosexuality in Western culture: The dilemma of identity and subculture in historical research. *Journal of Homosexuality, 10,* 29–43.

Stevenson, M. R. (1988). Promoting tolerance for homosexuality: An evaluation of intervention strategies. *The Journal of Sex Research, 25,* 500–511.

Stokes, J., McKirnan, D., & Burzette, R. (1993). Sexual behavior, condom use, disclosure of sexuality, and stability of sexual orientation in bisexual men. *The Journal of Sex Research, 30,* 203–213.

Suppe, F. (1984a). Classifying sexual disorders: The diagnostic and statistical manual of the American Psychiatric Association. *Journal of Homosexuality, 9,* 9–28.

Suppe, F. (1984b). In defense of a multidimensional approach to sexual identity. *Journal of Homosexuality, 10,* 7–14.

Terris, E. (1991). My life as a lesbian-identified bisexual fag hag. In L. Hutchins & L. Kaahumanu (Eds.), *Bi any other name: Bisexual people speak out* (pp. 56–59). Boston: Alyson.

Troiden, R. (1979). Becoming homosexual: A model for gay identity acquisition. *Psychiatry, 42,* 362–373.

Warren, C. (1974). *Identity and community in the gay world.* New York: Wiley-Interscience.

Watson, M., & Whitlock, F. (1982). *Breaking the bonds: The realities of sexually open relationships.* Denver, CO: Tudor House Press.

Weinberg, M., Williams, C., & Pryor, D. (1994). *Dual attraction: Bisexuality in the age of AIDS.* New York: Oxford University Press.

Weinrich, J. (1988). The periodic table model of the gender transpositions: Part II. Limerent and lusty sexual attractions and the nature of bisexuality. *The Journal of Sex Research, 24,* 113–129.

Wolf, T. (1985). Marriages of bisexual men. *Journal of Homosexuality, 11,* 135–148.

Wolf, T. (1987). Group psychotherapy for bisexual men and their wives. *Journal of Homosexuality, 14,* 191–199.

Woodard, V. (1991). Insights at 3:30 a.m. In L. Hutchins & L. Kaahumanu (Eds.), *Bi any other name: Bisexual people speak out* (pp. 83–86). Boston: Alyson.

Zinik, G. (1985). Identity conflict or adaptive flexibility? Bisexuality reconsidered. *Journal of Homosexuality, 11,* 7–19.

# Chapter 20

▼

# MENTAL HEALTH AND SEXUAL ORIENTATION

## John C. Gonsiorek

*Homosexuality first evolved as a medical "illness" in the late nineteenth or early twentieth century, depending on the country.[1] In 1973, however, the American Psychiatric Association removed homosexuality as a diagnosis of illness, replacing it with "ego-dystonic homosexuality," a vague and problematic concept that attempted to label dissatisfaction with same-sex orientation as an illness. In early 1975, the governing body of the American Psychological Association voted to support the 1973 action of the American Psychiatric Association. Ego-dystonic homosexuality was itself removed in 1986, probably because it created more confusion than illumination. Bayer (1987) reviewed the historical and political background of these changes.*

*This chapter focuses on a number of related questions:*

- What was the basis for the declassification of homosexuality as a mental illness and how did it come about?
- What does the declassification mean?
- What is our current understanding about the relationship between mental health problems and sexual orientation?
- Why do illness models of homosexuality persist despite this declassification?
- What concepts are replacing illness models of sexual orientation for developing a psychological understanding of gay, lesbian, and bisexual individuals?
- What are the implications of these new models and what are the most viable and important avenues for future research and theory development?

*Readers interested in a comprehensive understanding of the interplay between scientific knowledge about sexual orientation and public policy are directed to Gonsiorek and Weinrich (1991).*

## THE DEPATHOLOGIZING OF HOMOSEXUALITY

Prior to 1957, it had been an almost unquestioned article of faith among mental health professionals and researchers that homosexuality was a mental illness. Hooker (1957), a psychology faculty member at UCLA, empirically tested this in an elegantly simple research design that had far-reaching social and political ramifications. With a sample of 30 gay and 30 heterosexual men, she administered a battery of psychological tests specifically designed to measure psychopathology, gave the 60 test protocols to a panel of psychological test experts, and asked them to differentiate the two groups. They were unable to do so.

The choice of psychological testing as a vehicle for this research was not an accident. There have been and remain many controversies about the reliability of mental health diagnoses and the frequency of diagnostician bias. Psychological testing is specifically designed to provide an objective means of measuring mental health difficulties and thus drastically reduce measurement problems. Psychological testing, in reality, rarely measures diagnoses but instead generally assesses the symptom clusters that underlie most diagnostic formulations. This intrinsically more reliable level of measurement, plus the validity that empirically based testing offers, has generally made the use of well-validated psychological test instruments the most accurate means of measuring mental health problems. When Hooker was unable to effect the expected differentiation of homosexual from heterosexual samples using these instruments, the illness model of homosexuality became suspect.

During the next two and a half decades, a series of experiments using psychological testing attempted to distinguish homosexual from heterosexual samples. This literature has been summarized by a number of authors (Gonsiorek, 1977, 1982a, 1991; Hart et al., 1978; Meredith & Reister, 1980; Reiss, 1980; Reiss, Safer, & Yotive, 1974). The findings from these reviews are sufficiently consistent and compelling to conclude that theories—or individuals—that purport a scientific basis for an illness model of homosexuality represent egregious distortions of these data.

The research of Hooker and others was the empirical basis for the depathologizing of homosexuality in the early 1970s. It is important to note, however, that this level of "proof" is unnecessary to depathologize homosexuality.

The illness model of homosexuality maintains that the existence of persistent homoerotic feelings and/or behavior is in and of itself absolutely predictive of psychological disturbance. Findings supportive of *any* group of same-sex oriented individuals who are not psychologically disturbed refute this model. One could even contend that the comparative rates of psychological disturbance in homosexual and heterosexual populations are irrelevant to whether homosexuality is an illness. The only relevant issue is whether *any* nonpathological gay or lesbian individuals exist. The psychological test literature suggests that *many* nonpathological gay and lesbian individuals exist and that, in addition, they cannot be reliably differentiated from heterosexual individuals.

## The Meaning of the Depathologizing of Homosexuality

The depathologizing of homosexuality, in its most conservative form, means that homosexuality per se is not a sign or symptom of psychological disturbance. This does not imply that there are no disturbed gay or lesbian people, but that the proportion or base rate of disturbed individuals in homosexual and heterosexual populations is roughly equivalent. Using the following figures solely for illustrative purposes, if 5% of the general population is seriously psychologically disturbed, 10% moderately disturbed, 15% slightly disturbed, and 70% within the normal range, then the statement that homosexuality is not indicative of disturbance implies that there are as many disturbed gay and lesbian people as there are heterosexuals.

Further, there are compelling reasons, such as facing increased levels of external stress, to believe that certain measures of disturbance may be higher in subpopulations of lesbian women and gay men, as well as in other disparaged groups. If, as a group, lesbian women and gay men are subject to high levels of external stress, then a proper comparison group may not be heterosexuals in general, but heterosexuals with roughly equivalent external stress. As noted below, there are measures of psychological difficulties in which the two populations differ. This is intriguing and certainly requires explanation, but it is essentially irrelevant to the issue of the *inherent* psychopathology of homosexuality.

The illness model of homosexuality was based on a projection of societal bigotry in the guise of scientific research and mental health professionalism and is without empirical foundation. As erroneous as the illness model of homosexuality was, however, it represented a coherent view of understanding same-sex sexual orientation. During the same time frame in which the illness model of homosexuality was successfully challenged, sociologists noted that homosexuality is not related to major demographic or sociological variables, with some exceptions, such as gay and lesbian individuals tend to have fewer children than their heterosexual counterparts. With the demise of the illness model, a serious dilemma emerged: There was no clear way to understand sexual orientation from a traditional psychological perspective.

The questions that have emerged as central since the repudiation of the illness model of homosexuality include: Is there psychological consistency in the experiences of gay, lesbian, and bisexual individuals? Are the categories homosexual, bisexual, and heterosexual coherent in any scientifically meaningful way? Do gay, lesbian, and bisexual individuals experience unique psychological events, and, if so, what are their meanings? These questions have been the focus of recent scientific research and will be outlined below.

Before describing these, however, it is important to examine the scientific literature regarding possible mental health problems in some gay men and lesbian women. Initially, the findings were confusing when they were compared to the psychological test results because they indicated that subsets of gay and lesbian populations experience high levels of psychological difficulties despite the fact that as a group they are indistinguishable in terms of psychopathology.

Again, as is often true in the process of scientific discovery, this seeming contradiction is not a problem but a vehicle for understanding phenomena in a richer way.

## SEXUAL ORIENTATION AND MENTAL HEALTH DIFFICULTIES

In addition to the early research on psychological testing, researchers used psychiatric interviews to measure mental health and life functioning. Two of the earliest large-scale studies were conducted by Saghir, Robins, Walbran, & Gentry (1970a), who compared gay men and male heterosexuals and lesbian women and female heterosexuals (1970b). In the former study, the authors observed no differences between the groups on interview questions pertaining to drug use, antisocial features, mood disorders, anxiety, or phobias. The gay group, however, had a history of more suicide attempts, more excessive drinking, and greater utilization of psychotherapy services. In their matching research on women, they found no differences between lesbian and heterosexual women in the number of individuals seeking psychotherapy services and having mood disorders, anxiety, phobias, or antisocial personality features. However, lesbian women more often reported mental health difficulties and a history of drug use.

In a subsequent study, Saghir and Robins (1973) compared psychiatric and personal history information of males and females, both homosexual and heterosexual. They found virtually no differences in psychiatric symptomatology with the exception of greater alcohol abuse in the lesbian sample as compared to the female heterosexual sample.

Weinberg and Williams (1974) reported no differences in psychological problems between gay and heterosexual groups, and Pillard (1988), using a psychiatric questionnaire, found no differences between gay and heterosexual men on estimates of lifetime mental disorders. Bell and Weinberg (1978), however, reported higher rates of loneliness, depression, and attempted suicide in gay and lesbian samples compared to heterosexual samples.

The issue of higher rates of suicide or suicide attempts in gay and lesbian populations has attracted considerable research and, recently, political interest. Savin-Williams and Cohen ("Psychosocial Outcomes," this volume) and Gonsiorek (1991) examined this literature in detail. Perhaps the most accurate conclusion is that there appears to be a subset of gay men and lesbian women who, particularly in their adolescence, are at enhanced risk for suicide.

The rates of alcoholism and substance abuse have also been investigated. Mosbacher (1988) reviewed the literature and concluded that lesbian women are at greater risk than heterosexual women for alcohol abuse. Similarly, Anderson and Henderson (1985) and Kus (1988) concluded that there was an increased risk of alcoholism among lesbian women and gay men, respectively. Herek (1990), however, challenged these findings, raising questions about the representativeness of samples used in this research. He concluded that empirical support for a higher incidence of alcoholism among lesbian women and gay men is weak.

Ironically, given the military's history of denying that gay and lesbian people exist in military service and the attempted exclusion of them from its ranks, some of the most interesting research with large sample sizes originated from the United States Department of Defense. Two internal studies were leaked in recent debates about the suitability of gay, lesbian, and bisexual citizens in the U.S. military. McDaniel (1989) posed the question whether such individuals would be suitable for national security clearances. He collected information about educational experiences, alcohol and drug use, criminal activities, and other factors on a self-report inventory and then compared individuals who were discharged from the armed services for homosexuality versus other reasons. McDaniel found that lesbian women and gay men had better preservice adjustment than heterosexuals in areas related to school behavior; displayed greater levels of cognitive ability; and had greater problems with alcohol and drug abuse. With the latter exception, lesbian women and gay men resembled those who had successfully adjusted to military life more than those who had been discharged for being unsuitable. The study concluded that the adjustment of gay men tended to be better or equal to that of male heterosexuals and that lesbian women tended to score somewhat lower on preservice adjustment compared to female heterosexuals. Females as a whole, however, tended to have better preservice adjustment than did males; while having poorer adjustment than female heterosexuals, lesbian women had better adjustment than male heterosexuals.

In their summary of military suitability, Sarbin and Carols (1988) concluded that same-sex orientation is unrelated to military job performance and that the primary problem facing integration of lesbian and gay individuals into the military is maintaining group cohesion within the general military structure when an unpopular minority group is absorbed. Similarly, in his review of the social science data, Herek (1990) concluded that denial or restriction of government security clearances for lesbian and gay people has no rational or empirical justification. He also noted that they are no more likely than heterosexual personnel to be subject to blackmail or coercion, to be unreliable or untrustworthy, or to be disrespectful of or fail to uphold laws.

Another line of research findings is intriguing in this context. Weinberg and Williams (1974) examined factors that facilitate general adjustment to homosexuality and found that gay men who are well-adjusted rejected the idea that homosexuality is an illness, had close and supportive associations with other gay people, and were not interested in changing their homosexuality.

Other research has supported and amplified these findings. For example, Hammersmith and Weinberg (1973) found that positive commitment to homosexuality was related to good psychological adjustment and the existence of significant others who support that identity. Farrell and Morrione (1974), Jacobs and Tedford (1980), and Savin-Williams (1990) reported that membership in sexual-minority groups had positive psychological effects and was predictive of self-esteem. Similarly, the work of D'Augelli (1987; D'Augelli & Hart, 1987) supports the view that, among rural gay men and lesbian women, having a supportive community is psychologically beneficial.

In summary, the findings regarding mental health problems in nonheterosexual populations are somewhat complex. There is no indication that homosexuality in and of itself is predictive of mental illness. There are indications, however, that in a few subgroups of gay and lesbian individuals, there is an increase in substance abuse problems. Furthermore, during adolescence, a subgroup of youth who eventually become gay or lesbian appear to be at increased risk for attempted or completed suicide. Although general mental health problems are not related to sexual orientation, it is clear that positive attitudes toward one's homosexuality and implementing those attitudes through behaviors, such as maintaining relationships with other lesbian and gay individuals and becoming active in lesbian and gay communities, tend to increase psychological adjustment in gay and lesbian populations.

The end of the illness model of homosexuality does not mean that there is nothing of interest regarding mental health issues and sexual orientation. Although mental health problems are not related to an inherent psychopathology of homosexuality, it is important to explicate the meaning of this research. Before pursuing this matter, however, it is important to address the lingering persistence of illness models of homosexuality.

## Attempts to Repathologize Homosexuality

Unlike behavioral therapists who by and large discontinued their attempts to "cure" homosexuality after homosexuality was depathologized (Davison, 1982, 1991), some psychoanalysts have continued expounding an illness model of homosexuality (Socarides, 1978). This pathologizing of homosexuality was primarily rooted in psychoanalytic theorists (Bergler, 1956; Bieber et al., 1962; Caprio, 1954; Hatterer, 1970; Socarides, 1968) who described in detail the alleged psychopathology of lesbian and gay individuals. Their work was based on psychoanalytic speculations about populations of "troubled homosexuals" who presented for psychotherapy. Some of these theorists (e.g., Bieber et al., 1962) purported to conduct "research" that supported their views, although in fact it represents a parody of research.

For example, as noted elsewhere (Gonsiorek, 1977, pp. 12–13), the Bieber et al. research better serves as a case study in researcher bias. They compared male homosexual and heterosexual patients in psychoanalysis. The same group of psychoanalysts developed a theory about homosexuality; developed a questionnaire to test their theory; designed the research study; were analysts for the patients/subjects; served as raters in the research project on their patients; and interpreted the results. It is not surprising they concluded that their theory had been verified. It is difficult to build more potential for researcher bias into experimental procedures than that which is evident in the Bieber group.

Concurrent with these attempts, however, has been the development of fairly elaborate psychoanalytic models that do not view homosexuality as an illness but rather as a normal variant in the human condition. They describe the ways in which psychoanalytic methods can be useful in understanding and assisting gay, lesbian, and bisexual individuals who have difficulties. Chief among these is the work of Isay (1985, 1987, 1989) and contributions by Hencken (1982), Lewes (1988), and Friedman (1988), who have explicated theoretically rich gay and lesbian affirmative psychoanalytic perspectives. Unfortunately, their reception in mainstream psychoanalysis has been lukewarm. In many psychoanalytic circles, the illness model persists.

Other vocal attempts to repathologize homosexuality are perpetuated by fundamentalist "Christian" therapists. These are church-affiliated individuals who purport to "cure" homosexuality through religious exhortation, which is often intermingled with fragments of twelve-step self-help programs. Occasionally this literature reaches professional journals (e.g., Pattison & Pattison, 1980). The work of Cameron (1985, 1986, 1988) typifies the transparent misrepresentation and distortion of scientific literature that attempts to repathologize homosexuality and portrays gay men and lesbian women, particularly the former, as child molesters and willful spreaders of infectious disease. Herek (1991) and Gonsiorek and Weinrich (1991) have critiqued this work. In fact, Cameron was removed from American Psychological Association membership for his misuse of scientific information.

There are a number of common features of these religiously oriented repathologizing attempts. First, they focus on changing sexual orientation and do so almost exclusively with males. As Haldeman (1991) noted in his review, these efforts generally assert, based on no discernible data, that members have been "cured" of homosexuality. On closer examination many of the therapists acknowledge that same-sex desire remains, but the individuals have "chosen" to lead a "moral," heterosexual life. In effect, the Christian therapists are occasionally capable of utilizing group pressure and brainwashing to coerce gay men into not acting on same-sex feelings. It is a comment on the pervasive sexism of these groups that lesbian women are of little interest and rarely attract their "therapeutic" efforts. It appears that only males are important enough to warrant such interventions.

Another feature of this new fundamentalist repathologizing of homosexuality is the sudden appearance of "scientific" institutions and foundations. These often have substantial funding and are usually headed by obscure individuals who are proclaimed authorities in the field. They frequently have well-orchestrated media contacts, usually in the wake of a legislative or court controversy, and often disappear once a media splash has been made. The substantial funding, nationwide coordination, and well-executed access to media suggest that many, if not most, of these foundations are part of a coordinated right-wing effort to target sexual, ethnic, and racial minorities and women in attempts to manipulate public policy.

Another recent hybrid is the appearance of professional-appearing attempts to "cure" homosexuality, usually couched in a 1950s' style psychoanalytic approach. Case examples, but no scientific data, "prove" the authors' points. Most of these, on close examination, bear clear indications of their religious affiliation (e.g., Nicolosi, 1991). A common feature of this pseudoscientific, covertly religiously oriented approach is to ignore the scientific information discussed above and to re-pose questions regarding psychopathology and homosexuality that have been decisively answered under the guise of scientific inquiry and curiosity about these "unanswered" questions (e.g., Jones & Workman, 1989). Attempts are made to create false confusion regarding scientific information about homosexuality.

Homosexuality was depathologized because the scientific literature required it. Psychiatry was in danger of losing face by not being congruent with mental health research.[2] For purposes of this discussion, it is important to note that despite the new attempts to repathologize homosexuality, these efforts have not produced a shred of scientific data suggesting that the depathologizing of homosexuality requires revision. In fact, by their assiduous distortions of research from the late 1950s onward that was the basis for the depathologization and by their reversion to obsolete literature and ways of understanding sexual orientation, they effectively make the point that the depathologizing of homosexuality was a scientifically robust decision.

# THE NEW AFFIRMATIVE MODELS OF UNDERSTANDING MENTAL HEALTH CONCERNS AND SEXUAL ORIENTATION

Although much of the affirmative theorizing about the psychological lives of gay and lesbian individuals is recent, it has its roots in theories developed earlier. Allport (1954), in the wake of the Holocaust, the Second World War, and the early stirrings of the United States civil rights movement, examined the nature and effects of stereotyping and prejudice. He described personality characteristics that develop in individuals who are targets of prejudice, initially as coping mechanisms but that may over time become relatively stable personality traits.

Allport termed these "traits due to victimization" and believed that they were common in most persecuted groups. These traits include: excessive concern and preoccupation with minority or deviant group membership, feelings of insecurity, denial of membership in the group, withdrawal and passivity, self-derision, strong in-group ties coupled with prejudice against out-groups, slyness and cunning, self-hate, aggression against one's own group, militancy, enhanced striving, neuroticism, and acting out self-fulfilling prophecies about one's own inferiority.

Allport developed his ideas by observing the effects of prejudice against Blacks and Jews. His analysis did not include the then nearly invisible same-sex-oriented population. Yet, the personality traits and coping mechanisms he described closely paralleled descriptions of personality characteristics some psychoanalytic writers (Bergler, 1956; Bieber et al., 1962; Hatterer, 1970; Socarides,

1968) described as inherent pathological features of such individuals and "evidence" that homosexuality per se is a neurotic illness. This is a clear example of the same phenomenon being viewed as intrinsic by one school of thought and as reactive to an external situation by another theoretical perspective. As social psychological understanding of minority group membership, stereotyping, and prejudice evolved (Gonsiorek, 1982b; Herek, 1991), an appreciation emerged that these social psychological forces have powerful behavioral effects on both the targets and the conveyors of prejudice.

Concurrent with the evolution of these ideas, other clinicians and theorists observed the ways in which gay, lesbian, and bisexual individuals come to terms with their sexual orientations. They described a "coming-out" process (see Gonsiorek and Rudolph, 1991, for a review of these concepts) with an initial stage in which individuals block recognition of same-sex feelings through a variety of defensive strategies. These may exact a high psychological price for their maintenance. Some individuals use these defensive strategies indefinitely, constricting their same-sex feelings, consuming much psychological energy, and incurring impairment of general functioning and self-esteem. For many individuals, however, the gradual recognition of same-sex interest emerges and the presence of significant same-sex feelings are tolerated (see Cohen and Savin-Williams, "Coming Out," this volume, and Gonsiorek, 1988, for a detailed examination of the coming-out process).

This is usually followed by a period of emotional and behavioral experimentation with homosexuality and an increasing sense of normalcy with same-sex feelings. Some models postulate a second crisis after the dissolution of a first relationship in which a reemergence of negative feelings about being gay or lesbian occurs. As the individual again accepts his or her same-sex feelings, a sense of identity as gay or lesbian is successfully integrated and accepted as a positive aspect of the self.

This coming-out process represents a shift in the person's core sexual identity and may be accompanied by dramatic levels of emotional distress. An individual may temporarily display various psychiatric symptoms, especially if she or he is without adequate support or information about sexuality. In general, however, the best predictor of an individual's long-term development at this stage is not her or his presenting symptomatology but level of functioning prior to the coming-out process. Most gay and lesbian individuals weather the coming-out crises and emerge several years later with minimal or no symptomatology and with improved functioning.

Coming-out models are an important theoretical development because they essentially describe a developmental process unique to the lives of lesbian, gay, and bisexual individuals. Coming out occurs in addition to, not instead of, psychological processes and identity developments typical of adolescence and adulthood. Thus, coming out to self and others is filtered through other aspects of personality structure and personal and family history.

These theories, though useful in providing an initial description of the psychological processes of some individuals, did not articulate a substantive connection with the rest of the psychological life of the individual. The work of Malyon (1981, 1982a, 1982b) helped remedy this deficit. Malyon theorized that gay and lesbian persons, similar to heterosexuals, are raised with culturally sanctioned, antihomosexual biases. Such biases mobilize other psychological processes that extend beyond the development of prejudice. Children who will eventually be bisexual, lesbian, or gay often develop an awareness of being different at an early age. They may not understand the sexual nature or the precise meaning of their differentness, but they soon learn that it is negatively regarded. As these individuals develop and mature, they reach a fuller understanding of the nature of this difference and the considerable negative societal reaction to it. These negative feelings may be incorporated into the self-image, resulting in varying degrees of internalized homophobia. In turn, the negative feelings about one's sexual orientation may be overgeneralized to encompass the entire self, and the effects of this may range from a mild tendency toward self-doubt in the face of prejudice to overt self-hatred and self-destructive behavior. Other theoreticians tackled this problem in other ways.

Grace (1977) theorized that gay and lesbian adolescents generally do not partake in typical adolescent social and romantic experimentation, creating a sense of loss that predisposes some individuals to depression, despair, and self-esteem problems in adulthood. In another publication, I described how certain developmental routes can result in an overlay of other symptomatology that over time can become a more pronounced part of the personality structure (Gonsiorek, 1982c). Married or closeted men who covertly engage in anonymous same-sex behavior can develop an overlay of maladaptive coping mechanisms. Daher (1981) explicated how the sense of difference in gay adolescents can lead to the development of feelings of inferiority.

Perhaps the most elaborate explanatory theory yet developed that addresses the relationships among gay and lesbian identity formation, the wounds inflicted by societal bigotry, and psychological health draws on elements from Kohut's self-psychology (1971, 1977, 1984). Gonsiorek and Rudolph (1991) postulated that the experience of antihomosexual prejudice is an assault on the sense of self that occurs relatively late in childhood. Because many developmental patterns have been laid down in the individual prior to this late-occurring assault on the self, the ways in which this assault manifests itself will be heavily filtered through pre-existing personality structures.

An important implication of this theory is that it offers an explanation for why most individuals weather the coming-out process and internalized homophobia and emerge in adulthood without significant psychological difficulties. Yet, simultaneously, a subset of gay, lesbian, and bisexual individuals may be psychologically overwhelmed by these same experiences. This theory proposes that individuals who experienced difficulties in terms of their early developmental events, before the onset of antihomosexual prejudice in middle and late childhood, may experience internalized homophobia and the coming-out process as overwhelming—the latest in a long series of assaults. Individuals whose early developmental experiences were relatively benign will treat these same events as a developmental challenge to be mastered and will likely, as a result, success-fully manage them.

This and similar formulations begin to provide an in-depth understanding of the psychological experience of being gay, lesbian, or bisexual and reconnect gay, lesbian, and bisexual affirmative theories with traditional psychological theory. They also explain why non-heterosexual persons vary in their levels of adaptation and functioning. Finally, and perhaps most importantly, these formulations offer the best "fit" in explaining empirical data derived from psychological tests and the documented mental health problems of some gay, lesbian, and bisexual individuals.

# THE FURTHER DIVERSIFICATION OF AFFIRMATIVE MODELS

There is an important limitation to the theories described in this chapter. Virtually all were developed with the use of White, English-speaking, middle-class male samples, although there has been sufficient work with individuals of both genders so that sex differences can be described (see Gonsiorek, 1988, and Gonsiorek and Rudolph, 1991, for description and review). Allport's theory of prejudice and its effects and the self-psychology perspective of Gonsiorek and Rudolph describe the interplay between external stressors and individual development. One would expect this interplay to be highly sensitive to culture, class, socio-economic status, gender, race, and ethnicity. Therefore, developmental concepts described in these models should not be assumed to accurately portray individuals other than those on whom they were developed. The application of these identity/developmental perspectives to diverse populations represents, however, one of the most intriguing aspects of current research and theoretical efforts.

Several investigators have applied similar concepts to other populations. For example, Icard (1986) has examined U.S. Black males; Loiacano (1989), Black lesbian women and gay men; Greene (1986), U.S. Black lesbian women; Gock (1985), Asian and Pacific gay men; Allen (1984), Native American lesbian women; Wooden, Kawasaki, and Mayeda (1983), Japanese American gay men; Hidalgo (1984) and Hidalgo and Christiansen (1976/1977), Puerto Rican lesbian women in the United States; and Espin (1987), Latina lesbian women. Morales (1983) developed a model applicable to Third World gay men and lesbian women. Espin (1987) applied the minority identity development model of Atkinson, Morten, and Sue (1979) to understand identity development among Latina lesbian women.

Although the specifics of an identity/developmental perspective vary among populations, the general perspective appears to be broadly useful. Because this perspective stresses the relationship among social forces, the individual, and sense of self, these differing cultural perspectives are not variations on a theme epitomized by the White, middle-class, North American, English-speaking world. Rather, developmental processes and outcomes of the sense of self vary as greatly as the social forces that shape them.

For example, both the nature of homophobia and concepts of "maleness" and "femaleness" can be significantly different within U.S. Black and White communities, and the distinction between individual and family is less clearly drawn in the more cohesive multigenerational Hispanic communities than in the relatively atomized, one-generational Anglo family. In addition, pressures on gay and lesbian members of Asian families to avoid dishonor and loss of face for the family are especially high. In her research, Chan (1989) discovered a complex relationship: Asian lesbian women experienced more discrimination for being Asian, while Asian gay men experienced more discrimination for being gay. An identity/developmental perspective can accommodate cultural variations on identity development and sense of self (see also Manalansan, this volume).

The aforementioned writers generally agree that there is commonality in the psychological processes experienced by lesbian and gay members of racial and ethnic minorities. Many speak of double (in the case of lesbian women, triple) minority statuses. For example, Gock (1985) described the perceived choice of having to identify with the gay community, and thus address expressions of intimacy, versus the ethnic-minority community, and thus retain cultural groundedness. Morales (1983) termed this a "conflict of allegiance" and offered a four-stage model on how ethnic lesbian women and gay men resolve such conflicts of multiple identities.

Icard (1986; Icard & Traunstein, 1987) described the ways in which gay Black men are subject to an unusually harsh triple prejudice from the White heterosexual majority and the White gay and Black heterosexual minorities. The strong pressures for social sex-role conformity in Black communities further exacerbate these stresses. Sears (1989), in his study of growing up lesbian or gay in the United States South, described a "fragmentation of identity" when integrating multiple identities. He noted that ethnic identity acquisition occurs first, and therefore the later sexual identity can create a sense of betrayal to one's ethnic group.

As research on racial- and ethnic-minority groups continues, our understanding of sexual orientation and sexual-identity development will expand beyond the confines of nonrepresentative samples. The complex interactions among the individual, external social forces, and internal psychological development are better explicated with the addition of these studies.

# What Has Been Learned? Where Do We Go From Here?

The nearly four decades since Hooker's revolutionary research have produced dramatic changes in the psychological understanding of sexual orientations. Homosexuality per se is no longer viewed as an illness, and there is an appreciation that gay, lesbian, and bisexual individuals, similar to other minority group members who experience external prejudice, are vulnerable to the negative effects of such prejudice and that they express resulting wounds in a variety of ways. In particular, gay, lesbian, and bisexual individuals who experienced psychological difficulties prior to encountering antihomosexual prejudice are prone, especially during adolescence, to suicide attempts and substance abuse. Further, it is apparent that these developmental events are filtered through a series of lenses determined by gender, race, ethnicity, class, education, and socioeconomic status. Newly developed affirmative models attempt to understand and predict the ways in which individuals respond to these events.

In terms of public policy implications, a number of features are apparent. The use of scientific information from the behavioral and social sciences to maintain an illness model of homosexuality and to foster prejudice against gay men, lesbian women, and bisexuals is an egregious abuse of such information. The tolerance in mental health professions for its members continuing to exercise personal bigotry and prejudice as a professional prerogative in the way gay, lesbian, and bisexual clients are treated is an affront to professional ethics and standards of conduct. The mental health professions have an obligation, if they are to maintain their integrity, to integrate the information that has become available over the past four decades into practice standards. The effect should be to relegate prejudicial and biased treatment of gay, lesbian, and bisexual individuals to the same level of impropriety as prejudice based on race, ethnicity, gender, and religious persuasions and to help practitioners operate in the best interests of all clients. Prejudice against sexual minorities remains the only form of bigotry whose exercise is considered a professional prerogative in some mental health circles.

Finally, it is clear that there is a subgroup of gay, lesbian, and bisexual individuals who, similar to their counterparts in other disparaged groups, are vulnerable to mental health problems as a direct result of the interaction between the prejudice they endure and earlier negative psychological experiences that may be unrelated to their sexual orientations. Preventive mental health services to reduce problems in these populations should provide educational and supportive environments for individuals who are particularly vulnerable so that they can enter adulthood with an optimal level of psychological functioning.

## ▼    ENDNOTES    ▼

1. See Bérubé (1990) for discussion of the initial medicalization of homosexuality in the United States.

2. Silverstein (1991) describes psychiatry's struggles with these issues.

▼ **REFERENCES** ▼

Allen, P. G. (1984). Beloved women: The lesbian in American Indian culture. In T. Darty & S. Potter (Eds.), *Women-identified women* (pp. 83–96). Palo Alto, CA: Mayfield.

Allport, G. W. (1954). *The nature of prejudice.* Reading, MA: Addison-Wesley.

Anderson, S. C., & Henderson, D. C. (1985). Working with lesbian alcoholics. *Social Work, 31,* 518–525.

Atkinson, D. R., Morten, G., & Sue, D. W. (1979). *Counseling American minorities.* Dubuque, IA: Brown.

Bayer, R. (1987). *Homosexuality and American psychiatry: The politics of diagnosis* (2nd ed.). Princeton, NJ: Princeton University Press.

Bell, A. P., & Weinberg, M. S. (1978). *Homosexualities: A study of diversity among men and women.* New York: Simon & Schuster.

Bergler, E. (1956). *Homosexuality: Disease or way of life?* New York: Collier.

Bérubé, A. (1990). *Coming out under fire: The history of gay men and women in World War II.* New York: Free Press.

Bieber, I., Dain, H. J., Dince, P. R., Drellich, M. G., Grand, H. G., Gundlach, R. H., Kremer, M. W., Rifkin, A. H., Wilbur, C. B., & Bieber, T. B. (1962). *Homosexuality: A psychoanalytic study.* New York: Basic Books.

Cameron, P. (1985). Homosexual molestation of children/sexual interaction of teacher and pupil. *Psychological Reports, 57,* 1227–1236.

Cameron, P. (1986). AIDS in hemophiliacs and homosexuals. *Lancet, 1,* 36.

Cameron, P. (1988). Kinsey sex surveys. *Science, 240,* 867.

Caprio, F. S. (1954). *Female homosexuality: A modern study of lesbianism.* New York: Grove Press.

Chan, C. S. (1989). Issues of identity development among Asian-American lesbians and gay men. *Journal of Counseling and Development, 68,* 16–20.

Daher, D. (1981). The loss and search for the puer: A consideration of inferiority feelings in certain male adolescents. *Adolescence, 16,* 145–158.

D'Augelli, A. R. (1987). Social support patterns of lesbian women in a rural helping network. *Journal of Rural Community Psychology, 8,* 12–21.

D'Augelli, A. R., & Hart, M. M. (1987). Gay women, men, and families in rural settings: Toward the development of helping communities. *American Journal of Community Psychology, 15,* 79–93.

Davison, G. (1982). Politics, ethics and therapy for homosexuality. In W. Paul, J. D. Weinrich, J. C. Gonsiorek, & M. Hotvedt (Eds.), *Homosexuality: Social, psychological and biological issues* (pp. 89–98). Beverly Hills, CA: Sage.

Davison, G. (1991). Constructionism and morality in therapy for homosexuality. In J. C. Gonsiorek & J. D. Weinrich (Eds.), *Homosexuality: Research implications for public policy* (pp. 137–148). Newbury Park, CA: Sage.

Espin, O. M. (1987). Issues of identity in the psychology of Latina lesbians. In Boston Lesbian Psychologies Collective (Ed.), *Lesbian psychologies: Explorations and challenges* (pp. 35–51). Urbana, IL: University of Illinois Press.

Farrell, R. A., & Morrione, T. J. (1974). Social interaction and stereotypic responses to homosexuals. *Archives of Sexual Behavior, 3,* 425–442.

Friedman, R. C. (1988). *Male homosexuality: A contemporary psychoanalytic perspective.* New Haven, CT: Yale University Press.

Gock, T. S. (1985, August). *Psychotherapy with Asian/Pacific gay men: Psychological issues, treatment approach and therapeutic guidelines.* Paper presented at Asian-American Psychological Association, Los Angeles.

Gonsiorek, J. C. (1977). *Psychological adjustment and homosexuality* (Social and Behavioral Sciences Documents, MS 1478). San Raphael, CA: Select Press.

Gonsiorek, J. C. (1982a). Results of psychological testing on homosexual populations. In W. Paul, J. D. Weinrich, J. C. Gonsiorek, & M. Hotvedt (Eds.), *Homosexuality: Social, psychological and biological issues* (pp. 71–80). Beverly Hills, CA: Sage.

Gonsiorek, J. C. (1982b) Social psychological concepts in the understanding of homosexuality. In W. Paul, J. D. Weinrich, J. C. Gonsiorek, & M. Hotvedt (Eds.), *Homosexuality: Social, psychological and biological issues* (pp. 115–120). Beverly Hills, CA: Sage.

Gonsiorek, J. C. (1982c). The use of diagnostic concepts in working with gay and lesbian populations. In J. Gonsiorek (Ed.), *Homosexuality and psychotherapy: A practitioner's handbook of affirmative models* (pp. 9–20). New York: Haworth.

Gonsiorek, J. C. (1988). Mental health issues of gay and lesbian adolescents. *Journal of Adolescent Health Care, 9,* 114–122.

Gonsiorek, J. C. (1991). The empirical basis for the demise of the illness model of homosexuality. In J. C. Gonsiorek & J. D. Weinrich (Eds.), *Homosexuality: Research implications for public policy* (pp. 115–136). Newbury Park, CA: Sage.

Gonsiorek, J. C., & Rudolph, J. R. (1991). Homosexual identity: Coming out and other developmental events. In J. C. Gonsiorek & J. D. Weinrich (Eds.), *Homosexuality: Research implications for public policy* (pp. 161–176). Newbury Park, CA: Sage.

Gonsiorek, J. C., & Weinrich, J. D. (1991). The definition and scope of sexual orientation. In J. C. Gonsiorek & J. D. Weinrich (Eds.), *Homosexuality: Research implications for public policy* (pp. 1–12). Newbury Park, CA: Sage.

Grace, J. (1977, November). *Gay despair and the loss of adolescence.* Paper presented at Fifth Biennial Professional Symposium of the National Association of Social Workers, San Diego, CA.

Greene, B. A. (1986). When the therapist is White and the patient is Black: Considerations for psychotherapy in feminist heterosexual and lesbian communities. *Women and Therapy, 6,* 41–65.

Haldeman, D. C. (1991). Sexual orientation conversion therapy for gay men and lesbians: A scientific examination. In J. C. Gonsiorek & J. D. Weinrich (Eds.), *Homosexuality: Research implications for public policy* (pp. 149–160). Newbury Park, CA: Sage.

Hammersmith, S. K., & Weinberg, M. S. (1973). Homosexual identity: Commitment, adjustment and significant others. *Sociometry, 36,* 56–79.

Hart, M., Roback, H., Tittler, B., Weitz, L., Walston, B., & McKee, E. (1978). Psychological adjustment of nonpatient homosexuals: Critical review of the research literature. *Journal of Clinical Psychiatry, 39,* 604–608.

Hatterer, L. (1970). *Changing homosexuality in the male.* New York: McGraw-Hill.

Hencken, J. (1982). Homosexuality and psychoanalysis: Toward a mutual understanding. In W. Paul, J. D. Weinrich, J. C. Gonsiorek, & M. Hotvedt (Eds.), *Homosexuality: Social, psychological and biological issues* (pp. 121–148). Beverly Hills, CA: Sage.

Herek, G. M. (1990). Gay people and governmental security clearances: A social perspective. *American Psychologist, 45,* 1035–1042.

Herek, G. M. (1991). Stigma, prejudice and violence against lesbians and gay men. In J. C. Gonsiorek & J. D. Weinrich (Eds.), *Homosexuality: Research implications for public policy* (pp. 60–80). Newbury Park, CA: Sage.

Hidalgo, H. A. (1984). The Puerto Rican lesbian in the United States. In T. Darty & S. Potter (Eds.), *Women-identified women* (pp. 105–115). Palo Alto, CA: Mayfield.

Hidalgo, H. A., & Christensen, E. H. (1976/1977). The Puerto Rican lesbian and the Puerto Rican community. *Journal of Homosexuality, 2,* 109–121.

Hooker, E. A. (1957). The adjustment of the male overt homosexual. *Journal of Projective Techniques, 21,* 17–31.

Icard, L. (1986). Black gay men and conflicting social identities: Sexual orientation vs. racial identity. In J. Gripton & M. Valentich (Eds.), *Social work practice in sexual problems* (pp. 83–93). New York: Haworth.

Icard, L., & Traunstein, D. M. (1987). Black gay alcoholic men: Their character and treatment. *Social Casework: The Journal of Contemporary Social Work, 68,* 267–272.

Isay, R. A. (1985). On the analytic therapy of homosexual men. *The Psychoanalytic Study of the Child, 40,* 235–254.

Isay, R. A. (1987). Fathers and their homosexually inclined sons in childhood. *The Psychoanalytic Study of the Child, 42,* 275–294.

Isay, R. A. (1989). *Being homosexual: Gay men and their development.* New York: Farrar, Straus, & Giroux.

Jacobs, J. A., & Tedford, W. H. (1980). Factors affecting self-esteem of the homosexual individual. *Journal of Homosexuality, 5,* 373–382.

Jones, S. L., & Workman, D. E. (1989). Homosexuality: The behavioral sciences and the church. *Journal of Psychology and Theology, 17,* 213–225.

Kohut, H. (1971). *The analysis of the self.* New York: International Universities Press.

Kohut, H. (1977). *The restoration of the self.* New York: International Universities Press.

Kohut, H. (1984). *How does analysis cure?* Chicago: University of Chicago Press.

Kus, R. J. (1988). Alcoholism and nonacceptance of gay self: The critical link. *Journal of Homosexuality, 15,* 25–41.

Lewes, K. (1988). *The psychoanalytic theory of male homosexuality.* New York: Simon & Schuster.

Loiacano, D. K. (1989). Gay identity issues among Black Americans: Racism, homophobia and the need for validation. *Journal of Counseling and Development, 68,* 21–25.

Malyon, A. K. (1981). The homosexual adolescent: Developmental issues and social bias. *Child Welfare, 60,* 321–330.

Malyon, A. (1982a). Biphasic aspects of homosexual identity formation. *Psychotherapy: Theory, Research & Practice, 19,* 335–340.

Malyon, A. (1982b). Psychotherapeutic implications of internalized homophobia in gay men. In J. Gonsiorek (Ed.), *Homosexuality and psychotherapy: A practitioner's handbook of affirmative models* (pp. 59–69). New York: Haworth.

McDaniel, L. A. (1989). *Preservice adjustment of homosexual and heterosexual military accessions: Implications for security clearance suitability* (PERS-TR-89-004). Monterey, CA: Defense Personnel Security Research and Education Center.

Meredith, R. L., & Reister. R. W. (1980). Psychotherapy responsibility and homosexuality: Clinical examination of socially deviant behavior. *Professional Psychology, 11,* 174–193.

Morales, E. (1983, August). *Third world gays and lesbians: A process of multiple identities.* Paper presented at American Psychological Association, Anaheim, CA.

Mosbacher, D. (1988). Lesbian alcohol and substance abuse. *Psychiatric Annals, 18,* 47–50.

Nicolosi, J. (1991). *Reparative therapy of male homosexuality.* Northvale, NJ: Jason Aronson.

Pattison, E., & Pattison, M. (1980). Ex-gays: Religiously-mediated change in homosexuals. *American Journal of Psychiatry, 137,* 1553–1562.

Pillard, R. (1988). Sexual orientation and mental disorder. *Psychiatric Annals, 18,* 51–56.

Reiss, B. F. (1980). Psychological tests in homosexuality. In J. Marmor (Ed.),

*Homosexual behavior: A modern reappraisal* (pp. 296–311). New York: Basic Books.

Reiss, B. F., Safer, J., & Yotive, W. (1974). Psychological test data on female homosexuality. *Journal of Homosexuality, l,* 71–85.

Saghir, M. T., & Robins, E. (1973). *Male and female homosexuality: A comprehensive investigation.* Baltimore, MD: Williams & Wilkins.

Saghir, M. T., Robins, E., Walbran, B., & Gentry, K. A. (1970a). Homosexuality III: Psychiatric disorders and disability in the male homosexual. *American Journal of Psychiatry, 126,* 1079–1086.

Saghir, M. T., Robins, E., Walbran, B., & Gentry, K. A. (1970b). Homosexuality IV: Psychiatric disorders and disability in the female homosexual. *American Journal of Psychiatry, 127,* 147–154.

Sarbin, T. R., & Carols, K. E. (1988). *Nonconforming sexual orientation and military suitability* (PERS-TR-89-002). Monterey, CA: Defense Personnel Security Research and Education Center.

Savin-Williams, R. C. (1990). *Gay and lesbian youth: Expressions of identity.* New York: Hemisphere.

Sears, J. T. (1989). The impact of gender and race on growing up lesbian and gay in the South. *National Women's Studies Association Journal, 1,* 422–457.

Silverstein, C. (1991). Psychological and medical treatments of homosexuality. In J. C. Gonsiorek & J. D. Weinrich (Eds.), *Homosexuality: Research implications for public policy* (pp. 101–114). Newbury Park, CA: Sage.

Socarides, C. W. (1968). *The overt homosexual.* New York: Grune & Stratton.

Socarides, C. W. (1978). *Homosexuality.* New York: Aronson.

Weinberg, M. S., & Williams, C. J. (1974). *Male homosexuals: Their problems and adaptations.* New York: Oxford University Press.

Wooden, W. S., Kawasaki, H., & Mayeda, R. (1983). Lifestyles and identity maintenance among Japanese-American gay males. *Alternative Lifestyles, 5,* 236–243.

# Author Biographies

**J. Michael Bailey** received his Ph.D. in Clinical Psychology from the University of Texas, Austin. He is currently Assistant Professor of Psychology at Northwestern University in Evanston, Illinois. His primary research interests include the causes and development of sexual orientation, particularly childhood sex-typed behavior and the genetic basis of sexual orientation. He has recently published major research studies in professional journals such as the *Journal of Personality and Social Psychology, Developmental Psychology,* and *Archives of General Psychiatry.*

**Susan Miller Campbell** is Assistant Professor of Psychology at Middlebury College, where she teaches courses in social psychology and on the psychology of women and gender. She received her Ph.D. in Social Psychology from the University of California, Los Angeles. Her research interests include the study of gender and close relationships. She is currently studying the role of motives and cognition in determining marital happiness and has published articles and chapters on power in close relationships, the relation of gender and power to condom use and attitudes, and women's responses to infertility.

**Virginia Casper** received her Ph.D. in Developmental Psychology from Yeshiva University. She is a Developmental Psychologist on the graduate faculty of Bank Street College of Education and teaches courses in their Infant and Parent Development Program, specializing in children from birth to three years and their families. Casper coauthored a shorter article in Teachers College Record based on the study reported in this volume. Her current research interests include the ways in which young children conceptualize nontraditional family structures.

**Kenneth M. Cohen** is a Psychotherapist at Cornell University Psychological Services and teaches lifespan developmental psychology courses at Ithaca College. He received his B.A. in Psychology from McGill University and M.A. in Clinical Psychology from the University of Detroit, where he is currently a doctoral candidate. Cohen has pursued graduate work in Developmental Psychology at the University of Massachusetts, Amherst, where he researched newborn, infant, and toddler development. He has published in such journals as *Developmental Psychology* and *The Journal of the Acoustical Society of America.* His clinical and research interests include lesbian, bisexual, and gay youth, suicide, bereavement, and health psychology.

**Anthony R. D'Augelli** is Professor of Human Development in the Department of Human Development and Family Studies at the Pennsylvania State University. He received his Ph.D. from the University of Connecticut in Clinical/Community Psychology. He is interested in the application of community psychology to lesbian, gay, and bisexual development and has recently completed a research project on lesbian, gay, and bisexual youth, examining identity development, discrimination, and harassment. He is coeditor of *Lesbian, Gay, and Bisexual Identities Across the Life Span*.

**Lee Ellis** holds a Ph.D. from Florida State University and has been teaching sociology at Minot State University in Minot, North Dakota since 1977. His interests center around sex differences in behavior and the biological basis of sexual orientation and sex-typical behavior. Important publications include a *Psychological Bulletin* review article with Ames (1987) on the causes of human variations in sexual orientation as well as the books written or edited by Ellis: *Theories of Rape; Crime in Biological, Social, and Moral Contexts; Social Stratification and Socioeconomic Inequality* (Volumes 1 and 2); and *Research Methods in the Social Sciences*.

**Kristin G. Esterberg** received her Ph.D. in Sociology from Cornell University. She is Assistant Professor of Sociology and Director of the Women's Studies Program at the University of Missouri, Kansas City. She has published several articles on the homophile movement and on lesbian/bisexual identity and community, and she is currently working on a book examining the social construction of lesbian and bisexual identities.

**Nancy J. Evans** is Associate Professor in the Department of Counseling and Rehabilitation Education and Coordinator of the College Student Personnel Option at Pennsylvania State University. She received her Ph.D. in Counseling Psychology from the University of Missouri, Columbia. She is coeditor of the book *Beyond Tolerance: Gays, Lesbians and Bisexuals on Campus,* as well as numerous articles in student affairs journals. Her research interests include assessment of interventions designed to address homophobia; preparation of student affairs administrators regarding gay, lesbian, and bisexual issues; and homophobia in minority communities.

**Carla Golden** received her Ph.D. in Lifespan Developmental Psychology from Syracuse University. Currently an Associate Professor at Ithaca College, she has lectured widely and written on feminist psychoanalytic theories of gender, as well as on the development of sexual identity. Golden was a Danforth Associate for excellence in teaching and has travelled around the world with the University of Pittsburgh's Semester at Sea Program teaching courses on human sexuality and the psychology of women from an international perspective. Golden was Beatrice Bain Scholar at the University of California, Berkeley, where she conducted research on bisexual women and men. She is currently coediting a reader for McGraw-Hill on the psychology of women.

**John C. Gonsiorek** received his Ph.D. in Clinical Psychology from the University of Minnesota and holds a Diplomate in Clinical Psychology from the American Board of Professional Psychology. He is a Past-President of Division 44

(Society for the Psychological Study of Lesbian and Gay Issues) of the American Psychological Association and has published widely in the areas of sexual exploitation by psychotherapists, sexual orientation and sexual identity, and professional ethics. His books include *Psychotherapists' Sexual Involvement With Clients: Intervention and Prevention, Homosexuality: Research Implications for Public Policy, Male Sexual Abuse: A Trilogy of Intervention Strategies, Homosexuality and Psychotherapy: A Practitioner's Handbook of Affirmative Models,* and *The Breach of Trust: Sexual Exploitation by Health Care Professionals and Clergy.* He is a Clinical and Forensic Psychologist in private practice in Minneapolis and Clinical Assistant Professor in the Department of Psychology, University of Minnesota.

**Arnold H. Grossman** received his Ph.D. in Human Relations from New York University. He also holds M.S.W. and A.C.S.W. degrees and is Professor of Education in the Department of Health Studies, School of Education, at New York University, where he teaches classes about gays and lesbians. He is the Project Director of the NYU AIDS/SIDA Mental Hygiene Project and Co-Principal Investigator of the NYU HIV/AIDS Mental Health Training Center. In addition, he is a member of the Executive Committee of the Hetrick-Martin Institute (a social service organization serving lesbian, gay, and bisexual youth in New York City) and is the author of numerous articles related to gay, lesbian, and HIV/AIDS issues. He received the Diego Lopez Award for Outstanding Service to People with AIDS from the New York City Chapter of the National Association of Social Workers in 1993, and he is the 1994 recipient of NYU School of Education's Professor of the Year Award.

**Sharon Jacobson** is a doctoral candidate in the Department of Recreation and Leisure Studies at the University of Georgia. She has published in such journals as *Journal of Gerontological Social Work, Clinical Gerontologist,* and *Journal of Gay and Lesbian Social Services.* Her primary research interests are in aging and marginalized populations, including older lesbians, the elderly homeless, and older adults with developmental disabilities. Her scholarship has received both local and international recognition. In 1994, she was the recipient of the Tom and Ruth Rivers International Scholarship, presented by the World Leisure and Recreation Association, as well as the Robert P. Wray Award, presented by the Georgia Gerontology Society.

**Martin F. Manalansan IV** is a doctoral candidate in Social Anthropology at the University of Rochester. A native of the Philippines, he holds a Bachelor's degree (magna cum laude) from the University of the Philippines and a Master's degree from Syracuse University. His doctoral research focuses on issues of identity among Filipino gay men living in New York City. His research interests include sexuality and gender, immigration and diaspora, critical theory, language, cultural studies, AIDS prevention, and applied research methods. He is currently a Coordinator of Program Evaluation at the Gay Men's Health Crisis. He has published essays in *Journal of Homosexuality, Positions: East Asia Cultures Critique,* and *Amerasia*.

**Charlotte J. Patterson** is Associate Professor of Psychology at the University of Virginia. Since receiving her Ph.D. in Psychology at Stanford University, she has pursued research in developmental psychology and has published widely in the areas of social and personal development among children and adolescents. She has also served on the editorial boards of *Child Development, Developmental Psychology, Merrill-Palmer Quarterly of Human Development,* and the *Journal of Social and Personal Relationships.* Her research has been supported by the Alton Jones Foundation, the Society for Psychological Study of Social Issues, the National Science Foundation, the National Institute of Mental Health, and by the United States Department of Education. Her ongoing research explores the psychosocial development among children who were born to, or adopted by, lesbian mothers. Patterson coedited a book entitled *Lesbian, Gay and Bisexual Identities Across the Lifespan* and served as Guest Editor for a special issue of *Developmental Psychology* focusing on Sexual Orientation and Human Development.

**Jay P. Paul** is Associate Specialist at the University of California, San Francisco's Center for AIDS Prevention Studies. He received his Ph.D. in Clinical Psychology from the University of California, Berkeley, and has worked for over a decade as a psychotherapist with a primarily bisexual and gay male population. His research has been in the areas of substance abuse and sexual risk behavior, development of HIV risk-reduction interventions, and initiation of health care among at-risk populations. In addition, Paul has published several articles on conceptual issues in sexual orientation and bisexuality.

**Letitia Anne Peplau** received her Ph.D. in Social Psychology from the Social Relations Department at Harvard University. She is Professor of Psychology at the University of California, Los Angeles. Peplau's research focuses on the impact of gender and changing sex roles on close relationships. For her studies of the relationships of lesbians and gay men, she received the Outstanding Achievement Award of the Committee on Lesbian and Gay Concerns of the American Psychological Association and the Evelyn C. Hooker Award from the Gay Academics Union. Peplau is President-elect of the International Society for the Study of Personal Relationships.

**William B. Rubenstein** is Director of the Lesbian and Gay Rights and AIDS Projects at the National Office of the American Civil Liberties Union. He is a magna cum laude graduate of Yale University and Harvard Law School and was the recipient of a Harvard Fellowship in Public Interest Law. Rubenstein has lectured at Yale and Harvard Law Schools, where he teaches a course entitled Sexual Orientation and the Law. Rubenstein is the author of numerous publications including *Lesbians, Gay Men, and the Law; AIDS Agenda: Emerging Issues in Civil Rights;* and *The Rights of People with AIDS/HIV.* He serves as counsel on a variety of litigation aimed at combating discrimination against, and advocating equal rights for, gay men and lesbians. He argued the landmark case of *Braschi v. Stahl Associates Co.* before the New York Court of Appeals (the first time the highest court in any state had recognized a gay couple to be the legal equivalent of a family). Rubenstein has also engaged in litigation filed throughout the country by the AIDS Project concerning issues such as discrimination, quarantine, confidentiality, forced HIV testing, and access to health care.

**Ritch C. Savin-Williams** is Professor of Clinical and Developmental Psychology in the Department of Human Development and Family Studies at Cornell University. He received his Ph.D. from the University of Chicago's Committee on Human Development. His writings include two books, *Adolescence: An Ethological Perspective* and *Gay and Lesbian Youths: Expressions of Identity,* as well as numerous articles and book chapters. Most recently, his research focus has been on identity development among gay and bisexual male youth. He is currently writing a book on the developmental significance of sexual behavior among gay and bisexual youth and is teaching courses on sexual minorities.

**Steven Schultz** is on the graduate faculty of Bank Street College of Education. He received his M.Ed. from Wheelock College and Ed.D. from Teachers College, Columbia University. He recently coauthored an article on lesbian and gay parents and the schools and is working on a book about communication problems and routes between lesbian and gay parents and the schools. His research interests include the manifestation of, and precursors to, sexual orientation in young children and hidden curriculum as interpreted by social reproduction and resistance theories.

**Rosemary Catbagan Veniegas** obtained her B.A. in Psychology from the University of Hawaii. She is currently a graduate student in the Social Psychology program at University of California, Los Angeles. She has conducted research on ethnoviolence and sexual harassment and her current research focus is on the dynamics of power in same-sex friendships.

**Walter L. Williams** is Professor of Anthropology and the Study of Women and Men in Society at the University of Southern California. He received his Ph.D. from the University of North Carolina and teaches courses in Gay Studies, American Indian Studies, and Gender Studies. Williams was cofounder of the Committee on Lesbian and Gay History for the American Historical Association, President of the International Gay and Lesbian Archives, and a Fulbright scholar in Indonesia. He has published six books, the most notable of which is his award-winning *The Spirit and the Flesh* (1986). His most recent research investigates homosexuality in Southeast Asian and Polynesian cultures.

# INDEX